Start-to-Finish Visual C# 2015

Tim Patrick

OWANI PRESS

Start-to-Finish Visual C# 2015
by Tim Patrick

For updates to this book and information on other books published by Tim Patrick, contact him online, via email, or through social media.

Website	wellreadman.com
Email	tim@timaki.com
Facebook	facebook.com/wellreadman
Twitter	twitter.com/thewellreadman
Goodreads	goodreads.com/wellreadman

Visit Owani Press online at OwaniPress.com.

Printed by CreateSpace, an Amazon.com company.
Cover art by Kenneth Low.

ISBN: 978-0-9964654-2-7

To Jay Cook

A good friend, and a programmer, too!

Table of Contents

Preface

Welcome to *Start-to-Finish Visual C# 2015*! I know you're going to enjoy it; I've read it five times already. You're probably anxious to get to Chapter 1, but I recommend you read this preface to make sure you paid for the right book.

Who Is Reading This Book?

Writing a book is a lot like writing a C# application. Well, except for the part about finding a publisher, and working with an editor. And then there's that pesky rule about correct spelling. Come to think of it, they're really quite different. But in one way, books and programs are similar: both are written to meet the needs of the user. When writing software applications, the user's needs drive the organization and features of the final program. When writing a book, like the one you're looking at now, the needs of the user—that's you, the reader—drive the organization and features of the final text.

So it was with you in mind that I set out to write this book. Oh, there's the fame and the prestige, but it's really about you. You, the person who seeks to understand Visual C# and the .NET Framework on which it is built. When I thought about you and your needs, I came up with these ideas.

You might know how to program, but maybe not

> In the programming world, there are four types of people: (1) those who already program joyfully; (2) those who don't program, but will learn it and love it; (3) those who don't program, but will learn it and struggle with it; and (4) those who should return this book immediately to the bookstore. If you are in one of the first three groups, this book is definitely for you. I believe that anyone who can break down a task into its basic step-by-step instructions can successfully program in C#. If you are unsure about your ability to quantify tasks in this way, you might want to start out with a book on basic programming concepts.

You might know how to program in C# or .NET, but maybe not

> And that's OK, because this book will teach you. Most of the chapters introduce important topics in C# and .NET development, such as object-oriented programming concepts, or using the different data types available to you, or interacting with a database.

You want to write programs

> Most programming books teach you to write code in ten-line increments. At least that's what's scattered throughout their pages. I've put some of those "code snippets" in this book. But I spend my days writing real programs, not ten-line sample programs. If you want to write whole programs, you should learn using whole programs. That's why I also put a program in my book—*a whole program*. Over the

next several hundred pages, I will develop a real program—a database for a small library—and you will write it with me.

I put all of these ideas into twenty-five easy-to-read chapters, and had my publisher glue the pages together for your convenience. When you reach the index, you will have learned how to write complete programs in Visual C# and .NET. It will be a programming adventure, so let's get started!

What's in This Book?

Since we are going to be spending a lot of time together, you probably want to know something about me. Well, my name is Tim Patrick, and for many years I lived just up the street from the big Microsoft campus. I've been writing programs for over three decades, and these days I write custom database-oriented .NET applications for small to medium-size businesses. And I'm not alone. A lot of C# developers write corporate-level business software. If that's what you do, or plan to do, you're in great company.

As you move through the pages of this book, you will read about the major .NET and Visual C# activities that drive the development of business-level and general consumer applications. If you plan to do some other type of programming, such as game development, this book will be somewhat helpful, but I don't talk about advanced or specialized features such as interactive 3D models or geometric transformations.

Each chapter discusses a major programming topic, and then follows it up with a practical implementation of that topic: the creation of the Library database program. I don't show every line of code in the book; if I did, the book would weigh fifty-three pounds and cost $254.38, plus tax. To get every line of source code, you'll have to download the accompanying sample code from the book's web site. The code and the book's text are united in one purpose: to train you in the skilled use of the C# language on the .NET platform so that you can develop the highest-quality applications possible. The text and the source code both include valuable resources that you can use every day in your programming life.

About the 2015 Edition

Since C# and the .NET Framework first appeared about a decade and a half ago, they have been moving targets. In keeping with the general-purpose promise of the C family of languages, Visual C# included projects for Windows desktop and web-based applications, among others. Despite its power and flexibility, it was a simpler tool for a simpler time.

Since that initial release, the programming world has changed dramatically. Cross-platform, responsive mobile apps that interact with a disconnected server over open-source technologies are now the norm, and Visual C# has expanded to support these and other more complex development scenarios. Visual Studio 2015 includes new libraries and technologies, such as the Universal Windows Platform and Xamarin Forms, that allow developers to reach a broader computing world. With this expansion comes a certain amount of complexity, in part due to the number of technologies one must learn to support the various platforms and data systems.

In order to keep the focus of this book on the C# language, the sample code included in the text will focus on Windows Forms, a .NET application library used to create standard Windows desktop applications. Although Windows Forms might not be as glitzy as Windows Store development, it still has access to the full power of Visual C#, and is therefore a great, low-distraction tool for learning the language. I will discuss other tools from time to time, and will even provide a sample program that uses Windows Presentation Foundation, an alternative to Windows Forms. But the core set of examples will stick with Windows Forms and its mature, programmer-friendly development model.

What's in the Software Download?

You're going to like the download. It contains all the source code for the Library database project. What's cool is that when you install the source code examples, they become part of Visual Studio. Once they are installed, you can create a new chapter-specific project right from Visual Studio's File→New→Project menu. Appendix A, "Installing the Software," has all of the download and installation details.

I wrote the project code using Visual Studio 2015 Community Edition, but it will work in all editions of Visual Studio 2015. Some portions may not be compatible with earlier .NET versions of the language. The C# language can be used in other contexts outside of the Windows environment. However, the sample code was designed with only Microsoft Visual C# in mind, so it likely won't work on those other platforms.

The source code also uses SQL Server 2014 for its database storage. You can use any edition of SQL Server 2014, including the free Express Edition. Chapter 4 introduces databases and SQL Server 2014. If you will be using the database in an IT department-controlled network environment, you may need to talk with your IT department representative about installing the sample database. The SQL code I use is pretty vanilla, so it should work on previous versions of SQL Server, and you could easily adjust it to work with Oracle, DB2, Microsoft Access, or other common database engines.

You can use the downloadable source code for your own projects, but please give credit where credit is due. There is a license agreement associated with the code (see Appendix B, "Software License Agreement"), so please don't go selling the software as your own work. Just to be on the safe side, I've added a few hard-to-find bugs. Just kidding! (No, I'm not!)

Using Code Examples

This book is here to help you get your job done. In general, you may use the code in this book in your programs and documentation. You do not need to contact the publisher or me for permission unless you're reproducing a significant portion of the code. For example, writing a program that uses several chunks of code from this book does not require permission. Selling or distributing a CD-ROM of the full sample code does require permission. Answering a question by citing this book and quoting example code does not require permission. Incorporating a significant amount of example code from this book into your product's documentation requires that you abide by the terms of the software license agreement found in Appendix B, "Software License Agreement."

If you feel your use of code examples falls outside fair use or the permissions given here, feel free to contact me at tim@timaki.com.

Chapter 1

Introducing .NET

Welcome to .NET! I might as well have said, "Welcome to the universe," because like the universe, .NET is huge. And it's complex. And it's filled with black holes and other things that don't always make sense. Yet it (.NET, not the universe) turns out to be a fantastic system in which to develop software applications.

The .NET Framework was not developed in a vacuum (unlike the universe); Microsoft designed it and its related development languages—especially C# and Visual Basic—to address various issues that plagued Windows software developers and users. To fully understand why .NET was necessary, we need to take a short trip down computer memory lane.

Before .NET

Practical, general-purpose computers have been around since the mid-twentieth century. However, they were inaccessible to most people because (a) they cost millions of dollars; (b) they consumed gobs of electricity; (c) maintenance and programming could be done only by highly trained specialists; and (d) they tended to clash with the living room furniture.

Fast-forward about thirty years. IBM comes out with the "personal" computer. These "desktop" computers represented a great advance in technology, but only a minority of people ever used them. They continued to be expensive (thousands of dollars), and maintenance and programming still required significant investments in training. IBM PCs also looked hideous around the living room furniture.

Then came the Apple Macintosh. With its sleek design and its user-friendly functionality, it introduced the joy of computing to the masses. And while programming it was not always straightforward, it did give nice results. It's no wonder that Microsoft decided to copy—oops, I mean improve upon—its functionality.

Microsoft Windows 1.0 brought a greater level of usability to the IBM/Intel computing platform. But it wasn't a free ride for programmers. MS-DOS development was hard enough without the addition of the "message pumps" and the hundreds of Application Programming Interface (API) calls needed by Windows programs. Visual Basic 1.0, introduced in 1991, greatly simplified the development process, but with the advent of 32-bit systems, ActiveX and COM components, and the Web, even VB programmers soon felt overwhelmed.

Throughout the 1990s, the situation only seemed to worsen. Microsoft saw increased competition in the form of the Java™ language and the Linux operating system. Hackers were exploiting buffer overruns and other security issues present in the Windows platform. Users experienced myriad computer problems stemming from conflicting standards, competing data integration technologies, registry bloat, and "DLL hell." In frustration, an Excel user's group set fire to the entire Microsoft campus in Redmond.

Well, it didn't get that bad. But Microsoft did see that it needed to address the overall software development and usability issues on its beloved Windows platform. Its solution came in the form of the .NET Framework.

Back to Introducing .NET

When Microsoft announced its plans for .NET, it surprised many developers, including Windows programmers already using C and C++. Some derided it an attempt by Microsoft to play catch-up with Java, an admission that it was behind the times. But the release of the .NET Framework version 1.0 in 2002 did bring many needed benefits.

.NET introduced a unified programming environment

All .NET-enabled languages compile to Microsoft Intermediate Language before being assembled into platform-specific machine code. C#, Visual Basic, and other .NET languages are wrappers around this common .NET "language." Since all .NET-enabled compilers speak the same underlying language, they no longer suffer from the many data and language conflicts inherent in other cross-language component-based systems such as COM. The .NET version of Visual Studio also unified the standard user interface that lets programmers craft source code.

.NET committed developers to object-oriented technologies

Not only does .NET fully embrace the object-oriented programming paradigm, but *everything* in .NET is contained in an object: all data values, all source code blocks, and the plumbing for all user-initiated events. Everything appears in the context of an object.

.NET simplified Windows programming

Programming in C on Windows before .NET was not that hard, as long as you never needed to interact with the user. User interface development required a lot of dense, repetitive, boilerplate code, and access to convenient, centralized Windows features required the use of ever-evolving APIs and "magic numbers." With .NET, most of the regularly used APIs are replaced with a hierarchy of objects providing access to many commonly needed Windows features. Since the hierarchy is extensible, other vendors can add new functionality without disrupting the existing framework.

.NET enhanced security

Users and administrators can now establish security rules for different .NET features, to limit malicious programs from doing their damage. .NET's "managed" environment also resolves buffer overrun issues and memory leaks through features such as strong data typing and garbage collection.

.NET enhanced developer productivity through standards

The .NET Framework is built upon and uses many Internet-era standards, such as XML and SOAP. This enhances data interchange not only on the Windows platform, but also in interactions with other platforms and systems.

.NET enhanced web-based and mobile development

Until .NET, a lot of web-based development was done using scripting languages. .NET brings the power of compiled, desktop development to the Internet. As the framework has matured, its features have been extended to support mobile platforms, including on non-Microsoft operating systems.

If .NET is installed on a system, releasing a program can be as simple as copying its EXE file to the target system (although an install program is much more user-friendly). Features such as side-by-side deployment, ClickOnce deployment, the Windows Store, and Universal apps make desktop, web-based, and mobile deployments a snap.

If you didn't understand some of the terms used in this section, that's all right. You will encounter them again, with explanations, in later chapters.

The .NET Object

To fully understand software development in .NET, you must understand what an *object* is. (If you are familiar with object-oriented programming—OOP—you can probably skip down to the next section, although you will miss some really great content.) While some of this section's information will also appear in Chapter 8, it is so important to the discussion of .NET that a portion appears here as well.

Objects and Data

From a programming standpoint, a computer performs four basic tasks.

- It stores *data* in the computer's memory area.
- It supports processing of this *data* through basic operations, including addition and subtraction, Boolean algebra, and text string manipulation.
- It allows the user to interact with the *data* stored in memory.
- It provides a way to bring the *data* in and out of memory, through input and output devices such as keyboards and printers, and through long-term storage media such as hard drives.

The core of these four activities is *data*. Computers exist to manipulate data. Operating systems provide the basic foundation for these activities, but it is software applications that make these features—the ability to manipulate data—real and meaningful to the user. High-level programming languages are the primary tools used to develop these applications, each of which uses some general methods to make data manipulation features available to the programmer. Back in the good old days of assembly language development, if you knew the memory address of a piece of data, you could access and manipulate it directly. In early flavors of C and in most other "procedural" languages, data was accessed through *variables*.

As languages grew in complexity and purpose, so did their view of data. In the LISP (short for "*List Processing*" or "*Lots of Irritating Silly Parentheses*") language, for example, any data value exists within a larger *list* or *set* of data. But in .NET languages, data is viewed through the *object*.

Objects are collections of data values and associated source code. Dialects of the C language always included support for structures, which grouped related data elements together. But objects in OOP languages bring these structures alive by including embedded source code designed to manipulate the data values of that object.

Objects generally represent some *thing*, often a thing that has a real-world counterpart, whether physical or conceptual. For instance, your code may include a `House` object that has data *fields* or *properties* for the address, the exterior paint color, and the number of people living in the house. Associated source code could manage that data; a `Paint` *method* could alter the color value used for the exterior paint.

The data and code elements within an object are called *members*. Some members are hidden inside the object and can be accessed only by the object's source code. Other members are more public; any code in your application can use them, not just that subset of application code found inside the object. Consider a television as an object (see Figure 1-1).

Outside View   Inside View

Figure 1-1. A TV: it's an object, not just objectionable

The public members of a TV are generally easy to use: the power button, channel selector, volume control, and so on. They are the conduits through which the user controls the data values of the TV (its video and audio output). There are also hidden members inside the TV; you could use these members to impact the picture and sound quality, although this would be a bad idea for most users. You don't want me messing with the internal members of your TV set, trust me. In the same way, an object doesn't want code outside the object to mess with its internal members *except through the public members*. I don't care how a TV works internally, as long as I can get pictures and sound out of it by using the controls that are exposed (power, channel, volume).

Objects and Interfaces

The public members of an object represent its *interface*. If code outside the object wants to manipulate the data belonging to that object, it uses the members of the interface. It doesn't have to figure out the hidden members or how they work, and that's good. It's especially good if those internal members ever change for any reason, which happens more often than you think. Consider how the internals of TVs have changed just in the past few decades. Here's a drawing of the TV my family had when I was a kid. Compare it to modern flat-panel TVs available today (see Figure 1-2).

The TV of My Childhood   A New-Fangled Thing

Figure 1-2. Are those really TVs?

My family's TV was cool. It had an AM/FM stereophonic hi-fi radio, a turntable that could play 33-1/3, 45, and 78 rpm records, and a large 19-inch screen with a vivid, black-and-white, crystal-clear display. Two kids could hide behind it when playing hide-and-seek. And my friend who had the same model said that you could draw these really cool permanent lines on the screen with a magnet. Who cares that the speaker panels looked like vertical shag carpet? Who cares that the unit took up thirty percent of the floor space in the room? Who cares that you could cook sausages on top of it from the heat generated by the vacuum tubes? It was more than a TV; it was an *entertainment center*.

Now compare it to the wimpy little flat-panel job on its right. If you look closely, you find that the interface to the TV hasn't really changed much in four decades. There are still controls for power, volume, and channel selection (although Horizontal Hold and Vertical Hold are gone, sniff), although they are more commonly accessed via a handheld remote device rather than on the unit itself. What has changed is the internal configuration. Gone are the humming vacuum tubes, all replaced with efficient transistors and solid-state components. But it doesn't really make much difference to the TV viewer, since the public interface remains the same.

Objects in OOP development work in the same way. As long as the public interface remains the same, the object's actual code and internal data storage system—also known as the object's *implementation*—can change with no impact to the overall application.

Objects and Instances

The interface and implementation of an object really represent only its design; these are the parts the programmer creates through the source code. They exist even before the program is compiled and installed on the user's computer. In fact, at this level, objects really aren't even known as objects. In most languages (including C#), the word *class* indicates the implementation of an object's interface.

Once your application is installed on a computer and starts up, the code creates *instances* of the class to store actual data in memory. These instances are the true objects of OOP development. Depending on how your code is written, a single class implementation might be used to create one or even hundreds of objects in memory at the same time.

In .NET, all of your code and data values appear inside objects. Pretty much everything you see in a running .NET program is an object: a Windows form is an object; a list box control on that form is an object; and a single item in that list box is an object.

The Parts of the .NET Framework

Now you know all about objects, and you are probably thinking it's time to toss this book into the pile and start programming. But there are a few more parts of the .NET Framework still to discuss. These parts show up ad nauseam in the .NET documentation, and they each have a three-letter acronym (TLA), or thereabouts.

The Common Language Runtime

At the center of the .NET Framework is the *Common Language Runtime* (CLR), so named not because it is common or ordinary, but because all .NET-enabled languages share it in common. Everything you do in a .NET program is *managed* by the CLR. When you create a variable, thank the CLR and its data *management* system. When you say goodbye to a piece of data, thank the CLR and how it *manages* the release of data through its garbage collection system. Did you notice how the word *manage* keeps showing up in those sentences? My editor sure did. But "manage" is the mot juste, since that is what the CLR does. In fact, software written for the .NET Framework is called *managed code*. Any code that falls outside the CLR's control is known as *unmanaged code*. (C# allows you to write blocks of unmanaged code via its `unsafe` keyword. I won't be covering that feature in this book.)

The CLR is a lot like Los Angeles International Airport. If you have ever been to LAX, you know that there is a whole lot of activity going on. Airplanes arrive and depart each minute. Cars by the thousands enter and leave the two-level roadway and the central parking structures. People and pickpockets move constantly among the eight main terminals and the massive international terminal. There's a lot happening, but so much of it is managed. Planes cannot take off or land without approval from the control tower. Access points and gates manage the roadways and parking garages. Friendly, courteous TSA agents manage the flow of passengers and pickpockets into and out of the secure areas of the terminals.

The control and management structures in place at LAX ensure an orderly and secure flow of people between their planes and the city of Los Angeles. The control and management structures of the CLR ensure an orderly and secure flow of data between .NET code and the rest of the computer or connected network.

You'd probably like to know the secret of how the CLR is able to process programs written in any .NET language, including C#, Visual Basic, and FORTRAN. So would Microsoft's competitors. Actually, they do know, because there is no secret. All .NET-enabled languages convert (i.e., "compile") your source code into *Microsoft Intermediate Language* (or *MSIL*, pronounced "missile," and more commonly abbreviated as just *IL*). For those of you familiar with assembly language, it looks a lot like that. For those of you not familiar with assembly language, it looks a lot like gibberish. For example, here is some C# source code for a *console application* (a non-Windows text-based program, like the old MS-DOS programs) that simply outputs "Hello, World!" from a code procedure called *Main*.

```
namespace ConsoleApplication1
{
    class Program
    {
        static void Main(string[] args)
        {
            System.Console.WriteLine("Hello, World!");
        }
    }
}
```

That's the whole .NET program. When the Visual C# compiler converts it to MSIL, the *Main* procedure looks like this (slightly modified to fit on this page).

```
.method private hidebysig static
    void  Main(string[] args) cil managed
{
    .entrypoint
    // Code size       13 (0xd)
    .maxstack  8
    IL_0000:  nop
    IL_0001:  ldstr      "Hello, World!"
    IL_0006:  call
       void [mscorlib]System.Console::WriteLine(string)
    IL_000b:  nop
    IL_000c:  ret
} // end of method Program::Main
```

Yes, it is gibberish. But that's OK, because it fulfills the International Computer Book Association's requirement that every Chapter 1 include a "Hello, World" code sample. Also, the CLR understands it, and that's what really counts in .NET. As long as you can get your code into IL, .NET will process it. The Visual C# compiler just happens to generate IL for you. Other .NET language compilers, including Visual Basic, target IL as well. You can even write your own IL code, but you're probably reading the wrong book for that. Just to put your mind at ease, this will be the last bit of IL you will see in this book.

The Common Language Specification

Languages that claim to support .NET cannot just say so for any old reason. They truly have to be compatible with .NET and its workings. This is done through the *Common Language Specification* (CLS). The CLS defines a minimum set of features that a language must implement before it is considered to be .NET-compliant, or more accurately, CLS-compliant.

A language can go beyond that minimum if it wants, and .NET includes many additional features upon which language-specific features may be built. A language that implements only the minimum CLS-specified features may not be able to fully interact with components from languages that exceed the minimum specification. C# is, of course, CLS-compliant, and in fact it goes way beyond that minimum.

The Common Type System

Since the CLR is controlling your source code anyway, Microsoft thought it would be good to have it control the source code's data as well. The .NET Framework does this through its *Common Type System* (CTS), which defines all of the core data types and data mechanisms used in .NET programs. This includes all numeric, string, and Boolean value types. It also defines the *object*, the core data storage unit in .NET.

The CTS divides all objects into two buckets. The first bucket, called *value types*, stores actual data right in the bucket. If you have a 32-bit integer value, it gets put right in the value type bucket, ready for your immediate use. The other bucket contains *reference types*. When you look in this bucket, you see a map that tells you where to find the actual data somewhere else in the computer's memory. It seems like value types are easier to use, and they are, but they come with a few restrictions not imposed on reference types.

Programs and components written using the CTS standard can exchange data with one another without any hindrances or limitations. (A few .NET data types fall outside the core CTS types, but you need to avoid them only when you want to specifically interact with components that can use only the core CTS types.)

When you write your applications in Visual C#, most of your code will appear in *classes*. Classes are reference types that include both data values and associated code. The data values included in a class are most often the core CTS data types, but they can also contain objects that you design elsewhere in your application. C# also includes *structures*, the weaker yet quicker younger brother of classes. Structures implement value types, and also include both data and code.

Classes and structures are just two of the data/code types available in C#. *Interfaces* are class and structure skeletons; they include design details of what should appear in a related class or structure, but don't include any actual implementation or working code. *Delegates* define a procedure "signature" sans implementation, and are used to support *events*, those actions (initiated by the user, by the operating system, or by your code) that tell your code, "Get to work now!" *Sea otters* are aquatic mammals that are curiously related to the weasel, and like to eat sea urchins. *Enumerations* group a set of related integer values, generally for use as a list of choices.

In .NET parlance, all of these terms (class, structure, interface, delegate, and enumeration, but not sea otter) are known collectively as *types*. You probably already knew that .NET had some confusing elements in it; you wouldn't have bought a book about it if it were easy. But despite all the complex technology, it is this simple word, *type*, which causes the most confusion. You will likely experience some angst throughout this book each time you read it. The problem: it's too general. Not only does it refer to these core elements of the CTS, but it is also used when talking about just the C#-specific value types (more often called the C# "data types"). The nickname for structures is "user-defined types," yet another confusing use of "type." Arrrgh! Microsoft should have used some word other than *type* for the world of classes, interfaces, enumerations, and so on. "Banana" would have been a better choice since it is only sometimes used to discuss software. But "type" *is* the word, so you better get used to seeing it. I will try to include as much context as possible when using the word throughout this volume.

The members of a type usually consist of simple data fields and code procedures, but you can also include other types as members. That is, a class can include a *nested* class if it needs to. Only certain types support nesting—see Chapter 8 for details. I also talk about *access levels* in that chapter. Each member has an access level that says what code can use that member. There are five access levels, ranging from *public* (anybody and their brother can use the member) to *private* (you have to be inside the type to even know it's there).

Chapter 6 discusses the .NET type system in greater detail, including the information you crave on classes, structures, and other bananas.

.NET Class Libraries

Computers are actually quite stupid. Whereas I can count all the way to 17, a computer tops out at 1; it only knows the digits 0 and 1. The CPU includes a set of simple operators used to manipulate the digits 0 and 1, and a few more operators that compare 1s and 0s in complex ways. The computer's last great trick is its ability to move 0s and 1s into and out of memory, but whoop-de-doo. Sure it does these things at nearly the speed of light, but can it calculate π to three million decimal places?

Well, actually it can. Computers don't know anything about the letters of the alphabet, and they really can handle only the digits 0 and 1, yet here I am using a computer to write an award-winning book. It is the ability to combine the simple 1-bit data values and operators into increasingly complex *libraries* of functionality that makes useful computers possible.[1]

The .NET Framework is built upon decades of increasingly complex functionality. When you install the .NET Framework, the CLR and its associated type system represent the core of the framework. By itself, the framework includes all the basic functionality needed to let you add 2 and 2 together and correctly get 4. And as a business application developer, you spend a lot of time doing just that. But what if you want to do something more complex, something that you know some other programmer has already done, like sorting a list of names or drawing a colored circle on the screen? To get that answer, go to the *class libraries*, the .NET Class Libraries. These libraries, installed with the framework, include a lot of prewritten (increasingly complex) functionality that you don't have to write from scratch.

There are two key class libraries in .NET: the *Base Class Library* (BCL) and the *Framework Class Library* (FCL). The BCL is smaller, and contains the most essential features that a program just couldn't do without. It includes only those classes that are an absolute must for supporting applications on the framework if Microsoft were to, say, port the framework to Linux. (Good news! In 2015, Microsoft announced the availability of the .NET Framework on Linux and Mac OS platforms. This distribution uses a variation of the BCL called ".NET Core BCL.")

The FCL is larger, and includes everything else Microsoft thought you would want to have in your programs, but was not absolutely essential to have in the BCL. Don't even ask how many classes there are in the FCL; you don't want to know. I bet that Microsoft doesn't even really know the full number. I am convinced that those wacky pranksters at Microsoft have included gag classes in the FCL, but they are so deeply buried that few programmers ever encounter them.

With thousands (yes, thousands!) of classes, enumerations, interfaces, and other types included in the BCL and FCL, you would think that it would be hard to find just the class you need. But it's not that difficult, at least not overwhelmingly difficult. The .NET Framework includes a feature called *namespaces*. All types in .NET appear in a hierarchy—a tree-like structure—with just a few minimal entries at the root. Each *node* in the hierarchy is a namespace. You uniquely identify any class or other type in the libraries by naming all the namespaces, from the root down to the local namespace that contains the class, separating each node with a period (.).

Unlike most hierarchies that have all branches starting from a single root node, the .NET namespace hierarchy has multiple root nodes. The largest root namespace is named `System`. It includes many classes, but it also includes several next-tier hierarchy nodes (namespaces) designed for specific programming needs

---

[1] If you want to read a truly fascinating book on how complex software and hardware operations are formed from the most basic uses of 0 and 1, read Charles Petzold's *Code: The Hidden Language of Computer Hardware and Software* (Microsoft Press).

and targets. For instance, since the framework includes features for both Windows-based and web-based application development, there are namespaces that contain the Windows-specific and web-specific development features. These namespaces appear just within the *System* namespace, and are called *Windows* and *Web*. All code related to on-screen Windows Forms in the *Windows* namespace appears in the *Forms* namespace, and within this namespace is the actual class that implements a form, named *Form*. Figure 1-3 presents an image of this namespace subset.

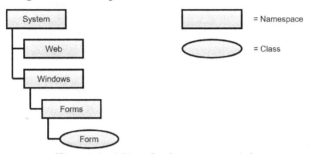

Figure 1-3. A hierarchy of namespaces and classes

In C#, you identify a class by qualifying it with all its namespaces, starting from its root namespace. The *Form* class has the following fully qualified name.

```
System.Windows.Forms.Form
```

All classes and types exist somewhere in the hierarchy, although not every class descends from *System*. When you create new projects in Visual C#, the name of the project is, by default, a new top-level node in the hierarchy. If you create a new Windows Forms application named *WindowsFormsApplication1*, the default *Form1* form has the following fully qualified name.

```
WindowsFormsApplication1.Form1
```

This new application's namespace is not just a second-class appendage hanging off the *System* namespace. It is fully integrated into the .NET namespace hierarchy; the *WindowsFormsApplication1* namespace is a root node, just like the *System* root node. Visual C# includes features that let you specify the namespace hierarchy for each class used in your application. You can even place your application's classes in a *System* namespace branch. Changing *WindowsFormsApplication1* to *System.MySuperApp* moves *Form1* to its new fully qualified location.

```
System.MySuperApp.Form1
```

If your application is actually a component or library destined for use in programs, your app's classes will appear in the namespace you specify when the other program loads your component into its application area. Your code will look like it is part of the Microsoft-supplied namespaces. Is that cool or what?

Although you can add your classes to the *System* namespace, you will incur the wrath of other .NET programmers. The *System* namespace is supposed to be for "system" (read: Microsoft-supplied) features, and that's it. Also, there's a chance that two vendors might use the same namespace path. So, to avoid potential namespace conflicts *and* dirty looks from other programmers, you should name your application's classes as follows.

```
CompanyName.ApplicationName.ClassName
```

A single class or other type cannot be split across multiple namespaces, even within the same hierarchy branch. However, two classes or types may share a common name in different namespaces, even within the same branch.

All classes of the BCL and FCL appear intermingled throughout the entire namespace hierarchy. This means that you cannot necessarily tell whether a particular class is from the BCL or the FCL. Frankly, it doesn't really matter; your code won't care which library a class comes from, as long as it is available for use on the user's workstation or device.

Several years ago, Microsoft made the source code for much of the Framework Class Library version 3.5 available for developers to review. This means that programmers who wanted to know how Microsoft sorted a list of names in memory or drew a colored circle on a display could get at least a partial glimpse of how it is done. In advance of the release of Visual Studio 2015, Microsoft announced that the entire .NET Framework library would become open-source, and available for both review and community-inspired updates. This release extended even to the source code for the Visual C# compiler itself.

Assemblies and Manifests

An *assembly* is a unit of deployment for the parts of a .NET application or library. In 99.9% of cases, an assembly is simply a .NET executable file (an *.exe* file, or platform-specific equivalent) or a .NET library of classes and other types (a *.dll* file). It is possible to split an assembly among multiple files, but usually it is one file for one assembly.

What makes an ordinary *.exe* or *.dll* file an assembly is the presence of a *manifest*. For single-file assemblies, the manifest appears right in the file; it can also appear in a file of its own. The manifest is a chunk of data that lists important details about the assembly, including its name, version information, default culture, information on referencing external assemblies and types, and a list of all the files contained in the assembly. The CLR will not recognize an assembly without its manifest, so don't lose it.

Assemblies can include an optional *strong name*. This helps to manage interactions between assemblies when one or more of them acts as a shared resource. The strong name uses public key cryptography to guarantee that the assembly is unique among similarly-named assemblies. Visual Studio and the .NET Framework include tools that let you add a strong name to an assembly.

When you deploy your application, you will normally place all assembly files, configuration files, and any related files specific to your application into the application's install directory (or into a deployment bundle for mobile distribution), just like in the old Jurassic days before .NET. Shared assemblies designed to be used by more than one application on a single machine can be stored in the *Global Assembly Cache* (GAC). All assemblies placed in the GAC must have strong names. Some systems may allow only the system administrator to add assemblies to the GAC.

Metadata and Attributes

Assemblies are brought to you by the letter *m*. In addition to manifests and type members, assemblies also contain *metadata*. The application code and data elements stored in an assembly parallel the code and data items found in the related C# source code; for each type and member in your source code, there is associated executable code in the deployed assembly. This makes sense, and is not much of a change from pre-.NET deployments. What is different is that the Visual C# compiler now attaches additional information—metadata—to each type and member in the assembly. This metadata documents the name of the associated content, information about required data types, information on class inheritance for the element, and security permissions required before the element can be used by the user or other software.

Your Visual C# source code can enhance the metadata for any element of your assembly through *attributes*. The metadata generated by an attribute is more than just some ID number. Attributes implement full .NET classes, with their own data values and associated logic. Any .NET code that knows how to process attributes can examine the attributes for a type or member and take action as needed. This includes Visual Studio, the Visual C# compiler, and your own custom applications.

How's this for a mundane example: the .NET Framework includes an attribute named *ObsoleteAttribute*. This attribute lets you mark types or members of your assembly as obsolete or no longer supported. (Visual Studio uses this attribute to display a warning whenever you attempt to use an out-of-date BCL or FCL feature.) To use the attribute, add it to a member of your application using square brackets.

```
class MyClassWithOldMembers
{
    [ObsoleteAttribute] public void DoSomeWork()
    {
    }
}
```

This code defines a single class (*MyClassWithOldMembers*) with a single member procedure (*DoSomeWork*), a procedure that clearly does some work. The procedure is tagged with the *ObsoleteAttribute* attribute. By custom, all attribute names end in the word *Attribute*. You can leave off this portion of the word if you wish, as long as the resultant word does not conflict with any C# language keyword.

```
[Obsolete] public void DoSomeWork()
{
}
```

When you compile the class and store it in an assembly, the *[ObsoleteAttribute]* attribute is stored as part of *DoSomeWork*'s definition. You can now write a separate Visual C# application that scans an assembly and outputs the name and status of every type and member it finds. When that analysis program encounters the obsolete member, it will detect *ObsoleteAttribute* in the metadata, and output the status.

```
DoSomeWork Procedure: Obsolete, don't use it!
```

Most attributes are designed with a specific purpose in mind. Some attributes instruct Visual Studio to display the members of a class in specific ways. You've probably already played with the form-editing features of Visual Studio to design a simple Windows desktop application. When you add a control (such as a button or a list box) to a form and select that control, Visual Studio lets you edit details of that control through the Properties panel area (see Figure 1-4).

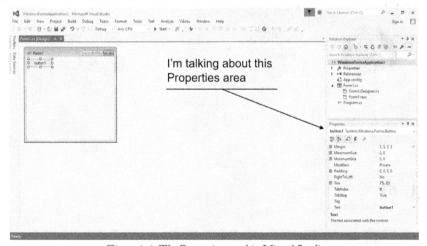

Figure 1-4. The Properties panel in Visual Studio

The Windows Forms `Button` control is implemented as a class, and many of its class members appear in the Properties panel, but not all of them. When the `Button` class was designed, attributes were added to its members that tell Visual Studio which members should appear in the Properties panel, and which should not. Visual Studio dutifully examines these attributes, and displays only the indicated properties.

Versioning

Like yours, my applications are perfect from their initial release, and I never have a reason to modify them or add features. But there are software development organizations—including one large company that, so as not to cause embarrassment, I will refer to only by its initial letter of *M*—that feel the need to one-up their competition by coming out with "improved" versions of their previously released software offerings. Let's say that "M" happened to have a popular word processor that includes version 1.0 of a spellcheck component. "M" also happens to sell an email tool that depends specifically on version 1.0 of that same shared component. If, in a show of competitive machismo, "M" releases an update to the word processor *and* the spellcheck component (now version 2.0), what happens to the email tool's spellchecking ability?

Not that this ever happens in real life. But if it did, the replacement of a vital shared component with a newer but somewhat incompatible version could cause real problems. A related problem is the deployment of multiple versions of a single component on the same workstation, all in different directories. Can any of them be safely deleted?

.NET solves these problems through *versioning*. All assemblies that use shared components identify exactly which versions of the shared components they require. Although an application can be reconfigured to use a later version, it will use only the originally specified version of a shared component by default.

Multiple versions of a single shared component can be added to the GAC, a feature called *side-by-side deployment*. The CLR ensures that the right application links up with the right component. You can even run applications simultaneously that use different versions of the same component.

From Source Code to EXE

Now you know pretty much everything there is to know about .NET except for that pesky programming thing. Before delving into some actual code, let's take a little snack break and examine the lifetime of an application, from start to finish (see Figure 1-5).

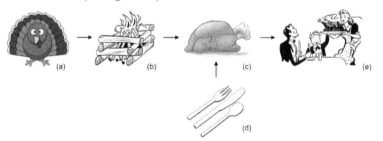

Figure 1-5. The real Visual C# development process

So, here's what happens, step by step.[2]

---

[2] The details of these steps differ somewhat when generating applications using Visual Studio's .NET Native technology.

1. You, as the programmer, are responsible for preparing the basic ingredients (a) of the application. For Visual C# programs, this means creating one or more source code files with a *.cs* extension. Your ingredients may also include other support files, such as resource files (text and graphics files, sometimes used for multi-language support).

2. Your application is cooked by the Visual C# compiler (b). The result is an assembly, complete with a manifest and metadata. The output is actually semi-compiled MSIL and includes ready-to-execute versions of the original source code's types and members, including all member and type names. All this content can be decompiled (returned back to full MSIL, although not to full C#) using a tool named *ildasm.exe* (the Microsoft Intermediate Language Disassembler), which is included with the .NET Framework. Since you probably don't want just anyone disassembling your application and looking at the code, Microsoft (and other third parties) also supplies an *obfuscator*, which sufficiently scrambles the content of your code to make it just difficult enough to discourage prying eyes.

3. The assembly (c) is deployed to the user's workstation or device. A few different methods are used to deploy the application, including (1) generating a standard Windows Installer setup package; (2) generating a ClickOnce deployment; (3) generating a Windows Store application package; or (4) performing an XCopy install, which involves nothing more than copying the EXE assembly itself to the destination machine. No matter which deployment method you choose, the core .NET components (d) must also be installed on the user's workstation or device.

4. The user eats—I mean runs—the program (e). The CLR does a final *just-in-time* (JIT) compile of the MSIL assembly, to prepare it for use on the local platform. It then presents the application to the user, and manages all aspects of the application while it runs. The user experiences a level of joy and satisfaction rarely encountered when using other software applications.

As with the preparation of a Thanksgiving meal, the actual development process is somewhat more involved than just reading a paragraph (or a recipe book) about it. But it's not so difficult that it can't be put in a book like this one.

What about Visual Studio?

Wait a minute, what about Visual Studio? That last section didn't even mention it. And it didn't need to, since *you do not need to use Visual Studio to develop, compile, deploy, or run Visual C# applications*. The entire .NET Framework—including the Visual C# compiler—is available for free from Microsoft's web site; download it and use it to develop and deploy applications that are every bit as powerful and complex as, well, Visual Studio.

The July 1983 issue of *Datamation* magazine includes an article from manly reader Ed Post, titled "Real Programmers Don't Use Pascal."[3] I highly recommend that you read this article, as it will help you quickly separate the real programmers from the "quiche eaters." And when you do, run away as fast as you can from the real programmers. Oh, sure, they can reconstruct your source code from the obfuscated .NET assembly, but they will be useless on a team project using Visual Studio.

A "real programmer" could code any .NET application using Notepad, and it would run. Actually, real programmers would use Emacs or vi instead of Notepad (since Windows does not include a keypunch interface), but the results would be the same. They would growl as you blissfully type away in Visual Studio's

---

[3] *Datamation* 29 (7): July 1983, pp. 263–265. I also found the text of the article on the Internet by doing a search on the title. A similar version of the text, with only minor editorial changes, also exists under the title "Real Programmers Don't Write Pascal."

elegant, well-designed, and fully customizable and extensible user interface. They would gripe and bare their cheese-cracker-with-peanut-butter-encrusted teeth at you while you use the IntelliSense and AutoCompletion features built into the Visual Studio code editor. They would consume another slice of quiche-shaped cold pizza while you drag-and-drop both Windows and web-based user interfaces.

Yes, the real programmer could generate full applications with just a text (or hex) editor and a .NET compiler, but you would get the glory, since you would be done in a fraction of the time it would take the FORTRAN lover to eek out his code. Fortunately, the decision to use Visual Studio is easy, especially since the Community Edition of Visual Studio 2015 is offered gratis by Microsoft. While it lacks some of the team-specific enterprise features of the full-price edition, it's sufficient for most individuals and small teams.

Visual Studio 2015

Since this is a book on Visual C# development and not on Visual Studio usage, I won't be delving too much into Visual Studio's features or its user interface elements. It is a great application, and its tight integration with the .NET Framework makes it the best tool for developing applications with .NET. But as the real programmer would tell you, it is really just a glorified text editor. Visual Studio hides a lot of the complexity of .NET code, and its automatic generation of the code needed to build your application's user interface is a must-have. Most of its features exist to simplify the process of adding code to your application.

Although I will not be including a twenty-page review of Visual Studio right here, you will find images of Visual Studio throughout the text, placed so as to advance your understanding of the topics under discussion in each chapter. When you fire up Visual Studio for the first time, it displays the Start Page. (See Figure 1-6. The screenshots in this book are taken from the Visual Studio 2015 Community Edition.)

Figure 1-6. The Visual Studio Start Page

Visual Studio 2015 is the eighth major release of the product since .NET's initial introduction in 2002. Each release corresponds to a related release of the .NET Framework (version 1.0 in 2002, up through version 4.6 in 2015) and the Visual C# compiler. The 2015 release of Visual Studio is major. It is packed with new usability features, a brand new compiler, and comes in three delicious flavors.

Visual Studio 2015 Community Edition

Before Visual Studio's 2015 release, the entry-level tier of the product ("Express Editions") existed for true beginners and hobbyists who just wanted to play around with .NET, or develop simple programs without the expense of the professional-level Visual Studio offerings. Because the many Express Editions included the core .NET Framework libraries and associated compilers, you could still create full-powered applications, but some of the advanced programmer-sustaining tools were absent. With the move to Visual Studio 2015 and its Community Edition starting point, many of those limits are gone. In fact, today's Community Edition is not that different from the costly Professional Editions of the past.

Microsoft still offers Express editions of the product, with distinct downloads for Desktop, Web, and Windows 10 ("Metro"-like) development targets. However, since the Community Edition is more powerful, more standardized to Visual Studio tools, and just as free, Microsoft doesn't really like to talk about the Express Editions anymore. Feel free to ignore them.

Visual Studio 2015 Professional Edition

The Professional Edition is the first paid tier of Visual Studio, available through a monthly subscription plan. It includes all of the core functionality from the Community Edition, and adds a portion of Microsoft's Team Foundation and Business Intelligence components. You also get Microsoft Office development components right in the box, which require a separate (though still free) download in the Community Edition. The Professional Edition also comes with CodeLens, a source code analysis tool integrated into Visual Studio that lets you see how every bit if source code is related to pretty much every other piece of source code in your project. When you are ready to leave the comfort of learning Visual C# and move on to the hard labor of getting paid to develop software in Visual Studio, it comes in handy.

Visual Studio 2015 Enterprise Edition

The crème de la crème of the Visual Studio product line is the Enterprise Edition. It includes features needed by development teams that work on projects together, features such as testing management and data architecture tools. Visual Studio Team Foundation Server 2015, a separate product, can be installed on a shared server, and enhances the features of the Enterprise Edition package.

Microsoft also offers a separate *Visual Studio Test Professional* product that includes some of the Enterprise Edition's testing functionality, but lacks the core programming elements that make this book such an awesome Visual Studio complement. *Visual Studio Code*, a new offering from Microsoft in 2015, is a cross-platform source code editor that runs on Windows, Mac OS, and Linux. It lets you edit source code from a variety of traditional and web-centric languages and data formats in a setting reminiscent of Visual Studio, but without a lot of the non-editor portions normally found in an integrated development environment.

Beyond the hype of having a shiny new 2015 edition of the product line, Visual Studio 2015 includes several new features that make it more useful than the previous 2013 release. Microsoft had released some of these new features as updates to earlier releases of Visual Studio, but they are now fully integrated into the 2015 product.

The Roslyn Compiler

Originally, the .NET language compilers were glorified meat grinders: stick source code in, get MSIL out. You didn't want to look too far inside the mechanics of how they worked, or worse, stick your fingers inside. That all changed with the Roslyn product. First announced in 2011, Roslyn is a new compiler technology that you can control, like a Lego set once the instructions have been lost. The C# and Visual Basic compilers have been completely rewritten as part of Roslyn, and you now have the ability to inject your own compilation rules into the code generation process. Not that you would want to, at least for most basic development tasks. But Roslyn also enables live scripting scenarios using the core .NET languages, and is the basis for many of the new code analysis features now included with Visual Studio.

Updates to Core Languages

Although distinct from Visual Studio itself, the core .NET languages (Visual Basic, C#, C++, and now F#) are typically updated in tandem with the Visual Studio release cycle. Microsoft used the integration of C# and Visual Basic with the Roslyn compiler to endow these languages with new features that developers had been clamoring for. You'll meet many of the new features specific to Visual C# through the pages of this book.

Enhanced Cross-platform Development Environment

A few months after taking over as Microsoft's CEO, Satya Nadella announced that it was pulling back on its Windows-first worldview, and soon began a series of product announcements that moved the focus away from Windows to other platforms like iOS and Android. This shift extends to Microsoft's development tools. Visual Studio 2015 includes new cross-platform development and debugging tools, enhanced by integrations with popular mobile platforms like Xamarin (for .NET development on non-Windows systems), Unity (for mobile game development), and Apache Cordova (for HTML and JavaScript applications). You can even develop and compile native applications for the iPhone using .NET, as long as you have access to a networked Macintosh.

Support for Universal Apps

A natural extension of Microsoft's new cross-platform push is its introduction of Universal Apps, programs that can run on a variety of formerly incompatible systems. The target systems include traditional Microsoft Windows PCs, Windows Phone platforms, and XBox systems, among others. Visual Studio 2015 targets the new Universal Windows Platform through new pan-platform project types.

Support for .NET Native

The managed elements of the .NET platform drive a lot of its functionality, but they also add a layer of complexity that can bog down large applications. In 2014, Microsoft introduced .NET Native, a variation of the C# and Visual Basic compilation processes that optimizes Windows Store apps so that they (in theory) run as fast as unmanaged programs developed in more traditional languages like C++.

New Code Analysis Tools

As discussed above, the Roslyn compiler enables new code analysis features that help programmers hunt, maim, and eventually murder code bugs. These tools include the aforementioned CodeLens integration, and a new "light bulb" feature that gives you code improvement hints as you type.

Despite all these great new features, Microsoft still refuses to implement the most requested Visual Studio feature, Procedure AutoCompletion, in which Visual Studio would create the entire content of a source code procedure based on your entry of its name and the use of the Ctrl-Space key combination. Instead, Microsoft fritters away its time on other so-called productivity features. With Procedure AutoCompletion, you could write entire applications in minutes. Until that feature becomes available, you and I will have to continue writing software, crafting the quality code that users have come to expect from our fingers.

Summary

Developers created applications for the Windows platform for years without realizing that they were doing it the hard way. When .NET appeared, it removed many of the complexities of Windows programming while retaining all of the power and flexibility. Visual C# 2015, through its association with the .NET Framework, provides access to the programming tools needed to develop quality applications for the Windows desktop, the Internet, mobile devices, and the upcoming Internet of Things (IoT).

And Microsoft is not halting this progress with the 2015 release. Now that the language compilers and framework are open source, the expanded collection of eyes peering at the central code will drive new innovations and features needed for the future of technology.

Project

Welcome to the Project section, the part of each chapter where you have an opportunity to get hands-on with Visual Studio 2015 and C#. Development of the Library Project, the main project focus of this book, formally begins in Chapter 3, but there's still project work to do in the meantime. In this chapter, I'll introduce you to the sample source code provided with this book, and we'll take a stab at using it.

Since most Project sections, including this one, will involve Visual Studio, make sure you have it installed and ready to use. Also, since each Project section is designed for you to use interactively with the supplied sample code, I will assume that you have downloaded and installed the source code (see Appendix A, "Installing the Software," for instructions), and are viewing the source code with one eye while you read this section with the other. I will print sections of the code in the book, but with tens of thousands of code lines in the Library Project, I will not be able to include every line here. You will certainly get a lot out of each Project section by simply reading it, but you will get even more if you have access to the full source code.

Visual Studio is abundantly configurable. It includes dozens of toolbars and information panels that you can show and hide to your heart's content, some of which I'll introduce here and in upcoming chapters. You can also adjust the main menus, keyboard shortcuts, display colors, and default settings in a way that will bring anyone who uses a different configuration to tears. Most of these settings are accessible through Visual Studio's Options form. While I use a fairly vanilla configuration that adheres closely to the default C# settings, I did made changes on the Options form that impact some of the step-by-step instructions I provide throughout the book. Feel free to make these changes in your edition of Visual Studio.

- Access the Options form by selecting the Tools→Options menu command. When the form appears, it includes a hierarchy of settings sections along the left side of the form.
- In the Projects and Solutions→General section, I cleared the Always Show Solution field. Visual Studio software projects appear within the context of *solutions*. Solutions are quite convenient in multi-project scenarios, but they are less useful for standalone projects. Since most of the projects we'll create in the book are independent, clearing this field hides some of the unnecessary solution features.
- On that same panel, I cleared the Save New Projects When Created field. Doing so lets you create temporary test projects in memory without clogging up your hard disk with all the files from these ephemeral projects.
- When you are finished with your option changes, click the OK button.

In this chapter's project, we'll load a sample program into Visual Studio and run it. There are two ways to do this. The first way is just to open the existing project directly from the installation directory. Browse to the directory where you installed this book's source code, open the Chapter 1 subdirectory, and double-click the *Chapter1.csproj* file. This will open the project directly in Visual Studio, ready to use.

The second way is to use the chapter-specific project templates to create new projects in Visual Studio. You copied these templates into your Visual Studio project templates folder during the book's software installation process, which in turn added new entries to Visual Studio's New Project dialog window. Each of these project templates can be used as the starting point for a new Visual C# project. To load the Chapter 1 sample program using the template, start Visual Studio. The Start Page will appear, as shown way back in Figure 1-6. From the File menu, select New, then Project to display the New Project dialog window (see Figure 1-7).

Figure 1-7. The New Project dialog window: so many choices

Your New Project dialog window may differ slightly depending on the features you chose to install with Visual Studio. A tree of template categories appears along the left side of the form, with individual project templates displayed in the main center list. Figure 1-8 shows the various default project types you can create in Visual C#, including Windows Forms Application (a standard desktop application for the Windows platform), Class Library (a DLL of class-defined features), and Console Application (command-line, text-based applications). To create a new application, first select the project category, select the template to use, and finally enter the name of the new project in the Name field. Clicking the OK button creates a new project.

To use the sample Chapter 1 project, select the *Start-to-Finish C# 2015* entry within the *Visual C#* template category, and then select *Chapter 01 Sample* from the list of templates (see Figure 1-8). Finally, click OK to create the new sample project.

Figure 1-8. Selecting the Chapter 1 Sample project

Once the project loads, access the program's main form by double-clicking on the *Form1.cs* file in the Solution Explorer (see Figure 1-9).

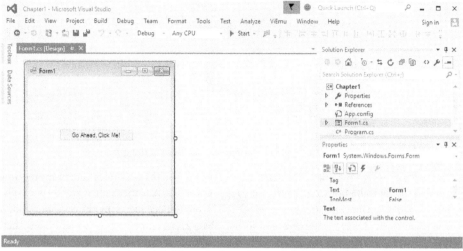

Figure 1-9. The main form of the sample application

This typical presentation of Visual Studio includes three editing components: (1) the main editing area, where the view of `Form1` appears; (2) the Solution Explorer panel, which provides access to all files included in the project; and (3) the Properties panel, which lets you edit various aspects of the currently selected item in the main editor area or elsewhere in the user interface.

The sample project is pretty basic. It includes one form with a single action button. Clicking this button in the running application displays a simple message. Run the project by pressing the F5 key. When the main form appears, clicking on the "Go Ahead, Click Me!" button displays the message in Figure 1-10 (goal, sweet goal).

Figure 1-10. Hello again, world!

So, what about all that complex code I had to write to develop this amazing form? It's all there for the viewing. From the Solution Explorer panel, right-click on the *Form1.cs* entry and select View Code from the shortcut menu. (For many of the source code samples presented in this book, I have had to slightly adjust the code so that it displays properly on the printed page. Generally, this involves splitting a long logical line into two or more shorter ones.)

```
using System;
using System.Windows.Forms;

namespace WindowsFormsApplication1
{
```

```csharp
public partial class Form1 : Form
{
    public Form1()
    {
        InitializeComponent();
    }

    private void button1_Click(object sender, EventArgs e)
    {
        MessageBox.Show("Hello, World!");
    }
}
```

We'll get into the intricacies of such code in later chapters, but here is the gist.

- The various *using* statements tell C# that you plan to use features from one or more namespaces, but don't want to be bothered typing the long, cumbersome names repeatedly throughout the file.
- The *namespace* line indicates where in the .NET namespace hierarchy the enclosed code appears.
- The main form, *Form1*, is represented in code by a class, named *Form1*. The boilerplate content that Visual Studio created for this default form includes initialization code.
- The form's declaration includes the word "Form" just after a colon on its first line. This colon establishes the inheritance relationship between this new Form1 class and the previously written *System.Windows.Forms.Form* class. (The "System.Windows.Forms" namespace prefix is left out since a *using* statement at the top of the file provides a shortcut.) *Form* is the base class and *Form1* is the derived class; *Form1* inherits all the functionality of the *Form* class, including its initial look and feel. I'll discuss these class relationships in more detail in Chapter 8.
- The form sports a command button named *button1* that exposes a *Click* event. This event is handled by the *button1_Click* procedure, a member of the *Form1* class.
- The *event handler*, *button1_Click*, includes a single statement, a call to the *MessageBox.Show* method. This statement presents the ever-friendly message box to the world.

That's all the code that I wrote for *Form1.cs*. It sure seems pretty short for all the work it does. There has to be more code hiding somewhere. And sure enough, a half dozen or so additional files are included in the project. Visual Studio positions these files within hierarchical groups, especially in cases where it manages content in subordinate files on your behalf. To view the subordinate files associated with *Form1*, expand it by clicking on the small triangle to the left of the *Form1.cs* item (see Figure 1-11).

Figure 1-11. Viewing subordinate files through the Solution Explorer

Double-click on the *Form1.Designer.cs* entry to see the code that Visual Studio automatically wrote for this form. (Dramatic pause.) Wow! Look at all that scary code. (If you don't see "all that scary code," click on the plus sign to the left of the "Windows Forms Designer generated code" message in the middle of the content.) Actually, it's not that bad. Here in Chapter 1, it's not really necessary to comprehend it all, but there are a few interesting lines to note. I'm including line numbers to make it easier to find the matching code in Visual Studio. If you want to view line numbers in Visual Studio, follow these steps.

1. Select the Tools→Options menu item to display Visual Studio's options.
2. Select Text Editor→C#→General from the tree view to the left.
3. Select (check) the Line Numbers field on the right.
4. Click OK to apply the changes.

If you're new to Visual C# or .NET programming, don't worry now if this code doesn't make sense; it will all become clear as you pass through the pages of this book.

```
03   partial class Form1
```

Did you see the word *partial* right there on line 03? I know I did. Hey, wait a minute; *partial class Form1* also appeared in the *Form1.cs* file, but with the *public* keyword in front of the *partial* keyword. Visual C# 2015 includes a feature that lets you divide a single class (*Form1* in this case) among multiple source code files by including the *partial* keyword before each part. Pretty cool, eh? It allows Visual Studio to add complex initialization code for your form (as found in this *Form1.Designer.cs* file) without it bothering your main source code file (*Form1.cs*).

```
58   private System.Windows.Forms.Button button1;
```

Line 58 defines the "Go Ahead, Click Me!" button that appears in the center of the form. All controls that appear on your form are separate instances of classes. (*private* is a declaration statement described in Chapter 6.) This line doesn't actually create an instance of the *Button* class; that happens back on line 31.

```
31   this.button1 = new System.Windows.Forms.Button();
```

The *new* keyword creates new instances of classes. In this case, that new instance is assigned to the *button1* class member defined on line 58. At this moment, *button1* is a default instance of the *Button* class; it doesn't have any of its custom settings, such as its size and position, or the "Go Ahead, Click Me!" display text. All of that is set in lines 36 to 41.

```
36   this.button1.Location = new System.Drawing.Point(64, 104);
37   this.button1.Name = "button1";
38   this.button1.Size = new System.Drawing.Size(152, 23);
39   this.button1.TabIndex = 0;
40   this.button1.Text = "Go Ahead, Click Me!";
41   this.button1.UseVisualStyleBackColor = true;
42   this.button1.Click +=
         new System.EventHandler(this.button1_Click);
```

The last line in this block, line 42, establishes the link between the button's *Click* event and the *button1_Click* event handler procedure that appears in the main *Form1.cs* file. Without this connection, nothing would happen when the user clicked the button.

Finally, the button is glued onto the form on line 49.

```
49   this.Controls.Add(this.button1);
```

This adds the *button1* instance to the list of controls managed by *Form1*. The *this* keyword used throughout this code refers to the *Form1* class itself, so *this.button1* refers to the *button1* class member specifically in the current *Form1* class.

Most of the code in this file appears in the *InitializeComponent* member procedure.

```
29   private void InitializeComponent()
30   {
        ...
54   }
```

When Visual C# creates an instance of *Form1* to display on the screen, it calls the *InitializeComponent* procedure to do the work of adding the controls to the form. Actually, Visual C# calls the form's *constructor*, which in turn calls *InitializeComponent*. Constructors are special class members that perform any needed initialization on a class instance. They are called automatically by .NET each time a class instance is created. In C#, all constructors share the name of the class that defines them, as with the following code.

```
public class ClassWithConstructor
{
    public ClassWithConstructor()
    {
        // ----- All initialization code goes here.
    }
}
```

You might have seen something like that before. Actually, I know you did, if you looked through the code for *Form1.cs*. The form's main code includes the constructor, which in turn calls *InitializeComponent*.

```
public partial class Form1 : Form
{
    public Form1()
    {
        InitializeComponent();
    }
```

Speaking of initializing things, one wonders, as one often does at times like this, what prompted the initialization of *Form1* in the first place. Since the constructor is only called when a class is instantiated, what instantiated *Form1*? One need only look in another of the project's source files, *Program.cs*. Like the console application we looked at earlier, this file includes a *Main* procedure, a requirement in all C# programs (at least for Windows desktop and console apps), and the starting point for these programs. *Main* contains the startup code for the program, including the code that instantiates a *Form1* object.

```
static void Main()
{
    Application.EnableVisualStyles();
    Application.SetCompatibleTextRenderingDefault(false);
    Application.Run(new Form1());
}
```

I'll talk more about this startup code in Chapter 7, and the general topic of constructors in Chapter 8.

Well, that's pretty much the entire code, at least the part that matters to us now. Although we will rarely, if ever, examine the Visual Studio-generated code for the forms in the Library Project, it's good to see what's going on behind the scenes. The crazy part to understand is that, even though you can drag-and-drop a form and its user interface controls using a mouse, Visual Studio generates standard C# source code behind the scenes. This code, not some magic image creator, produces what you see on screen. You could craft this code yourself if you really wanted to, but it's nice to have a computer do most of the work for you. That's why we created them.

Now, turn to Chapter 2, where I delve into the C# language itself.

Introducing C#

In the beginning was C. C came from B, and B from BCPL, so how can C be the beginning? And yet, here we are, learning a language that is based on the famous C Programming Language. Originally created in 1972 as the core development language for Bell Labs' UNIX operating system, C went on to enjoy a long and successful life, and begot many language offspring, including C++, Java, Objective-C, Perl, and even parts of Visual Basic. Oh yeah, and also C#.

C was an important general purpose "procedural" programming language, and continues in use to this day. Syntactically, it was bare-bones and simplistic. And yet that very simplicity made it a great starting point for more feature-rich languages. C# is one of those feature-laden languages, enhancing C's procedural syntax with object-oriented, functional, and dynamic programming methodologies, features that we'll learn about throughout these pages. Despite all of these enhancements, C# is still a straightforward, general-purpose language, and a good tool for creating desktop, web-based, and mobile applications.

A Brief History of C#

Anders Hejlsberg and his team at Microsoft began work on the C# language in 1999, as part of Microsoft's overall vision for the .NET platform. Initially called "Cool" (for "C-like Object Oriented Language"), C# came into being to help overcome some of the problems inherent in Windows platform development. C was one of the main languages for Windows development back then, and despite C's simplicity (or because of it), the language was a playground for all types of bugs, especially those related to loose memory management policies. C#'s *managed* approach to data—the language itself controlled the lifecycle of all data values used by an application—brought a new level of safety in programming, freeing developers to focus more on an application's overall logic and less on the boilerplate nature of data management.

Microsoft officially unleashed C# to the world in 2002 as part of its initial Visual Studio .NET rollout. The language was tightly bound to the .NET Framework, and as .NET has improved over the years, C# has improved with it, gaining amazing new abilities every two or three years. Visual Studio 2015 includes version 6.0 of the C# language. It's packed full of features, many of which you will discover in these chapters. But Microsoft isn't resting on its laurels, as painful as that would be. Version 7.0 is already under development, and this time around, the changes are open to public scrutiny. As part of its move to a more collaborative strategy, Microsoft has made the C# language and its underlying "Roslyn" compiler open-source. You can follow the changes on the compiler's GitHub web site, https://github.com/dotnet/roslyn. But enough fawning. Let's start learning about the language.

C# from the Inside Out

As a general-purpose development language, Visual C# includes gobs of features that allow you to develop just about any type of application supported by the Microsoft Windows platform, plus some new targets outside the Microsoft family. As such, all of its features could never be covered in a concise, twenty- or thirty-page chapter, and I won't try. What I will do in this chapter is introduce you to the basics of the language, and its core features. Features not covered in this chapter are discussed throughout the rest of the book. It has to be that way, since I don't want you to finish this chapter and then say to yourself, "That Tim Patrick is so amazing. I learned all I needed to know about Visual C# in one chapter; I didn't even have to read the rest of the book." My publisher would not be amused.

In the remainder of this chapter, I will take the from-the-inside-out approach, starting the discussion with the core concepts of logic and data, and adding layer after layer of C# functionality as you turn the pages.

The Basics of Logic and Data

Lest you forget it, let me remind you again: computers are not really very smart. They know how to do only the simplest of tasks. If you want them to do anything remotely complex, you have to give precise, step-by-step instructions down to moving individual bits of data—only 1s and 0s, remember—around in memory. Fortunately, most of the code you would ever need at that low level has already been written for you, and incorporated into the Windows operating system and the .NET Framework. Microsoft- and third-party-supplied code libraries give you a lot of prewritten functionality that's available for use in your own programs. And that's good, because you would rather be hurtled into space on a giant bungee cord than have to write business applications at the *machine code* level all day long.

Even though you have all this great prewritten code in your arsenal, you still have to tell the computer precisely what you want it to do, in fine detail, or it won't do it. And that's where *high-level languages* like C# come in. They provide the grammar you need to communicate with the computer. For any given task that the computer needs to perform, your job as a programmer is to determine the individual steps to accomplish that task—the *logic*—and translate those steps into computer-ese using the programming language.

As an example, let's say you receive a request from the sales department for a program that will reverse all the letters in any chunk of text provided to the program. "Our customers are clamoring for this; we need it by Tuesday," they say. OK, so first you figure out the logic, and then you implement it in C#. Using *pseudocode*, an artificial programming language that you make up yourself to help you write programs, you can sketch out the basics of this task (with leading line numbers).

```
01  Obtain the original text (or string) from the user.
02  If the user didn't supply any content, then quit now.
03  Prepare a destination for the reversed string, empty for now.
04  Repeat the following until the original string is empty:
05  [Start of repeat section]
06    Copy the last character from the remaining original string.
07    Put that character onto the end of the destination string.
08    Shorten the original string, dropping the last character.
09  [End of repeat section]
10  Show the user the destination string.
```

You could write this logic in many ways; this is just one example. You can now convert this pseudocode into your language of choice; in this case, C# (don't worry about the syntax details for now).

```
01   originalText = GetUserInput("Enter text to reverse.");
02   if (originalText.Length == 0)
        return;
03   finalText = "";
04   while (originalText != "")
05   {
06      oneCharacter = originalText[originalText.Length - 1];
07      finalText += oneCharacter;
08      originalText = originalText.Substring(0,
            originalText.Length - 1);
09   }
10   MessageBox.Show("The reverse is: " + finalText);
```

This *source code* is now ready to be used in a Visual C# program. And it also demonstrates several essential aspects of coding.

- The individual steps of the step-by-step instructions are called *statements*. In C#, each statement typically appears on a line by itself, terminated by a semicolon. More complex statements appear on a single line, followed by a subordinate statement, or by a group of statement lines within curly braces. But like driving on the road instead of the sidewalk, this is a tradition-only rule. C# is completely hands-off when it comes to enforcing the line-statement rule. Statements are based on syntax, and the use of semicolons and curly braces. You could place the entire block of code above on a single physical line and it would still work. You could also put each space-separated element on a line all its own and the compiler would not complain. Notice how line 08 is split across two physical lines. You could also have broken it out like this.

  ```
  originalText              =
  originalText      .Substring(
  0,                originalText.
  Length                    - 1
  )                         ;
  ```

  Ugly yet valid.[4] When a single statement is spread across multiple lines in this manner, the entire statement is sometimes called a *logical line*. Since a single logical line often includes only a single primary C# action (such as the `if` or `while` action, or the various assignment actions using the equals sign [=]), these actions are also referred to as statements.

- The statements in the code are processed one at a time, from top to bottom. However, certain statements alter the normal top-to-bottom flow of the program, as is done with the `while` block on lines 04 through 09 of the sample code. Such statements are called *flow control* statements, and include loops (repeating a block of code), conditions (optionally processing a block of code based on a comparison or calculated result), and jumps (moving immediately to some other section of the code).

- Data can be stored in *variables*, which are named containers for data values. The sample code block includes three variables: *originalText*, *oneCharacter*, and *finalText*, all of which store text (string or character) data. The .NET Common Type System (CTS) allows you to create variables for four primary types of basic data values: text (both single characters and longer strings), numbers (both integer and decimal values), dates (and times), and Booleans (true or false values). You can also build more complex types of data by grouping the basic types.

---

[4] In the C programming community, the International Obfuscated C Code Contest is an annual contest that offers prizes based on the ability to manipulate style and logic in ways that confound and amaze other developers. Visit the ioccc.org web site for examples.

- Data is stored in a variable through an *assignment*. Generally, this involves placing a variable name on the left side of an = assignment operator, and putting the data or calculation to store in that variable on the right side of that same equals sign. The statement `finalText = ""` on line 03 stores an empty string (`""`) in the variable `finalText`. The `+=` assignment operator on line 07 shows a slightly different assignment syntax.
- Statements can include *function calls*, blocks of prewritten functionality, all squished down into a single name. Function calls do a bunch of work, and then *return* a final result, a data value. Function names are followed by a set of parentheses, which may include zero or more *arguments*, additional data values supplied by the calling code that the function uses to generate its result.

    The sample code includes some examples of function calls, including the `GetUserInput` function on line 01. This function, which I would need to create elsewhere in the code, supposedly displays a form into which the user types a response, which is then returned for use by the calling code. In the sample, the response from the user is stored in the `originalText` variable. As shown in this sample, it accepts a single argument: the message string that informs the user how to respond to the `GetUserInput` prompt. How this function works internally is irrelevant to the statement on line 01. All that matters is that the message passed into it gets displayed to the user, and any data supplied by the user comes back.

    When you use a function in your source code, the function acts a little like a variable; all the text of the function call, from the start of its name to the end of its closing parenthesis, could be replaced by a variable that contained the same resulting data. Function calls cannot appear on the left-hand side of an assignment statement, but they can appear almost anywhere else that a variable can appear. For example, consider the following code that tests the result of a function call.

    ```
    success = DoSomeWork(targetDate);
    if (success == false)
        MessageBox.Show("Fail.");
    ```

    This code could be compressed in a way that makes the `success` variable unnecessary, using the output of the `DoSomeWork` function itself like a variable.

    ```
    if (DoSomeWork(targetDate) == false)
        MessageBox.Show("Fail.");
    ```

- In addition to functions, C# also includes procedures. *Procedures* bundle up prewritten code in a named package, just like functions, but they don't return a value. They must be used as standalone statements; you cannot use them where you would use a variable or a function call. The call to `MessageBox.Show` on line 09 is a typical example of a procedure call in use. (`MessageBox.Show` is actually a function, but in this code it is masquerading as a procedure; more on that later.)
- The sample code makes frequent use of class members to process its data. The `Length` property on line 02 and the `Substring` method on line 08 are members of the string data class, of which `originalText` is an instance. Members are always accessed by hanging them off the object that defines them, separated by a period ("`.`").

The sample code listed previously could be made a little more efficient. But it would still use the same basic syntax of statements, members, and assignments that appear in the current code.

Data Types and Variables

Take my data . . . please! Ha, ha, that one always cracks me up. But it's actually what I ask my Visual C# application to do: take data from some source (keyboard, hard disk, Internet, etc.) and present it in some useful way. All programs I write will actively manage at least some data in memory. Each data value is stored in a specific area of the computer's memory, as determined by the Common Language Runtime (CLR). The statements in C# exist primarily to manage and manipulate this data in useful and complex ways.

All data managed by the CLR is stored in the computer's memory, with each data value separated and protected from all others. It's as though each data value had its own individual teacup, as in Figure 2-1.

Figure 2-1. All types of teacups and data

All data values managed by the CLR have *content* and *type*. Content is the actual data: the text string "abc," the number 5, a sales invoice, orange pekoe. Whatever you put in the teacup, that's the content. In some cases, .NET allows you to store absolutely nothing in the teacup (for reference types as described shortly, or nullable value types as described in Chapter 6).

Type indicates the kind of content stored in the teacup. In Figure 2-1, this is shown by the shape of each teacup. Each teacup has limits on the type of data that can be poured into the teacup: a text string, an integer number, a customer invoice.

Literals

Some basic data values, such as numbers and text strings, can be entered into your source code and used just as they are. For instance, the *MessageBox.Show* procedure displays a window with a supplied text message.

```
MessageBox.Show("The answer is " + 42);
```

This statement includes a *literal string*, "The answer is," and a *literal integer* value, 42. (The "+" symbol is an operator that connects two values together into a new string.) Literals are used once, and then they're gone. If I wanted to show the same "The answer is 42" message again, I would have to once again type the same literal values into a different part of the source code.

C# supports several types of basic literals. *String literals* are always surrounded by quote marks. If you want to include a quote mark itself in the middle of a string, put a backslash symbol before it.

```
"This is \"literally\" an example."
```

The backslash syntax enables a few more special features, but I'll fill you in on those details in Chapter 6. String literals can be really, really long, up to about two billion characters in length; if you were to type just one character per second, it would take more than sixty-three years to reach the maximum string length. C# also includes a *character literal* that is exactly one character in length; if you were to type just one character per second, well, never mind. These character literals use single quotes instead of the double quotes of full text strings. The character literal "A" is entered as follows.

```
'A'
```

Eleven different kinds of numeric data values—both integers and floating-point values—make up the core set of numeric teacups. And who needs more than eleven? With these eleven teacups, you can manage numbers from zero all the way to 1×10^{300} and beyond. To use a numeric literal, type the number right in your code, like *27*, or *3.1415926535*. C# also lets you specify which of the eleven numeric teacups to use for a number, by appending a special character to the end of the number. Normally, *27* is an integer 27. To make it a currency-focused decimal value, append the letter *M*.

When I talk about data types in full detail in Chapter 6, I will list the different special characters, like M, that set the data type for literal numbers.

The third and final type of Visual C# literal is the Boolean literal. Boolean values represent the simplest type of computer data: the bit. Boolean values are either true or false, on or off, yes or no, delicious or disgusting, cats or dogs, zero or nonzero. Booleans always represent any two opposite values or states. Back in the 1800s, George Boole invented *Boolean algebra*, a language he used to represent logic statements as mathematical equations. It just so happens that computers *love* Boolean algebra. All the basic operations of a computer, such as addition, are implemented using Boolean functionality.

Visual C# includes the Boolean literals `true` and `false`. No quotes; no trailing letters—just the words *true* and *false*. Question: is Tim Patrick telling the truth about this? Here is the answer.

```
true
```

In certain cases, you can treat numbers as Boolean values. I'll talk about it more later on, but for now just know that `false` equates to zero (0), and `true` equates to everything else (although generally, 1 is used for "everything else").

Variables

Literal data values are all well and good, but they are useful only once, and then they're gone. Each time you want to use a literal value, you must retype it. It's as though the data values are stored in disposable cups instead of fine china teacups. And besides, only programmers enter literal values, not users, so they are of limited use in managing user data.

Variables are not simply disposable cups; they are reusable. You can keep putting the same type of tea over and over into the teacup. A string variable teacup can hold a string for reuse over and over. For instance, in this block of code, `response` holds the various strings assigned to it.

```
01   response = "A";
02   MessageBox.Show("Give me an 'A'!");
03   MessageBox.Show(response);
04   MessageBox.Show("Give me another 'A'!");
05   MessageBox.Show(response);
06   MessageBox.Show("What's that spell?");
07   response = new String('A', 2);
08   MessageBox.Show(response);
```

The variable *response* is assigned twice with two different strings: an "A" (line 01) and then "AA" (line 07). It keeps whatever value was last assigned to it; both lines 03 and 05 display "A" in a message box window. And you don't have to assign just literal strings to it; anything that generates a string can assign its result to *response*. Line 07 uses a special string-creation constructor syntax to return the two-character string "AA" and assign it to *response*.

Using variables is a two-step process. First you must *declare* the variable, and then you *assign* a value to it. In C#, declaration takes place by stating the *type* of the variable, followed by its *name*, as a single statement.

```
string response;
```

In this declaration, *response* is the name of the variable and *string* is its type. Assignment occurs using the = assignment operator.

```
response = "The answer";
```

A single variable can have new values assigned to it over and over again. For those times when you want your variable to have some specific value immediately upon declaration, you can combine declaration and assignment into a single statement.

```
string response = "The answer";
```

Of course, you're not limited to just a single declaration; you can create as many variables as you need in your code. Each one normally appears as its own distinct statement.

```
string question;
string answer;
```

You also can combine these into a single statement, although I think it's just plain ugly.

```
string question, answer;
```

See, I told you it was ugly. This is just the start of what's possible with variable declaration. I'll get into more details as the chapter progresses.

Value Types and Reference Types

I talked about *value types* and *reference types* in Chapter 1. Value type variables store an actual value; the tea in a value type teacup is the content itself. All of the literal data values I mentioned previously, except for strings, are value types.

Reference type variables store a *reference* to the actual data, data found somewhere else in memory. When you look into a reference type teacup, you have to read the tea leaves at the bottom to determine where the real data resides.

Either reference types have data or they don't. In the absence of data, a reference type has a value of `null`, a C# keyword that indicates no data. Value types are never `null`; they always contain some value, possibly the default value for that type (such as zero for numeric types). A special *nullable* type does let you assign `null` to a value type, allowing you to implement the same "is there any data here at all" logic that exists with reference types. I'll talk about nullable types in Chapter 6.

Data Types

The `string` data type is useful, but it's only one of the teacup shapes at your disposal. The .NET Framework defines several core *data types*. Each data type is implemented as a specific class within the `System` namespace. The most basic data type, a large teacup that can hold any type of data, is called `Object`. More than just an object, this is object with a capital O. In the .NET Class Library namespace hierarchy, it's located at `System.Object`. It is the mother of all classes in .NET; all other classes, structures, enumerations, and delegates, no matter where they reside in the namespace hierarchy, whether they are written by Microsoft or by you, derive from `System.Object`. There's no getting around it; you cannot create a type that ultimately derives from anything else.

So, back to these core data types I've been hinting at. They match the three types of literal data values I listed before, plus one for chronographic data: strings, dates, numbers, and Boolean values. Table 2-1 lists these core data types. Each type (except for the date/time type) also has a Visual C#-specific name that you can (and should) use instead.

Table 2-1. Core .NET and Visual C# data types

C# name	.NET name	Description
bool	Boolean	The `bool` data type supports only values of `true` and `false`. It's possible to convert numbers to Boolean values: 0 becomes `false` and everything else becomes `true`. When you convert a Boolean back to a number, `false` becomes 0 and `true` becomes 1.

C# name	.NET name	Description
byte	Byte	A numeric data type, byte stores single-byte (8-bit) unsigned integers, ranging from 0 to 255. The byte data type is pretty useful for working with non-text data, such as graphical images.
char	Char	The char data type holds exactly one text character. Each char data value represents two bytes (16 bits) of storage, so it can manage *double-byte character sets*, providing support for languages such as Japanese that have a large number of characters. Although it is used to store single text characters, internally the char data type maintains the characters as integer values, ranging from 0 to 65,535.
N/A	DateTime	This date and time data type handles all dates between January 1, 1 AD and December 31, 9999 AD, in the Gregorian calendar. The time can be included as well; if no time is specified, midnight is used. Internally, the DateTime data type stores the date and time as the number of "ticks" since midnight on January 1, 1 AD. Each tick is 100 nanoseconds. C# does not include its own language keyword for this type.
decimal	Decimal	The decimal data type is designed with currency in mind. It is very accurate in mathematical calculations, and has a pretty good range, supporting numbers just beyond 79-octillion, positive or negative. (Did he say 79-octillion?) That's twenty-nine digits long, and that's important to remember, since you get only twenty-nine digits total on both sides of the decimal point. That 79-octillion number comes with the limitation of no digits to the right of the decimal point. If you want one decimal position, you have to give up one to the left (the mantissa) and only keep numbers up to 7.9-octillion. If you want twenty-nine digits after the decimal, you get a big fat zero for the mantissa.
double	Double	The double data type handles the largest possible numbers of all the core numeric data types. Its range is about 4.94×10^{-324} to $1.798 \times 10^{+308}$ for positive numbers, with a similar range for negative values. While you may think you are in giganto-number heaven, it's not all harps and wings. The double data type is notoriously inaccurate in complex calculations. Sometimes a calculation that should result in zero will actually calculate as something like 0.00000000000005434, which is close. But comparisons of this number with zero will fail, since it is not zero.
int	Int32	The int data type is a 4-byte (32-bit) signed integer type. It handles numbers from −2,147,483,648 to 2,147,483,647.
long	Int64	The long data type is even bigger than int; it's an 8-byte (64-bit) signed integer type. It handles numbers from −9,223,372,036,854,775,808 (wow!) to 9,223,372,036,854,775,807 (wow! wow!).
object	Object	object is the core type for all .NET types. It sits at the top of the class and type hierarchy; it is the ultimate base class for all other classes. It is a reference type, although value types eventually derive from it, too.

C# name	.NET name	Description
sbyte	SByte	A numeric data type, *sbyte* stores single-byte (8-bit) signed integers, ranging from −128 to 127. It is the signed version of the unsigned *byte* data type.
short	Int16	The *short* data type is a 2-byte (16-bit) signed integer type. It stores numbers from −32,768 to 32,767.
float	Single	The *float* data type is pretty much like the *double* data type, only smaller. Its range for positive numbers is about 1.4×10^{-45} to $3.4 \times 10^{+38}$, with a similar range for negative numbers. Like the *double* data type, the *float* data type suffers from slight inaccuracies during calculations.
string	String	The *string* data type is a reference type that stores up to about two billion characters of text. It stores *Unicode* characters, which are 2-byte (16-bit) characters capable of managing text from most languages in the world, including languages with large alphabets, such as Chinese.
uint	UInt32	*uint* stores 4-byte (32-bit) unsigned integers, ranging from 0 to 4,294,967,295. It is the unsigned version of the signed *int* data type.
ulong	UInt64	*ulong* stores 8-byte (64-bit) unsigned integers, ranging from 0 to 18,446,744,073,709,551,615. It is the unsigned version of the signed *long* data type.
ushort	UInt16	*ushort* stores 2-byte (16-bit) unsigned integers, ranging from 0 to 65,535. It is the unsigned version of the signed *short* data type.

The Microsoft developers in charge of Visual C# data types lucked out on that job since all core C# data types are simply wrappers for specific data types implemented by .NET. The Visual C# names given for each of these core data types are fully interchangeable with the .NET names. For example, *int* is fully equivalent to *System.Int32*. When writing C# code, it is better to use the C# synonyms, since most Visual C# developers expect these data type names in the code they read and write. The lone exception is *System.DateTime*, which though as common as the others, has no intrinsic C# equivalent.

Except for *object* and *string*, all of these data types are value types. All value types are derived from *System.ValueType* (which in turn derives from *System.Object*).

Unlike the other core data types, the *sbyte*, *uint*, *ulong*, and *ushort* data types are not CLS-compliant; that is, they cannot be used to interact with .NET components and languages that limit themselves to just the very core required features of .NET. Generally this is not much of a limitation, but be on your guard when working with third-party components or languages.

Advanced Declaration

Value types must have a value assigned to them before they can be used in other things.

```
int notYetReady;        // You can't use this yet
int readyForUse = 0;    // But this one is ready

result = notYetReady + readyForUse;  // This fails
notYetReady = 10;
result = notYetReady + readyForUse;  // Now it works
```

Value types take on whatever value you assign to them, but they also have a *default* value, which is typically some form of zero. You could assign zero to an integer to initialize it, and I typically do that. But C# also includes a `default` keyword that sets a variable to its default value without you needing to wrack your brain to recall what that value is.

```
int trueDefault = default(int);
```

For value types, declaration and assignment are all you need to do before you start using those variables in other code. Reference types require one additional step: *instantiation*. Consider the following assignments done with both value types and reference types.

```
// ----- Assume firstValue already existed.
int secondValue = firstValue;

// ----- Assume firstReference already existed.
object secondReference = firstReference;
```

When assigning a value type, the destination variable receives a fresh copy of that variable. If you adjust *secondValue*, it will have no impact on *firstValue*. However, when you assign an existing reference type to another reference type variable, the destination variable will contain the exact same reference. That is, *firstReference* and *secondReference* both contain the same set of instructions on where to find the true data in memory. This means that certain changes made to *secondReference* will impact *firstReference*, and vice versa, since they refer to the identical piece of data.

If you have a piece of reference type data and you want it shared by two variables in this manner, that's fine. But it's hard to see how you could write a useful program that just kept assigning the same piece of data to a lot of different variables. At some point, the original reference type data has to be brought into existence. That's where instantiation comes in. To create a new bit of reference type data out of thin air, you instantiate it using the *new* keyword, followed by the name of data type you want to create.

```
// ----- Instantiate as part of declaration.
object secondReference = new object();

// ----- Or, instantiate after declaration.
object secondReference;          // Declaration
secondReference = new object();  // Instantiation and assignment
```

Now *secondReference* points to a brand new object; now the *secondReference* teacup has something fresh inside it, although since it is just *System.Object*, it doesn't have much in the way of flavor. Strings are a little more interesting, and they also have more interesting *constructors*.

As you may recall from way back in Chapter 1, a constructor is a block of initialization code that runs when you create a new data value or object. Some objects allow you to supply extra information to a constructor, additional information that is used in the initialization process. A *default constructor* doesn't allow you to supply any extra information; it just works on its own, initializing data like it was nobody's business. The instantiation of the *secondReference* variable just above uses a default constructor, with just an empty pair of parentheses after the type name. There is no limit on the number of constructors in a class, but each one must vary in the type of extra information passed to it.

So, back to strings. In C#, when you want to initialize a string variable to an empty (zero-length) string, you set it equal to a string literal with no content between the quotation marks.

```
string worldsMostBoringString = "";
```

Setting a reference type to its most elementary, default content is exactly what a default constructor exists for, and since Strings are reference types, you should expect that its default constructor would likewise initialize a variable to an empty string.

```
string worldsMostBoringString = new string();
```

Now, nobody ever does this, because it doesn't work. The *string* data type, for reasons I don't fully understand, turned off its default constructor, probably since the two-quote syntax is just so fun to type. If you want to use a constructor to create a zero-length string instance, you need to use one of the *string* type's non-default constructors, the ones that put something between the parentheses. How about this?

```
string worldsMostBoringString = new string('x', 0);
```

One of the *string* type's constructors accepts two arguments, a character to use in the initial string, and a count that indicates how many of that character to include. The code just above creates a string instance made up of exactly zero of the "x" character. That's not very practical. Here's a better use for that constructor, using it to create a new string with the character "M" appearing twenty-five times.

```
string mmGood = new string('M', 25);
```

I'll delve into the details of constructors in Chapter 8.

Constants

Literals don't change, but you can use them only once in your code. *Constants* are a cross between a literal and a variable; they have a single, never-changing value just like data literals, but they also have a name that you can use over and over again, just like variables.

You declare constants using the *const* keyword just before the type name in a declaration.

```
const int SpeedOfLight = 186000;
```

Actual assignment of the value to the constant occurs in the statement itself, with the value following the = operator. Once your constant is declared and assigned, it's available for use in actual statements of your actual code.

```
MessageBox.Show("Lightspeed in miles/second: " + SpeedOfLight);
```

Local Declaration and Fields

In the real world, you need to keep some data private, for your use only. Your neighbors have other juicy bits of data and information that they share among themselves. And then there is public data that isn't hidden from anyone. But it's not just this way in the real world; the fake world of Visual C# has different levels of access and privacy for your data.

A little later in the chapter, we'll see that your application's logic code will always appear in procedures, named blocks of source code. You declare *local variables* (and constants) in these same procedures when you need a short-lived and personal variable that is only for use within a single procedure. Other variables (and constants) can appear outside procedures, but still within the context of a class or similar type. These *fields*, whether variable or constant, are immediately available to all the different procedures that also call the current class home.

As shown a bit earlier, you define all local variables by stating the target data type followed by the variable name. This syntax works for field definitions as well, but it's more common to prefix these declarations with special *access modifier* keywords. These modifiers determine what code can access the fields, from *private* (used only by code inside the class) to *public* (also available outside the class).

```
private int ForInClassUseOnly;
```

There are five access modifiers in all. I'll talk more about them and about fields in general in Chapter 6.

Intermission

That was a lot to take in. Getting your mind around data and variables is probably the most complex part of programming in C#. Once you have the data in variables, it's pretty easy to manipulate.

Although the thought of a cup of tea may cause you to run out of the room like a raving lunatic, you might want to take a few minutes, grab a cup, glass, saucer, or mug of your beverage of choice, and relax. I'll see you in about twenty or thirty minutes.

Comments

If you're an opera fan, you know how exciting a good opera can be, especially a classic work presented with the original foreign language libretto. If you're not an opera fan, you know how irritating it can be to listen to several hours of a foreign language libretto. With the advent of "supra titles" conveying the English-language interpretation of the content, those who until now have gotten little joy out of the opera experience will still find it repulsive, only this time in their native tongue. But at least now they will know why they don't enjoy the story.

That's really what comments do: tell you in your own language what is actually going on in a foreign language. In this book, the foreign language is C#, and English is the vernacular. You may find a particular block of Visual C# code to be poorly written or even detestable, but if the accompanying comments are accurate, you can be disgusted in your own language, with a human-language understanding of the process.

Comments normally appear on lines by themselves, but you may also attach a comment to the end of an existing code line. If a logical line is broken into multiple physical lines, comments can also appear at the end of each physical line component.

```
// ----- This is a standalone comment, on a line by itself.
int counter = default(int);   // This is a trailing comment.
MessageBox.Show("Counter starts at " +  // A mid-statement comment.
    counter);  // One final comment for the road.
```

Comments begin with the comment marker, a set of two forward-slash characters (//). Any text following the comment marker is a comment, and is ignored when your code is compiled into a usable application. Any set of slashes that appears within a literal string is not recognized as a comment marker.

```
MessageBox.Show("No //comments// in this text.");
```

C# also supports a more aggressive comment syntax that uses a start and end marker, can appear anywhere that any otherwise-ignored space characters would appear, and can run on for any length, including across hundreds of lines. The start symbol is a slash-asterisk pair (/*), and the ending symbol is its reverse, an asterisk-slash pair (*/).

```
/* ----- I'm demonstrating a multi-line comment
 *       because it's the right thing to do.
 */
int position;  /* <-- That's a declaration */
position /* This is assignment --> */ = 100;
```

Although this start-symbol, end-symbol comment syntax is great for multi-line comments, you will find that most C# programmers still use the double-slash syntax, starting each line with its own comment symbol.

```
/* ----- This is a multi-line
 *       comment that works well. */
```

```
// ----- Yet many programmers
//       use this form instead.
```

Basic Operators

Visual C# includes several basic operators that let you do what your code really wants to do: manipulate data. To use them, just dial zero from your phone. No, wait; those operators let you place operator-assisted calls for only $2.73 for the first minute. The C# operators let you perform mathematical, logical, bitwise, and string management functions, all at no additional cost.

The most basic operator is the assignment operator, represented by the equals sign (=). You've already seen this operator in use in this chapter. Use it to assign some value to a variable (or constant); whatever appears to the right of the operator gets assigned to the reference type or value type variable on the left. This statement assigns a value of *25* to the variable *fiveSquared*.

```
fiveSquared = 25;
```

Most operators are *binary operators*—they operate on two distinct values, one to the operator's left and one to the right; the result is a single calculated value. It's as though the calculation is fully replaced by the calculated result. The addition operator is a binary operator.

```
seven = 3 + 4;
```

When processed by Visual C#, it's as if the operator and its left and right *operands* are replaced with the result of the operation before the final application of the assignment (=) operator.

```
seven = 7;
```

A *unary operator* appears just to the left of its operand. For instance, the unary negation operator turns a positive number into a negative number.

```
negativeSeven = -7;
```

I'll comment on each operator in detail in Chapter 6. But we'll need a quick summary for now so that we can manipulate data before we get to that chapter. Table 2-2 lists the main Visual C# operators and briefly describes the purpose of each one.

Table 2-2. Visual C# operators

Operator	Description
+	The addition operator adds two numbers together. When used with two strings, the plus symbol acts as the concatenation operator, joining two string operands together and returning the combined results.
+	The unary plus operator retains the sign of a numeric value. It's not very useful until you get into operator overloading, something covered in Chapter 12.
++	The increment operator is a unary operator that adds one to its associated integer operand. For example, if an integer variable named *position* has a value of *5*, the following expression changes its value to *6*. `    ++position` The increment operator can appear as *prefix* (before its operand) or *postfix* (after its operand). While the position has no impact on the target variable, it does impact other code that surrounds the expression. When used in prefix notation, the operand variable is updated, and then the new value is communicated to the surrounding code. In the following code, both *position* and *newValue* will be *10* after the statements complete.

Operator	Description

	`position = 9; newValue = ++position;`
	 When used in postfix notation, the operands current value is communicated, and then it is incremented. In the following code, `newValue` will be 9, and `position` will be 10 after the statements complete.
	 `position = 9; newValue = position++;`
	 Unlike other operators, the increment operator (and the related decrement operator) is *destructive*, because it alters the value of its operand. Other operators return a new value without impacting the original.

−	The subtraction operator subtracts the second operand from the first.
−	The unary negation operator reverses the sign of its associated numeric operand.
−−	The decrement operator is a unary operator that subtracts one from its associated integer operand. See the ++ operator entry above for information about using this operator in prefix and postfix notation.
~	The bitwise complement operator reverses the value of each bit within an integer operand. If any bit is 0 (zero), it will be changed to 1 (one), and vice versa.
*	The multiplication operator multiplies two numeric values together.
/	The division operator divides the first numeric operand by the second, returning the quotient.
%	The modulo operator divides the first numeric operand by the second, and returns only the remainder as an integer value.
&	The conjunction operator returns `true` if both Boolean operands are also `true`. When used with integer operands, the operator performs a bitwise operation. If the corresponding bits in both operands are both 1 (one), the result of the expression will include a 1-bit in that position. Otherwise, the returned bit is 0 (zero).
&&	This operator is just like the & operator when used with Boolean operands, but it doesn't examine or process the second operand if the first one is `false`. This operator is not valid with integer operands.
|	The disjunction operator returns `true` if either of the Boolean operands is also `true`. When used with integer operands, the operator performs a bitwise operation. If either of the corresponding bits in the operands are 1 (one), the result of the expression will include a 1-bit in that position. Otherwise, the returned bit is 0 (zero).
||	This operator is just like the | operator when used with Boolean operands, but it doesn't examine or process the second operand if the first one is `true`. This operator is not valid with integer operands.
!	The negation operator returns the opposite of a Boolean operand.
^	The exclusive-or operator returns `true` if exactly one of the operands is also `true`. When used with integer operands, the operator performs a bitwise operation. If exactly one of the corresponding bits in the operands is 1 (one), the result of the expression will include a 1-bit in that position. Otherwise, the returned bit is 0 (zero).
<<	The shift-left operator shifts the individual bits in an integer operand to the left by the number of bit positions in the second operand.
>>	The shift-right operator shifts the individual bits of an integer operand to the right by the number of bit positions in the second operand.
==	The equal-to comparison operator returns `true` if the operands are equal to each other.
<	The less-than comparison operator returns `true` if the first operand is less than or comes before the second.

Operator	Description
`<=`	The less-than-or-equal-to comparison operator returns `true` if the first operand is less than or equal to the second.
`>`	The greater-than comparison operator returns `true` if the first operand is greater than or comes after the second.
`>=`	The greater-than-or-equal-to comparison operator returns `true` if the first operand is greater than or equal to the second.
`!=`	The not-equal-to comparison operator returns `true` if the first operand is not equal to (or in some cases, not equivalent to) the second.
`?:`	The conditional operator returns one of two expressions based on a Boolean test expression. It is sometimes called the *ternary* operator, because it includes three operands: (1) a Boolean test expression, (2) a value to return if the test is `true`, and (3) a value to return if the test is `false`. In the following code, `result` will be AM or PM depending on the hour. `result = startTime.Hour < 12 ? "AM" : "PM";`
`??`	The coalescence operator is a binary operator that normally returns its first operand. However, if that first operand is `null`, it returns the second operand instead. The following code sets `displayName` to *Unknown* if `customerName` is `null`. `displayName = customerName ?? "Unknown";`

As powerful as operators are, they possess even more power when you combine them. This works because any of the operands can be a complex *expression* that includes its own operands. Parentheses grouped around clauses in operands ensure that values are processed in the order you expect.

```
percentChange = (original - final) / final;
```

In this statement, the first operand of the / division operator is another expression, which includes its own operator.

Using Functions and Subroutines

Years ago I worked for a software company that sometimes published software developed outside the organization, all for a non-Windows platform. While most of these programs were written in the C language, we also published software written in Pascal, assembly language, and good ol' BASIC. I inherited one such external application written entirely in BASIC, a program that assisted the user in 3D modeling and graphics rendering. It was a complex program, containing about 30,000 lines of source code. The problem was that it was one large block of 30,000 source code lines. No comments, no variable names longer than a few characters, no extra-strength buffered aspirin product. Just thousands of lines of code with flow control statements jumping this way and that. And, of course, it had a bug.

I was able to move past that event in my life without too much therapy, but at the time it was a shock to see code in that condition. And it was so unnecessary, since that flavor of BASIC was a *procedural language*, just like C and Pascal. Procedural languages allow you to break your code into named blocks of logic, called procedures. These procedures let you take a divide-and-conquer approach to programming; you write procedures that accomplish a specific logical portion of the code within your entire application, and then access these procedures from other procedures.

Visual C# includes three types of procedures.

Subroutines

These procedures, sometimes called *void functions*, do a bunch of work and then return to the calling procedure. Data can be sent into the subroutine through its *argument list*, and some values may come back through that same list, but the procedure does not send an official final result back. A subroutine does its work, and once it is complete, the calling code continues on its merry way.

Functions

Functions are just like subroutines, with one additional feature: you can return a single value or object instance from the function as its official result. Usually, the calling code takes this *return value* into consideration when it completes its own logic.

Properties

When used, properties actually look like variables. You assign and retrieve values to and from properties just like you would for a variable. However, properties include hidden code, often used to validate the data being assigned to the property.

Subroutines, functions, and properties are the code members of each class or similar type. I'll delay discussion of properties until a little later in the chapter. For now, let's enjoy functions and subroutines, which together are also known as *methods*. Let's start with subroutines. To call a subroutine, type its name as a statement, followed by a set of parentheses. Any data you need to send to the subroutine goes in the parentheses. For instance, the following subroutine call does some work, passing the ID number of a customer, and a starting date.

```
DoSomeWork(customerID, startDate);
```

Each subroutine defines the data type and order of the arguments you pass. This argument list may include one or more *optional arguments*, which are assigned default values if you don't include them. A subroutine might also be *overloaded*, defining different possible argument lists based on the number and data type of the arguments. We'll encounter a lot of these later.

Functions are a little more interesting since they return a usable value. Often, this value is assigned to a variable.

```
bool balanceDue;
balanceDue = HasOutstandingBalance(customerID);
```

Then you can do something with this result. If you want, you can ignore the return value of a function, and we already have. The *MessageBox.Show* function used earlier returns the identity of the on-screen button clicked by the user to close the message box. If you include only an OK button (the default), you probably don't care which button the user clicks.

```
MessageBox.Show("Go ahead, click the OK button.");
```

But you can also capture the result of the button click.

```
whichButton = MessageBox.Show("Click Yes or No.",
    "Please Choose", MessageBoxButtons.YesNo);
```

In this case, *whichButton* will be either *DialogResult.Yes* or *DialogResult.No*, two of the possible results defined by the *MessageBox.Show* function.

Conditions

Sometimes you have to make some choices, and conditional expressions will help you do just that. Visual C# includes support for *conditions*, which use data tests to determine which code should be processed next.

If Statements

The most common conditional statement is the `if` statement. It is equivalent to English questions in the form "If such-and-such is true, then do so-and-so." For instance, it can handle "If you have $20, then you can buy me dinner," but not "If a train departs Chicago at 45 miles per hour, when will it run out of coal?"

`if` statements have a syntax that spans multiple source code lines.

```
01  if (hadAHammer == true)
02  {
03      DoHammer(inTheMorning, allOverThisLand);
04      DoHammer(inTheEvening, allOverThisLand);
05  }
06  else if (hadAShovel == true)
07      DoShovel(inTheNoontime, allOverThisLand);
08  else
09      TakeNap(allDayLong, onMySofa);
```

The `if` statement lets you define *branches* in your code based on conditions. It is built from three main components.

Conditions

> The expression found within parentheses just after the `if` keyword is the condition. The sample includes two conditions, on lines 01 and 06. Conditions may be simple or complex, but they must always result in a Boolean `true` or `false` value. They can include calls to other functions and multiple logical and comparison operators.

```
if (((PlayersOnTeam(homeTeam) >= 9) &
      (PlayersOnTeam(visitingTeam) >= 9)) |
     (justPracticing == true))
    PlayBall();
else
    StadiumLights(turnOff);
```

> The original condition always follows the `if` keyword. If that conditions fails, you can specify additional conditions following an `else if` keyword pair, as on line 06. You may include as many `else if` clauses as you need. The optional `else` condition, when included within an `if` statement, doesn't let you specify a test expression. Instead, it matches everything not yet caught by the earlier `if` clauses. Only one plain `else` clause is allowed per `if` statement.

Branches

> Each condition is followed by one or more C# statements that are processed if the associated condition evaluates to `true`. When just a single statement is needed within a conditional branch, it can appear by itself, terminated by standard statement-ending semicolon. Lines 07 and 09 show such single-statement branches.

> If you need to include more than one statement within a branch, as is the case with lines 03 through 04, you must surround all of those statements within a set of curly braces. You may include any number of statements in a branch block, including additional subordinate `if` statements. In the sample code, branch lines 03 and 04 are processed if the original `hadAHammer` condition is `true`. Line 07 is

processed instead if the original condition fails, but the second *hadAShovel* condition passes. If none of the conditions are *true*, the *else*'s branch, on line 09, executes.

Statement keywords

The *if* statement is one of several multiline statements in C#. (I use the term "multiline" loosely, since in C#, you can put as many statements as you want on a single physical line. But by tradition, statements like the *if* statement are split across multiple lines.) The *if* statement's keywords, which give the statement its structure, include *if* and *else*. Also, every condition must be enclosed in a set of parentheses. All *else* clauses and related branches are optional. The simplest *if* statement includes only an *if* branch.

```
if (phoneNumberLength == 10)
    DialNumber(phoneNumber);
```

if statements are cool because they make your code more than just a boring set of linear step-by-step instructions that never deviate for any reason. Software is written to support some real-world process, and real-world processes are seldom linear. The *if* statement makes it possible for your code to react to different data conditions, taking the appropriate branch when necessary.

Once the entire *if* block completes, processing continues with the next statement that follows the final conditional branch.

Switch Statements

Sometimes you might write an *if* statement that tests a variable against one possible value, then another, then another, then another, and so on.

```
if (billValue == 1)
    presidentName = "Washington";
else if (billValue == 2)
    presidentName = "Jefferson";
else if (billValue == 5)
    presidentName = "Lincoln";
...
```

And on it goes, through many more *else if* clauses. It's effective, but a little tedious, as your code must specifically test every case. The *switch* statement provides a cleaner alternative for simple value comparisons against a list.

```
01  switch (billValue)
02  {
03      case 1:
04          presidentName = "Washington";
05          break;
06      case 2:
07          presidentName = "Jefferson";
08          break;
09      case 5:
10          presidentName = "Lincoln";
11          break;
12      case 20:
13          presidentName = "Jackson";
14          break;
15      case 50:
16          presidentName = "Grant";
17          break;
```

```
18     case 10:
19     case 100:
20         presidentName = "!! Non-president";
21         break;
22     default:
23         presidentName = "!! Invalid value";
24         break;
25  }
```

Unlike the *if* statement, which checks for a Boolean result, *switch* compares a single value against a set of test case values. In the example, the *billValue* variable is compared against the different values identified by each *case* clause. All code that follows a *case* clause (until the next *case* clause) is the branch that is processed when a match is found. An optional *default* condition (line 22) catches anything that is not matched by any other *case*. If none of the test cases match and there is no *default* block, the entire *switch* statement gets skipped.

Normally, one *case* clause maps to a single branch of code. You can bunch several *case* clauses together, and they will all map to the branch that follows them, as shown in lines 18 to 21. No matter what code a branch contains, you must intentionally exit it by using a branch-terminating statement. The *break* statement is normally used for this purpose. When the code encounters the *break* statement, execution immediate jumps to the line just after the entire *switch* statement.

Loops

Visual C# includes three major types of loops: *for*, *foreach*, and *while*. Just as conditions allow you to break up the sequential monotony of your code through branches, loops add to the usefulness of your code by letting you repeat a specific block of logic a fixed or variable number of times.

for Loops

The *for* loop typically uses a numeric counter that increments from a starting value to an ending value, processing the code within the loop once for each incremented value.

```
int whichMonth;
for (whichMonth = 1; whichMonth <= 12; whichMonth++)
    ProcessMonthlyData(whichMonth);
```

This sample loops twelve times, once for each month, from 1 to 12. It determines this by using the three semicolon-delimited rules that follow the *for* keyword. The first portion is the *initializer*, which sets the initial value of the loop management variable. In the sample, the pre-declared *whichMonth* variable is set to *1*. You can also declare the variable as part of the loop syntax.

```
for (int whichMonth = 1; whichMonth <= 12; whichMonth++)
```

The second portion of the loop declaration is the *condition*. It defines a Boolean expression that, when true, allows the loop to continue. In the sample above, the loop will continue for as long as the *whichMonth* variable is less than or equal to *12*.

The third semicolon-delimited loop component is the *iterator*. It includes an expression that is processed after each pass through the loop, adjusting the loop management variable as needed for comparison with the test condition. The sample loop uses a postfix increment operator to bump *whichMonth* up by *1* each time through the loop.

As with all loops in C#, the *for* loop must be followed by a subordinate statement, either a single semicolon-terminated statement, or a block of statements contained within curly braces.

```
for (int whichMonth = 1; whichMonth <= 12; whichMonth++)
{
    ProcessMonthlyData(whichMonth);
    UpdateStatusDisplay();
}
```

The initializer-condition-iterator syntax of the *for* loop allows for much flexibility. You can specify any starting value you wish, use complex conditions that involve non-loop variables, and even employ non-numeric "counters" for loop management, although a *while* loop is often a better choice when using a non-numeric loop variable.

```
// ----- Loop from 10 to 1.
for (int level = 10; level >= 1; level--)

// ----- Use a string as the loop variable.
For (string process = ""; process.Length <= 10; process += ".")
```

foreach Loops

A variation of the *for* loop, the *foreach* loop scans through a set of ordered and related items, from the first item until the last. Arrays and collection objects also work, as does any object that supports the *IEnumerable* interface (all these topics are covered in Chapter 6). The syntax is simpler than that of the standard *for* statement, and the loop variable must always be declared as part of the loop syntax.

```
foreach (Customer oneRecord in setOfRecords)
    ProcessRecord(oneRecord);
```

In this sample, the loop variable *oneRecord* (an object of type *Customer*) scans through all of the available customer records within the *setOfRecords* collection. The body of the loop, a single statement in this case, gets processed each time through the loop.

while Loops

Sometimes you want to repeat a block of code as long as a certain condition is true, or only until a condition is true. The *while* structure performs both of these tasks. The statement includes a conditional expression that specifies when execution should continue through the loop. For instance, the following statement does some processing for a set of dates, from a starting date to an ending date.

```
DateTime processDate = new DateTime(2000, 1, 1);
while (processDate < new DateTime(2000, 2, 1))
{
    // ----- Perform processing for the current date.
    ProcessContent(processDate);

    // ----- Move ahead to the next date.
    processDate = processDate.AddDays(1);
}
```

Processing in this sample will continue until the *processDate* variable meets or exceeds 2/1/2000, which indicates the end of processing. Make the included condition as simple or as complex as you need. Putting the *while* clause at the bottom of the loop guarantees that the statements inside the loop will always be processed at least once. In this syntax, the loop requires an initial *do* keyword.

```
do {
    ...
} while (processDate < #2/1/2000#)
```

If the loop condition is never met, the loop will continue forever. So, if you want your loop to exit at some point (and usually you do), make sure the condition can eventually be met.

break Statement

Normally, when you enter a loop, you have every intention of looping for the full number of times specified by the initial conditions of the loop. For *for* and *foreach* loops, you expect to continue through the entire numeric range or collection of elements. In *while* loops, you plan to keep the loop going as long as the exiting condition has not yet been met. But there may be loops that you want to exit early. You accomplish this using a *break* statement.

```
while (someCondition == true)
{
    // ----- Some code here, then...
    if (someOtherCondition == true)
        break;
    // ----- More code might appear here.
}
// ----- Code continues here no matter how the loop was exited.
```

Processing continues with the line immediately following the loop. This *break* statement is the same *break* statement we met earlier as part of the *switch* statement.

In a *break* statement within *nested loops* (where one loop appears within another), only the loop that immediately contains the statement is exited.

```
for (int whichMonth = 1; whichMonth <= 12; whichMonth++)
{
    for (int whichDay = 1; whichDay <= DaysInMonth(whichMonth);
        whichDay++)
    {
        if (ProcessDailyData(whichMonth, whichDay) == false)
            break;
    }
    // ----- The break statement jumps to this line.
    //       Processing continues with the next month.
}
```

continue Statement

Since exiting a loop abandons all remaining passes through the loop, you may miss out on important processing that would have happened in subsequent passes. Visual C# includes a *continue* statement that lets you abandon only the current pass through the loop.

Since the loop conditions are re-evaluated when using the *continue* statement, there are times when *continue* may cause the loop to exit, such as when it had been the final pass through the loop already.

In this example, the *continue* statement skips processing for months that have no data to process.

```
for (int whichMonth = 1; whichMonth <= 12; whichMonth++)
{
    if (DataAvailable(whichMonth) == false)
        continue;
    RetrieveData(whichMonth);
    ProcessData(whichMonth);
    SaveData(whichMonth);
}
```

Creating Your Own Procedures

All logic statements in your code must appear within a procedure, whether in a subroutine, a function, or a property. Although there are thousands of prewritten procedures for you to choose from in the .NET Framework libraries, you can also add your own.

Subroutines

Subroutines begin with the *void* keyword, which indicates that the method returns a void of data, absolutely nothing. The routine name soon follows with its parameters, and then the body of the procedure in a now-familiar set of curly braces.

```
01  void ShowIngredients(char gender)
02  {
03     string theMessage = "Unknown.";
04     if (gender == 'M')
05        theMessage = "Snips and snails and puppy dog tails.";
06     else if (gender == 'F')
07        theMessage = "Sugar and spice and everything nice.";
08     MessageBox.Show(theMessage);
09  }
```

Line 01 shows the subroutine's declaration line in its simplest form; throughout the book, you will find that there are additional keywords that decorate procedure declarations to change their behavior. The statement begins with the *void* keyword, followed by the name of the procedure, *ShowIngredients*.

The parentheses following this name contain the subroutine's *parameters*. Parameters allow another block of code that will use this procedure to pass data into the procedure, and optionally receive data back. You can include any number of parameters in the subroutine definition; simply separate them by commas. Each parameter specifies the name as it will be used in the procedure (*gender* in the sample) and its data type (*char*). The arguments are treated as declared variables within the procedure, as is done with *gender* on lines 04 and 06.

The values supplied by the calling code are known as *arguments*. All arguments are passed *by value* or *by reference*. In the sample code, the argument passed into *gender* will be passed by value, the default passing method. The alternative, pass by reference, uses the *ref* keyword before the declared parameter, and before the argument in the code that calls this method.

```
// ----- The 'ref' keyword makes it pass-by-reference.
void ShowIngredients(ref char gender)...

// ----- Elsewhere, calls to ShowIngredients use 'ref' as well.
ShowIngredients(ref targetGender);
```

The passing method impacts whether changes made to the argument within the local procedure are propagated back to the calling code. However, the ability to update the original data is also influenced by whether the data is a *value type* or a *reference type*. Table 2-3 indicates the behavior for each combination of passing method and data type.

Table 2-3. Updating data, the .NET way

Passing method	Data type	Behavior
By value	Value type	Changes made to the local version of the argument have no impact on the original version.

Passing method	Data type	Behavior
By value	Reference type	Changes made to *members* of the data object immediately impact the original data object. However, the object itself cannot be changed or replaced with a completely new data object.
By reference	Value type	Changes made to the local version are returned to the calling procedure, and permanently impact the original data value.
By reference	Reference type	Changes made to either the data object or its members are also changed in the original. It is possible to fully replace the object sent into the procedure.

In most cases, if you are interested in modifying the value of a parameter and having the changes return to the caller, use pass-by-reference; otherwise, use the default pass-by-value system.

A variation of the `ref` keyword, `out`, is used when a return value will come from the procedure through the indicated parameter. No data is passed in through this variable; its direction is out only.

Lines 03 through 08 in the sample code above comprise the *body* of the procedure, where all your logic appears. Any variables to be used solely in the routine are also defined here, as with the `theMessage` variable on line 03.

Functions

The syntax of a function differs only slightly from subroutines, to support a return value.

```
01  bool IsPrime(long source)
02  {
03     // ----- Determine whether source is a prime number.
04     if (source < 2)
05        return false;
06     else if (source > 2)
07     {
08        for (long testValue = 2;
09           testValue <= source / 2L; testValue++)
10        {
11           if ((source % testValue) == 0L)
12              return false;
13        }
14     }
15     return true;
16  }
```

As with subroutines, the function's declaration line appears first (line 01), followed by the body (lines 03 through 15) wrapped in curly braces (lines 02 and 16). The declaration line replaces the emotionally empty `void` keyword with the data type of the final value to be returned by the code, in this case `bool`. Use this return value in the calling code just like any other value or variable. For example, the following line calls the `IsPrime` function and stores its Boolean result in a variable.

```
primeResult = IsPrime(23);
```

To indicate the value to return, use the `return` statement (described later in the chapter). The sample code does this on lines 05, 12, and 15.

Properties

A little earlier I mentioned fields, which are variables or constants that appear within a class, but outside any procedure definition.

```
01   class PercentRange
02   {
03      public int Percent;
04   }
```

Properties are similar to fields; they are used like class-level variables or constants. But they are programmed like functions, accepting parameters, having return values, and including as much logic as you require.

Properties are often used to protect private class data with logic that weeds out inappropriate values. The following class defines a single property that provides access to the related hidden field.

```
01   class PercentRange
02   {
03      // ----- Stores a percent from 0 to 100 only.
04      private int SavedPercent = 0;
05      public int Percent
06      {
07         get
08         {
09            return SavedPercent;
10         }
11         set
12         {
13            if (value < 0)
14               SavedPercent = 0;
15            else if (value > 100)
16               SavedPercent = 100;
17            else
18               SavedPercent = value;
19         }
20      }
21   }
```

The *Percent* property (lines 05 to 20) protects access to the *SavedPercent* field (line 04), correcting any caller-supplied values that exceed the 0-to-100 range. Properties include separate assignment and retrieval components, called *accessors*. The *get* accessor (lines 07 to 10) returns the property's monitored value to the caller. The *set* accessor (lines 11 to 19) lets the caller modify the value of the property.

The property declaration statement (line 05) includes a data type that matches the data type passed into the *set* accessor, silently through an invisible parameter named *value*. This is the data type of the value set or retrieved by the caller. To use this sample *Percent* property, create an instance of the *PercentRange* class, and then use the property.

```
PercentRange activePercent = new PercentRange();
activePercent.Percent = 107;      // An out-of-range integer
MessageBox.Show(activePercent.Percent); // Displays "100", not "107"
```

You can create read-only or write-only properties by omitting the unneeded *get* or *set* accessor.

Properties do not need to be tied to fields. You can use properties to get and set any type of value, and store it or act upon it in any manner you wish.

Where to Put Your Procedures

All Visual C# procedures must appear within a defined class (or a structure).

```
class Employee
{
   public void StartVacation()
   {
      ...
   }

   public double TotalVacationTaken()
   {
      ...
   }
}
```

When you create instances of your class later in code, the methods can be called directly through the object instance.

```
Employee executive = new Employee();
...
executive.StartVacation();
```

Chapter 8 shows you how to use and build classes.

Other Flow Control Features

The loops and conditional statements available in C# let you reroute your code based on data. The language includes a few other statements that let you control the action in a more direct manner.

The goto Statement

The *goto* statement lets you jump immediately to some other location within the current procedure. The destination of a jump is always a *line label*, a named line position in the current procedure. Line labels traditionally appear at the start of a logical line, and end with a colon.

```
PromptUser:
   GetValuesFromUser(numerator, denominator);
   if (denominator == 0)
      goto PromptUser;
   quotient = numerator / denominator;
```

In this sample, the *goto* statement jumps back to the *PromptUser* label when the code detects invalid data. Processing continues with the line immediately following the *PromptUser* label. You can't use the same label name twice in the same procedure, although you can reuse label names in different procedures. If you want, include another logic statement on the same line as your label, right after the colon, although your code will be somewhat easier to read if you keep labels on their own lines.

```
LabelAlone:
   MessageBox.Show("It's all alone.");
LabelAndCode: MessageBox.Show("Together again.");
```

It's all right to include as many labels in your code as you need, but the *goto* statement is one of those elements of Visual C# that is monitored closely by pesky international software agencies, such as the International Committee to Keep Goto Always Gone (ICK-GAG). That group also scans computer books looking for derogatory references to its organization name—not that it would find anything like that in this book. But its core issue is that overuse of *goto* statements can lead to *spaghetti code*, such as the following.

```
string importantMessage = "Do";
goto Step2;
Step6: importantMessage += "AG!";
goto Step7;
Step3: importantMessage += "wit";
goto Step4;
Step2: importantMessage += "wn ";
goto Step3;
Step5: importantMessage += "CK-G";
goto Step6;
Step4: importantMessage += "h I";
goto Step5;
Step7: MessageBox.Show(importantMessage);
```

Some people say that such code is hard to read. Others call it job security. No matter what you call it, it does make code very hard to maintain and review. You should probably keep an eye on your use of *goto* statements; if you don't, someone else might.

Visual C# itself places some limits on the use of *goto*. You cannot jump into or out of certain multiline statements that would result in improperly initialized code or data values. For instance, you cannot jump into the body of a *for* loop from outside the loop, since the loop counter variable would not be properly initialized.

```
// ----- This goto statement will fail.
goto InsideTheLoop;
for (int counter = 1; counter <= 10; counter++)
{
InsideTheLoop:
    MessageBox.Show("Loop number: " + counter);
}
```

However, once you are inside the loop, you can jump to line labels that also appear in the loop, and it's acceptable to jump out of the loop using *goto*. Some other multiline structures impose similar restrictions.

The return Statement

Not only can you jump around within a procedure using *goto*, but you can also jump right out of a procedure anytime you want using the *return* statement. Normally, a procedure exits when processing reaches the last line of code in the procedure; processing then continues with the code that called the procedure. The *return* statement provides a way to exit the procedure before reaching the end.

In subroutines and property get accessors, the *return* statement appears by itself as a standalone statement.

```
return;
```

In functions and property set accessors, the statement must include the value to be returned to the calling code: a variable, a literal, or an expression that must match the specified return value data type of the function.

```
return 25;
```

Events and Event Handlers

Visual C# is an *event-driven language*. This is especially true of programs written to run on the Windows desktop. After some important initialization, the user is generally in control of all actions in the program. Who knows what the crazy user will do? He might click here. She might type there. It could be all mayhem and bedlam. But whatever the user does, your program will learn about it through *events*.

Since the first days of Windows, desktop programs have used a *message pump* to communicate user and system actions to your code. Mouse and keyboard input, system-generated actions, and other notifications from external sources flow into a program's common *message queue*. The message pump draws these messages out one by one, examines them, and feeds them to the appropriate areas of your code.

In traditional Windows programming, you craft the message pump yourself, including code that makes direct calls to event-handling procedures based on the message type. In a Visual C# program, the framework provides the message pump for you. It analyzes the messages as they are pumped out of the message queue, and directs them to the appropriate code. In .NET, this code appears within classes. Once a class has a chance to analyze the message, it can generate an event, which is ultimately processed by an *event handler*, a subroutine you write to respond to the action. This calling of the event handler is known as *firing an event*. So, there are two parts of an event: (1) some code that decides to fire the event; and (2) an event handler that responds to the fired event.

Events are really just indirect calls to a procedure. Instead of having the main code call another subroutine directly, it asks .NET to call the other subroutine for it, passing specific arguments that the calling code may wish to include. So, why would you want to do this instead of just making the subroutine call directly? For one thing, this indirect method lets you add event handlers long after the initial event-firing code was written. This is good, since the event-firing code may be in a third-party assembly that was written years ago. A second benefit is that one event can target multiple event handlers. When the event fires, each event handler will be called, and each can perform any custom logic found in the handler subroutine.

The code that fires the event passes event-specific data to the target event handler(s) through the handler's parameter list. For the indirect subroutine call to work, the event handler needs to contain the correct number of arguments, in the right order, each of a specific and expected data type. Declaring such an event is a two-step process.

1. Indicate the parameter list and return value of the event by creating a *delegate*.
2. Use the delegate to declare an *event*.

These two steps use the `delegate` and `event` declarations, respectively.

```
// ----- First, define the delegate.
public delegate void SalaryChangedDelegate(decimal newSalary);

// ----- Then define the event.
public event SalaryChangedDelegate SalaryChanged;
```

This `event` declaration defines an event named `SalaryChanged` that takes its structure from the `SalaryChangedDelegate` delegate definition. That delegate indicates that the event will accept a single parameter, a `decimal` value. Any event handler wishing to monitor the event must match its delegate definition.

```
void EmployeePayChanged(decimal updatedSalary)...
```

Events can occur for any reason you deem necessary; they need not be tied to user or system actions. In this sample class, an event fires each time a change is made to the employee's salary. The actual firing of the event occurs by calling the event as if it was a true procedure, although you need to do a check first to see if the event is *null*. If it is, that means that no event handlers are attached. Include any arguments in parentheses just after the event name.

```
public class Employee
{
    public string Name;
    private decimal CurrentSalary;

    public decimal Salary
    {
        get
        {
            return CurrentSalary;
        }
        set
        {
            CurrentSalary = value;
            if (SalaryChanged != null)
                SalaryChanged(CurrentSalary);
        }
    }

    public delegate void
        SalaryChangedDelegate(decimal newSalary);
    public event SalaryChangedDelegate SalaryChanged;
}
```

In this code, it looks like you are "calling the event." Actually, you are calling a delegate, which is a reference to a procedure. In this case, that reference refers to the event itself. You can make this a little clearer if you create a delegate variable and use that to trigger the event.

```
SalaryChangedDelegate theCaller;
theCaller = SalaryChanged;  // A delegate to the event
if (theCaller != null)
    theCaller(CurrentSalary);
```

Since this need to perform a check of the event delegate before calling it is universal, C# developers typically embody this boilerplate sanity-check code in a separate procedure within the class, calling it "On" followed by the event name.

```
protected virtual void OnSalaryChanged(decimal newSalary)
{
    SalaryChangedDelegate theCaller = SalaryChanged;
    if (theCaller != null)
        theCaller(newSalary);
}
```

Don't worry about terms like *protected* and *virtual* for now. They will be covered in later chapters.

In our sample *Employee* class, this lets us simplify the *set* accessor for the *Salary* property, removing the need for that code to worry about whether any other code has attached itself to the event.

```
set
{
    CurrentSalary = value;
```

```
        OnSalaryChanged(CurrentSalary);
    }
```

The event handlers are not added directly to the class code. Instead, they are attached to an instance of the class, an instance that is typically created in some other code block outside of the class exposing the event. An event handler must be declared using the same *argument signature* (parameter list and return value) as the event's delegate.

```
// ----- Looks like the SalaryChangedDelegate delegate.
private void CelebrateSalaryChange(decimal newSalary)
{
    MessageBox.Show("Good Job!");
}
```

Then you can connect this event handler to the event exposed by a class instance. The following code creates an *Employee* object for someone named John, and connects that object's *SalaryChanged* event to the *CelebrateSalaryChange* handler.

```
Employee johnDoe = new Employee();
johnDoe.Name = "John";

// ----- This next line won't trigger an event, since we
//       haven't connected any handlers yet.
johnDoe.Salary = 0M;

// ----- Now connect a handler. The Salary update will then
//        trigger the event and the handler code.
johnDoe.SalaryChanged += CelebrateSalaryChange;
johnDoe.Salary = 50000M;
```

Every time that John gets a raise, a celebration occurs in the event handler, called indirectly through the *Salary* property's *set* accessor and its call to the *OnSalaryChanged* procedure.

The events built into the Windows Forms classes in .NET work just like this, but instead of watching with me for a salary increase, they are watching for mouse clicks and keyboard clacks. All of these system events use a common parameter delegate.

```
public delegate void EventNameDelegate(object sender, EventArgs e);
```

(The framework also provides parallel *EventName* event declarations and *OnEventName* procedures for each event.) The *sender* argument identifies the instance of the object that is firing the event, in case the caller needs to examine its members. The *e* argument is an object that lets the caller send event-specific data to the handler through a single class instance. The *System.EventArgs* class doesn't have much in the way of members, but many events use a substitute class that is derived from *System.EventArgs*.

As we pass through the chapters of this book, there will be no end to the number of event examples you will see and experience. I will save the more involved and interesting samples until then.

Namespaces

Classes, structures, enumerations, interfaces, and delegates—the major .NET types—don't just float around in the code of your application. They must all be grouped and managed into *namespaces*. As described in Chapter 1, namespaces provide a hierarchy for your types, sort of a tree-shaped condominium where each type has a home. Some of those homes (or nodes), such as *System*, get pretty crowded with all those type families living there. Others, such as *System.Timers*, may have only a few types dwelling in their ample abodes. But every type must live in the hierarchy; none of the types is adventurous enough to strike out on its own and build a ranch house.

At the very root of the hierarchy is `global::`, not a node itself, but a Visual C# keyword that indicates the root of all roots. You can include `global::` when referencing your namespaces, but its use is required only when leaving it out would cause confusion between two namespace branches.

Directly under `global::` are the few top-level namespaces, including *System* and *Microsoft*. Each top-level namespace contains subordinate namespaces, and each of those can contain additional third-level namespaces, and so on. Namespace nodes are referenced relative to one another using a "dot" notation.

```
System.Windows.Forms
```

This specifies the third-level *Forms* namespace. You could also have typed the following.

```
global::System.Windows.Forms
```

Relative namespaces are also supported.

```
Forms
```

However, to use relative namespaces, you must tell your C# code to expect them. There are so many namespaces out there, and there may be several *Forms* namespaces somewhere in the hierarchy.

Referencing Namespaces

Before namespaces can be used in your code, they must be *referenced* and optionally *imported*. The act of referencing is done by adding type libraries to the References branch of your project within the Solution Explorer (see Figure 2-3). To add a new reference, right-click on the References node and select Add Reference from the shortcut menu.

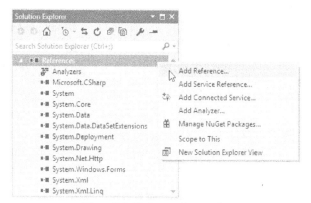

Figure 2-3. References for a project

Referencing a namespace identifies the DLL assembly file that contains that namespace's types. Actually, you are not referencing the namespaces in the DLL, but rather the types, all of which happen to live in specific namespaces. However, for the core type DLLs supplied with the .NET Framework, it feels like the same thing. In fact, Microsoft even named many of the DLLs to match the namespaces they contain. *System.dll* contains types within the *System* namespace. *System.Windows.Forms.dll* includes types specific to Windows Forms applications, and all of these types appear in the *System.Windows.Forms* namespace or one of its subordinates.

If you don't reference a DLL in your project, none of its types will be available to you in your code. Visual Studio loads several references into your project automatically based on the type of project you create. Figure

2-3 shows the eleven default references included within a Windows Forms application: *Microsoft.CSharp*, *System*, *System.Core*, *System.Data*, *System.Data.DataSetExtensions*, *System.Deployment*, *System.Drawing*, *System.Net.Http*, *System.Windows.Forms*, *System.Xml*, and *System.Xml.Linq*.

Once you have referenced a library of classes (or other types) in your code, access any of its classes by specifying the full namespace to that class. For instance, the class for an on-screen form is referenced by *System.Windows.Forms.Form*. That's three levels down into the hierarchy, and some classes are even deeper. I hope that your health insurance plan covers carpal tunnel syndrome.

To avoid typing all those long namespaces over and over again, Visual C# includes an *imports* feature. Imports are namespace-specific; once a namespace has been imported, you can access any of the types in that namespace without specifying the namespace name. If you import the *System.Windows.Forms* namespace, you only have to type "Form" to access the *Form* class.

Imports are managed on a per-file basis within your source code. To enable an import in code, add the *using* directive to the very start of a source code file.

```
using System.Windows.Forms;
```

The *using* directive supports namespace abbreviations, short names that represent the full namespace in your code. The following directive lets you reference the *Form* class as *Fred.Form*.

```
using Fred = System.Windows.Forms;
```

Because imports are processed on a per-file basis, you must add them to each file where you wish to access types relative to the imported namespaces.

Namespaces in Your Project

By default, all the classes and types in your project appear in a top-level namespace that, by default, is the same as the name of your project. For a Windows Forms application, this root namespace is called *WindowsFormsApplication1*. Each time you add a new file to your project, Visual Studio automatically includes code that specifies this namespace.

```
// ----- using directives appear here, then...
namespace WindowsFormsApplication1
{
    // ----- File-specific code appears here.
}
```

To specify a different default root namespace for newly added project files, change the Default Namespace field on the Application tab of the project's properties. For existing files, you can change this default by simply replacing whatever namespace already appears in the *namespace* statement. There is no requirement that every file use the same namespace, but it is typical that the same root namespace is used throughout an entire project.

All the types in your project appear within a *namespace* statement. If you specify an existing Microsoft-supplied namespace in a file's code, all your types in that code will appear in that specified namespace, mixed in with the preexisting types. For standalone applications, this mixture will be visible only from your code.

Namespaces can be nested, either by including a multi-part namespace as part of the *namespace* statement, or by nesting multiple *namespace* statements.

```
namespace WindowsFormsApplication1
{
    // ----- Code here appears in the indicated namespace.
}

namespace WindowsFormsApplication1.AdminFeatures
{
    // ----- Code here apears in the second-tier namespace.
}

// ----- Two-level namespace using nested statements.
namespace WindowsFormsApplication1
{
    // ----- Code here appears in the root namespace.

    namespace AdminFeatures
    {
        // ----- Code here appears in the second-tier namespace.
    }
}
```

Any types you create within the *namespace* statement will be contained in that namespace. For example, if your namespace is *WindowsFormsApplication1*, the following statements create a class whose full name is *WindowsFormsApplication1.WorkArea.BasicStuff.BusyData*.

```
namespace WindowsFormsApplication1
{
    namespace WorkArea.BasicStuff
    {
        class BusyData
        {
            ...
        }
    }
}
```

Summary

Sadly, this chapter has reached its conclusion. You may feel that it went by all too fast; you may feel that you didn't really learn how to write Visual C# programs; you may feel that a mild sedative would be right just about now. But don't fret. This chapter served as an introduction to the syntax and major features of Visual C#. Now begins the deeper training. As we start this book's main focus—the Library Project—you will encounter specific examples of all features covered only briefly in this chapter.

Project

In this chapter, we will use the Code Snippets feature of Visual Studio to insert source code into a basic sample code framework. Code Snippets is essentially a hierarchical database of saved source code text. If you installed the code for this book, you will find code snippets for most chapters included right in Visual Studio. In this chapter's project, I will show you how to use them to add chapter-specific code into your project.

Since we haven't officially started the Library Project, this chapter's project will extend the "Hello, World!" project we developed in Chapter 1, but with fun parts added. I will include some of the language features we discovered throughout this chapter.

> **Project Access**
> Load the "Chapter 2 (Before) Code" project, either through the New Project templates or by accessing the project directly from the installation directory. To see the code in its final form, load "Chapter 2 (After) Code" instead.

Each chapter's sample code includes a "Before" and "After" version. The After version represents the code as it will look when all the changes in that chapter's "Project" section have been applied. The Before version doesn't have any of the chapter's project changes included, just placeholders where you will insert the code, one block at a time.

Like the project in Chapter 1, this chapter's project includes a basic Windows form with a single button on it. Clicking the button displays the same "Hello, World!" message. However, this time, the message starts in an encoded form, and a separate class decodes the message and triggers an event that displays the result.

Once the project is open, view the source code attached to *Form1*. It should look somewhat like the following.

```
namespace WindowsFormsApplication1
{
    public partial class Form1 : Form
    {
        // ***** Insert Code Snippet #2 here.

        public Form1()
        {
            InitializeComponent();
        }

        private void Button1_Click(object sender, EventArgs e)
        {
            // ***** Insert Code Snippet #3 here.

        }

        // ***** Insert Code Snippet #4 here.

    }
}

// *** Insert Code Snippet #1 here.
```

This sample uses a separate class to process the displayed message. The code for this class appears as Snippet 1. To insert the snippet, move the cursor *just after* the #1 snippet marker line.

```
// *** Insert Code Snippet #1 here.
```

To insert a snippet through the Visual Studio menus, select Edit→IntelliSense→Insert Snippet. The equivalent default keyboard sequence is Ctrl-K, Ctrl-X. You can also right-click where you want the snippet to appear, then select Insert Snippet from the shortcut menu. Any of these methods displays the first level of snippets (see Figure 2-4).

```
// ***** Insert Code Snippet #1 here.
```

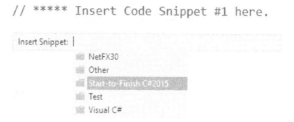

Figure 2-4. Snip, snip, snip

From the snippet list, select *Start-to-Finish C#2015*, and then select *Chapter 02*. A list of the available snippet items for this chapter appears (see Figure 2-5).

```
// ***** Insert Code Snippet #1 here.
```

Insert Snippet: Start-to-Finish C#2015   Chapter 02

     Item 1
     Item 2
     Item 3

Figure 2-5. Item, item, item

Finally, select *Item 1*. The content magically appears within the source code. All insertions of code snippets throughout this book occur in exactly this way.

Snippet 1 inserts the *SayHello* class, part of the *HelloStuff* namespace, a portion of which appears here.

```csharp
namespace HelloStuff
{
    internal class SayHello
    {
        private string SecretMessage;
        private bool ReverseFlag;
        private bool Decoded;

        public delegate void MessageDecodedDelegate(
            string decodedMessage);
        public event MessageDecodedDelegate MessageDecoded;
        protected virtual void OnMessageDecoded(
            string decodedMessage)
            ...

        public SayHello(string codedMessage, bool reverseIt)
            ...

        public void DecodeMessage(int rotationFactor)
            ...

        public void ReportMessage()
            ...
    }
}
```

The *SayHello* class includes three private fields (*SecretMessage*, *ReverseFlag*, and *Decoded*), which monitor the current status of the display message. A constructor allows the user to create a new instance of *SayHello* with an initial message text, and a flag that indicates whether the text should be reversed before display. The *DecodeMessage* subroutine converts each letter of the encoded message to its final form by shifting each letter a *rotationFactor* number of places. If the letter *E* appears and *rotationFactor* is 3, the letter *E* is shifted three spaces forward, to *H*. A negative rotation factor shifts the letters lower in the alphabet. The alphabet wraps at the A-Z boundary. Only letters are rotated, and uppercase and lowercase letters are handled independently.

The *ReportMessage* method calls *OnMessageDecoded*, which in turn fires the *MessageDecoded* event, sending the previously decoded message to the event handler as an argument. So, where is this event handler? It's attached to an instance of *SayHello* that will be created when the user clicks the trigger button on *Form1*. Let's add that code now. It appears in the button's click event handler.

Insert Snippet
Insert Chapter 2, Snippet Item 2.

```
HelloStuff.SayHello helloDecoder;

helloDecoder = new HelloStuff.SayHello("!iqwtB ,tqqjM", true);
helloDecoder.MessageDecoded += ReceiveDecodedMessage;
helloDecoder.DecodeMessage(-5);
helloDecoder.ReportMessage();
```

The *helloDecoder* variable holds an instance of the *HelloStuff.SayHello* class that we just wrote. After the initial declaration line, the code creates that instance using the *new* keyword, and stores it in the *helloDecoder* variable. Can't read the first argument in the constructor? It's encoded! It's a secret! And the *true* flag says that it's been reversed to make it an even bigger secret (you don't know what it is!). The *DecodeMessage* call removes the secrets by shifting each letter as needed, although the reversal doesn't happen until the call to *ReportMessage*.

The *+=* operator used about halfway through the code is what connects the decoder's *MessageDecoded* event with our custom-written event handler, which we will custom write in just a custom second, through our third snippet.

Insert Snippet
Insert Chapter 2, Snippet Item 3.

```
private void ReceiveDecodedMessage(string decodedMessage)
{
    // ----- Show the decoded message.
    MessageBox.Show(decodedMessage);
}
```

The decoded message comes into the handler through the *decodedMessage* argument, and is splashed all over the screen with a simple yet powerful call to the *MessageBox.Show* function.

That's it for the sample code. Now it's time to roll up your sleeves and embark on a full Visual C# 2015 project.

Chapter 3

Introducing the Project

You're sitting in your office, surfing the...I mean reading up on the latest technology issues most pressing to software developers. You're minding your own business, when *boom*, someone walks up to your desk and offers to pay you money to write a program. It happens every day, all over corporate America, and sometimes it just makes me sick.

But enough about my health problems. This desk-hovering somebody informs you that you must develop a software application, possibly a database application with a user-friendly interface. Although the feature set will be specified by the primary users, you, as the lead (or only) programmer, will design, document, develop, and deliver discs dripping with distinguished, dazzling, and dynamic digital...um...software. (Darn.)

Well, that's what happened to me. A client of mine had a large collection of books that they needed to organize as a traditional library. Seeing that I was a reasonably codependent software architect, the client asked me to develop some software to manage the books and such. Out of this request came the *Library Project*.

As you read through this chapter, you will have to keep my day job in mind. Back then, I spent most of my day writing custom .NET applications for small to medium-size organizations. Most of the projects were sized so that I could complete them by myself, including all design and documentation requirements, in less than a year. All my projects involved a *key user*, one person—or sometimes a very small group—who spoke for the user community. Those projects also involved someone who had *signature authority*, a person authorized to pay for the project, or decide on its continued existence. This individual may be the same as the key user.

If you were developing, say, a replacement for Microsoft Word, you would likely lack a key user. To obtain the specific requirements for the project, you may have to conduct general user interviews with dozens of user candidates. Or you might create a *persona*, a fictional person who represents your intended target audience. (For Visual Studio, Microsoft used three personas named Einstein, Elvis, and Mort.) Whichever method applies to you, the general discussion in this chapter should guide you to the happy conclusion: a design document that you will use to build the application.

The Library Project

My client needed a program that would manage a database of books and media items, and control how those items moved between bookshelves and patrons. The software needed to have both patron- and administrator-focused features. It would include various reports, including the printing of a receipt of checked-out items for the patron. And most of all, it needed to both print and read barcodes.

It sounds like a lot for one man to do, and it is a sizable project. But I don't have to do it alone; you will help me. Together, through the pages of this book, you and I will design that program, and develop that code, and bring joy to the users, and collect that paycheck. Actually, I will collect the paycheck, although it wouldn't hurt to ask your boss to pay you to read this fine book.

The remainder of this section documents the key features of the Library management application.

Library Item Features

The Library system will manage an inventory of books and other media items, locate them, and manage the details and status of each copy of an item. To make this a reality, the Library program will do the following.

- Allow patrons or administrators to search for items currently in inventory. The program allows searches based on several different properties of each item.
- Support multiple search methods, including by title, by author name, by subject or topic, by a miscellaneous keyword, by the name of the related publisher, by the name of a series or group that contains the item, or by a barcode number attached to the actual item.
- Limit search results by the location of the item, or by the type of media (book, CD, DVD, etc.).
- Support the definition and use of distinct physical locations. The client has books and media stored at three different sites within their building, including a storage closet for seldom-accessed items.
- Display the details of a retrieved item in a familiar browser-style interface. For instance, when looking up a book by title, the user clicks on the author's name to access all other items by that same author.
- Allow access to each library item through a barcode scan. As is common in most libraries today, the items in this library's collection each have a barcode affixed, which serves as a unique identifier for the individual item copy.

Patron Features

In addition to books and other items, the program manages a list of patrons, the "customers" of the library who are permitted to check out items. To support interaction with patrons, the application will include these patron-specific features.

- Items can be checked out to patrons, and checked back into the library inventory.
- All patrons are assigned a PIN code that acts as a password.
- Patrons can check out items without librarian and administrator assistance. They can use a barcode scanner to scan a patron library card and library items.
- The media type of an item determines its checkout (and subsequently its renewal) duration.
- Patrons can view their library record, including all books currently checked out, and a list of fines owed to the library.
- If permitted on a specific item, the patron can renew an item he has currently checked out.
- Patron-centric online help is available through the standard F1 key. This help file includes no information on administrative features, so as to reduce experimentation.
- Patrons can be divided into patron groups for the reporting and processing convenience of the administrative staff.

Administrative Features

Administrators include librarians, IT staff, and others who need advanced access to application features. They are the primary users of the system, not the patrons. The application includes the following administrator-specific features.

- A login feature provides access to the administrative features of the application. Only authorized users can log in through an assigned password. The login feature is normally hidden from view from ordinary patrons.

- Administrators can view patron details just like patrons can, but they also have access to additional patron details. Specifically, administrators can add new patrons and manage their identities and demographic details. Administrators can also disable a patron record to prevent further item checkouts.
- Administrators collect and manage patron fines, including the ability to add nonstandard fines or to dismiss unpaid fines.
- Administrators define the records for each item managed by the system's inventory database. This includes the basics of each item, such as title and authors. Each item includes one or more copies, which represent physical items that can be checked out. Barcodes are assigned to copies.
- Beyond the items and copies, administrators define all supporting values and lists, including author names and categories, the list of media types, publishers, book series names, status codes that identify the disposition of each item copy, and locations.
- Designated administrators can add, edit, and remove the accounts of other administrators. Each account includes feature-specific authorization settings (group rights).
- In addition to the scanning of barcodes, the program can assist administrators in the design and printing of both patron and item barcodes.
- A simple program-managed process allows the administrative staff to process overdue items and fines on a regular basis.
- The application allows holidays to be added and maintained. When a patron checks out a book, the program adjusts the due date of the item to avoid holidays.
- Administrator-centric online help provides assistance to the enhanced features of the application through the same F1 key available to patrons.
- The application includes some basic administrative reports, and the ability to plug-in reports as needed in the future without the need to update the program itself.

The Application as a Whole

Beyond the basic features of the program as experienced by the patrons and administrators, there are a few other requirements.

- The program is user-friendly and easy to navigate, especially for patrons, without much training or assistance.
- The application stores its data in a SQL Server database.
- Distribution of the application is done by administrative staff that has local administrative privileges, so a standard Windows installation package is sufficient.
- Configuration of the application uses standard XML methods.

Except for these general and feature-specific requirements, I was given design freedom. But where did the listed requirements come from? They came from the users, the masters of the application. It was their *needs*—the needs of my customers and theirs, who would be using the product day in and day out—that determined the list of requirements.

The Needs of the Users

Back in the old days of computers, there were no users. Who needed users? The only ones manly enough to approach the hallowed inner sanctum of the computing systems were the programmers. Only they touched the vacuum tubes, connected the cables, toggled the front panels, and fondled the punch cards that provided access to the heart of the machine. These programmers were tough, and their programs, tougher. "We don't need no stinking users" was their mantra.

Then came the 1980s, with its *Greatest American Hero*-inspired attitude and its personal "personal" computers. Now there were users everywhere. They were like the Blob, only with fewer computing skills. But they were the masters because most programs were written for them. Programmers rarely used the programs they wrote; they were simply the interface between the user and the heart of the computer. Programmers provided the element of *control* needed by both the computer and the users. In fact, that is a programmer's job: to provide highly controlled access to the computer and the data it contains.

Users have a lot of needs, most of which can't be met by a computer. But for those that can, the needs come in five parts: data and information, process, usability, commonality, and project-specific needs. The design process involves an examination of these needs and the subsequent massaging of those needs into a software product. By examining the current data and procedures, conducting user interviews, and performing other need-extraction methods, you gather the details you require to craft the right solution.

Data and Information

Your ability to provide convenient and specific access to the data and information required by the user is what makes you, the programmer, so lovable. Most users got along just fine before computers. They kept their information on 3×5 index cards, or on legal pads, or on scrolls of parchment, or in hermetically sealed mayonnaise jars. But they had a reason to move to a computer-based storage medium: the convenience.

Data is the raw information stored by your program: names, numbers, images, or any other standalone values. *Information* is data in context: a customer record, an order, a slide show. When you provide a quality program that moves data up to the level of information, you are providing the level of convenience the user needs to move from mayonnaise jars to silicon chips.

Process

When the user demands her data back from the computer, you have three options.

- Dump every single byte of data to the screen, printer, or disk, and let the user sort it out. Actually, this is the system that some users had before they started using a computer.
- Protect the data from user access, insisting that the supplied password is invalid or expired, or that the data is unavailable. "Abort, Retry, Fail" anyone? Actually, this is the system that some other users had before they started using a computer.
- Present the data as information, in a format that is both usable and accessible.

Although the first two choices are indeed tempting, the third option is the best. And given the amount of data that your application will likely manage, you will have to dole out the interaction with it a bit at a time, and in an appropriate sequence. This is *process*.

Through the implementation of a valid process, you control not only the user's data, but also the orderly interaction with that data. Most users need to supply or retrieve only a small portion of their data at a time. But when they do, it will usually be in the context of some process. For instance, in an order-taking situation, the user (1) enters or confirms the customer's contact information; (2) enters or updates the order details; and (3) prints or electronically communicates the order information so that it can be fulfilled. Your application (surprise!) manages this three-step process.

Usability

If your program presents data and information to the user, and in a specific arrangement or order, but it is difficult to use, your users will hate you. They will loathe you. They will spread mean stories about you, true or not. And when they appear in groups, their vehemence can get downright ugly. I heard this story about an Excel user's group...but perhaps it was just a rumor.

As a programmer, it is your job to make the computer, and the software that runs on it, as usable as possible. And although you may not be able to control many of the basic system features, you are the king when it comes to your own software.

The more ease and usability you design into your programs, the happier your users will be. But I must warn you, ease of use for the user *always* means more work for the developer. *Always.* It's one of those unfair laws of the universe, and there is no way around it. But sometimes we try—to the user's peril.

Many, many years ago, I wrote some programs to demonstrate a hot new version of BASIC that ran on the Motorola 6809 processor. This release could handle programs that were twice the size of the previous version: a whopping 32 KB of source code. I was charged with testing the system, writing "big" programs that would show off the new functionality. I set to work in a fever of activity, but as my program approached about 27 KB, things started to happen, things that involved a shaking table and the smell of smoke. Seriously!

Since then, I have subconsciously feared the development of programs that I felt were too large for a particular system. So, when I went to work on Windows flavor of that same language—Visual Basic—I brought to my projects some of this apprehension. I tried to make my programs easy to use, but I also held back on the number of forms I would add to my projects. It wasn't an irrational fear; the original versions of Visual Basic (before .NET) did impose limits on code size, the number of unique variable names, and the maximum number of forms. I once hit the limit on the number of unique variable names, but I never came close on the number of forms. Still, I held back. I was sure that if I added too many forms, my users would require medical attention for smoke inhalation.

Unfortunately, my users were still suffering. I had put too much data on each form, to the point where they were no longer communicating information. My phone would ring constantly with the same user-sponsored question: "How do I use the fields on such-and-such a form?" Of course, I always said, "Why don't you press the F1 key?" But it didn't make a bit of difference, since my online help pages were as long and complex as the forms they sought to simplify.

There did come a day when I escaped my phobia of form-laden applications. And on that day, I came up with the following rules for my own programs.

- Don't put too much information on a single form. When in doubt, move some information to another form.
- Present only the most necessary information and data to the user by default. Show additional information only if the user requests it.
- Make it easy for the user to access the enhanced data, but allow the program to run properly without it.
- Use text, graphics, and colors to the user's advantage.
- Simplify the application so that user documentation becomes unnecessary.
- Always provide user documentation. Make it simple enough so that calls to technical support become unnecessary.

These rules are generic enough to work with any type of application, and they are in-your-face enough to make them meaningful to us, the programmers, and to them, the users.

Commonality

Microsoft constantly touts *innovation*, and the ability to innovate has moved software products forward at a tremendous pace. But unfortunately, users can handle only so much innovation at a time. Consider the telephone. I inherited an old oak-boxed telephone from my grandparents (see Figure 3-1).

Figure 3-1. What a great phone!

It's a fun phone and so simple to use. When you want to make a call, you pick up the handset and crank the handle on the side of the unit for about three or four seconds. When the operator comes on the line, you tell her who you wish to call. What could be simpler? What could be more user-friendly? What could be more expensive than an operator-assisted call? But it was simple, and everyone instinctively knew how to use it.

Today's phones use buttons and touch screens instead of cranks. Most of the buttons on the keypad are simple digits that let you directly dial a specific phone number. But there are other buttons as well: Mute, Redial, Pause, Flash, #, and *. I'm afraid to push the Flash button, and what was the deal with the SND and CLR buttons on those older cell phones? The problem is not the buttons themselves, but that every phone has a different selection of buttons. They have lost the *commonality* that made crank phones easy to use. Sure, they have many more features, but if the average person can't figure out how to use that functionality, what is the benefit?

Getting back to software: even new and innovative programs must retain some commonality with the operating system, and with other installed programs. As you speak to users about their needs and think about the great advancements in software technology you will provide, don't forget about commonality. Don't forget about one of the core needs of users: the need to not be overwhelmed by new ways of doing tasks they thought they already could do. Users need consistency.

Project-Specific Needs

Beyond the general user needs required of every project, there are needs specific to each project. As an application designer or software architect, this is where you spend most of your time. If you have a lot of programming experience, you may be able to fulfill the other needs without ever meeting with a user. But the project-specific needs require an understanding of the tasks that the user needs to accomplish with the proposed application.

Once the users discover that you have a real interest in their needs, they may dump on you. They might start listing off a whole wish list of features, more features than they could ever use. That's OK. When they hear how much time it will take or how much it will cost to implement, they may back off on a few requests. The important thing is to *document everything*. Write down what the user asks for, combine it with a reasonable time schedule (always) and cost estimate (if required), and return it to the key user for confirmation. If possible, have the user sign a document that says he agrees with the specific requirements listed in the document.

It is essential that there be *agreement* on the project design, at least for the initial phase or release. Since users' needs are so often a moving target, it is vital that an agreement on the project exist at some point in time. Later, after you have begun work on the project, the user will come to you, probably on a daily basis, and say, "Hey, that's not what I asked for." When that happens, point to the agreement and say, "Hey, yes it is." Changes will occur; I'll discuss how to handle those a little later in this chapter.

The Life of a Project

Projects have a lifetime all their own. Some are short-lived; I've written programs that were used for two weeks and then discarded when the business project was complete. Some programs go on forever, with continual improvements made over a series of version iterations. I'm typing into such a program right now.

As a developer, you should be aware of the lifetime of your project. Once you understand the lifetime, you can apply business processes to each major phase of the project's life. The skills needed to guide a project to its conclusion, or through each successive version of the project, are collectively called *project management*. Many organizations have dedicated project managers, especially for larger projects. For small projects, the programmer may have to carry the project management burden alone.

Fortunately, most project managers don't just make things up as they go (although I have met some who did). They work within a system, a *project methodology framework*, a management system that keeps the project plan on track. I will hit the highlights of a typical framework in the remainder of this chapter. If you go back to the bookstore where you received a discount on this book, you will find a full shelf of project methodology framework resources. Microsoft even has its own recommended framework, called the Microsoft Solutions Framework (MSF). Because most of the projects Microsoft develops are renewed through successive versions, the MSF is *cyclical* or *iterative*. For applications that, at least for now, will have only one major release, a *linear* approach works well. (See Figure 3-2 for both approaches.)

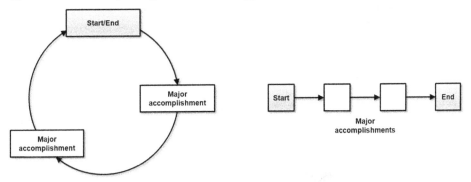

Figure 3-2. Two basic approaches to project management

Since this book will end with a completed project, and neither the next edition nor the movie rights have been arranged yet by my publisher, I will use the linear approach. Whichever approach you use, several major events happen between the start and end of the line or iteration, beginning with the project kickoff.

Project Kickoff

Once everyone agrees that there should be a project, they all come to a big meeting to get things started. Everyone who is considered to be in charge of any part of the project is there: the technical lead (you), the key user, the project manager, and the person with signature authority. If you're writing a program for yourself, only you will be in the room, but you can still provide bagels. This event, the *project kickoff*, marks the official start of the project. This meeting of the minds usually determines the initial schedule for information and resource gathering.

Documentation

It's important to document everything as you go through the entire project, especially in the early design stages. Not only will this help you recall essential aspects of the project later during the development phase, but it will also help you keep all involved parties informed about the status of the project. Imagine this conversation with your boss.

Boss:

Management is asking about the status of the Hazel Project. Do you have anything up-to-date that I can give them?

You:

Sure, I've got the project plan right here. I'll print you off a copy.

Boss:

That'd be great. Hey, did you see the new car Bernie in accounting just got?

You:

I know! How does an accountant afford a car like that?

Boss:

Beats me. It makes you wonder if he's cooking the books or something.

You:

Hey author, weren't we talking about documentation?

Oh yeah, documentation. Proper and complete documentation is important in any project. Precise documentation will keep Bernie from accounting out of the big house. And it will keep you in step with the project from initial kickoff to final delivery.

Depending on the scope of the project and the requirements of your organization, your project may need just some basic documentation, or it may need several three-inch binders filled with design documents that examine every nook and cranny of the system. Some project management documents require a signature before the project can continue. Others are informational only. As a programmer, the two most important documents are the main *project design* document (from which you will build the application) and the *schedule* (that lets you gauge progress during the project).

Project Goals

The first important item you will document is the set of *project goals*. If a project (or iteration) has a definite end, it should be possible to identify the major accomplishments needed for that ending event. These goals should be broad, and concerned with the final project *deliverables*. Deliverables are those items that are produced as a result of a project. They generally include software, user and technical documentation, installation processes, and related materials. They can also include contractual and project management items, such as a proposed schedule for the next phase or iteration of the project.

The project's goals help determine its *scope*, the extent of the features and supporting materials that will be produced during the project's lifetime. Determining scope is important because it sets the constraints, the limits that will keep the project from going out of control. Although some aspects of the project may change throughout its lifetime, if you allow a project to continue without restraint, you will find yourself months or even years behind the original schedule.

Design and Planning

My mother once gave me a rather old piece of paper with a drawing of a house floor plan. As I examined this paper in more detail, I found that the design matched the house in which I grew up, a house that is, alas, no longer part of the vast Patrick family real estate holdings. Yet it is still part of the vast Patrick family memory cells, and the home I remembered from my childhood was remarkably similar to the simple sketch.

Some forgotten builder was able to take that sketch, add wood and windows and doors and red shag carpeting and an avocado-green refrigerator, and turn it into a home.

Home builders don't work off rough sketches. Between the sketch and the builder was an *architect*, a designer who set down on paper precise details on how to build the house. An architect provides a lot of detail, although not everything. The builder still has the choice of basic materials and construction methodology. But without the project plan—the blueprints—the builder would just be hammering boards together at random, and applying red shag carpet where it didn't belong.

During the design phase, you play the role of an architect, crafting the user's dreams and wishes into a design that can then be turned into a software creation. The level of detail required in these *specifications* will vary by project and organization. For the Library Project, the bullet items listed at the start of this chapter comprise the bulk of the design detail. (It parallels the level of detail my clients have agreed to in similar projects.) Other organizations require excruciating detail, demanding flowcharts and functional specifications, diagrams, and pseudocode that is nearly as detailed as the final source code. For projects that include multiple programmers, you will likely have to specify the interfaces, the function or class member details that allow the code written by two different programmers to communicate accurately.

Whatever level of detail you include in your plan, you will also document certain key events that will happen throughout the entire project schedule. These *milestones* identify interim deliverables, results expected at specified moments throughout the timeline of the project. Comparing the milestone schedule against the actual results produced during development provides an overall view of how the project is progressing over time. Failing to meet several milestone deadlines may require an adjustment in the project schedule, cost, or scope.

Project Approval

A design document gives both the programmer and the user a point of agreement. Both sides can look at the design and say, "Yes, this is it; this is the plan." If the completed program is different from the proposed design, the user can say, "Hey, that wasn't what we agreed to." Sometimes the opposite happens; the programmer develops the application according to the plan, but the user claims that she requested something different. When this happens, the programmer can point to the design and say politely, "This is what we agreed to, and this is what was built."

To provide additional stability, the completed design usually includes a *project approval* document. This paper, signed by both the user representative and the development representative, says that (1) both sides have read the design document; (2) they agree with what it says; and (3) they commit to seeing the project through to completion as designed. As each representative *signs off* on the document, they pledge to give their support to the project.

The approval process also covers the *project cost and schedule*. A realistic estimate of the total time and costs needed to complete the project is as important as the project design itself. Any adjustments in the time and cost throughout the lifetime of the project can also provide valuable feedback on the progress being made.

Software and Other Development

Software development usually consumes most of a project's lifetime. Although the majority of work is done by the programmer or programming team, the user sometimes has a role in this step. By reviewing *prototypes* of specific portions of the application and testing *beta versions* of the nearly completed product, the user remains an active participant in this long project phase.

Changes to the Project

In general, developers always complete projects on time, under budget, and with all features included, and the satisfied user joyfully installs the software, using it daily to meet his demanding business challenges.

Ha, ha. Now that you've had a good laugh, let's continue with the chapter. Many projects do go well, and generally stick to the plan agreed to by the user and the developer. But other projects don't. Somewhere in the middle of the project's life, a change occurs. It may be due to difficulties in building the project, resulting in a *schedule change*. It may be due to new requirements in the user's needs (or desires), or in the related business process, resulting in a *scope change*.

Minor project changes may happen that neither the user nor the programmer is overly concerned about. But other changes can have a significant impact on cost or schedule, or both. Such changes can be documented and agreed to by both sides through a scope change document, sometimes called a *change order*. If the development team must adjust the schedule, or reduce or change the included features of the application, communicating this to the user through a scope change document keeps the user from being surprised at the ever-advancing end of the project.

Using scope change documents, and requiring sign-off from both sides, also helps prevent *scope creep*, the continual adjustment or expansion of software features included in the final product. As users see the progress you are making on the project, and what a great job you are doing, they may show their confidence in you by adding to the project, certain that you can complete the additional work well within the original timeline. Funneling all change requests through the scope change process provides a reality check to the user, giving him a sense of the effort (in terms of cost and schedule) required to develop software.

Acceptance Criteria Testing

There will come a day when you will say, "There, that's the last line of code I need to write for this project." Of course, you will be wrong, but it will feel good to say it. The real last day of coding won't be for several more weeks, after all of the testing is done.

Unit testing concentrates on the individual components, even down to the class and method levels. It ensures that each component or code block returns expected results when given specific input. Both good and bad inputs are sent into the components, and the results analyzed. Unit testing is actually the most cost-effective form of testing, since it is not concerned with the complex interactions of the various components that make up the entire system.

Interface testing is concerned with these interactions. Components that interact with one another are tested as a group, to make sure they work and play well together. Components that expose public interfaces are also tested for consistent results and secure access. *System testing* gives a chance for users to interact with the product, doing all they can to certify that the entire application works in a real-life setting. *Beta testing* is part of the system testing process. System testing may also involve *stress testing*, where the system is tested in extreme computing conditions to see whether it can support the load. Testing various installation scenarios ensures that the new software does not negatively impact other software or operating system components. *Regression testing* is a type of double testing. It involves retesting previously stable code to determine whether subsequent coding changes have introduced direct or indirect bugs into that code.

All of these testing phases are important, but there is one more type of testing that has a direct impact on the progression of the project: *acceptance criteria testing*. This involves a checklist of testable items that both the user and the programmer agree must pass successfully before the project is considered complete. This phase may cover items found in the other phases of testing, but it might also check for basic elements and features, such as the inclusion of quality documentation, or the delivery of the software on a certain medium, such as a CD-ROM. Once acceptance criteria testing is complete, the user signs off on that phase, and the project moves to final acceptance.

Project Acceptance

You've worked long and hard. It's been difficult at times, and perhaps you weren't sure whether you would ever finish. And I'm just talking about this chapter. Some projects take quite a while to complete, and by the end everyone should be ready to see the fruits of his or her labor. The final step in the agreement portion of the project is the *project acceptance* document. This paper, signed by the user, says that the project was completed as requested (or as modified through change orders). Once this document is signed, the project is officially complete. The programmer is now handsomely paid, and takes a well-deserved three days off.

Deployment and Distribution

The project is now ready for installation on each user's workstation. The method of distribution and delivery depends on the project and target audience. Whether it's an internal network distribution, CD distribution to a small number of locations, web-based presentation to the general public, or a mobile app for sale in a platform-specific app store, the programming team usually has limited interaction with the target workstations. Of course, that can change quickly once the technical support phone line is plugged in.

Ongoing Support

After the product has been in use by the user population for a while, reports of application errors or desired enhancements may trickle in to the development team. These can be collected for consideration in a future versioned release, or acted on immediately in *service release* updates of the product. As you may have multiple versions of the product in use within the user community, it is essential that you are able to identify and test against any particular release. *Source code control* systems allow you to maintain version-specific images of the source code. You can also maintain an archive of release executables and other files for later testing.

If your application was written for a single customer or organization, there may be a *warranty period* during which some or all errors that are reported during the length of the warranty are fixed free of charge.

Summary

Projects are more than just source code. From design documents to project management tools to online help integration to web-based support functionality, a project encompasses resources that go way beyond the basic task of coding. If you are a lone developer, you will have to wear many hats to fully support the application. Those who are part of a larger product team don't have to worry about every possible component of the project, but they also lose out on some of the joy that comes with working on every aspect of a project.

Project

There are many tasks to complete before coding begins in a large project. The actual coding of the Library Project starts in Chapter 5. For this chapter, we will complete the project agreement document that describes the Library Project features.

This chapter does not include a Visual Studio project template that you can load and examine in Visual Studio. Instead, you must access the Chapter 3 subdirectory from the book's installation directory. This subdirectory contains three Microsoft Word files.

Project Agreement.docx

> This is the primary project document that identifies the features of the completed project. It is agreed upon by both the developer and user representatives. Deviation from this document occurs only through the Change Order process.

Change Order.docx

This file is used to modify the original project through the Change Order process. When using this document, include a description of the change to be made to the project, and any schedule and cost impacts.

Project Acceptance.docx

This file is used when the project is complete, and the user is ready to accept the finished product. This document combines the "Acceptance Criteria Testing" and "Project Acceptance" elements described earlier in the chapter.

Please feel free to use these documents to support your own projects. These documents are meant as examples only. You should talk to a lawyer in your state or country if you wish to craft your own documents similar to these and have them be contractually binding.

The remainder of this section presents a portion of the Project Agreement document, the "Project Estimate and Timetable" portion that shows the expected work hours and costs needed to complete the project. The table uses the major sections of the Library Project design elements listed earlier in this chapter, assigning a number of hours for each section. For demonstration purposes, I have used an hourly rate of $25.00.

Task Description	Hourly Rate	Time Estimate	Price Estimate
1. Library Item Features	$25.00	30 hours	$750.00
2. Patron Features	$25.00	35 hours	$875.00
3. Administrative Features	$25.00	100 hours	$2,500.00
4. Application As a Whole	$25.00	35 hours	$875.00
Task Subtotal		**200 hours**	$5,000.00
5. SQL Server (estimate only)			$5,000.00
Project Total			**$10,000.00**

Chapter 4

Designing the Database

Data. Databases. It just kind of makes sense. If you have data, you need to put it somewhere. And what better place to put it than in a "data" base?

Just to make sure I had all the "bases" covered, I did a quick search on the Internet for a useful definition. What a shock. According to virtually every web site I found, a database is "a collection of data organized for easy retrieval by a computer." With a definition like that, pretty much everything I put on my system is stored in a database. All my disk files are organized for easy access. My saved emails can be sorted by subject or date received or sender, so they must be in a database, too. Even this document can be searched and sorted in any manner I wish. Is it a database?

Relational Databases

Perhaps that definition is too broad. These days, when we think of a database, it's generally a *relational database* system. Such databases are built on the "relational model" designed by Edgar Codd of IBM. In 1970, he issued "A Relational Model of Data for Large Shared Data Banks," the seminal paper on relational modeling, and later expanded on the basic concepts with C. J. Date, another real programmer. Upon reading that 1970 paper—and if you have a free afternoon, you would really benefit from spending time with your family or friends rather than reading that paper—you will enter a world of n-tuples, domains, and expressible sets. Fortunately, you don't need to know anything about these terms to use relational database systems.

The relational databases that most programmers use collect data in *tables*, each of which stores a specific set of unordered *records*. For convenience, tables are presented as a grid of data values, with each *row* representing a single record and each *column* representing a consistent *field* that appears in each record. Table 4-1 presents a table of orders, with a separate record for each line item of the order.

Table 4-1. Boy, a lot of people drink coffee and tea

Record ID	Order ID	Customer ID	Customer Name	Product ID	Product	Price	Quantity
92231	10001	AA1	Al Albertson	BEV01COF	Coffee	3.99	3
92232	10001	AA1	Al Albertson	BRD05RYE	Rye bread	2.68	1
92233	10002	BW3	Bill Williams	BEV01COF	Coffee	3.99	1
92234	10003	BW3	Will Williams	BEV01COF	Tea	3.99	2
92235	10004	CC1	Chuck Charles	CHP34PTO	Potato chips	0.99	7

Putting all of your information in a table is really convenient. The important data appears at a glance in a nice and orderly arrangement, and it's easy to sort the results based on a particular column. Unfortunately, this table of orders has a lot of repetition. Customer names and product names repeat multiple times. Also, although the product ID "BEV01COF" indicates coffee, one of the lines lists it as "Tea." A few other problems are inherent in data that's placed in a single *flat file* database table.

Mr. Codd, the brilliant computer scientist that he was, saw these problems, too. But instead of just sitting around and complaining about them like I do, he came up with a solution: *normalization*. By breaking the data into separate tables with data subsets, assigning a unique identifier to each record/row in every table (a *primary key*), and making a few other adjustments, the data could be *normalized* for both processing efficiency and data integrity. For the sample orders in Table 4-1, the data could be normalized into three separate tables: one for customers, one for products, and one for order line items (see Table 4-2, Table 4-3, and Table 4-4, respectively). In each table, I've put an asterisk next to the column title that acts as the primary key column.

Table 4-2. The table of customers

Customer ID *	Customer Name
AA1	Al Albertson
BW3	Bill Williams
CC1	Chuck Charles

Table 4-3. The table of products

Product ID *	Product Name	Unit Price
BEV01COF	Coffee	3.99
BRD05RYE	Rye bread	2.68
BEV01COF	Coffee	3.99
CHP34PTO	Potato chips	0.99

Table 4-4. The table of order line items

Record ID *	Order ID	Customer ID	Product ID	Quantity
92231	10001	AA1	BEV01COF	3
92232	10001	AA1	BRD05RYE	1
92233	10002	BW3	BEV01COF	1
92234	10003	BW3	BEV01COF	2
92235	10004	CC1	CHP34PTO	7

To get combined results from multiple tables at once, *join* (or link) their matching fields. For instance, you can link the `Customer ID` field in the table of line items with the matching `Customer ID` primary key field in the table of customers. Once joined, the details for a single combined line item record can be presented with the matching full customer name. It's the same for direct joins with any two tables that have linkable fields. Figure 4-1 shows the relationships between the customer, product, and order line tables.

Figure 4-1. Three tables, and yet they work as one

To join tables together, relational databases implement *query languages* that allow you to manipulate the data using *relational algebra* (from which the term *relational database* derives). The most popular of these languages,

---

SQL, uses simple English-like sentences to join, order, summarize, and retrieve just the data values you need. The primary statement, *SELECT*, provides basic data selection and retrieval features. Three other common statements, *INSERT*, *UPDATE*, and *DELETE*, let you manipulate the records stored in each table. Together, these four statements make up the primary *data manipulation language* (DML) commands of SQL. SQL also includes *data definition language* (DDL) statements that let you design the tables used to hold the data, as well as other database features. I'll show examples of various SQL statements later in this chapter.

Vendor-specific systems such as Microsoft's SQL Server, Oracle's Oracle, Microsoft's Access, and IBM's DB2 extend these core DDL and DML features through additional data analysis and management tools. They also battle one another over important features such as data replication, crash-proof data integrity, the speed at which complex queries return the requested results, and who has the biggest private jet.

SQL Server 2014

Microsoft's primary business-level database tool is SQL Server. Although it began its life as a derivative of Sybase (another relational database), it has been given the Microsoft touch. Unlike Access (Microsoft's other relational database product), SQL Server includes advanced data management and analysis features, and a nifty price tag to go along with those features. Although Microsoft was somewhat late in joining the relational database game, it has done a pretty good job at playing catch-up. Oracle still gets high marks for at least its perception of being the most robust, the most stable, and the most platform-independent of the various players. But SQL Server scores big as well, especially with its somewhat lower costs and its more intuitive visual tools.

Originally, Microsoft touted SQL Server as a business-minded tool for business-minded people with their business-minded agendas and their business-minded three-piece poly-knit double-breasted suits, and it is still viewed in this way. But Microsoft is increasingly identifying the database as a development tool. One of the SQL Server 2014 product editions is known as the Developer Edition, which has all the power of the high-end versions of the products, but licensed for a lone programmer at a very low cost (a few dozen dollars as opposed to around $15,000 or more for the highest Enterprise Edition). For those just looking to kick the database tires, the free Express Edition sports the core features, but with limits on database size and functionality.

SQL Server, as the name implies, is a "server" product. It runs in the background on a system and communicates with you, the user, by having you first establish a standard network connection with the server engine. This is true even if the SQL Server engine runs on your own workstation. Watching a server product is about as exciting as reading some of those other Visual C# 2015 tutorial books that you wisely avoided, so Microsoft provides various client tools that let you manage databases, tables, and other relational database properties. SQL Server Management Studio is the standard enterprise-level client tool for managing SQL Server databases, and is included with all variations of SQL Server 2014, even the Express Edition (see Figure 4-2). This tool lets you manage databases and process DDL and DML statements.

> **Note**
> All SQL statements (both DDL and DML) presented in this book and in the Library Project's source code will work with any edition of SQL Server 2014. Although Microsoft does offer a stripped-down version of SQL Server Management Studio, the examples in this book use the full edition that gets installed with SQL Server 2014.

Although Microsoft continues to update and sell Microsoft Access, it is recommending more and more that professional developers use and distribute databases in SQL Server format. Microsoft will even permit you to redistribute SQL Server 2014 Express Edition with your application.

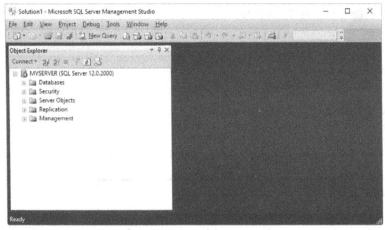

Figure 4-2. SQL Server Management Studio

SQL

Conducting business in Japan is pretty easy—once you know the language. The same is true of SQL Server: it's pretty easy to manipulate and access data, once you know the language. In this case, the language is SQL, or *Structured Query Language*. Originally developed by IBM, SQL has since become a standard across the database industry. Well, kind of. As with America and England, Microsoft's SQL Server and Oracle's Oracle are two relational databases that are divided by a common language. The core parts of the SQL language are pretty consistent between vendors, but each supplier adds a lot of extra features and syntax variations designed by Edgar Codd wannabes.

This section describes those DDL and DML statements that will be most useful in our development of the Library program. You'll be glad to know that SQL isn't too picky about the formatting of the various statements. Upper- and lowercase distinctions are ignored; `SELECT` is the same as `select` is the same as `SeLeCt`. (Traditional SQL code is mostly uppercase. I use uppercase for all keywords, and mixed case for tables, fields, and other custom items. Whatever you choose, consistency is important.) Also, employ whitespace as you see fit. You can put statements on one gigantic line, or put every word on a separate line. The only time whitespace and case matter is in the actual data text strings; whatever you type, that's how it stays.

SQL statements normally end with a semicolon, but some tools do not require you to include the semicolon, and other tools require that you exclude it. When using SQL Server Management Studio to process queries, semicolons are optional, but it's a good idea to include them when you are using multiple statements together, one after another. SQL statements used in Visual C# code never include semicolons.

Later, when you look at a SQL script I wrote, you will see the word `GO` from time to time. In SQL Server, this command says, "For all of the other statements that appeared so far, go ahead and process them now."

DDL Statements

This may come as a shock to you, but before you can store any data in a table, you have to create that table. SQL has just the tool to do this: the `CREATE TABLE` statement. It's one of the many DDL statements. The basic syntax is pretty straightforward.

```
CREATE TABLE tableName
(
```

```
    fieldName1    dataType    options,
    fieldName2    dataType    options,
    and so on...
)
```

Just fill in the parts and you're ready to populate (data, that is). *Table names* and *field names* are built from letters and digits; you can include spaces and some other special characters, but it makes for difficult coding later on. Each vendor has its own collection of *data types*; I'll stick with the SQL Server versions here. The *options* let you specify things such as whether the field requires data, whether it represents the table's primary key, and other similar *constraints*. Extensions to the syntax let you set up constraints that apply to the entire table, *indexes* (which let you sort or search a specific column more quickly), and data storage specifics.

Here's a sample *CREATE TABLE* statement that could be used for the table of order line items (refer to Table 4-4).

```
CREATE TABLE LineItems
(
    RecordID     bigint          IDENTITY PRIMARY KEY,
    OrderID      bigint          NOT NULL,
    CustomerID   varchar(20)     NOT NULL
            REFERENCES Customers (CustomerID),
    ProductID    varchar(20)     NOT NULL,
    Quantity     smallint        NOT NULL
)
```

The *IDENTITY* keyword lets SQL Server take charge of filling the *RecordID* field with data; it will use a sequential counter to supply a unique *RecordID* value with each new record. The *PRIMARY KEY* clause identifies the *RecordID* field as the unique identifying value for each record in the table. The *bigint* and *smallint* data types indicate appropriately sized integer fields, and the *varchar* type provides space for text, up to the maximum length specified in the parentheses (twenty characters). The *REFERENCES* option clause identifies a relationship between this *LineItems* table and another table named *Customers*; values in the *LineItems.CustomerID* field match the key values from the *Customers.CustomerID* field. (Note the "dot" syntax to separate table and field names. It shows up everywhere in SQL.) References between tables are also known as *foreign references*.

If you need to make structure or option changes to a table or its fields after it is created, SQL includes an *ALTER TABLE* statement that can change almost everything in the table. Additionally, there is a related *DROP TABLE* statement used to get rid of a table and all of its data. You might want to avoid this statement on live production data, as users tend to get a bit irritable when their data suddenly disappears off the surface of the earth.

Table 4-5 summarizes the available data types used in SQL Server.

Table 4-5. SQL Server data types

Data type	Description
bigint	An 8-byte (64-bit) integer field for values ranging from −9,223,372,036,854,775,808 to 9,223,372,036,854,775,807.
binary	Fixed-length binary data, up to 8,000 bytes in length. You specify the length through a parameter, as in binary(100).
bit	Supports three possible values: 1, 0, or NULL. Generally used for Boolean values. Internally, SQL Server stores multiple bit fields from a single record in a merged integer field.

Data type	Description
char, nchar	Fixed-length standard (char) or Unicode (nchar) strings, up to 8,000 characters in length. You specify the length through a parameter, as in char(100).
cursor	This data type is used within *stored procedures* (custom procedures that you create within SQL Server), and cannot be used to create a column.
datetime	A general date and time field for dates ranging from January 1, 1753 AD to December 31, 9999 AD. Time accuracy for any given value is within 3.33 milliseconds. Other related data types in SQL Server include: date (dates without times), time (times without dates), datetime2 (same as datetime, but with a larger range and accurate to 100 nanoseconds), smalldatetime (has a smaller range and a one-minute granularity), and datetimeoffset (date and time ranges).
decimal	A fixed-precision and scale decimal field. You specify the maximum number of digits to appear on both sides of the decimal point (the precision) and the maximum number of those digits that can appear on the right side of the decimal point (the scale). For instance, a setting of decimal(10,4) creates a field with up to ten total digits, four of which may appear after the decimal point. The maximum precision value is 38. numeric is a synonym for decimal, as is dec.
float	A floating-point decimal field with variable storage. You can specify the number of bits used to store the value, up to 53. By default, all 53 bits are used, so a setting of float is equivalent to float(53). The pseudo-data type real is equivalent to float(24). The values stored are on the order of $\pm 1.0 \times 10^{\pm 38}$; the exact range and precision vary by the bits used for storage. This data type is susceptible to minor calculation errors.
hierarchyid	This data type supports querying of hierarchical and tree-shaped data.
int	A 4-byte (32-bit) integer field for values ranging from −2,147,483,648 to 2,147,483,647.
money	An 8-byte (64-bit) high-accuracy field for storing currency values, with up to four digits after the decimal point. Stored data values range from −922,337,203,685,477.5808 to 922,337,203,685,477.5807.
rowversion	This data type is used to record modification events on records. There are restrictions on its use, and it is not guaranteed to be unique within a table. timestamp is a synonym for rowversion, but that term might be removed in a future release of SQL Server.
smallint	A 2-byte (16-bit) integer field for values ranging from −32,768 to 32,767.
smallmoney	A 4-byte (32-bit) high-accuracy field for storing currency values, with up to four digits after the decimal point. Stored data values range from −214,748.3648 to 214,748.3647.
sql_variant	A generic type that stores values from many other type-specific fields.
table	A special field that temporarily stores the results of a query in a compacted table format. Defining a table field is somewhat complex, and its use naturally carries with it certain restrictions.
tinyint	A 1-byte (8-bit) unsigned integer field for values ranging from 0 to 255.
uniqueidentifier	A 16-byte globally unique identifier (GUID). The related NEWID function generates values for this field.

Data type	Description
varbinary	Variable-length binary data, up to 8,000 bytes in length. You specify the length through a parameter, as in varbinary(100). The field only consumes space for the actual content currently stored in the field. A special setting of varbinary(max) allows entry of up to about two billion bytes. Another data type, image, holds similar data, but is slated for removal from SQL Server.
varchar, nvarchar	Variable-length standard (varchar) or Unicode (nvarchar) strings, up to 8,000 characters in length. You specify the length through a parameter, as in varchar(100). The field only consumes space for the actual content currently stored in the field. A special setting of varchar(max) allows entry of up to about two billion characters. Two other data types, text and ntext, hold similar data, but are slated for removal from SQL Server.
xml	Provides storage for typed and untyped XML data documents, up to two gigabytes.

DML Statements

Although DDL statements are powerful, they aren't used that much. Once you create your database objects, there's not much call for tinkering. The DML statements are more useful for everyday data surfing.

The *INSERT* statement adds data records to a table. Data is typically added to a table one record at a time, although there are multi-record syntax options. To use the *INSERT* statement, specify the destination table and fields, and then list the individual values to put into each field. One data value corresponds to each specified data column name.

```
INSERT INTO LineItems
    (OrderID, CustomerID, ProductID, Quantity)
    VALUES (10002, 'BW3', 'BEV01COF', 1)
```

Assuming this statement goes with the *CREATE TABLE* statement written earlier, this insert action will add a new record to the *LineItems* table with five new field values—four specified fields, plus the primary key automatically added to the *RecordID* field (since it was marked as *IDENTITY*). SQL Server also does a variety of data integrity checks on your behalf. Each data field you add must be of the right data type, but you already expected that. Since we designed the *CustomerID* field to be a reference to the *Customer* table, the insert will fail if customer BW3 does not already exist in the *Customer* table.

Numeric literals can be included in your SQL statements as needed without any additional qualification. String literals are always surrounded by single quotes, as is done for the customer and product IDs in the sample *INSERT* statement above. If you need to include single quotes in the literal, enter them twice.

```
'John O''Sullivan'
```

Surround literal date and time values with single quotes.

```
'7-Nov-2015'
```

Such date and time values accept any recognized format, although you should use a format that is not easy for SQL Server to misinterpret.

Many field types support an unassigned value, a value that indicates that the field contains no data at all. This is known as the "null" value, and is specified in SQL Server using the *NULL* keyword. You cannot assign *NULL* to primary key fields, or to any field marked with the *NOT NULL* option.

To remove a previously added record, issue the *DELETE* statement.

```
DELETE FROM LineItems WHERE RecordID = 92231
```

The *DELETE* statement includes a *WHERE* clause (the *WHERE RecordID = 92231* part). *WHERE* clauses let you indicate one or more records in a table by making comparisons with data fields. Your *WHERE* clauses can include *AND* and *OR* keywords to join multiple conditions, and parentheses for grouping.

```
DELETE FROM LineItems WHERE OrderID = 10001
    AND ProductID = 'BRD05RYE'
```

A *DELETE* statement may delete zero, one, or thousands of records, so precision in the *WHERE* clause is important. To delete all records in the table, exclude the *WHERE* clause altogether.

```
DELETE FROM LineItems
```

The *UPDATE* statement also uses a *WHERE* clause to modify values in existing table records.

```
UPDATE LineItems SET Quantity = 4
    WHERE RecordID = 92231
```

Assignments are made to fields with the *SET* clause; put the field name (*Quantity*) on the left side of the equals sign, and the new value on the right (*4*). To assign multiple values at once, separate each assignment with a comma. You can also include formulas and calculations.

```
UPDATE LineItems SET Quantity = Quantity + 1,
    ProductID = 'BEV02POP'
    WHERE RecordID = 92231
```

As with the *DELETE* statement, the *UPDATE* statement may update zero, one, or many records based on which records match the *WHERE* clause. Omitting the *WHERE* clause updates all records.

The final DML statement, and the one most often used, is *SELECT*.

```
SELECT ProductID, Quantity FROM LineItems
    WHERE RecordID = 92231
```

SELECT scans a table (*LineItems*), looking for all records matching a given criterion (*RecordID = 92231*), and returns a smaller table that contains just the indicated fields (*ProductID* and *Quantity*) for the matching records. The most basic query returns all rows and columns.

```
SELECT * FROM LineItems
```

This query returns all records from the table in no particular order. The asterisk (*) means "include all fields."

The optional *ORDER BY* clause returns the results in a specific order.

```
SELECT * FROM LineItems
    WHERE Quantity > 5
    ORDER BY ProductID, Quantity DESC
```

This query returns all records that have a *Quantity* field value of more than 5, and sorts the results first by the *ProductID* column (in ascending order) and then by the numeric quantity (in descending order, specified with *DESC*).

Aggregate functions and grouping features let you summarize results from the larger set of data. The following query documents the total ordered quantity for each product in the table.

```
SELECT ProductID, SUM(Quantity) FROM LineItems
    GROUP BY ProductID
```

You can use *joins* to link together the data from two or more distinct tables. The following query joins the *LineItems* and *Customer* tables on their matching *CustomerID* columns. This *SELECT* statement also demonstrates the use of table abbreviations (the "LI" and "CU" prefixes) added through the *AS* clauses; they aren't usually necessary, but they can help make a complex query more readable.

```
SELECT LI.OrderID, CU.CustomerName, LI.ProductID
   FROM LineItems AS LI
   INNER JOIN Customer AS CU ON LI.CustomerID = CU.CustomerID
   ORDER BY LI.OrderID, CU.CustomerName
```

This table uses an inner join, one of the five main types of joins, each of which returns different sets of records based on the relationship between the first (left) and second (right) tables in the join.

Inner join

Returns only those records where there is a match in the linked fields. This type of join uses the `INNER JOIN` keywords.

Left outer join

Returns every record from the left table and only those records from the right table where there is a match in the linked fields. If a left table record doesn't have a match, it acts as though all the fields in the right table for that record contain `NULL` values. This type of join uses the `LEFT JOIN` keywords. One use might be to join the `Product` and `LineItems` tables. You could return a list of the full product name for all available products, plus the total quantity ordered for each one. By putting the `Product` table on the left of a left outer join, the query would return all product names, even if that product had never been ordered (and didn't appear in the `LineItems` table).

Right outer join

This works just like a left outer join, but all records from the right table are returned, and just the left table records that have a match. This type of join uses the `RIGHT JOIN` keywords.

Full outer join

Returns all records from the left and right tables, whether they have matches or not. When there is a match, it is reflected in the results. This type of join uses the `FULL JOIN` keywords.

Cross join

Also called a *Cartesian join*. Returns every possible combination of left and right records. This type of join uses the `CROSS JOIN` keywords.

Joining focuses on the relationship that two tables have. (This use of "relationship," by the way, is not the basis for the term *relational database*.) Some tables exist in a parent-child relationship; one "parent" record has one or more dependent "child" records in another table. This is often true of orders; a single order header has multiple line items. This type of relationship is known as *one-to-many*, since one record is tied to many records in the other table. And the relationship is unidirectional; a given child record does not tie to multiple parent records.

A *one-to-one* relationship ties a single record in one table to a single record in another table. It's pretty straightforward, and is often used to enhance the values found in the original record through a supplementary record in a second table.

In a *many-to-many* relationship, a single record in one table is associated with multiple records in a second table, *and* a single record in that second table is also associated with multiple records in the first table. A real-world example would be the relationship between teachers and students in a college setting. One teacher has multiple students in the classroom, but each student also has multiple teachers each semester. Practical implementations of many-to-many relationships actually require three tables: the two related tables, and a go-between table that links them together. I will show you a sample of such a table in the upcoming "Project" section of this chapter.

Beyond Basic SQL

The sample statements I listed here only scratch the surface of the data manipulation possibilities available through SQL. By now you should have noticed that SQL is remarkably English-like in syntax. In fact, the original name for the language—SEQUEL—was an acronym for "Structured *English* Query Language." As the SQL statements get more complex, they will look less and less like an eighth-grade essay and more like random collections of English words.

The goal here is to introduce you to the basic structure of SQL statements. Most of the statements we will encounter in the Library Project will be no more complex than the samples included here. If you're hungry for more, access the "Books Online for SQL Server 2014" documentation on Microsoft's MSDN web site. Several good books on the ins and outs of SQL, including vendor-specific dialects, are also available.

Using Databases in Visual C#

Visual C# can interact with data stored in a database in a few different ways.

- Use ADO.NET, the primary data access technology included in the .NET Framework, to interact with database-stored content. This is the method used throughout the Library program to interact with its database. ADO.NET is discussed in Chapter 10, with examples of its use. I will also introduce ADO.NET-specific code into the Library Project in that chapter.

- Use the *data binding* features available in Visual C# and Visual Studio. Binding establishes a connection between an on-screen data control or similar data-enabled object and content from a database. Code written for you by Microsoft takes care of all the communication work; you can even drag and drop these types of interactions. Although I will discuss data binding in Chapter 10 (since binding is based on ADO.NET), I tend to avoid it since it reduces the amount of control the programmer can exert on user data management. Data binding will not be used in the Library program.

- Extract the data from the database into a standard file, and use file manipulation features in .NET to process the data. Hmm, that doesn't seem very useful, but I have actually had to do it, especially in the old days when some proprietary databases could not interact easily with C# code.

- Each time you need some of the data, tell the user that somehow the data has been lost, and that it must be reentered immediately. If you have ever been curious to know what the inside of an unemployment office looks like, this could be your chance.

Documenting the Database

Technical content that describes the tables and fields in your application's database represents the most important piece of documentation generated during your application's lifetime. In fact, the need for good documentation is the basis for one of my core programming beliefs: project documentation is as important, and sometimes more important, than source code.

You may think I'm joking about this. Although you will (hopefully) find a lot of humor in the pages of this book, this is something I don't joke about. If you are developing an application that centers on database-stored user content, complete and accurate documentation of every table and field used in the database is a must. Any lack in this area will—not might, not perhaps, but will—lead to data integrity issues and a longer-than-necessary development timeline. Figure 4-3 puts it another way.

This is your application.

This is your application without database documentation.

This is your application with database documentation.

Figure 4-3. Any questions?

Why do I think that database documentation is even more important than user documentation or functional specifications? It's because of the impact the document will have on the user's data. If you have a documented database, you can make guesses about the functional specification, and probably come pretty close. If you lack user documentation, you can always write it when the program is done (as though there was any other way?). But if you lack database documentation, you are in for a world of hurt.

If you haven't worked on large database projects before, you might not believe me. But I have. I once inherited an existing enterprise-wide database system written in Visual Basic 3.0. The source code was bad enough, but the associated undocumented 100-table database was a mishmash of inconsistently stored data values. The confusing stored procedure code wasn't much better. Since there wasn't a clear set of documentation on each field, the six programmers who originally developed the system had each made their own decisions about what range of data would be allowed in each field, or about which fields were required or not.

Tracing back through the uncommented 100,000 lines of source code to determine what every field did was not fun, and it took a few months to complete it with accuracy. Since the customer had paid for and expected a stable and coherent system, most of the extra cost involved in replacing the documentation that should have been there in the first place was borne by my development group. Don't let this happen to you!

Summary

Most Windows applications target the business world and are designed to interact with some sort of database. Understanding the database system used with your application is important; even more important is documenting the specific database features you incorporate into your application.

Because of the influence of relational databases and the SQL language on the database industry, it won't be hard to find a lot of resources to assist you in crafting SQL statements and complex data analysis queries. The Library Project in this book uses SQL Server 2014, but because of the generally consistent use of the core SQL language features, the application could just as easily have used Oracle, Microsoft Access, or any of a number of other relational databases.

Project

To assist in my development of Visual C# database projects, I always write a "Technical Resource Kit" document before I begin the actual coding of the application. The bulk of this word processing document consists of the table- and field-level documentation for the application's associated database. Also included are the formats for all configuration and custom data files, documentation on exposed API functions and data expectations, and information about third-party products used in the application. Depending on the type of application, my expectations for the user, and the terms of any contract, I may supply none, some, or all of the Resource Kit's content to the user community.

Let's begin the Technical Resource Kit for the Library Project by designing and documenting the database tables to be used by the application. This Resource Kit appears in the book's installation directory, in the Chapter 4 subdirectory, and contains the following three files.

ACME Library Resource Kit.docx

A Microsoft Word version of the technical documentation for the project

ACME Library Resource Kit.pdf

A second copy of the Technical Resource Kit, this time in Adobe Acrobat (PDF) format

Database Creation Script.sql

A SQL Server database script used to build the actual tables and fields in the database

Database Table Documentation

The bulk of the Technical Resource Kit documents each database table, showing the column names, data types, and expected data values that will appear in each table in the Library database. For example, the `NamedItem` entry describes the table that manages the list of library items, such as books, CDs, and magazines. It lists the table's fourteen columns, including its automatically assigned primary key field, ID.

Table 4-6. The NamedItem table

Field	Type	Description
ID	bigint	Primary key; automatically assigned. Required.
Title	varchar(150)	Title of this item. Required.
Subtitle	varchar(150)	Subtitle of this item. Optional.
Description	varchar(max)	Full description of this item. Optional.
Edition	varchar(10)	Edition number for this item. Optional.
Publisher	bigint	This item's publisher. Foreign reference to `Publisher.ID`. Optional.
Dewey	varchar(20)	Dewey decimal number. Use / for line breaks. Optional.
LC	varchar(25)	Library of Congress number. Use / for line breaks. Optional.
ISxN	varchar(20)	ISBN, ISSN, or other standardized number of this item. Optional.
LCCN	varchar(12)	Library of Congress control number. Optional.
Copyright	smallint	Year of original copyright, or of believed original copyright. Optional.
Series	bigint	The series or collection in which this item appears. Foreign reference to `CodeSeries.ID`. Optional.
MediaType	bigint	The media classification of this item. Foreign reference to `CodeMediaType.ID`. Required.
OutOfPrint	bit	Is this title out of print? *0* for False, *1* for True. Required.

This table is just one of two key tables involved in tracking library items. The other, `ItemCopy`, stores details about individual copies of each book. For example, if the library contains two identical copies of *The Count of Monte Cristo*, the `NamedItem` table will contain one record that describes the book, and the `ItemCopy` table will contain two distinct records, one for each physical, optionally barcoded copy.

Table 4-7. The ItemCopy table

Field	Type	Description
ID	bigint	Primary key; automatically assigned. Required.
ItemID	bigint	The related named item record. Foreign reference to *NamedItem.ID*. Required.
CopyNumber	smallint	Numbered position of this item within the set of copies for a named item. Required, and unique among items with the same *ItemID* field value.
Description	varchar(max)	Comments specific to this copy of the item. Optional.
Available	bit	Is this copy available for checkout or circulation? *0* for False, *1* for True. Required.
Missing	bit	Has this copy been reported missing? *0* for False, *1* for True. Required.
Reference	bit	Is this a reference copy? *0* for False, *1* for True. Required.
Condition	varchar(30)	Any comments relevant to the condition of this copy. Optional.
Acquired	datetime	Date this copy was acquired by the library. Optional.
Cost	money	Value of this item, either original or replacement value. Optional.
Status	bigint	The general status of this copy. Foreign reference to *CodeCopyStatus.ID*. Required.
Barcode	varchar(20)	Barcode found on the copy. At this time, only numeric barcodes are supported. Optional.
Location	bigint	The site or room location of this item. Foreign reference to *CodeLocation.ID*. Optional.

The link occurs between the *NamedItem.ID* and *ItemCopy.ItemID* fields. Together, the records form a one-to-many relationship: one *NamedItem* record that links to many (two, in this case) *ItemCopy* records.

Another table relationship described earlier in the chapter is the many-to-many relationship, such as the association between teachers and students across multiple classrooms. In the Library database, one such relationship appears when dealing with book authors, like me. In the database, each book can have multiple authors. Also, one specific author can be associated with (be the author of) multiple books. This many-to-many relationship requires three tables. The first is the *NamedItem* table, shown above, representing the book side of the association. The *Author* table handles the other side, listing individual authors, illustrators, performers, and others who create or contribute to media items typically found in libraries.

Table 4-8. The Author table

Field	Type	Description
ID	bigint	Primary key; automatically assigned. Required.
LastName	varchar(50)	Last name of this author. Required.
FirstName	varchar(30)	First name of this author. Optional.
MiddleName	varchar(30)	Middle name or initial of this author. Optional.
Suffix	varchar(10)	Name suffix, such as "Jr." Optional.
BirthYear	smallint	Year of birth. Use negative numbers for BC. Optional.
DeathYear	smallint	Year of death. Use negative numbers for BC. Optional.
Comments	varchar(250)	Miscellaneous comments about this author. Optional.

The connection between a given book and a given author exists through the `ItemAuthor` table. Each record in this table identifies a single `NamedItem` record by its `ID` (through the `ItemID` field in the `ItemAuthor` table), and also a single `Author` record by its `ID` (through the `AuthorID` field in the `ItemAuthor` table).

Table 4-9. The ItemAuthor table

Field	Type	Description
ItemID	bigint	Primary key. The associated named item. Foreign reference to `NamedItem.ID`. Required.
AuthorID	bigint	Primary key. The author associated with the named item. Foreign reference to `Author.ID`. Required.
Sequence	smallint	Relative order of this author among the authors for this named item. Authors with smaller numbers appear first. Required.
AuthorType	bigint	The specific type of contribution given by this author for this named item. Foreign reference to `CodeAuthorType.ID`. Required.

An interesting aspect of this linking table is its primary key. Other tables we've seen so far, such as the `Author` table, had a single primary key field: the `ID` field. The database automatically generated values for these key fields, and each `ID` value in the table was guaranteed to be unique, a requirement for any primary key. In the `ItemAuthor` table, the primary key moniker applies to two fields: `ItemID` and `AuthorID`. As with the `ID` field in the other tables, this *two-part key* uniquely identifies each record in the table. Only one record can ever have a specific combination of a given `ItemID` and a given `AuthorID`. Additionally, the databases does not generate these values automatically. Instead, they are specified as part of an `INSERT` statement when creating new linking records.

As an example, consider two movies starring Harrison Ford: the original *Star Wars*, directed by George Lucas; and *Raiders of the Lost Ark*, directed by Steven Spielberg. Both movies share a common performer: Harrison Ford. But each one has a distinct record. Establishing these relationships for the DVD editions of these movies in the Library database requires nine records: two `NamedItem` records, three `Author` records, and four `ItemAuthor` records.

Table 4-10. Sample NamedItem records

ID	Title
1	Star Wars
2	Raiders of the Lost Ark

Table 4-11. Sample Author records

ID	LastName	FirstName
1	Ford	Harrison
2	Lucas	George
3	Spielberg	Steven

Table 4-12. Sample ItemAuthor records (with comments)

ItemID	AuthorID	What it Links
1	1	*Star Wars* with Ford
1	2	*Star Wars* with Lucas
2	1	*Raiders* with Ford
2	3	*Raiders* with Spielberg

In this sample, there is nothing that indicates that Harrison Ford is an actor, or that George Lucas isn't an actor. These types of "author" descriptions (author, illustrator, actor, director, editor, and so on) appear in one of the Library database's many code tables. In this case, it's the `CodeAuthorType` table that lists the possible contributor types.

Table 4-13. The CodeAuthorType table

Field	Type	Description
ID	bigint	Primary key; automatically assigned. Required.
FullName	varchar(50)	Name of this type of author or contributor. Required.

All of the code tables in the database have more or less the same structure: a generated `ID` field and a `FullName` description field. This common structure makes it easy to create shared editing code when it comes time to develop the application logic for maintaining the table's records.

Most of the tables in the Library database exist to manage items tracked by the library: books, authors, patrons, administrators, publishers, and so on. There is one table that exists for the benefit of the developer, and it is named `SystemValue`.

Table 4-14. The SystemValue table

Field	Type	Description
ID	bigint	Primary key; automatically assigned. Required.
ValueName	varchar(50)	Name of this value. Required.
ValueData	varchar(100)	Information associated with this entry. Optional.

The records of this table contain configuration items that are shared among all users of the application within a library system. In each record, the `ValueName` field specifies the name of the configuration element, and `ValueData` contains its actual value. The Technical Resource Kit describes each possible `ValueName` that may appear in this table, along with a complete description of the data values allowed for that entry. For example, a record with a `ValueName` of "PatronCheckOut" allows the following content in its associated `ValueData` field, as documented in the Resource Kit.

> Indicates whether patrons can check out items without being logged in as an administrative user. Use a value of `0` (zero) to indicate no checkout privileges, or any nonzero value to allow patron checkout (-1 is preferred). If this value is missing or empty, patrons will not be allowed to check out items without administrator assistance.

Beyond the tables described here, the Library database contains nearly two dozen other tables. Be sure to read the complete Technical Resource Kit document provided with the downloaded source code to understand all of the structural elements that make up the Library database.

Creating the Database

Adding the database to SQL Server is almost as easy as documenting it; in fact, it requires less typing. The `CREATE TABLE` statements are straightforward, and they all pretty much look the same. I'm going to show only a few of them here. The *Database Creation Script.sql* file in this chapter's sample code directory includes the full script content.

If you haven't done so already, install your preferred edition of SQL Server 2014 (or whichever version of the database you will be using; the script will work for all versions going back to at least SQL Server's 2005 release). SQL Server 2014 Management Studio should be installed as well as part of the normal SQL Server installation process.

Most of the tables in the Library Project are simple data tables with a single primary key. Their code is straightforward. The `Author` table is a good example.

```
CREATE TABLE Author
(
    ID           bigint         IDENTITY PRIMARY KEY,
    LastName     varchar(50)    NOT NULL,
    FirstName    varchar(30)    NULL,
    MiddleName   varchar(30)    NULL,
    Suffix       varchar(10)    NULL,
    BirthYear    smallint       NULL,
    DeathYear    smallint       NULL,
    Comments     varchar(250)   NULL
);
```

The fields included in each *CREATE TABLE* statement appear as a comma-delimited list, all enclosed in parentheses. Each field includes either a *NULL* or a *NOT NULL* option that indicates whether *NULL* values may be used in that field. The *PRIMARY KEY* option automatically specifies *NOT NULL*.

Some statements create tables that link two other tables in a many-to-many relationship. One example is the *GroupActivity* table, which connects the *GroupName* table with the *Activity* table.

```
CREATE TABLE GroupActivity
(
    GroupID      bigint     NOT NULL,
    ActivityID   bigint     NOT NULL,
    PRIMARY KEY (GroupID, ActivityID)
);
```

The *Author* table had a single primary key, so the *PRIMARY KEY* option could be attached directly to its *ID* field. Since the *GroupActivity* table has a two-part primary key, the *PRIMARY KEY* option is specified as an entry all its own, with the key fields included as a parentheses-enclosed, comma-delimited list.

Earlier in this chapter, I showed how you could establish a reference to a field in another table by using the *REFERENCES* constraint as part of the *CREATE TABLE* statement. You can also establish them after the tables are already in place, as I do in the script. Here is the statement that establishes the link between the *GroupActivity* and *GroupName* tables.

```
ALTER TABLE GroupActivity
    ADD FOREIGN KEY (GroupID)
    REFERENCES GroupName (ID);
```

Since I've already written the entire SQL script for you, I'll just have you process it directly using Microsoft SQL Server 2014 Management Studio. Before adding the tables, we need to create a database specific to the Library Project. Start Microsoft SQL Server 2014 Management Studio and connect to the target instance.

To add a new database for the Library Project, right-click on the Databases folder in the Object Explorer, and select New Database from the shortcut menu. On the New Database form that appears, enter `Library` in the Database Name field, and then click OK.

The Library database is a shell of a database; it doesn't contain any tables or data yet. Let's use the *Database Creation Script.sql* file from the book's installation directory to generate the tables and initial data. In Management Studio, select the File→Open→File menu command, and locate the *Database Creation Script.sql* file. (You may be prompted to log in to SQL Server again.) Opening this file places its content in a new panel within Management Studio.

All that's left to do is to process the script. In the toolbar area, make sure that "Library" is the selected database (see Figure 4-4). Then click the Execute toolbar button, or press the F5 key. It's a small script with not a lot going on (at least from SQL Server's point of view), so it should finish in just a few seconds.

Figure 4-4. If you don't select "Library," your tables will go somewhere else

That's it! Close the script panel. Then, back in the Object Explorer, right-click on the *Library* database folder and select Refresh from the menu. If you then expand the Library database branch and its Tables sub-branch, you will see all the tables created by the script (see Figure 4-5).

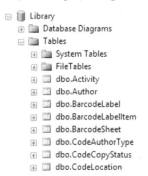

Figure 4-5. Partial list of database tables

With the database done, it's time to start programming.

Chapter 5

.NET Assemblies

The mere mention of the word *assembly* takes me back to my days as a high school freshman. The assembly was actually held in the school gym, with 2,000 screaming adolescents filling the bleachers around the basketball court. Since this was a school function, I naturally thought of an experience packed with fresh educational opportunities. School, education—the words just seem to go together. But then came the marching band, and the football players, and the cheerleaders, and the school mascot (a horse). For the next thirty minutes, the principal whipped the students into a controlled frenzy, attempting to prove the institution's place as the number-one school in the city. I still don't know what area we were supposed to be number one in, but it was all very exciting.

.NET assemblies are not that exciting. In fact, they're just files, executable and DLL files, and without you to activate them, they just sit there taking up disk space. And as they are not doing anything else, let's take a moment to examine what they are and what they contain.

What Is an Assembly?

As I already mentioned in Chapter 1, an assembly is a *unit of deployment*, which in most cases is just a file. An assembly is a repository for compiled .NET application code; any code you write will eventually be stored in some application file (such as an *.exe* file) or a code library file (a *.dll* file). Everything that .NET needs to know to load and run your application is stored in the assembly.

Assemblies are either private or public. *Private assemblies* are designed for use in a single application only. If there aren't any supporting library assemblies, then the executable assembly *is* the application. Private assemblies appear in their own directory, the *installation directory* of the application or library. You can run two different private assemblies at the same time, and they won't bother each other. This is true even if each assembly uses the same combination of namespace and class names for its coded elements. If two application assemblies each implement a class named `WindowsFormsApplication1.Class1`, they will not interfere with each other when running; they are private, and private means private.

Public assemblies are designed for shared use among multiple .NET applications. Public assemblies differ from private assemblies in two major ways.

- Public assemblies always have a *strong name*, an encrypted digital signature that is attached to an assembly to guarantee that it came from its named vendor or source. (Private assemblies can also include a strong name, but they don't have to.) The strong name is built from the assembly's name, version number, culture information, a public key, and a digital signature generated from the assembly file that contains the manifest (described later). The .NET Framework includes a strong name generation tool (*sn.exe*) that assists in this process, and Visual Studio includes options that let you add a digital signature during the compilation process. (It's on the Signing tab of the project's properties.)

The strong name of an assembly should be (and better be) unique; if two assemblies share a common strong name, they are copies of the same assembly.

- Public assemblies appear in the Global Assembly Cache (GAC). Although you can put a copy of your shared component in your application's install directory, it will only truly be shared once it reaches the GAC directory. The GAC lives in a directory named *assembly* within the computer's Windows directory. (On my system, it's in *c:\windows\assembly*.) Once a .NET assembly has a strong name applied, you can add it to the GAC by either dragging the file into the *assembly* directory or by using the Global Assembly Cache Tool (*gacutil.exe*). Don't worry about your file being lonely if it's not communing with your other installed files. On my freshly installed copy of .NET, I found over a hundred files already in the GAC directory, including all the DLLs for the Framework Class Library (FCL).

.NET lets you install multiple versions of an assembly on a system and use them at the same time (a process called *versioning*). This applies both to applications and libraries, and to private assemblies and shared assemblies in the GAC. The GAC may also contains identically named assembly files that differ by things like target platform (x86 vs. AMD, for instance), language culture, or version number. Don't believe me? Open up the GAC's *assembly* folder, set the Explorer folder to a Details view, and then sort by Assembly Name. If you scroll down, you'll see the same file show up multiple times. Figure 5-1 shows a part of the cache. But each one has a different target or use in mind.

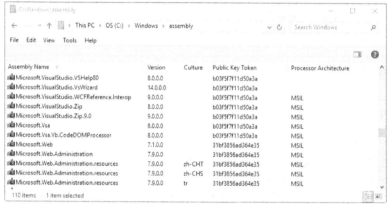

Figure 5-1. The GAC has this duplication under control

Although there is usually a one-to-one relationship between files and assemblies, there may be cases when an assembly is made up of multiple files. For instance, an application might include an external graphics file in its assembly view. .NET keeps a close watch on these files. If any of the files are modified, deleted, or otherwise maimed, you will hear about it. For the purposes of discussion, the rest of this chapter considers only single-file assemblies.

What's Inside an Assembly?

An assembly file is a standard Portable Execution (PE) file, the same file format used for non-.NET Windows executables and code libraries (pretty much any Windows *.exe* or *.dll* file). What makes .NET PE files different is all the extra stuff found inside. As a general word, *assembly* indicates a gathering together of various parts into a single unit. In a .NET assembly, these "various parts" are specifically designed for use with .NET.

A .NET PE file contains three main parts.

A PE header

Required of all PE files, this section identifies the locations of the other sections of the file.

The MSIL code section

The actual code associated with the assembly is stored as semi-compiled Microsoft Intermediate Language (MSIL) code. Unfortunately, the CPU in your computer is apparently too brainless to process MSIL code directly (what were they thinking?), so the .NET Framework includes a platform-specific *just-in-time* (JIT) compiler that can convert MSIL to native code at a moment's notice. The type of native code emitted will vary depending on where the executable is used (Windows, mobile, non-Microsoft, etc.).

The Metadata section

All of the extra detail that .NET needs to rummage through to know about your assembly appears in this essential section. Some of these items, when taken together, make up the assembly's manifest, a type of document that completely describes the assembly to the world. In the following list of metadata elements, I've noted which items appear in the manifest.

The name of the assembly

(Part of the manifest.) This is defined on the Application tab of the project's properties.

The version number of the assembly

(Part of the manifest.) That's the four-part version number, as in 1.2.3.4. You've probably been wondering all day how you could set this number in your own projects. Your patience will be rewarded in this chapter's "Project" section, where I will demonstrate not just one, but two ways to set the assembly version number.

Strong name content

(Part of the manifest.) This includes the publisher's public key.

Culture and language settings

(Part of the manifest.) This is especially useful when you need to create language-specific resource files.

Assembly file listing

(Part of the manifest.) Single-file assemblies will show only the assembly filename, but some assemblies may include several files in this section. All files in an assembly must appear within the same directory, or in a directory subordinate to the assembly file that contains the manifest.

Exported type information

(Part of the manifest.) Some assemblies export some of their types for use outside the application. The details of those types appear here.

References

(Part of the manifest, but in multi-file assemblies, each file will contain its own list of references.) The metadata includes a listing of all external assemblies referenced by your application, whether they are private or appear in the GAC. This list indicates which specific version, culture, and platform-target of the external assembly your assembly expects.

Internal type information

(Not part of the manifest.) All types crafted in your assembly are fully described within the metadata. Also, any additional metadata you added to your types through Visual C#'s attribute feature appear here.

In multi-file assemblies, the manifest-specific elements appear only in the main file of the assembly.

The manifest is a subset of the metadata within your assembly. I hate to say that it's the most important part of the metadata—but it is. The manifest is the public expression of your assembly, and the only way that .NET knows whether it is legit. It's sort of like the "Nutrition Facts" label put on American food packaging (see Figure 5-2).

Assembly Facts

Serving Size   1 assembly
Files Per Assembly   1

Amount Per Assembly

Exported Types   12

	% Daily Value*
References 5	50%
Cultures 3	300%
Version 1.0.0.4	
Vitamin C#	100%
Vitamin VB	0%

* Percent Daily Values are based on a Core i5 with 8GB memory. Your daily needs may be lower, but I doubt it.

Figure 5-2. Is that really good for me?

When you look at the food label, you know what the food package contains—although no one really knows what *riboflavin* is. When you look at the manifest for an assembly, you know at a glance what the assembly contains, and what requirements it has before it can be loaded and run.

Even before .NET burst onto the scene, executables and libraries already contained some metadata, such as the version number of the file. But this data wasn't used to manage access between software components, nor was it organized in a generic and extensible way. The metadata in .NET embodies all of these attributes.

The presence of both the MSIL and metadata in each assembly makes these files very readable and understandable. With the right tools, even I seem to understand them. And if I can, anyone can, which leads to a big problem. Companies invest a lot of time and money in their software development efforts, and they don't want any rinky-dink two-bit startup reverse-engineering their code and getting all their algorithmic secrets. To prevent this casual reading of any .NET application, Microsoft and other third parties include *obfuscators*, software programs that scramble the contents of an assembly just enough so that it's hard for humans to understand, but not for the .NET Framework. I'll talk more about obfuscation in Chapter 22.

Reflection

It may be a bad thing for people to access the content of an assembly, but it's great when the code in an assembly can access itself. .NET includes a feature called *reflection* that lets you examine the contents of an assembly. You generally use this feature to access metadata in your own assembly, but it also works with any available assembly. Most reflection-related features appear in the `System.Reflection` namespace.

Through reflection, you can extract pretty much anything stored in the metadata of an assembly, including details on all types, their members, and even the parameters included with function members. This is why obfuscation is so important to vendors; between the compiled MSIL and the metadata, you can virtually regenerate the entire source code for an application from just its executable. The source code would be in MSIL, but it wouldn't be that tough for someone to massage much of it back into C# or Visual Basic.

Assemblies and Applications

.NET applications are an instance of an assembly. But a single application can include multiple assemblies; it fact, it almost always does. I wrote a little program that uses reflection to list all assemblies actively being used by the program itself. I gave the program the default name of *WindowsFormsApplication1*. When I ran the program against itself, it generated the following list.

```
mscorlib
Microsoft.VisualStudio.HostingProcess.Utilities
System.Windows.Forms
Microsoft.VisualStudio.HostingProcess.Utilities.Sync
System
Microsoft.VisualStudio.Debugger.Runtime
vshost32
System.Core
System.Xml.Linq
System.Data.DataSetExtensions
Microsoft.CSharp
System.Data
System.Deployment
System.Drawing
System.Net.Http
System.Xml
WindowsFormsApplication1
Accessibility
```

Wow! Eighteen assemblies, including *WindowsFormsApplication1*, the main program. Most of the assemblies are framework-supplied DLLs. For `Microsoft.CSharp`, it's the *Microsoft.CSharp.dll* assembly; for `System`, it's the *System.dll* assembly. All of the assemblies (except the main program assembly) are shared libraries from the GAC. The application can also support private assemblies loaded from local DLL files.

The .NET Framework automatically loaded these assemblies for me when *WindowsFormsApplication1* started up; it figured out which ones needed to be loaded by looking in the manifest for *WindowsFormsApplication1*. When the framework loaded each assembly, it checked to see whether those assemblies in turn needed additional assemblies loaded, and so on. Pretty soon, your once-simple application becomes a dumping ground for assemblies all over the GAC. But that's OK, since the purpose of .NET is to manage it all.

Directives and Assemblies

Directives are Visual C# statements—but then again, they're not. The key directives—`#define`, `#undef`, and `#if` (and its related `#elif`, `#else`, and `#endif` directives)—provide instructions to the compiler on how to handle a block of Visual C# source code. (Another common directive, `#region`, helps to visually present source code within Visual Studio, but it has no impact on the compiler or the final compiled application. It shows up regularly in the Visual Studio-generated designer files for your forms.) By using directives, you can tell the compiler to include or exclude specific chunks of source code from the final project. So, they aren't really C# source code statements, but they are available only in Visual C#.

Why would you want to include or exclude code in an application? Well, I can think of several good reasons, some of which involve the CIA and former Federal Reserve chairman Alan Greenspan. But the most common use is when you want to produce two different versions of your application, based on some condition. For example, you may sell an "express" version and a "professional" version of a product. Much of the code is identical for the two versions, but the professional version would include features not available in the express version. Also, the express version may include a simplified presentation for a feature that has a more complex usage in the professional edition.

Some software products fulfill this need by using standard C# conditions.

```
if (professionalVersion == true)
    ShowWhizBangFeatures();
else
    ShowLaughableFeatures();
```

This, of course, works just fine. But the express application still contains all the enhanced features. Since it can't access any of that code, why even include it in the installation package? If you use directives, you can mark down that problem as solved. Directives use conditional expressions, much like the `professionalVersion == true` condition in the preceding block of code. But they are defined with the `#define` statement, and are called *compiler constants*.

```
#define fullVersion
```

This statement defines a Boolean compiler constant. The constant can be used only with directives; if you try to use `fullVersion` in a standard C# statement, the compiler will complain. But it will work just fine in the `#if` directive.

```
#if (fullVersion)
    ShowWhizBangFeatures();
#else
    ShowLaughableFeatures();
#endif
```

This code looks a lot like the previous code block, but with the added # signs. It looks the same but it's not. With the plain `if` statement, the following code gets compiled into the final application.

```
if (professionalVersion == true)
    ShowWhizBangFeatures();
else
    ShowLaughableFeatures();
```

Yeah, the whole block of code. But with the directives, what gets included in the compiled application depends on the state of `fullVersion`. If `fullVersion` is defined with the `#define` directive, this gets compiled into the compiled application.

```
ShowWhizBangFeatures();
```

The other lines are gone; they've vanished...into thin air, as though they never existed. But in this case, it's a good thing. The goal was to have a version of the assembly completely devoid of the undesired code, and that's what happened.

To set the *fullVersion* compiler constant to generate the full version, you include this line at the top of each source code file that includes conditional *#if* code blocks.

```
#define fullVersion
```

When you're ready to generate the express version, just remove the line, or use the *#undef* directive to make it clear that *fullVersion* is false.

```
#undef fullVersion
```

Somehow, changing this line in every source code file that needs it seems like a lot of work, and it is. And what happens if I forget to set one of them to the right directive? No good, I can tell you.

To keep Visual C# developers from running down the halls screaming more than they normally would, Visual Studio provides a few different ways to set compiler constants once, and have them apply to every part of the application. The most common way to do this is through the project properties' Build panel (see Figure 5-3). Add your global compiler constants to the Conditional Compilation Symbols field. If you exclude a symbol from this list, the compiler acts as if you used *#undef* with the symbol.

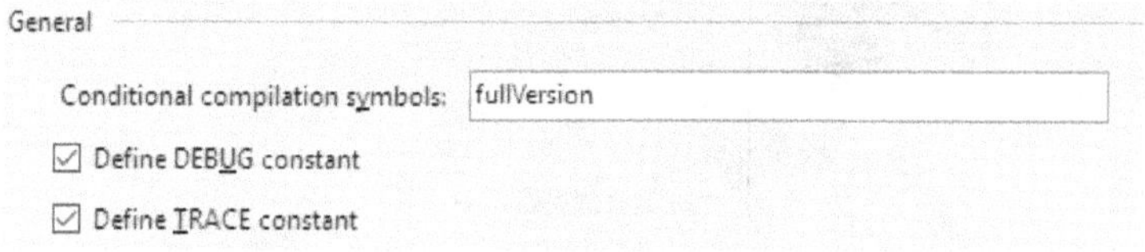

General ────────────────────────────────

Conditional compilation symbols: fullVersion

☑ Define DEBUG constant

☑ Define TRACE constant

Figure 5-3. This is a whole lot easier than all that typing

Now, by either including or omitting *fullVersion* from this field, you can build different versions of the application. The Visual C# compiler also provides features that let you set up different compile scripts for your project. I won't talk about it in this book, but you can read up on the MSBuild tool in the MSDN documentation if you need this level of control.

Compiler constants come in handy when you develop mobile applications using the Xamarin.Forms library included with Visual Studio. This library lets you target Windows Phone, iOS, and Android platforms from a single application. When writing your code for such apps, much of the code will be common to all platforms. For those sections that are platform-specific, *#if* blocks allow you, for example, to exclude iOS code from the Android version.

Summary

Assemblies aren't just souped-up *.exe* or *.dll* files; they contain gobs of metadata, including the manifest, that make .NET applications *self-describing*. The compiler uses this information to correctly configure and process the managed MSIL code in each assembly.

Although not actually parts of an assembly, this chapter also discussed directives, a feature that impacts what code gets included in your assembly.

Project

This chapter's project officially kicks off the coding of the Library Project (muted applause). We'll start off with something simple: building the About form that provides basic information about the application, including its version number.

> **Project Access**
> Load the "Chapter 5 (Before) Code" project, either through the New Project templates or by accessing the project directly from the installation directory. To see the code in its final form, load "Chapter 5 (After) Code" instead.

Our goal is a pleasant form that conveys basic information about the program, a form that looks something like Figure 5-4.

Figure 5-4. Everything you wanted to know about the program

Like any Visual C# application for Windows, the creation of this form involves two steps: (1) adding controls to the form; and (2) writing the related code.

Adding Controls

If there is one area where Visual C# excels, it is in creating desktop application forms. Programs can be crafted by the simple dragging and dropping of prebuilt controls onto the surface of a prebuilt form. It's all done from the comfort and convenience of the Visual Studio Integrated Development Environment (IDE).

The displayed environment includes four key areas, which I've labeled with letters in Figure 5-5.

A. The toolbox

This listing of controls includes not only display controls, but also controls that expose no specific user interface, such as the `Timer`. (If you don't see the toolbox, select the View→Toolbox menu command.) To add a control to a form, double-click the control in the toolbox, drag it from the toolbox to the form, or draw the control on the form after first selecting it from the toolbox.

B. The form surface

Place any control that exposes a user interface here. The form is WYSIWYG, so you can see the final result as you design the form.

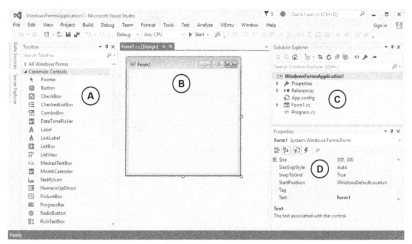

Figure 5-5. The Visual Studio environment

C. The Solution Explorer

All files related to your project appear here. For the current project, the key elements you will see are the *Properties* entry, the *Program.cs* file that contains the startup code, and an entry for the form, *Form1.cs*. There are actually more files. If you click the Show All Files toolbar button located on the top of the Solution Explorer, it will show you additional files, most of which are managed by Visual Studio on your behalf.

D. The Properties panel

When you select a control on your form surface, or the form surface itself, or an item in the Solution Explorer, the properties of the selected item appear in this area. You can alter the settings of many properties by typing in the new setting. Some properties include special tools to assist you in setting the property value.

If you haven't done so already, open the form *Form1.cs* in design view by double-clicking it in the Solution Explorer. We'll add eight text labels, three shape and line elements, two web-style hyperlinks, a command button, and a picture to the form's surface. I've already added the picture to the form for you, with an image of some books, naming it `SideImage`.

Set up the form by adjusting the following properties from their defaults. Click on the form surface, and then modify these property values using the Properties panel. (NOTE: All sizes assume that your display is scaled to 100% of the Windows standard.)

Property	Setting
(Name)	AboutProgram
ControlBox	False
FormBorderStyle	FixedDialog
Size	450, 318
StartPosition	CenterScreen
Text	About the Library Project

Next, add the eight basic text labels to the form's surface using the `Label` control. You'll find this control in the toolbox. As you add each `Label` control, use the following list of settings to update the properties for each label. The included text matches my situation, but feel free to modify the content as needed.

Label name	Property settings
ProgramName	(Name): ProgramName AutoSize: True Font/Bold: True Location: 136, 16 Text: The Library Project
ProgramVersion	(Name): ProgramVersion AutoSize: True Location: 136, 32 Text: Version X.Y Revision Z
LicenseInfo	(Name): LicenseInfo AutoSize: False Location: 136, 48 Size: 280, 48 Text: Unlicensed
DevelopedBy	(Name): DevelopedBy AutoSize: True Location: 136, 104 Text: Developed By
DeveloperName	(Name): DeveloperName AutoSize: True Location: 160, 128 Text: Tim Patrick
DeveloperBook	(Name): DeveloperBook AutoSize: True Location: 160, 144 Text: Start-to-Finish Visual C# 2015
DeveloperProject	(Name): DeveloperProject AutoSize: True Location: 160, 160 Text: In-book Project
CompanyCopyright	(Name): CompanyCopyright AutoSize: True Location: 136, 224 Text: Copyright (c) 2016 by Tim Patrick.

Let's add some lines and colored sections to the form. Unfortunately, Windows Forms does not include distinct shape controls for lines, rectangles, and ellipses. Instead, you have to add them by hand using source-code-specified drawing commands. But we can simulate lines and rectangles using the standard Label control, sans the text.

Label name	Property settings
VersionDivider	(Name): VersionDivider AutoSize: False BackColor: Black Location: 136, 96 Size: 280,1 Text: [Don't add any text]
BackgroundSide	(Name): BackgroundSide AutoSize: False BackColor: White Location: 0, 0 Size: 120, 296

Label name	Property settings
	Text: *[Don't add any text]*
BackgroundDivider	(Name): BackgroundDivider AutoSize: False BackColor: Black Location: 120, 0 Size: 1, 296 Text: *[Don't add any text]*

If the BackgroundSide label obscures the graphic, right-click on the label and select Send To Back from the shortcut menu that appears.

The LinkLabel control is similar to the more basic Label control, but you can include hypertext links in the text, clickable sections that are similar to the links on a web page. We'll use these to display the web site and email address. Add two LinkLabel controls to the form and use the following settings to configure each control's properties.

LinkLabel name	Property settings
CompanyWeb	(Name): CompanyWeb AutoSize: True LinkBehavior: HoverUnderline Location: 160, 176 Text: http://www.owanipress.com
CompanyEmail	(Name): CompanyEmail AutoSize: True LinkBehavior: HoverUnderline Location: 160, 192 Text: tim@timaki.com

The final control to add is a button that lets the user close the form. Add a Button control to the form with the following properties.

Button name	Property settings
ActClose	(Name): ActClose DialogResult: Cancel Location: 344, 240 Size: 80, 24 Text: Close

Forms can be configured so that a press of the Esc key triggers a Button control on the form, as though the user was clicking on the button instead of pressing the Esc key. To do this, click on the form surface, and then set its CancelButton property to ActClose. We had to delay this step until the button was actually added to the form; the CancelButton property would not have allowed a setting for a nonexistent button.

Well, the form should look pretty good by now. The last thing I like to do is to set up the *tab order*, the order in which the user accesses each field on the form when pressing the Tab key on the keyboard. To edit the tab order, select the form surface and then select the View→Tab Order menu command. Each control on the form that can be given a tab order value will suddenly have a tab order number next to it. Click on each number or control in order until you get the arrangement you want. (See Figure 5-6 to view how I ordered the controls.) Finally, select the View→Tab Order menu command again, or press the Esc key, to leave the tab ordering process.

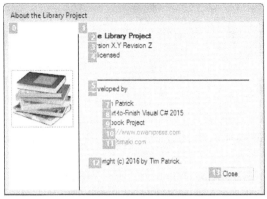

Figure 5-6. Nice and orderly

You can also set the tab order for each control by modifying its `TabIndex` property using a zero-based numbering system. However, it's usually faster to set these values by clicking on each control in order.

Adding the Code to the Form

Now it's time to add some real Visual C# code. Not that we haven't added any until now. Everything we did on the form, although we didn't see it happen, was converted into C# source code. Let's take a quick look. In the Solution Explorer, click on the triangle next to *Form1.cs*, then double-click *Form1.Designer.cs* (see Figure 5-7).

Figure 5-7. Accessing the hidden, secret, forbidden code—yeah, it's out there

Since it's more than 200 lines of source code bliss, I won't be printing it here. But look it over; it's all pretty interesting. As you dragged-and-dropped controls on the form and modified its properties, Visual Studio edited this file on your behalf. It's part of your form's class (all forms are classes that derive from `System.Windows.Forms.Form`), although just a part of it. You can tell that by the `partial` keyword at the top.

```
partial class AboutProgram
```

Most of the action happens in the `InitializeComponent` procedure. When you are finished looking it all over, close up the designer code and return to the form surface. To make our form a real and interesting form, we need it to do three things.

- Show the actual version number of the application. This should be determined and displayed right when the form first appears.

- Jump to the appropriate web site or email recipient when clicking on the link labels. These events get processed in response to a user action.
- Close the form when the user clicks the Close button. This is also a user-driven event.

Let's start with the easy one, closing the form. I'm sure you remember about event handlers from Chapter 1. Event handlers are blocks of code that are processed in response to something happening, most often a user action such as a mouse click. All of the actions we want to perform on this form will be in response to a triggered event (lucky us). The easiest way to get to the default event handler for a control is to double-click the control. Try it now; double-click the Close button. When you do, the IDE opens the source code view associated with the form, and adds an empty event handler (the *ActClose_Click* subroutine).

```
Private void ActClose_Click(object sender, EventArgs e)
{
}
```

Every forms-based event (and in fact, most other types of events) in .NET has pretty much the same arguments: (1) a *sender* argument that indicates which object triggered this event; and (2) the e argument, which allows *sender* to supply any additional information that may be useful in the event. In this case, the *sender* argument will be a reference to the *ActClose* button, since that's the object that will generate the *Click* event. A button's *Click* event doesn't have any more useful information available, so e is the default object type, *System.EventArgs*, which is pretty much just a placeholder, and the object from which all of the more interesting e argument types derive.

The name of this event handler is *ActClose_Click*, but if you want to change it to *FredAndWilma*, that's fine; the procedure name for an event handler isn't magic. What is magic is the link between the generating event and the event handler. Visual Studio added that link in the designer file, in the *InitializeComponent* method we looked at earlier. If you open the *Form1.Designer.cs* file again and scroll down to the section that describes the *ActClose* button, you will see the code line that establishes the link.

```
this.ActClose.Click += new
    System.EventHandler(this.ActClose_Click);
```

If you have a compelling need to rename the handler *FredAndWilma*, you have to update this connection line as well.

Close the designer file and return to the *ActClose_Click* event handler. The code to close the form is extremely simple. Enter it now, either by using the first code snippet for this chapter or by typing it directly.

Insert Snippet
Insert Chapter 5, Snippet Item 1.

```
// ----- Close the form.
this.Close();
```

This statement says, "I'm the *AboutProgram* form/object, and I command myself to close." If you run the program right now (press the F5 key), you close the form by clicking on the Close button. Since the *AboutProgram* form was the only form in the application, closing it automatically ended the entire application, no questions asked.

OK, back to the second item, the web-style links. Double-clicking on a control to access the default event handler is fine, but it's an imprecise method, especially if you don't want the default handler. To add a handler for any event supported by a control, you can use the Events view on the Properties panel for the form.

Let's try that now with the *CompanyWeb* control that we added to the form's surface, the one that displays a web page link. On the form's surface, select that control. The on the Properties panel, click the Events toolbar button, the one that looks like a lightning bolt (see Figure 5-8).

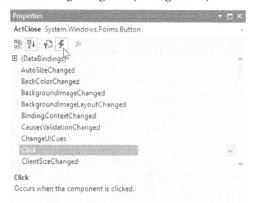

Figure 5-8. The Properties panel's Events button and view

Clicking that button converts the list of properties to a list of event names. Any previously added handlers would appear to the right of the event name. For the *CompanyWeb* control, we want to respond to the *LinkClicked* event, which occurs when the user clicks on the linked part of the text with the mouse. To generate the handler for this event, double-click on the LinkClicked name in event list. Visual Studio returns to the code for the form and adds the appropriate event handler shell.

```
private void CompanyWeb_LinkClicked(
    object sender, LinkLabelLinkClickedEventArgs e)
{
}
```

This template's argument list is a little more interesting, since its *e* argument is an object of type *System.Windows.Forms.LinkLabelLinkClickedEventArgs*. The *LinkLabel* control allows you to have multiple web-style links in a single control, interspersed among regular text. The *e* argument has a *Link* property that tells you which of the links in the control the user clicked. Since our labels have only a single link, we won't bother to check it. We'll just show the web page immediately anytime the link gets clicked.

Insert Snippet
Insert Chapter 5, Snippet Item 2.

```
// ----- Show the company web page.
Process.Start("http://www.owanipress.com");
```

The *Process* object is part of the *System.Diagnostics* namespace, and *Start* is one of its shared members that lets you start up external applications and resources. You pass it any valid URL and it will run using the user's default browser or application for that URL.

The third way to add an event handler, and the most boring of the three normal options, is to type the handler procedure declaration from memory, remembering to use the correct type for the *e* argument. This seems like the wrong way of doing things, but since I'm having you add entire handlers using code snippets from time to time, this method will get some action. Go ahead and add the handler for the *CompanyEmail*'s *LinkClicked* event by adding the entire procedure snippet

---

```
private void CompanyEmail_LinkClicked(
    object sender, LinkLabelLinkClickedEventArgs e)
{
    // ----- Send email to the company.
    Process.Start("mailto:tim@timaki.com");
}
```

The problem with this option is that it doesn't establish the link between the control's event and the handler, the part that Visual Studio normally added to the designer file on your behalf. You must add this link as an extra step. There are two ways you can do this. The first is to return to the form's surface, select the *CompanyEmail* control, and then select or type "CompanyEmail_LinkClicked" in the space to the right of the *LinkClicked* item in the Properties panel's event list. (NOTE: Do not double-click as you did before, since Visual Studio is not fully featured enough to figure out that you want to use the existing handler with the default procedure name. You must select or type the name instead.)

Another way to establish the link is to hand-type it yourself, just like you hand-typed the entire procedure shell and content. You can type the code in the designer file, just like Visual Studio does. Or, you can add the linking statement to the form's constructor (that's the procedure named "*void AboutProgram*"), just after the call to *InitializeComponent*. That seems like the right place for us.

```
this.CompanyEmail.LinkClicked += new System.Windows.Forms.
    LinkLabelLinkClickedEventHandler(
    this.CompanyEmail_LinkClicked);
```

The last event to design is one of the first events called in the lifetime of the form: the *Load* event. It's called just before the form appears on the screen. Double-clicking on the surface of the form creates an event handler template for the *Load* event. If you prefer to use the Properties-panel-event-list option instead, that's fine. Either way will create the following handler skeleton.

```
private void AboutProgram_Load(object sender, EventArgs e)
{
}
```

Let's add code to this event handler that displays the correct version number, using the version information found in the core assembly identifying fields.

```
// ----- Prepare the form.
Assembly currentAssembly;
Version versionInfo;

// ----- Update the version number.
currentAssembly = Assembly.GetEntryAssembly();
if (currentAssembly == null)
    currentAssembly = Assembly.GetCallingAssembly();
versionInfo = currentAssembly.GetName().Version;
```

```
ProgramVersion.Text = string.Format(
    "Version {0}.{1} Revision {2}", versionInfo.Major,
    versionInfo.Minor, versionInfo.Revision);
```

The logic needed to suss out the version information is fairly esoteric, and required several minutes clicking hyperlinks in the MSDN documentation for the .NET Framework's class libraries. Eventually, you end up with the *versionInfo* variable, an instance of a *System.Version* class, which exposes the individual components of the version number as properties.

This code uses the *string.Format* method to construct a formatted string from a template and data parts. The placeholders in the string appear in zero-based, numbered braces, like *{0}*, each of which corresponds to the comma-delimited arguments that follow the formatting string: *{0}* goes with the *Major* property, *{1}* with *Minor*, and *{2}* with *Revision*.

Setting the Version Number

If you run the program, it will display the currently defined version number, "1.0 Revision 0," as shown in Figure 5-9.

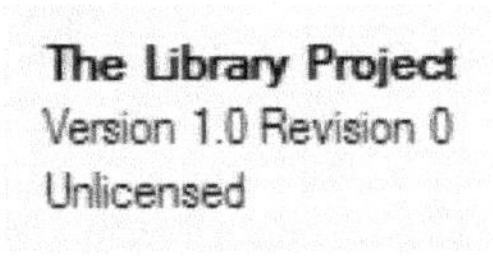

The Library Project
Version 1.0 Revision 0
Unlicensed

Figure 5-9. The version number from the AboutProgram form

My question—and I hope I can answer it before the paragraph is finished—is, "Where is that version number defined, and how can it be changed?" It turns out that I do know the answer: the version values are stored as metadata within the assembly. Visual Studio includes a form that lets you modify the basic informational metadata stored in the assembly. To access the form, display the project's properties (double-click on Properties in the Solution Explorer), select the Application tab, and then click on the Assembly Information button (see Figure 5-10).

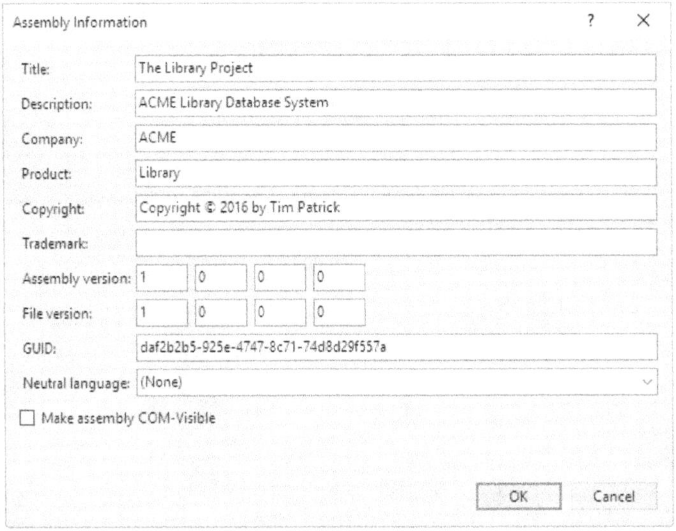

Figure 5-10. The Assembly Information form, filled out with some relevant values

Our *AboutProgram* form displays the assembly's version number, which is set using the four text fields next to the Assembly Version label. Those four fields represent the Major, Minor, Build, and Revision numbers of the assembly. Go ahead, set them to some other values, click OK, and run the program again.

Although this form is convenient, it's just another example of Visual Studio writing some of your project's code on your behalf. Every field on this form gets saved in a source code file included with your project. To view it, expand the Properties item in the Solution Explorer hierarchy, and then double-click on the *AssemblyInfo.cs* item. This file defines several assembly-specific attributes (which we'll explore in Chapter 18), including the following informational entries.

```
[assembly: AssemblyTitle("The Library Project")]
[assembly: AssemblyDescription("ACME Library Database System")]
[assembly: AssemblyCompany("ACME")]
[assembly: AssemblyProduct("Library")]
[assembly: AssemblyCopyright("Copyright © 2016 by Tim Patrick")]
[assembly: AssemblyTrademark("")]
[assembly: AssemblyVersion("1.0.0.0")]
[assembly: AssemblyFileVersion("1.0.0.0")]
```

You see the *AssemblyVersion* attribute defined here. If you modify these values, the changes will be reflected in the Assembly Information form, and also in your running application and final compiled assembly. Thank you Visual Studio!

The last thing we will do for now to the *AboutProgram* form is to give it a meaningful filename. Currently, it is named *Form1.cs*, but *AboutProgram.cs* would be much more descriptive. To change the name, select *Form1.cs* in the Solution Explorer, and modify the File Name property to *AboutProgram.cs* in the Properties panel. If you have the file in the Solution Explorer expanded and showing its subordinate files, you will see Visual Studio also update the names of those two files: the designer file (*AboutProgram.Designer.cs*) and the resource file (*AboutProgram.resx*).

Now would be a great time to save your work (File→Save All).

Adding the Main Form

As useful and full featured as the *AboutProgram* form is, such forms are seldom the core focus of an application. In the Library Project, this form will be displayed only when triggered from the Main form, so let's add a simple Main form now. In Visual Studio, select the Project→Add Windows Form menu command. (If you don't see this menu item, try selecting the Solution Explorer panel first.) When the Add New Item form appears, select Windows Form from the list of available items, and give it a name of *MainForm.cs* before clicking the Add button.

When the new form appears, adjust the following properties as indicated.

Property	Setting
(Name)	MainForm
FormBorderStyle	FixedSingle
MaximizeBox	False
Size	586, 466
Text	The Library Project

From the toolbox, add a *Button* control to the form with the following properties.

Property	Setting
(Name)	ActHelpAbout
Size	80, 24

Property	Setting
Text	&About...

The special & character in the button's *Text* property sets the "shortcut" for the button. When you press the Alt key and the letter that follows & (in this case, A), the program acts as though you clicked on the button with the mouse.

Double-click the button and add the following code to the *Click* event procedure.

Insert Snippet

Insert Chapter 5, Snippet Item 6.

```
// ----- Show the About form.
(new AboutProgram()).ShowDialog();
```

This code creates an instance of the *AboutProgram* form/class, and then calls the public *ShowDialog* method, a member that the *AboutProgram* class inherited from its *Form* class base.

If you run the program, it will still show only the *AboutProgram* form. That's because the *AboutProgram* form is specifically mentioned in the startup code in the *Program.cs* file. Open that file and you will see the following line near the end of the *Main* method.

```
Application.Run(new AboutProgram());
```

This line tells the program to start the Windows message pump with the *AboutProgram* form as the focus of all activity. To make the main form be the focus instead, replace *AboutProgram* with *MainForm* on that code line.

```
Application.Run(new MainForm());
```

Since the *AboutProgram* form is now being shown as a *dialog* form (through a call to its *ShowDialog* method), its behavior is somewhat different. Each form includes a *DialogResult* property whose value is returned by the *ShowDialog* method when the form closes. Each button on your form can be configured to automatically set this property. The Close button on the *AboutProgram* form does just that; its own *DialogResult* property is set to *Cancel*, which is assigned to the form's *DialogResult* property when the user clicks the Close button. As a side effect of this assignment, the form closes.

The upshot of that drawn-out paragraph is that you can now delete the event handler for the Close button's *Click* event, and the button will still close the form. The removal is a multi-step process: you need to tell both the main source code and the designer file that the handler is going away. The easiest way to remove the event handler connection from the designer file is to return to the form surface, select the *ActClose* button, access the Properties panel, switch it into the event list view, locate the Click line in that list, and then remove the "ActClose_Click" text from the Click line's value field. Actually, that doesn't seem easy at all. If only someone could invent a computer that could perform these steps for us. Oh well. The alternative is to open the *AboutProgram.Design.cs* file and manually delete the line that adds the event handler link.

Once the handler connection is gone, you can remove the *ActClose_Click* procedure itself from the form's source code. Once you've done that, run the program and see what happens. The Close button still closes the form, even without the event handler.

You could also have left the procedure and the designer-file connection statement in place, cleared the Close button's *DialogResult* property, and added the following statement to that button's event handler.

```
this.DialogResult = DialogResult.Cancel;
```

That brings to three the number of different ways we can close the *AboutProgram* form. It's the flexibility of .NET at work; there are many different ways to accomplish the same task. So, be creative!

Extra Credit: Adding an Icon

If you've still got a little energy left, we can make one more change before this chapter runs out of paper: adding a custom icon to the main form. Just follow these step-by-step instructions.

1. Display the main form by double-clicking on the *MainForm.cs* item in the Solution Explorer.

2. Select the form's surface.

3. Select the form's Icon property in the Properties panel.

4. Click the "..." button in this property, and search for the *Book.ico* file in the *Chapter 5 Before* subdirectory of the book's installation directory. You can also use any other *.ico* file.

Save Your Work

Make sure you always save changes. By default, Visual Studio is configured to save your changes every time you run your program, but I like to save often just in case.

This chapter included a lot of manual instruction because there were so many cool Visual Studio features to play with; I just couldn't help myself. We'll probably keep up this pace somewhat for a few chapters, but eventually there will be so much code that a lot of it will come from the code snippets.

Chapter 6

Data and Data Types

Data is a funny word—although not as funny as *datum*. Our minds are filled with data: the useful and useless trivia that clogs thought; the millions of memories that keep superficial conversations going strong. But the word *data* rarely comes up in conversation. Unless you are a computer junkie, or you hang around the office all hours of the day or night waiting for reports of crunched numbers, you never have a need to use the term. I have never been asked to lend someone a cup of data. My friends never try to judge my health by asking, "How's your data going?" And you almost never hear it used as a character name in popular science fiction television shows.

Despite its lack of usage in everyday communication, data is extremely important. In the programming world, it is everything. In this chapter, we will discuss how Visual C# uses and manipulates data within your applications, and how you can master the tools that make this manipulation possible.

The Nature of Computer Data

In Chapter 2, I mentioned how all data in a computer eventually breaks down to individual bits, electrical impulses that represent either 1 or 0, on or off, true or false. Since our decimal number system requires more than just those two values, computers work in the world of binary—a number system limited to only the numbers 0 and 1. Fortunately, it's pretty easy to represent basic decimal-system integers using binary notation. You probably remember Mrs. Green back in second grade telling you about the different place values of multi-digit numbers, shown in Figure 6-1.

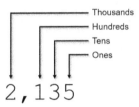

Figure 6-1. The fruits of Mrs. Green's labors

The same type of diagram can be used for binary numbers; only the position names and values are changed. For convenience, we call these positions by their decimal names, or use the related powers of two. All of this is shown in Figure 6-2.

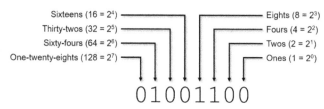

Figure 6-2. The positions of an "8-bit" (8-digit) binary number

To figure out what this number is in decimal, just add up the columns. Let's see, there's one each of fours, eights, and sixty-fours, and none of the rest; 4 + 8 + 64, that's 76. Since any binary digit can never be more than 1, the counting is pretty simple. I showed an 8-bit (8-digit) binary example here—which can handle the decimal numbers 0 through 255—but you can represent larger decimal numbers by adding more binary digits.

That's just fine for integer values, but how do you represent fractional numbers? What about negative numbers; where do they fit in this binary system? And it's not just numbers. My computer can process text data, arrays of numbers, graphical images, and customer records. How are those stored in binary form?

To handle myriad data forms, every computer includes a small community of Lilliputians who are good at math, language, and art. No wait, I think that's from a story I read to my son when he was young. Oh yes, now I remember. Computers implement *data types* to handle all the various forms of data to be managed. Each data type acts as an interpreter between a collection of bits and a piece of information that a computer user can better utilize and understand.

All data types ultimately store their content as individual bits of data, but they differ in how those bits get interpreted. Imagine a data type named `Vitamin` that indicated which vitamins were included in a food product. Figure 6-3 shows how the 8 bits used earlier could be assigned and interpreted as vitamins.

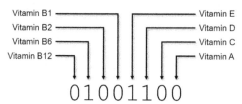

Figure 6-3. Loaded with vitamins B6, D, and E

With such a data type, you could assign vitamin values to food items tracked in your application. (This is just a sampling of vitamins; you would require more bits to handle all of the vitamins. This example should not be construed as an offer of medical services. Consult your doctor.)

For an example that is more in tune with Visual C#, take that number 76 we were discussing earlier. It's easy enough to convert it to binary representation, as in 01001100. The .NET Framework includes a few data types that do this conversion automatically, varying only by the number of binary digits (bits) they can handle. In the computer world, 76 also represents a letter of the alphabet—the capital letter *L*. That's because there's a data type that establishes a dictionary between binary values and alphabetic (and other) characters. Windows programs have long used *ASCII* (American Standard Code for Information Interchange) as its number-to-character dictionary. This 8-bit system documents how to convert the numbers 0 through 255 into all the various characters used in English, including punctuation and other miscellaneous characters. Another dictionary, *Unicode*, uses sixteen bits of data to handle around 65,000 different characters. .NET uses Unicode for its character and text-string data types.

Another rule-bearing data type is Boolean, which uses a single bit to represent either true (a bit value of *1*) or false (*0*). Negative integers, floating-point and fixed-point decimal values, and dates and times round out the kinds of basic data most often managed by computers and their applications. More complex *data structures* can be built up from these basic types.

Data in .NET

All data types in .NET are implemented as classes within the *System* namespace. One such data type is *System.Byte*, which implements an 8-bit integer value, just like we discussed earlier. It holds integer values from 0 to 255. These values are always stored using eight bits of binary data, but they magically appear in decimal form whenever you ask them to be presented.

The .NET Framework includes fifteen core interpretive data types: eight for integers, three for decimal numbers, two for character data, a combined data type for dates and times, and a Boolean data type.

Integer Data Types

Based on the number of available data types (eight out of the fifteen core types), you would think that most programmers worked with integers all day long—and you'd be right. Whether it's actual user data or loop counters or status codes or the storage method for enumerated data types, integers show up everywhere in .NET code.

The range of values for an integer data type depends directly on the number of binary digits managed by that data type; the more digits, the bigger the range. Also, half of the integer data types store both positive and negative values (called "signed" integers), whereas the other half support only positive numbers ("unsigned"). Table 6-1 lists the eight integer data types included with .NET, and their associated ranges.

Table 6-1. Integer data types in .NET

.NET data type	Bits	Style	Range of values
System.Byte	8	Unsigned	0 to 255
System.SByte	8	Signed	-128 to 127
System.Int16	16	Signed	-32,768 to 32,767
System.UInt16	16	Unsigned	0 to 65,535
System.Int32	32	Signed	-2,147,483,648 to 2,147,483,647
System.UInt32	32	Unsigned	0 to 4,294,967,295
System.Int64	64	Signed	-9,223,372,036,854,775,808 to 9,223,372,036,854,775,807
System.UInt64	64	Unsigned	0 to 18,446,744,073,709,551,615

Looking at these types another way, Table 6-2 shows the relationship between the types and their number of bits and range style.

Table 6-2. Bits and signed status for integer .NET data types

	8-bits	16-bits	32-bits	64-bits
Signed	SByte	Int16	Int32	Int64
Unsigned	Byte	UInt16	UInt32	UInt64

Decimal Data Types

Once upon a time, life was happy. Strangers said hello when they met you on the street. Succulent fruit burst forth from the trees. In short, God was in His heaven, and everything was right with the world—and then along came fractions. At first, they didn't seem that bad, since so many of them could be easily converted into a plain numeric form by inserting a decimal point in the number: ½ became 0.5; ¼ became the longer yet smaller 0.25; ⅓ became 0.333333333333333333333333333333333333333333333333333333333333333333 33333333333333333333333333333333333333333333333333333333333333333333333333333333333... hey, what's going on here? I can't write all those 3s. The book would be 2,000 pages, or more. Eventually people discovered that in many cases, it just wasn't worth the bother of writing out all the 3s, so they just stopped at some point, as in 0.33333333. It wasn't perfectly accurate, but it was good enough.

This is what life is like for computer-based fractional values. You can have perfect accuracy—up to a point. After that, you have to settle for good enough. The .NET Framework includes three fractional decimal data types. One type has perfect accuracy, but its range is somewhat limited. The other two offer limited accuracy in exchange for a larger range of values. Table 6-3 documents these three types.

Table 6-3. An accurate list of the inaccurate decimal data types

.NET data type	Description
System.Decimal	The Decimal data type provides around twenty-eight combined digits on both sides of the decimal point. Although it may truncate after the last available digit position, it is accurate within those digits. Because of this, it is perfect for working with money. The more digits you have on the left of the decimal, the fewer you have available to the right of the decimal, and vice versa. For numbers with no decimal portion, the range is from $-79{,}228{,}162{,}514{,}264{,}337{,}593{,}543{,}950{,}335$ to $79{,}228{,}162{,}514{,}264{,}337{,}593{,}543{,}950{,}335$. (That's twenty-nine digits, but who's counting?) For numbers with only zero (0) to the left of the decimal, the range is $-0.0000000000000000000000000001$ to $0.0000000000000000000000000001$.
System.Single	The Single data type offers a much larger range than Decimal does, but it does have some accuracy problems. Sometimes when you do a complex calculation that you know should result in zero, the actual calculated result might be 0.0000000000023. It's close to zero, but not exactly zero. But you can use very large or very small numbers. For negative values, the range is -3.402823E^{+38} to -1.401298E^{-45}; for positive values, its range is 1.401298E^{-45} to 3.402823E^{+38}.
System.Double	The Double data type is just like the Single data type, but with a bigger attitude—I mean a larger range. For negative values, the range is $-1.79769313486231\text{E}^{+308}$ to $-4.94065645841247\text{E}^{-324}$; for positive values, the range is $4.94065645841247\text{E}^{-324}$ to $1.79769313486232\text{E}^{+308}$.

Character Data Types

Hey, check this out. *ktuefghbiokh*. Pretty cool, eh? That's the power of a computer in action managing text data. So efficient; so graceful; so *lskjdfljsdfjl*. Although computers are really number machines, they handle text just as well. Of course, it's really just you doing all the wordsmithing. In fact, the computer isn't even smart enough to tell the difference between numbers and letters; it's all bits to the CPU. Pretty mindless, if you ask me. I mean, what's the use of having all that computing power if you can't even think?

Despite all their speed and technology, computers are still just lumps of silicon wrapped up in a nice package. The computer I'm typing on doesn't even know that I'm insulting it; I can type these things on and on, and there's nutten that thiz komputre cann due about itt.

The .NET Framework includes two text-related data types: System.Char and System.String. The Char data type holds a single character, no more, no less. At 16 bits, it holds any of the thousands of Unicode characters.

The *String* data type allows up to about two billion Unicode characters to be "strung" together into one long text block. Strings in .NET are immutable; once you create a string, it cannot be changed in any way. If you want to add text to an existing string, .NET will instead create a brand new string built from the original two immutable strings.

Although *Char* and *String* are different data types, you can easily move data back and forth between them, since they are both based on basic Unicode characters.

Date and Time Data Type

The *System.DateTime* data type lets you store either date or time values (or both) as data. Internally, *DateTime* is just a simple integer counter that displays a converted date or time format when needed. As a number, it counts the number of "ticks" since 12:00 a.m. on January 1, 1 AD. Each tick is exactly 100 nanoseconds, so it's pretty precise. The maximum allowed date is December 31, 9999 in the Gregorian calendar.

Boolean Data Type

The *System.Boolean* data type represents the true essence of computer data: the bit. It holds one of two possible values: *true* or *false*. Shockingly, the data type actually requires between 2 and 4 bytes of data space to keep track of that single bit of data.

It turns out that Boolean values are very important in programs. As a developer, you are always testing to see whether various conditions are met before you process a block of code. All of these conditions eventually boil down to Boolean values and operations. .NET even has ways to easily migrate data between integer values and the Boolean data type. In such conversions, 0 becomes *false*, and the world of all other possible values becomes *true*. When moving from Boolean to an integer equivalent, *false* becomes 0 and *true* becomes 1. (If you ever use the Visual Basic language, you'll find that it converts *true* to −1, not 1. Internally in .NET, *true* does convert to 1, but for historical reasons, Visual Basic uses −1. This difference normally isn't a problem unless you store Boolean values as integers in a disk file and expect both Visual Basic and C# programs to interpret the data correctly.)

The System.Object Class

You already knew that .NET is an object-oriented development environment. What you probably didn't know is that some pranksters at Microsoft placed a bet to see whether they could make the entire .NET system one big derived class. Well, the group that said it could be done won the bet. Everything in .NET— all code and all data—is derived from a single base class: *System.Object*. By itself, this class doesn't have too many features. It can tell you its name, its type, and whether two instances of an object are in fact the same object. Other than that, it isn't useful for much except to be used as a starting point for all other classes and types.

Because all classes in .NET—including all data types—derive from *System.Object*, you can treat an instance of any class (or data type) as *Object*. The data will remember what type it really is, so if you have a *System.Int32* posing as *System.Object*, you can change it back to *System.Int32* later.

Value Types and Reference Types

Back in Chapter 1, you read about the difference between *value types* and *reference types*: Value types are buckets that contain actual data, and reference types contain instructions on where you can find the actual data. In general, value types contain simple and small data values, whereas reference types point to large and complex data blocks. This isn't always true, but for most data you work with, it will be true.

System.Object is a reference type from which all other types and classes derive. This includes all the core data types, so you would think that they would be reference types as well. But there is another class stuck in between *System.Object* and most of the .NET data types. This class, *System.ValueType*, implements the basic definition and usage of a value type. Table 6-4 lists some of the differences between value and reference types.

Table 6-4. Value type and reference type usage

Value types	Reference types
Ultimately derive from `System.ValueType`, which in turn derives from `System.Object`.	Ultimately derive from `System.Object`.
Derived core data types: `Boolean`, `Byte`, `Char`, `DateTime`, `Decimal`, `Double`, `Int16`, `Int32`, `Int64`, `SByte`, `Single`, `UInt16`, `UInt32`, `UInt64`.	Derived core data type: `String`.
Provide support for C# structures.	Provide support for C# classes.
Value types cannot derive from other classes or structures, nor can further structures derive from them.	Reference types can be derived from other classes, and can be used as base classes.
Instances cannot be set to `null`. (Using a nullable type overcomes this limitation.)	Instances can be set to `null`.
Instances can only contain data of the specified type. For instance, `System.Int32` instances can only contain 32-bit signed integer data.	Instances usually refer to data of their defined type, but an instance can also point to a derived type. For example, an instance of `System.String` could refer to any data that used `System.String` as a base class.
Do not go through the full .NET garbage collection process.	Are destroyed through garbage collection.

A value type can only contain data of its own type, but reference types can point to derived instances. This is important in .NET, since it was designed to allow a `System.Object` instance to refer to any data in an application. `System.Object` instances can refer to either value type or reference type data. For reference types, this is easy to understand since that instance will just point to some derived instance of itself. But if you assign a value type to a `System.Object` reference, .NET has to mark that instance in a special way to indicate that a reference type contains a value type. This process is called *boxing*, and the reverse process is called *unboxing*. Although boxing is useful, and sometimes essential, it comes with a substantial performance hit.

Visual C# Data Types

All the data types implemented in the C# language are wrappers for the core .NET data types. Only some of the names have been changed to protect the innocent. Table 6-5 lists the Visual C# data types and their .NET equivalents.

Table 6-5. Visual C# data types and related .NET types

Visual C# type	.NET type
`bool`	`System.Boolean`
`byte`	`System.Byte`
`char`	`System.Char`
No equivalent	`System.DateTime`
`decimal`	`System.Decimal`
`double`	`System.Double`
`int`	`System.Int32`

Visual C# type	.NET type
long	System.Int64
object	System.Object
sbyte	System.SByte
short	System.Int16
float	System.Single
string	System.String
uint	System.UInt32
ulong	System.UInt64
ushort	System.UInt16

All the Visual C# data types are fully interchangeable with their .NET equivalents. Any instance of *System.Int32* can be treated as though it were an instance of *int*, and vice versa. For reasons that elude technical book authors like myself, C# does not include its own intrinsic equivalent for the *System.DateTime* type. If you want to include a date or time variable in your code, you must rely on the framework's *DateTime* value type directly.

Literals

The quickest way to include values of a particular data type in your Visual C# code is to use a *literal*. You've already seen literals in action in this book. Chapter 1 included a literal in its sample project.

```
MessageBox.Show("Hello, World!");
```

This call to the *MessageBox.Show* function includes a *string literal*. String literals always appear within a set of double quotes. Most numeric literals appear with a data-type-defining character on the end of the literal, but there are other variations. Table 6-6 lists the different literal values you can include in your code.

Table 6-6. Literals supported by Visual C#

Literal type	Example	Description
bool	true	The *bool* data type supports two literal values: *true* and *false*.
char	'Q'	Single-character literals appear in a set of single quotes. A literal of type *char* is not the same as a single-character literal of type *string*.
decimal	123.45M	Floating-point values of type *decimal* are followed by the letter *M*, upper or lower case.
double	123.45D	Floating-point values of type *double* are followed by *D* or *d*. Also, if you use a numeric literal with a decimal portion, but with no trailing data type character, that literal will be typed as a *double*.
Hexadecimal	0xABCD	You can include hexadecimal literals in your code by starting the value with the *0x* (zero-x) character sequence, followed by the hex digits.
int	123	Any non-decimal numeric literal that is small enough to fit inside the *int* data type is automatically an *int*.
long	123L	Integral values of type *long* are followed by *L* or *l*. Also, if you use a numeric literal that falls in the range of a *long* and outside the range of an *int*, but with no trailing data type character, that literal will be typed as a *long*.
float	123.45F	Floating-point values of type *float* are followed by *F*.

Literal type	Example	Description
string	`"A \"B\" C"`	String literals appear within a set of double quotes. Precede a double-quote mark with a backslash (\) within the string literal to embed a single quotation mark. Strings can span multiple physical lines, and the line breaks will be part of the resulting string literal.
uint	`123U`	Unsigned integer literals are followed by the letter *U*.
ulong	`123UL`	Unsigned long literals are followed by the letters *UL*.

Literal strings require a little more explanation. The example in Table 6-6 shows that you can include quotation mark inside the string by *escaping* it with a backslash. There are actually several such *escape sequences* available within string literals, each starting with the backslash character. Table 6-7 lists these sequences.

Table 6-7. String escape sequences

Sequence	Description
`\'`	Single quote character
`\"`	Double quote character
`\\`	Backslash character
`\0`	Null character (ASCII 0), which is not the same as a null string
`\a`	Alert symbol (ASCII 7)
`\b`	Backspace symbol (ASCII 8)
`\f`	Form feed symbol (ASCII 12)
`\n`	New line symbol (ASCII 10)
`\r`	Carriage return symbol (ASCII 13)
`\t`	Horizontal tab symbol (ASCII 9)
`\u`	Unicode escape sequence. The sequence is followed by four hex digits identifying the character.
`\U`	Unicode escape sequence used to access supplementary planes through surrogate pairs. The sequence is followed by the hex digits identifying the Unicode content.
`\v`	Vertical tab symbol (ASCII 11)
`\x`	Unicode escape sequence. This is the same as `\u`, except a variable number of hex digits can follow `\x`.

Any of these sequences can also be used as *char* literals by including them in single quotes.

```
string indentedText = "\t\tTwo Tabs";
char justTab = '\t';
```

These special characters provide a convenient way to embed commonly used but difficult-to-type characters in your strings. However, they can sometimes become cumbersome. A key example is the extra work needed to include backslashes in file paths.

```
' ----- All backslashes are doubled.
path = "C:\\temp\\WorkFile.txt";
```

To simplify such strings, C# includes another string literal format called *verbatim strings*. These strings begin with an at-sign, forgo all escape sequences, and double-up on quotation marks when an embedded quote is needed.

```
path = @"C:\temp\WorkFile.txt";
famousQuote = @"I'm ""famous"".";
```

Constants

Literals are nice, but it isn't always clear what they mean. Encountering the number 12 in a formula, for instance, might cause the formula to generate correct results, but it would still be helpful to know what 12 means. Is it the number of months in a year, the number of hours in a day, the minimum number of teeth in a mouth to eat steak, or something even more sinister?

Constants provide a way to assign meaningful names to literal values. They are treated a lot like literal values, but once defined, they can be used over and over again in your code. Each use of a literal value, even if it has the same value, represents a distinct definition and instance of that value.

In Visual C#, constants are defined using the *const* keyword.

```
const short MonthsInYear = 12;
```

This constant definition has the following parts.

A name

> In this case, the name is *MonthsInYear*.

A data type

> This example defines a *short* constant. The data type always follows the *const* keyword. Any of the intrinsic C# data types can be used as constants, or the name of an enumeration (discussed in the next section).

An initializer

> The initializer assigned here is *12*. Once assigned, this value cannot be altered while your code is running. Initializers are usually simple literals, but you can also include basic calculations.
>
> ```
> const int Seven = 3 + 4;
> ```

An access level

> The definition of *MonthsInYear* listed here represents the typical format of a constant definition included within a code procedure. You can also define constants outside of procedures, but still within a class or other type. When you do this, you generally add an access modifier keyword just before the *const* keyword. This keyword indicates how much code will be able to use the constant. I'll describe access modifiers a little later, in the section on variables. Constants defined within a procedure can only be used within that procedure.

Once you define a constant, you can use it anywhere you would use an equivalent literal.

```
const string GreatGreeting = "Hello, World!";
...Later...
MessageBox.Show(GreatGreeting);
```

Enumerations

Enumerations, one of the core .NET types, allow you to group together named, related integer values as a set. Once bound together, the enumeration can be used like any other data type; you can create variables that are specific instances of an enumeration.

Enumerations are a multiline construct; the first line defines the name and underlying data type of the enumeration. Each enumeration member appears on a separate line, ending with a final closing *End Enum* line.

```
01    enum CarType : int
02    {
03        Sedan = 1,
04        StationWagon = 2,
05        Truck = 3,
06        SUV = 4,
07        Other = 5
08    }
```

The declaration line (line 01) includes the *enum* keyword, the name of the enumeration (*CarType*), and the underlying data type (*int*). The data type (and the colon that precedes it) is optional; if you leave it off, the enumeration defaults to *int*. If you do supply a data type, it must be one of the following: *byte*, *int*, *long*, *sbyte*, *short*, *uint*, *ulong*, or *ushort*.

Each comma-delimited member of the enumeration (lines 03 to 07) must include at least a member name (such as *Sedan*). You can optionally assign a numeric value to some or all of the members, as I have done in the sample. If a member lacks an assignment, it is set to one more than the previous member. If none of the members have an assigned value, the first is assigned *0*, the next *1*, and so on.

Once defined, enumeration members act a lot like integer constants; you can use them anywhere you would normally use a literal or constant. When referencing the members of an enumeration in your code, include both the enumeration name and the member name.

```
CarType.Sedan
```

The *enum* statement cannot be used within a method or procedure. Instead, you define an enumeration as a member of a type (class or structure), or as its own standalone type, just like a class. The .NET Framework includes many useful predefined enumerations intended for use with framework features. For instance, the *System.DayOfWeek* enumeration includes members for each day of the week.

Variables

Literals are nice, and constants and enumerations are nicer, but none of them can be altered once your program starts. This tends to make your application rigid and inflexible. If all your customers are named Fred, and they only place orders for $342.34, it probably won't be much of a limitation. But most users want more variety in their software. *Variables* are named containers for data, just like constants, but their contents can be modified throughout the run of an application. Also, they can contain both value types and reference types. Here's the basic syntax for defining a new variable.

```
string customerName;
```

The data type of the new variable begins the declaration, followed by the variable name. In this case, the declaration creates a variable named *customerName* with a data type of *string*. This named container is ready to hold any *string* value; assign to it string literals, other string variables, or the return value from functions that generate strings. Since it is a reference type, it can also be set to *null*, a special C# value and keyword that means "this reference type is empty, really empty."

```
customerName = null;          // No data
customerName = "";            // Blank zero-length string
customerName = "Fred";        // Literal
```

```
customerName =
    GetCustomerName(customerID); // Function result
```

All variables are undefined until set to something. You cannot ask that a variable return its value if that value has never been set up. If you want to use the official default value as the initial setting for a variable, use the default operator, passing it the data type name.

```
position = default(int);   // Set to default, that is, zero
position = 0;              // This also initializes to zero
```

You can include this initialization as part of the declaration itself. Put the initial value just after an equals sign.

```
short countdownSeconds = 60;
DateTime processingDate = DateTime.Today;
string customerName = GetCustomerName(customerID);
```

The last line in that code block shows a reference type—*string*—being assigned the *string* result of a function. You can also assign a brand-new instance of a reference type to a reference type variable. And it's new. That is, it uses the special *new* keyword, which says, "I'm creating a new, basically empty instance of the specific data type." You can include the initial assignment with the declaration or keep it separate, but both methods produce the same result.

```
// ----- One-line variation.
Employee someEmployee = new Employee();

' ----- Two-line variation.
Employee someEmployee;
someEmployee = new Employee();
```

Remember that reference types are buckets that contain directions for locating the actual data. A reference variable that has not yet had anything assigned to it (other than *null*) is empty. That is, the bucket contains no instructions at all since there is no related data stored anywhere. When you assign a new instance to a reference type variable, that instance gets stored somewhere in memory, and instructions for locating that data are dumped into the bucket. In the previous code block, each use of the *new* keyword creates a new data instance somewhere in memory. This data's location is then assigned to the *someEmployee* variable.

Many classes include one or more *constructors*, initialization routines that set up the initial values of the instance. You can call a specific constructor through the *new* clause. The *string* data type includes constructors that let you build an initial string. One of these special constructors lets you create a new string containing multiple copies of a specific character. The following statement assigns a string of twenty-five asterisks to the *lotsOfStars* variable.

```
string lotsOfStars = new String('*', 25);
```

Constructors are discussed in detail in Chapter 8.

Variable declarations can appear anywhere in a procedure, but by tradition they appear right at the start of a procedure, before any other logic statements.

```
void MyProcedure()
{
    int myVariable;
    // ----- Additional code goes here...
}
```

As with constants, variables can be defined either within a procedure, or outside a procedure but within a type. (Variables and constants declared outside a procedure are known as *fields*. Variables and constants declared inside a procedure are known as *local variables* and *local constants*, respectively.) At the type level, the declaration is typically prefixed by one of the following *access modifiers*.

private

> `private` variables can be used by any member or procedure within the type, but nowhere else. If you derive a new class from a base class that includes a private type variable, the code in that derived class will have no access at all to that `private` variable; it won't even know it exists.

internal

> `internal` variables are private to an assembly. They can be used by any code in their containing types, but also by any code anywhere in the same assembly.

public

> `public` variables are available everywhere. It is possible to write an application or component that exposes its types to code beyond itself. Anything marked `public` can be exposed in this way.

protected

> `protected` variables are like `private` type variables, but code in derived classes can also access them. You can use the `protected` keyword only in a class definition; it doesn't work in a structure.

protected internal

> `protected internal` variables combine all the features of `internal` and `protected`. This modifier can be used only in classes.

A single class or type may contain fields, local variables, and constants.

```
class MyClass
{
    // ----- Here's a field.
    private bool InternalUseOnly;

    void MyProcedure()
    {
        // ----- Here's a local variable.
        int myVariable;
    }
}
```

There are other syntax variations in declaration statements, some of which I will discuss later in this chapter and in other chapters.

Scope and Lifetime

When you define a variable within a procedure, it has *procedure-level scope*. This means you can use the variable anywhere within that procedure. Your procedure will likely have *block statements*, those statements, such as `for` and `if` when followed by curly braces, that require more than one line of source code to complete. If you declare a variable within a set of curly braces for one of these statements, that declared variable will have only *block-level scope*. It will be available only within that block of the procedure.

```
for (int counter = 1; counter <=10; counter++)
{
    int processResult;
    // ----- More code here.
}
```

```
MessageBox.Show(processResult);   // This line will fail
```

This code declares *processResult* within the *for* block. So, it's available only for use inside that block; any attempted use of *processResult* outside the *for* block generates an immediate error.

The C# language allows you to start a new set of curly braces even if there is no statement (such as *for* or *if*) introducing it. You can declare variables within such blocks, and those variables will have block-level scope as well.

```
// ---- No statement here. And then...
{
    int justBecauseICan;
}
```

The *lifetime* of a procedure-level variable begins when the code first enters that procedure, and ends when the code exits the procedure. For block-level variables, the lifetime of the variable is the entry into and exit from that block. Each time you enter the procedure or block that contains a variable declaration, that variable will be initialized according to the code you provide.

For fields (class-level variables), the scope depends on the access level used when declaring the variable. The lifetime of a field begins when the class instance is created in code, and ends when the instance is destroyed or goes completely out of use.

Variable and Constant Naming Conventions

The names that you give to your variables will not have that much impact on how your application runs on the user's workstation, but they can affect the clarity of the source code. In the days before .NET, many Windows programming languages used a system called *Hungarian Notation* to craft variable names. Such names helped to communicate information about the data type and usage of a variable to anyone reading the source code. Unfortunately, the rules used to define Hungarian variable names were somewhat complex, and varied not only among programming languages, but also among programmers using the same language.

When Microsoft released .NET back in 2002, its documentation included various programming recommendations. One of those recommendations was "Stop using the Java programming language." Another recommendation encouraged programmers to cease from using Hungarian Notation, and instead embrace a new system that used casing rules to differentiate variables. The rules state that all variable names should employ mixed-case names (where each logical word in the variable name starts with a capital letter and continues with lowercase letters). The only differentiation comes in the capitalization of the initial letter.

- Set the first letter of all local variables and all method parameters to lowercase. This is known as *Camel Casing*.
- Set the first letter of all fields, methods, type members (including controls), and types to uppercase. This is known as *Pascal Casing*.

In the interest of full disclosure, I must tell you that I modified the original recommendations slightly from the documentation supplied with Visual Studio. The original rules were a little more complex when it came to field and method parameter names. Personally, I find the two rules listed here to be adequate for my needs.

You might give a local variable a name like *lookInThisVariable*, which capitalizes the first letter of each word, but not the initial letter. If you defined this variable as a field instead, you would change its name to *LookInThisVariable*, capitalizing the first letter.

Local Type Inference

C# is a *strongly typed language*. This means that all data values are either `int`, or `short`, or `string`, or some other specific data type. Even the default `object` data type is considered strong. To create a variable without a data type would be weak, and Visual C# programmers are anything but weak.

Normally, you specifically tell Visual C# what data type to use for a variable. But there are times when you may want a variable's data type determined by context. This process, called *local type inference*, lets the Visual C# compiler join in the fun of assigning data types to variables. And what fun it is!

In standard variable declaration, the intended data type starts the declaration process.

```
string whatAmI;
whatAmI = "You're a string, and nothing but a string.";
```

But with local type inference, Visual C# will figure out the data type all on its own when you replace the data type with the `var` keyword, and include an initialization expression.

```
var thing1 = "This is a string.";
var thing2 = 25;
MessageBox.Show(thing1.GetType().ToString());
MessageBox.Show(thing2.GetType().ToString());
```

When you run this code, two messages appear to tell you the strong-type-name of each thing: `System.String` and `System.Int32`, respectively. (Don't worry about the "GetType" stuff for now. It just identifies the true type of the things.) Visual C# acts as though the first two lines looked like this.

```
string thing1 = "This is a string.";
int thing2 = 25;
```

Once C# identifies the data type for one of the somewhat untyped variables, that variable is glued to that type. The following code will fail.

```
var thing1 = "This is a string.";
thing1 = 25;  // This fails, since thing1 is a string.
```

As the name implies, local type inference works only with local variables. Class fields must be declared with a specific data type. Other restrictions apply. See dealer for details.

Type inference exists to support the LINQ features discussed in Chapter 17. Although you can let Visual C# infer most or all of the variables in your application, it is not a good thing to do in practice. As smart as the compiler is, it doesn't think deeply about the overall logic of your application, and it may make different data typing choices than you would. For instance, Visual C# may infer a variable as `int`, even though you plan to stuff large `long` values into it later. If you have the opportunity to include meaningful and accurate data types in your declarations, do it. Because I said so. Because it's the right thing to do.

Operators

Visual C# includes a variety of *operators* that let you manipulate the values of your variables. You've already seen the *assignment operator* (=), which lets you assign a value directly to a variable. Most of the other operators let you build up *expressions* that combine multiple original values in formulaic ways for eventual assignment to a variable. Consider the following statement.

```
squareArea = length * width;
```

This statement includes two operators: assignment and multiplication. The multiplication operator combines two values (`length` and `width`) using multiplication, and the assignment operator stores the product in the *squareArea* variable. Without operators, you would be hard-pressed to calculate an area or any complex formula.

There are two formats of non-assignment operators: *unary* and *binary*. Unary operators work with only a single value, or *operand*. Binary operators require two operands, but result in a single processed value. Operands include literals, constants, variables, and function return values. Table 6-8 lists the different operators with usage details.

Table 6-8. Visual C# non-assignment operators

Operator	Description
+	Addition. Adds two operands together, producing a sum. It also doubles as the *string concatenation* operator, joining two string operands into a new, longer string. Syntax: *operand1 + operand2* Numeric Example: *2 + 3* String Example: *"O" + "K"*
+	Unary plus. Ensures that an operand retains its current sign, either positive or negative. Since all operands automatically retain their sign, this operator is usually redundant. It may come in handy when we discuss operator overloading in Chapter 12. Syntax: *+operand* Example: *+5*
++	Increment. Increments the associated operand and returns the new value. This operator is *destructive*, since it modifies the operand itself. The operator can occur before (prefix) or after (postfix) the operand. When it appears before, the value is returned after it has been modified. In its postfix form, the original value is returned to the surrounding expression first, and then the operand itself is incremented. Syntax: *++operand* Syntax: *operand++* Example: *++position*
−	Subtraction. Subtracts one operand (the second) from another (the first), and returns the difference. Syntax: *operand1 - operand2* Example: *10 - 4*
−	Unary negation. Reverses the sign of its operand. When used with a literal number, it results in a negative value. When used with a variable that contains a negative value, it produces a positive result. Syntax: *-operand2* Example: *-34*
--	Decrement. Decrements the associated operand and returns the new value. It is similar to the *++* operator, in that it is destructive, and can appear in prefix or postfix orientations. Syntax: *--operand* Syntax: *operand--* Example: *--remaining*
*	Multiplication. Multiplies two operands together, and returns the product. Syntax: *operand1 * operand2* Example: *8 * 3*
/	Division. Divides one operand (the first) by another (the second), and returns the quotient. If the second operand contains zero, a divide-by-zero error occurs. (When

Operator	Description
	working with *float* and *double* values, divide-by-zero actually returns special infinity or not-a-number indicators.) Syntax: *operand1 / operand2* Example: *9 / 3*
%	Modulo. Divides one operand (the first) by another (the second), and returns the remainder as an integer value. If the second operand contains zero, a divide-by-zero error occurs. (See the caveat listed with the / operator.) Syntax: *operand1 % operand2* Example: *10 % 3*
&	Conjunction, sometimes called the "and operator." Performs a logical or bitwise conjunction on two operands, and returns the result. For logical (Boolean) operations, the result will be *true* only if both operands evaluate to *true*. For bitwise (integer) operations, each specific bit in the result will be set to *1* only if the corresponding bits in both operands are *1*. Syntax: *operand1 & operand2* Example: *isOfficer & isGentleman*
|	Disjunction, sometimes called the "or operator." Performs a logical or bitwise disjunction on two operands, and returns the result. For logical (Boolean) operations, the result will be *true* if either operand evaluates to *true*. For bitwise (integer) operations, each specific bit in the result will be set to *1* if the corresponding bit in either operand is *1*. Syntax: *operand1 | operand2* Example: *enjoyMountains | enjoySea*
&&	Short-circuited conjunction. This operator is equivalent to the logical version of the & operator, but if the first operand evaluates to *false*, the second operand will not be evaluated at all. This operator does not support bitwise operations. Syntax: *operand1 && operand2* Example: *isOfficer && isGentleman*
||	Short-circuited disjunction. This operator is equivalent to the logical version of the | operator, but if the first operand evaluates to *true*, the second operand will not be evaluated at all. This operator does not support bitwise operations. Syntax: *operand1 || operand2* Example: *enjoyMountains || enjoySea*
!	Negation. Performs a logical negation on a single operand. The operator returns a *true* result if the operand evaluates to *false*, and *false* if the operand evaluates to *true*. Syntax: *!operand1* Example: *!readyToSend*
~	Bitwise complement. Performs a bitwise complement on a single operand. Each specific bit in the result will be set to *1* if the corresponding integer operand bit is *0*, and set to *0* if the operand bit is *1*. Syntax: *~operand1* Example: *~readyToSend*
^	Exclusion, sometimes called the "exclusive-or (or Xor) operator." Performs a logical or bitwise exclusive-or operation on two operands, and returns the result. For logical (Boolean) operations, the result will be *true* only if the operands have different logical

Operator	Description
	values (`true` or `false`). For bitwise (integer) operations, each specific bit in the result will be set to `1` only if the corresponding bits in the operands are different. Syntax: `operand1 ^ operand2` Example: `chickenDish ^ beefDish`
`<<`	Shift-left. Shifts the bits of the first operand to the left by the number of positions specified in the second operand, and returns the result. Bits pushed off the left end of the result are lost; bits added to the right end are always `0`. This operator works best if the first operand is an unsigned integer value. Syntax: `operand1 << operand2` Example: `0x25 << 3`
`>>`	Shift-right. Shifts the bits of the first operand to the right by the number of positions specified in the second operand, and returns the result. Bits pushed off the right end of the result are lost; bits added to the left end are always the same as the bit originally in the leftmost position. This operator works best if the first operand is an unsigned integer value. Syntax: `operand1 >> operand2` Example: `0x25 >> 2`
`?:`	Conditional, sometimes called the "ternary operator." This operator takes three operands. If the first operand evaluates to `true`, the second operand is returned by the operator. If instead the first operand is `false`, the third operand is returned. The operator is short-circuiting in that it will not attempt to evaluate the operand that is not returned. Syntax: `operand1 ? operand2 : operand3` Example: `(result > 10) ? failureCode : successCode`
`??`	Coalescence. Returns the first operand. However, if that first operand is `null`, the second operand is returned instead. Syntax: `operand1 ?? operand2` Example: `customerName ?? "Unknown"`
`==`	Equals (comparison). Compares two operands and returns `true` if they are equal in value. Syntax: `operand1 == operand2` Example: `expectedAmount == actualAmount`
`!=`	Not equals. Compares two operands and returns `true` if they are not equal in value. Syntax: `operand1 != operand2` Example: `startValue != endValue`
`<`	Less than. Compares two operands and returns `true` if the first is less in value than the second. When comparing string values, the return is `true` if the first operand appears first when sorting the two strings. Syntax: `operand1 < operand2` Example: `raiseRate < inflationRate`
`>`	Greater than. Compares two operands and returns `true` if the first is greater in value than the second. When comparing string values, the return is `true` if the first operand appears last when sorting the two strings. Syntax: `operand1 > operand2` Example: `raiseRate > inflationRate`
`<=`	Less than or equal to. Compares two operands and returns `true` if the first is less than or equal to the value of the second.

Operator	Description
	Syntax: *operand1 <= operand2* Example: *raiseRate <= inflationRate*
>=	Greater than or equal to. Compares two operands and returns *true* if the first is greater than or equal to the value of the second. Syntax: *operand1 >= operand2* Example: *raiseRate >= inflationRate*
is	Type comparison. Returns *true* if the first operand is of the data type specified in the second operand. Syntax: *operand1 is typeOperand* Example: *someVariable is Customer*
typeof	Type retrieval. Returns an instance derived from the *System.Type* class for the data type operand. Syntax: *typeof(operand1)* Example: *typeof(int)*
as	Type conversion. Returns the first operand after it has been converted into the compatible data type indicated by the second operand. See the discussion on data conversion later in this chapter for more information. Syntax: *operand1 as typeOperand* Example: *someManager as Employee*

Non-assignment operators use their operands to produce a result, but they do not cause the operands themselves to be altered in any way (except for the *++* and *--* operators). The assignment operator does update the operand that appears on its left side. In addition to the standard assignment operator, Visual C# includes several operators that combine the assignment operator with some of the binary operators. Table 6-9 lists these assignment operators.

Table 6-9. Visual C# assignment operators

Operator	Based on
=	Standard assignment operator
+=	+ (addition)
-=	− (subtraction)
*=	* (multiplication)
/=	/ (division)
%=	% (modulo)
&=	& (conjunction)
|=	| (disjunction)
^=	^ (exclusion)
<<=	<< (shift-left)
>>=	>> (shift-right)

These assignment operators are just shortcuts for the full-bodied operators. For instance, to multiply a numeric variable by 2, you can use either of these two statements.

```
// ----- Multiply levelSoFar by 2.
levelSoFar = levelSoFar * 2;

// ----- Another way to multiply levelSoFar by 2.
levelSoFar *= 2;
```

Arrays

Software applications often work with sets of related data, not just isolated data values. Visual C# includes two primary ways of working with such sets of data: collections (discussed in Chapter 16) and arrays. An *array* assigns a numeric position to each item included in the set, starting with *0* and ending with one less than the number of items included. An array of five items has elements numbering from *0* to *4*.

As an example, imagine that you are developing a zoo simulation application. You might create an array named *animals* that includes each animal name in your zoo.

- Animal #0: Aardvark
- Animal #1: Baboon
- Animal #2: Chimpanzee
- Animal #3: Donkey
- ...and so on...

Visual C# identifies array elements by a number in square brackets after the array name. For our animals, a simple assignment puts the *string* name of each animal in an array element.

```
animal[0] = "Aardvark";
animal[1] = "Baboon";
animal[2] = "Chimpanzee";
animal[3] = "Donkey";
```

Using each array element is just as easy.

```
MessageBox.Show("The first animal is: " + animal[0]);
```

Each element of an array is not so different from a standalone variable. In fact, you can consider the set of animals in the example code to be distinct variables: a variable named *animal[0]*, another variable named *animal[1]*, and so on. But they are better than ordinary variables because you can process them as a set. For instance, you can scan through each element using a *for* loop. Consider an *int* array named *eachItem* with elements numbered from *0* to *2*. The following code block adds up the individual items of the array as though they were distinct variables.

```
int totalAmount;
totalAmount = eachItem[0] + eachItem[1] + eachItem[2];
```

But since the items are in a numbered array, you can use a *for* loop to scan through each element, one at a time.

```
int totalAmount = 0;
for (int counter = 0; counter <= 2; counter++)
{
    // ----- Keep a running total of the items.
    totalAmount += eachItem[counter];
}
```

Before you assign values to array elements, or retrieve those elements, you must declare and size the array for your needs.

```
string[] animal = new string[25]; // 25-element array, 0 to 24
string[] moreAnimals;             // An undefined array
moreAnimals = new string[25];     // Now it has elements
```

Each element of the array is an independent object that can be assigned data as needed. In this example, each element is a *string*, but you can use any value type or reference type you wish in the array declaration.

If you create an array of *object* elements, you can mix and match the data in the array; element *0* need not contain the same type of data as element *1*.

The array itself is also an independent object—a class instance that manages its set of contained elements. If you need to specify the entire array, and not just one of its elements (and there are times when you need to do this), use its name without any brackets or positional values.

Multidimensional Arrays

Visual C# arrays support more than one *dimension* (or *rank*). The dimensions indicate the number of independent ranges supported by the array. A one-dimensional array, like the *animal* array earlier, includes a single range. A two-dimensional array includes two comma-delimited ranges, forming a grid arrangement of elements, with separate ranges for rows and columns.

```
char[,] ticTacToeBoard = new char[3, 3];  // 3 × 3 board
```

An array can have up to sixty different dimensions, although there are usually better ways to organize data than breaking it out into that many dimensions.

Array Boundaries

The *lower bound* of any array dimension is usually *0*. There are a few special cases where nonzero lower bounds are allowed, such as when working with older COM-generated arrays. But the standard Visual C# declaration syntax does not allow you to create arrays with nonzero lower bounds.

To determine the current lower or upper bound of an array dimension, use the *GetLowerBound* and *GetUpperBound* methods. (I discuss methods in detail in Chapter 8.) You must indicate which dimension as an argument; you always pass *0* for single-dimension arrays.

```
MessageBox.Show(string.Format("The board is {0} by {1}",
    ticTacToeBoard.GetUpperBound(0) + 1,
    ticTacToeBoard.GetUpperBound(1) + 1));
```

Initializing Arrays

Once you've declared your array elements, you can store and retrieve elements whenever you need. It's also possible to store elements in your array right at declaration time. The list of new array elements appears in a set of curly braces.

```
int[] squares = {0, 1, 4, 9, 16, 25};
```

The *squares* array shown here will have elements numbered 0 to 5.

Nullable Types

Value types are hard-working variables, maintaining their data values throughout their lives. Reference types work hard, too, but they can be filled with *null* and get some time off. This difference has long been a thorn in the side of value types. Is it too much to ask to give these working-class variables a little down time?

Well, Microsoft has heard this plea, and allowed value types to be assigned with *null*. These *nullable types* are essential when you want to have an undefined state for a standard value type (especially useful when working with database fields). Consider this class that manages employee information.

```
public class Employee
{
    public string Name;
    public DateTime HireDate;
    public DateTime FireDate;
```

```
    public Employee(string employeeName, DateTime dateHired)
    {
        this.Name = employeeName;
        this.HireDate = dateHired;
        this.FireDate = DateTime.MinValue;
    }
}
```

This class works well, except that *FireDate* is not really correct. By default, *FireDate* will be set to the minimum-allowed date for the *DateTime* type, which is January 1, in the year 1, at midnight. You could use that date as your "never fired" date. But what happens if your company really did fire someone just at that moment, more than two thousand years ago?

To resolve this issue, nullable types let you assign and retrieve *null* from value type variables. These vitamin-enriched value types are declared using a special question-mark syntax.

```
    public DateTime? FireDate;
```

Once it's declared, a value type can take either standard data or *null*.

```
    this.FireDate = null;
    this.FireDate = new DateTime(2015, 7, 18);

    // ----- Test for valid content.
    if (this.FireDate == null)...

    // ----- This is another way of testing.
    if (this.FireDate.HasValue == false)...
```

There is a special syntax used to define your own custom value types as nullable, but since it employs Visual C#'s generics feature, I'll wait until Chapter 16 to introduce it.

Casting and Conversion

Integers are the blue-collar workers of the data world. But even ordinary numbers want to get fancied up once in a while and experience the life of a decimal value. Fortunately, C# includes *conversion* and *casting* features that let you move data into other compatible formats.

Some conversions happen automatically, such as when you want to use an integer as a long integer.

```
    int smallerValue = 10;
    long largerValue;
    largerValue = smallerValue;   // This just works
```

Such *implicit* conversions occur without you doing anything extra. C# already knows how to convert an *int* to a *long*, and it doesn't expect any problems doing so, so it goes ahead and does it without complaint. The move from *int* to *long* is a *widening conversion*, which means that every possible value in the *int* range will fit inside of the *long* range. No data loss will ever occur, so the conversion is made as easy as possible.

Other conversions are not so easy. Moving data from *long* to *int*, for instance, is fraught with problems.

```
    long largerValue = 5000000000;
    int smallerValue;
    smallerValue = largerValue;   // Oops
```

The *int* data type cannot hold a value of five billion. The *long*-to-*int* direction represents a *narrowing conversion*, since there may be values of the larger type that won't fit into the smaller type. Visual C# knows about this possibility for failure, and it forbids you from performing the conversion implicitly. But sometimes you know that a conversion will work.

```
long largerValue = 5;
int smallerValue;
smallerValue = largerValue;   // Why not?
```

C# will still prevent this code from compiling, even though there is no data-specific reason to restrict it. It is this type of impediment to data movement that led to the eventual downfall of the rigid class system in Great Britain.

Fortunately, Visual C# provides several features that let you move data between types, even in cases where the language might feel uncomfortable doing so. The most direct means is known as casting. To perform a cast, you insert the destination data type within a set of parentheses just before the source expression.

```
smallerValue = (int)largerValue;   // This will compile
```

In this statement, you are telling C# *explicitly* to make the conversion happen. Visual C# shows its trust in you, by allowing the conversion even though it knows there could be problems. And its concerns are warranted. If `largerValue` contains that five billion data value, the statement will generate a *runtime error*. But C# transfers the responsibility for the safety of this conversion to you.

Casting works between any two data types for which C# understands the rules of conversion. Usually, these are straightforward conversions: `char` to `string`, `int` to `float`, `double` to `decimal`. Casting works between any base and derived types, which means that anything can be cast as `object`, since everything derives from `object`.

Although basic casts work well, more complex migrations of data often require a true conversion. A cast will convert a long value to an integer, but it won't convert a text string containing a number to an integer. That operation requires features that know how to interpret more complex data. One such feature is the `System.Convert` class and its type-specific members, such as `ToInt32`. This function is able to transform numeric strings into actual numbers because it contains the logic needed to examine and migrate string-based numeric data.

```
int dest;
string source = "123";
dest = (int)source;   // This fails
dest = Convert.ToInt32(source);   // This works
```

The `System.Convert` class includes conversion methods for most of the core data types: `ToBoolean`, `ToByte`, `ToChar`, `ToDateTime`, `ToDecimal`, `ToDouble`, `ToInt16`, `ToInt32`, `ToInt64`, `ToSByte`, `ToSingle`, `ToString`, `ToUInt16`, `ToUInt32`, and `ToUInt64`. They each accept a variety of compatible source expressions. We'll use both casting and these conversion methods regularly in the Library Project.

We will also have the opportunity to use the `Parse` and `TryParse` methods that are part of each core .NET data type. Like many of the `System.Convert` methods, these methods take content from a string and convert it to a target data type. For example, the following statement converts a numeric string to its `decimal` data type equivalent.

```
string source = "123.45";
decimal dest = decimal.Parse(source);
```

This code still generates a runtime error of the source string is not in a valid decimal format. Runtime errors are obnoxious, but you can avoid them by using the `TryParse` method instead. Instead of erroring out, `TryParse` returns a `true` or `false` value indicating whether the conversion succeeded. The output variable is sent to the method as an argument, proceeded by the `out` keyword, which indicates that data will only be coming out through that argument, not sent in.

```
string source = "123.45";
decimal dest;
if (decimal.TryParse(source, out dest) == false)
    dest = 0M;
```

Visual C#'s `as` operator is as gentle as `TryParse`. It works much like a standard parenthesized cast. However, if the cast fails for any reason, the result of the expression is `null` instead of an exception.

```
dest = source as Customer;
if (dest == null)...
```

One final conversion feature isn't a true conversion, but an ability of any .NET object to represent itself as a string. Every instance exposes a `ToString` method that returns its string form. The precise form is up to the data type of the expression or variable. Some `ToString` methods accept arguments that lets you adjust the returned content.

```
decimal source = 123.45M;
display = source.ToString();        // Returns: "123.45"
display = source.ToString("0.0");   // Returns: "123.4"
```

String Interpolation

String concatenation provides a basic way to create complex strings from constituent parts.

```
ageMessage = "I am " + age.ToString() + " years old.";
```

As mentioned in the "Project" section in Chapter 5, the `string.Format` method lets you achieve similar results using a string template, where placeholders are replaced with positional values.

```
ageMessage = string.Format(
    "I will be {0} years old on {1:M/d/yyyy}.",
    age, nextBirthday);
```

Visual C# 2015 adds a new feature called *string interpolation* that condenses the string template and positional references into a single string syntax. In such strings, each numeric placeholder is replaced with an expression that otherwise would follow the template within the source code. A dollar sign ($) symbol always appears immediately before an interpolated string.

```
ageMessage = $"I will be {age} years old " +
    $"on {nextBirthday:M/d/yyyy}.";
```

Useful Data Type Features

The core data type classes include many useful properties, methods, and helper classes that help you manage and manipulate the data values they contain. I'll mention a few of them here, broken up by the type of data.

Numeric Features

The `System.Math` class exposes several methods that increase your number-working prowess. To use them, pass your data as an argument to the method, and use the result in any way that seems well-rounded to you. Speaking of well-rounded, the `Round` method rounds a number to a specific number of decimal places.

```
// ----- Round to two decimal places.
dollarsAndCents = Math.Round(price * discount, 2);
```

If you leave off the second argument, the method rounds to zero decimal places.

Most of the other `Math` class members work just like this. They typically return the same data type of the value that you pass in. Table 6-10 lists other key members that you will find useful in your calculations.

Table 6-10. Useful Math class members

Member	Description
Abs	Returns the absolute value of the supplied argument.
Floor	Returns the largest integer that is at or below the passed-in value. That is, it rounds toward negative infinity.
Ceiling	Returns the largest integer that is at or above the passed-in value. That is, it rounds toward positive infinity.
Min	This method accepts two arguments, and returns the one that has the lower numeric value.
Max	Like `Min`, this method accepts two arguments, but returns the higher-valued one.
Pow	Raises a number (the first argument) to the power indicated by the second argument.
Sign	Returns a simplified value indicating the positive or negative state of the original value: -1 for negative, 1 for positive, or 0 if the source value was zero.
Sqrt	Returns the square root of the source value.
PI	Returns a representation of π.
Trig methods	The `Math` class has all of your favorite high school era trig functions: `Sin`, `Sinh`, `Cos`, `Cosh`, `Tan`, `Tanh`, `Asin`, `Acos`, `Atan`, and `Atan2`.

String Features

Variables created as *string* each include several properties and methods that let you manipulate text strings in useful ways. Because strings are immutable, any method that returns a string returns a completely new string, and the original string is left intact.

Most of the methods are used from an existing instance of the string.

```
result = originalText.ToLower();
```

Table 6-11 lists some of the *string* class methods that I use regularly.

Table 6-11. Useful string class members

Member	Description
ToUpper	Returns an uppercase version of the source string. The parallel `ToLower` method does the same, but to lowercase.
Trim	Removes excess whitespace (spaces, tabs, and so on) from the start and end of a string. If you only want to remove whitespace from the start or end of the string, but not both, use `TrimStart` or `TrimEnd` instead.
Substring	Returns a portion of a string, using a zero-based starting index, plus an optional length. The following statement returns the second through fourth characters from the original string. That is, it returns 3 characters starting at position 1. `    result = origText.Substring(1, 3);` If you leave off the length argument, all content until the end of the string is returned. Substring is not very smart about detecting the edges. If you request a section of string that goes beyond the length of the source string, an error occurs.

Member	Description
`Split`	Splits a string into multiple parts using a delimiter, and returns an array of the split pieces. The following statement returns an array containing "One," "Two," and "Three," but with the commas removed. `parts = "One,Two,Three".Split(',');`
`Join`	The opposite of `Split`, this method connects array parts into a single string. You can indicate a string to stick in between each joined pair.
`IndexOf`	Returns the zero-based position of a substring when found within a larger string. If the substring doesn't exist, the method returns -1. The related `LastIndexOf` method finds the last such match instead of the first.
`Replace`	Replaces all occurrences of one substring within another inside of a larger string.
`StartsWith`	Returns `true` if the string starts with a provided substring. The related `EndsWith` method does the same, but it checks for matches on the string's tail.
`Contains`	Returns `true` if the string contains the indicated substring.
`Length`	This property (not a method) returns the current character length of the string.

Another useful method is *Format*, which we already learned about in Chapter 5 and earlier in this chapter.

Date and Time Features

Although it is not one of the core Visual C# data types, the `System.DateTime` type is still an important and regular part of C# applications, especially enterprise or line-of-business apps. This class has a bunch of date- and time-specific members that detail or manage calendar data.

There are individual properties for date and time components: `Year`, `Month`, `Day`, `Hour`, `Minute`, `Second`, `DayOfWeek`, plus a few others. These properties are read only. If you want to alter a date, you use the various `Add...` methods to return the modified date or time: `AddHours`, `AddDays`, `AddMilliseconds`, and so on. Each method accepts a positive or negative count, so you can advance or reverse time, just like a real time machine.

The `TimeSpan` type helps you examine the differences between two times or dates. There are various ways to generate one of these objects, but the easiest is to subtract one date or time from another. In the following statement, the parenthesized portion is an instance of `TimeSpan`.

```
double delay = (endTime - startTime).TotalSeconds;

// ----- You can also store the time span.
TimeSpan difference = endTime - startTime;
double delay = difference.TotalSeconds;
```

Summary

When you're working with Visual C#, you're working with data. The data types included with C# are simply wrappers for the core data types in .NET, but Visual C# also adds many options and features that enhance your ability to manage and organize data.

Project

You look tired. Why don't you take a five-minute break, and then we'll dive into the project code.

Welcome back! In this chapter, we'll use the data types and features we read about to design some general support routines that will be used throughout the Library program. All of this code will appear in a Visual C# class named *General*, all stored in a project file named *General.cs*.

Project Access

Load the "Chapter 6 (Before) Code" project, either through the New Project templates or by accessing the project directly from the installation directory. To see the code in its final form, load "Chapter 6 (After) Code" instead.

I've already added the *General.cs* file with its class declaration.

```
internal static class General
```

I'll introduce you to the *static* keyword more formally in Chapter 8. For now, just know that when you define a class as *internal static*, you are typically establishing a repository of common procedures that you can use throughout your application without creating a specific instance of the class. For example, if you added a method to this *General* class named *GetSomeInfo*, you could access it anywhere in your code using the following statement.

```
essentialInfo = General.GetSomeInfo();
```

We'll do this a lot throughout the Library Project, so much so that we are going to get sick and tired of the *General* prefix real fast. You might recall that we had this discussion already, when we talked about the repetitive use of namespaces. The solution was to add a *using* directive to the top of each source file.

```
using System.Windows.Forms;
```

Unfortunately, the standard *using* directive only works with namespaces, not classes. But starting with Visual C# 2015, Microsoft added a variation that works with static classes.

```
using static Library.General;
```

When this directive appears in a source file, the code in that file can reference members of the *General* class without having to include the "General" part. It would be meaningless to add that line to *General.cs*, but we'll include it in most of the other code files throughout the project.

For now, let's add some general constants that will be used throughout the program. Add the following code just after the opening curly brace for the *General* class.

Insert Snippet

Insert Chapter 6, Snippet Item 1.

```
// ----- Public constants.
public const string ProgramTitle = "The Library Project";
public const string NotAuthorizedMessage =
   "You are not authorized to perform this task.";
public const int UseDBVersion = 1;

// ----- Constants for the MatchingImages image list.
public const int MatchPresent = 0;
public const int MatchNone = 1;

public enum LookupMethods: int
{
   ByTitle = 1,
   ByAuthor = 2,
```

```
      ...remaining items excluded for brevity...
   }

   public enum LibrarySecurity: int
   {
      ManageAuthors = 1,
      ...remaining items excluded for brevity...
      ViewAdminPatronMessages = 23
   }
   public const LibrarySecurity MaxLibrarySecurity =
      LibrarySecurity.ViewAdminPatronMessages;
```

These constants and enumerations are pretty self-explanatory based on their Pascal-cased names. *UseDBVersion* will be used to ensure that the application matches the database being accessed when multiple versions of each are available. The *MatchPresent* and *MatchNone* constants will be used for library item lookups.

The two enumerations define codes that specify the type of library item lookup to perform (*LookupMethods*), and the security codes used to limit the features that a specific administrator will be able to perform in the application (*LibrarySecurity*).

It's time to add some methods. The first method, *CenterText*, centers a line of text within a specific width. For instance, if you had the string *"Hello, World"* (twelve characters in length) and you wanted to center it on a line that could be up to forty characters long, you would need to add fourteen spaces to the start of the line (determined by subtracting twelve from forty, and then dividing the result by two). The routine uses features of the *string* data type (such as *Trim*, *Substring*, and *Length*) to manipulate and test the data.

Insert Snippet

Insert Chapter 6, Snippet Item 2.

```
public static string CenterText(string origText, int textWidth)
{
   // ----- Center a piece of text in a field width.
   //       If the text is too wide, truncate it.
   string resultText;

   resultText = origText.Trim();
   if (resultText.Length >= textWidth)
   {
      // ----- Truncate as needed.
      return origText.Substring(0, textWidth).Trim();
   }
   else
   {
      // ----- Start with extra spaces.
      return new string(' ',
         (textWidth - origText.Length) / 2) + resultText;
   }
}
```

The function starts by making a copy of the original string (*origText*), removing any extra spaces with the *Trim* method. It then tests that result to see whether it will even fit on the line. If not, it chops off the trailing characters that won't fit, and returns that result. For strings that do not completely fill a line *textWidth* characters wide, the function adds the appropriate number of spaces to the start of the string, and returns the result.

Snippet 2 also added a function named *LeftAndRightText*. It works just like *CenterText*, but it puts two distinct text strings at the extreme left and right ends of a text line. Any questions? Great. Let's move on.

Snippet 3 adds a routine named *DigitsOnly*. It builds a new string made of just the digits found in a source string, *origText*. It does this by calling *IsDigit*, one of the useful methods of the *char* data type, for each character in *origText*. Each found digit is then concatenated to the end of *destText*.

Insert Snippet
Insert Chapter 6, Snippet Item 3.

```
public static string DigitsOnly(string origText)
{
    // ----- Return only the digits found in a string.
    string destText;

    // ----- Examine each character.
    destText = "";
    for (int counter = 0; counter < origText.Length; counter++)
    {
        if (char.IsDigit(origText[counter]) == true)
            destText += origText[counter];
    }
    return destText;
}
```

Snippet 3 also added a handful of methods that check for valid data within a text string. The *CheckDateTime*, *CheckDecimal*, *CheckInt*, and *CheckLong* methods confirm that a string contains valid *DateTime*, *decimal*, *int*, or *long* content, respectively. Each one returns the Boolean result from the relevant type's *TryParse* method, as in this line from the *CheckDateTime* procedure.

```
return DateTime.TryParse(content, out result);
```

One final method in that snippet, *GetBoolean*, converts a string that contains a number or the words "true" or "false" to their *bool* data type equivalents. This procedure also uses *TryParse* to make sure the incoming data is valid.

The last two functions, *CountSubStr* and *GetSubStr*, count and extract substrings from larger strings, based on a delimiter. The *string* data type's *Substring* method also extracts content from larger strings, but it is based on the position of the substring. The *CountSubStr* and *GetSubStr* functions examine substrings by first using a delimiter to break the larger string into pieces.

Insert Snippet
Insert Chapter 6, Snippet Item 4.

The *CountSubStr* function counts how many times a given substring appears in a larger string. It uses the *string* data type's *IndexOf* function to find the location of a substring (*subText*) in a larger string (*mainText*). It keeps doing this until it reaches the end of *mainText*, maintaining a running count (*totalTimes*) of the number of matches.

```
public static int CountSubStr(string mainText, string subText)
{
    // ----- Return a count of the number of times that
    //       a subText occurs in a string (mainText).
    int totalTimes;
```

```
        int startPos;
        int foundPos;

        if ((mainText == null) || (mainText.Length == 0))
            return 0;
        if ((subText == null) || (subText.Length == 0))
            return 0;
        totalTimes = 0;
        startPos = 0;

        // ----- Keep searching until we don't find it no more!
        do
        {
            // ----- Search for the subText.
            foundPos = mainText.IndexOf(subText, startPos);
            if (foundPos == -1)
                break;
            totalTimes += 1;

            // ----- Move to just after the occurrence.
            startPos = foundPos + subText.Length;
        } while (true);

        // ----- Return the count.
        return totalTimes;
    }
```

Just to be more interesting than I already am, I used a different approach to implement the *GetSubStr* function. This function returns a delimited section of a string. For instance, the following statement gets the third comma-delimited portion of *bigString*.

```
bigString = "abc,def,ghi,jkl,mno";
MessageBox.Show(GetSubStr(bigString, ",", 3)); // Displays: ghi
```

I used the *string* data type's *Split* function to break the original string (*origString*) into an array of smaller strings (*stringParts*), using *delim* as the breaking point. Then I return element number *whichField* from the result. Since *whichField* starts with 1 and the array starts at 0, I must adjust the position to return the correct element.

```
public static string GetSubStr(string origString,
    string delim, int whichField)
{
    // ----- Extracts a delimited string from
    //       another larger string.
    string[] stringParts = null;

    // ----- Handle some errors.
    if (whichField < 0)
        return "";
    if ((origString == null) || (origString.Length == 0))
        return "";
    if ((delim == null) || (delim.Length == 0))
        return "";

    // ----- Break the string up into delimited parts.
    stringParts = origString.Split(
```

```
        new[] {delim}, StringSplitOptions.None);

    // ----- See if the part we want exists and return it.
    if (whichField > stringParts.Length)
        return "";
    else
        return stringParts[whichField - 1];
}
```

The delimiter passed to the *Split* method must be part of an array, which the curly braces around the *delim* variable make possible. I don't know why Microsoft didn't allow a simple string to be passed instead, but it's these types of traumas that programmers must deal with every day.

If these functions seem simple to you, great! Most Visual C# code is no more difficult than these examples. Sure, you might use some unfamiliar parts of the FCL, or interact with things more complicated than strings and numbers. But the overall structure will be similar. Most source code is made up of assignment statements, tests using the *if* statement, loops through data using a *for* or similar statements, and function calls. And that's just what we did in these short methods.

Chapter 7

Windows Forms

William Shakespeare wrote, "All the world's a form, and all the controls and labels merely players: they have their exit events and their entrance events; and one control in its time exposes many properties" (from *As You Code It*, Act 2.7.0). Although .NET was still in beta when he penned these words, they apply perfectly to pretty much any .NET application you write, even today.

The .NET technology known as *Windows Forms* includes all the classes and features needed to develop standard "desktop" applications for Microsoft Windows. In the early days of Windows, this was pretty much the only type of program you could write for the platform. But now it is just one of many application types, along with console applications, ASP.NET web applications, Windows Store applications, cross-platform mobile applications, and services.

Inside a Windows Application

If you're new to development on the Windows system, writing applications in the .NET Framework may keep you from a full appreciation of what really happens inside a Windows desktop program, and from being involuntarily committed to an asylum. That's because the internals of Windows applications are no fun.

Windows was originally developed as an application running within MS-DOS, and this had a major impact on the design of Windows and of any applications running within its pseudo-operating-system environment. The latest releases of Windows are true operating systems, no longer dependent on MS-DOS. But the programming methodology was left unchanged for backward compatibility. Applications written in Visual C# still use this Windows 1.0 technology internally, but it is mostly hidden by the many well-designed classes of the Windows Forms package.

Everything Is a Window

Rumors abound about why Microsoft attached the name "Windows" to its flagship product. Some say it represented the "Windows of Usability and Opportunity" that users would gain through the enhanced graphical interface. Some believe it represented the building cavity through which Microsoft executives promised to toss several key developers and managers if the product bombed. But the name actually refers to the different elements that appear on-screen when using Windows and its included applications. In short, everything you see on the screen either is a window or appears within a window: all forms, all controls, all scroll bars, and all display elements. Figure 7-1 points out some of the windows within a typical Microsoft Windows 2.0 display.

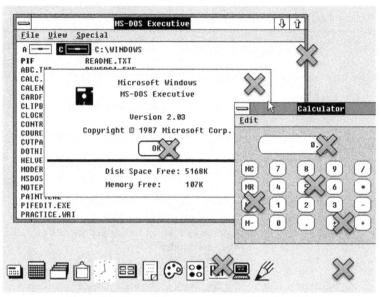

Figure 7-1. Some of the many windows of Windows 2.0

Every main application window was clearly a "window," as were all push buttons, text entry fields, checkbox and radio selection buttons, list boxes, and combo boxes (with a separate window for the drop-down portion). Static text and graphical images were drawn on a window's surface, and did not embody windows by themselves. But certainly hundreds of windows could be on display at any one time.

Although the original developers on the Windows project team suffered from a deplorable lack of originality in the area of feature naming, Microsoft compensated for this somewhat with its release of Visual Basic 1.0, one of the ancestors of today's Visual Studio. In that system, though everything was still a window internally, Microsoft divided the public world of Visual Basic windows into two hemispheres: *forms* and *controls*. There were always some internal differences between these two types of windows, and the new names did a lot to bring normalcy to the Windows application development situation. Microsoft elected to keep these useful monikers when it used Visual Basic as a foundation for the .NET Windows Forms package.

Messages and the Message Pump

When you interact with Windows, it's pretty easy for you (as a human) to detect the different forms and controls on the screen. The image of Windows 2.0 I showed you in Figure 7-1 looks like a typical Windows screen, with its ability to interact with the keyboard and mouse, but it isn't. Go ahead; try to tap Figure 7-1 with your finger. You can tap all day long, but except for putting a hole in the page and not being able to get your money back on the book, nothing else will happen. But while you're tapping, you could shout out, "I just tapped on the OK button" or "I just tapped on the 4 button of the Calculator window."

This is what Microsoft Windows does for you. Windows keeps a list of all "windows" displayed on the screen, how they overlap and obscure each other, and which application each window belongs to. (Some applications are broken into multiple *threads* that all run at the same time. In such programs, Windows keeps track of all windows on a per-thread basis, not just on a per-application basis.) Each user input action (such as mouse clicks and key presses) gets placed in the *system message queue* by the related device driver. As you click on the screen with your mouse, Windows extracts the system message from this queue, determines where you clicked, tries to figure out which window the mouse-click occurred on, and then informs that window's application about the mouse click by adding a *message* to the application's *message queue*. It does the same thing for keyboard input and other actions that a window might need to know about.

To function within the Windows environment, your application (or a specific thread within your application) includes a *message pump*, a block of code that monitors the message queue. Each incoming message includes the ID number of the intended window. The code extracts the message from the queue, and routes it to the *window procedure* (also called a *WndProc*) of the appropriate window for final processing. In the C language, which was the dominant language in early Windows development, the message pump looked somewhat like this.

```
while (!done)
{
    /* ----- Extract and examine the next message. */
    MSG msg;
    if (GetMessage(&msg, NULL, 0, 0))
    {
        /* ----- WM_QUIT means it's time to exit the program. */
        if (msg.message == WM_QUIT)
            done = true;

        /* ----- Send the message to the right window. */
        TranslateMessage(&msg);
        DispatchMessage(&msg);
    }
}
```

Each application (actually, each thread within an application) has one message pump, but multiple window procedures. The message pump exists to route incoming messages to the correct window procedure.

Window Procedures

Just as the message pump dispatches messages to distinct window procedures, the WndProc routine directs processing to individual code blocks or procedures based on the type of incoming message. Here's a general logic outline (pseudocode) that shows the structure of a typical window procedure.

```
if (message type is a mouse click)
    Do mouse-click related code
else if(message type is a key press)
    Do key-press related code
else if (message type is a window resize)
    Do window-resizing-related code
else...
```

(The pseudocode uses successive *if* statements, but an actual window procedure would more commonly use a *switch* type of statement to process the incoming message.) The window procedure is like a vending machine. If the customer pushes the cola button, do the processing that returns a can of cola. If the customer presses the chewing gum button, do the processing that returns chewing gum. If the customer presses the coin return button, keep the money.

For each type of message (at least those that the program wants to handle), some related code gets processed when a message arrives. Boy, that really sounds familiar, but I just can't seem to recall what ... *events*! This sounds just like events in Visual C#. And so it does. Even way back in Visual Basic 1.0 of the early 1990s, all generated applications included a message pump and WndProc procedures for each window, all hidden from view. The primary task of these WndProc procedures was to call the code in your event handlers.

Windows in .NET

Take it from someone who used to write Windows applications in the C language: writing message pumps and window procedures isn't a lot of fun. Microsoft did try to mask some of the tedium with a variety of technologies, including "Message Crackers" and "MFC." It was Visual Basic, and later .NET, that finally succeeded in burying the complexity under a programmer-friendly logical system.

The .NET Framework continues to have WndProc call custom event handlers written by you. It bundles up all this power and simplicity in a technology called Windows Forms. All of its classes appear in the `System.Windows.Forms` namespace. Many of these classes implement specific types of windows, such as ordinary main windows, buttons, text boxes, drop-down combo box lists, and so on.

If you really want to, you can still access the message pump and the various WndProc routines. Each window-specific class includes a `WndProc` method that you can override and craft yourself. The message pump is found in the `System.Windows.Forms.Application.Run` method. You could commandeer any of these components and control the whole ball of wax yourself, but you'll soon find out that the Windows Forms development process is so pleasant, you will work hard to forget what "message pump" even means.

Forms and Controls

In .NET, windows are grouped into *forms* and *controls*. But they are still all windows, built from the same core components. If you don't believe me, check out the classes for the various forms and controls in .NET. Both forms and controls derive from the common `System.Windows.Forms.Control` class, which abstracts the core Windows "window" functionality.

Some of the controls supplied with .NET don't actually implement on-screen window elements. These controls—such as the Timer control—include no user interface experience, but do provide a programming experience that is similar to that of the visible controls. I'll list the specific controls a little later in this chapter, and indicate which ones are not user interface controls.

Designing Windows Forms Applications

Creating a Windows Forms application in Visual C# is easy. Let's try it. Start Visual Studio and select the File→New→Project menu command. The New Project form appears, as shown in Figure 7-2.

Figure 7-2. Visual Studio's New Project form

On the project template tree along the left side of the form, expand the Templates branch, then choose Visual C# below it. From the list of templates that appears, choose the Windows Forms Application template. Give the project any name you want in the Name field, and then click OK. The new project has a single form (`Form1`) ready for you to use. At this point, Visual Studio has already added about 200 lines of source code to your application. If you browse through the Solution Explorer panel and open the various files in the project, you can see the code for yourself. Some of the most interesting code is in the *Form1.Designer.cs* file, slightly edited here.

```
namespace WindowsFormsApplication1
{
    partial class Form1
    {
        private System.ComponentModel.IContainer
            components = null;

        protected override void Dispose(bool disposing)
        {
            if (disposing && (components != null))
            {
                components.Dispose();
            }
            base.Dispose(disposing);
        }

        private void InitializeComponent()
        {
            this.components = new
                System.ComponentModel.Container();
            this.AutoScaleMode =
                System.Windows.Forms.AutoScaleMode.Font;
            this.Text = "Form1";
        }
    }
}
```

All the code that implements a form's behavior appears in the `Form` class in the `System.Windows.Forms` namespace. This project's initial form, `Form1`, inherits from that base form, receiving all of `Form`'s functionality and default settings. Any custom design-time changes made to `Form1`'s user interface, such as adding child controls, are added to the `InitializeComponent` procedure automatically as you use Visual Studio. Check out the routine periodically to see how it changes.

Most programs will have multiple forms. I suppose that .NET could select one of the forms at random to display when a program first runs. That would be fun and unpredictable. But it doesn't work that way. Instead, you indicate the starting form through code in the projects *Main* procedure, found in the *Program.cs* file.

```
namespace WindowsFormsApplication1
{
    static class Program
    {
        [STAThread]
        static void Main()
        {
            Application.EnableVisualStyles();
            Application.
                SetCompatibleTextRenderingDefault(false);
            Application.Run(new Form1());
        }
    }
}
```

When a .NET application begins, the framework calls the *Main* method, which dictates the first moments of your custom application. The first two lines in that routine set up some user interface techie stuff that doesn't concern our C# language learning. But that third line is the important one: it's the message pump.

```
Application.Run(new Form1());
```

Do you see the pump? No? Well, it is somewhat hidden away. But you can see what happens when that line is gone. As a test, comment out that line, and add a new line that simply displays a new copy of the *Form1* form.

```
(new Form1()).Show();
// Application.Run(new Form1());
```

Run the program by pressing the F5 key, and then watch carefully. Very carefully! If you blink, you might miss it. *Form1* appears, but it disappears a fraction of a second later. What?

Each window (or form or control) has a distinct WndProc procedure, but there is only one message pump for each application or thread. In this simple program, *Form1* has its own WndProc procedure, but it doesn't control the message pump by itself. You have to specifically tell the program to start running the message pump. Since the standard message pump for Windows Forms applications appears in the *System.Windows.Forms.Application.Run* method, altering the *Main* code to put it back in will enable the pump and keep *Form1* displayed until the user closes the form or accidentally kicks the power cord out of the outlet.

Put the *Main* code back to the way it was originally, and then try running the program again. This time, *Form1* will stick around for as long as you want.

You can add all sorts of initialization code to your *Main* procedure, and show the main form only when your code is ready to interact with the user. We'll make several changes to this startup method as the Library program grows.

If you need to add a new form to your application, use the Project→Add Windows Form menu command.

Working with Forms

In .NET, all forms are simply classes, variations of the *System.Windows.Forms.Form* class. Each time you create a new form, you are creating a derived class based on that common *Form* class. And your new class is loaded with functionality; it includes all the fields, methods, bugs, properties, and events that make up the *Form* class. Visual Studio takes these elements and presents them in a way that makes it easy to program a form, both through source code and through the drag-and-drop interface of the Visual Studio Forms Designer.

When you first add a form to your application, it's kind of plain and boring. Use the Properties panel (see Figure 7-3) to adjust the form to your liking. This panel shows the principle properties for the currently selected item within the Visual Studio environment. It includes a separate entry for each property setting, most of which can be updated through simple text entry. For instance, you can alter the caption displayed at the top of the form by changing the content of the *Text* property from *Form1* to *CoolForm*.

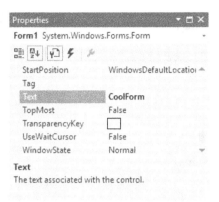

Figure 7-3. The properties of your form

Table 7-1 lists some of the more interesting form properties and their uses.

Table 7-1. Form properties

Property	Description
(Name)	This is the name of the form, or more correctly, of the class that is the form. By default, it is named *Formx*, where *x* is some number. It needs to be changed to something informative.
AcceptButton	Indicates which *Button* control already placed on the form should be triggered when the user presses the Enter key.
AutoScroll	If you set this field to *True*, the form automatically adds scroll bars that move around the contents of the form if the form is sized too small to show everything.
BackColor	The background color. Uses a specific or general system color.
BackgroundImage	Use this property, along with the *BackgroundImageLayout* property, to place a graphic on the background of the form.
CancelButton	This is just like the *AcceptButton* property, but the assigned button is triggered by the Esc key, not the Enter key.
ContextMenuStrip	This property lets you create a custom shortcut menu that appears when the user right-clicks on the background of the form. *ContextMenuStrip* refers to a separate control that you add to the form.
ControlBox	You hide or show the control box in the upper-left corner of the form through this property setting.
Cursor	Indicates the style of mouse cursor that appears when the mouse is over the form. This property demonstrates one of the many editors that appear within the properties window. If you click the down arrow at the right of the property setting, it displays a graphical list of all included mouse cursors. Click an image to get the one you want. (Other properties include custom editors designed for their type of content.) This list includes only the built-in cursors. You can also modify this property in the form's source code if you need to set the cursor to a custom graphic.
FormBorderStyle	This property indicates the type of form to display. The default is *Sizable*, which lets the user resize the form by dragging the bottom-right corner. If you set this property to *None*, the form's title bar and borders disappear. You

Property	Description
	could use this setting for an application's "Splash" welcome form, which normally has no form border.
Icon	Sets the graphic displayed in the upper-left corner of the form's border.
IsMdiContainer	Enables "multiple document interface" support on this form. This allows a master form to contain multiple child document forms.
KeyPreview	If you set this property to *True*, the form's *KeyDown* and *KeyPress* events will get to process any keys entered by the user, even if those keys were destined for a control contained on the form. This is useful when you need to capture keys that apply to the entire form, such as using the F1 key to trigger online help.
Location	Sets the top and left positions of the form on the screen. The *StartPosition* property also impacts the location of the form.
MainMenuStrip	Identifies the *MenuStrip* control to use for the form's main menu. The referenced *MenuStrip* control is added separately to the form.
MaximizeBox	Indicates whether the maximize box (button) appears in the upper-right corner of the form. This box lets the user show a form in "full-screen" mode.
MinimizeBox	Indicates whether the minimize box (button) appears in the upper-right corner of the form. This box lets the user send the form to the system task bar.
MinimumSize	On forms that can be resized, this property indicates the minimum allowed size of the form. The user will not be able to size the form any smaller than this. This property, like some of the others, is a *composite property*, built by merging two or more other properties. In this case, it is built from distinct *Width* and *Height* sub-properties.
Opacity	Allows you to specify the level of transparency for a distinct color that appears on the form (set via the *TransparencyKey* field). Setting this field to 100% means that that color is fully displayed with no transparency; setting it to 0% makes that color fully transparent. You can set this property anywhere from 0% to 100%. Anything that appears behind the form will be partially or completely visible through the transparent portions of this form.
ShowInTaskbar	Specifies whether this form should appear as an item in the system task bar.
Size	Indicates the current size of the form through distinct *Width* and *Height* sub-properties.
StartPosition	Specifies how the form should be placed on the screen when it first appears. It is set through a list of predefined values, which actually link to an enumeration.
Tag	You can put any type of data you want in this property; it's there for your use.
Text	The form's display caption is set through this property.
TopMost	When set to *True*, this form will appear on top of all others, even when it is not the active form.
TransparencyKey	Indicates the color to use for transparency when the *Opacity* field is other than 100%.
WindowState	Identifies the current state of the window: normal, maximized, or minimized.

I listed only about half of the available properties; clearly you have a lot of control over the form and how it is presented to the user. What's really interesting is that many of these properties are not limited to just forms. Some of these properties come from the *System.Windows.Forms.Control* class, and also appear in all other controls that use that same base class. This includes properties such as *Location*, *BackColor*, and *Text*. Although the text displayed in a form's caption and the text displayed on a command button differ significantly in their presentation, the usage through code is identical.

```
Form1.Text = "This is a form caption.";
button1.Text = "This is a button caption.";
```

Although you can set all of the properties in Table 7-1 through the Properties panel, you can also update and view them through code. In fact, if you've modified any of the properties through the Properties panel, you've already updated them through source code, since Visual Studio is just updating your code for you. Try it out! Set the form's *TopMost* property to *True*, and then view the *InitializeComponent* routine in the *Form1.Designer.cs* file. You'll find the following new statement near the bottom of the method.

```
this.TopMost = true;
```

I know what you're thinking: "I'm a programmer, but my text editor is having all the programming fun. When do I get a chance to modify properties through code?" That's a fair question. Properties are pretty easy to modify. You just name the object to be modified along with the property name and its new value, as Visual Studio did with the *TopMost* property.

```
this.Text = "The Library Project";
```

You can also retrieve the property values by naming them.

```
MessageBox.Show("The form's caption is: " + this.Text);
```

You access the form's various methods in much the same way. For instance, the *Close* method closes the form.

```
this.Close();
```

Of course, these statements need to appear within some valid procedure, such as an event handler. Let's add some code to the form's *Click* event so that when the user clicks on the form, the new code will alter the form's caption, remind us what that caption is, and close the form, causing the program to exit. What a great program! Create the event handler by selecting the form's surface, displaying the Events in the Properties panel (by clicking the "lightning bolt" icon on that panel), and double-clicking on the Click item in that events list. The form's code appears with a *Click* event handler skeleton in place (see Figure 7-4).

```
Form1.cs  ↔ ✕  Form1.cs [Design]
C# WindowsFormsApplication1          ⌐ ⁀⁙ WindowsFormsApplication1.Form1          ⌐ ⚙ₐ Form1_Click(object sender, EventArgs e)          ⌐
    namespace WindowsFormsApplication1
    {
        public partial class Form1 : Form
        {
            public Form1()
            {
                InitializeComponent();
            }

            private void Form1_Click(object sender, EventArgs e)
            {
                █
            }
        }
    }
```

Figure 7-4. Adding a Click event to the form

Modify the event handler so that it displays the code listed here.

```
private void Form1_Click(object sender, EventArgs e)
{
```

```
        this.Text = "The Library Project";
        MessageBox.Show("The form's caption is: " + this.Text);
        this.Close();
    }
```

If you run this code and click on the form's surface, a message box appears with the form's caption just before the application exits (see Figure 7-5).

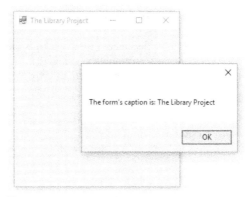

Figure 7-5. A program that communicates when clicked

Adding Controls

New forms are like blank canvases, and like the great painters who came before us, we have a large palette of colorful tools at our disposal. In Visual Studio, these tools are called *controls*, .NET classes designed specifically for use on form surfaces. Visual C# and .NET include dozens of Windows Forms controls, and more are available from third parties. You can even build your own controls, either by deriving them from existing control classes, or by implementing them completely from scratch.

Visual Studio's Toolbox includes all the basic controls you need to build high-quality, or even pathetic low-quality, software applications. Return to the design surface for the *Form1* form, and then access the Toolbox, part of which appears in Figure 7-6, through the View→Toolbox menu command.

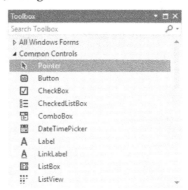

Figure 7-6. Visual Studio's Toolbox with Windows Forms controls

There are five ways to add a control to a form.

- Double-click on a control in the Toolbox. An instance of the control appears on the form in its default location with all of its default settings.
- Drag-and-drop a control from the Toolbox to the form.

- Click on a control in the Toolbox, and then use the mouse to draw the rectangular area on the form where the control will appear. Some controls, such as the *ComboBox* control, have limits on their width or height; they will not necessarily size themselves as you intend.
- Ask someone else to add the control to the form. This option is for the faint of heart. If you are reading this book, this option is not for you.
- Add the control to the form using Visual C# source code. As you add controls to the form in Visual Studio, it is writing source code for you on your behalf. There is no reason why you can't add such code yourself. Although there are warnings in the *Form1.Designer.cs* file telling you not to edit the file, you can hand-modify the *InitializeComponent* routine if you properly conform to the code style generated by Visual Studio. You can also add controls in other areas of your code, such as in the form's *Load* event handler or its constructor. Adding controls dynamically is beyond the scope of this book, but go ahead, experiment.

Some controls have no true user-interface presence in a running application. These controls, when added to your form, appear in a panel just below the form's design surface. You can still interact with them just like form-based controls.

Once a control appears on the form, use the mouse to move the control, or resize it using the resizing anchors that appear when the control is selected. A few of the controls are limited in their resizing options. The *ComboBox* control, for instance, can only be resized horizontally; its vertical size is determined by things such as the font used in the control. Other controls let you resize them, but only sometimes. The *Label* control can be manually resized only when its *AutoSize* property is set to *False*.

Some controls include a small *Smart Tags* arrow button, often near the upper-right corner of the control. Clicking the Smart Tag glyph provides access to useful features associated with the control, as shown in Figure 7-7.

Figure 7-7. The Smart Tag for a ComboBox control

Table 7-2 lists some of the more commonly used controls, all included in the Toolbox by default with a new Windows Forms application. If you create applications using templates other than Windows Forms, the available controls will differ from this list.

Table 7-2. Windows Forms controls available in Visual Studio

Icon	Control	Description
	BackgroundWorker	.NET includes support for multithreaded applications. The *BackgroundWorker* control lets you initiate a background task right from the comfort of your own form. It's especially useful when you wish to update form-based display elements interactively with another "worker" thread. You kick off the new work task through this control's *RunWorkerAsync* method, and perform the actual work via its *DoWork* event.
	Button	A standard push button. A button's *Click* event is its most common programmatic feature, although you can also use its *DialogResult* property to trigger a dialog-specific action.

Icon	Control	Description
☑	CheckBox	This control implements a two-way (on, off) or three-way (on, off, other) checked selection field. The ThreeState property indicates the total number of choices. Use the Checked Boolean property for two-way checkboxes, or the CheckState property for three-way checkboxes.
	CheckedListBox	The CheckedListBox control combines the best of the ListBox and CheckBox worlds, giving you a list where each item can be checked in a two-way or three-way manner. The GetItemChecked and GetItemCheckState methods (and their "Set" counterparts) provide one of the many ways to examine the status of items in the list.
	ColorDialog	Displays the standard Windows form used for color selection by the user. Display the color dialog using this control's ShowDialog method, getting the result via the Color property.
	ComboBox	This control implements the standard Windows drop-down ComboBox control, in all its various styles. The list of items can include any objects you wish; it is not just limited to text strings. You can also provide custom "owner draw" code that lets you draw each list item yourself.
	ContextMenuStrip	This control lets you design a *shortcut* (or *context*) menu, to be displayed when the user right-clicks on the form or the control of your choice. It is designed and used in much the same way as the standard MenuStrip control.
	DataGridView	The DataGridView control implements a standard table-like grid used to display or edit data in individual cells. It is loaded with more display options than you can shake a stick at. The displayed data can be bound to some external data source, or you can make it up on the fly. A virtual-data mode also lets you load data only as needed.
	DateTimePicker	The DateTimePicker control lets the user enter a date, a time, or both, through either basic text entry or mouse-based controls. You can set minimum and maximum boundaries on the user's selection. The MonthCalendar control provides an alternative interface for date-specific selection.
	DomainUpDown	Through this control, the user selects one from among a list of choices that you define, choices that have a specific inherent order. Use this control as an alternative to a ComboBox or TrackBar control when warranted.
	FolderBrowserDialog	Displays the standard Windows form used for directory or folder selection by the user. Display the selection dialog using this control's ShowDialog method, getting the result via the SelectedPath property.
	FontDialog	Displays the standard Windows form used for font selection by the user. Display the selection dialog using this control's ShowDialog method, getting the result via the Font property.

Icon	Control	Description
		Other properties provide access to components of the selected font.
	GroupBox	The *GroupBox* control provides a simple way to visibly group controls on a form. Subordinate controls are drawn or pasted directly onto the *GroupBox* control. To access similar functionality without the visible border or caption, use the *Panel* control.
	HelpProvider	The *HelpProvider* control lets you indicate online help details for other controls on the form. When used, it adds several extra "Help" pseudoproperties to each of the other form controls through which you can supply the help context details. When implemented properly, the indicated online help content will display when the user presses the F1 key in the context of the active control.
	HScrollBar	This control implements a horizontal scroll bar, allowing the user to scroll among a display region or list of choices. For a vertical implementation of this control, use the *VScrollBar* control. Several other controls include their own copies of these scroll bars.
	ImageList	The *ImageList* control encapsulates a set of small graphics or icons for use by other controls that support image lists. Image lists are commonly used by *ListView*, *Toolbar*, and *TreeView* controls.
A	*Label*	This control displays static text on a form. By using the various border and background properties, you can display simple lines and rectangles on a form.
A	*LinkLabel*	The *LinkLabel* control implements a static label that includes one or more links within the text content. These links are similar to the standard text links that appear in web browser content. The control calls its *LinkClicked* event handler when the user clicks on any of the embedded links.
	ListBox	This control implements the standard Windows list box control, displaying a list of items from which the user can select zero or more. The list of items can include any objects you wish; it is not just limited to text strings. You can also provide custom owner-draw code that lets you draw each list item yourself.
	ListView	The *ListView* control presents a set of items with optional display properties. It is somewhat similar to the Windows File Explorer with its various display modes. You can add column-specific data for the details view. The items in the control appear as a set of *ListViewItem* class objects.
(.).	*MaskedTextBox*	This variation of the standard text field helps the user enter formatted numeric or text data by displaying an entry template or mask. For instance, you can force the user to enter a telephone number in "xxx-xxx-xxxx" format by using a numeric mask with embedded hyphen characters.

Icon	Control	Description
	MenuStrip	This control lets you design standard form menus, which are displayed along the top of the user area of the form. Menus within the menu strip are implemented through ToolStripMenuItem class instances. The menu strip is a toolbar-like implementation of a standard Windows menu. You can add other types of controls to the menu, including toolbar-specific ComboBox controls. Context-sensitive menus, displayed when the user right-clicks on the form or a control, are implemented through the ContextMenuStrip control.
	MonthCalendar	The MonthCalendar control displays a subset of a calendar, focusing on a month-specific view. More than one month can be displayed at a time, in vertical, horizontal, or grid configurations. The DateTimePicker control provides an alternative interface for date-specific selection.
	NotifyIcon	The NotifyIcon control lets you place an icon in the system tray area of the Windows task bar, and communicate important messages to the user through this interface. Since this control has no form-specific display presentation, it is possible to use it without having a standard form displayed.
	NumericUpDown	Allows the user to select a numeric value using a scrollable up/down selection method. Use this control as an alternative to HScrollBar, TextBox, TrackBar, or VScrollBar controls when warranted.
	OpenFileDialog	Displays the standard Windows form used for open-file selection by the user. The user can select one or more existing files from local or remote filesystems. Display the selection dialog using this control's ShowDialog method, getting the result via the FileName and FileNames properties. The OpenFile method provides a quick way to open the selected file.
	PageSetupDialog	Displays the standard Windows form used for printed page configuration by the user. Display the configuration dialog using this control's ShowDialog method, getting the results via the PageSettings and PrinterSettings properties.
	Panel	The Panel control logically groups controls on a form. Subordinate controls are drawn or pasted directly onto the Panel control. To access similar functionality with a visible border and user-displayed caption, use the GroupBox control.
	PictureBox	This control displays an image in a variety of formats.
	PrintDialog	Displays the standard Windows form used for document printing and print property selection by the user. Display the dialog using this control's ShowDialog method. This control is used in conjunction with an instance of the System.Drawing.Printing.PrintDocument class, which is created through code or via the PrintDocument control.

Icon	Control	Description
	PrintDocument	This control is used as part of the print and print preview process. It adds a wrapper around your custom print implementation, providing a consistent method of selecting and printing document pages.
	PrintPreviewDialog	This control provides a standardized interface for print preview, implementing all elements of the entire print preview dialog. When used with a PrintDocument class or control, it displays on-screen precisely what will appear on the final printed page. In fact, your printing code doesn't necessarily know whether it is printing to the printer or to the print preview display.
	ProgressBar	The ProgressBar provides graphical feedback to the user for a task completion range. Normally, the range goes from 0% to 100%, but you can supply a custom range. The Value property indicates the current setting between the Minimum and Maximum range limits.
	PropertyGrid	The PropertyGrid control allows the user to graphically edit specific members of an attached class instance. The Properties panel within the Visual Studio environment is an instance of this control. This control makes heavy use of class-based attributes to manage the display and modification of properties. Chapter 18 uses this control to support barcode label management in the Library Project.
	RadioButton	This control implements the standard Windows radio selection button. Although the circular-point display is most common, the control can also appear as a toggle button by setting the Appearance property appropriately. The Checked property indicates the current value of a control. All RadioButton controls that appear within the same group context act in a mutually exclusive manner. Use the Panel and GroupBox controls to enforce specific group contexts.
	SaveFileDialog	Displays the standard Windows form used for save-file selection by the user. The user can indicate a new or existing file from local or remote filesystems. The control optionally prompts the user to overwrite existing files. Display the selection dialog using this control's ShowDialog method, getting the result via the FileName property. The OpenFile method provides a quick way to open or create the indicated file.
	SplitContainer	This control adds a split bar by which you can divide your form into multiple sizable regions, each of which contains a Panel control. Use the Orientation property to alter the direction of the split. The order in which you add SplitContainer controls to a form will impact the usability of the splits; experimentation is recommended.
	StatusStrip	This control displays a status bar, usually along the bottom edge of a form, through which you can display status and other

Icon	Control	Description
		context-sensitive information to the user. The strip can contain multiple *ProgressBar*, *StatusStripPanel*, and *ToolStripLabel* controls.
▬	*TabControl*	The *TabControl* control lets you divide the controls of your form into multiple tabbed regions. Each named tab has an associated *TabPage* control, which works a lot like the *Panel* control. Add or paste subordinate controls directly to each *TabPage* control.
abl	*TextBox*	This control implements the standard Windows text box, in both its single-line and multi-line styles. The main body content is set through the *Text* property. The *PasswordChar* and *UseSystemPasswordChar* properties allow you to mask the input when accepting a user-supplied password.
⏱	*Timer*	This control triggers a timed event at an interval you specify. The size of the interval, in milliseconds, is set through the *Interval* property. If the *Enabled* property is set to *True*, the *Tick* event handler will be called at each met interval. Although you can set the interval as small as one millisecond, it is unlikely that you will achieve this frequency with today's hardware.
▦	*ToolStrip*	The *ToolStrip* control implements a toolbar on which other controls appear. It comes with a set of associated controls and classes that provide advanced rendering and user interaction features.
☐	*ToolStripContainer*	The *ToolStripContainer* control provides a convenient way to add *MenuStrip*, *StatusStrip*, and *ToolStrip* controls to the edges of a form.
⬓	*ToolTip*	The *ToolTip* control lets you indicate a tool tip for other controls on the form. When used, it adds a *ToolTip* pseudoproperty to each of the other form controls, through which you can supply the associated tool tip text. When the mouse hovers over a control with an assigned tool tip text, a small text window appears temporarily over the control to provide meaningful information to the user.
⬚	*TrackBar*	The *TrackBar* control allows the user to make a selection from among a small number of related and ordered values. Its real-world counterpart is the volume control on a radio. Use this control as an alternative to an *HScrollBar*, *NumericUpDown*, or *VScrollBar* control when warranted.
⁝≡	*TreeView*	The *TreeView* control presents a set of items in a hierarchical arrangement. It is quite similar to the Navigation Panel portion of the Windows File Explorer. Each item in the tree is a "node" that can have zero or more child nodes.
⬍	*VScrollBar*	This control implements a vertical scroll bar, allowing the user to scroll among a display region or list of choices. For a horizontal implementation of this control, use the

Icon	Control	Description
		HScrollBar control. Several other controls include their own copies of these scroll bars.
	*WebBrowser*	Implements a web browser within your application. You can use the standard web-based navigation features available within Internet Explorer for URL-based access, or provide your own custom HTML content through the *DocumentText* property or related properties.

Although there is no reasonable limit on the number of controls you can add to a form, there is a limit on how much information the user can experience on a single form without a direct wired connection to the brain. Don't get too wild.

Events and Delegates

Each form and control in a .NET application contains its own WndProc window procedure, and as it processes each incoming message from the message pump, it translates those messages into events. An *event* is the standard .NET technique that controls—and all other classes—use to say, "Hey, something is happening, and you might want to do something about it." When you include a form or control in your application, you can monitor one, some, or all of these events, and write custom code that responds appropriately. The custom code you write for each event appears in an *event handler*. But what actually happens between the finger of the user on the mouse and the logic in your custom event handler? Figure 7-8 shows you graphically what occurs between action and custom logic.

1. The user clicks on a button.   2. Magic happens.   3. The event handler runs.

```
private void button1_Click(
    object sender, EventArgs e)
{
    // ----- Code here.
}
```

Figure 7-8. What really happens when the user clicks a button

Clearly, there is still some mystery surrounding event processing.

Controls—and all classes—determine which events they will make available. For controls, many of the events parallel user-initiated actions: *Click*, *MouseDown*, *KeyPress*, and *SizeChanged*. But there are also many events that could be triggered only by modifications to the control through your source code: *TabIndexChanged* (when the tab-key order of the controls changes), *BackgroundImageChanged*, and *CursorChanged* are just three of the many events that the user cannot trigger directly. A few final events tie to system-level changes, such as the *SystemColorsChanged* event, which fires when the user modifies the system-wide color scheme through the Windows settings panel.

Each event has not only a name (such as *Click*), but also a set of parameters that the event handler will receive when called. Here's a typical event handler for a *Button* control.

```
private void button1_Click(object sender, EventArgs e)
{
}
```

This event handler receives two arguments from the triggering event: a *System.Object* instance (*sender*) and a *System.EventArgs* instance (*e*). Other event handlers may use a slightly different set of arguments, so how do you know what to use? Any events defined within a control class must also indicate the number and type of arguments it will send to the event handler. Visual C# includes an *event* declaration that, when used together with the *delegate* declaration, defines events. Although I didn't peer inside of the code for the *Button*'s *Click* event system, here is a possible look at what that event definition might look like.

```
public delegate void ButtonClickDelegate(
    System.Object sender, System.EventArgs e);
public event ButtonClickDelegate Click;
```

The delegate in this definition sure looks a lot like the event handler, and it should. A delegate is a way of declaring the parameters and return value of a method without actually defining the method. Like a method, it has a return value (*void* in this case), a name (*ButtonClickDelegate*), and zero or more parameters (*sender* and *e*). What it lacks is a method body, since it's not a real method. It's simply the promise of a method to come.

By invoking a specific delegate definition, the *event* declaration establishes a parameter-passing contract between the control and any code that wants to receive event notifications. In this case, the *Click* event promises to send two arguments to the event handler. The first, *sender*, is a reference to the object that the event refers to. For *Button* controls, this parameter receives a reference to the *Button* instance itself. The second parameter, *e*, provides a method for passing an entire object of additional information. The *System.EventArgs* class doesn't have much information, but some events use an expanded derivative of the core *System.EventArgs* class.

Thanks to its affiliated *delegate* declaration, the *event* declaration has a firm grasp on what data it needs to send to any listening event handlers. And it sends those arguments by treating the event as a pseudo-procedure, appending a set of parentheses-enclosed arguments that show up as parameters in the event handler. Let's trace this process down for the *Button* control's *Click* event. When the user clicks on the button, the message pump finds a way to get a message to the WndProc procedure for the *Button* control. That procedure examines the message, sees it is a mouse click, and decides to tell event handlers about it. Then, from within the WndProc code, it raises the event.

```
ButtonClickDelegate theCaller = Click;
if (theCaller != null)
    theCaller(theButtonControl, new System.EventArgs());
```

We'll just pretend that *theButtonControl* correctly refers to the target button. The *e* argument for a *Button* control's *Click* event contains no information beyond the default fields included in a *System.EventArgs* instance, so WndProc just sends a new empty instance. Controls with other event arguments would have created an instance first, filled it in with the relevant data, and passed that instance to the event handler.

If an event fires in an application, and there is no event handler to hear it, does it make a sound? Perhaps not. There is no requirement that an event have any active handlers listening. But when we do want to listen for an event, how do we do it? The standard way to do this in a Windows Forms application is a two-step process. First, you create the procedure that will handle the event, and then you use syntactic epoxy to bind the event and the handler together.

The first part is easy to complete; we've encountered such procedures many times already, including just a few paragraphs before this one.

```
private void button1_Click(object sender, EventArgs e)
{
}
```

C#'s *+=* operator provides the special glue that binds an event to its handler. As mentioned in earlier chapters, Visual Studio uses this operator behind the scenes when it hooks up event handlers in the designer

---

file. For example, here's some typical Visual Studio-generated designer code for a button control. (I've included line numbers, but stripped out most of the code not specific to the button control.)

```
01  partial class Form1
02  {
03      private void InitializeComponent()
04      {
05          this.button1 = new Windows.Forms.Button();
06          this.button1.Location = new Drawing.Point(48, 16);
07          this.button1.Name = "button1";
08          this.button1.Size = new Drawing.Size(75, 23);
09          this.button1.TabIndex = 0;
10          this.button1.Text = "button1";
11          this.button1.UseVisualStyleBackColor = true;
12          this.button1.Click +=
                new EventHandler(this.button1_Click);
13          this.Controls.Add(this.button1);
14      }
15      private System.Windows.Forms.Button button1;
16  }
```

The code in the *InitializeComponent* method in *Form1.Designer.cs* creates the *Button* control instance (line 05), modifies its properties to get just the look we want (lines 06 to 11), and attaches it to the form (line 13). The button instance variable itself is defined outside of the initialization method, on line 15.

The line we care about for event processing is line 12, which uses the += operator to connect *button1*'s *Click* event to the *button1_Click* procedure. That line includes a reference to *EventHandler*, which is a delegate defined by Windows Forms that looks just like the *ButtonClickDelegate* delegate we created above. So many of the Windows Forms events look exactly the same (with a set of *object* and *EventArgs* parameters) that Microsoft decided to create a generic *EventHandler* delegate instead of building an identical but specially named delegate for every possible event.

C# can also figure out the delegate stuff from the context. As long as the original event and the event handler procedure do in fact share the same set of parameters, you don't have to be so explicit about the delegate, although explicit is typically a good thing. The following two lines establish the same event connection.

```
// ----- With an explicit delegate.
this.button1.Click += new EventHandler(this.button1_Click);

// ----- Without an explicit delegate.
this.button1.Click += this.button1_Click;
```

Just as the delegate can be generic and multiuse, an event handler procedure can be multiuse as well. If you want events from several different controls to all do the same thing, you can have them all point to the same event handler code. Normally, each event would have its own personal event handler.

```
this.button1.Click += this.button1_Click;
this.button2.Click += this.button2_Click;
this.button3.Click += this.button3_Click;
```

But if the three *buttonX_Click* routines all contain the exact same code, there is no reason they can't exist as one procedure.

```
this.button1.Click += this.ManyButtons_Click;
this.button2.Click += this.ManyButtons_Click;
this.button3.Click += this.ManyButtons_Click;
```

You can accomplish this by creating the `ManyButtons_Click` procedure (or whatever you want to call it) in your form's code, and then putting the name "ManyButtons_Click" into the Click item on the Events view of the form's Properties panel, doing this for each selected button control.

You don't need to limit yourself to just `Click` events in this sharing. If two different types of events use the same underlying delegate to define the argument signature, they can share an event procedure, although it's not a good idea to go overboard on this sharing for seemingly unrelated events.

Another variation is to have multiple event handlers monitor a single event, although Visual C# gets to decide which handler to call first.

```
this.button1.Click += this.FirstRoutine;
this.button1.Click += this.SecondRoutine;
```

These connections can appear anywhere in your code, not just in the designer file. You can add new event connections whenever you want, and you can also *remove* connections whenever you want. The `-=` operator does the opposite of the `+=` operator.

```
this.button1.Click -= this.SecondRoutine;
```

Naturally, this only works if you connected the event to the handler in some earlier block of code.

A lot of complicated steps take you from an initial user or system action to the code in an event handler. I've spent a big chunk of chapter space discussing exactly how events work, but with good reason. Events and event processing are core features of .NET application development. Eventually, you will spend so much time writing event handlers that it will all become second nature to you. But I also went into all of this detail so that you could take full advantage of this technology. Not only does Visual C# let you monitor controls for events, it also lets you design new events into your own classes. You can use the `delegate` and `event` declarations for your own custom events, triggered by whatever conditions you choose. If you have a class that represents an employee, you can have it trigger a `Fired` event whenever the employee loses his job. By adding custom events, you make it possible for custom code to attach itself to your class logic, even if a programmer doesn't have access to your class's source code.

Making Forms Useful

The form passed to the `Application.Run` call in your `Main` procedure appears automatically when the program begins. All other forms need to be displayed manually, using either the `Show` or the `ShowDialog` method of that form. For instance, if you have a form called `Form2`, you can display it by creating an instance of its class, then calling its `Show` method.

```
(new Form2()).Show();
```

The `Show` method displays a *modeless form*. Modeless forms can be accessed independently from all other forms in the running application. All modeless forms can be activated at any time just by clicking on them; the form you click on will come to the front of the others and receive the input focus. A program might have one, two, or dozens of modeless forms open at once, and the user can move between them freely.

Modal forms take control of all input in the application for as long as they appear on-screen. Modal forms are commonly called *dialogs*. The user must dismiss a modal form before any other open forms in the application can be accessed. The message box window that appears when you use the `MessageBox.Show` function is a common modal dialog window. (Despite having the name `Show` instead of `ShowDialog`, it nonetheless presents a modal form. Inconsistent, right?) A form's `ShowDialog` method displays that form modally, and lets you return a value from that form. The values returned are the members of the `System.Windows.Forms.DialogResult` enumeration.

If you think of forms as works of literature by Alexandre Dumas, modeless forms would be a lot like *The Three Musketeers*: "All for one and one for all." They work with one another in support of the entire application. Modal forms are akin to *The Count of Monte Cristo*. Yes, there are other forms/characters in the application/story, but they are nothing when the Count is in view.

To display the Count—that is, a modal form—use the form's *ShowDialog* method, and optionally capture its return value.

```
DialogResult theResult = (new Form2()).ShowDialog();
```

Modal dialogs are useful for editing some record that requires a click on the OK button when changes are complete. Let's say you were writing an application that displayed a list of books by Alexandre Dumas. It might include two forms: (1) a "parent" form that displays the list of books; and (2) a "child" form that lets you type the name of a single book to be added to the parent list. Wouldn't it be great if you could return the name of the book (or, perhaps, an ID number of a record for the book as stored in a database) instead of a *DialogResult* value?

If the *ShowDialog* method, a public method of the underlying *Form* class, can return a result code, perhaps we can add another public method to a form that will return a result code that has actual meaning. Indeed, we can. Consider the child form (named *BookEntry*) with a data entry field (*BookTitle*), and OK (*ActOK*) and Cancel (*ActCancel*) buttons, as shown in Figure 7-9.

Figure 7-9. Book title entry form

When empowered with the following code, this simple form returns whatever is typed in the field when the user clicks OK (first rejecting blank values), or returns a blank string when the Cancel button is used.

```
public partial class BookEntry : Form
{
    public Form1()
    {
        InitializeComponent();

        // ----- I added these here just to remind you that
        //       the event handlers need to be connected up.
        //       Normally, these lines would appear in the
        //       designer file.
        this.ActOK.Click += this.ActOK_Click;
        this.ActCancel.Click += this.ActCancel_Click;
    }

    public string EditTitle()
    {
        // ----- Show the form, return what the user enters.
        if (this.ShowDialog() == DialogResult.OK)
            return BookTitle.Text.Trim();
        else
            return "";
    }
```

```
        private void ActCancel_Click(object sender, EventArgs e)
        {
            // ----- Return a blank title for "Cancel."
            this.DialogResult = DialogResult.Cancel;
            // ----- Continue with EditTitle()
        }

        private void ActOK_Click(object sender, EventArgs e)
        {
            // ----- Only accept valid titles.
            if (BookTitle.Text.Trim().Length == 0)
                MessageBox.Show("Please supply a valid title.");
            else
            {
                this.DialogResult = DialogResult.OK;
                // ----- Continue with EditTitle()
            }
        }
    }
```

To use this form, the parent form calls the *EditTitle* method, which returns the book title entered by the user.

```
    string newTitle = (new BookEntry()).EditTitle();
```

The *EditTitle* routine shows the form modally with the *ShowDialog* method, and then just sits there until the user closes the form. Closing the form is done through the OK or Cancel button events; setting the form's *DialogResult* property has the side effect of closing the form. Great!

Once the form closes, execution returns to *EditTitle*, which does a quick status-check before returning the final value. And there we have it: a new public interface for a form's most important return value. We'll use this method a lot in the Library Project application.

Summary

Windows programming really hasn't changed much since Windows 1.0. It still does everything through messages, message queues, and window procedures. What has changed is the way the code is abstracted for the benefit of the programmer. The .NET Framework's package for traditional Windows programming, Windows Forms, makes Windows development easy and—dare I say it—fun!

Project

This chapter's project code implements the Library Project's basic Main form, as well as the Splash form that appears when the project first starts up. We'll also take some time to make the program a *single instance* application, which will prevent two copies of the program from running at the same time on a single computer.

Project Access
Load the "Chapter 7 (Before) Code" project, either through the New Project templates or by accessing the project directly from the installation directory. To see the code in its final form, load "Chapter 7 (After) Code" instead.

Configuring the Splash Screen

I've already added a new form file to the project, named *Splash.cs* (the form itself is named `Splash`), including some simple display elements to gussy it up. Check out the graphic on the form. It's presented through a `PictureBox` control, but it's stored in the application as a *resource*, a collection of strings and images attached to your source code. The *Resources* folder in the Solution Explorer includes this image file. It's linked into the picture box through that control's `Image` property. And it sure makes the form look pretty. Your job will be to attach this form into the startup sequence of the application and make it informative.

Let's start with the easy part, showing the version number and copyright information on the splash form. You might remember some of this code from Chapter 5, when we displayed the version number on the About form. The version code this time around is exactly the same. What's new is the copyright code, although it's the same type of code. Go ahead and add that code now to the `Splash_Load` event handler procedure.

> **Insert Snippet**
> Insert Chapter 7, Snippet Item 1.

Here's the portion of that snippet that displays the copyright message on the form.

```
// ----- Show the copyright information.
object[] attrSet = currentAssembly.GetCustomAttributes(
    typeof(AssemblyCopyrightAttribute), inherit:true);
if (attrSet.Length != 0)
    ProgramCopyright.Text =
        ((AssemblyCopyrightAttribute)attrSet[0]).Copyright;
```

This code...is complicated. It uses features we won't talk about for a while, and even then, it's advanced. Basically, it asks the current assembly—that's our running Library program—to look in its collection of assembly-level attributes and return all of the attributes defined by the `AssemblyCopyrightAttribute` class. If you expand the Properties item in the Solution Explorer and double-click on the *AssemblyInfo.cs* file, you can see where this was added to the assembly.

```
[assembly: AssemblyCopyright(
    "Copyright © 2016 by Tim Patrick")]
```

Fortunately, that's the only one we added to the assembly, so when the call to `GetCustomAttributes` returns all items matching that attribute, it returns just one instance. That instance includes a property named `Copyright` that contains the content we seek, and that we assign to the `ProgramCopyright` label's `Text` property.

Now comes the hard part: determining how long to keep the Splash form on the screen before showing the main Library form. Zero seconds seemed a little short to me, and three minutes is certainly too much. I compromised and decided on two seconds. If you look near the top of code in *Splash.cs*, you'll see these class-level declarations.

```
private const int DisplaySeconds = 2;
private DateTime OpenTime;
```

The `OpenTime` field will keep track of when we first displayed the splash screen, and we'll add our two seconds to that to determine when to close the form. In the form's constructor, add the code that records the starting time. That way, it will be set immediately upon creation of the form class.

> **Insert Snippet**
> Insert Chapter 7, Snippet Item 2.

```
    this.OpenTime = DateTime.Now;
```

So that's the birth of the form. Now for its demise. Let's add a method that lets the caller know when the two-second delay is complete, so that it can close the form. Add the new *ShowAwhile* method to the form's class code now.

Insert Snippet

Insert Chapter 7, Snippet Item 3.

```
public void ShowAwhile()
{
    // ----- Show the form for up to two seconds.
    DateTime currentTime = DateTime.Now;
    if (currentTime >= this.OpenTime.AddSeconds(DisplaySeconds))
        return;
    System.Threading.Thread.Sleep(
        this.OpenTime.AddSeconds(DisplaySeconds) - currentTime);
    return;
}
```

The routine compares the time the form first appeared (*this.OpenTime*) with the *currentTime*. If we've already gone past the *DisplaySeconds* timeout, then the routine exits right away, since there is no need to wait any longer. If not, it generates a *TimeSpan* instance through time subtraction, and uses that to take a nap (*Thread.Sleep*) for that remaining amount of time.

This isn't actually the best way to implement a splash screen delay, since it can make the program appear unresponsive. However, since the only thing going on at this point is the display of the splash screen, and since we haven't yet learned about the typical features used to manage such delays, this will be good enough for our needs. And it's only a two second delay. The invention of the microwave oven has really made us an impatient culture.

The splash screen is ready, but we still need to show it. We'll do that from *Main*, the program's core startup routine. Open the *Program.cs* file and add the following code to the Main method, just before the call to *Application.Run*.

Insert Snippet

Insert Chapter 7, Snippet Item 4.

```
// ----- Show the splash screen.
Splash splashScreen;
splashScreen = new Splash();
splashScreen.Show();
splashScreen.Refresh();

// ----- Close the splash screen after a reasonable delay.
splashScreen.ShowAwhile();
splashScreen.Close();
```

This code seems a bit useless, opening and closing the splash screen in quick succession, albeit with a two-second delay coded in. In a later chapter, we'll add code before the *ShowAwhile* call that will make this block seem more logical.

Configuring the Main Form

Although we designed a main form in an earlier chapter, it was pretty sparse, including only an About button. This chapter's project adds all the user interface elements to the form. In fact, I've already added that form's controls to its surface for you (see Figure 7-10).

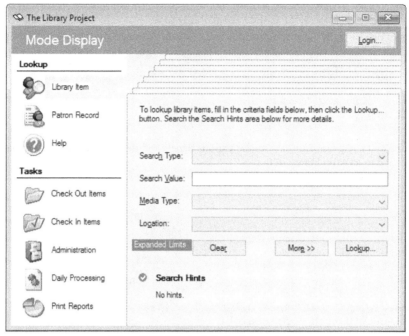

Figure 7-10. The basic look of the main form

The main form looks scary and complex, but looks can be deceiving. To the human eye, there is a mish-mash of elements. But from Visual C#'s perspective, it is nice and orderly: multiple labels, buttons, text entry boxes, and a few other control types appear in their designated spots, some visually overlapping others. For example, the set of icons and labels down the left side of the form ("Library Item," "Patron Record," and so on) are made up of label and picture box controls, the same controls we added to the About form back in Chapter 5.

The only tricky thing on the form is the collection of panel controls that appears on the right half of the form. The *Panel* control, introduced earlier in this chapter, is somewhat like a form itself, in that you can place other controls directly on it. Once placed, those controls stay stuck to the panel, and when you move the panel round, its contained controls move with it. The main form includes eight such panels, one for each of the sections represented by the feature icons. The panel out in front, *PanelLibraryItem*, contains eight *Label* controls, three *ComboBox* controls, one *TextBox* control, and three *Button* controls. I added the *Panel* control to the form first, and then after resizing it how I liked it, I added each of the subordinate controls to that panel.

You must be a little careful when using panel controls, since anything you drag-and-drop onto them becomes subordinate to them. This includes other panel controls. If you drag one of the eight main panel controls on top of another panel control, the destination control will "eat" the one you are dragging, and make it a subordinate control. To move a panel safely, I found that clicking on the panel and then using either the arrow keys or the *Location* property in the Properties panel worked best. If you do accidentally drag a control onto a panel, you can drag it back out onto the main form surface to remove it from the panel.

All the general event code for the form appears in the next code snippet.

Insert Snippet
Insert Chapter 7, Snippet Item 5.

Most of this code exists to move things around on the display. For example, the user can access different features of the form by clicking on the icons or related text labels along the left side of the form. Each icon and label triggers one of eight common routines that exist to rearrange the furniture. The upper-left icon, *PicLibraryItem*, calls the common *TaskLibraryItem* routine when clicked.

```
private void PicLibraryItem_Click(object sender, EventArgs e)
{
    // ----- Library Item mode.
    TaskLibraryItem();
}
```

The *TaskLibraryItem* procedure adjusts the various panels and fields on the display so that the user sees those fields needed to look up library items.

```
private void TaskLibraryItem()
{
    // ----- Library item task.

    // ----- Update the display.
    AllPanelsInvisible();
    PanelLibraryItem.Visible = true;
    ActLibraryItem.BackColor = SystemColors.Control;
    LabelSelected.Location =
        new Point(LabelSelected.Left, PicLibraryItem.Top);
    this.AcceptButton = ActSearch;

    // ----- Get ready for a new search.
    if (SearchText.CanFocus)
        SearchText.Focus();
}
```

The *AllPanelsInvisible* routine also does some on-screen adjustments.

I like to have the existing text in a *TextBox* field selected when it becomes the active control. Each text control includes a *SelectAll* method that accomplishes this feat. We'll call that method during each *TextBox* control's *Enter* event, an event that occurs when a control receives the keyboard input focus.

```
private void SearchText_Enter(object sender, EventArgs e)
{
    // ----- Highlight the entire text.
    SearchText.SelectAll();
}
```

Using the mouse to access the different features of the form is good, but I'm a keyboard person. To deal with keyboard users like me, the code adds support for feature access using the F2 through F9 keys.

```
private void MainForm_KeyDown(object sender, KeyEventArgs e)
{
    // ----- The keys F2 through F9 access the
    //       different sections of the form.
    switch (e.KeyCode)
    {
```

```
            case Keys.F2:
                TaskLibraryItem();
                e.Handled = true;
                break;
            case Keys.F3:
                TaskPatronRecord();
                e.Handled = true;
                break;
            case Keys.F4:
                // ----- Allow form to handle Alt+F4.
                if (e.Alt == true)
                    this.Close();
                else
                    TaskHelp();
                e.Handled = true;
                break;
            case Keys.F5:
                TaskCheckOut();
                e.Handled = true;
                break;
            case Keys.F6:
                TaskCheckIn();
                e.Handled = true;
                break;
            case Keys.F7:
                TaskAdmin();
                e.Handled = true;
                break;
            case Keys.F8:
                TaskProcess();
                e.Handled = true;
                break;
            case Keys.F9:
                TaskReports();
                e.Handled = true;
                break;
        }
    }
```

As each keystroke comes into the *KeyDown* event handler, the *switch* statement examines it. When a matching *case* entry is found, the code within the *case* block executes. Pressing the F2 key triggers the code in the *case Keys.F2* block. *Keys* is one of the many built-in enumerations that you can use in your .NET applications. Notice the special code for the F4 key. It allows the Alt+F4 key combination to exit the application, which is the standard key combination for exiting Windows programs.

Normally, all keystrokes go to the active control, not to the form. To enable the *MainForm.KeyDown* event handler, the form's *KeyPreview* property must be set to *True*. Set this property back in the form designer.

If you were to run the program right now, most of the mouse clicks and keyboards actions I mentioned wouldn't work. That's because we haven't glued the events to their event handlers. Using the Events list on the Properties panel allowed us to create event handlers already connected to the events through designer-file code. But we did a basic cut-and-paste into the form's code, so Visual Studio didn't know it needed to create the event connections. We could use the Events list to manually establish the links, but it's faster to paste the needed connection code. Return to the form's constructor and past the following code just after the call to *InitializeComponent*.

```
this.ActAdmin.LinkClicked += this.ActAdmin_LinkClicked;
this.ActCheckIn.LinkClicked += this.ActCheckIn_LinkClicked;
this.ActCheckOut.LinkClicked += this.ActCheckOut_LinkClicked;
this.ActHelp.LinkClicked += this.ActHelp_LinkClicked;
this.ActLibraryItem.LinkClicked +=
    this.ActLibraryItem_LinkClicked;
this.ActPatronRecord.LinkClicked +=
    this.ActPatronRecord_LinkClicked;
this.ActProcess.LinkClicked += this.ActProcess_LinkClicked;
this.ActReports.LinkClicked += this.ActReports_LinkClicked;
this.ActSearchLimits.Click += this.ActSearchLimits_Click;
this.CheckInBarcode.Enter += this.CheckInBarcode_Enter;
this.CheckOutBarcode.Enter += this.CheckOutBarcode_Enter;
this.KeyDown += this.MainForm_KeyDown;
this.Load += this.MainForm_Load;
this.PicAdmin.Click += this.PicAdmin_Click;
this.PicCheckIn.Click += this.PicCheckIn_Click;
this.PicCheckOut.Click += this.PicCheckOut_Click;
this.PicHelp.Click += this.PicHelp_Click;
this.PicLibraryItem.Click += this.PicLibraryItem_Click;
this.PicPatronRecord.Click += this.PicPatronRecord_Click;
this.PicProcess.Click += this.PicProcess_Click;
this.PicReports.Click += this.PicReports_Click;
this.SearchText.Enter += this.SearchText_Enter;
```

Two of the connections are to events for the main form (*KeyDown* and *Load*), and naturally lack a specific control name before the event name.

Although I had you add these lines manually to the form's constructor, if you open the project in Chapter 8 and later, you'll find that they've been moved to their appropriate positions in the designer file.

Making the Program Single-Instance

The Library Project is designed for use only within a small library; it will run on only a few workstations at a time, perhaps up to ten at most. And there's no need to run more than one copy on a single workstation, since each copy includes all the available application features. We can restrict multiple simultaneous uses of the program by making it a *single-instance application*, one that enforces the one-at-a-time run policy on each workstation.

There are a few different ways to create a single-instance app, but they all follow a general pattern. When the program begins, it grabs a unique token, or locks a specific file, or reserves a portion of memory, or in some other way gains access to something that there can only be one of. If that one thing isn't available, it means that some other program already has it. The .NET Framework includes a feature known as a *mutex* that implements this sort of "it's mine, all mine" system.

Mutexes take care of conflict management between multiple applications. They do this via string tokens. When you create a mutex, you pass it a string that all the apps wishing to avoid conflict agree to. If the creation of the mutex doesn't work, that means that another process created a mutex using that token.

```
// ----- Assumes: "using System.Threading;"
Mutex justMe = new Mutex(true, "Agreed-Upon Token");
If (justMe == null)
    Application.Exit();  // Someone else has the token.
```

We'll use a mutex in the Library program. When the program starts, if it detects another instance already holding the token, the new app will shut down. But first, we want that new app to send a message to the first instance, telling that other copy to bring itself to the top-most position on-screen so that the user can see it. This is actually the more difficult part, and we have to employ features outside of .NET to communicate between instances. C# includes an *extern* keyword that works somewhat like a delegate, in that it points to a method defined somewhere else. In the case of *extern*, that method exists in a non-.NET DLL declared somewhere outside of the active .NET application.

The Library Project includes a new file named *NativeMethods.cs* that defines two such *extern* declarations.

```
[DllImport("user32.dll", SetLastError=true,
    CharSet=CharSet.Auto)]
public static extern bool PostMessage(IntPtr hWnd,
    int Msg, IntPtr wParam, IntPtr lParam);

[DllImport("user32.dll", EntryPoint="RegisterWindowMessageW",
    SetLastError=true, CharSet=CharSet.Unicode)]
public static extern int RegisterWindowMessage(string message);
```

This code locates two external methods, both in the Microsoft-supplied *user32.dll* system library.[5] The *RegisterWindowMessage* method defines a sort of mailbox address to which we can send messages from one program to another. The related *PostMessage* method sends the message to that postbox. *NativeMethods.cs* includes a few other declarations that support this message delivery system.

Don't you feel like a spy, with all of these secret messages and single-use tokens? Now that we have enough deep background, it's time to code the mutex. Return to the *Program.cs* file and add the code that tries to create the mutex, right at the top of the *Main* routine.

Insert Snippet
Insert Chapter 7, Snippet Item 7.

```
// ----- Perhaps another copy is already running.
//       Use a mutex shared among all copies of the
//       app to see if another copy exists.
Mutex librarySync;
librarySync = new Mutex(true, "ACME.Library.CoreApp");
if ((librarySync == null) || (librarySync.WaitOne(
    TimeSpan.Zero, true) == false))
{
    // ----- Send a message to the other copy.
    NativeMethods.PostMessage(
        (IntPtr)NativeMethods.HWND_BROADCAST,
        NativeMethods.WM_LibraryNotify,
        IntPtr.Zero, IntPtr.Zero);
    Application.Exit();
```

---

[5] Don't worry too much about all of the attributes and syntax for these statements. Most *externs* are added to a program via cut-and-past. I use a combination of Microsoft's MSDN web site and the community-supported www.pinvoke.net site when searching for the right external declaration.

```
        return;
    }
```

This block attempts to create a mutex using "ACME.Library.CoreApp" as the token. If it isn't able to obtain the mutex for its own, it sends a message to the token owner via the *PostMessage* external method. Then it quits, using .NET's *Application.Exit* method. Bye bye.

If the program is able to grab the token, it is responsible for releasing it later so that it no longer blocks future uses of the app. Add that code to the very end of the *Main* method.

Insert Snippet

Insert Chapter 7, Snippet Item 8.

```
// ----- Let another copy run later.
librarySync.ReleaseMutex();
```

The last step is to add some code that intercepts and acts on those secret messages we sent when there was a mutex token conflict. The message that got sent was a standard Windows message, the same type of message used to manage mouse clicks and system color palette changes. The application's message pump will intercept this message, and pass it on to relevant windows procedures. To process the message, we need to add code to the main form's WndProc. Since each form already includes a WndProc, all we need to do is override the existing procedure, something we'll talk more about in the next chapter.

Open the code for the *MainForm.cs* file and add the following method to the form's class code.

Insert Snippet

Insert Chapter 7, Snippet Item 9.

```
protected override void WndProc(ref Message m)
{
    // ----- Watch for messages from other copies
    //       of the application.
    if (m.Msg == NativeMethods.WM_LibraryNotify)
    {
        // ----- Focus on this form.
        if (this.WindowState == FormWindowState.Minimized)
            this.WindowState = FormWindowState.Normal;
        this.Activate();
    }
    base.WndProc(ref m);
}
```

This code specifically handles the *WM_LibraryNotify* message, which we defined in the *NativeMethods.cs* file. We still need to let the form handle all other messages it was already dealing with before we got involved. We condescend to grant that permission through the last line in the method, the call to *base.WndProc*, which runs the WndProc for the underlying base implementation that we replaced when using the *override* keyword.

That's all the changes for this chapter. See you on the next page.

Chapter 8

Classes and Inheritance

How many .NET programmers does it take to change a light bulb? None—they call a method on the light bulb object, and it changes itself. Ha, ha, ha! That's funny, but only if you understand the *object-oriented programming* (OOP) concepts that are the basic foundation of the .NET system. (Actually, it's not even that funny if you do understand OOP.) Without OOP, it would be difficult to support core features of .NET, such as the central `System.Object` object, which is the basic foundation of the .NET system. Also, productivity would go way down among Windows developers, who are the basic foundation of the .NET system.

Although I briefly mentioned OOP development concepts in Chapter 1 and Chapter 2, it was only to provide some context for other topics of discussion. But in this chapter, I hold back no longer. After a vigorous discussion of general OOP concepts, I'll discuss how you can use these concepts in your .NET code.

Object-Oriented Programming Concepts

If you've read this far into the book, it's probably OK to let you in on the secret of object-oriented computing. The secret is: it's all a sham, a hoax, a cover-up. That's right, your computer does not really perform any processing with objects, no matter what their orientation. The CPU in your computer processes data and logic statements the old-fashioned way: one step at a time, moving through specific areas in memory as directed by the logic, manipulating individual values and bits according to those same logic statements. It doesn't see data as collective objects; it sees only bits and bytes.

One moment, I've just been handed this important news bulletin. It reads, "Don't be such a geek, Tim. It's not the computer doing the object-oriented stuff, it's the programmer." Oh, sorry about that. But what I said before still stands: the final code as executed by your CPU isn't any more object-oriented than old MS-DOS code. But *object-oriented language compilers* provide the illusion that OOP is built into the computer. You design your code and data in the form of objects, and the compiler takes it from there. It reorganizes your code and data, adds some extra code to do the simulated-OOP magic, and bundles it all up in an executable file. You could write any OOP program using ordinary procedural languages, or even assembly language. But applications that focus on data can often be written much more efficiently using OOP development practices.

The Object

The core of object-oriented programming is, of course, the *object*. An object is a person, place, or thing. Wait a minute, that's a noun. An object is *like* a noun. Objects are computer data-and-logic constructs that symbolize real-world entities, such as people, places, or things. You can have objects that represent people, employees, dogs, sea otters, houses, file cabinets, computers, strands of DNA, galaxies, pictures, word processing documents, calculators, office supplies, books, soap opera characters, space invaders, pizza slices, majestic self-amortizing canals, plantations of ripening tea, a few of my favorite things, and sand.

Objects provide a convenient software means to describe and manage the data associated with one of these real-world objects. For instance, if you had a set of objects representing DVDs in your home video collection, then you would really need to sign up for some sort of video streaming service. And also, each object in the set could manage features of the DVD, such as its title, the actors performing in the content, the length of the video in minutes, whether the DVD was damaged or scratched, its cost, and so on. If you connected your application to the optical drive in your system, your object could even include a Play feature that (assuming the DVD was in the drive) would begin to play the movie, possibly from a timed starting position or DVD chapter.

Objects work well because of their ability to simulate the features of real-world counterparts through software development means. They do this through the four key attributes of objects: *abstraction*, *encapsulation*, *inheritance*, and *polymorphism*.

Throughout this chapter, the term *object* usually refers to an *instance* of something, a specific in-memory use of the defined element, an instance with its own set of data, not just its definition or design. *Class* refers to the design and source code of the object, comprising the *implementation*.

Abstraction

An abstraction indicates an object's limited view of a real-world object. Like an abstract painting, an abstracted object shows just the basic essentials of the real-world equivalent (see Figure 8-1).

ORIGINAL   *Abstract*

Figure 8-1. Actually, the one on the left is kind of abstract, too

Objects can't perfectly represent real-world counterparts. Instead, they implement data storage and processes on just those elements of the real-world counterpart that are important for the application. Software isn't the only thing that requires abstraction. Your medical chart at your doctor's office is an abstraction of your total physical health. When you buy a new house, the house inspector's report is an abstraction of the actual condition of the building. Even the thermometer in your back yard is an abstraction; it cannot accurately communicate all of the minor temperature variations that exist just around the flask of mercury. Instead, it gathers all the information it can, and communicates a single numeric result.

All of these abstract tools record, act on, or communicate just the essential information they were designed to manage. A software object, in a similar way, only stores, acts on, or communicates essential information about its real-world counterpart. For instance, if you were designing an object that monitored the condition of a building, you might record the following.

- Building location and address
- Primary construction material (wood, concrete, steel-beam, etc.)
- Age (in years)
- General condition (from a list of choices)
- Inspector notes

Although a building would also have color, a number of doors and windows, and a height, these elements may not be important for the application, and therefore would not be part of the abstraction. Those values that are contained within the object are called *properties*. Any processing rules or calculations contained within the object that act on the properties (or other supplied internal or external data) are known as *methods*. Taken together, methods and properties make up the *members* of the object.

Encapsulation

The great advantage of software is that a user can perform a lot of complex and time-consuming work quickly and easily. Actually, the software takes care of the speed and the complexity on behalf of the user, and in many cases, the user doesn't even care how the work is being done. "Those computers are just so baffling; I don't know and I don't care how they work as long as they give me the results I need" is a common statement heard in management meetings. And it's a realistic statement too, since the computer has *encapsulated* the necessary data and processing logic to accomplish the desired tasks.

Encapsulation carries with it the idea of *interfaces*. Although a computer may contain a lot of useful logic and data, if there was no way to interact with that logic or data, the computer would basically be a useless lump of plastic and silicon. Interfaces provide the means to interact with the internals of an object. An interface provides highly controlled entries and exits into the data and processing routines contained within the object. As a consumer of the object, it's really irrelevant how the object does its work internally, as long as it produces the results you expect through its publicly exposed interfaces.

Using the computer as an example, the various interfaces include (among other things) the keyboard, display, mouse, power connector, USB ports, speakers, microphone jack, and power button. Often, the things I connect to these interfaces are also *black boxes*, encapsulations with well-defined public interfaces. A printer is a mystery to me. How the printer driver can send commands down the USB cable and eventually squirt ink onto 24-pound paper is just inexplicable, but I don't know and I don't care how it really works, as long as it does work.

Inheritance

Inheritance in .NET isn't like inheritance in real life; no one has to die before it works. But as in real life, *inheritance* defines a relationship between two different objects. Specifically, it defines how one object is descended from another.

The original class in the object relationship is called the *base class*. It includes various and sundry interface members, as well as internal implementation details. A *derived class* is defined using the base class as the starting point. Derived classes *inherit* the features of the base class. By default, any publicly exposed members of the base class automatically become publicly exposed members of the derived class, including the implementation. A derived class may choose to *override* one, some, or all of these members, providing its own distinct or supplementary implementation details.

Derived classes often provide additional details specific to a subset of the base class. For instance, a base class that defines *animals* would include interfaces for the common name, Latin species name, number of legs, and other typical properties belonging to all animals. Derived classes would then enhance the features of the base class, but only for a subset of animals. A *mammal* class might define gestation time for birthing young, whereas a parallel *avian* derived class could define the diameter of an egg. Both *mammal* and *avian* would still retain the name, species name, and leg count properties from the base *animal* class. An instance of *avian* would be an *animal*; an instance of *mammal* would be an *animal*. However, an instance of *avian* would not be a *mammal*. Also, a generic instance of *animal* could be considered as an *avian* only if it was originally defined as an *avian*.

Even though a base and derived class have a relationship, implementation details that are *private* to the base class are not made available to the derived class. The derived class doesn't even know that those private members exist. A base class may include *protected* members that, although hidden from users of the class, are visible to the derived class. Any member defined as *public* in the base class is available to the derived class, and also to all users of the base class. (Visual C# defines another level named *internal*. Members marked as internal are available to all code in the same assembly, but not to code outside the assembly. Public members can be used by code outside the defining assembly.)

Examples of inheritance do exist in the real world. A clock is a base object from which an alarm clock derives. The alarm clock exposes the public interfaces of a clock, and adds its own implementation-specific properties and methods. Other examples include a knife and its derived Swiss Army knife, a chair and its derived recliner, and a table and its derived Periodic Table of the Chemical Elements.

Polymorphism

The concepts introduced so far could be implemented using standard procedural programming languages. Although you can't do true inheritance in a non-OOP language such as C, you can simulate it using flag fields: if a flag field named "type" in a non-OOP class-like structure was set to "mammal," you could enable use of certain mammal-specific fields. There are other ways to simulate these features, and it wouldn't be too difficult.

Polymorphism is a different avian altogether. Polymorphism means "many forms." Because a derived class can have its own (overridden) version of a base class's members, if you treat a *mammal* object like a generic *animal*, there could be some confusion as to which version of the members should be used, the *animal* version or the *mammal* version. Polymorphism takes care of figuring all this out, on an ad hoc basis, while your program is running. Polymorphism makes it possible for any code in your program to treat a derived instance as though it were its base instance. This makes for great coding. If you have a routine that deals with *animal* objects, you can pass it objects of type *animal*, *mammal*, or *avian*, and it will still work. This type of polymorphism is known as *subtyping polymorphism*, but who cares what its name is.

Another variation of polymorphism is *overloading*. Overloading allows a single class method (forget about derived classes for now) to have multiple forms, but still be considered as a single method. For instance, if you had a `House` object with a `Paint` method (that would change the color of the house), you could have one `Paint` method that accepted a single color (paint the house all one color) and another `Paint` method that accepted two colors (the main color plus a trim color). When these methods are overloaded in a single class, the compiler determines which version to call based on the data you include in the call to the method.

Interfaces and Implementation

OOP development differentiates between the public definition of a class, the code written to implement that class, and the resultant in-memory use of that class as an object. It's similar to how, at a restaurant, you differentiate between a menu, the cooking of your selection, and the actual food that appears at your table.

- The description of an item on the menu is (to some extent) its *interface*; it describes what the real object will expose publicly in terms of taste, smell, and so on.
- The method used by the kitchen staff to make the food is the *implementation*; it's how the meal is prepared. There may be different implementations by different restaurants for the same menu item. In objects, the implementation is hidden from public view; in a restaurant, food preparation is thankfully hidden from view or no one would ever eat there.

- The food you receive from the kitchen is—ta-da!—the object, the actual *instance* of what the menu described. Many hungry customers may each order the same menu item, and each would receive a distinct instance of the food.

OOP in Visual C# and .NET

Conceptually, OOP really isn't that complex. Since both humans and programmers interact with real-world objects and instances every day, it's pretty easy to wrap their minds around the idea of programming with objects. But how easy is it to communicate these object concepts to the computer through the Visual C# compiler and the .NET Framework? Can it be done without weekly sessions on a shrink's comfy sofa? Duh! It's Visual C#; of course it's easy.

One reason objects are so easy in .NET is that they have to be. Everything in your .NET program is part of an object, and if everything about .NET was hard, you'd be reading a book on Macintosh development right about now. But it's not too hard because the C# implementation of objects parallels the conceptual ideas of objects.

Classes

Visual C# uses *classes* and *structures* to define objects. I'll talk about structures a little later in the chapter. The `class` keyword starts the definition of a class.

```
class Superhero
{
    // ----- Class-related code goes here.
}
```

That's most of it: the `class` keyword, and a name for the class ("Superhero," in this case). All classes reside in a namespace (discussed way back in Chapter 1). A surrounding `namespace` statement provides a container for the classes and other types in your project. By default, each file's namespace matches the name of the application, configured through the project properties.

```
namespace WindowsFormsApplication1
{
    class Superhero
    {
    }
}
```

The class in this sample code is identified as *WindowsFormsApplication1.Superhero*. You can add any number of classes to a namespace. Classes that use the same name, but that appear in different namespaces, are unrelated.

After the initial class declaration, the members of a class appear between a set of curly braces. You can also split a class's definition into multiple source code files. If you do split up a class like this, each part includes the keyword *partial* in the definition.

```
partial class Superhero
```

As with field definitions, classes are defined using one of the access modifier keywords: *public*, *private*, *protected*, *internal*, or *protected internal*. Flip back to Chapter 6, in the "Variables" section, if you need a refresher course.

The .NET Framework Class Library (FCL) is simply loaded with classes and objects, and they are all pretty much defined with this simple keyword: *class*.

Class Members

Calling your class `Superhero` won't endow it with any special powers if you don't add any *members* to the class. All class members must appear between the class's curly braces, although if you use the `partial` feature to break up your class, you can sprinkle the members among the different class parts in any way you wish.

You can include thirteen different kinds of members in your Visual C# classes. Other books or documents may give you a different number, but they're wrong, at least if they organize things the way I do here.

Variable fields

Value type and reference type variables can be added directly to your class as top-level members. As full class members, they are accessible by any code defined in the same class, and possibly by code that uses your class. As with local variables, field variables are defined using the data type, optionally prefixed by one of the access modifiers. If you omit the modifier, `private` is assumed.

```
class Superhero
{
    public string Name;
    protected string TrueIdentity;
}
```

Variable fields are quick and convenient to add to classes, but sometimes they are a little too freewheeling. Public fields can be modified at will, without any limitations, even if you desire to limit the allowed range of a field. Also, fields don't work directly with all Visual C# features, including some LINQ-specific features. When problems such as these arise, you can use property members instead of variable field members. I'll introduce properties in just a few paragraphs.

Constant fields

You define constants just like variable fields, but include the `const` keyword. As with local procedure-level constants, you must assign a value to the constant immediately in source code, using literals or simple non-variable calculations.

```
private const int BaseStrengthFactor = 1;
```

Enumerations

Enumerations define related integral values. Once defined, you can use them in your code just like other integer values.

```
private enum GeneralSuperPower
{
    Flight,
    Speed,
    VisionRelated,
    HearingRelated,
    WaterRelated,
    TemperatureRelated,
    ToolsAndGadgets,
    GreatCostume
}
```

Enumerations can also be defined at the namespace level, outside any specific class.

Sub methods

Classes include two types of methods: subs and functions. All logic code in your application appears in one of these method types or in properties, so don't bother looking for such code in an enumeration. Sub methods include the *void* keyword to indicate no return value. They perform some defined logic, optionally working on data passed in as *arguments*.

```
public void DemonstrateMainPower(int strengthFactor)
{
    // ----- Logic code appears here.
}
```

The *DemonstrateMainPower* method, as a public member of your class, can be called either by code within the class, or by any code referencing an instance of your class. This method includes a single parameter, *strengthFactor*, through which calls to the method send in data arguments.

You can jump out of a sub method at any time using the *return* statement.

Function methods

Function methods are just like sub methods, but they support a return value that the calling code can intercept and use. The data type of the return value goes in place of the sub's *void* keyword. The *return* statement from the sub method is still there, but it now includes a return value, an expression that appears just after the *return* keyword.

```
public string GetSecretIdentity(string secretPassword)
{
    if (secretPassword == "Krypton")
    {
        // ----- I created a class field named
        //       TrueIdentity earlier.
        return this.TrueIdentity;
    }
    else
        return "FORGET IT BAD GUY";
}
```

Properties

Properties combine the ideas of fields and methods. You can create read-write, read-only, or write-only properties through the *get* and *set* accessors. The following code defines a write-only property by excluding the *get* portion.

```
public string SecretIdentity
{
    set
    {
        this.TrueIdentity = value;
    }
}
```

As mentioned above, sometimes you need to add a property to a class instead of a variable field to support LINQ or some other Visual C# feature that expects a property. If you don't require any of the advanced features of a property, and simply want to assign or retrieve a basic variable-like value, then you can create an *auto-implemented property*, which has a greatly condensed syntax.

```
// ----- Standard auto-implemented property.
public string Name { get; set; }

' ----- Read-only auto-property with initialization.
public int Maximum { get; } = GetConfiguredMaximum();
```

Indexers

An indexer allows a type to be treated like an array, with the ability to retrieve and update collection values based on an index. It uses the `this` keyword as a property name, and includes an index value for reference into the collection or pseudo-collection of accessible values. For example, consider a *BaseballTeam* class that includes a collection of team member names.

```
class BaseballTeam
{
    public string TeamName;
    public string CoachName;
    private Dictionary<string, string> Players =
        new Dictionary<string, string>();

    public string this[string index]
    {
        get
        {
            // ----- Return indexed member.
            if (Players.ContainsKey(index))
                return Players[index];
            else
                return "";
        }
        set
        {
            // ----- Update indexed member.
            //       First, validate position.
            string[] ValidPlayers =
                { "1B", "2B", "3B", "SS", "LF",
                  "CF", "RF", "P", "C" };
            if (!ValidPlayers.Contains(index))
                return;

            // ----- Update the player.
            if (Players.ContainsKey(index))
                Players[index] = value;
            else
                Players.Add(index, value);
        }
    }
}
```

Instances of *BaseballTeam* can now be treated like an index without using a specific member name.

```
BaseballTeam abbottsTeam = new BaseballTeam();
abbottsTeam.TeamName = "St. Louis";
abbottsTeam["1B"] = "Who";
abbottsTeam["2B"] = "What";
abbottsTeam["3B"] = "I Don't Know";
```

Indexers typically use an integer value for the index, just like traditional arrays. But as in the case of the *BaseballTeam* class, you can use any type you wish for both the index and the value that the collection manages.

Delegates

Delegates define arguments and return values for a method, and encase them in a single object all their own. They are generally used to support the event process, callback procedures, and indirect calls to class methods.

```
public delegate void GenericPowerCall(int strengthFactor);
```

Events

Adding events to your class allows consumers of your class to react to changes and actions occurring within a class instance. The syntax works in tandem with a delegate, which supplies the argument and return value structures of the event.

```
public event GenericPowerCall PerformPower;
```

Iterators

Iterators are special function methods or (typically read-only) properties that return a set of results, one element at a time. They are commonly used in *foreach* loops, or in any situation where a sequential set of results needs to be processed. Jump ahead to Chapter 16 to learn about iterators right now, this very second. Or stay here to keep reading about classes. It's your choice.

Externs

The *extern* declaration lets you call code defined in external DLL files, although it works only with traditional (non-.NET) DLL calls. The syntax for declares closely resembles the syntax used to define methods. A supporting attribute indicates the name of the original DLL.

```
[DllImport("evil.dll")]
public static extern string TalkToBadGuy(string message);
```

Once defined, an externally declared sub or function can be used in your code as though it were a built-in .NET sub or function definition. The .NET Framework does a lot of work behind the scenes to shuttle data between your program and the DLL. Still, care must be taken when interacting with such external unmanaged code, especially if the DLL is named *evil.dll*.

Interfaces

Interfaces allow you to define abstract classes and, in a way, class templates. A section near the end of this chapter discusses interfaces. Interfaces can also be defined at the namespace level, and usually are.

Nested types

Classes can include other subordinate classes (or structures) for their own internal or public use. If you make such a nested class public, you can return instances of these classes to code that uses the outer class.

```
class Superhero
{
   class Superpower
   {
   }
}
```

You can nest classes to any depth, but don't go overboard. Creating multiple classes within the same namespace will likely meet your needs without making the code overly complex. But that's just my idea; do what you want. It's your code after all. If you want to throw your life away on a career in the movies, that's fine with me.

Adding a nice variety of members to a class is a lot of fun. You can add class members in any variety, in any order, and in any quantity. If you add a lot of members, you might even get a quantity discount on Visual Studio from Microsoft, but don't hold your breath.

Shared Class Members

Normally, objects (class instances) are greedy and selfish; they want to keep everything to themselves and not share with others. That's why each instance of a class you create has its own version of the data elements defined as class members. Even class methods and properties give the appearance of being distinct for each class instance. It's as though each object was saying, "I've got mine; get your own." It's this attitude that has led to what is now commonly called "class warfare."

In an attempt to promote affability among software components and push for "kinder and gentler" classes, Microsoft included the *static* keyword in its class design. The *static* keyword can be applied to variable field, sub method, function method, and property members of your class. When defined, a *static member* can be used *without the need to create an instance of that class*. You reference these static members using just the class name and the member name.

```
class ClassWithSharedValue
{
    public static int TheSharedValue;
}
...later, in some other code...
ClassWithSharedValue.TheSharedValue = 10;
```

Static members are literally shared by all instances of your class, and if public, by code outside the class as well. Since they don't require an object instance, they are also limited to just those resources that don't require an object instance. This means that a static method cannot access a non-static variable field of the same class. Any class members that are not marked with *static* are known as *instance members*.

Overloaded Members and Optional Arguments

Overloading of a method occurs when you define two methods with the same name, but with different sets of parameters.

```
class House
{
    public void PaintHouse()
    {
        // ----- Use the same color(s) as before.
    }

    public void PaintHouse(Color baseColor)
    {
        // ----- Paint the house a solid color.
    }

    public void PaintHouse(Color baseColor, Color trimColor)
    {
        // ----- Paint using a main and a trim color.
    }
```

```
    public void PaintHouse(Color baseColor, int coats)
    {
        // ----- Paint house with many coats, of paint
        //       that is, not of fabric.
    }
}
```

When you call the *PaintHouse* method, you must pass arguments that match one of the overloaded versions. Visual C# determines which version to use based on the argument signature. If you pass the wrong type or number of arguments, the program will refuse to compile.

Two of the overloaded members in this class look alike, except for the second *coats* argument.

```
    public void PaintHouse(Color baseColor)
```

```
    public void PaintHouse(Color baseColor, int coats)
```

Instead of defining two distinct methods, I could have combined them into a single method, and declared an *optional argument* for the *coats* parameter. Adding an assignment to a parameter enables this feature.

```
    public void PaintHouse(Color baseColor, int coats = 1)
```

Any number of parameters can be optional, but no non-optional parameters can appear after them; the optional arguments must always be last in the list. Although the calling code might not pass a value for *coats*, .NET still requires that every parameter receive an argument value. Therefore, each optional argument includes a *default value* using a simple assignment within the parameter definition. The optional argument *coats* uses a default value of *1* whenever the calling code omits the *coats* argument.

Inheritance

Visual C# supports inheritance, the joining of two classes in an ancestor-descendant relationship. By default, classes don't indicate any such relationships.

```
    class AllAlone
    {
    }
```

This class gives the appearance of independence. And yet it does have a relationship to another class: *System.Object*. All classes ultimately derive from this core class, even if they don't want to talk about it. But some classes might want to brag about it, and C# includes a colon-based syntax that lets them do just that.

```
    class NotAlone : System.Object
    {
    }
```

By adding a reference to *System.Object* after the colon, the declaration makes it clear what *NotAlone*'s relationship is with that base class. Of course, this isn't needed with *System.Object*. But this same syntax can be used to indicate that another class (the "base" class) is the immediate ancestor of the one being declared (the "derived" class).

```
    class Animal
    {
        // ----- Animal class members go here.
    }
```

```
    class Mammal : Animal
    {
        ' ----- All members of Animal are automatically
```

```
'       part of Mammal. Add additional Mammal
'       features here.
}
```

In this example, *Mammal* derives from *Animal*; *Animal* is the base class. The base-class declaration syntax allows exactly one class to be specified as the immediate base class. If you split up your derived class using the *partial* keyword, you only need to add the base class indictor to one of the parts. Although a derived class can only have a single base class, the base class itself can be used in several different derived classes, and the derived class can further be used as a base class for other derived classes.

Derived classes automatically inherit all defined members of the base class. If a derived class needs to provide special functionality for a member defined in the base class, it *overrides* that member. This is a two-step process: (1) the base class must allow its member to be overridden with the *virtual* keyword; and (2) the derived class must supply the overriding code using the *override* keyword.

```
class Animal
{
    public virtual void Speak()
    {
        MessageBox.Show("Grrrr.");
    }
}

class Canine : Animal
{
    public override void Speak()
    {
        MessageBox.Show("Bark.");
    }
}
```

Any class that derives from *Animal* can now supply its own custom code for the *Speak* method. But the same is true for classes derived from *Canine*; the *virtual* keyword is passed down to each generation. If you need to stop this attribute at a specific generation, use the *sealed* keyword. This keyword is valid only when used in a derived class since base class members are non-overridable by default.

```
class Canine : Animal
{
    public sealed override void Speak()
    {
        MessageBox.Show("Bark.");
    }
}
```

There are times when it is not possible to write a truly general method in the base class, and you want to require that every derived class define its own version of the method. Using the *abstract* keyword in the base member definition enables this requirement.

```
class Animal
{
    public abstract void DefenseTactic();
}
```

Members marked as *abstract* include no implementation code of their own, since it would go unused. (Also notice that *DefenseTactic* has no curly braces.) Because there is no code associated with this member, the entire *Animal* class has a deficiency. If you created an instance of *Animal* and called its

DefenseTactic method, panic would ensue within the application. Therefore, it is not possible to create instances of classes that contain *abstract* members. To note this limitation, the class is also decorated with the *abstract* keyword.

```
abstract class Animal
{
    public abstract void DefenseTactic();
}
```

It won't be possible to create an instance of *Animal* directly, although you can derive classes from it, and create instances of those classes. Also, you can create an *Animal* variable (a reference type) and assign an instance of an *Animal*-derived class to it.

```
Animal zooMember;
Simian monkey = new Simian();  // Simian is derived from Animal
zooMember = monkey;
```

Such code doesn't really seem fair to the base class. I mean, it defined all the core requirements for derived classes, but it doesn't get any of the credit since it can't be directly instantiated. But there is a way for a base class to control its own destiny, to take all the glory for itself. It does this by applying the *sealed* keyword to the class itself.

```
sealed class Animal
{
}
```

The only way to use a *sealed* class is to create an instance of it; you cannot use it as the base class of another derived class. (If your non-inheritable class contains static members, they can be accessed without the need to create an instance.)

Base-class indicators, *abstract*, *sealed*, *override*, *virtual*—there's a whole lot of family-relationship terminology being thrown around. And there's still one more of these inimitable keywords: *new*, known also as the shadowing keyword. This isn't *new* as in "create a new instance." This is *new* as in "I'm defining something new, and I don't care who I confuse in the process." When you override a base class member, the new code must use a definition that is identical to the one provided in the base class. That is, if you override a function method with two *string* arguments and an *int* return code, the overriding code must use that same signature. Shadowed members have no such requirements. A shadowed member matches an item in the base class in name only; everything else is up for grabs. You can even change the member type. If you have a sub method named *PeanutButter* in a base class, you can shadow it in the derived class with a variable field (or constant, or enumeration, or nested class) also named *PeanutButter*.

```
class Food
{
    public void PeanutButter()
    {
    }
}
class Snack : Food
{
    public new string PeanutButter;
        // Hey, it's not even a method.
}
```

Without the *new* keyword in the *Snack* class, a compile-time error would occur.

Creating Instances of Classes

Step one: designing classes. Step two: deriving classes. Step three: creating class instances. Step four: cha-cha-cha. Visual C# uses the *new* keyword to create instances of your custom classes.

```
Animal myPet = new Animal();
// ----- Or...
Animal myPet;
myPet = new Animal();
```

The instance can then be used like any other .NET instance variable. Member access occurs using "dot" notation.

```
myPet.Name = "Fido";
```

You can also (within reason) pass instance variables between their base and derived variations.

```
Animal myPet;
Canine myDog;
myDog = new Canine();
myDog.Name = "Fido";
myPet = myDog;          // Since Canine derives from Animal
MessageBox.Show(myPet.Name);  // Displays "Fido"
```

Some data movement between related types is just this simple. The assignment of *myDog* (*Canine*) to *myPet* (*Animal*) just happened without question. But the other way won't be this easy.

```
myDog = myPet;  // This won't compile
```

That line fails because Visual C# is not completely sure that the movement of data from *myPet* to *myDog* is valid. *Canine* derives directly from *Animal*, Visual C# knows that every possible instance of *Canine* will fit into an *Animal* variable, since all *Canine* instances are, in fact, *Animal* instances. That's what it means to be derived. But every possible instance of *Animal* is not necessarily an instance of *Canine*. If you derived a *Simian* class from *Animal*, it would be incompatible with the parallel *Canine* class, also derived from *Animal*. Since the Visual C# compiler can't be sure that you won't be sneaking a *Simian* instance into the *myDog* variable, it complains.

```
Animal myPet;
Canine myDog;
Simian myMonkey;
myMonkey = new Simian();
myPet = myMonkey;  // A Simian is an Animal
myDog = myPet;  // A Simian is not a Canine: Failure!
```

In this code, *myPet* will contain a *Simian* instance, even though it is an *Animal* variable. Visual C# never forgets the true type of an instance. So if you try to assign that *Simian* instance to a *Canine* variable, problems will occur. That's why C# rejects the code at compile time.

But even if Visual C# assumes the movement of data can fail, you as the programmer might understand the overall logic of the code, and that a worrisome conversion will, in fact, work out just fine. In such situations, you can force the movement of an *Animal* instance to a *Canine* variable by using a cast.

```
myDog = (Canine)myPet;
```

Referring to class instances is simply a matter of referring to the variable or object that contains the instance. That is true for code that uses an instance from outside the class itself. For the code within your class (such as in one of its methods), you refer to members of your instance as though they were local variables (with no qualification), or use the special *this* keyword.

```
class Animal
{
    public string Name;
    public void DisplayName()
    {
        // ----- Either of these lines will work.
        MessageBox.Show(Name);
        MessageBox.Show(this.Name);
    }
}
```

The *base* keyword references elements of the base class from which the current class derives. It references only the closest base class; if you have a class named *Class5* that derives from *Class4*, which in turn derives from *Class3*, which derives from *Class2*, which derives from *Class1*, which eventually derives from *System.Object*, references to *base* in the code of *Class5* refer to *Class4*. Well, that's almost true. If you try to use *base.MemberName*, and *MemberName* doesn't exist in *Class4*, *base* will search back through the stack of classes until it finds the closest definition of *MemberName*.

```
class Animal
{
    public virtual void ObtainLicense()
    {
        // ----- Perform Animal-specific licensing code.
    }
}

class Canine : Animal
{
    public override void ObtainLicense()
    {
        // ----- Perform Canine-specific licensing code, then...
        base.ObtainLicense();  // Calls code from Animal class
    }
}
```

Constructors and Destructors

Class instances have a lifetime: a beginning, a time of activity, and finally, thankfully, an end. The beginning of an object's lifetime occurs through a *constructor*; its final moments are dictated by a *destructor* before passing into the infinity of the .NET garbage collection process.

Each class includes at least one constructor, whether explicit or implicit. If you don't supply one, .NET will at least perform minimal constructor-level activities, such as reserving memory space for each instance variable field of your class. If you want a class to have any other startup-time logic, you must supply it through an explicit constructor.

Constructors in C# are similar to sub methods, but omit the *void* keyword, and use the class's name as the method name. A constructor with no arguments acts as the *default constructor*, called by default whenever a new instance of a class is needed.

```
class Animal
{
    public string Name;
    public Animal()
    {
        // ----- Every animal must have some name.
```

```
            this.Name = "John Doe of the Jungle";
        }
    }
```

Without this constructor, new instances of *Animal* wouldn't have any name assigned to the *Name* field. A default constructor gives you a chance to provide at least the minimum needed data and logic for a new instance.

You can provide additional custom constructors by adding more constructor methods, each with a different argument signature.

```
class Animal
{
    public string Name;
    public Animal()
    {
        // ----- Every animal must have some name.
        this.Name = "John Doe of the Jungle";
    }
    public Animal(string startingName)
    {
        // ----- Use the caller-supplied name.
        this.Name = startingName;
    }
    public Animal(int startingCode)
    {
        // ----- Build a name from a numeric code.
        this.Name = $"Animal Number {startingCode}";
    }
}
```

The following code demonstrates each constructor.

```
MessageBox.Show((new Animal()).Name);
    // Displays "John Doe of the Jungle"

MessageBox.Show((new Animal("Fido")).Name);
    // Displays "Fido"

MessageBox.Show((new Animal(5)).Name);
    // Displays "Animal Number 5"
```

You can force the consumer of your class to use a custom constructor by excluding a default constructor from the class definition.

When you create an instance of a derived class, the new instance first accesses the default constructor of its base class. After that base constructor runs, the local instance constructor gets processed. For example, if you create an instance of an *Animal*-derived *Canine* class, the constructor for *Animal* gets processed, followed by the constructor for *Canine*. Normally, the default constructor for the base class is used. However, if the base has an overloaded constructor—one with custom parameters—you can force the use of that alternate constructor by using the *base* keyword as part of the constructor definition.

```
class Animal
{
    public Animal(string Name)
    {
        // ----- Do something with Name argument.
```

```
    }
}
class Canine : Animal
{
    public Canine(string Name) : base(Name)
    {
        // ----- Animal's Name-based constructor
        //       has already been called at this point.
    }
}
```

Similar, you can use another constructor *in the same class* as the starting point by using the *this* keyword.

```
class Canine : Animal
{
    public Canine(string Name) : base(Name)
    {
    }
    public Canine(string Name, int age) : this(Name)
    {
        // ----- Name dealt with in other constructor.
        //       Deal with age here.
    }
}
```

Killing a class instance is not as easy as it might seem. When you create local class instances in your methods, they are automatically *destroyed* when that method exits *if you haven't assigned the instance to a variable outside the method*. If you create an instance in a method and assign it to a class member, it will live on in the class member for the lifetime of the class, even though the method that created it has exited.

But let's think only about local instances for now. An instance is destroyed when the routine exits. You can also destroy an instance immediately by setting its variable to *null*.

```
myDog = null;
```

Setting the variable to a new instance will destroy any previous instance stored in that variable.

```
myDog = new Canine();
myDog.Name = "Fido";
myDog = new Canine();   // Sorry Fido, you're gone
```

When an object is destroyed, .NET calls a special method called a *destructor*, if present, to perform any final cleanup before removing the instance from memory. Destructors appear as methods that use the class name, prefixed with a tilde (~). Destructors never use access modifiers, parameters, or return values.

```
class Animal
{
    ~Animal()
    {
        // ----- Put final cleanup code here.
    }
}
```

So, what's with that crack about killing instances being so hard? The problem is that .NET controls the calling of the destructor; it's part of the garbage collection process. The framework doesn't continually clean up its garbage. It's like the service at your house; it gets picked up by the garbage truck only once in a while. Until then, it just sits there, rotting, decaying, decomposing, and not having its destructor called. For most objects, this isn't much of a problem; who cares if the memory for a string gets released now or thirty seconds from now. But there are times when it is important to release acquired resources as quickly as possible. For instance, if you acquire a lock on an external hardware resource and release it only in the destructor, you could be holding that lock long after the application has exited. Talk about a slow death.

There are two ways around this problem. One way is to add a separate cleanup method to your class that you expect any code using your class to call. This will work—until some code forgets to call the method. The second method is similar, but it uses a framework-supplied interface called *IDisposable*. (I'll talk about interfaces in a minute, so don't get too worried about all the code shown here.)

```
class Animal : IDisposable
{
    void IDisposable.Dispose()
    {
        // ----- Cleanup code here. Then...
        base.Dispose();    // Only if base needs it
        System.GC.SuppressFinalize(this);
    }
}
```

The *SuppressFinalize* method tells the garbage collector, "Don't do the cleanup process; I've already done it." Any code that uses your class will need to call its *Dispose* method to perform the immediate cleanup of resources. So, it's not too different from the first way I talked about, but it does standardize things a bit. Also, it enables the use of the C# *using* statement. This block statement provides a structured method of cleaning up resources.

```
using (Animal myPet = new Animal())
{
    // ----- Code here uses myPet.
}
// ----- At this point, myPet is destroyed, and Dispose is
//       called automatically when using{} exits.
```

Interfaces

The *abstract* keyword forces derived classes to implement specific members of the base class. But what if you want the derived class to implement *all* members of the base class? You could use *abstract* next to each method and property, but a better way is to use an *interface*. Interfaces define true abstract classes, classes consisting only of definitions, no implementation. (OOP purists will point out that a class with the *abstract* keyword attached to even a single member is also an abstract class. Fine.) Interfaces create a *contract*, an agreement that the implementing class or structure agrees to carry out.

The *interface* statement begins the interface definition process. By convention, all interface names begin with the capital letter *I*.

```
interface IBuilding
{
    double FloorArea();
    void AlterExterior();
}
```

As you see here, the syntax is a somewhat simplified version of the class definition syntax. All interface members are automatically public, so access modifiers aren't included. Only the definition line of each member is needed since there is no implementation. In addition to function and sub methods, interface members also include properties and events. Interfaces can also derive from other interfaces (using a colon syntax just after the declaration), and automatically include all the members of the base interface.

```
interface IBuilding : IMasonry
{
    // ----- Classes that implement IBuilding will also
    //       need to implement IMasonry members.
}
```

You attach interfaces to a class the same way you specify a base class: using a post-colon identifier. Class members that use the same name as an interface member automatically implement that member, but you can also prefix the class member name with the name of the interface.

```
class House : IBuilding
{
    public double FloorArea()
    {
        // ----- This method implicitly implements
        //       the IBuilding.FloorArea member.
    }

    public void IBuilding.AlterExterior()
    {
        // ----- This method explicitly implements
        //       the IBuilding.FloorArea member.
    }
}
```

Classes can only inherit from a single base class, but there is no limit on the number of interfaces that a class can implement.

```
class House : IBuilding, IDisposable
```

That post-colon list can also include a single base class.

```
class House : Ediface, IBuilding, IDisposable
```

So, why use interfaces? Interfaces provide a generic way to access common functionality, even among objects that have nothing in common. Classes named *Animal*, *House*, and *Superhero* probably have nothing in common in terms of logic, but they may all need a consistent way to clean up their resources. If they each implement the *IDisposable* interface, they gain that ability without the need to derive from some common base class.

Structures

Classes in C# implement reference types. Another core type, the *structure*, implements value types. All structures derive from *System.ValueType* (which in turn derives from *System.Object*). As such, they act like the core Visual C# data types, such as *int*. You can create instances of a structure through the same syntax used to create class instances. However, you cannot use a structure as the base for another derived structure. And although you can include a constructor in your structure, destructors are not supported.

Because of the way that structures are stored and used in a .NET application, they are well suited to simple data types. You can include any number of members in your structure, but it is best to keep things simple. The *struct* keyword declares a structure.

```
struct SimpleType
{
    public string BasicName;
    public int BasicNumber;
}
```

The *partial* keyword, when applied to a class, allows you to split the class implementation across multiple source code files. That same *partial* keyword can be applied to structure declarations.

Static Classes

We've already seen how a static class member can be used without creating a specific instance of the class. A natural extension of this idea is the *static class*, a class that itself is marked as static, and where every member is also static. Such classes cannot be instantiated, since there would be no point in doing so. Instead, they just sit there, making their members available without comment or concern. To create as static class, attach the *static* keyword to the class and all of its members.

```
internal static class GenericDataAndCode
{
    // ----- Application-global constant.
    public const string AllDigits = "0123456789";

    // ----- Application-global function.
    public static string GetEmbeddedDigits(string sourceString)
    {
    }
}
```

Static classes are useful for gathering common utility routines into one place for easy access. They are also great for storing application-wide constants and *global variables*, values that are accessible throughout your entire application.

```
// ----- In some method...
string startDigits = GenericDataAndCode.AllDigits;
```

When accessing these static members, you reference the class name and the member name, as shown in this sample. If you use these static members all over your code, repeating the class name all the time can get a little dull. C# includes a variation of the *using* directive that lets you use these class members sans their class names. To enable this feature, add the *static* keyword once again to the *using* directive. You need to include the relevant namespace before the class name.

```
using static WindowsFormsApplication1.GenericDataAndCode;
```

Then you can update your method code to exclude the class name.

```
// ----- Same as before, just shorter.
string startDigits = AllDigits;
```

Partial Methods

Partial classes and structures are especially common in code created by code generators. Visual Studio is, in part, a code generator; as you drag-and-drop controls on your form, it generates code for you in a partial *Form* class. In such cases, partial classes have two authors: the automated generator and you.

Partial methods are also used by code generators, although you are free to employ them yourself. They are particularly useful when some automatically generated class wants to give its second author (you) the ability to supply some optional logic that will enhance the automatically generated logic. Partial methods might be more accurately called "optional methods," since you have the option to implement them or not.

Partial methods have two parts: (1) an unimplemented half; and (2) an optional implemented half. The two halves appear in different parts of a partial class. A partial method is never split between a base and derived class; they have nothing to do with inheritance.

The unimplemented half of a partial method looks like an empty sub method definition, but with the *partial* keyword added. No access modifiers are allowed, since partial methods are implicitly private.

```
partial void ImplementIfYouDare();
```

Partial methods must always be sub methods, never functions. If you supply any parameters, they cannot include the *out* keyword. Boy, that's a lot of restrictions.

The implemented half looks really familiar, except for the presence of a method body. It sure looks good with real code between its jaws.

```
partial void ImplementIfYouDare()
{
    MessageBox.Show("I did it, so there.");
}
```

So, what's the big deal with these partial methods? Perhaps not much, but looking at an example might help. Let's return to our living, breathing *Animal* class, this time with a partial method included. Let's start with the auto-generated side of the world.

```
partial class Animal
{
    public void Move()
    {
        // ----- Interesting movement code, then...
        MoveSideEffects();
    }

    partial void MoveSideEffects();
}
```

Sometimes when an animal moves, it has side effects, such as scaring other animals. As the second half of the implementation team, you could program these side effects by completing the other half of the partial method. But if there were no side effects for this particular implementation, you could just leave the partial method unfinished. It's optional.

Yawn, yawn, snore, snore. "Get to the point, Tim," you say. The point is that if you never write the second half of a partial method, the Visual C# compiler will leave out both halves, generating code as though the unimplemented half was never auto-generated in the first place. Also, it changes code in the *Move* method.

```
partial class Animal
{
    public void Move()
    {
        // ----- Interesting movement code, then...
    }
}
```

Not only did the partial method definition disappear, but the call to that method inside the *Move* routine disappeared as well.

As a lone programmer writing lonely code, you will probably never craft a partial method; the event system is a much better way to generically respond to actions within a class. But you might have a chance to write the implementation side of a partial method when using some third-party components.

Object Initializers

When creating an object instance that sports public fields and properties, a typical scenario involves creating the instance, then assigning a value to each member in a distinct statement.

```
someDog = new Animal();
someDog.Name = "Rover";
someDog.LegCount = 4;
```

For such basic initialization, it is absolutely a waste of valuable hard disk space to spread the source code across so many lines. Fortunately, Visual C# offers an *object initializer* syntax that combines instantiation and member initialization into a single statement. This format includes member assignments in a set of curly braces.

```
someDog = new Animal() { Name = "Rover", LegCount = 4 };
```

Related Issues

Let me take a few moments here before getting into the project code to discuss some issues that don't really fit into any particular chapter discussion, but that you might end up using in your own applications.

The MessageBox.Show Method

Although I've used it on practically every page of this book so far, I have never formally introduced you to the `MessageBox.Show` method. Part of the `System.Windows.Forms` namespace, `MessageBox.Show` displays a simple message window, including a selection of response buttons and an optional icon. As a function, it returns a code indicating which button the user clicked to close the form, one of the `DialogResult` enumeration values. Here is the typical syntax, as a function declaration.

```
public DialogResult Show(
    string text, string caption = null,
    MessageBoxButtons buttons = MessageBoxButtons.OK,
    MessageBoxIcon icon = MessageBoxIcon.None)
```

The `text` parameter accepts a string for display in the main body of the dialog; `caption` accepts a custom window title for those times when you want to provide some additional context; `buttons` indicates which acceptance buttons to display; and `icon` specifies the standardized Windows notification icon to include in the dialog. The following statement displays the window in Figure 8-2.

```
DialogResult result = MessageBox.Show(
    "It's safe to click; the computer won't explode.",
    "Click Something", MessageBoxButtons.YesNoCancel,
    MessageBoxIcon.Question);
```

Figure 8-2. Communicating an important message

Parameter Array Arguments

Any method can enable optional arguments, and the calling code can choose to include or exclude those arguments. But what if you wanted to add an unlimited number of optional arguments to a method? How could you write, for instance, a function that would return the average of all supplied arguments, with no limit on the number of arguments? Although you could accept an array variable with the source data values, you can also use a *parameter array argument*, enabled via the `params` keyword.

As with optional arguments, parameter array arguments must appear at the end of a method's argument list, and there can be only one, because one is more than enough for any method. Parameter array arguments use the `params` keyword just before the argument name.

```
public decimal CalculateAverage(params decimal[] sourceData)
{
    // ----- Calculate the average for a set of numbers.
    decimal runningTotal = 0M;

    if (sourceData.GetLength(0) == 0)
        return 0M;
    else
    {
        foreach (decimal singleValue in sourceData)
            runningTotal += singleValue;
        return runningTotal / sourceData.GetLength(0);
    }
}
```

Calls to the `CalculateAverage` function now accept any number of decimal values.

```
MessageBox.Show(CalculateAverage(
    1, 2, 3, 4, 5).ToString()); // Displays: 3
```

Null Propagation Operator

Visual C#'s *null-propagation operator*, new with the 2015 release of the language, lets you get around the troubling problem of the `null`. Consider the following block of code.

```
// ----- Method returns null when user abandons lookup.
customerRecord = LetUserLookupCustomer();
customerName = customerRecord.LastName;
```

The `LetUserLookupCustomer` method does some user interface magic to prompt the user for a customer record, and returns the contents of that record in an object. The code then proceeds to use that returned record. But what happens to the `customerName` record when the lookup routine returns `null`? Visual C# does not let you access the members of an object that is undefined, so the code above would generate a runtime error, and your program would crash, and your user would cry.

The `?.` null-propagation operator gets around this by taking `customerRecord`'s current setting of `null`, and propagating it to its members on access. In the code above, changing the dot symbol to a question-dot pair causes the `LastName` member to return `null` when the object itself is `null`.

```
// ----- customerName will become null.
customerRecord = null;
customerName = customerRecord?.LastName;
```

Mind you, this still isn't great code. The `customerName` variable still doesn't contain much that is useful. But you can combine it with other language features to help ensure data integrity in your code.

```
customerName = customerRecord?.LastName ?? "Unknown";
```

As you recall from Chapter 2, the *??* coalescence operator returns the second argument if the first one is *null*. This ensures that the *customerName* variable always has a readable value, even if the customer record doesn't exist. It's still not amazing code, but it does save on typing. The statement above replaces the following verbose block.

```
if (customerRecord == null)
   customerName = "Unknown";
else
   customerName = customerRecord.LastName;
```

Null propagation will do its nullifying magic for any depth of object members.

```
customerCity = customerRecord?.Address?.City;
```

That's an amazing time saver, but use the feature with caution, as it can mask bugs that stem from having uninitialized variables romping around in your code.

Summary

The ability to extend classes through inheritance is truly the foundation on which complex yet manageable programs are built in .NET. And they are not overly complex, either. Classes are simple containers for their members, and the variety and complexity of the available members are not that vast. So, it's really amazing that you can write almost any type of program, and implement any number of features, using these simple foundational tools. Oh yeah, the C# language helps, too.

As we add code to the Library Project throughout this book, you will become more and more familiar with classes, structures, and their members. Soon you will be adding properties, methods, events, fields, and other members to classes like you were born with the ability.

Project

This chapter's code implements two features of the Library Project: (1) a simple helper class used with *ListBox* and *ComboBox* controls to manage text and data; and (2) a set of generic forms used to edit lookup tables in the Library, such as tables of status codes.

Supporting List and Combo Boxes

The Windows Forms' *ComboBox* and *ListBox* controls display a list of text strings to the user for single or multiple selection. But you aren't just limited to string instances. Each control allows you to add any type of data items to the control, in any combination: strings, integer, dates and times, customer records, or whatever.

Let's see a *ListBox* in action. Add a new *ListBox* to a form, and then add the following code to the form's *Load* event handler.

```
private void Form1_Load(object sender, EventArgs e)
{
   listBox1.Items.Add(1);
   listBox1.Items.Add("Easy");
   listBox1.Items.Add(new DateTime(2016, 5, 3));
}
```

Running this code displays the form in Figure 8-3.

Figure 8-3. A simple ListBox with three different items

So, how does a *ListBox* control know how to display text for any mixture of objects? By default, the control calls the *ToString* method of the object. *ToString* is defined in *System.Object*, and you can override it in your own class. The *ListBox* control also includes a *DisplayMember* property that you can set to the field or property of your class that generates the proper text, although this only works if all items added to the list share a common structure that exposes the indicated member.

In the Library project, we'll use *ListBox* and *ComboBox* controls to display database records: books, patrons, publishers, media formats, overdue items, and dozens more. In most cases, these records have a unique ID that is used as the primary key in the underlying database table. If you select, say, a book name from a list of books, the associated ID for the book can be used to access the full record from just the name. But showing a list item string in the format "War and Peace (ID=525)" doesn't seem very user friendly. The pre-.NET version of the Visual Basic development system, which was used as part of the inspiration for Windows Forms, included *ListBox* and *ComboBox* controls that paired a display value with a long integer ID value for each item in the list. They always traveled together, which was convenient for record access. Sadly, .NET lacks this parallel ID field.

Actually, it's not sadly at all. While the *ListBox* control might lack a specific item field that tracks a database ID, each item added to the control can be anything you want. A simple string works as a list item, but so does a large object with dozens or hundreds of data properties. Instead of just adding a book title to a list, you could add a *Book* instance that contains title, author, publisher, copyright date, description, book cover image, and page count properties. As long as the object's *ToString* method returned the book's title (or you set the control's *DisplayMember* property appropriately), it wouldn't matter how much content each list item contained.

Storing entire records in a *ListBox* or *ComboBox* control is pretty wasteful. It's usually much better to store just a display name and an ID number, and use the ID as a lookup into a database. That's what we'll do in the Library Project. To support this, we'll create a simple class that will expose a text and data value pair. First, let's go back into the Library code.

Let's put the class in a source code file all its own. Add a new class file through the Project→Add Class menu command. Name the file *ListItemData.cs* and click the Add button. The following code appears automatically.

```
public class ListItemData
{
}
```

This class will be pretty simple. As for data members, it will include the display name and ID value members I just described, named *ItemText* and *ItemData*, respectively. I will also include a third public data member named *TextCode* that will be used in cases where a single text character is a better lookup value than a numeric ID. To avoid the time and expense of setting the *ListBox* or *ComboBox*'s *DisplayMember* property, we'll also include an override to the *ToString* function, some other supporting infrastructure, and two custom constructors that makes initialization of the members easier. Add the following code to the body of the class.

Insert Snippet
Insert Chapter 8, Snippet Item 1.

```
public string ItemText;
public long ItemData;
public char TextCode;
private bool UseChar;

public ListItemData(string displayText, long itemID)
{
    // ----- Initialize the record for long codes.
    ItemText = displayText;
    ItemData = itemID;
    TextCode = '\0';
    UseChar = false;
}

public ListItemData(string displayText, char itemCode)
{
    // ----- Initialize the record for char codes.
    ItemText = displayText;
    ItemData = -1L;
    TextCode = itemCode;
    UseChar = true;
}

public override string ToString()
{
    // ----- Display the basic item text.
    return ItemText;
}

public override bool Equals(object obj)
{
    // ----- Allow IndexOf() and Contains() searches by ItemData.
    if ((UseChar == false) & (obj is long))
        return (Convert.ToInt64(obj) == ItemData);
    else if ((UseChar == true) & (obj is char))
        return (Convert.ToChar(obj) == TextCode);
    else
        return base.Equals(obj);
}

public override int GetHashCode()
{
    // ----- Use the data or code value as the hash.
    if (UseChar == false)
        return this.ItemData.GetHashCode();
```

```
        else
            return this.TextCode.GetHashCode();
    }
```

Later, when it's time to populate a *ListBox*, we can use this object to add the display and identification values.

```
listBox1.Items.Add(New ListItemData("Item Text", 25L));
```

The override of the *Equals* method allows us to quickly look up items already added to a *ListBox* (or similar) control using features of the control. The *ListBox* control's *Items* collection includes an *IndexOf* method that returns the position of a matching item. Normally, this method will match only the object itself; if you pass it a *ListItemData* instance, it will report whether that item is already in the *ListBox*. The updated *Equals* code will also return *true* if we pass a *long* value that matches a *ListItemData.ItemData* member for an item already in the list.

```
int itemPosition = SomeListBox.Items.IndexOf(5L);
```

If we search for a *char* value, it will compare against the *ListItemData.TextCode* member instead. The related *GetHashCode* override helps the class do a better job at processing *IndexOf* requests. I wasn't that interested in figuring out custom logic for that method, so I passed processing on to the identically named method for the field used as the record identifier.

Editing Code Tables

Back in Chapter 4, when we crafted the database for the Library Project, several of the tables were created to fill simple *ComboBox* lists in the application. All of these tables begin with the prefix "Code," and contain records that rarely, if ever, change in the lifetime of the application. One such table is *CodeCopyStatus*, which identifies the current general condition of an item in the library's collections.

Field	Type	Description
ID	Long - Auto	Primary key; automatically assigned. Required.
FullName	Text(50)	Name of this status entry. Required.

Since all of these tables have basically the same format—an ID field and one or more content fields—it should be possible to design a generic template to use for editing these tables. A base (class) form would provide the basic editing features, to be developed in full through derived versions of the base form.

For the project, we will add two forms: a summary form (that displays a list of all currently defined codes) and a detail form (that allows editing of a single new or existing code). To make things even simpler, we will include only the most basic record-management functionality in the summary form. Most of the code needed to edit, display, and remove codes will appear in the detail forms.

The Generic Detail Form

Add a new form to the project (Project→New Windows Form), naming it *BaseCodeForm.cs*. Alter the following properties as indicated.

Property	Setting
(Name)	BaseCodeForm
ControlBox	False
FormBorderStyle	FixedDialog
ShowInTaskbar	False
Size	416, 180
StartPosition	CenterScreen
Text	Code Form

Now access the source code for this class (View→Code). The code will never create instances of this generic form directly, so let's disallow all direct instantiation by including the *abstract* keyword.

```
public abstract partial class BaseCodeForm : Form
{
    ...
}
```

The main features of the form will be the adding of new code records, the editing of existing code records, and the removal of existing records. Add three function skeletons that support these features. We could have made them *abstract* as well, but as you'll see later, we will want the option to keep the default functionality from the base generic form.

Insert Snippet

Insert Chapter 8, Snippet Item 2.

```
public virtual long AddRecord()
{
    // ----- Prompt to add a new record. Return the
    //       ID when added, or -1 if cancelled.
    return -1L;
}

public virtual bool DeleteRecord(long recordID)
{
    // ----- Prompt the user to delete a record.
    //       Return True on delete.
    return false;
}

public virtual long EditRecord(long recordID)
{
    // ----- Prompt the user to edit the record. Return
    //       the record's ID if saved, or -1 on cancel.
    return -1L;
}
```

The detail form will take responsibility for filling the *ListBox* control on the summary form with its items. Two methods will handle this: one that adds all items, and one that updates a single item. The derived class will be required to supply these features.

Insert Snippet

Insert Chapter 8, Snippet Item 3.

```
// ----- Fill a ListBox control with existing records.
public abstract void FillListWithRecords(
    ListBox destList, ref bool exceededMatches);

// ----- Return the formatted name of a single record.
public abstract string FormatRecordName(long recordID);
```

The detail form must also display the proper titles and usage information on the summary form.

Insert Snippet

Insert Chapter 8, Snippet Item 4.

```
// ----- Return a description of this editor.
public abstract string GetEditDescription();

// ----- Return the title-bar text for this editor.
public abstract string GetEditTitle();
```

Although most of the tables will supply a short list of alphabetized codes, some tables will include a large number (possibly thousands) of codes. The summary form will support a search method, to locate an existing code quickly. Since only certain derived forms will use this feature, we won't include *abstract*.

Insert Snippet
Insert Chapter 8, Snippet Item 5.

```
public virtual void SearchForRecord(
   ListBox destList, ref bool exceededMatches)
{
   // ----- Prompt the user to search for a record.
   return;
}
```

Finally, the detail form will indicate which of the available features can be used from the summary form. The summary form will call each of the following functions, and then enable or disable features as requested.

Insert Snippet
Insert Chapter 8, Snippet Item 6.

```
public virtual bool CanUserAdd()
{
   // ----- Check the security of current user
   //       to see if adding is allowed.
   return false;
}

public virtual bool CanUserEdit()
{
   // ----- Check the security of the user
   //       to see if editing is allowed.
   return false;
}

public virtual bool CanUserDelete()
{
   // ----- Check the security of the user
   //       to see if deleting is allowed.
   return false;
}

public virtual bool UsesSearch()
{
   // ----- Does this editor support searching?
   return false;
}
```

That's it for the generic detail form. Later on in the book, we'll create derived versions for each of the code tables.

The Generic Summary Form

The summary form is a little more straightforward, since it is just a plain form. When it starts up, it uses an instance of one of the derived detail forms to control the experience presented to the user. I've already added the form to the project; it's called *ListEditRecords.cs*, and it looks like Figure 8-4.

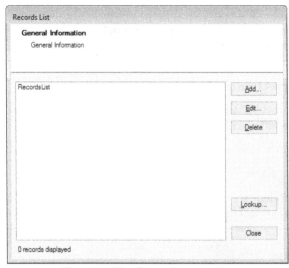

Figure 8-4. The Generic Summary form

A large `ListBox` control fills most of the form, a control that will hold all existing items. There are also buttons to add, edit, delete, and search for items in the list. There's a lot of code to manage these items; I've already written it in a code snippet. Switch to the form's source code view, and add the source code just after the class constructor.

Insert Snippet
Insert Chapter 8, Snippet Item 7.

The first line of the added code defines a private instance of the generic detail form we just designed.

```
private BaseCodeForm DetailEditor;
```

This field holds an instance of a class derived from *BaseCodeForm*. That assignment appears in the public method *ManageRecords*.

```
public void ManageRecords(BaseCodeForm useDetail)
{
   // ----- Set up the form for use with this code set.
   bool exceededMatches = false;

   DetailEditor = useDetail;
   RecordsTitle.Text = DetailEditor.GetEditTitle();
   RecordsInfo.Text = DetailEditor.GetEditDescription();
   this.Text = DetailEditor.GetEditTitle();
   ActAdd.Visible = DetailEditor.CanUserAdd();
   ActEdit.Visible = DetailEditor.CanUserEdit();
   ActDelete.Visible = DetailEditor.CanUserDelete();
   ActLookup.Visible = DetailEditor.UsesSearch();
```

```
    DetailEditor.FillListWithRecords(
        RecordsList, ref exceededMatches);
    RefreshItemCount(exceededMatches);
    this.ShowDialog();
}
```

The code that calls *ManageRecords* passes in a form instance, one of the forms derived from *BaseCodeForm*. Once assigned to the internal *DetailEditor* field, the code uses the public features of that instance to configure the display elements on the summary form. For instance, the detail form's *CanUserAdd* function, which sports a *bool* return value, sets the *Visible* property of the *ActAdd* button. The *FillListWithRecords* method call populates the summary *ListBox* control with any existing code values. After some more display adjustments, the *this.ShowDialog* method displays the summary form to the user.

Although the user will interact with the controls on the summary form, most of these controls defer their processing to the detail form, *DetailEditor*. For example, a click on the Add button defers most of the logic to the detail form's *AddRecord* method. The code in the summary form doesn't do much more than update its own display fields.

```
private void ActAdd_Click(object sender, EventArgs e)
{
    // ----- Let the user add a record.
    long newID;
    int newPosition;

    // ----- Prompt the user.
    newID = DetailEditor.AddRecord();
    if (newID == -1L)
        return;

    // ----- Add this record to the list.
    newPosition = RecordsList.Items.Add(
        (new ListItemData(DetailEditor.FormatRecordName(
        newID), newID)));
    RecordsList.SelectedIndex = newPosition;
    RefreshButtons();
    RefreshItemCount(false);
}
```

Most of the remaining code in the summary form either is just like this (for edit, delete, and search features), or is used to refresh the display based on user interaction with the form. Be sure to examine the code to get a good understanding of how the code works.

The previous snippet added some event handlers, but they haven't been connected to their events. Add those connections how to the end of the form's constructor.

Insert Snippet
Insert Chapter 8, Snippet Item 8.

As when we added these connections in a previous chapter, I will eventually move these code lines out of the constructor and put them in the form's designer file where they normally exist.

In later chapters, when we add actual detail forms, we'll see this form's code in action, including all its calls to the detail form's members.

Chapter 9

Functional Programming

In this chapter, we'll cover three major Visual C# programming topics: *lambda expressions*, *asynchronous processing*, and *error handling*. All are mysterious, one because it uses a Greek letter in its name and the others because they might as well be in Greek for all the difficulty programmers have with them. Lambda expressions in particular have to do with the broader concept of *functional programming*, the idea that every computing task can be expressed as a function and that functions can be passed around willy-nilly within the source code. Visual C# is not a true functional programming language, but the inclusion of lambda expressions in C# brings some of those functional ways and means to the language.

Lambda Expressions

Lambda expressions are named for *lambda calculus* (or λ-calculus), a mathematical system designed in the 1930s by Alonzo Church, certainly a household name between the wars. Although his work was highly theoretical, it led to features and structures that benefit most programming languages today. Specifically, lambda calculus provides the rationale for the Visual C# functions, arguments, and return values that we've already learned about. So, why add a new feature to C# and call it "lambda" when there are lambda things already in the language? Great question. No answer.

Lambda expressions let you define an object that contains an entire function. Although this is a somewhat newer feature in Visual C#, the core idea of a lambda expression has been around for decades. I found an old manual from the very first programming language I used, BASIC PLUS on the RSTS/E timeshare computer. It provided a sample of the *DEF* statement, which let you define simple functions. Here is some sample code from that language that prints a list of the first five squares.

```
100   DEF SQR(X)=X*X
110   FOR I=1 TO 5
120      PRINT I, SQR(I)
130   NEXT I
140   END
```

The function definition for *SQR()* appears on line 100, returning the square of any argument passed to it. It's used in the second half of line 120, generating the following output.

```
1          1
2          4
3          9
4          16
5          25
```

Lambda expressions in Visual C# work in a similar way, letting you define a delegate variable as a simple function. Here's the C# equivalent for the preceding code.

```
delegate int SqrDelegate(int i);

// ----- Later, in a method...
SqrDelegate sqr = (x) => x * x;
for (int counter = 1; counter <= 5; counter++)
   Console.WriteLine("{0}\t{1}", counter, sqr(counter));
```

The actual lambda expression is on the second line.

```
(x) => x * x
```

The => operator defines the lambda expressions, with a set of parameters just before the operator, and the logic immediately after. That logic uses the passed-in arguments to generate some final result. In this case, the result is the value of *x* multiplied by itself. In the single-line lambda format, there is no specific `return` statement. Instead, the return value just seems to fall out of the expression naturally. Multi-line lambdas exhibit a more traditional function format, complete with `return` statements and as much logic as you can cram in before the closing curly brace.

```
SqrDelegate sqr = (x) => {
   return x * x;
};
```

Inferring Lambdas

Inserting an ad hoc function into your method is great, but having it tied to a predefined delegate can be a burden, right? There is a way around this, a means of creating a lambda function that figures out the delegate on its own—sort of. To infer a lambda function variable, use the *Func* delegate—so original. (This delegate is actually an example of *generics*, something we won't cover until Chapter 16. For now, just pretend it's a magical part of the language.)

When using a *Func* delegate, the data type pseudo-argument list within angle brackets matches the argument list of the actual lambda expression, but with an extra data type thrown in at the end that represents the return value's data type. Here's a lambda expression that checks whether an `int` argument (represented by *x*) is even or not, returning a Boolean result. Inside the angle brackets, the `int` datatype ties to the *x* parameter, while the `bool` type indicates the return value.

```
public void TestNumber()
{
   Func<int, bool> IsEven =
      new Func<int, bool>((x) => (x % 2) == 0);

   MessageBox.Show("Is 5 Even? " + IsEven(5));
}
```

This code displays a message that says, "Is 5 Even? False." Behind the scenes, Visual C# is generating an actual function, and linking it up to the variable using a delegate. The following code is along the lines of what the compiler is actually generating for the previous code sample.

```
private bool HiddenFunction1(int x)
{
   return (x % 2) == 0;
}

private delegate bool HiddenDelegate1(int x);

public void TestNumber()
{
```

```
    HiddenDelegate1 IsEven = HiddenFunction1;
    MessageBox.Show("Is 5 Even? " + IsEven(5));
}
```

In this code, the lambda expression and related *IsEven* variable have been replaced with a true function (*HiddenFunction1*) and a go-between delegate (*HiddenDelegate1*). Although lambdas entered the language in 2008, this type of equivalent functionality has been available since the first release of Visual C#. Lambda expressions provide a simpler syntax when the delegate-referenced function is just returning a result from an expression.

Inline Lambdas

As we learned way back in some long forgotten chapter, delegates allow you to treat functions like any other type of data: you can store them in variables, or pass them to other functions. For example, consider the following method, which accepts a tax calculation function through a delegate parameter.

```
private void AnnouncePrice(decimal subtotal,
    Func<decimal, decimal> taxCalculator)
{
    MessageBox.Show(string.Format(
        "Subtotal: {0:C}\r\n" +
        "Sales Tax: {1:C}\r\n" +
        "----------------\r\n" +
        "Total: {2:C}",
        subtotal, taxCalculator(subtotal),
        subtotal + taxCalculator(subtotal)));
}
```

The *taxCalculator* parameter is a delegate, and is called as a function twice within the method to calculate sales tax on some subtotal. If you live in a state that charges sales tax, you could use the following sample code to call the *AnnouncePrice* method. After creating a lambda function that calculates a five-percent tax amount, the code passes this function and a subtotal to the *AnnouncePrice* method.

```
Func<decimal, decimal> fivePercent =
    new Func<decimal, decimal>((x) => x * 0.05M);
AnnouncePrice(10M, fivePercent);
```

Figure 9-1 shows the announced output.

Figure 9-1. That sales tax isn't too bad

There are better ways to accomplish this particular example in .NET, but passing a tax calculation engine to the *AnnouncePrice* method does work. Still, you could make the calling code even simpler. That's because Visual C# allows you to use lambda expressions inline, without creating separate variables for them. Here's a single-line version of that same five-percent display code that dispenses with the *fivePercent* variable altogether.

```
AnnouncePrice(10M, (x) => x * 0.05M);
```

This line builds a tax calculation function on the fly, and passes it as data into the awaiting *AnnouncePrice* method. We'll see in Chapter 17 that this is a somewhat common way of interacting with LINQ.

Statement Lambdas

Lambdas that skip the return-value part of the logic also exist, and use delegates that include *void* as the return type instead of some actual data type.

```
delegate void DblDelegate(int x);

// ----- Later, in a method...
DblDelegate writeDouble =
    (baseValue) => Console.WriteLine(baseValue * 2);

' ----- Or, put more statements inside...
DblDelegate RunProcessTwice = (processKey) =>
    {
        ExternalProcess(processKey);
        ExternalProcess(processKey);
    };
```

Variable Lifting

Although you can pass arguments into a lambda expression, you may also use other variables that are within the scope of the lambda expression.

```
private void NameMyChild()
{
    Func<string, string> nameLogic = GetChildNamingLogic();
    MessageBox.Show(nameLogic("John"));  // Displays: Johnson
}

private Func<String, String> GetChildNamingLogic()
{
    string nameSuffix = "son";
    Func<string, string> newLogic =
        (baseName) => baseName + nameSuffix;
    return newLogic;
}
```

The *GetChildNamingLogic* function returns a lambda expression. That lambda expression is used in the *NameMyChild* method, passing *John* as an argument to the lambda. And it works. The question is how. The problem is that *nameSuffix*, used in the lambda expression's logic, is a local variable within the *GetChildNamingLogic* method. All local variables are destroyed whenever a method exits. By the time the *MessageBox.Show* function is called, *nameSuffix* will be long gone. Yet the code works as though *nameSuffix* lived on.

To make this code work, Visual C# uses a feature called *variable lifting*. Seeing that *nameSuffix* will be accessed outside the scope of *GetChildNamingLogic*, Visual C# rewrites your source code, changing *nameSuffix* from a local variable to a variable that has a wider scope.

In the new version of the source code, Visual C# adds a *closure class*, a dynamically generated class that contains both the lambda expression and the local variables used by the expression. When you combine these together, any code that gets access to the lambda expression will also have access to the "local" variable.

```
private void NameMyChild()
{
```

```csharp
    Func<string, string> nameLogic = GetChildNamingLogic();
    MessageBox.Show(nameLogic("John"));  // Displays: Johnson
}

public class GeneratedClosureClass
{
    public string nameSuffix;
    public string newLogic(string baseName)
    {
        return baseName + this.nameSuffix;
    }
}

private Func<string, string> GetChildNamingLogic()
{
    GeneratedClosureClass localClosure =
        new GeneratedClosureClass();
    localClosure.nameSuffix = "son";
    return localClosure.newLogic;
}
```

The actual code generated by Visual C# is more complex than this, but this is the basic idea. Closure classes and variable lifting are essential features for lambda expressions since you can never really know where your lambda expressions are at all hours of the night.

Asynchronous Processing

A core software development activity involves breaking a task down into minute step-by-step actions that, when taken together, accomplish something amazing. But sometimes, this one-thing-at-a-time *synchronous* way of doing things isn't good enough. To fulfill this need for more, .NET offers several options for *threading*, the ability for your software to perform two or more distinct *asynchronous* paths of coded logic at the same time. For example, the word processor I am using at this very second is (1) displaying words as I type them, and (2) scanning the entire document looking for and finding an embarrassing number of spelling and grammar errors.

I already mentioned one such "multithreading" feature in passing. In Chapter 7, I listed out the most common Windows Forms controls, one of which was the `BackgroundWorker` control. Through this tool, doing extra work in the background is as close as an event handler. A more traditional way of kicking off background tasks is to use .NET's `Thread` class, found in the `System.Threading` namespace. This class has features galore that let you manage the full asynchronous experience, with members that let distinct threads communicate with each other. It's all very convenient for your data, and so very, very inconvenient for the programmer.

Here comes Visual C# to the rescue. Starting in the 2012 edition of the language, C# gained two new keywords that help simplify the asynchronous programming experience: `async` and `await`. The `async` keyword, when applied to a method declaration, indicates that the method will do something asynchronously. Within that method, the `await` keyword says to Visual C#, "Hey, I know I told you to do something in the background. Pause here a bit until that background work completes, but by all means, *let the user keep doing other stuff!*"

The most elementary use of these asynchronous features involves kicking off a background task without locking up the rest of the application. This lets the user keep on accessing other parts of the program while

something else happens in the background. The following method starts the long-winded *DoGobsOfWork*
process, but in a way that doesn't hinder other parts of the program from working.

```
public async void StartBackgroundTask()
{
    // ----- Start DoGobsOfWork in the background using
    //       a lambda expression. Assumes DoGobsOfWork
    //       is an existing Sub method.
    await Task.Run(() => DoGobsOfWork());

    // ----- The following message appears when
    //       DoGobsOfWork is done, even though the
    //       user was free to click on other buttons
    //       and controls while it was working.
    MessageBox.Show("Finished gobs of work.");
}
```

If that method had left out the *async* and *await* elements, the user interface of the program would have
halted while *DoGobsOfWork* did its gobbing work. That's because your code normally does only one thing
at a time, and in this case, *DoGobsOfWork* would be that one thing. But by sprinkling the new asynchronous
keywords in the right places, the user interface (or other code you indicate) keeps running in the foreground
while the designated logic moves to the background.

The *async* and *await* keywords make use of the *Task* class, from the *System.Threading.Tasks*
namespace. It's a generic type, something we won't learn about until Chapter 16. Asynchronous
programming is an advanced topic with many variations and options. I won't cover it beyond this brief
section. You can read about it for hours in Microsoft's MSDN documentation.

Error Handling in Visual C#

Debugging and error processing are two of the most essential programming activities you will ever perform.
There are three absolutes in life: death, taxes, and software bugs. Even in a relatively bug-free application,
there is every reason to believe that a user will just mess things up royally. As a programmer, your job is to
be the guardian of the user's data as managed by the application, and to keep it safe, even from the user's
own negligence (or malfeasance), and also from your own source code.

I once spoke with a developer from a large software company headquartered in Redmond, Washington; you
might know the company. This developer told me that in any given application developed by this company,
more than fifty percent of the code is dedicated to dealing with errors, bad data, system exceptions, and
failures. Certainly, all this additional code slows down each application and adds a lot of overhead to what
is already called "bloatware." But in an age of hackers and data entry mistakes, such error management is an
absolute must.

Testing—although not a topic covered in this book—goes hand in hand with error management. Often, the
report of an error will lead to a bout of testing, but it should really be the other way around: testing should
lead to the discovery of errors. A few years ago, NASA's *Mars Global Surveyor*, in orbit around the red planet,
captured images of the *Beagle 2*, a land-based research craft that crashed into the Martian surface in 2003. An
assessment of the *Beagle 2*'s failure pinpointed many areas of concern, with a major issue being inadequate
testing.

> This led to an attenuated testing programme to meet the cost and schedule constraints, thus inevitably
> increasing technical risk. (From Beagle 2 ESA/UK Commission of Inquiry Report, April 5, 2004, Page 4)

Look at all those big words. Boy, the Europeans sure have a way with language. Perhaps a direct word-for-word translation into American English will make it clear what the commission was trying to convey.

They didn't test it enough, and probably goofed it all up.

The Nature of Errors in Visual C#

You will deal with three major categories of errors in your Visual C# applications.

Compile-time errors

Some errors are so blatant that Visual C# will refuse to compile your application. Generally, such errors are due to simple syntax issues that can be corrected with a few keystrokes. For instance, implicit narrowing conversions will generate compile-time errors.

```
long bigData = 5L;
int smallData;
// ----- The next line will not compile.
smallData = bigData;
```

Visual Studio 2015 includes features that help you locate and resolve compile-time errors. Such errors are marked with a red squiggle below the offending syntax. Some errors also prompt Visual Studio to display corrective options through a pop-up window, as shown in Figure 9-2.

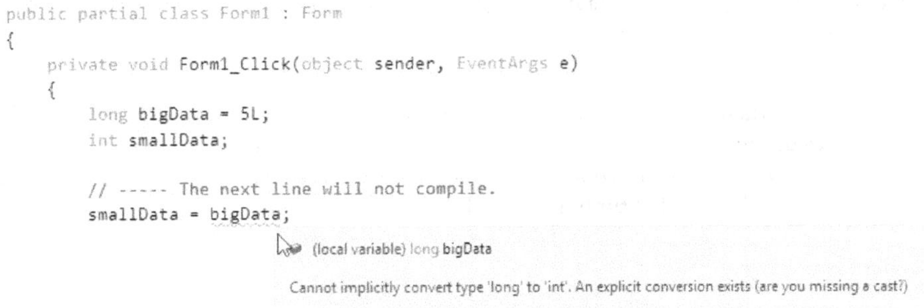

```
public partial class Form1 : Form
{
    private void Form1_Click(object sender, EventArgs e)
    {
        long bigData = 5L;
        int smallData;

        // ----- The next line will not compile.
        smallData = bigData;
                    (local variable) long bigData

        Cannot implicitly convert type 'long' to 'int'. An explicit conversion exists (are you missing a cast?)
```

Figure 9-2. Error correction options for a narrowing conversion

Runtime errors

Runtime errors occur when a combination of data and code causes an invalid condition in what otherwise appears to be valid code. Such errors frequently occur when a user enters incorrect data into the application, but your own code can also generate runtime errors. Adequate checking of all incoming data will greatly reduce this class of errors. Consider the following block of code.

```
public int GetNumber()
{
    // ----- Prompt the user for a number.
    //       Return zero for invalid numbers.
    string userInput;
    string justDigits = "";

    // ----- Assume that InputBox will return a string
    //       with whatever the user types in.
    userInput = InputBox("Enter number.");
```

```
        // ----- Keep only the digits.
        for (int counter = 0;
            counter < userInput.Length; counter++)
        {
            if (char.IsDigit(userInput[counter]))
                justDigits += userInput[counter];
        }

        // ----- See if there are any digits left.
        if (justDigits.Length > 0)
        {
            // ----- Convert to an integer and return it.
            return Convert.ToInt32(justDigits);
        }
        else
        {
            // ----- Invalid data. Return zero.
            return 0;
        }
    }
```

This code looks pretty reasonable, and in most cases, it is. It prompts the user for a number, grabs any digits it finds in the user's input, and converts that to a true integer value. The *justDigits.Length* test will weed out any input that contains no digits. Assuming that you've crafted the *InputBox* method elsewhere, this function will, in fact, return valid integers for entered content, and zero for input with no digits.

But what happens when a fascist dictator tries to use this code? As history has shown, a fascist dictator will enter a value such as "342304923940234." Because it's filled with digits, it will pass the *justDigits.Length* test with flying colors, but since it exceeds the size of the *System.Int32* data type, it will generate the dreaded runtime error shown in Figure 9-3.

Figure 9-3. An error message only a fascist dictator could love

Without additional error-handling code or checks for valid data limits, the *GetNumber* routine generates this runtime error, and then causes the entire program to abort. Between committing war crimes and entering invalid numeric values, there seems to be no end to the evil that fascist dictators will do.

Logic errors

Logic errors are the third, and the most insidious, type of error. They are caused by you, the programmer; you can't blame the user on this one. From process-flow issues to incorrect calculations, logic errors are the bane of software development, and they result in more required debugging time than the other two types of errors combined.

Logic errors are too personal and too varied to address directly in this book. You can force many logic errors out of your code by adding sufficient checks for invalid data, and by adequately testing your application under a variety of conditions and circumstances.

You won't have that much difficulty dealing with compile-time errors. A general understanding of C# and .NET programming concepts, and regular use of the tools included with Visual Studio 2015, will help you quickly locate and eliminate them.

The bigger issue is: what do you do with runtime errors? Even if you check all possible data and external resource conditions, it's impossible to prevent all runtime errors. You never know when a network connection will suddenly go down, or the user will trip over the printer cable, or a scratch on a DVD will generate data corruption. Anytime you deal with resources that exist outside your source code, you are taking a chance that runtime errors will occur.

Figure 9-3 showed you what Visual C# does when it encounters a runtime error: it displays to the user a generic error dialog, and offers a chance to ignore the error (possible corruption of any unsaved data) or exit the program immediately (complete loss of any unsaved data).

Although both of these user actions leave much to the imagination, they don't instill consumer confidence in your coding skills. Trust me on this: the user will blame you for any errors generated by your application, even if the true problem was far removed from your code.

Fortunately, Visual C# includes two tools to help you deal completely with runtime errors, if and when they occur. These C# features—structured error handling and unhandled error handling—can be used in any Visual C# application to protect the user's data—and the user—from unwanted errors.

Structured Error Handling

Visual C#'s key technology for managing runtime errors goes by the name of *structured error handling*. Like everything else in C#, it's filled with object-oriented goodies, using standard objects to communicate errors in a way that is tightly integrated with the code it monitors.

Structured error handling naturally uses a structured, multiline statement to document error issues, specifically the *try...catch...finally* set of statements.

```
try
{
   // ----- Add error-prone code here.
}
catch (Exception ex)
{
   // ----- Error-handling code here.
}
finally
{
   // ----- Cleanup code goes here.
}
```

The try Clause
The *try* statement is designed to monitor smallish chunks of code. Although you could put all the source code for your procedure within the *try* block, it's more common to put within that section only the statements that are likely to generate errors.

```
try
{
    System.IO.File.Move(oldLocation, newLocation);
}
catch...
```

"Safe" statements can remain outside the *try* portion of error management block. Exactly what constitutes a safe programming statement is a topic of much debate, but two types of statements are generally unsafe: (1) those statements that interact with external systems, such as disk files, network or hardware resources, or even large blocks of memory; and (2) those statements that could cause a variable or expression to exceed the designed limits of the data type for that variable or expression.

The catch Clause

The *catch* clause defines an error handler. You can include one global error handler in a *try* statement, or you can include multiple handlers for different types of errors. Each handler includes its own *catch* keyword.

```
catch (ErrorClass ex)
```

The *ex* identifier provides a variable name for the active error object that you can use within the *catch* section. You can give it any name you wish; it can vary from *catch* clause to *catch* clause, but it doesn't have to.

ErrorClass identifies an exception class, a special class specifically designed to convey error information. The most generic exception class is *System.Exception*; other, more specific exception classes derive from *System.Exception*. The .NET Framework includes many predefined exception classes already derived from *System.Exception* that you can use in your application. For instance, *System.DivideByZeroException* catches any errors that (obviously) stem from dividing a number by zero.

```
try
{
    result = firstNumber / secondNumber;
}
catch (DivideByZeroException ex)
{
    MessageBox.Show("Divide by zero error.");
}
catch (OverflowException ex)
{
    MessageBox.Show("Divide resulting in an overflow.");
}
catch (Exception ex)
{
    MessageBox.Show("Some other error occurred.");
}
```

When an error occurs, your code tests the exception against each *catch* clause until it finds a matching class. The *catch* clauses are examined in order from top to bottom, so make sure you put the most general one last; if you put *System.Exception* first, no other *catch* clauses in that *try* block will ever trigger because every exception matches *System.Exception*. How many *catch* clauses you include, or which exceptions they monitor, is up to you. If you leave out all *catch* clauses completely, the *try* statement will gobble up the error like it never happened. When this happens, all remaining statements in the *try* block

---

will be skipped. Execution continues with the *finally* block, and then with the code following the entire *try* statement.

The finally Clause

The *finally* clause represents the "do this or die" part of your *try* block. If an error occurs in your *try* statement, the code in the *finally* section will always be processed after the relevant *catch* clause is complete. If no error occurs, the *finally* block will still be processed before leaving the *try* statement. If you issue a *return* statement somewhere in your *try* statement, the *finally* block will still be processed before leaving the routine. (This is getting monotonous.) If, while your *try* block is being processed, your boss announces that a free catered lunch is starting immediately in the big meeting room and everyone is welcome, the *finally* code will also be processed, but you might not be there to see it.

The *finally* clause is optional, so you include one only when you need it. The only time that *finally* clauses are required is when you omit all *catch* clauses in a *try* statement.

Unhandled Errors

I showed you earlier in the chapter how unhandled errors can lead to data corruption, crashed applications, and spiraling, out-of-control congressional spending. All good programmers understand how important error-handling code is, and they make the extra effort to include meaningful error-handling code. Yet there are times when I, even I, as a programmer, think, "Oh, this procedure isn't doing anything that could generate errors. I'll just leave out the error-handling code and save some typing time." And then it strikes, seemingly without warning: an unhandled error. Crash! Burn! Another chunk of user data confined to the bit bucket of life.

Normally, all unhandled errors bubble up the call stack, looking for a procedure that includes error-handling code. For instance, consider this code.

```
private void Level1()
{
    try
    {
        Level2();
    }
    catch (Exception ex)
    {
        MessageBox.Show(ex.Message);
    }
}

private void Level2()
{
    Level3();
}

private void Level3()
{
    // ----- The throw statement triggers an error
    //       immediately that your code must handle.
    //       It is explained later in this chapter.
    throw new Exception("Something bad happened.");
}
```

When the error occurs in *Level3*, the application looks for an active error handler in that procedure, but finds nothing. So, it immediately exits *Level3* and returns to *Level2*, where it looks again for an active error handler. Such a search will, sadly, be fruitless. Heartbroken, the code leaves *Level2* and moves back to *Level1*, continuing its search for a reasonable error handler. This time it finds one. Processing immediately jumps down to the *catch* block and executes the code in that section.

If *Level1* didn't have an error handler, and no code farther up the stack included an error handler, the user would see the Error Message Window of Misery (refer to Figure 9-3), followed by the Dead Program of Disappointment.

Fortunately, you can add a catchall error handler to your Visual C# project that traps such unmanaged exceptions and lets you do something about them. Your program exposes a thread-specific event that tells anyone listening when an unhandled error occurs. As with other events, you can plug your own event handler procedure into this event and taken action when something bad does occur.

In Windows Forms projects, I normally add my global error handler to the *Program.cs* file, in the same class that contains the *Main* starting routine. Since it's a standard .NET event handler, it uses the typical *sender* and e parameters that you've already seen in other handlers. The procedure name can be whatever you want.

```
private static void GlobalErrorHandler(
    object sender, ThreadExceptionEventArgs e)
{
}
```

Add your special global error-handling code to this routine. The e event argument includes an *Exception* member that provides access to the details of the error via a *System.Exception* object.

To connect this handler to the unhandled-error event, add the following code to your *Main* startup routine.

```
Application.ThreadException += GlobalErrorHandler;
Application.SetUnhandledExceptionMode(
    UnhandledExceptionMode.CatchException);
```

Even when the program does stay running, you will lose the active event path that triggered the error. If the error stemmed from a click on some button by the user, that entire *Click* event, and all of its called methods, will be abandoned immediately, and the program will wait for new input from the user.

Managing Errors

In addition to simply watching for them and screaming "Error!" there are a few other things you should know about error management in Visual C# programs.

Generating Errors

Believe it or not, there are times when you might want to generate runtime errors in your code. In fact, many of the runtime errors you encounter in your code occur because Microsoft wrote code in the Framework Class Library (FCL) that specifically generates errors. This is by design.

Let's say that you had a class property that accepts percentage values from 0 to 100, but as an *int* data type.

```
private int StoredPercent;
public int InEffectPercent
{
    get
    {
        return this.StoredPercent;
```

```
    }
    set
    {
        this.StoredPercent = value;
    }
}
```

Nothing is grammatically wrong with this code, but it will not stop anyone from setting the stored percent value to either 847 or −847, both outside the desired range. You can add an *if* statement to the *set* accessor to reject invalid data, but properties don't provide a way to return a failed status code. The only way to inform the calling code of a problem is to generate an exception.

```
set
{
    if ((value < 0) |(value > 100))
    {
        throw new ArgumentOutOfRangeException("value",
            value, "The allowed range is from 0 to 100.");
    }
    else
        this.StoredPercent = value;
}
```

Now, attempts to set the *InEffectPercent* property to a value outside the 0-to-100 range will generate an error, an error that can be caught by *catch* error handler blocks. The *throw* statement accepts a *System.Exception* (or derived) object as its argument, and sends that exception object up the call stack on a quest for an error handler.

The System.Exception Class

The *System.Exception* class is the base class for all structured exceptions. When an error occurs, you can examine its members to determine the exact nature of the error. You also use this class (or one of its derived classes) to build your own custom exception in anticipation of using the *throw* statement. Table 9-1 lists the key properties of this object.

Table 9-1. Members of the System.Exception class

Property	Description
Data	Provides access to a collection of key-value pairs, each providing additional exception-specific information.
HelpLink	Identifies online help location information relevant to this exception.
InnerException	If an exception is a side effect of another error, the original error appears here.
Message	A textual description of the error.
Source	Identifies the name of the application or object that caused the error.
StackTrace	Returns a string that fully documents the current stack trace, the list of all active procedure calls that led to the statement causing the error.
TargetSite	Identifies the name of the method that triggered the error.

Classes derived from *System.Exception* may include additional properties that provide additional detail for a specific error type.

The Debug Object

The *System.Diagnostics* namespace includes a *Debug* object that can help you diagnose issues in your application. It includes a *WriteLine* method that outputs content to Visual Studio's Immediate Window panel while your program is running.

```
// Assumes: using System.Diagnostics;
Debug.WriteLine("Reached point G in code");
```

Everything you output using the *WriteLine* method goes to a series of "listeners" attached to the *Debug* object. You can add your own listeners, including output to a work file. But the *Debug* object is really used only when debugging your program. Once you compile a final release, none of the *Debug*-related features work anymore, by design.

Summary

The best program in the world would never generate errors, I guess. But come on, it's not reality. If a multimillion-dollar Mars probe is going to crash on a planet millions of miles away, even after years of advanced engineering, my customer-tracking application for a local widget shop is certainly going to have a bug or two. But you can mitigate the impact of these bugs using the error-management features included with Visual C#.

Project

This chapter's project code will be somewhat brief. Error-handling code will appear throughout the entire application, but we'll add it in little by little as we craft the project. For now, let's focus on the central error-handling routines that will take some basic action when an error occurs anywhere in the program. I'll show some lambda expression project code in a later chapter. The Library Project does not include any asynchronous logic.

General Error Handler

As important and precise as error handling needs to be, the typical business application will not encounter a large variety of error types. Applications such as the Library Project are mainly vulnerable to three types of errors: (1) data entry errors; (2) errors that occur when reading data from, or writing data to, a database table; and (3) errors related to printing. Sure, there may be numeric overflow errors or other errors related to in-use data, but it's mostly interactions with external resources, such as the database, that concern us.

Because of the limited types of errors occurring in the application, it's possible to write a generic routine that informs the user of the error in a consistent manner. Each time a runtime error occurs, we will call this central routine, just to let the user know what's going on. The code block where the error occurred can then decide whether to take any special compensating action, or continue on as though no error occurred.

Project Access

Load the "Chapter 9 (Before) Code" project, either through the New Project templates or by accessing the project directly from the installation directory. To see the code in its final form, load "Chapter 9 (After) Code" instead.

In the project, open the *General.cs* class file, and add the following code as a new method to the *General* class.

Insert Snippet

Insert Chapter 9, Snippet Item 1.

```
public static void GeneralError(
    string routineName, Exception theError)
{
    // ----- Report an error to the user.
    MessageBox.Show(
```

```
    "The following error occurred at location '" +
    routineName + "':" + Environment.NewLine +
    Environment.NewLine + theError.Message,
    ProgramTitle, MessageBoxButtons.OK,
    MessageBoxIcon.Exclamation);
}
```

Not much to that code, is there? So, here's how it works. When you encounter an error in some routine, the in-effect error handler calls the central *GeneralError* method.

```
try
{
    // ----- Lots of code here.
}
catch (Exception ex)
{
    GeneralError("RoutineName", ex);
}
```

The purpose of the *GeneralError* global method is simple: communicate to the user that an error occurred, and then move on. It's meant to be simple, and it is simple. You could enhance the routine with some additional features. Logging of the error out to a file (or any other active log listener) might assist you later if you needed to examine application-generated errors. But for now, error management in the program is fairly basic.

Unhandled Error Capture

As I mentioned earlier, it's a good idea to include a global error handler in your code, in case some error gets past your defenses. To include this code, open the *Program.cs* file, then add the following code to the *Program* class.

Insert Snippet
Insert Chapter 9, Snippet Item 2.

```
private static void GlobalErrorHandler(
    object sender, ThreadExceptionEventArgs e)
{
    // ----- Some unhandled error occurred. Just report
    //       the error and keep the program running.
    GeneralError("Library.UnhandledError", e.Exception);
}
```

To attach this handler to the program, add the following code to the *Main* method, just before the code that displays the splash screen.

Insert Snippet
Insert Chapter 9, Snippet Item 3.

```
// ----- Add the global event handler for uncaught errors.
Application.ThreadException += new
    ThreadExceptionEventHandler(GlobalErrorHandler);
Application.SetUnhandledExceptionMode(
    UnhandledExceptionMode.CatchException);
```

That's it for functional and error-free programming. In the next chapter, which covers database interactions, we'll make frequent use of this error-handling code.

Chapter 10

ADO.NET

Before .NET, life for Windows database developers was traumatic. It wasn't due to programming language issues, nor with the choice of underlying database platform. Instead, the trouble stemmed from the layer that appeared between the application source code and the database of choice: the database library. Before the dawn of .NET in 2002, Microsoft released a steady stream of database technologies every two years or so.

- ODBC—Open DataBase Connectivity
- ISAM—Indexed Sequential Access Method
- DAO—Data Access Objects
- RDO—Remote Data Objects
- OLE DB—Object Linking and Embedding for Databases
- ADO—ActiveX Data Objects

When you look at this list, you might think, "Wow, that's great. There were so many options to choose from." You would be foolish to think this. This list isn't great; it's terrible. Imagine, just for a moment, that we weren't talking about database interfaces, but about other, more practical issues. What if you had to replace the engine in your car every two years? What if the steering column had to be replaced annually? What if you had to replace the oil every 3,500 miles or three months, whichever came first? Could you imagine life in such a world?

Whenever Microsoft introduced a new database object technology into the mix, it was quickly followed by a flurry of reprogramming to bring legacy applications up to the latest database technology. This wasn't always possible, as time and budget constraints kept organizations on older platforms. For nearly a decade I maintained a quarter-million-line application using DAO. Although the later ADO technology was better in terms of programming flexibility and application performance, the company that owned the program didn't want to spend the money rewriting what was essentially working code. (They eventually skipped over ADO and went right to ADO.NET as part of an overall .NET migration.)

So far, it seems that *ADO.NET*, Microsoft's database library for .NET, is different. It's been out for more than a decade (as of this writing), and Microsoft hasn't yet teased programmers with a replacement. ADO.NET is quite flexible, and that flexibility will hopefully allow it to stretch itself over new advances in technology for the foreseeable future.

What Is ADO.NET?

ADO.NET is a set of classes, included with the .NET Framework, that represent the primary method by which .NET applications interact with relational databases and other open and proprietary data management systems. But it's not just for interaction; ADO.NET is, in reality, a partial in-memory relational database all by itself. You can create tables and relationships (joins) with ADO.NET objects, add and remove records, query tables based on selection criteria, and do other simple tasks that are typical of standalone relational database systems.

All classes included with ADO.NET appear in the `System.Data` namespace; other subordinate namespaces provide derived classes geared toward specific database platforms or technologies. For instance, the `System.Data.SqlClient` namespace targets SQL Server databases, and `System.Data.EntityClient` focuses on interactions with .NET's Entity Framework technology. Other database providers can develop streamlined implementations of the various ADO.NET classes for use with their own systems or tools, and supply them as a separate namespace.

ADO.NET implements a *disconnected* data experience. In traditional database programming, especially in desktop applications, the connection between an application and its database was fixed and long-term. When the program started up, the connection started up. When the program exited many hours later, the connection finally ended. But in a world of massively scalable web sites, keeping a database connected for hours on end is sometimes wasteful and often impossible.

ADO.NET encourages you to open data connections just long enough to get the data that fulfills your immediate needs. Once you have the data, you drop the connection until the next time you need to retrieve, insert, or update database content.

```
SELECT * FROM Customer WHERE BalanceDue > 0
```

In this SQL statement, you have a choice of (1) scanning through all the records once in a quick and simple manner; or (2) loading the data into an in-memory table-like object, closing the connection, and working with the loaded records as though they were the originals. If you use the first method, you can take your sweet time waltzing through the records, spending many minutes to process each one. But ADO.NET frowns upon this type of selfish behavior. The goal is to get in and get out as quickly as you can.

Because of the disconnected nature of ADO.NET, some techniques common in database applications need to change. For instance, the long-term locking of database records during a user modification (known as *pessimistic concurrency*) is difficult to accomplish in ADO.NET's disconnected environment. You will have to use other methods, such as transactions or atomic stored procedure features, to accomplish these same goals.

Overview of ADO.NET

ADO.NET divides its world into two hemispheres: *providers* and the *data set*. Imagine your kitchen as the world of ADO.NET, with your refrigerator representing the provider, and the oven as the data set. The provider "provides" access to some content, such as food, or a SQL Server database (which normally appears in the meat-and-cheese drawer). It's a long-term storage facility, and content that goes in there usually stays in there for quite a while. If something is removed, it's because it is no longer valid, or has become corrupted.

A data set, like an oven, prepares (cooks) and presents content originally obtained from the long-term storage. Once presented, it will either be consumed, or be returned to the refrigerator for more long-term storage. This analogy isn't perfect; in fact, something just doesn't smell right about it. But it conveys the basic idea: providers give you access to stored data, some of which can be moved into and processed through an application and its data set on a short-term basis.

Providers

Large database systems, such as SQL Server, are standalone "servers" (hence the "SQL *Server*" name) that interact with client tools and applications only indirectly. These systems generally accept network connections from clients through a TCP/IP port or similar connection. Once authenticated, the client makes all its requests through this connection before disconnecting from the system.

Back in the early 1990s, Microsoft implemented *ODBC* (based on other existing standards) as a common system through which clients would connect to database servers, as well as other simpler data sources. Clients no longer had to worry about all the networking protocols needed to talk with a database; all that code was included in the ODBC driver.

Microsoft later released a similar data connection system called *OLE DB*, based on ActiveX technology. OLE DB drivers for common systems soon appeared, although you could still get to ODBC resources through a generic ODBC driver built into OLE DB.

In .NET, both ODBC and OLE DB are replaced by *providers*, libraries of code that manage all the communication between the database and your application. Providers are an integral part of ADO.NET, and you will have to use them to get to your databases. Fortunately, you can find providers for the most popular database systems, and a generic OLE DB provider exists for systems without their own providers.

Four primary classes make up the programmer's view of the provider.

The Connection *class*

> This class directs communication between your program and the data source. It includes properties and methods that let you indicate the location or connection parameters for the data source. Multi-command transactions are managed at this object level.

The Command *class*

> This class takes the SQL statement you provide, and prepares it for transport through the Connection object. You can include parameters in your command for stored procedure and complex statement support.

The DataReader *class*

> The DataReader provides a simple and efficient way to retrieve results from a data query, one record at a time. Other objects in ADO.NET use it to receive and redirect data for use within your program, but your code can use it directly to process the results of a SELECT statement or other data retrieval action.

The DataAdapter *class*

> This class is what makes communication between a data set and the rest of a provider possible. One of its primary jobs is to modify data manipulation statements (the SELECT, INSERT, UPDATE, and DELETE statements) generated by a data set into a format that can be used by the related data source.

Using these classes is a little involved, but not hard to understand. To connect to a typical relational database, such as SQL Server, and process data, follow these steps.

1. Establish a connection to your data source using a Connection instance.
2. Wrap a SQL statement in a Command object.
3. Execute that Command in the context of the established Connection.
4. If any results are to be returned, use either a DataReader to scan through the records, or a combination of a DataAdapter and DataSet (or DataTable) to retrieve or store the results.
5. Close all objects that you opened to process the data.

Although the .NET Framework includes data providers for a few different data targets, the remainder of this chapter's discussion focuses only on the SQL Server provider, exposed through the *System.Data.SqlClient* namespace.

> **Note**
> SQL Server 2014 includes support for a feature called "User Instances," for use with SQL Server 2014 Express Edition databases. This feature allows a low-privilege user to access a specific SQL Server Express database file without the need for an administrator to establish SQL Server security settings for that user. This feature is useful in environments where the related software was installed through the ClickOnce deployment method (discussed in Chapter 24) without administrator involvement. It also requires specific reconfiguration of the SQL Server Express installation before use. For more information on this feature, search for "SQL Server User Instances" in Microsoft's MSDN documentation.

Data Sets

If you are going to do more than just quickly scan the data that comes back from a *DataReader* query, you will probably use a *data set* to store, manage, and optionally update your data. Each data set provides a generic disconnected view of data, whether it is data from a provider, or data that you build through code. Although each provider is tied to a specific database platform (such as SQL Server) or communication standard (such as OLE DB), the objects in the data set realm are generic, and can interact with any of the platform-specific providers.

Three main classes make up the world of data sets.

The DataSet *class*

> Each *DataSet* instance acts like a mini database. You can add as many tables to a *DataSet* as you like, and establish foreign-key relationships between the fields of those tables. The internals of each *DataSet* are an unfathomable mystery, but you can export an entire *DataSet* to XML, and load it back in again later if you must.

The DataTable *class*

> Each table in your *DataSet* uses a separate *DataTable* object, accessible through the *DataSet*'s *Tables* collection. The *DataTable* is also useful as a standalone object. If you plan to add only a single table to your *DataSet*, you might opt just to use a *DataTable* object alone without a *DataSet*. Within each *DataTable* object, separate *DataColumn* and *DataRow* objects establish the field definitions and the actual data values, respectively.

The DataRelation *class*

> Use *DataRelation* objects, stored within a *DataSet*'s *Relations* collection, to establish field-level relationships and constraints between columns in your *DataTable* objects.

Although data sets are most often used with providers, you can use them independently to build your own in-memory collection of tables and relationships.

> **Note**
> Visual C# includes "Typed DataSets," a feature used to integrate a *DataSet* with a specific data or record format. You may find them useful in your applications, but I won't be discussing them in this book. LINQ uses a similar feature to help establish relationships between LINQ and database tables.

Data Sets Versus No Data Sets

When used together, providers and data sets give an end-to-end interface to individual data values, from the fields in your database tables to the in-memory items of a *DataRow* record. Figure 10-1 shows this object interaction.

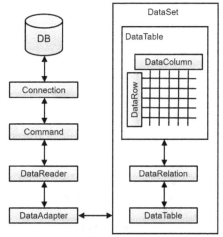

Figure 10-1. Providers and data sets in action

When you interact with data from an external database, you always use the provider classes, but it's up to you whether you want to also use data sets. There are pros and cons with both methods, some of which appear in Table 10-1.

Table 10-1. The pros and cons of using data sets

Without data sets	With data sets
You must supply all SQL statements, in the format the provider expects. This is true for all *SELECT*, *INSERT*, *UPDATE*, and *DELETE* requests.	The *DataSet* and *DataAdapter* work together to craft many of the SQL statements on your behalf.
Data retrieved through the *DataReader* is read-only. You must issue separate commands to update data.	Data read from the database can be modified in-memory, and updated as a batch with a single method call.
Data transfers are very efficient, since no overhead is needed to move data into a complex data set structure.	There may be a performance hit as the data set builds the necessary objects required for each transferred record.
Memory allocation is limited to a single record's worth of data fields, plus some minimal overhead.	Memory allocation is required for the entire result set, plus overhead for every table, field, column, and row in the result set.
In general, only a single *DataReader* can be open at a time.	Any number of data sets can be in use at once.
A live connection to the database exists as long as a *DataReader* is in use. If it takes you five minutes to scan a result set because you are doing a lot of per-record analysis, the connection will be active for the full five minutes.	Data connections are maintained only long enough to transfer data from or to the database.

Without data sets	With data sets
`DataReader`s present one record at a time. The records must be processed in the order they arrive.	You can jump around the records in a data set, and reorganize them to meet your needs.
You spend a lot of time working with strings (for SQL statements) and raw data fields.	All data fields are organized logically, just like they are in the actual database. You can interact with them directly.
Each `Command` and `Connection` works with a single provider-supported data source.	Different `DataTable`s within your `DataSet` can connect to distinct data sources. Also, you can hand-craft data so that each `DataRow` contains data from different sources.
Because you manage all SQL statements, you have a (relatively) high level of control over the entire data interaction process.	Because the view of the data is abstracted, you have a (relatively) limited level of control over the entire data interaction process (although advanced use of data sets does give you some additional control).

Although the speed and low overhead of `DataReader` objects are compelling reasons to eschew data sets, I like the convenience of data sets and the database-like tables they contain. In the Library Project, I avoid the `DataReader` system altogether, but still try to keep things simple by using a `DataAdapter` to generate single `DataTable` objects as needed, without an enveloping `DataSet`. I will also use these objects in a way that keeps as much control over the process as possible in the application's code, instead of delegating full control to ADO.NET. I'll have more to say about that later in this chapter.

Connecting to SQL Server with Visual Studio

Visual Studio has many built-in tools that make working with data as simple as drag-and-drop. Well, it's not really that quick. But by answering a few questions and dragging and dropping one item, you can build an entire application that lets you edit data in your database. Let's try it together.

Creating a Data Source

Start up a new Windows Forms project in Visual Studio—just a plain Windows Forms project, not one of the Library-specific projects. Selecting the View→Other Windows→ Data Sources menu command brings up the Data Sources panel, as shown in Figure 10-2.

Figure 10-2. Where are the data sources?

New projects don't include any data sources by default, so we need to add one. Click on the Add New Data Source link in the Data Sources panel. The Data Source Configuration Wizard guides you through the data source creation process.

1. The first step asks, "Where will the application get data from?" Select Database and click the Next button.

2. The second steps asks, "What type of database model do you want to use?" You will probably only see the Dataset option, so select it and click the Next button.

3. The third step asks, "Which data connection should your application use to connect to the database?" We'll create a new connection for the Library database we designed way back in Chapter 4. Click the New Connection button.

4. The Choose Data Source dialog appears. Select Microsoft SQL Server from the Data Source list, and then click the Continue button. If you have accessed this dialog before and checked the Always Use This Selection field, it's possible that this dialog will not appear at all.

5. The Add Connection dialog appears to collect the details of the new connection. If the Data Source field contains something other than "Microsoft SQL Server," click the Change button to alter the connection type using the dialog mentioned in step 4.

6. Back on the Add Connection form, fill in the Server Name field with the name of your SQL Server instance. Hopefully, this drop-down list already has the instances listed, but if not, you'll have to enter it yourself. The default for SQL Server Express is the name of your computer, with "\SQLEXPRESS" attached. If your computer name is "MYSYSTEM," the instance name would be "MYSYSTEM\SQLEXPRESS." Non-Express or "Default" database instances will often use just the server name, without the "\SQLEXPRESS" suffix.

7. Configure your authentication settings in the Log On to the Server section. I used standard Windows authentication, but it depends on how you set up the database in Chapter 4.

8. In the Connect to a Database section, either select or type in *Library* for the database name.

9. Click the Test Connection button to make sure it all works. When you're finished, click the OK button to create the new connection.

10. OK, we're back on the Data Source Configuration Wizard form. The connection we just created should now appear in the list, as shown in Figure 10-3. Click Next.

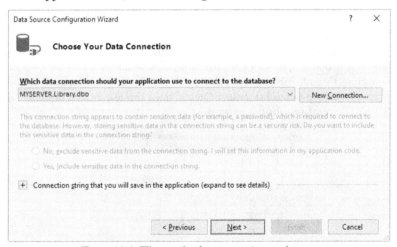

Figure 10-3. The new database connection, ready to use

11. The next panel asks whether this data source should become part of the configurable settings for this project. We'll get into the settings features of Visual C# in Chapter 14. For now, just accept the default and click Next.

12. We're almost there. Only twenty-seven more steps to go! Just kidding. This is the last step in creating the data source. The final panel shows a list of the data-generating features in the Library database. Open the Tables branch and select Activity, as shown in Figure 10-4. Then click Finish.

Figure 10-4. The final step is to select the Activity table

Check out the Data Sources panel shown in Figure 10-5. It includes the new *LibraryDataSet* data source with its subordinate *Activity* table.

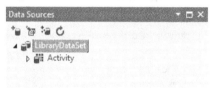

Figure 10-5. Finally, a real data source

Using a Data Source

So, what is this data source anyway? It is simply a link to some portion of your database, wrapped up in a typical .NET object. Now that it's part of your project, you can use it to access the data in the *Activity* table through your project's code, or by drag-and-drop. In the Data Sources panel, you will find that the Activity entry is actually a drop-down list. Select Details from the list, as I've done in Figure 10-6. (The surface of *Form1* must be displayed for this to work.)

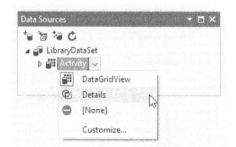

Figure 10-6. Select the Details view instead of DataGrid

Finally, drag-and-drop the Activity entry onto the surface of *Form1*. When you let go, Visual Studio will add a set of controls to the form, plus a few more non-user-interface controls just below the form (see Figure 10-7).

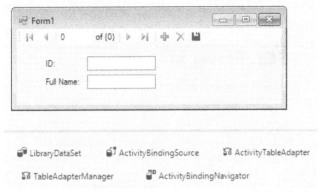

Figure 10-7. A complete program without writing a single line of code

By just dragging-and-dropping, Visual Studio added all the necessary controls and links to turn your form into a turbo-charged *Activity* table editor. Try it now by pressing the F5 key. In the running program, you can use the Microsoft Access-style record access "VCR" control to move between the records in the *Activity* table. You can also modify the values of each record, add new records, or delete existing records (but please restore things back to their original state when you are done; we'll need all the original records later). Talk about power! Talk about simplicity! Talk about unemployment lines! Who needs highly paid programmers like us when Visual Studio can do this for you?

Data Binding

In reality, Visual Studio isn't doing all that much. It's using a feature called *data binding* to link the on-form fields with the data source, the Library database's *Activity* table. Data binding is a feature built into Windows Forms controls that allows them to automatically display and modify values in an associated data source, such as a database. It's all sorted out through the properties of the control.

Select the *FullNameTextBox* control added to this project's form, and then examine its properties. Right at the top is a property section named "(DataBindings)." Its *Text* subproperty contains "ActivityBindingSource - FullName," a reference to the *ActivityBindingSource* non-user-interface control also added by Visual Studio. *ActivityBindingSource*, in turn, contains a reference to the *LibraryDataSet* object, the data source we created earlier. That data source links to SQL Server, to the Library database, and finally to the *Activity* table and its *FullName* field. Piece of cake!

If you count up all the objects involved in this data-binding relationship, you come up with something like 5,283 distinct objects. It's no wonder that Visual Studio did so much of the work for you. Data binding provides a lot of convenience, but it also takes away a lot of your *control* as a developer. Although there are properties and events that let you manage aspects of the data binding and its update process, most of the essential code is hidden away inside the data-binding portions of .NET. You may not touch, taste, fold, spindle, or mutilate it, and that's just bad. A quick look at one of my core programming beliefs says it all: *good software includes maximum control for the developer, and minimum control for the user.*

Part of your job as a developer is to provide a highly scripted environment for the user to access important data. This requires that you have control over the user's experience through your source code. Certainly, you will defer much of that control to others when you use any third-party supplied tools. As long as those tools allow you to control the user experience to your level of satisfaction, that's great. But I've always been disappointed with data binding, except when implementing a read-only display of data from the database. (Newer WPF and XAML applications make extensive use of data binding, but it is often for more localized control over the user interface, and not primarily as a database management tool.)

Fortunately, if you eschew the data-binding features, Visual C# will pass to you the responsibility of managing all interactions between the database and the user.

Interacting with SQL Server in Code

Communicating with a database yourself is definitely more work than dragging-and-dropping data sources, but whoever said programming was a cakewalk?

Building the Connection String

The first step on the road to the data-controlling lifestyle is to connect to the database using a connection string. Sadly, it is through connection strings that Microsoft keeps a tight rein on Windows developers. It's not that the strings are complex; they are nothing more than lists of semicolon-separated parameters. But the parameters to include, and their exact format, are the stuff of legend. The MSDN documentation does provide some examples of connection strings, but not much detail. A third-party resource, http://www.connectionstrings.com, also provides numerous examples of valid connection string formats.

The connection string we will use to connect to the Library database, fortunately, isn't overly complex. If you use your Microsoft Windows login to connect to the database, the following string will meet your needs (as one unbroken line).

```
Data Source=instance_name;Initial Catalog=Library;
    Integrated Security=true
```

instance_name is replaced by the name of your SQL Server instance or data source. Typically, this is the name of the system, but SQL Server Express instances usually add "\SQLEXPRESS" to the data source name, as in "MYSYSTEM\SQLEXPRESS."

To use SQL Server user IDs and passwords, try this format (also entered as one unbroken line).

```
Data Source=instance_name;Initial Catalog=Library;
    User ID=sa;Password=xyz
```

Of course, replace the user ID (*sa*) and password (*xyz*) with your own settings.

> **Note**
> Other connection string options let you connect to a SQL Server Express (SSE) database file directly, alter the "user instancing" method (often used with ClickOnce-deployed databases), and make other adjustments. Although they are somewhat scattered about, you can find these options detailed in the MSDN documentation.

Establishing the Connection

Now we're ready to use the connection string to create a *SqlConnection* object and open the connection. Create a brand-new Windows Forms application in Visual Studio. Add a *Button* control to the surface of *Form1*. Double-click the button to access its *Click* event handler. Then add the following code to that handler.

```
// ----- Assumes:
//          using System.Data.SqlClient;
SqlConnection libraryDB = new SqlConnection(
    "Data Source=MYSYSTEM;" +
```

```
    "Initial Catalog=Library;Integrated Security=true");
  libraryDB.Open();
```

Make sure you replace "MYSYSTEM" with your own target server name or database instance. This entire block of code sure seems a lot easier to me than those ten or fifteen steps you had to follow earlier when setting up the connection through Visual Studio.

Using SQL Statements

Once the connection is open, you can issue *SELECT*, *INSERT*, *UPDATE*, *DELETE*, or any other data manipulation language (DML) or data definition language (DDL) statement accepted by the database. A *SqlCommand* object prepares your SQL statement for use by the open connection. Here's a statement that returns the description for entry number *1* in the *Activity* table.

```
SELECT FullName FROM Activity WHERE ID = 1
```

Creating a *SqlCommand* object that wraps around this statement is easy. The constructor for the *SqlCommand* object takes a SQL statement, plus a *SqlConnection* object. Add the following code to the end of your *button1_Click* event handler.

```
SqlCommand sqlStatement = new SqlCommand(
    "SELECT FullName FROM Activity WHERE ID = 1", libraryDB);
```

Processing the Results

The only thing left to do is to pass the SQL statement to the database, via the connection, and retrieve the results as a *SqlDataReader* object. (An alternative would be to use a *SqlDataAdapter* with a *DataSet* or *DataTable* target. We'll use such code in this chapter's "Project" section.) Once the data arrives from the database, process each record using that object's *Read* method. You access individual fields by name through the data reader's default item collection. Add this additional code to the end of your *button1_Click* event handler.

```
SqlDataReader sqlResults = sqlStatement.ExecuteReader();
sqlResults.Read();
MessageBox.Show(sqlResults["FullName"].ToString());
```

Taking all these blocks of code together displays the message shown in Figure 10-8.

Figure 10-8. Basic data retrieved from a database

When you're finished, make sure you close all the connections you opened. Add this last bit of code to the end of your *button1_Click* event handler.

```
sqlResults.Close();
libraryDB.Close();
```

Modifying Data

Making changes to database tables is coded just like data retrieval, but no *SqlDataReader* is needed. Instead of using the *ExecuteReader* method, use the *ExecuteNonQuery* method, which returns no results.

```
SqlCommand sqlStatement = new SqlCommand(
    "UPDATE Activity SET FullName = 'Sleeps all day' " +
    "WHERE ID = 1", libraryDB);
sqlStatement.ExecuteNonQuery();
```

SQL Server 2014 has a convenient feature that will return a single field from a new record created via an *INSERT* statement. If you look back at the Library Project's database design, you will see that the ID fields in many of the tables are generated automatically. Traditionally, if you wanted to immediately retrieve the ID field for a new record, you first had to *INSERT* the record, and then perform a separate *SELECT* statement, returning the new record's ID field.

```
INSERT INTO CodeSeries (FullName)
    VALUES ('Children''s Books')

SELECT ID FROM CodeSeries
    WHERE FullName = 'Children''s Books'
```

SQL Server's *OUTPUT INSERTED* clause combines both of these statements into a single action.

```
INSERT INTO CodeSeries (FullName)
    OUTPUT INSERTED.ID
    VALUES ('Children''s Books')
```

When the *INSERT* is complete, SQL Server returns the ID field as a result set, just as though you had issued a separate *SELECT* statement. The *SqlCommand*'s *ExecuteScalar* method is a simple way to retrieve a single value from a SQL query.

```
sqlStatement = new SqlCommand(
    "INSERT INTO CodeSeries (FullName) " +
    "OUTPUT INSERTED.ID VALUES ('Children''s Books')",
    libraryDB);
long newID = Convert.ToInt64(sqlStatement.ExecuteScalar());
```

Using Parameters

Building up SQL statements from basic string components is easy, but there are negatives as well. For example, when crafting long queries, you will be doing a truckload of concatenating and formatting as you mix query keywords and data together. Also, by including record-specific data in your query text, you miss out on some of the efficiencies that databases like SQL Server apply to more generic queries. Most importantly, allowing unwashed user data to be inserted directly into your query strings can open your application up to SQL Injection attacks and other similar query-based dangers.

To alleviate these problems, ADO.NET includes support for *parameterized queries*. In such queries, you include data placeholders in the query text, and transmit the actual data alongside the query as a data processing package. The placeholder format varies by target database, but for SQL Server, each named placeholder begins with an @ sign, as with the *@SeriesName* placeholder in the following query text.

```
sqlStatement = New SqlCommand(
    "INSERT INTO CodeSeries (FullName) " +
    "OUTPUT INSERTED.ID VALUES (@SeriesName)",
    libraryDB);
```

Once your query string is peppered with placeholders, you can add *SqlParameter* objects to the *SqlCommand* instance, each of which contains the actual data value for a given placeholder. The *AddWithValue* method provides the quickest means of adding parameters to a query.

```
sqlStatement.Parameters.AddWithValue(
    "SeriesName", "Children's Book");
```

Although parameters require a little more coding, they keep things clean by providing a distinct separation between code and data, which is great since they sometimes like to fight with each other. You might have seen another benefit in this sample: the replacement of the two single-quote marks in the "Children's Book" data content with just a single (normal) single quote. Parameters take care of all special formatting needs for you. All you need to do is provide your data in a parameter, and ADO.NET figures out how to make it fit into the query.

Database Transactions

Transactions enable all-or-nothing actions across multiple SQL statements. Once started, either all the SQL statements issued within the context of the transaction complete, or none of them complete. If you have ten data updates to perform, but the database fails after only five of them, you can *roll back* the transaction. The database reverses the earlier statements, restoring all records to what they were before the transaction began. (Updates from other users are not affected by the rollback.) If all statements succeed, you can *commit* the entire transaction, making all of its changes permanent.

For SQL Server databases, transactions are managed through the provider's *SqlTransaction* object. Like the other ADO.NET features, it's easy to use. A transaction starts with a *BeginTransaction* method call on the connection.

```
SqlTransaction atomicSet = libraryDB.BeginTransaction();
```

To include a SQL statement in a transaction, assign the *SqlTransaction* object to the *SqlCommand* object's *Transaction* property.

```
sqlStatement.Transaction = atomicSet;
```

Then call the appropriate *Execute* method on the command. When all commands complete, use the transaction's *Commit* method to make the changes permanent.

```
atomicSet.Commit();
```

If, instead, you need to abort the transaction, use the *Rollback* method.

```
atomicSet.Rollback();
```

ADO.NET Entity Framework

ADO.NET includes a database interaction library known as the ADO.NET Entity Framework. Part entity-relationship modeling tool, part code generator, this new technology helps you craft logical data views of the data stored in your relational database or other data source.

The Entity Framework lets you design three types of objects based on your stored data: *entities* (similar to tables), *relationships* (database joins), and *entity sets* (related entities). Each type is represented by objects that expose the members of your core database in a more programmable fashion. For instance, you can design an entity object representing a table in your database, and the object's members can represent the fields in a single record.

"So what," you say? It sounds like the same features built into ADO.NET's *DataTable* object? But wait, there's more. What makes the Entity Framework so useful is (1) its mapping of physical data to logical views; (2) its support for entity inheritance; and (3) its ability to act as an ADO.NET provider.

Data mapping

The mapping of data is similar to creating a *view* in a traditional relational database; you can create entities that are built up from multiple source records spread across multiple database tables. This includes parent-child views of data; you can create an `Order` entity that refers to both the main order record and the multiple order line items included in the order. Logically, this new entity is treated as a single queryable element. When you request data through the new entity, you don't have to teach it each time how to join and relate the various source pieces of data.

Entity inheritance

Once you have an entity defined, you can extend the structure of the entity through inheritance. For instance, you might want to create an entity called `InternalOrder` based on your original `Order` entity, adding members that track data specific to internal orders. These new fields might be in a specialized table, or identified by a Boolean flag on the main table of orders. But that doesn't matter: it can all be hidden by the logic of the entity itself. When you request an instance of `InternalOrder`, it will just know that you mean only the special internally flagged type of order, and not standard orders.

ADO.NET provider support

Once you've created your entities and related mapping logic, you can connect to the entities as though they were stored in their own database. Instead of connecting up to SQL Server and querying tables directly, you connect to the mapping context and query against the new logical view of your data.

I'll have a little more to say about the Entity Framework in Chapter 17, when I discuss interactions between that framework and LINQ.

Summary

There are programmers in this world who never have to access a database, who never worry about connections or transactions or record locking or `INSERT` statements or referential integrity. Yes, there are such programmers in the world—five, maybe six at last count. All other programmers must include code that manages external data of some sort, whether in a relational database, or an XML file, or a configuration file. ADO.NET is one of the .NET tools that make such data management easy. When I consider the power and flexibility of ADO.NET, I can't help feeling sorry for those six programmers who never use databases.

Project

It's likely that more than fifty percent of the code in the Library Project will directly involve database access, or manipulation of the data retrieved through ADO.NET. Constantly creating new `Command` and `Connection` objects, although simple, is pretty hard on the fingers. Since so much of the code is repetitive, the code in this chapter's project will try to centralize some of that basic, boilerplate code.

Project Access
Load the "Chapter 10 (Before) Code" project, either through the New Project templates or by accessing the project directly from the installation directory. To see the code in its final form, load "Chapter 10 (After) Code" instead.

Connecting to the Database

Most of the new code for this chapter appears in the *General.cs* file, so open it now. The first step in communicating with SQL Server is to establish a connection to the database. In a later chapter, we'll store the connection information in a configuration file and retrieve it before making the initial connection. Let's create a storage variable for that connection string right now to the top of the *General* class.

Insert Snippet
Insert Chapter 10, Snippet Item 1.

```
private static string ActiveConnectionString = "";
```

The *ConnectDatabase* procedure contains all the code needed to create a database link based on the connection string's configuration details. Add the following routine to your *General* class. Make sure you change the reference to "MYSYSTEM" to whatever is needed on your own system.

Insert Snippet
Insert Chapter 10, Snippet Item 2.

```
public static SqlConnection ConnectDatabase()
{
    // ----- Connect to the database.
    //       Throw exception on failure.
    SqlConnection libraryDB;

    // ----- Build the connection string.
    // !!! WARNING: Hardcoded for now.
    if (ActiveConnectionString.Length == 0)
        ActiveConnectionString = "Data Source=MYSYSTEM;" +
            "Initial Catalog=Library;Integrated Security=true";

    // ----- Attempt to open the database.
    libraryDB = new SqlConnection(ActiveConnectionString);
    libraryDB.Open();

    // ----- Success.
    return libraryDB;
}
```

In a later chapter, we'll replace the hardcoded database location with an entire configuration form and settings system.

Managing Parameterized Data

The *SqlParameter* object is simple to use, but it is really a low-level tools that provides a thin layer between your code and SQL Server. Also, its *AddWithValue* method lacks some of the fine control needed for specific types of data. For the Library Project, we'll create a query management class that provides a more programmer-friendly and data-friendly interface for parameterized query creation. The class is named *DataCommand*. Add it now to the end of the *General.cs* file.

Insert Snippet
Insert Chapter 10, Snippet Item 3.

After creating an instance of this class with a query string, you can use data-type-specific methods to build up the collection of parameters.

```
DataCommand sqlRun = new DataCommand(
    "INSERT INTO CodeSeries (FullName) " +
    "OUTPUT INSERTED.ID VALUES (@SeriesName)");
sqlRun.AddText("SeriesName", "Children's Books");
```

Other methods exist for Boolean, numeric, and date/time parameters. The class's `GetCommandObject` method builds a `SqlCommand` instance ready for processing with a data adapter.

Working with Transactions

As we did with parameters, we'll create a custom class that hides some of the details of transaction management. Add the new `LibraryTransaction` class to the end of the *General.cs* file.

> **Insert Snippet**
> Insert Chapter 10, Snippet Item 4.

The class is pretty basic, really just a wrapper around a connection and transaction pair. To deal with transactions through the program, we also need to add begin, commit, and rollback methods that know about this new transaction management class. Add the new `TransactionBegin`, `TransactionCommit`, and `TransactionRollback` methods to the `General` class.

> **Insert Snippet**
> Insert Chapter 10, Snippet Item 5.

Since transactions are all-or-nothing events, atomic database updates will typically be bundled within a single error handler, with rollback processing appearing in the error handler.

```
LibraryTransaction transInfo;
try
{
    transInfo = TransactionBegin();

    // ----- Insert dangerous statements here, then...
    TransactionCommit(transInfo);
}
catch (Exception ex)
{
    TransactionRollback(transInfo);
    // ----- Other needed error processing.
}
```

One thing you might notice about this code is that there is no database connection information specified anywhere. ADO.NET is designed to be as disconnected as possible from the database, and therefore all connections are postponed for as long as possible. We'll see the actual calls to `ConnectDatabase` in the next section when we add in the query processing routines.

Processing Queries

The next code block adds in routines that create `DataTable` objects from SQL Server queries, or that process arbitrary SQL code, with or without the return of a static value from that query. Add them to the `General` class.

> **Insert Snippet**
> Insert Chapter 10, Snippet Item 6.

This snippet adds the following twelve routines.

`CreateDataTable` *method (four variations)*

Given a SQL statement, retrieve its results from the database, and put it all in a `DataTable` object. A `SqlDataAdapter` connects a `SqlCommand` (generated by the `DataCommand` class that we added just above) to the *DataTable*. The four variations of this method take into account the parameter and transaction opportunities available with each query.

ExecuteSQL *method (four variations)*

Send a SQL statement to the database for processing.

ExecuteSQLReturn *method (four variations)*

Send a SQL statement to the database for processing, returning a single result value.

All of these routines throw any generated exceptions back to the calling code instead of handling such errors locally. This lets the calling routine take specific action based on the type of error generated. All of these routines are pretty similar to one another. Here is the code for retrieving a table of results using a parameterized query.

```
public static DataTable CreateDataTable(DataCommand theAction)
{
   // ----- Given a SQL statement with parameters,
   //       return a data table.
   SqlCommand dbCommand;
   SqlDataAdapter dbAdapter;
   DataTable dbTable;
   SqlConnection localConnection = null;

   // ----- Connect to the database, if not yet done.
   //       Throw exception on failure.
   if (theAction.Connection == null)
      localConnection = ConnectDatabase();

   // ----- Try to run the statement.
   //       Throw exception on failure.
   try
   {
      dbCommand = theAction.GetCommandObject();
      if (localConnection != null)
         dbCommand.Connection = localConnection;
      dbAdapter = new SqlDataAdapter(dbCommand);
      dbTable = new DataTable();
      dbAdapter.Fill(dbTable);
   }
   catch
   {
      // ----- Reissue error after Finally clause.
      throw;
   }
   finally
   {
      // ----- Disconnect if needed.
      if (localConnection != null)
         localConnection.Close();
   }
   return dbTable;
}
```

Retrieving Data Values

Although you can configure your ADO.NET queries so that they pick up the data type details from the queries they process, this can add a lot of configuration code and processing time to your query management. Another option is to have the calling code already be aware of the types of data coming back from a query. For example, a routine that retrieves the name of a book from the database should understand that this book name is text, and not an integer. I think that's a fair assumption, so it's the method we'll employ in the Library Project.

To assist with the retrieval of such typed data, we'll add a handful of helper routines that make sure the incoming data is usable in our expected format.

Insert Snippet

Insert Chapter 10, Snippet Item 7.

Six of the methods added here retrieve data from a database field in the appropriate target format. For example, the *DBGetBool* function returns a Boolean value from a retrieved database record. The other functions return other types of field values, differentiated by data type: *DBGetDate* (dates and times), *DBGetDecimal* (decimal values), *DBGetInteger* (smaller integer values), *DBGetLong* (larger integer values), and *DBGetText* (text strings). Here's the code for the *DBGetText* method, which is quite similar to the others.

```
public static string DBGetText(
   object dataField, string defaultText = "")
{
   // ----- Return the text equivalent of an
   //       optional database field.
   if (Convert.IsDBNull(dataField) == true)
      return defaultText;
   else
      return Convert.ToString(dataField);
}
```

One final method added in this step, *DBComboParam*, is used to help populate query parameters based on items stored in *ComboBox* controls.

System-Level Configuration

The last blocks of code support the quick update and retrieval of system-wide configuration values stored in the *SystemValue* table of the Library database. The *GetSystemValue* routine returns the current setting of a configuration value when supplied with the value name. *SetSystemValue* updates (or adds, if needed) a named configuration value. Both of these routines appear in the *General* class.

Insert Snippet

Insert Chapter 10, Snippet Item 8.

```
public static string GetSystemValue(string valueName)
{
   // ----- Return the data portion of a system
   //       value name-data pair.
   string sqlText;
   DataCommand sqlRun;

   // ----- Retrieve the value.
   sqlText = "SELECT ValueData FROM SystemValue " +
      "WHERE UPPER(ValueName) = @TestName";
```

```
    sqlRun = new DataCommand(sqlText);
    sqlRun.AddText("TestName", valueName.ToUpper());
    try
    {
        return DBGetText(ExecuteSQLReturn(sqlRun));
    }
    catch (Exception ex)
    {
        GeneralError("GetSystemValue", ex);
        return "";
    }
}

public static void SetSystemValue(
    string valueName, string valueData)
{
    // ----- Update a record in the SystemValue table.
    string sqlText;
    DataCommand sqlRun;

    try
    {
        // ----- See if the entry already exists.
        sqlText = "SELECT COUNT(*) FROM SystemValue " +
            "WHERE UPPER(ValueName) = @TestName";
        sqlRun = new DataCommand(sqlText);
        sqlRun.AddText("TestName", valueName.ToUpper());
        if (DBGetInteger(ExecuteSQLReturn(sqlRun)) > 0)
        {
            // ----- Value already exists.
            sqlText = "UPDATE SystemValue " +
                "SET ValueData = @NewData " +
                "WHERE UPPER(ValueName) = @TestName";
            sqlRun = new DataCommand(sqlText);
            sqlRun.AddText("NewData", valueData);
            sqlRun.AddText("TestName", valueName.ToUpper());
        }
        else
        {
            // ----- Need to create value.
            sqlText = "INSERT INTO SystemValue " +
                "(ValueName, ValueData) " +
                "VALUES (@NewName, @NewData)";
            sqlRun = new DataCommand(sqlText);
            sqlRun.AddText("NewName", valueName);
            sqlRun.AddText("NewData", valueData);
        }

        // ----- Update the value.
        ExecuteSQL(sqlRun);
    }
    catch (Exception ex)
    {
        GeneralError("SetSystemValue", ex);
```

```
        }
    }
```

The *GetSystemValue* routine is clear. It simply retrieves a single value from the database. *SetSystemValue* has to first check whether the configuration value to update already exists in the database. If it does, it modifies the records. Otherwise, it adds a full new record. To determine whether the record exists, it requests a count of records matching the system value name. It queries the database through our new *ExecuteSqlReturn* method, which returns a single value from a query. In this case, the value is the count of the matching records.

```
sqlText = "SELECT COUNT(*) FROM SystemValue " +
    "WHERE UPPER(ValueName) = @TestName";
sqlRun = new DataCommand(sqlText);
sqlRun.AddText("TestName", valueName.ToUpper());
if (DBGetInteger(ExecuteSQLReturn(sqlRun)) > 0)
```

Using the *GetSystemValue* routine is easy, so let's use it right now. Go back to the *Main* startup routine in *Program.cs*, and add the following code near the end of the routine, just before dismissing the splash screen.

Insert Snippet
Insert Chapter 10, Snippet Item 9.

```
// ----- Check the database version.
if (int.TryParse(GetSystemValue("DatabaseVersion"), out
productionDBVersion) == false)
    productionDBVersion = 0;
if (productionDBVersion != UseDBVersion)
{
    splashScreen.Close();
    MessageBox.Show(
        "The program cannot continue due to an " +
        "incompatible database. The current database " +
        $"version is '{productionDBVersion}'. " +
        $"The application version is '{UseDBVersion}'.",
        ProgramTitle, MessageBoxButtons.OK,
        MessageBoxIcon.Error);
    librarySync.ReleaseMutex();
    Application.Exit();
    return;
}
```

Once in a while, I found it necessary to modify the structure of a database to such an extent that older versions of an application either crashed, or would cause major data headaches. To prevent this, I added a database version setting, *DatabaseVersion*, and use this code block to test against it. If the program doesn't match the expected database version, it will refuse to run.

This all assumes that we can access the database in the first place. Before we check the database version, we need to establish a valid connection to the data store. Add the following code before the block we just inserted.

Insert Snippet
Insert Chapter 10, Snippet Item 10.

```
// ----- Make sure we can connect to the database.
testConnect = ConnectDatabase();
```

```
if (testConnect == null)
{
    splashScreen.Close();
    librarySync.ReleaseMutex();
    Application.Exit();
    return;
}
testConnect.Dispose();
```

Now that we have some basic database access tools, we're ready to start adding some real data interaction code to the Library application.

Chapter 11

Security

Secrets are funny things. With billions of people on the planet, there is no shortage of really interesting events and stories, but none of them will hold our interest if there is a secret to be discovered somewhere else. For instance, former associate director of the FBI, W. Mark Felt, revealed himself to be the famous Deep Throat of Watergate fame, but not before thirty years of speculation and whispering about this secret identity had passed by. Other secrets are just as intriguing, even if we are in on the secret. Superman is fascinating in part due to his secret alter ego, Clark Kent. Many books include the word *Secret* in their titles to make them and their topics more interesting. If I had been thinking more clearly, I would have named this book *Secret Start-to-Finish Visual C# 2015*.

In this era of information overload and increasingly permissive moral standards on television, secrets seem to be scarce. But everyone has important information that needs to be protected from others, and that includes the users of your programs. Fortunately, .NET programs and related data can be as secure as you need, if you use the security features available to you in the .NET Framework.

Here's a secret that I'll tell right now: I really don't know that much about computer security issues. Back in the early 1980s, I worked for a computer vendor that was coming out with its own Unix System V implementation. The company needed to confirm that its product would be sufficiently secure for governmental sales, and I was tasked with building a bibliography of computer security resources, including the famous Orange Book, a government security standards document whose title has no rhyme.

Although I don't recall many of the security details, I do remember that it would take several city garbage trucks to haul away all the available materials on computer security. The bibliography I developed was more than forty pages long! And that was just the table of contents. One article that I do recall was quite interesting. It discussed password encryption in Unix systems, at least back when AT&T was in charge. The interesting part was that the entire algorithm was printed in a publicly available book. Anyone could examine the book and see how the passwords were secreted away. And if you were familiar with Unix, you knew that each user's encrypted password was stored in plain text in the file */etc/passwd*. But it wasn't a big deal. Although the method for enciphering the password was public knowledge, and although you could see everyone's encrypted password, Unix was still considered secure enough for use even in the military.

Security Features in .NET

Security in .NET involves many features, but they fall generally into three major areas.

Internal security

> Classes and class members in .NET can be protected via user-based or role-based security. This *Code Access Security* (CAS) exists to keep unauthorized users from reaching powerful libraries of .NET features. Only those users meeting a minimum or specific set of rights can use those protected features.

External security

Since anyone can develop and distribute a .NET application, it's important to protect system resources from malicious code. This is a big issue, especially with the ongoing reports of hackers taking advantage of buffer-overrun problems in released software from Microsoft and other vendors. Just as CAS keeps code from accessing certain features of a class, it interacts with the operating system to keep rogue code from accessing some or all files and directories, registry entries, network resources, hardware peripherals, or other .NET assemblies based on in-effect security policies.

Data security

Programs and computer resources aren't the only things that need to be protected. Some highfalutin users think their precious data is so important that it deserves to be protected through "special" software means. Encryption, digital signatures, and other cryptographic features provide the special support needed for such data.

Because the Library Project interacts with a major external resource—a SQL Server database—it does deal with external security issues, although indirectly through ADO.NET and system security policies. Still, because of this book's focus on typical business application development, this chapter will not discuss either internal security or external security issues. Instead, it will focus on data security topics, especially the encryption of data.

Cryptography and Encryption

Knowing a secret is one thing. Keeping it safe and protected from others is another. Making sure an enemy doesn't alter it while we're blabbing—I mean, confiding—it to someone else is still another issue. Confirming that a secret coming from someone else is reliable is yet another issue. Making sure that I get the best deal on car insurance is again another issue entirely.

Clearly, data security is about more than just keeping a piece of data protected from prying eyes. And it's not only prying eyes that concern us. A while back, I experienced the Windows Blue Screen of Death when I tried to synchronize the data on my desktop system with my first electronic handheld scheduler. The potential for data corruption through the normal everyday use of technology is vast. Fortunately, the word processor I am using to type this chapter is frëë fR̂ôm su©h ¢θr®µptioñ¡

Keeping Secrets

When people think about encryption and data security, they generally focus on the "Keeping Secrets" aspect. The ability to cryptographically encode content, keep it from an adversary, and still have it decoded by you or an associate at some later time is important. Encryption techniques range from simple language aberrations (such as pig Latin) and replacement ciphers (letter substitutions, used in cryptogram puzzles) to complex enigma-machine-quality encoding systems.

Software-enabled encryption is now a part of our everyday experience. When you make credit card purchases from web sites, the chance is pretty good that your credit card information is encrypted and transferred in 256-bit secret fidelity.

Typical encryption methods make use of one or more *keys*, plus a combination of *hashing functions* and *encryption algorithms*, to convert sensitive content into a form that is not easily accessible without the original or related key. *Symmetric cryptography* is the name used for encryption methods using a single secret key.

Public-key encryption—also known as *asymmetric cryptography*—uses a pair of keys to encrypt and decrypt data. One of the keys, a *public key*, can be given to anyone who cares about communicating with you securely. You can even give it to your enemies; it's public. The related *private key* is kept safe for your use; you never show it to anyone, not even your mother. Content encrypted using one of the keys (and an encryption algorithm) can only be decrypted later using the other key. If your friend encrypts some information using the public key, nobody except you will be able to decrypt it, and it will require your private key. You can also encrypt data with your private key, but anyone would be able to decrypt it with the public key. We'll see uses for this seemingly insecure action a little bit later.

Data Stability

Data encryption helps to ensure the integrity of a block of data, even if that data is not encrypted. If you send someone an email during a lightning storm, there is certainly the chance that some or all of the email content could be electronically altered before it reaches the recipient. Let's say that some static in the transmission line just happens to cause one sentence of the content to be duplicated. Let's say that some static in the transmission line just happens to cause one sentence of the content to be duplicated. How would you know whether it was the author trying to make some clever point, or simply a computer glitch?

Including a *checksum* with the content can help to identify data problems during transmission. A checksum—sometimes called a *hash value*—takes the original content and passes it through a function that generates a short value that represents the original data. Good checksum functions (or *hashing algorithms*) are very sensitive to even single-byte changes in the content, whether that single byte was altered, repositioned, added, or removed from the original data. By generating a checksum both before and after data transmission, you can determine whether the content changed at all during the transfer.

Checksums represent a *unidirectional encryption* of the original data. It is impossible to use the checksum to obtain the original data content. That's all right, though, since the purpose of a checksum is not to deliver content secretly, but to deliver it unchanged. *Bidirectional encryption* is what I talked about in the "Keeping Secrets" section. If you have the right key and the right algorithm, bidirectional encryption restores original content from encrypted content.

Identity Verification

Let's say that you receive an email from your boss that says, "Order fifty copies of Tim Patrick's newest book, and hurry." How do you know this message is reliable, or really from your boss? In this case, the content alone should prove that it is trustworthy. But if you really wanted to verify the source, and your boss was unavailable, you could employ *digital signatures* to confirm the identity of the sender.

One method of using digital signatures employs public-key encryption to transmit an agreed-upon password or message, and passes that encrypted content along with the larger email. For instance, your boss could encrypt the text "I'm the boss" using his private key. When you receive the email, you could decrypt the digital signature using your boss's public key. If the decryption resulted in the "I'm the boss" message, you would know that the message did, in fact, come from your boss.

Encryption in .NET

The data encryption and security features included with .NET appear in the `System.Security.Cryptography` namespace. Most of the classes in this namespace implement various well-known encryption algorithms that have been accepted by organizations and governments as dependable encryption standards. For instance, the `DESCryptoServiceProvider` class provides features based on the Data Encryption Standard (DES) algorithm, an algorithm originally developed by IBM in the mid-1970s.

Symmetric Cryptography

Symmetric cryptography uses a single secret key to both encrypt and decrypt a block of data. Although these algorithms are often quite fast (when compared to asymmetric cryptography), the need to provide the full secret key to others to share data may make them inherently less secure. Still, for many applications, "secret key encryption" is sufficient.

The .NET Framework includes support for five symmetric encryption algorithms.

- *Advanced Encryption Standard (AES)*, a variable bit (between 128 and 256 bits) block cipher with primary support through the *AesManaged* and *AesCryptoServiceProvider* classes. This is the algorithm recommended by the United States government, replacing its older preference for DES.
- *Data Encryption Standard (DES)*, a 56-bit block cipher with primary support through the *DESCryptoServiceProvider* class. This algorithm is generally secure, but due to its small key size (smaller keys are more easily compromised), it is inappropriate for highly sensitive data.
- *RC2 (Rivest Cipher number 2)*, a 56-bit block cipher with primary support through the *RC2CryptoServiceProvider* class. Lotus originally developed the cipher for use in its Lotus Notes product. It is not excitingly secure, but for this reason, it was given more favorable export freedoms by the U.S. government.
- *Rijndael* (derived from the names of its two designers, Daemen and Rijmen), a variable bit (between 128 to 256 bits) block cipher with primary support through the *RijndaelManaged* class. It is closely related to AES algorithm, and is the most secure of the secret key algorithms provided with .NET.
- *Triple DES*, a block cipher that uses the underlying DES algorithm three times to generate a more secure result, with primary support through the *TripleDESCryptoServiceProvider* class. Although more secure than plain DES, it is still much more vulnerable than the Rijndael or AES standard.

The various "provider" classes are tools that must be used together with other cryptography classes to work properly. For instance, this sample code (based on code found in the MSDN documentation) uses the *DESCryptoServiceProvider* and *CryptoStream* classes, both members of the *System.Security.Cryptography* namespace, to jointly encrypt and decrypt a block of text.

```
using System;
using System.IO;
using System.Text;
using System.Security.Cryptography;

class CryptoMemoryStream
{
    public static void Main()
    {
        // ----- Encrypt then decrypt some text.
        DESCryptoServiceProvider key =
            new DESCryptoServiceProvider();
        byte[] encryptedVersion;
        string decryptedVersion;

        // ----- First, encrypt some text.
        encryptedVersion = Encrypt("This is a secret.", key);

        // ----- Then, decrypt it to get the original.
        decryptedVersion = Decrypt(encryptedVersion, key);
    }
```

```
public static byte[] Encrypt(string origText,
      SymmetricAlgorithm key)
{
   // ----- Uses a crytographic memory stream and a
   //       secret key provider (DES in this case)
   //       to encrypt some text.
   MemoryStream baseStream = new MemoryStream();
   CryptoStream secretStream;
   StreamWriter streamOut;
   byte[] encryptedText;

   // ----- A memory stream just shuffles data from
   //       end to end. Adding a CryptoStream to it
   //       will encrypt the data as it moves through
   //       the stream.
   secretStream = new CryptoStream(baseStream,
      key.CreateEncryptor(), CryptoStreamMode.Write);
   streamOut = new StreamWriter(secretStream);
   streamOut.WriteLine(origText);
   streamOut.Close();
   secretStream.Close();

   // ----- Move the encrypted content into a useful
   //       byte array.
   encryptedText = baseStream.ToArray();
   baseStream.Close();
   return encryptedText;
}

public static string Decrypt(byte[] encryptedText,
      SymmetricAlgorithm key)
{
   // ----- Clearly, this is the opposite of the
   //       Encrypt() function, using a stream reader
   //       instead of a writer, and the key's
   //       "decryptor" instead of its "encryptor."
   MemoryStream baseStream;
   CryptoStream secretStream;
   StreamReader streamIn;
   string origText;

   // ----- Build a stream that automatically decrypts
   //       as data is passed through it.
   baseStream = new MemoryStream(encryptedText);
   secretStream = new CryptoStream(baseStream,
      key.CreateDecryptor(), CryptoStreamMode.Read);
   streamIn = new StreamReader(secretStream);

   // ----- Move the decrypted content back to a string.
   origText = streamIn.ReadLine();
   streamIn.Close();
   secretStream.Close();
   baseStream.Close();
   return origText;
```

```
        }
    }
```

This code combines a DES encryption class with a *stream*, a common tool in .NET applications for transferring data from one state or location to another. (Streams are a primary method used to read and write files.) Streams are not too hard to use, but the code still seems a little convoluted. Why doesn't the `DESCryptoServiceProvider` class simply include `Encrypt` and `Decrypt` methods? That's my question, at least. I'm sure it has something to do with keeping the class generic for use in many data environments. Still, as chunky as this code is, it's sure a lot easier than writing the encryption code myself. And it's general enough that I could swap in one of the other secret key algorithms without making too many changes in the code.

Asymmetric Cryptography

In secret key cryptography, you can use any old key you wish to support the encryption and decryption process. As long as you keep it a secret, the content of the key itself isn't really too important. The same cannot be said, though, of *asymmetric* (public key) *cryptography*. Because separate keys are used to encrypt and decrypt the data, the private and public keys must be crafted specifically as a pair. You can't just select random public and private keys and hope that they work together.

The components used to support asymmetric cryptography include *generators* that emit public and private key pairs. Once generated, these keys can be used in your code to mask sensitive data. And due to the large key size, it's very difficult for anyone to hack into your encrypted data.

Public key encryption is notoriously slow; it takes forever and a day to encode large amounts of data using the source key. This is one of the reasons that the founding fathers didn't use public key encryption on the Declaration of Independence. Because of the sluggish performance of asymmetric encryption, many secure data systems use a combination of public-key and secret-key encryption to protect data. The initial authorization occurs with public-key processes, but once the secure channel opens, the data passed between the systems gets encrypted using faster secret-key methods.

.NET includes three public key cryptography classes for your encrypting and decrypting pleasure.

- *The Digital Signature Algorithm (DSA)*, an algorithm designed by the U.S. government for use in digital signatures, with primary support through the `DSACryptoServiceProvider` class.
- *The Elliptic Curve Digital Signature Algorithm (ECDSA)*, an alternative to DSA that uses the structure of an elliptic curve in a way that allows for smaller cryptographic keys, with primary support through the `ECDsaCng` class. A related *Elliptic Curve Diffie-Hellman* class supports interchanges between two parties that wish to use ECDSA keys.
- *The RSA algorithm* (named after its founders, Ron Rivest, Adi Shamir, and Len Adleman), an older though generally secure asymmetric algorithm, with primary support through the `RSACryptoServiceProvider` class.

We will be using asymmetric encryption in the Library Project, but not until a later chapter. Even then, I won't be getting into too much detail about how asymmetric encryption works. Although the background information on prime number generation and large number factorization is fascinating, such discussions are beyond the scope of this book.

Hashing

Although *hashing* algorithms do not give you the ability to encrypt and decrypt data at will, they are useful in supporting systems that secure and verify data content. We will perform some hashing of data in the project code for this chapter, so stay alert.

Coming up with a hashing algorithm is easy. It took the best minds of the National Security Agency and the Massachusetts Institute of Technology to come up with reliable secret-key and public-key encryption systems, but you can develop a hashing algorithm in just a few minutes. A few years ago, I wrote my own hashing algorithm that I used for years in business applications. That fact alone should prove how simple and basic they can be. Here's a hashing algorithm I just made up while I was sitting here.

```
public long HashSomeText(string origText)
{
    // ----- Create a hash value from some data.
    long hashValue = 0L;

    for (int counter = 0;
        counter <= origText.Length - 1; counter++)
    {
        hashValue += (long)(char)origText[counter];
        if (hashValue > (long.MaxValue * 0.9))
            hashValue /= 2;
    }
    return hashValue;
}
```

In the code, I just add up the Unicode values of each character in the text string, and return the result. I do a check in the loop to make sure I don't exceed ninety percent of the maximum *long* value; I don't want to overflow the *hashValue* variable and generate an error. Although *HashSomeText* does generate a hashed representation of the input data, it also has some deficiencies.

- It's pretty easy to guess from the hash value whether the incoming content was short or long. Shorter content will usually generate small numbers, and larger output values tend to indicate longer input content.
- It's not very sensitive to some types of content changes. For instance, if you rearrange several characters in the content, it probably won't impact the hash value. Changing a character will impact the value, but if you change one character from *A* to *B* and another nearby letter from *T* to *S*, the hash value will remain unchanged.
- The shorter the content, the greater the chance that two inputs will generate the same hash value.

Perhaps you want something a little more robust. If so, .NET includes several hashing tools.

- *Hash-based Message Authentication Code* (HMAC) is calculated using the Secure Hash Algorithm Number 1 (SHA-1) hash function, made available through the *HMACSHA1* class. It uses a 160-bit hash code. There are no specific restrictions on the length of the secret key used in the calculation. Although suitable for low-risk situations, the SHA-1 algorithm is susceptible to attack.
- *Message Authentication Code* (MAC) is calculated using the Triple-DES secret key algorithms (described earlier), made available through the *MACTripleDES* class. The secret key used in the calculation is either 16 or 24 bytes long, and the generated value is 8 bytes in length.
- *Message-Digest algorithm number 5* (MD5) hash calculation, made available through the *MD5CryptoServiceProvider* class. MD5 is yet another super-secret algorithm designed by Ron Rivest (that guy is amazing), but it has been shown to contain some flaws that could make it an encoding security risk. The resultant hash value is 128 bits long.
- *RIPEMD-160* was designed by a team in the European Union to replace MD5 and similar hashes. Primary support is through the *RIPEMD160Managed* class.
- Like the *HMACSHA1* class, the *SHA1Managed* class computes a hash value using the SHA-1 hash function. However, it is written using .NET managed code only. *HMACSHA1* and some of the other

cryptographic features in .NET are simply wrappers around the older *Cryptography API* (CAPI), a pre-.NET DLL. *SHA1Managed* uses a 160-bit hash code.

- Three other classes—*SHA256Managed*, *SHA384Managed*, and *SHA512Managed*—are similar to the *SHA1Managed* class, but use 256-bit, 384-bit, and 512-bit hash codes, respectively.

Each of these algorithms uses a secret key that must be included each time the hash is generated against the same set of input data. As long as the input data is unchanged, and the secret key is the same, the resultant hash value will also remain unchanged. By design, even the smallest change in the input data generates major changes in the output hash value.

The SecureString Class

It's amazing that with all of these advanced tools, programmers still spend much of their time building and parsing string data. Fortunately, .NET includes a plethora of useful string manipulation tools. Unfortunately, they aren't very secure. You may recall that .NET strings are immutable; once created, they are never changed. Eventually, they will be destroyed by the garbage collection process. But until then, they sit around in memory, just waiting to be scanned by some hacker-designed code. Internally, string data is stored as plain text, so if someone can get to the memory, a copy of the content can be extracted for nefarious purposes.

SecureString to the rescue! The *System.Security.SecureString* class lets you store strings and get them back, but internally, the content of the string is encrypted. If anyone obtained the internal content of a class instance, it would look like gibberish.

Summary

When you write a business application for some organization or department, you might not care all that much about the security and integrity of the data managed by the software tool. As long as the data gets from the user's fingertips to the database and back, it's all hunky-dory.

Although such views may work for many applications, there are systems and users that expect much more in the way of security. Sometimes you need to ensure the security and integrity of the data managed by the application, especially if it will leave the confines of your software or associated database. The security features found in the *System.Security.Cryptography* namespace provide a fun variety of data hiding and restoration options.

Project

This chapter will see the following security-focused features added to the Library Project.

- The login form, which authenticates librarians and other administrative users
- Security group and user management forms
- A function that encrypts a user-supplied password
- Activation of some application features that depend on user authentication

Project Access
Load the "Chapter 11 (Before) Code" project, either through the New Project templates or by accessing the project directly from the installation directory. To see the code in its final form, load "Chapter 11 (After) Code" instead.

Authentication Support

Since all of the library's data is stored in a SQL Server database, we already use either Windows or SQL Server security to restrict access to the data itself. But once we connect to the database, we will use a custom authentication system to enable and disable features in the application. It's there that we'll put some of the .NET cryptography features into use.

Before adding the interesting code, we need to add some global variables that support security throughout the application. All of the global elements appear in the *General.cs* file, within the *General* class.

Insert Snippet

Insert Chapter 11, Snippet Item 1.

```
public static long LoggedInUserID;
public static string LoggedInUserName;
public static long LoggedInGroupID;
public static bool[] SecurityProfile =
    new bool[(int)MaxLibrarySecurity + 1];
```

Although we added it in a previous step, the *LibrarySecurity* enumeration is an important part of the security system. Its elements match those found in the *Activity* table in the Library database. Each enumeration value matches one element in the *SecurityProfile* array that we just added to the code.

```
public enum LibrarySecurity : int
{
    ManageAuthors = 1,
    ManageAuthorTypes = 2,
    ...more here...
    ManagePatronGroups = 22,
    ViewAdminPatronMessages = 23
}
public const LibrarySecurity MaxLibrarySecurity =
    LibrarySecurity.ViewAdminPatronMessages;
```

All of the newly added global variables store identity information for the active administrator. When a patron is the active user, the program sets all of these values to their default states. Since this should be done when the program first begins, we'll add an *InitializeSystem* routine that is called on startup. It also appears in the *General* class.

Insert Snippet

Insert Chapter 11, Snippet Item 2.

```
public static void InitializeSystem()
{
    // ----- Initialize global variables here.

    // ----- Clear security-related values.
    LoggedInUserID = -1L;
    LoggedInUserName = "";
    LoggedInGroupID = -1L;

    for (int counter = 1; counter <=
            (int)MaxLibrarySecurity; counter++)
        SecurityProfile[counter] = false;
}
```

(The *SecurityProfile* array has items that range from *0* to *MaxLibrarySecurity*, but the loop at the end of this code starts from element *1*. Because the *Activity* table starts its counting at *1*, I decided to just skip element *0*.) The *InitializeSystem* method is called from the *Main* startup procedure in the *Program.cs* file, just before the check for the correct database version. Let's add that code now.

Insert Snippet

Insert Chapter 11, Snippet Item 3.

```
// ----- Perform general initialization.
InitializeSystem();
```

Each time an administrator tries to use the system, and each time the administrator logs off and returns the program to patron mode, all of the security-related global variables must be reset. This is done in the *ReprocessSecuritySet* method, added to the *General* class.

Insert Snippet

Insert Chapter 11, Snippet Item 4.

```
public static void ReprocessSecuritySet()
{
    // ----- Reload in the security set for the current user.
    //       If no user is logged in, clear all settings.
    string sqlText;
    DataCommand sqlRun;
    DataTable dbInfo = null;

    // ----- Clear out the existing items.
    for (int counter = 1; counter <=
            (int)MaxLibrarySecurity; counter++)
        SecurityProfile[counter] = false;

    // ----- Exit if there is no user logged in.
    if ((LoggedInUserID == -1L) | (LoggedInGroupID == -1L))
        return;

    try
    {
        // ----- Load in the security elements for this user.
        sqlText = "SELECT ActivityID FROM GroupActivity " +
            "WHERE GroupID = @RecordID";
        sqlRun = new DataCommand(sqlText);
        sqlRun.AddLong("RecordID", LoggedInGroupID);
        dbInfo = CreateDataTable(sqlRun);
        foreach (DataRow dbRow in dbInfo.Rows)
            SecurityProfile[DBGetLong(dbRow["ActivityID"])] = true;
    }
    catch (Exception ex)
    {
        // ----- Some database-related error.
        GeneralError("ReprocessSecuritySet", ex);

        // ----- Un-login the administrator through recursion.
        LoggedInUserID = -1L;
        LoggedInGroupID = -1L;
        ReprocessSecuritySet();
```

```
    }
    finally
    {
        if (dbInfo != null)
            dbInfo.Dispose();
        dbInfo = null;
    }
}
```

This routine uses code built in Chapter 10 and other earlier chapters. When it detects an authorized user (the *LoggedInUserID* variable), it retrieves a *DataTable* object containing that user's allowed security features, and stores those settings in the *SecurityProfile* array. Once it is loaded, any array element that is *true* represents an application feature that the administrator is authorized to use. I'll discuss the *GroupActivity* table a little later in this chapter.

If a database error occurs during processing, the code resets everything to patron mode, making a *recursive* call to *ReprocessSecuritySet* to clear the *SecurityProfile* array. (Recursion occurs when a routine directly or indirectly calls itself.)

Encrypting Passwords

The entire content of this chapter has been building to this very moment, the section where I reveal the winner of the next presidential election. Wait! Even better than that, I will use one of the .NET hashing methods to encrypt an administrator-supplied password before storing it in the database. One of the tables in the Library database, the *UserName* table, stores the basic security profile for each librarian or other administrative user, including a password. Since anyone who can get into the database will be able to see the passwords stored in this table, we will encrypt them to make them a little less tempting. (For patrons simply using the program, there shouldn't be any direct access to the database apart from the application, but you never know about those frisky patrons.)

To keep things secure, we'll scramble the user-entered password, using it to generate a hash value, and store the hash value in the database's password field for the user. Later, when an administrative user wants to gain access to enhanced features, the program will again convert the entered password into a hash value, and compare that value to the on-record hashed password.

Each .NET hashing function depends on a secret code. Since the Library Project will only perform a unidirectional encryption, and it will never ask any other program to re-encrypt the password, we'll just use the user's login name as the secret key. I decided to use the *HMACSHA1* hashing class, mostly for its ability to accept a variable-size key. Although it is reported to have security issues, that shouldn't be a problem for the way that we're using it. I mean, if someone actually got into the database trying to decrypt the passwords stored in the *UserName* table, she would already have full access to everything in the Library system.

Of course, the encryption code requires references to the *System.Security.Cryptography* namespace. We'll also need a reference to *System.Text* for some of the support code. Add the relevant *using* directives to the top of the *General.cs* code file.

Insert Snippet
Insert Chapter 11, Snippet Item 5.

```
using System.Text;
using System.Security.Cryptography;
```

The actual jumbling of the password occurs in the *EncryptPassword* routine, making its entrance in the *General* class.

```
public static string EncryptPassword(
    string loginID, string passwordText)
{
    // ----- Given a username and a password, encrypt the
    //       password so that it is not easy to decrypt.
    //       There is no limit on password length since
    //       it is going to be hashed anyway.
    HMACSHA1 hashingFunction;
    byte[] secretKey;
    byte[] hashValue;
    string result = "";

    // ----- Prepare the secret key. Force it to uppercase
    //       for consistency, and then stuff it in a byte array.
    secretKey = (new UnicodeEncoding()).GetBytes(
        loginID.ToUpper());

    // ----- Create the hashing component using Managed SHA-1.
    hashingFunction = new HMACSHA1(secretKey, true);

    // ----- Calculate the hash value. One simple line of code.
    hashValue = hashingFunction.ComputeHash(
        (new UnicodeEncoding()).GetBytes(passwordText));

    // ----- The hash value is ready, but I like things in
    //       plain text when possible. Let's convert it to a
    //       long hex string.
    for (int counter = 0;
         counter < hashValue.Length; counter++)
        result += Convert.ToString(
            hashValue[counter], 16).ToUpper();

    // ----- Stored passwords are limited to 20 characters.
    if (result.Length > 20)
        result = result.Substring(0, 20);
    return result;
}
```

The primary methods of interacting with the security providers in .NET are via a byte array or a stream. I opted to use the byte array method, converting the incoming string values through the *UnicodeEncoding* object's *GetBytes* method. Once stored as a byte array, I pass the login ID and password as arguments to the *HMACSHA1* class's features.

Although I could store the output of the *ComputeHash* method directly in a database field, I decided to convert the result into readable ASCII characters so that things wouldn't look all weird when I issued SQL statements against the *UserName* table. My conversion is basic: convert each byte into its printable hexadecimal equivalent using the *Convert.ToString* method, passing *16* as the second argument to indicate hexadecimal (16-bit) format. Then just string the results together. The *UserName.Password* database field holds only twenty characters, so I chop off anything longer.

Just to make sure that this algorithm generates reasonable output, I called *EncryptPassword* with a few different inputs.

```
MessageBox.Show(string.Format(
    "Alice/none:     {0}\r\n" +
    "Alice/password: {1}\r\n" +
    "Bob/none:       {2}\r\n" +
    "Bob/password:   {3}",
    EncryptPassword("Alice", ""),
    EncryptPassword("Alice", "password"),
    EncryptPassword("Bob", ""),
    EncryptPassword("Bob", "password")));
```

This code generates the following message.

```
Alice/none:     6570FC214A797C023F40
Alice/password: 4AEC6C914C65D88BD082
Bob/none:       7F544120E3AB9FB48C32
Bob/password:   274A56F047293EA0B97E
```

Undoing Some Previous Changes

The *UserName*, *GroupName*, and *GroupActivity* tables in the database define the security profiles for each administrative user. Every user (a record in *UserName*) is part of one security group (a *GroupName* record). Each group includes access to zero or more enhanced application features; the *GroupActivity* table identifies which features match up to each security group record.

To manage these tables, we need to add property forms that edit the fields of a single database record. We already wrote some of the code a while back. Chapter 8 defined the *BaseCodeForm.cs* file, a template for forms that edit single database records. That same chapter introduced the *ListEditRecords.cs* file, the parent form that displays a listing of already-defined database records. Our record editors for both users and security groups will use the features in these two existing forms.

> **Note**
> Your friendly author, Tim Patrick, is about to rant on and on about something that really bugs him.
> Why not join him in this rant?

When we designed the code for *BaseCodeForm.cs* in Chapter 8, my goal was to show you the *abstract* class and member features included with Visual C#. They are pretty useful features. Unfortunately, they just don't mix well with user interface elements, and here's why: Visual Studio actually creates instances of your forms at design time so that you can interact with them inside the editor. If you were to delve into the source code for, say, a *TextBox* control, you would find special code that deals with design-time presentation of the control. Interesting? Yes. Flexible? Yes. Perfect in all cases? No.

The problem—and *problem* is putting it mildly—is that Visual Studio won't (actually, can't) create an instance of a class defined as *abstract*. That's because you *must inherit it through another class first before you create instances*. What does this mean to you? It means that if you try to design a form that inherits from an *abstract* form template, Visual Studio will not present the user interface portion of the form for your editing enjoyment. You can still access the source code of the form, and if this is how you want to design the inherited form, that's fine. But you and I are looking for simplicity in programming, and we plunked down good money or even no money for Visual Studio, so we're certainly going to use its visual tools to edit our visual forms.

The upshot of all this ranting—and I'm almost at the end of my rant, but you can keep on going if you want—is that we must change the *BaseCodeForm.cs* file, removing the *abstract* keywords, and making other appropriate adjustments. I've already made the changes to both the before and after templates of the Chapter 11 code.

This is part of the reality of programming in a complex system such as Visual Studio. Sometimes, even after you have done all your research and carefully mapped out the application features and structure, you run into some designer- or compiler-specific behavior that forces you to make some change. Once you learn to avoid the major issues, you find that it doesn't happen too often. But when it does occur, it can be a great time to rant.

Managing Security Groups

So, back to our *GroupName* record editor. I haven't added it to the project yet, so let's add it now. Because it will inherit from another form in the project, we have to allow Visual Studio to instantiate the base form by first compiling the application. This is easily done through the Build→Build Library menu command.

To create the new form, select the Project→Add Windows Form menu command. When the Add New Item window appears, select Windows Forms from the Categories list, followed by Inherited Form from the Templates list. Enter *GroupName.cs* in the Name field, and then click the Add button. When the Inheritance Picker form appears (see Figure 11-1), select BaseCodeForm from the list, and click OK. The new *GroupName* form appears, but it look remarkably like the *BaseCodeForm* form.

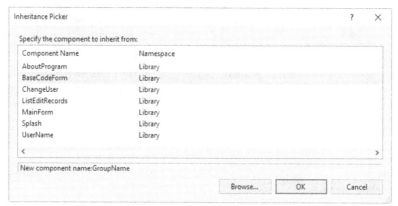

Figure 11-1. Who says you can't pick your own relatives?

Add two *Label* controls, one *TextBox* control, two *Button* controls, and a *CheckedListBox* control from the toolbox, and set their properties using the following settings.

Control type	Property settings
Label	(Name): LabelFullName AutoSize: True Location: 8, 10 Text: &Security Group Name:
TextBox	(Name): RecordFullName Location: 128, 8 MaxLength: 50 Size: 248, 20
Label	(Name): LabelActivity AutoSize: True Location: 8, 34 Text: &Allowed Activities:
CheckedListBox	(Name): ActivityList

Control type	Property settings
	Location: 128, 32
	Size: 248, 244
Button	(Name): ActOK
	Location: 208, 288
	Size: 80, 24
	Text: OK
Button	(Name): ActCancel
	DialogResult: Cancel
	Location: 296, 288
	Size: 80, 24
	Text: Cancel
Form (GroupName)	(Name): GroupName
	AcceptButton: ActOK
	CancelButton: ActCancel
	Size: 402, 358
	Text: Edit Security Group

Don't forget to adjust the tab order of the controls on the form.

Let's add the code all at once. Add the next code snippet to the class source code body.

> **Insert Snippet**
> Insert Chapter 11, Snippet Item 7.

Hey, that's over 400 lines of source code. Good typing. We also need to add the event handler hookups to the end of the *InitializeComponent* method.

> **Insert Snippet**
> Insert Chapter 11, Snippet Item 8.

Finally, add a using directive to the top of the file to support some shortcuts included in the code.

> **Insert Snippet**
> Insert Chapter 11, Snippet Item 9.

```
using static Library.General;
```

The class includes two private members. *ActiveID* holds the ID number of the currently displayed *GroupName* database record, or −1 when editing new records. The *StartingOver* flag is a little more interesting. Remember that we are using a shared summary form to display all of the already-entered *GroupName* records. To allow this generic form, *ListEditRecords.cs*, to work with the different record editors, we pass an instance of the detail form (*GroupName.cs* in this case) to the summary form.

```
(new ListEditRecords()).ManageRecords(new GroupName());
```

Within the *ListEditRecords* form's code, the instance of *GroupName* is used over and over, each time the user wants to add or edit a *GroupName* database record. If the user edits one record, and then tries to edit another, the leftovers from the first record will still be in the detail form's fields. Therefore, we will have to clear them each time we add or edit a different record. The *StartingOver* flag helps with that process by resetting the focus to the first detail form field in the form's *Activated* event.

```
private void GroupName_Activated(object sender, EventArgs e)
{
    // ----- Return the focus to the main field.
```

```
    if (StartingOver)
        RecordFullName.Focus();
    StartingOver = false;
}
```

The related *PrepareFormFields* private method does the actual clearing and storing of data with each new Add or Edit call. For new records, it simply clears all entered data on the form. When editing an existing record, it retrieves the relevant data from the database, and stores saved values in the various on-form fields. The following statements display the stored group name in the *RecordFullName* field, a *TextBox* control.

```
sqlText = "SELECT FullName FROM GroupName " +
    "WHERE ID = @RecordID";
sqlRun = new DataCommand(sqlText);
sqlRun.AddLong("RecordID", ActiveID);
RecordFullName.Text = DBGetText(ExecuteSQLReturn(sqlRun));
```

Most of the routines in the *GroupName* form provide simple overrides for base members of the *BaseCodeForm* class. The *CanUserAdd* method, which simply returns *false* in the base class, includes actual logic in the inherited class. It uses the *SecurityProfile* array we added earlier to determine whether the current user is allowed to add group records.

```
public override bool CanUserAdd()
{
    // ----- Check the user for security access: add.
    return SecurityProfile[(int)LibrarySecurity.ManageGroups];
}
```

If you look through the added code, you'll find overrides for all of the *BaseCodeForm* members except for the *UsesSearch* and *SearchForRecord* methods. The derived class accepts the default action for these two members.

The user adds, edits, and deletes group name records through the *AddRecord*, *EditRecord*, and *DeleteRecord* overrides, respectively, each called by code in the *ListEditRecords* form. Here's the code for *EditRecord*.

```
public override long EditRecord(long recordID)
{
    // ----- Edit an existing record.
    ActiveID = recordID;
    PrepareFormFields();
    this.ShowDialog();
    if (this.DialogResult == DialogResult.OK)
        return ActiveID;
    else
        return -1L;
}
```

After storing the ID of the record to edit in the *ActiveID* private field, the code loads the data through the *PrepareFormFields* method, and prompts the user to edit the record with the *this.ShowDialog* call. The form sticks around until some code or control sets the form's *DialogResult* property. This is done in the *ActOK_Click* event, and also through the *ActCancel* button's *DialogResult* property, which Visual C# will assign to the form automatically when the user clicks the *ActCancel* button.

The *AddRecord* routine is just like *EditRecord*, but it assigns −1 to the *ActiveID* member to flag a new record. The *DeleteRecord* routine is more involved, and uses some of the database code we wrote in the last chapter.

```
public override bool DeleteRecord(long recordID)
{
    // ----- The user wants to delete the record.
    string sqlText;
    DataCommand sqlRun;
    LibraryTransaction transInfo = null;

    // ----- Confirm with the user.
    if (MessageBox.Show(
        "Do you really wish to delete the security group?",
        ProgramTitle, MessageBoxButtons.YesNo,
        MessageBoxIcon.Question) != DialogResult.Yes)
        return false;

    // ----- Make sure this record is not in use.
    sqlText = "SELECT COUNT(*) FROM UserName " +
        "WHERE GroupID = @RecordID";
    sqlRun = new DataCommand(sqlText);
    sqlRun.AddLong("RecordID", recordID);
    try
    {
        if (DBGetInteger(ExecuteSQLReturn(sqlRun)) > 0)
        {
            MessageBox.Show("You cannot delete this " +
                "record because it is in use.",
                ProgramTitle, MessageBoxButtons.OK,
                MessageBoxIcon.Exclamation);
            return false;
        }
    }
    catch (Exception ex)
    {
        GeneralError("GroupName.DeleteRecord.Check", ex);
        return false;
    }

    // ----- Delete the record.
    try
    {
        transInfo = TransactionBegin();

        sqlText = "DELETE FROM GroupActivity " +
            "WHERE GroupID = @RecordID";
        sqlRun = new DataCommand(sqlText);
        sqlRun.AddLong("RecordID", recordID);
        ExecuteSQL(sqlRun, transInfo);

        sqlText = "DELETE FROM GroupName " +
            "WHERE ID = @RecordID";
        sqlRun = new DataCommand(sqlText);
        sqlRun.AddLong("RecordID", recordID);
        ExecuteSQL(sqlRun, transInfo);
```

```
        TransactionCommit(transInfo);
    }
    catch (Exception ex)
    {
        if (transInfo != null)
            TransactionRollback(transInfo);
        GeneralError("GroupName.DeleteRecord.Delete", ex);
        return false;
    }

    // ----- Success.
    return true;
}
```

After confirming the delete with the user, a quick check determines whether the group is still being used somewhere in the *UserName* table. If everything checks out fine, the record is deleted using a SQL *DELETE* statement. Since we need to delete data in two tables, I wrapped it all up in a transaction. If an error does occur, the error handler at the end of the block will roll back the transaction through *TransactionRollback*.

Database Integrity Warning

If you have a background in database development, you have already seen the flaw in the delete code. Although I take the time to verify that the record is not in use before deleting it, it's possible that some other user will use it between the time I check the record's use and the time when I actually delete it. Based on the code and database configuration I've presented so far, it would indeed be an issue. When I designed this system, I expected that a single librarian would manage administrative tasks such as this, so I didn't worry about such conflicts and "race conditions."

If you are concerned about the potential for deleting in-use records through code like this, you can enable *referential integrity* on the relationships in the database. I established a relationship between the *GroupName.ID* and *UserName.GroupID* fields, but it was for informational purposes only. You can reconfigure this relationship to have SQL Server enforce the relationship between the tables. If you do this, it will not be possible to delete an in-use record; an error will occur in the program when you attempt it. That sounds good, and it is, but an overuse of referential integrity can slow down your data access. I will leave this configuration choice up to you.

When the user is done making changes to the record, a click on the OK button pushes the data back out to the database. The *ActOK_Click* event handler verifies the data, and then saves it.

```
if (ValidateFormData() == false)
    return;
if (SaveFormData() == false)
    return;
this.DialogResult = DialogResult.OK;
```

The *ValidateFormData* method does some simple checks for valid data, such as requiring that the user enter the security group name, and that it is unique. If everything looks good, the *SaveFormData* routine builds SQL statements that save the data. Here's the core update code from that routine, with the error handling and transaction code removed so it's easier to read on this page.

```
// ----- Save the data.
if (ActiveID == -1L)
{
    // ----- Create a new entry.
    sqlText = "INSERT INTO GroupName (FullName) " +
```

```
            "OUTPUT INSERTED.ID VALUES (@NewName)";
        sqlRun = new DataCommand(sqlText);
        sqlRun.AddText("NewName", RecordFullName.Text.Trim());
        newID = DBGetLong(ExecuteSQLReturn(sqlRun, transInfo));
    }
    else
    {
        // ----- Update the existing entry.
        newID = ActiveID;
        sqlText = "UPDATE GroupName SET FullName = @NewName " +
            "WHERE ID = @RecordID";
        sqlRun = new DataCommand(sqlText);
        sqlRun.AddText("NewName", RecordFullName.Text.Trim());
        sqlRun.AddLong("RecordID", ActiveID);
        ExecuteSQL(sqlRun, transInfo);
    }

    // ----- Clear any existing security settings.
    sqlText = "DELETE FROM GroupActivity " +
        "WHERE GroupID = @RecordID";
    sqlRun = new DataCommand(sqlText);
    sqlRun.AddLong("RecordID", newID);
    ExecuteSQL(sqlRun, transInfo);

    // ----- Save the selected security settings.
    foreach (ListItemData itemChecked
        in ActivityList.CheckedItems)
    {
        sqlText = "INSERT INTO GroupActivity (GroupID, " +
            "ActivityID) VALUES (@NewGroup, @NewActivity)";
        sqlRun = new DataCommand(sqlText);
        sqlRun.AddLong("NewGroup", newID);
        sqlRun.AddLong("NewActivity", itemChecked.ItemData);
        ExecuteSQL(sqlRun, transInfo);
    }

    // ----- This change may affect this user.
    if (LoggedInGroupID == newID)
        ReprocessSecuritySet();

    // ----- Success.
    ActiveID = newID;
    return true;
```

Be sure to check out the other routines in the *GroupName* form; they exist to support and enhance the user experience.

Managing Users

We also need a form to manage records in the *UserName* table. Since the code for that form generally follows what we've already seen in the *GroupName* form, I won't bore you with the details. I've already added *UserName.cs* to your project, but to prevent bugs in your code while you were in the middle of development, I disabled it (at least in the Before version of the code). To enable it, select the file in the Solution Explorer window. Then in the Properties panel, change the Build Action property from None to

Compile. Visual Studio will hopefully change its subordinate *UserName.Designer.cs* file to Compile as well, but if it doesn't, don't forgot to change that file also.

The only interesting code in this form that is somewhat different from the `GroupName` form is the handling of the password. To keep things as secure as possible, I don't actually load the saved password into the on-form password field. It wouldn't do any good anyway since I've stored a hashed version in the database.

Since I use the user's Login ID as the secret key when encrypting the password, I must regenerate the password if the user ever changes the Login ID. The private `OrigLoginID` field keeps a copy of the Login ID when the form first opens, and checks for any changes when resaving the record. If changes occur, it regenerates the password.

```
passwordResult = EncryptPassword(RecordLoginID.Text.Trim(),
    RecordPassword.Text.Trim());
```

Using the `UserName` and `GroupName` editing forms requires some additional code in the main form. Add this code to the body of the `MainForm` class.

Insert Snippet
Insert Chapter 11, Snippet Item 10.

Also add some event hook-up code to the `InitializeComponent` method in that class.

Insert Snippet
Insert Chapter 11, Snippet Item 11.

The `AdminLinkGroups` and `AdminLinkUsers` controls are web-style link labels that we added to the program a few chapters back. The `LinkClicked` event—not the `Click` event—triggers the display of the code editor. Here's the code to edit the `GroupName` table.

```
private void AdminLinkGroups_LinkClicked(object sender,
    LinkLabelLinkClickedEventArgs e)
{
    // ----- Let the user edit the list of security groups.
    if (SecurityProfile[
        (int)LibrarySecurity.ManageGroups] == false)
    {
        MessageBox.Show(NotAuthorizedMessage, ProgramTitle,
            MessageBoxButtons.OK, MessageBoxIcon.Exclamation);
        return;
    }

    // ----- Edit the records.
    (new ListEditRecords()).ManageRecords(new GroupName());
}
```

Per-User Experience

Now that we have all of the security support code added to the project, we can start using those features to change the application experience for patrons and administrators. It's not polite to tempt people with immense power, so it's best to hide those features that are not accessible to the lowly and inherently less powerful patron users.

First, let's provide the power of differentiation by adding the administrative login form, shown in Figure 11-2.

Figure 11-2. The official Library Project administrative login form

I've already added the *ChangeUser.cs* form to the project. If you're using the Before version of this chapter's code, select *ChangeUser.cs* in the Solution Explorer. Then change its Build Action property (in the Properties panel) from None to Compile, just as you did with the *UserName.cs* form. Confirm that its subordinate *ChangeUser.Designer.cs* file also had its Build Action changed to Compile.

All of the hard work occurs in the form's `ActOK_Click` event handler. If the user selects the Return to Patron Mode option, all security values are cleared, and the main form hides most features (through code added later).

```
LoggedInUserID = -1L;
LoggedInUserName = "";
LoggedInGroupID = -1L;
ReprocessSecuritySet();
```

This form gets connected into the application through the main form's `ActLogin_Click` event. Open up the *MainForm.cs* file, double-click on the Login button in the upper-right corner, and add the following code to the `Click` event template that appears.

Insert Snippet
Insert Chapter 11, Snippet Item 12.

```
// ----- Prompt the user for patron or administrative mode.
ShowLoginForm();
```

That wasn't much code. Add the *ShowLoginForm* method's code to the form as well.

Insert Snippet
Insert Chapter 11, Snippet Item 13.

```
private void ShowLoginForm()
{
    // ----- Prompt the user for patron or
    //       administrative mode.
    DialogResult userChoice;

    // ----- Prompt the user.
    userChoice = (new ChangeUser()).ShowDialog();
    if (userChoice == DialogResult.OK)
        UpdateDisplayForUser();
}
```

Let's also enable the F12 key to act as a login trigger. Add the following code to the `switch` statement in the *MainForm_KeyDown* event handler.

```
case Keys.F12:
    // ----- Prompt the user for patron or administrative mode.
    ShowLoginForm();
    e.Handled = true;
    break;
```

The *ShowLoginForm* routine calls another method, *UpdateDisplayForUser*, which hides and shows various display elements on the main form based on the security profile of the current user. Add it to the *MainForm* class code. I won't show the code here, but basically it looks at the *LoggedInUserID* variable, and if it is set to −1, it hides all the controls for advanced features.

Currently, when you run the application, all the advanced features appear, even though no administrator has supplied an ID or password. Calling *UpdateDisplayForUser* when the main form first appears solves that problem. Add the following code to the end of the *MainForm_Load* method.

```
// ----- Prepare for a patron user.
UpdateDisplayForUser();
```

The last update (five updates, actually) involves limiting the major sections of the form to just authorized administrators. For instance, only administrators who are authorized to run reports should be able to access the reporting panel on the main form. Locate the *TaskReports* method in the main form, and find the line that displays the panel.

```
PanelReports.Visible = true;
```

Replace this line with the following code.

```
if (SecurityProfile[(int)LibrarySecurity.RunReports])
    PanelReports.Visible = true;
```

We need to do the same thing in the *TaskCheckOut*, *TaskCheckIn*, *TaskAdmin*, and *TaskProcess* methods. In each case, look for the following line.

```
Panel???.Visible = true;
```

Replace each line with code that checks the security settings before showing the panel.

- Use Snippet 18 for *TaskCheckOut*.
- Use Snippet 19 for *TaskCheckIn*.
- Use Snippet 20 for *TaskAdmin*.
- Use Snippet 21 for *TaskProcess*.

Run the program and you'll see that it's starting to look like a real application. If you want access to the enhanced features, try a Login ID of "admin" with no password. You can change that through the *UserName* form if you want!

Since we have a way to secure access to the data and features of the Library Project, let's move to the next chapter and start focusing on the data, the focal point of any business application.

Chapter 12

Overloads and Extensions

Do you ever wish you could do things beyond what people were designed to do? Like flying? We all dream about it, but we can't do it without several hundred pounds of jet fuel. Or what about bending steel in our bare hands? Does that sound like anyone you know? Then there's breathing underwater, doing long division in your head, speaking a foreign language fluently without much study, and having a successful career as an author of popular computer books. Ah, one can dream.

It's not that we want to do all of these things, but once in a while it would be nice to be *slightly enhanced* with the ability to do one or two of the things that are beyond our natural abilities. Unfortunately, it doesn't work for humans very often, but could it work for .NET operators?

You probably didn't even know that the humble C# addition operator (+) had dreams of flying, or of speaking Hungarian, or of bending steel. Well, operators are people, too. And now their dreams can be fulfilled because Visual C# supports *operator overloading*.

This chapter will show how you can direct the body-building enhancement process for the various Visual C# operators. I'll also introduce *extension methods*, which let you similarly enhance classes, even if you don't have access to the original source code for those classes.

What Is Operator Overloading?

Operator overloading allows your code to enhance the basic C# operators, and endow them with abilities not previously granted to them by the compiler. Overloading doesn't change the syntax used when employing operators, but it does change the types of objects that each operator can manage. For instance, the multiplication operator (*) normally interacts only with numbers, but you can augment it to work with your own custom *Bumblebee* class.

```
Bumblebee swarm;
Bumblebee oneBumblebee = new Bumblebee();
Bumblebee twoBumblebee = new Bumblebee();
swarm = oneBumblebee * twoBumblebee;
```

The meaning you apply to the overloaded operator is up to you. Although you would normally want to retain the additive nature of the addition operator when overloading it, you don't have to. In fact, you could overload the addition operator so that it subtracts one value from another. But I'd fire you if you did that working for me. Just so you know.

All operator overloading features tie directly to one or more of your classes. Overloaded features look curiously like standard function members, and appear as members of your classes.

Visual C# includes two types of operators: *unary* and *binary*, defined based on the number of operands recognized by the operator. (There is a single "ternary" operator, one with three operands, but it doesn't participate in operator overloading.) Unary operators accept a single operand, which always appears to the right of the operator name or symbol. The logical ! ("not") operator is a unary operator.

```
oppositeValue = !originalValue;
```

Binary operators accept two operands, one on each side of the operator. The multiplication operator is a binary operator.

```
ten = two * five;
```

The nature of an operator is that once it has done its work, the operator and its input operand(s) are, in effect, fully replaced by the calculated result. The expression "10/5" is replaced by the calculated "2" result, and this result is used to complete whatever statement or expression the original operation appeared in. It works just like a function.

```
// ----- These two lines (probably) place the same
//       calculated result in theAnswer.
theAnswer = 2 * 5;
theAnswer = DoubleIt(5);
```

To get ready for operator overloading, alter your mind to see operators as functions. Look past the confines of your operator universe, and open yourself to the truth that operators and functions are one. If you've ever programmed in LISP, I truly feel sorry for you. But you also already understand operators as functions. In LISP, everything is a function. To multiply two numbers together in LISP, you use "prefix" syntax, where the operator name comes first. The expression "seven times three" uses this syntax.

```
(* 7 3)
```

Once complete, the entire parenthesized expression is replaced, function-like, by its answer.

```
(+ 2 (* 7 3))
```

This slightly more complex LISP function reduces to a simpler form after the multiplication operator does its work.

```
(+ 2 21)
```

This in turn gets replaced with the result of the addition operator.

```
23
```

Defining overloaded operators in Visual C# is somewhat similar. If you were to translate the definition of integer multiplication into C# function-ese, it might look like this.

```
public static int *(int firstOperand, int secondOperand)
{
}
```

The operator (*) becomes a function name, with operands playing the role of function parameters, ultimately generating a value exposed through the function's return value. Although intrinsic operators aren't defined as functions in this way in Visual C#, overloads of those operators are.

To overload the multiplication operator in our imaginary *Bumblebee* class, we use the *operator* keyword to define a multiplication function for operands of the *Bumblebee* class.

```
partial class Bumblebee
{
```

```
public static Bumblebee operator *(
     Bumblebee operand1, Bumblebee operand2)
{
   // ----- Multiply two bumblebees together.
   Bumblebee finalResult = new Bumblebee();

   // ----- Add special multiplication code here, then...
   return finalResult;
}
}
```

Now, when you multiply two *Bumblebee* instances together with the multiplication operator, Visual C# recognizes the "operand1 * operand2" pattern as matching a multiplication operator overload with two *Bumblebee* arguments, and calls this class-based *operator* function to get the result.

All *operator* declarations must include the *public* and *static* keywords. If they weren't static, Visual C# would be required to create an extra instance of the class just to access the operator overload code, and that wouldn't be very efficient.

What Can You Overload?

You can overload pretty much any of Visual C#'s standard operators, plus a few other features. This section describes each overloadable operator, grouped by general type. Each section includes a table of operators. To overload an operator in a class, use the name in the Operator column as the function name. If there were an operator named *XX*, the matching *operator* statement would be as follows.

```
public static ReturnType operator XX(...)
{
}
```

Mathematical Operators

Visual C# defines nine mathematical or pseudo-mathematical operators. In their traditional forms, they all manipulate numbers, although one of them (+) does double duty concatenating strings.

Two of the operators, plus (+) and minus (–), are both unary and binary operators. The minus sign (–) works as a unary negation operator (as in "−5") and as a binary subtraction operator (the common "5 - 2" syntax). When overloading these operators, the difference lies in the number of arguments included in the argument signature.

```
public static SomeClass operator -(
     SomeClass operand1, SomeClass operand2)
{
   // ----- This is the binary subtraction version.
}

public static SomeClass operator -(operand1 As SomeClass)
{
   // ----- This is the unary negation version.
}
```

Table 12-1 lists the mathematical operators that support overloading.

Table 12-1. The overloadable mathematical operators

Operator	Type	Comments
+	Unary	The unary plus operator. You can already use this operator with numbers, as in "+5." But if you enter this value in Visual Studio, the plus operator gets stripped out since it is considered redundant. However, if you overload this operator on a class of your own, Visual Studio will retain the unary form of this operator when used in code. ``` Bumblebee oneBuzz = new Bumblebee(); Bumblebee moreBuzz = +oneBuzz; ``` Since this is a unary operator, include only a single argument when defining the *operator* method.
+	Binary	The standard addition operator. Remember, just because the operator is called the addition operator doesn't mean that you have to retain that connotation. The *string* data type already treats it like an overload for its own purposes, and you can do the same.
−	Unary	This is the unary negation operator that comes just before a value or expression.
−	Binary	The subtraction operator, although if you can figure out how to subtract one bumblebee from another, you're a better programmer than I am.
*	Binary	The multiplication operator.
/	Binary	The division operator.
%	Binary	The modulo operator, sometimes called the remainder operator since it returns the remainder of a division action.
++	Unary	The increment operator, which can appear before or after its operand.
--	Unary	The decrement operator.

Comparison Operators

Visual C# includes six basic comparison operators, most often used in *if* statements and similar expressions that require a *bool* conditional calculation. The *operator* methods for these comparison operators have the same syntax as is used for mathematical operators, but most of them must be implemented in pairs. For example, if you overload the less than (<) operator, Visual C# requires you to overload the greater than (>) operator within the same class, and for the same argument signature.

All comparison operators are Boolean operators. Although you can alter the data types of the arguments passed to the operator, they must all return a *bool* result.

```
public static bool operator <=(
    SomeClass operand1, SomeClass operand2)
{
    // ----- The <= operator returns a Boolean result.
}
```

Table 12-2 lists the overloadable comparison operators. Each entry includes a "buddy" value that identifies the matching operator that must also be overloaded.

Table 12-2. The overloadable comparison operators

Operator	Buddy	Comments
==	!=	The equal-to operator compares two operands for equivalence, returning *true* if they are equal.
!=	==	The not-equal-to operator compares two operands for non-equivalence, and returns *true* if they do not match.

Operator	Buddy	Comments
<	>	The less-than operator returns *true* if the first operand is less than (or before) the second.
>	<	The greater-than operator returns *true* if the first operand is greater than (or after) the second.
<=	>=	The less-than-or-equal-to operator returns *true* if the first operand is less than or equal to the second. Aren't you getting tired of reading basically the same sentence over and over again?
>=	<=	The greater-than-or-equal-to operator returns *true* if the first operand is greater than or equal to the second.

Bitwise and Logical Operators

Among the logical and bitwise operators included in Visual C#, three already act as overloaded operators. The bitwise &, |, and ^ operators accept integer operands, generating numeric results with values transformed at the individual bit level. They also work as logical operators, accepting and returning Boolean values, most often in conditional statements. But they can handle the stress of being overloaded a little more.

When you do overload these three operators, you are overloading the bitwise versions, not the logical versions. Basically, this means that you have control over the return value, and aren't required to make it Boolean.

Table 12-3 lists the nine overloadable bitwise and logical operators.

Table 12-3. The overloadable bitwise and logical operators

Operator	Comments

<<	The shift-left operator performs bit shifting on a source integer value, moving the bits to the left by a specified number of positions. Although you do not have to use this operator to perform true bit shifting, you must accept a shift amount (an *int*) as the second operand.
	```public static Bumblebee operator <<(```
	``` Bumblebee operand1, int operand2)```
	``` {```
	``` // ----- Add shifting code here.```
	``` }```

>>	The shift-right operator performs bit shifting just like the shift-left operator, but it moves the bits to the right. I guess that would make those bits more conservative. Your code can make the return value more liberal if you want, but as with the shift-left operator, you must accept an *int* as the second operand.
!	The logical negation operator, a unary operator that need not retain any semblance of "logical," since it will not be working with Boolean values.
~	The bitwise complement operator is unary, and like the ! operator, is completely free to disregard its numeric roots.
&	The bitwise conjunction operator sets a bit in the return value if both equally positioned bits in the source operands are also set.
		The bitwise disjunction operator sets a bit in the return value if either of the equally positioned bits in the source operands is set.
^	The bitwise exclusion operator sets a bit in the return value if only one of the equally positioned bits in the source operands is set.

Operator	Comments
`true`	Overloading the | operator does not automatically overload the related || operator. To use ||, you must also overload the special `true` operator. It's not a real Visual C# operator, and you can't call it directly even when overloaded. But when you use the || operator in place of an overloaded | operator, Visual C# calls the `true` operator when needed. There are a few rules you must follow to use the `true` overload. • The overloaded | operator must return the class type of the class in which it is defined. If you want to use || on the `Bumblebee` class, the overload of the | operator in that class must return a value of type `Bumblebee`. • The overloaded `true` operator must accept a single operand of the containing class's type (`Bumblebee`), and return a `bool`. • You must also overload the `false` operator. How you determine the truth or falsity of a `Bumblebee` is up to you.
`false`	The `false` overload works just like `true`, and has similar rules, but it applies to the `&` and `&&` operators.

The Custom Conversion Operator

A special variation of the `operator` declaration lets you create custom and special conversions between data types that don't seem compatible. The following method template converts a value of type `Bumblebee` to an `int`. The source type (`Bumblebee`) appears in the argument list, and the return type (`int`) is used as the method name, just after the `operator` keyword.

```
public static operator int(Bumblebee operand1)
{
    // ----- Perform conversion here, returning an int.
}
```

If you try to type that last block of code into Visual Studio, it will complain that you are missing the `explicit` keyword, although it should say that you are missing either that keyword or the related `implicit` keyword (see Figure 12-1).

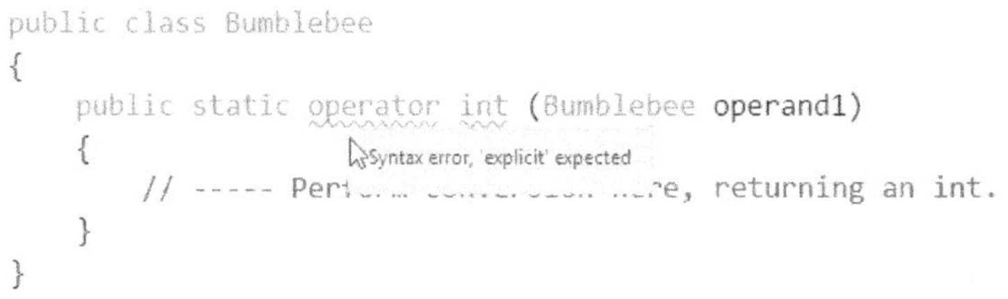

```
public class Bumblebee
{
    public static operator int (Bumblebee operand1)
    {                          Syntax error, 'explicit' expected
        // ----- Per.... ......... ....e, returning an int.
    }
}
```

Figure 12-1. Visual C# complains about all things implicit and explicit

When you convert between some core data types in C#, there is a chance that it will sometimes fail because the source value cannot fit into the destination value. This is true when converting a `short` value to a `byte`.

```
short quiteBig = 5000;
byte quiteSmall;
// ----- This line will fail.
quiteSmall = (byte)quiteBig;
```

And it's obvious why it fails: A `byte` variable cannot hold the value `5000`. But what about this code?

```
short quiteBig = 5;
byte quiteSmall;
```

```
        // ----- This line will succeed.
        quiteSmall = (byte)quiteBig;
```

It will run just fine, since *5* fits into a *byte* variable with room to spare. Still, there is nothing to stop me from reassigning a value of *5000* to *quiteBig* and trying the assignment again. It's this *potential* for failure during conversion that is the issue.

When a conversion has the potential to fail due to the source data not being able to fully fit in the target variable, it's called a *narrowing conversion*. Narrowing conversions are a reality, and as long as you have checked the data before the conversion, there shouldn't be any reason to permanently restrict such conversions.

Widening conversions go in the opposite direction. They occur when any source value in the original data type will always fit easily in the target type. A widening conversion will always succeed as long as the source data is valid.

Visual C# allows widening conversions to occur automatically, implicitly. You don't have to explicitly use a cast to force the conversion. If you had a widening conversion from *Bumblebee* to *int*, the following code would work just fine.

```
Bumblebee sourceValue = new Bumblebee();
int destValue = sourceValue;
```

If the conversion from *Bumblebee* to *int* was narrowing, you would have to force the conversion using a cast so that Visual C# would be sure you really wanted to do this.

```
Bumblebee sourceValue = new Bumblebee();
int destValue = (int)sourceValue;
```

When you create custom conversions with the *operator* declaration, you must inform Visual C# whether the conversion is widening or narrowing by inserting either *implicit* (for widening) or *explicit* (for narrowing) between the *static* and *operator* keywords.

```
public static explicit operator int(Bumblebee operand1)
{
    // ----- Perform narrowing conversion here.
}
```

Other Operator Overloading Issues

There are a few other rules you must follow when overloading operators, but first let's look at a semi-useful *Bumblebee* class.

```
class Bumblebee
{
    public int Bees;

    public Bumblebee()
    {
        // ----- Default constructor.
        this.Bees = 0;
    }

    public Bumblebee(int startingBees)
    {
```

```
        // ----- Assign an initial number of bees.
        this.Bees = startingBees;
    }

    public static Bumblebee operator +(
            Bumblebee operand1, Bumblebee operand2)
    {
        // ----- Join bumblebee groups.
        Bumblebee newGroup = new Bumblebee();
        newGroup.Bees = operand1.Bees + operand2.Bees;
        return newGroup;
    }

    public static Bumblebee operator -(
            Bumblebee operand1, Bumblebee operand2)
    {
        // ----- Separate bumblebee groups.
        Bumblebee newGroup = new Bumblebee();
        newGroup.Bees = operand1.Bees - operand2.Bees;
        if (newGroup.Bees < 0)
            newGroup.Bees = 0;
        return newGroup;
    }

    public static Bumblebee operator *(
            Bumblebee operand1, Bumblebee operand2)
    {
        // ----- Create a swarm.
        Bumblebee newGroup = new Bumblebee();
        newGroup.Bees = operand1.Bees * operand2.Bees;
        return newGroup;
    }

    public static implicit operator int(Bumblebee operand1)
    {
        // ----- Perform conversion here.
        return operand1.Bees;
    }
}
```

The class is pretty simple; it exists to maintain a count of bees. But by overloading the addition, subtraction, and multiplication operators, plus an integer conversion, we can use instances of bees with a more natural syntax.

```
Bumblebee studyGroup1 = new Bumblebee(20);
Bumblebee studyGroup2 = new Bumblebee(15);
Bumblebee swarmGroup = studyGroup1 * studyGroup2;
MessageBox.Show(string.Format(
    "The swarm contains {0} bees.", (int)swarmGroup));
```

Running this code correctly generates a 300-bee swarm and the message in Figure 12-2.

Figure 12-2. Bees sure know how to multiply

Including a custom conversion overload that generates an *int* allowed me to convert a *Bumblebee* using the *(int)* cast. I could also have changed the last line to use the *Convert.ToInt32* method.

```
MessageBox.Show(string.Format(
    "The swarm contains {0} bees.",
    Convert.ToInt32(swarmGroup)));
```

Declaration Requirements

As mentioned earlier, you must always make *operator* methods *public static*. And because the overloaded operators need some sort of intimate connection to their containing class, at least one of the operands or the return value must match the type of the containing class. (In some overloads, Visual C# requires that it be one of the operands that match.) Either of the two following overloads will work just fine, since *Bumblebee* is used for one of the operands.

```
public static bool operator <=(
        Bumblebee operand1, int operand2)
{
    // ----- Compare a bumblebee to a value.
}

public static bool operator <=(
        DateTime operand1, Bumblebee operand2)
{
    // ----- Compare a date to a bumblebee.
}
```

However, you cannot set both operands to a non-*Bumblebee* type at the same time and still keep the overload in the *Bumblebee* class.

```
class Bumblebee
{
    public static bool operator <=(
            DateTime operand1, int operand2)
    {
        // ----- This will not compile.
    }
}
```

Overloading Overloads

You can overload overloaded operators. No, dear editor, I didn't type the same word twice by mistake. You can add multiple argument-and-return-value signature variations of an overloaded operator to a single class.

```
public static implicit operator int(Bumblebee operand1)
{
    // ----- Perform conversion to int here.
}
```

```
public static implicit operator DateTime(Bumblebee operand1)
{
    // ----- Perform conversion to DateTime here, somehow.
}
```

As long as the argument signatures or return values differ, you can add as many overloads of an operator as you want..

Be Nice

That's right. Be nice. Just because you have the power to redefine addition to be division, you don't have to be so shocking. Don't make the maintenance programmers who have to modify your code later work harder because of your mischievous operator overloads. When you add overloads, let the meaning of the new feature at least have the feeling of the original operator. My fellow maintenance programmers and I will thank you.

Extension Methods

What if you want to modify the behavior of a class, but you don't have access to the source code? You could derive from it and build a new class, but that's not always convenient. You could call up the original developer and beg for the code, but some of those programmers are tight-fisted when it comes to their software.

Another option is to use *extension methods*. Here's how it works.

1. You decide which class you want to extend (that is, to enhance) with new methods.
2. You write those methods within a standard *static class* in your source code.
3. You start using the new methods as though they were included in the class definition.

The *string* data type includes several built-in methods that return a modified version of a string instance. One such method is *ToUpper*.

```
string bossyString = "are you talking to me?";
MessageBox.Show(bossyString.ToUpper());
```

The text that appears in the message box will be all uppercase because the *ToUpper* method returns a new uppercase version of the original string instance. A matching *ToLower* method works the other way, but what I really want is a *ToTitle* method that capitalizes just the first letter of each word.

```
MessageBox.Show(bossyString.ToTitle());
```

The *string* class doesn't include a *ToTitle* method, but we can add it thanks to extension methods. To create an extension method, create a method within a static class that accepts the target data type as its first parameter. Just before that parameter, insert the *this* keyword.

```
// ----- Assumes: using System.Globalization;
public static class UtilityFunctions
{
    public static string ToTitle(this string sourceText)
    {
        TextInfo changer = new CultureInfo(
            "en-US", false).TextInfo;
        return changer.ToTitleCase(sourceText);
    }
}
```

Normally, you would call this function as is, passing in the original string.

```
MessageBox.Show(ToTitle(bossyString));
```

And that code does work, but the addition of the *this* keyword turns *ToTitle* into an extension method, extending the *string* data type. Your code isn't really modifying *string*. Behind the scenes, the Visual C# compiler is converting the new method-like syntax into the old function-like syntax on each use of *ToTitle*.

By themselves, extension methods don't do much. Calling *ToTitle(bossyString)* is not that different from *bossyString.ToTitle()*. But as with so many of the features that Visual C# acquired over the years, extension methods were added just to raise the price of the product. Just kidding! Actually, the extension methods functionality is an important support for LINQ technology.

Summary

Operator overloading is a pretty neat feature, but you don't really need it. Anything you can do by overloading the addition operator you can also do by adding an *Append* method to a class. But operator overloading does allow you to bring your classes more into the mainstream of C# syntax usage.

Extension methods can also be replicated using standard method code, but there are some features of LINQ that specifically take advantage of extension methods.

When you do overload your operators or use extension methods, make sure you include sufficient documentation or comments to make it clear what it means to left-shift a customer, *Normalize()* a *string*, or multiply a bank account. Hey, I'd like to know about that last one.

Project

This chapter's project will add a lot of code to the Library application, as much as twenty-five percent of the full code base. Most of it is identical to code we added in earlier chapters, so I won't print it all here. There's a lot to read here, too, so I won't overload you with pasting code snippets right and left. But as you add each new form to the project, be sure to look over its code to become familiar with its inner workings.

> **Project Access**
> Load the "Chapter 12 (Before) Code" project, either through the New Project templates or by accessing the project directly from the installation directory. To see the code in its final form, load "Chapter 12 (After) Code" instead.

Overloading a Conversion

Operator overloading is a useful tool, and I have grown especially fond of developing custom conversion overloads. Let's add some custom conversions to a class we first designed back in Chapter 8: *ListItemData*. This class exposes both *ItemText* and *ItemData* properties, providing access to the textual and numeric aspects of the class content. (The *TextCode* property replaces the *ItemData* property when using a character instead of a number as the tracked key for a record.) Its primary purpose is to support the tracking of ID numbers (or characters) in *ListBox* and *ComboBox* controls. If we need to know the ID number of a selected item in a *ListBox* control (let's name it *SomeList*), we use code similar to the following.

```
long recordID =
    ((ListItemData)SomeList.SelectedItem).ItemData;
```

There's nothing wrong with that code. But I thought, "Wouldn't it be nice to convert the `ListItemData` instance to a *long* directly, and not have to mess with member variables like *ItemData*?"

```
long recordID =
    (long)(ListItemData)SomeList.SelectedItem;
```

Hmm. The code's not that different. But hey, why not? Let's do it. To support this conversion, we need to add custom conversion overload to the `ListItemData` class, plus a second conversion to support similar *char*-based conversions for the *TextCode* field. Open that class's file, *ListItemData.cs*, and add the following code as a member of the class.

Insert Snippet

Insert Chapter 12, Snippet Item 1.

```
public static implicit operator long(
    ListItemData sourceItem)
{
    // ----- To convert to long, simply
    //       extract the numeric element.
    return sourceItem.ItemData;
}

public static implicit operator char(
    ListItemData sourceItem)
{
    // ----- To convert to char, simply
    //       extract the text element.
    return sourceItem.TextCode;
}
```

That's pretty simple. This implicit widening conversion from *ListItemData* to *long* just returns the *long* portion of the instance, and the *char* conversion does the same with the *TextCode* field. There are only about four or five places in the current Library Project that directly access the *ItemData* member, and it's not that important to go back and change them. But we'll use these conversion overloads frequently in the new code added in this chapter.

Global Support Features

We need to add a few more global variables and common global routines to support various features used throughout the application. Two new global variables will track settings stored in the database's *SystemValue* table. Add them as members to the *General* class (in *General.cs*).

Insert Snippet

Insert Chapter 12, Snippet Item 2.

```
public static long DefaultItemLocation;
public static int SearchMatchLimit;
```

The Library program identifies books and other items as stored in multiple locations, such as in branches or storage rooms. *DefaultItemLocation* indicates which one of these locations, from the *CodeLocation* table, is the default. The *DefaultLocation* entry of the *SystemValue* database table stores this value permanently.

When searching for books, authors, or other things that could result in thousands of matches, the *SearchMatchLimit* indicates the maximum number of matches returned by such searches. It's stored as the *SearchLimit* system value.

Since we're already in the *General* class, add two more helper functions.

Insert Snippet
Insert Chapter 12, Snippet Item 3.

ConfirmDefaultLocation

This routine verifies that a valid *DefaultLocation* entry exists in the *SystemValue* table. It returns *true* on success.

GetCopyDisposition

This routine provides a short description for the current status of a specific library item copy. It analyzes the item's and patron's records, and returns one of the following status code strings: *New Item Copy*, *Checked In*, *Checked Out*, *Overdue*, *Missing*, or *Reference*.

Extending a Framework-Supplied Class

What's in a name? Well, if it's the author names in the Library Project, they might include first and last names, prefixes (such as "Dr.") and suffixes ("Jr."), and dates for birth and death. Some of those parts are optional, so formatting the author name is a multistep process. Since the application will need to format author names in several places throughout the code, let's add a central routine, *FormatAuthorName*, which does the work for us.

Insert Snippet
Insert Chapter 12, Snippet Item 4.

```
public static string FormatAuthorName(this DataRow dbRow)
{
    // ----- Given an author record,
    //       return the formatted name.
    string authorName;

    // ----- Format the name.
    authorName = DBGetText(dbRow["LastName"]);
    if (Convert.IsDBNull(dbRow["FirstName"]) == false)
    {
        authorName += ", " + DBGetText(dbRow["FirstName"]);
        if (Convert.IsDBNull(dbRow["MiddleName"]) == false)
            authorName += " " + DBGetText(dbRow["MiddleName"]);
    }
    if (Convert.IsDBNull(dbRow["Suffix"]) == false)
        authorName += ", " + DBGetText(dbRow["Suffix"]);

    // ----- Add in the birth and death years.
    if ((Convert.IsDBNull(dbRow["BirthYear"]) == false) |
        (Convert.IsDBNull(dbRow["DeathYear"]) == false))
    {
        authorName += " (";
        if (Convert.IsDBNull(dbRow["BirthYear"]) == true)
            authorName += "????";
        else
        {
            authorName += Math.Abs(DBGetInteger(
                dbRow["BirthYear"])).ToString();
```

```
            if (DBGetInteger(dbRow["BirthYear"]) < 0)
                authorName += "BC";
        }
        authorName += "-";
        if (Convert.IsDBNull(dbRow["DeathYear"]) == false)
        {
            authorName += Math.Abs(DBGetInteger(
                dbRow["DeathYear"])).ToString();
            if (DBGetInteger(dbRow["DeathYear"]) < 0)
                authorName += "BC";
        }
        authorName += ")";
    }

    // ----- Finished.
    return authorName;
}
```

This routine is an extension method that extends the *DataRow* class. The *this* keyword in the parameter list activates the connection between our custom extension and the framework-defined *DataRow* class. Given a *DataRow* (part of a *DataTable*) built from records in the *Author* table, the function formats and returns a friendly author name in the format "Public, John Q, Jr. (1900–1999)." Elsewhere in the application, it's called as though it were a member of the data row instance.

```
dbRow.FormatAuthorName()
```

We could have left out the extension method features altogether by simply omitting the *this* keyword. Then, calls for author formatting would look like this.

```
FormatAuthorName(dbRow)
```

Record Editors and Supporting Forms

Now things really start to hop. We'll add twenty-three new forms to the application in this chapter. Most of them implement basic code editors, similar to the *UserName.cs* and *GroupName.cs* files we built in Chapter 11. Other forms exist to provide additional support for these record editors. I won't reprint anything I've gone over before, but I'll point out some interesting new code on our way through each of these forms.

If you're following along in the Before version of this chapter's project, you will need to enable each form (and its subordinate designer file) as you encounter it. To do this, select the file in the Solution Explorer panel, and change the file's Build Action property (in the Properties panel) from None to Compile. Then do the same for its related designer file, *<formname>.Designer.cs*.

Search-limiting forms

The first four forms allow the librarian to limit the information overload that comes through using a database with thousands of books, publishers, and authors. You probably remember that the generic *ListEditRecords* form displays all existing records from a table of records by default. This works fine for the security groups stored in the *GroupName* table since you probably won't have even a dozen of those. But listing all books in even a small library can generate quite an imposing list. And depending on the speed of your workstation, it can take a while to load all book titles into the list.

The four search-limiting forms help to reduce the number of records appearing in the list at once. When the librarian accesses the list of books and other library items, the *ItemLimit* form (see Figure 12-3) provides a quick search prompt that reduces the listed results.

Figure 12-3. The ItemLimit form acts like a bar-room bouncer for items

The form lets the user retrieve all records, or specific items, based on item name (with wildcard support). Once the matches are loaded, the user can access this form again by clicking on the Lookup button on the `ListEditRecords` form for those types of code editors that support lookups (authors, items, patrons, and publishers).

We are ready to include these four search-limiting forms in the project.

AuthorLimit.cs

This form limits author records as loaded from the `Author` table.

ItemLimit.cs

This is the form we just talked about. It limits the display of library items from the `NamedItem` table.

PatronLimit.cs

Just in case patrons are flocking to your library, this form lets you limit the records loaded from the `Patron` table.

PublisherLimit.cs

This form limits records from the `Publisher` table.

Keyword and subject editors

Although most record editors provide a full editing experience through the `ListEditRecords` form, some are subordinate to other editor forms. Keywords and subjects are a good example. Though each has its own independent table (`Keyword` and `Subject`), I chose to allow editing of them through the form that edits individual library items, the `NamedItem` form (added later). That form manages all interactions between the `Keyword` and `Subject` records and the `NamedItem` table, all through the intermediate many-to-many tables `ItemKeyword` and `ItemSubject`.

The `KeywordAdd` and `SubjectAdd` forms provide a simple text entry form for a single keyword or subject. Include each of these forms now in the project.

- *KeywordAdd.cs*
- *SubjectAdd.cs*

More named item support forms

As we'll see later, the `NamedItem` form is one of the most complex forms added to the Library Project so far. It manages everything about a generalized library item (such as a book). Each item can have multiple copies, authors, keywords, subjects, and so on. It's simply too much editing power to include on a single form. We already added two of the subordinate forms: *KeywordAdd* and *SubjectAdd*. Let's add five additional support forms.

AuthorAddLocate.cs

This form presents a wizard-like interface that lets the user add a new or existing author record to an item. *Author* in the Library program is a generic term that refers to authors, editors, illustrators, performers, and so on. This form's three wizard steps let the user (1) indicate the type of author via the *CodeAuthorType* table; (2) perform a search for an existing author by name; and (3) select from a list of matching author names. If the desired author isn't yet in the database, the last step allows a new author to be added. Figure 12-4 shows the first two of these steps.

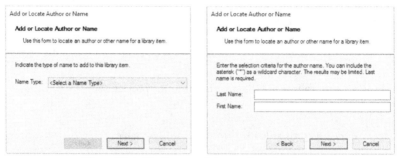

Figure 12-4. The first two of three author wizard steps

Most of the logic is controlled through the Next button's event handler. The logic in this routine varies based on the current wizard panel in view (as indicated by the *ActivePanel* class-level variable). Here's the code that runs when the user clicks Next after selecting the author type.

```
// ----- Make sure a name type is selected.
if ((long)(ListItemData)NameType.SelectedItem == -1L)
{
    MessageBox.Show(
        "Please select a name type from the list.",
        ProgramTitle, MessageBoxButtons.OK,
        MessageBoxIcon.Exclamation);
    NameType.Focus();
    return;
}
```

Did you see the first logic line in that code? We used a series of casts to get an *ItemData* value from a list item. This calls our *long*-based custom conversion operator in the *ListItemData* class.

PublisherAddLocate.cs

This form is just like the *AuthorAddLocate* form, but focuses on publishers. Its wizard has only two steps since publishers are not grouped by type. It locates or adds records in the *Publisher* table. When it's time to add a publisher to an item, the item editor form calls the public *PublisherAddLocate.PromptUser* function. This function returns the ID of the selected publisher record, or *-1* to abort the adding of a publisher. A return value of *-2* clears any previously selected publisher ID.

SeriesAddLocate.cs

This form is similar to the *PublisherAddLocate* form, but it prompts for records from the *CodeSeries* table.

Once an author has been added to an item, the only way to change it to a different author is to remove the incorrect author, and add the correct author separately through the `AuthorAddLocate` form. But if the user simply selected the wrong author type (such as "Editor" instead of "Illustrator"), it's kind of a burden to search for the author name again just to change the type. The `ItemAuthorEdit` form lets the user modify the type for an author already added to an item. It modifies the `ItemAuthor.AuthorType` database field.

ItemCopy.cs

A library will likely have multiple copies of a particular book, CD, or other item. In the Library program, this means that each `NamedItem` record can have more than one `ItemCopy` record attached to it. Each copy is edited through the `ItemCopy` form (see Figure 12-5).

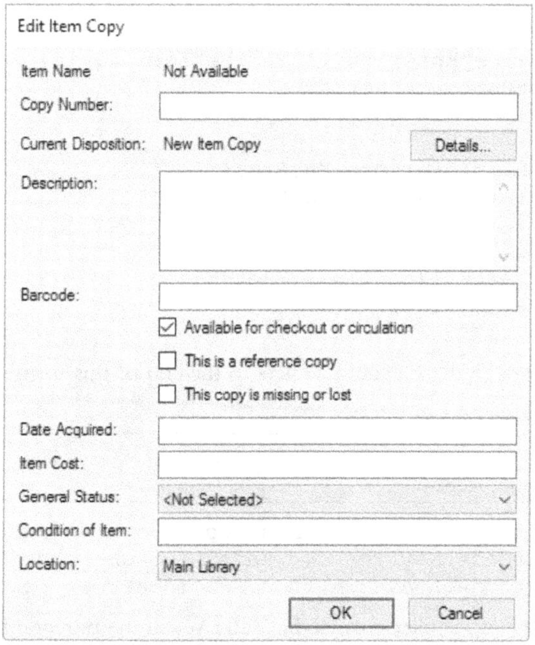

Figure 12-5. Details only a librarian could love

Although this code does not inherit from `BaseCodeForm` as other record editors do, it still has many of the features of those forms, including a `SaveFormData` routine that writes records to the database.

One interesting thing that this form does have is support for reading barcodes. Many barcode readers act as a "wedge," inserting the text of a scanned barcode into the keyboard input stream of the computer. Any program monitoring for barcodes simply has to monitor normal text input.

Barcode wedge scanners append a carriage return (the Enter key) to the end of the transmitted barcode. This lets a program detect the end of the barcode number. But in most of the Library program's forms, the Enter key triggers the OK button and closes the form. We don't want that to happen here. To prevent this, we'll add some code to this form that disables the auto-click on the OK button whenever the insertion point is in the Barcode text entry field.

```
private void RecordBarcode_Enter(
    object sender, EventArgs e)
{
    // ----- Highlight the entire text.
    RecordBarcode.SelectAll();

    // ----- Don't allow Enter to close the form.
    this.AcceptButton = null;
}

private void RecordBarcode_Leave(
    object sender, EventArgs e)
{
    // ----- Allow Enter to close the form again.
    this.AcceptButton = ActOK;
}

private void RecordBarcode_KeyPress(
    object sender, KeyPressEventArgs e)
{
    // ----- Ignore the enter key.
    if (e.KeyChar == (char)Keys.Return)
        e.Handled = true;
}
```

Also add the connections to these event handlers to the end of this form's *InitializeComponent* method.

```
this.RecordBarcode.Enter += this.RecordBarcode_Enter;
this.RecordBarcode.KeyPress += this.RecordBarcode_KeyPress;
this.RecordBarcode.Leave += this.RecordBarcode_Leave;
```

With these additions, when the user presses the Enter key in the Barcode field manually, the form will not close. But it's a small price to pay for barcode support.

Inherited code editors

Twelve of the forms added in this chapter inherit directly from the *BaseCodeForm* class. Add them to the project as I review each one.

Author.cs

The *Author* form edits records in the *Author* database table. As a typical derived class of *BaseCodeForm*, it overrides many of the public elements of its base class. Two overrides that we haven't yet used in earlier chapters are the *UsesSearch* and *SearchForRecord* methods. These allow the user of the *ListEditRecords* form to limit the displayed authors through the prompting of the *AuthorLimit* form described earlier in this chapter. (The *FillListWithRecords* override also calls *SearchForRecord* to prompt the user for the initial list of authors to display.)

In *SearchForRecord*, the call to `AuthorLimit.PromptUser` returns a comma-separated string in "Last, First" format.

```
// ----- Prompt the user for the limited author name.
exceededMatches = false;
userLimit = (new AuthorLimit()).PromptUser();
if (userLimit.Length == 0)
    return;
```

The user can include the asterisk (*) character as a wildcard in the first or last name parts. The asterisk has become a common character to use in all types of wildcard searches. Unfortunately, it is not supported in SQL Server *SELECT* statements. SQL Server uses the percent (%) character for a wildcard instead (as do many other SQL-compliant database platforms). As *SearchForRecord* extracts the first and last names, it ensures that the right wildcard character is used.

```
// ----- Use the limits to help prepare the search text.
limitLast = userLimit.GetSubStr(",", 1).Trim();
limitFirst = userLimit.GetSubStr(",", 2).Trim();
if ((limitLast + limitFirst).Length == 0)
    return;
if (limitLast.Contains("*") == false)
    limitLast += "*";
if (limitFirst.Contains("*") == false)
    limitFirst += "*";
limitLast = limitLast.Replace("*", "%");
limitFirst = limitFirst.Replace("*", "%");
```

This code uses our custom *GetSubStr* routine already added to the *General* static class. Once the name parts are extracted, the *string* type's *Replace* method replaces all instances of * with %. You'll find similar code in the other record editors that allow limits on the list of records, such as the *Publisher* form added later.

The *Author* form has one more notable element. A Name Matches label appears near the bottom of the form, as shown in Figure 12-6.

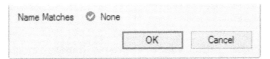

Figure 12-6. The bottom of the Author form showing Name Matches

This field helps the user avoid adding the same author to the database twice. As changes are made to the Last Name and First Name fields, the Name Matches field gets refreshed with matching author names found in the *Author* table. The *RefreshMatchingAuthors* routine counts the number of matching authors through the following code.

```
sqlText = "SELECT COUNT(*) AS TheCount FROM Author " +
    "WHERE LastName LIKE @TestLast";
if (RecordFirstName.Text.Trim().Length != 0)
    sqlText += " AND FirstName LIKE @TestFirst";
sqlRun = new DataCommand(sqlText);
sqlRun.AddText("TestLast", RecordLastName.Text.Trim());
if (RecordFirstName.Text.Trim().Length != 0)
    sqlRun.AddText("TestFirst",
        RecordFirstName.Text.Trim().Substring(0, 1) + "%");
matchCount = DBGetInteger(ExecuteSQLReturn(sqlRun));
```

This is similar to the lookup code in the *SearchForRecord* routine, but it only adds a wildcard to the first name before doing the search.

CodeAuthorType.cs

The *CodeAuthorType* form edits records in the related *CodeAuthorType* table. Who knew?

CodeCopyStatus.cs

This form edits records in the *CodeCopyStatus* database table.

CodeLocation.cs

As expected, this form edits records in the *CodeLocation* table. Once you've added at least one record to that table, you'll be able to set the default location for the database. I'll discuss this again a little later in this chapter.

CodeMediaType.cs

The *CodeMediaType* form, which edits records in the *CodeMediaType* table, includes a few more fields than the other code-table editors. Most of the fields accept numeric input. Although I do a final check for valid numeric data just before writing the record to the database, I try to prevent any non-numeric data from showing up in the first place by restricting the acceptable keystrokes. For instance, the *RecordCheckoutDays* text field's *KeyPress* event includes this code.

```
// ----- Only allow digits and backspaces.
if ((e.KeyChar.ToString() == "\b") |
        (Char.IsDigit(e.KeyChar) == true))
    return;
e.Handled = true;
```

Setting the *e.Handled* property to *true* stops Visual C# from doing anything else (pretty much) with the entered key. It's a quick and easy way to dispose of a user-entered keystroke.

CodePatronGroup.cs

This form edits records in the *CodePatronGroup* table.

CodeSeries.cs

This editor manages records in the *CodeSeries* table. Earlier I mentioned how series names and keywords are subordinate to named items. But it made sense to me to also provide direct management for series names, in case you wanted to build up a common list before adding individual library items. So, this form performs double duty: you can access it as a standard record editor through the *ListEditRecords* form, and it's also used for a specific named item through the not-yet-added *NamedItem* form.

When editing item-specific series names, the user first gets to search for a series name by typing it. Since I don't want the user to have to retype the series name again in this editor form, I wanted to pass the typed series name into the *CodeSeries* form, but none of the overridden public methods supported this. So, we'll need to add a new method that will accept the typed name. The *AddRecord* member already overrides the base function of the same name.

```
public override long AddRecord()
{
    // ----- Add a new record.
    ActiveID = -1L;
    PrepareFormFields();
```

```
    this.ShowDialog();
    if (this.DialogResult == DialogResult.OK)
       return ActiveID;
    else
        return -1L;
}
```

Let's add an overload to this function that includes a string parameter. The caller will pass the originally typed text to this parameter. We'll assign it to the *RecordFullName* control's *Text* property so that it shows up automatically when the form opens.

Insert Snippet

Insert Chapter 12, Snippet Item 7.

```
public long AddRecord(string seriesText)
{
    // ----- Add a new record, but use a starting
    //       value previously entered by the user.
    ActiveID = -1L;
    PrepareFormFields();
    RecordFullName.Text = seriesText;
    this.ShowDialog();
    if (this.DialogResult == DialogResult.OK)
       return ActiveID;
    else
        return -1L;
}
```

Yes, we could have used some name other than *AddRecord* for this function and avoided adding an overload. But it's nice to keep things consistent.

Holiday.cs

This form manages the records in the *Holiday* table. In a later chapter, we'll add a cache of holidays within the program for quick access.

Patron.cs

The *Patron* form provides editing services for records in the *Patron* table, and appears in Figure 12-7.

This form includes a *TabControl* to help break up the number of fields the user has to experience at once. This control manages all of the panel-switching logic automatically when the user selects a different tab. Each panel is a separate *TabPage* class instance. In your code, forcing the tab control to display a different tab is as easy as assigning the appropriate *TabPage* instance to the *TabControl* object's *SelectedTab* property, as with this code line from the *ValidateFormData* function.

```
TabPatron.SelectedTab = TabGeneral;
```

Although this form looks quite complex, it's made up almost entirely of code we've seen in other forms. Beyond the standard overrides of *BaseCodeForm* members, this form includes barcode scanning support borrowed from the *ItemCopy* form, password logic stolen from the *UserName* form, and name-matching code similar to that used in the *Author* form.

Figure 12-7. Most of the Patron form (Messages tab details are hidden)

I included a Manage Patron's Items button on the form, but we won't add its logic until a later chapter. An extra public function, `EditRecordLimited`, becomes important at that time.

Publisher.cs

The `Publisher` form lets the user edit the records in the `Publisher` table. It's a pretty simple form with only two data entry fields. A Status field indicates how many `NamedItem` records link to this publisher. A small button appears to the right of the text entry field for the publisher's web site. This is the "show me the web site" button, and when clicked, it brings up the supplied web page in the user's default browser. To enable this button, add the following code to the `ShowWeb` button's `Click` event handler.

Insert Snippet

Insert Chapter 12, Snippet Item 8.

```
// ----- Show the web site displayed in the field.
ProcessStartInfo newProcess;

if (RecordWeb.Text.Trim().Length == 0)
   return;
try
{
   newProcess = new ProcessStartInfo(
      RecordWeb.Text.Trim());
   Process.Start(newProcess);
}
catch
{
   // ----- Ignore errors.
}
```

This code editor manages items in the *SystemValue* table. Although we will connect it to a link on the main Library form in this chapter, we will change this access method in a future chapter.

Well, that's eleven of the twelve derived forms. The last one is the *NamedItem* form, shown in Figure 12-8.

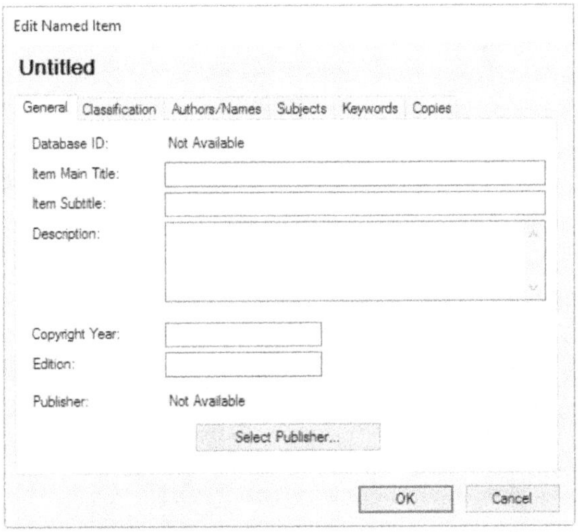

Figure 12-8. The NamedItem form with the General tab active

The *NamedItem* form is the largest and most complex of the forms that derive from *BaseCodeForm*. It edits primary library items recorded in the *NamedItem* database table. It's complex because it also directly manages records in other subordinate tables: *ItemAuthor*, *ItemCopy*, *ItemKeyword*, *ItemSubject*; and indirectly: *Author*, *Keyword*, *Publisher*, and *Subject*.

All of the fields on the General and Classification tabs are basic data entry fields that flow directly into the *NamedItem* table, just as is done with the other record-editing forms. The Publisher and Series fields use separate selection forms (*PublisherAddLocate* and *SeriesAddLocate*) to obtain the ID values stored in *NamedItem*. Here's the code that looks up the publisher.

```
// ----- Prompt the user.
newPublisher = (new PublisherAddLocate()).PromptUser();
if (newPublisher == -1L)
    return;

// ----- Check to clear the publisher.
if (newPublisher == -2L)
{
    RecordPublisher.Text = "Not Available";
    PublisherID = -1L;
    return;
}
```

The other four tabs—Authors/Names, Subjects, Keywords, and Copies—manage subordinate records. The code is pretty consistent among the four different tabs, so I'll limit my comments to the Authors/Names tab (see Figure 12-9).

Figure 12-9. The NamedItem form with the Authors/Names tab active

The controls on this tab are quite similar to those on the *ListEditRecords* form; they exist to manage a set of records in a table. In this case, it's the *ItemAuthor* table. For the presentation list, I chose to use a *ListView* control instead of a standard *ListBox* control. By setting a *ListView* control's *View* property to *Details*, setting its *FullRowSelect* field to *True*, and modifying its *Columns* collection (see Figure 12-10), you can quickly turn it into a multicolumn list box.

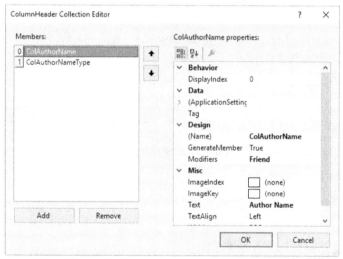

Figure 12-10. The ColumnHeader editor for a ListView control

When you add an item to this list, you also have to add sub-items to have anything appear in all but the first column.

```
ListViewItem newItem =
    AuthorsList.Items.Add("John Smith");
newItem.SubItems.Add("Illustrator");
```

The Add button brings up the *AuthorAddLocate* form, whereas the Properties button displays the *ItemAuthorEdit* form instead.

Before any of the subordinate records can be added, the parent record must exist in the database. That is because the child records include the ID number of the parent record, and without a parent record, there is no parent ID number. If you look in each of the Add button routines on this form, you will find code such as the following.

```
// ----- The record must be saved first.
if (ActiveID == -1L)
{
    // ----- Confirm with the user.
    if (MessageBox.Show(
            "The item must be saved to the database before " +
            "authors or names can be added. Would you like " +
            "to save the record now?", ProgramTitle,
            MessageBoxButtons.YesNo, MessageBoxIcon.Question)
            != DialogResult.Yes)
        return;

    // ----- Verify and save the data.
    if (ValidateFormData() == false)
        return;
    if (SaveFormData() == false)
        return;
}
```

If this is a brand-new *NamedItem* record (*ActiveID == -1L*), this code will save it before allowing the user to add the subordinate record. Any invalid data that prevents the record from being saved will be caught in the call to *ValidateFormData*.

Actually, the calls to both *ValidateFormData* and *SaveFormData* are the same ones that occur when the user clicks on the OK button. Normally, that triggers a return of the new record's ID number to the calling form. But what if *SaveFormData* gets called by adding an author, but then the user clicks the Cancel button (which normally returns a *-1* value to indicate "no record added")? To avoid that, the *SaveFormData* function sets a class-level variable named *SessionSaved*.

```
SessionSaved = true;
```

This flag is cleared when the form first opens, but is set to *true* pretty much anytime a subordinate record changes. The *NamedItem* form's overridden *AddRecord* and *EditRecord* functions check for this flag before returning to the calling form.

```
if ((this.DialogResult == DialogResult.OK) |
        (SessionSaved == true))
    return ActiveID;
else
    return -1L;
```

There are lots of other interesting code blocks in the *NamedItem* form. But at around 1,800 lines (not counting the related designer code), I'll have to let you investigate it on your own.

Connecting the Editors to the Main Form

OK, take a breath. That was a lot of code to go through. But if you run the program now, you won't see any difference at all. We still need to connect all of the record editors to the main form. They all connect through the *LinkLabel* controls on the main form's Administration panel (*PanelAdmin*). We need to add twelve *LinkClicked* event handlers to access all of the new and various forms. Go ahead and add them now to the *MainForm* class.

Also add the related event handler hookups to the end of the form's *InitializeComponent* method.

Each of the *LinkClicked* event handlers is almost a mirror image of the others, except for a few object instance names here and there. Here's the code that handles a click on the Publisher link label.

```
private void AdminLinkPublishers_LinkClicked(
   object sender, LinkLabelLinkClickedEventArgs e)
{
   // ----- Make sure the user is allowed to do this.
   if (SecurityProfile[(int)LibrarySecurity.
      ManagePublishers] == false)
   {
      MessageBox.Show(NotAuthorizedMessage, ProgramTitle,
         MessageBoxButtons.OK, MessageBoxIcon.Exclamation);
      return;
   }

   // ----- Let the user edit the list of publishers.
   (new ListEditRecords()).ManageRecords(new Publisher());
}
```

After doing a quick security check, the code calls up the standard *ListEditRecords* form, passing it an instance of the record editor it is to use.

There are still a few inactive links on the Administration panel that we'll enable in later chapters.

Setting the Default Location

The program is now ready to run with all of its new features in place. Since we added only administrative features, you must click the Login button in the upper-right corner of the main form before gaining access to the Administration panel and its features. Unless you changed it, your login username is "admin" with no password.

Although you can now run the program and access all of the record editors, you won't be able to add new item copies until you set a default location. Follow these steps to set the default location.

1. Add at least one location through the Locations link on the Administration panel.

2. Obtain the ID number of the *CodeLocation* record you want to be the default. You can use SQL Server Management Studio Express's query features to access the records in this table. If this is the first time you've added records to the *CodeLocation* table, the first item you add will have an ID value of *1*.

3. Back in the Library program, edit the *SystemValue* table through the System Values link on the Administration panel.

4. Add or modify the "DefaultLocation" system value, setting its value to the ID number of the default location record.

Alternatively, you can update the *DefaultLocation* record in the *SystemValue* table directly using SQL Server Management Studio. If the ID of the location to use is *1*, use this SQL statement to make the change.

```
UPDATE SystemValue
    SET ValueData = '1'
    WHERE ValueName = 'DefaultLocation'
```

In a future chapter, we'll add a more user-friendly method to update this default location.

Speaking of user-friendly, we're about to enter the not-user-friendly but logic-friendly world of text-structured data: XML.

Chapter 13

XML

Because computers are computers and people are people, they generally have different requirements when it comes to getting their data into a usable format. XML is an attempt to arrange data in a structure that is usable for both people and software.

XML has really come into vogue in recent years, but its roots are quite old. It's derived from SGML (Standard Generalized Markup Language), as is HTML (cousins!). SGML in turn came from GML (Generalized Markup Language), a *metalanguage* (a language that describes another language) designed by IBM back in the 1960s. So, blame IBM if you want to, but either way, you will come in regular contact with XML as you develop .NET applications.

I might as well tell you right from the start: either you will love XML, or you will hate it, but probably both. It's a strange beast, this XML, as you would expect from any acronym that takes letters from the middle of the words it represents ("eXtensible Markup Language"). XML represents an alphabet of data manipulation technologies, an alphabet which strangely has seven Xs. But enough of the teasing; let's *extend* our understanding of this basic .NET technology.

What Is XML?

XML is nothing more than a data format that is both human-readable and machine-readable. Have you ever tried to open a Microsoft Word document with Notepad? Good luck (see Figure 13-1). Before Microsoft's switch to the Office Open XML format in 2007, you could sometimes sift out the main text of a document, though most of what you saw was gobbledygook. That's because it was in a *proprietary binary* format. It was *proprietary* because, frankly, you shouldn't be poking your fingers in there. That's what Microsoft Word is for. And it was *binary* because you could store a lot of information conveniently in a little bit of disk space. With such a file, I can store my data any way I choose. If fact, I can write my data out willy-nilly, and not have to get permission from anyone, because it's mine, mine, all mine.

Binary files are great for storing any kind of data: numbers, strings, base-64 encrypted images, streams of networking data chatter, anything. The problem is that unless you know the exact structure you used to write it out, there is little chance of ever getting the data back. This is good if your goal is secrecy, but if you ever need to share that data with another person or program, or worse yet, debug the output from your errant program, you're in for a tough time. If one little byte gets messed up, the whole file might be useless.

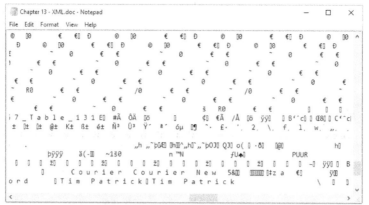

Figure 13-1. This chapter in Notepad

There are, of course, other ways to store your data. For programs that store records of data, tab-delimited and CSV (comma-separated value) files provide a convenient transfer medium, in a more human-friendly format. For instance, consider this data from Microsoft's old Access-centric "Northwind Traders" database, stored as comma-separated values.

```
ProductID,ProductName,SupplierID,Category,UnitPrice,Available
"1","Chai","652","Beverages","$18.00","Yes"
"2","Chang","9874","Beverages","$19.00","No"
"3","Aniseed Syrup","9874","Condiments","On Sale","Yes"
```

Now that's better. This data is pretty easy to understand. Each piece of data is grouped by commas, and the first row indicates what each column contains. And the best part is that many programs already know how to read files in this format. If you save this data in a text file with a *.csv* extension, and open it in Microsoft Excel, the data automatically appears in columns.

But it could be better. For instance, what do those "652" and "9874" values refer to anyway? And is it correct that the unit price of Aniseed Syrup is "On Sale?" Sure, I can load this data into my program, but can I do anything with it? At least it's an easy read for both people and computer programs, and isn't that what I said XML was all about?

Well, yes. Although XML includes rules and features that make it more flexible than your average text data file, it's not that different. For all the hype, XML is just a way of storing data. Any of the fancy-schmancy XML traits discussed in this chapter could be performed easily with data stored in simpler text or binary proprietary formats. In fact, it is often quicker and more convenient to develop using a proprietary format, because your data will contain exactly and only what you need, without any fluff.

That being said, XML does include many aspects that make it a strong contender when considering a data format.

It's straightforward to read

Each data element includes a type of title. Good titles make for good reading.

It's easy to process

All data includes starting and ending tags, so a program can process the data without much effort. And one bad element won't necessarily ruin the whole file.

It's flexible

You can store any type of data in XML. It is just a text file, after all. If you have a certain XML file format used in version 1 of your program, and you add features to it in version 2, you can do it in a way that still allows version 1 programs to use version 2 files without breaking.

It's self-describing

XML includes several features that let you describe the content of a given XML file. Two of the most popular are DTD (Document Type Definition, although this standard is less popular now) and XSD (XML Schema Definition, much more common in modern XML). You use these tools to indicate exactly what you expect your data file to contain. Additionally, XML allows you to embed comments in the content without impacting the actual data.

It's self-verifying

Tools are available, including tools in .NET, which can confirm the integrity and format of an XML file by comparing the content to the associated DTD or XSD. This lets you verify a file before you even process it.

It's an open standard

XML has gained widespread acceptance, even across divergent computer platforms.

It's built into .NET

This is going to be the biggest reason for using it. In fact, you won't be able to get away from XML in .NET, even if you try. It's everywhere.

But there's bad news, too.

It's bulky

XML content contains a lot of repetitive structural information, and generally lots of whitespace. You could abbreviate many of the structure elements, and remove all the whitespace (XML doesn't require it), but that would remove the human-readable aspects of the data. Some platforms, such as cell phone browsers, like to keep data small. XML is anything but small.

It's text

Wait a minute, this is a good thing—most of the time. Sometimes you just need to store binary data, such as pictures. You can't really store true binary data in an XML file without breaking one of the basic rules about XML: text only! Often, binary data is encoded in a text-like format, such as base-64 (which uses readable characters to store binary data).

It's inefficient

This comes from having data in a verbose semi-human-readable format, rather than in a terse, compact binary form. It simply takes longer for a computer to scan text looking for matching start and end tags than it does to move a few bytes directly from a lump of binary data into a location in memory.

It's human-readable

There are not many secrets in an XML file. And although you could encrypt the data elements in the file, or the entire file for that matter, that would kind of ruin the human-readable aspect of using XML.

It's machine-readable

If you are expecting the average Joe to pick up an XML printout and read it in his easy chair, think again. XML is not appropriate for every type of data file.

It's not immune to errors

As I keep repeating, XML is just a text file. If you open it in Notepad and let your five-year-old pound on the keyboard, the content will have problems. XML is not a panacea; it's just a useful file format.

The XML Rule

Before we look at some actual XML, you need to know *The Rule*. You must obey *The Rule* with every piece of XML text you write.

> **The Rule**
> If you open it, close it.

That's it. Don't forget it. Obey it. Live it. I'll explain what it means later.

XML Content

There's no better way to learn about XML than to start looking at it. If you've never used XML, but you've written some HTML, this should look somewhat familiar.

Some Basic XML

Here's a simple chunk of XML for you to enjoy.

```
<?xml version="1.0"?>
<hello>
   <there>
      <!-- Finally, real data here. -->
      <world target="everyone">think XML</world>
      <totalCount>694.34</totalCount>
      <goodbye />
   </there>
</hello>
```

Hey, I didn't say it was going to be interesting. As I mentioned before, it's just data, but it is useful data, and here's why.

It's obviously XML

This is clear from the first line, which always starts with `<?xml` . . . . This line also indicates the XML version number, which tells XML processing routines (parsers) to adjust behavior if needed. That's foresight.

It's structured

XML is a hierarchical data structure. That is, you can have data *elements* embedded inside other data elements to any depth you want. Every element is bounded by a set of *tags*. In this sample, the tags are `hello`, `there`, `world`, `totalCount`, and `goodbye`. Tags always appear inside `<angle brackets>`, and always appear in pairs, as in `<hello>...</hello>`. (This is where *The Rule*, "If you open it, close it," comes in.) Don't forget the `/` just before the tag name in the closing bracket. This syntax lets you organize your data into specifically arranged named units. For tag pairs that have nothing in between them, you can use the shortened syntax $< tagname />$, as I did with the *goodbye* tag. By the way, XML tags are case-sensitive, so type carefully.

It's readable

It's human-readable, thanks to all the whitespace, although you could remove it all and still have XML. It's also computer-readable because of the consistent use of tags.

It's a single unit of data

All XML files have a single *root element* in which all other elements must appear. In the sample, `<hello>` is the root element. Once that element is closed (through its ending tag) you can't add any additional elements. Nope. Nada.

It's got comments

See that `<!--...-->` line? That's a comment. You can stick comments here and there just like they were free-floating tags.

It's got attributes

XML supports two varieties of data: real data and attributes. Real data values come between the innermost tag pairs, as with *think XML* and *694.34* in the sample. Attributes provide extended information about the tags themselves. I included an attribute named *target* in the *world* element. The content of all attributes must be in quotes. I could have made this attribute a sub-element instead, and a lot of people do. There is disagreement among programmers as to when data should be an element or an attribute. Let your conscience be your guide.

So, there you have it—some clean, clear XML data.

Some Basic—and Meaningful—XML
Let's see what that comma-delimited data that I listed previously could look like in XML.

```
<?xml version="1.0"?>
<productList>
   <supplier ID="652" fullName="Beverages R Us">
      <product ID="1" available="Yes">
         <productName>Chai</productName>
         <category>Beverages</category>
         <unitPrice>18.00</unitPrice>
      </product>
   </supplier>
   <supplier ID="9874" fullName="We Sell Food">
      <product ID="2" available="No">
         <productName>Chang</productName>
         <category>Beverages</category>
         <unitPrice>19.00</unitPrice>
      </product>
      <product ID="3" available="Yes" onSale="true">
         <productName>Aniseed Syrup</productName>
         <category>Condiments</category>
         <unitPrice>12.00</unitPrice>
      </product>
   </supplier>
</productList>
```

Moving the data to XML has greatly increased the size of the content. But with an increase in size comes an increase in processing value. I was immediately able to get some benefit from the hierarchical structure of XML. In the original data, supplier was just another column. But in the XML version, all the data is now grouped into supplier sections, which makes sense (at least, if that is how I was planning to use the data).

You can also see that I followed *The Rule*. Every opening tag has a matching closing tag. Whatever you do, don't forget *The Rule*.

Now, you're saying to yourself, "Tim, I could have grouped the data by supplier once I loaded the comma-delimited data into my program." And to that I say, "You're right." I told you that XML was just another data format. By itself, the XML content is not all that sexy. It's really the tools that you use with your XML data that make it zoom. Because XML uses a consistent yet generic structure to manage data, it was a snap to develop tools that could process consistent yet generic data in ways that look interesting and specific.

What about the Human-Readable Part?

One of the tools used with XML is *XSLT*, which stands for XSL Transformations (XSL stands for eXtensible Stylesheet Language). XSLT is a hard-to-use scripting language that lets you transform some XML data into whatever other data or output format you want. It's just one of a handful of XSL-related languages created to manipulate XML data in complex ways. Ready for some hands-on XSL fun? Take the useful chunk of XML listed previously (the `<productList>` sample), and replace the first `?xml` line with the following two lines.

```
<?xml version="1.0"?>
<?xml-stylesheet type="text/xsl" href="hello.xsl"?>
```

Save all of that beautiful XML text to a file on your desktop as *hello.xml*. Next, put the following XSLT script into another file on your desktop named *hello.xsl*.

```
<?xml version="1.0"?>
<xsl:stylesheet
      xmlns:xsl="http://www.w3.org/1999/XSL/Transform"
      version="1.0">
  <xsl:template match="/">
    <html><head><title>Products</title></head><body>
    <xsl:text>
ProductID,ProductName,SupplierID,Category,UnitPrice,Available
    </xsl:text><br/>
    <xsl:apply-templates/>
    </body>
    </html>
  </xsl:template>

  <xsl:template match="supplier">
    <xsl:variable name="supID" select="@ID"/>
    <xsl:for-each select="product">
      "<xsl:value-of select="@ID"/>",
      "<xsl:value-of select="productName"/>",
      "<xsl:value-of select="$supID"/>",
      "<xsl:value-of select="category"/>",
      "<xsl:choose>
        <xsl:when test="@onSale='true'">On Sale</xsl:when>
        <xsl:otherwise>
          $<xsl:value-of select="unitPrice"/>
        </xsl:otherwise>
      </xsl:choose>",
```

```
        "<xsl:value-of select="@available"/>"
        <br/>
      </xsl:for-each>
    </xsl:template>
  </xsl:stylesheet>
```

I told you it was hard to use, and even harder to look at. OK, now for the show. Open the *hello.xml* file in your browser, and *voilà*, the following beautifully formatted text should appear.

```
ProductID,ProductName,SupplierID,Category,UnitPrice,Available
"1","Chai","652","Beverages","$18.00","Yes"
"2","Chang","9874","Beverages","$19.00","No"
"3","Aniseed Syrup","9874","Condiments","On Sale","Yes"
```

Note

Your results may vary. When I viewed the results in Internet Explorer, Firefox, and Chrome, the output appeared as above. However, the display in Microsoft's Edge browse was markedly different, showing its own interpretation of the original XML content, and ignoring the stylesheet completely. Beware!

Now that's more like it. XML and XSLT together have made this advance in data technology possible. But seriously, although I was able to generate a comma-separated data set presentation with XSLT, more common tasks for XSLT include generating nicely formatted HTML based on XML data, or generating a new XML document with a specific alternative view of the original data. How does it work? Basically, the `<xsl:template>` elements tell the parser to look for tags in the XML document that match some pattern (such as "supplier"). When it finds a match, it applies everything inside the `<xsl:template>` tags to that matching XML tag and its contents. The pattern specified in the `match` attributes uses an XML technology called *XPath*, a pattern language used to generically search for matching tags within your XML document.

Sounds confusing? Well, it is, and don't get me started on how long it took to write that short little XSLT script. XSLT scripting is, blissfully, beyond the scope of this book. Of course, tools are available to make the job easier. But XSLT is useful only if the XML data it manipulates is correct. You could write an XSL Transformation to report on data inconsistencies found in an XML document, but it won't work if some of the tags in your document are misspelled or arranged in an inconsistent manner. For that, you need another advancement in XML technology: XSD.

XML Schemas

XSD (XML Schema Definition) lets you define the *schema*—the language or vocabulary—of your particular XML document. Remember, XML is a wide-open generic standard; you can define the tags any way you want and nobody will care, at least until you have to process the tags with your software. If they aren't correct, your processing will likely fail. XSD lets you define the rules that your XML document *must* follow if it is to be considered a valid document for your purposes. (DTD, or Document Type Definition, is a similar, though older, technology. It's widely supported by XML tools, but it is not as flexible as XSD. There are also other schema definition languages similar to XSD, but since XSD is included in .NET, we'll focus on that.)

XSD schemas are every bit as endearing as XSLT scripts. Let's create an XSD for our original sample `<productList>` XML listed previously. First, we need to change the top of the XML to let it know that an XSD schema file is available. Here are the top two lines from the original products file.

```
<?xml version="1.0"?>
<productList>
```

Replace those two lines with the following enhanced version.

```
<?xml version="1.0"?>
<productList xmlns="SimpleProductList"
        xmlns:xsi="http://www.w3.org/2001/XMLSchema-instance"
        xsi:noNamespaceSchemaLocation="hello.xsd">
```

These directives tell the XML parser to look in *hello.xsd* for the schema. They also define a namespace; more on that later. The *hello.xsd* file contains the following schema.

```
<xs:schema xmlns:xs="http://www.w3.org/2001/XMLSchema"
    targetNamespace="SimpleProductList">
  <xs:element name="productList" type="ProductListType"/>

  <xs:complexType name="ProductListType">
    <xs:sequence>
      <xs:element name="supplier" type="SupplierType"
        maxOccurs="unbounded"/>
    </xs:sequence>
  </xs:complexType>

  <xs:complexType name="SupplierType">
    <xs:sequence>
      <xs:element name="product" type="ProductType"
        maxOccurs="unbounded"/>
    </xs:sequence>
    <xs:attribute name="ID" type="xs:integer"/>
    <xs:attribute name="fullName" type="xs:string"/>
  </xs:complexType>

  <xs:complexType name="ProductType">
    <xs:sequence>
      <xs:element name="productName" type="xs:string"/>
      <xs:element name="category" type="xs:string"/>
      <xs:element name="unitPrice" type="xs:decimal"/>
    </xs:sequence>
    <xs:attribute name="ID" type="xs:integer"/>
    <xs:attribute name="available" type="YesOrNoType"/>
    <xs:attribute name="onSale" type="xs:boolean"/>
  </xs:complexType>
  <xs:simpleType name="YesOrNoType">
    <xs:restriction base="xs:string">
      <xs:enumeration value="Yes"/>
      <xs:enumeration value="No"/>
    </xs:restriction>
  </xs:simpleType>
</xs:schema>
```

It looks nasty, doesn't it? Actually, it's more straightforward than XSLT. Basically, the schema says that for each element (or tag or node) in my XML document, here are the subordinate elements and attributes they contain, and the data type of each of them. You can even create your own pseudo-data types (actually, limiting factors on existing data types), as I did with the *YesOrNoType* data type, which limits the related value to the strings *Yes* and *No*.

You can look at the XML file with the attached XSD schema in your browser, but it wouldn't be all that interesting. It just shows you the XML. But schemas will be useful when you need to assess the quality of XML data coming into your software applications from external sources.

XML Namespaces

The product list XML shown earlier is nice, but someone else could come up with a product list document that is just as nice, but with different naming and formatting rules. For instance, someone might create a document that looks like this.

```
<?xml version="1.0"?>
<allProducts>
    <vendor ID="652" vendorName="Beverages R Us">
        <item ID="1" available="Yes">
            <itemName>Chai</itemName>
            <group>Beverages</group>
            <priceEach>18.00</priceEach>
        </item>
    </vendor>
</allProducts>
```

All of the data is the same, but the tags are different. Such a document would be incompatible with software written to work with our original document. Running the document through our XSD would quickly tell us that we have a bogus data set, but it would be nicer if something told us that from the start. Enter *namespaces*. Namespaces provide a convenient method to say, "This particular tag in the XML document uses this XSD-defined language." Notice the start of the XSD schema shown previously.

```
<xs:schema xmlns:xs="http://www.w3.org/2001/XMLSchema">
```

This line sets up a namespace named *xs* by using the *xmlns* attribute. (The *:xs* part tells XML what you want to call your namespace locally, within the file.) The value of the attribute is a Uniform Resource Identifier (URI), just a unique value that you are sure no one else is going to use. Typically, you use a web site address for your own company; the web site doesn't have to exist. You could even put your phone number there, just as long as it is unique, and unlikely to conflict with identifiers supplied by other organizations.

The most common way to use a namespace is to prefix the relevant tags in your XML document with the new namespace name, as in *xs:schema* instead of just *schema*. This tells the parser, "If you are checking my syntax against an XSD schema, use the one that I defined for the *xs* namespace." You can also use a default namespace for a given element and all its descendants by including the *xmlns* attribute in the outermost element. Then all elements within that outermost element will use the specified namespace. I used this method in one of the preceding examples.

```
<productList xmlns="SimpleProductList"...
```

For basic XML files that will only be used by your program, you may not need to bother with namespaces. They really come in handy when you are creating XML data that uses some publicly published standard. There are also instances where a single XML file might contain data related to two or more distinct uses of XML. In this case, different parts of your XML file could refer to different namespaces.

As with other parts of the XML world, XSD and namespaces are not all that easy to use, but they are flexible and powerful. As usual, there are tools, including tools in Visual Studio, which let you build all of this without having to think about the details.

As I keep saying, XML is just data, and if your program and data don't understand each other, you might as well go back to chisel and stone. XML and its related technologies provide a method to help ensure that your data is ready to use in your application.

Using XML in .NET: The Old Way

Visual C# includes two primary methods for working with XML content: the old way and the new way. The old way uses classes from the *System.Xml* namespace, and provides traditional object-based access to XML tags, attributes, and data. The new way, introduced in the 2008 release, uses classes in the *System.Xml.Linq* namespace, and provides a more fluid declaration syntax for new XML content. I'll discuss both methods in this chapter, starting with the old way.

Since XML is no fun to manage as a big chunk of text, .NET includes several classes that manage XML data. All of these tools appear in the *System.Xml* namespace and its subordinate namespaces.

System.Xml

    The main collection of old-way XML-related classes.

System.Xml.Linq

    Classes that integrate XML with LINQ technologies. This is the new way that I'm going to talk about later.

System.Xml.Schema

    Classes that create and use XSD schemas.

System.Xml.Serialization

    Classes that read and write XML documents via a standard .NET stream.

System.Xml.XPath

    Classes that implement the XPath technology used to search XML documents.

System.Xml.Xsl

    Classes that enable XSL Transformations.

The features included in each class tie pretty closely to the structure of XML and related technologies such as XSD and XSLT.

The Basic XML Classes, Basically

The *System.Xml* namespace includes the most basic classes you will use to manage XML data. An *XmlDocument* object is the in-memory view of your actual XML document.

```
XmlDocument myData = new XmlDocument();
```

Your document is made up of declarations (that `<?xml...?>` thing at the top), data elements (all the specific tags in your document), attributes (inside each starting element tag), and comments. These are represented by the *XmlDeclaration*, *XmlElement*, *XmlAttribute*, and *XmlComment* classes, respectively. Together, these four main units of your document are called *nodes*, represented generically by the *XmlNode* class. (The four specific classes all inherit from the more basic *XmlNode* class.) When you build an XML document by hand in memory, you use the individual classes such as *XmlElement*. Later on, when you need to scan through an existing document, it is easier to use the generic *XmlNode* class.

Let's build a subset of our sample XML product data.

```
<?xml version="1.0"?>
<productList>
   <!-- We currently sell these items. -->
   <supplier ID="652" fullName="Beverages R Us">
```

```
        <product ID="1" available="Yes">
           <productName>Chai</productName>
           <category>Beverages</category>
           <unitPrice>18.00</unitPrice>
        </product>
     </supplier>
</productList>
```

Declare all the variables you will use, and then use them.

```
XmlDocument products;
XmlDeclaration prodDeclare;
XmlElement rootSet;
XmlElement supplier;
XmlElement product;
XmlElement productValue;
XmlComment comment;

// ----- Create the document with a valid declaration.
products = new XmlDocument();
prodDeclare = products.CreateXmlDeclaration("1.0",
   null, string.Empty);
products.InsertBefore(prodDeclare,
   products.DocumentElement);

// ----- Create the root element, <productList>.
rootSet = products.CreateElement("productList");
products.InsertAfter(rootSet, prodDeclare);

// ----- Add a nice comment.
comment = products.CreateComment(
   " We currently sell these items. ");
rootSet.AppendChild(comment);

// ------ Create the supplier element, <supplier>.
//        Include the attributes.
supplier = products.CreateElement("supplier");
supplier.SetAttribute("ID", "652");
supplier.SetAttribute("fullName", "Beverages R Us");
rootSet.AppendChild(supplier);

// ----- Create the product element, <product>, with the
//        subordinate data values.
product = products.CreateElement("product");
product.SetAttribute("ID", "1");
product.SetAttribute("available", "yes");
supplier.AppendChild(product);

productValue = products.CreateElement("productName");
productValue.InnerText = "Chai";
product.AppendChild(productValue);

productValue = products.CreateElement("category");
productValue.InnerText = "Beverages";
product.AppendChild(productValue);
```

```
productValue = products.CreateElement("unitPrice");
productValue.InnerText = "18.00";
product.AppendChild(productValue);
```

It really works, too. To prove it, put this code in the *Click* event of a button, and end it with the following line.

```
products.Save(@"c:\products.xml");
```

Run the program and view the *c:\products.xml* file to see the XML product data. There are many different ways to use the XML classes to create an XML document in memory. For instance, although I used the *SetAttribute* method to add attributes to the supplier and product nodes, I could have created separate attribute objects, and appended them onto these nodes, just like I did for the main elements.

```
XmlAttribute attrData;
attrData = products.CreateAttribute("ID");
attrData.Value = "652";
supplier.SetAttributeNode(attrData);
```

So, this is nice and all, but what if you already have some XML in a file, and you just want to load it into an *XmlDocument* object? Simply use the *XmlDocument* object's *Load* method.

```
XmlDocument products;
products = new XmlDocument();
products.Load(@"c:\products.xml");
```

For those instances where you just want to read or write some XML from or to a file, and you don't care much about manipulating it in memory, the *XmlTextReader* and *XmlTextWriter* classes let you quickly read and write XML data via a text stream. But if you are going to do things with the XML data in your program, the *Load* and *Save* methods of the *XmlDocument* object are a better choice.

Finding Needles and Haystacks

In our sample data, all of the products appear in supplier groups. If we just want a list of products, regardless of supplier, we ask the *XmlDocument* object to supply that data via an *XmlNodeList* object.

```
XmlNodeList justProducts;

// ----- First, get the list.
justProducts = products.GetElementsByTagName("product");

// ----- Then do something with them.
foreach (XmlNode oneProduct in justProducts)
{
    // ----- Put interesting code here.
}
MessageBox.Show("Processed " +
    justProducts.Count.ToString() + " product(s).");
```

For a more complex selection of nodes within the document, the *System.Xml.XPath* namespace implements the XPath searching language, which gives you increased flexibility in locating items. The MSDN documentation describes the methods and searching syntax used with these classes.

Schema Verification

An *XmlDocument* object can hold any type of random yet valid XML content, but you can also verify the document against an XSD schema. If your XML document refers to an XSD schema, includes a DTD, or uses XDR (XML Data Reduced schemas, similar to XSD), an *XmlReader*, when configured with the appropriate *XmlReaderSettings*, will properly compare your XML data against the defined rules, and throw an exception if there's a problem.

```
XmlDocument products = new XmlDocument();
XmlTextReader xmlRead;
XmlReaderSettings withVerify = new XmlReaderSettings();
XmlReader xmlReadGood;

// ----- Open the XML file and process schemas
//       referenced within the content.
withVerify.ValidationType = ValidationType.Schema;
xmlRead = new XmlTextReader(@"c:\products.xml");
xmlReadGood = XmlReader.Create(xmlRead, withVerify);

// ----- Load content, or throw exception on
//       validation failure.
products.Load(xmlReadGood);

' ----- Clean up.
xmlReadGood.Close();
xmlRead.Close();
```

XML Transformations

XSL Transformations are no more difficult than any of the other manipulations of XML. Just as there are many ways to get XML source data (from a file, building it by hand with *XmlDocument*, etc.), there are many ways to transform the data. If you just want to go from input file to output file, the following code provides a quick and efficient method. It uses a *System.Xml.Xsl.XslCompiledTransform* instance to perform the magic.

```
// ----- Assumes: using System.Xml.Xsl;
XslCompiledTransform xslTrans;

// ----- Open the XSL file as a transformation.
xslTrans = new XslCompiledTransform();
xslTrans.Load(@"c:\convert.xsl");

// ----- Convert and save the output.
xslTrans.Transform(@"c:\input.xml", @"c:\output.txt");
```

Using XML in .NET: The New Way

In the old-way section a few pages ago, I showed you some code that created the XML product list for "Chai." The XML content was eleven lines long, but it took nearly fifty lines of source code to produce it. But you can build that same XML content using the new way in pretty close to the final eleven lines.

```
XDocument chaiItem = new XDocument(
    new XDeclaration("1.0", "utf-8", "yes"),
    new XElement("productList",
        new XComment("We currently sell these items."),
        new XElement("supplier",
            new XAttribute("ID", 652),
            new XAttribute("fullName", "Beverages R Us"),
            new XElement("product",
                new XAttribute("ID", 1),
```

```
            new XAttribute("available", "Yes"),
            new XElement("productName", "Chai"),
            new XElement("category", "Beverages"),
            new XElement("unitPrice", 18M)
        )
      )
    )
  );
```

The content gets stored in the new *XDocument* object, part of the *System.Xml.Linq* namespace. Just like the *XmlDocument* class, the *XDocument* class includes *Load* and *Save* methods to manage file-based XML, plus other features that let you manipulate and examine XML content.

Summary

There are a lot of useful features in the various *System.Xml* namespaces, and you can manage complex data in very effective ways. It's not always the most efficient way to manage data, but if you have structured hierarchical data, it may be the most direct and clearest method.

Although XML lurks everywhere in the .NET Framework, and in all applications written using .NET, you could actually write large and interesting applications without looking at a single line of XML content. Even if your application needs to interact with XML content, the XML features included in Visual C# make managing XML only slightly more complicated than typing the content directly into Notepad.

XML is a very useful and flexible data format that is here to stay. Although it will always lack the speed of more compact data standards, its benefits are numerous. There has been talk of introducing a "binary XML" format as a standard, although nothing concrete has come of it yet. If binary XML does become a standard, you will likely continue to use the same classes and methods introduced in this chapter, with the possible addition of an *OutputFormat* ("Text" or "Binary") property.

Project

The administrator of the Library system will want to see statistics and information at a glance, or run various reports that provide meaningful summary or detail views of system data. Although as a programmer I could try to add every conceivable type of report that the user may need, I have learned from experience that this is not possible. Users always want the moon, usually in the form of some weird esoteric report that I know they will use once and never look at again (although they will call once a year asking for the same report to be written again). I don't like recompiling and rereleasing the entire application every time a user needs a new report. Instead, I keep the reports outside the application, stored as separate programs. Then, from one form in the main application, I make all of those external reports available in a nice convenient list.

To implement this generic feature, I use a report configuration file, a simple XML file that contains information about the available reports, and how to run them. I want my selection list to have indented items so that I can visibly group reports for convenience. To do this, I will make my XML file into an unlimited depth hierarchy, with each level representing a further level of displayed indent. For instance, let's say I wanted the following outline of reports (with report group titles in bold).

Detail Reports

Daily Report

Monthly Reports

Monthly Value

Monthly Inventory

Summary Reports

Inventory Summary

The XML configuration would follow this structure.

```
<Group name="Detail Reports">
   <Item name="Daily Report"/>
   <Group name="Monthly Reports">
      <Item name="Monthly Value"/>
      <Item name="Monthly Inventory"/>
   </Group>
</Group>
<Group name="SummaryReports">
   <Item name="Inventory Summary"/>
</Group>
```

Of course, this is greatly simplified (not to mention noncompliant) XML. In addition to the hierarchy, I also want to include support for a variety of reporting methods. To keep things simple, the Library Project will include three types of reports.

Built-in reports

The application includes a limited number of reports that are permanently built into the main application (assembly). The reports are numbered, starting from 1, and at this time I have five reports in mind. The designer of the XML configuration file can choose to include these in the display of reports or not by simply including or not including them in the file. In the absence of a configuration file, these reports will appear in the list by default. In addition to the report number (1 to 5), each entry has a display text and a long description.

Application reports

These reports are separate and distinct EXE files, and are started via standard application initiation methods. Each entry includes a display text, the full path to the application, optional arguments, a flag to pass the identity of the user initiating the report, and a long description.

URL reports

These reports are simple calls to web pages, or any other valid URL. For instance, you could include a report entry that does a "mailto:" to the local organization's help desk. Each entry includes the display text, the URL itself, and a long description.

The project activities in this chapter involve both coding and documentation of the new external resource (the XML file format).

Update Technical Documentation

First, let's add clear documentation on the structure of the XML configuration file. There is no easy way to communicate the structure of an XML file to an ordinary user. Although such documentation is a requirement, hopefully the application will also include a tool to let an administrator build the configuration file. Such a program, sadly, is not included in this book's project. It is left as an exercise for the reader. (I always wanted to say that.)

I've updated the Resource Kit for the Library Project, and placed a new copy of that document (in Microsoft Word and PDF formats) in the *After* folder for this chapter. For your convenience, I'm including here the content from the new "Report Confirmation File" section of that document.

The library application can be configured to run any number of reports through the *Reports* form. The list of available reports is managed through an XML report configuration file, a file describing report groups and items. All items are reports, and appear within a group. You can nest groups within groups to any depth, and the list of reports displayed in the Library program will indent each subordinate group to help the user see the organization of the reports. There is no limit to the nesting of groups.

The root element of the XML file must be named `<reportList>`, and it may contain any number of `<reportGroup>` and `<reportItem>` data elements.

- `<reportItem>`: Represents a single report entry. This entry has one required attribute, and up to five subordinate data elements depending on the setting of the attribute.
  - *type* (attribute): Set to one of the following values.
    - `built-in`: Run one of the built-in programs. This type of report uses the `<displayText>`, `<reportPath>`, and `<description>` data elements.
    - `program`: Runs a separate EXE program. This type of report uses the `<displayText>`, `<reportPath>`, `<reportArgs>`, `<reportFlags>`, and `<description>` data elements.
    - `url`: Starts a URL, such as a web page or a "mailto" email to a recipient address. This type of report uses the `<displayText>`, `<reportPath>`, and `<description>` data elements.
  - `<displayText>`: A short name or description for this report, as it will appear in the list of report choices. This element is required for all types of reports.
  - `<reportPath>`: The full path, URL, or number of the report, depending on the type of report. For program (EXE) reports, this is the full UNC or driver letter-based path to the report, without additional arguments. For built-in reports, this is a report number, from 1 to 5 (values and their meanings are listed later in this section). For URL reports, this is the actual URL, as in "http://example.com/myreport.htm" or "mailto:helpdesk@example.com." This element is required for all types of reports.
  - `<reportArgs>`: For program (EXE) reports, this entry includes any command-line arguments to be included when running the program. This element is valid only for program (EXE) reports, and is always optional.
  - `<reportFlags>`: For program (EXE) reports, this entry indicates the optional flags that should be appended to the application command as arguments. At this time, the only flag is the *U* flag. When this element is set to *U*, the argument `-u userid` is appended to the command string (where *userid* is the user's login ID, from the database field

UserName.LoginID). This element is valid only for program (EXE) reports, and is always optional.

  ○ *<description>*: This is a longer, verbose description of the report, up to about 200 characters, which will appear on the Report form when the user selects the report from the list. This description should assist the user in selecting the right report. This element is valid for all types of reports, but is always optional.

 • *<reportGroup>*: Represents a category group, used to visibly group and indent reports in the display list. This element must contain exactly one *<displayText>* element, but may contain any number of *<reportItem>* or *<reportGroup>* elements.

  ○ *<displayText>*: A short name or description for this group, as it will appear in the list of report choices. This element is required.

When using the built-in report type, the *<reportPath>* element is set to one of the following integer values.

 • 1—Items Checked Out Report
 • 2—Items Overdue Report
 • 3—Items Missing Report
 • 4—Fines Owed by Patrons Report
 • 5—Library Database Statistics Report

Create Report Entry Class

With .NET's ability to store whole objects as *ListBox* items, we can create a custom class that contains all the information needed to select and run a report from the list of reports. This class is fairly simple, with nothing but basic public fields, plus an overridden *ToString* function, used by the *ListBox* control to properly display each list item.

In the Library Project, add a new class file named *ReportItem.cs* through the Project→Add Class menu command. Add the following enumeration to the file, but add it outside the boundaries of the *ReportItem* class. This enumeration indicates what type of entry each list item represents.

Insert Snippet
Insert Chapter 13, Snippet Item 1.

```
public enum ReportItemEnum : int
{
    // ----- The type of item in the report select list.
    GroupLabel = 0,
    BuiltInCheckedOut = 1,
    BuiltInOverdue = 2,
    BuiltInMissing = 3,
    BuiltInFinesOwed = 4,
    BuiltInStatistics = 5,
    ExeProgram = 6,
    UrlProgram = 7
}
```

To this same file, add the members of the *ReportItem* class. This class contains all the information we need to run reports loaded from the configuration file.

Insert Snippet
Insert Chapter 13, Snippet Item 2.

```
// ----- Instance of report selection items used
//       in the ReportSelect form.
public ReportItemEnum ItemType;
public int Indent;          // Indent level. Starts with 0.
public string DisplayText;
public string ReportPath; // ExeProgram / UrlProgram only
public string ReportArgs; // ExeProgram only
public string Description;

public override string ToString()
{
    // ----- Display an indented string. Prepend with spaces.
    return (new string(' ', Indent * 5)) + DisplayText;
}
```

Design the Report Form

Librarians and administrators use the Select Report form (see Figure 13-2) to view reports. The form includes a *ListBox* control that displays all reports and report groups, a Run button that starts a report, and a Close button that returns the user to the main form. A label displays the full description of a report, when available, just below the *ListBox*.

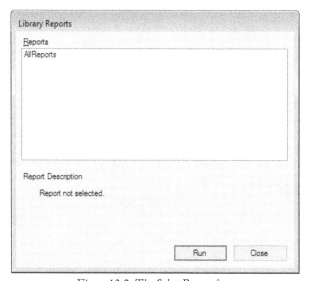

Figure 13-2. The Select Report form

Add a new form file named *ReportSelect.cs* through the Project→Add Windows Form menu command. Add the controls and settings as listed in Table 13-1.

Table 13-1. Controls and settings for the Select Report form

Control/form	Type	Settings
LabelReports	Label	(Name): LabelReports Location: 8, 8 Text: &Reports
AllReports	ListBox	(Name): AllReports Location: 8, 24 Size: 392, 160

Control/form	Type	Settings
LabelDescription	Label	(Name): LabelDescription Location: 8, 200 Text: Report Description
FullDescription	Label	(Name): FullDescription AutoSize: False Location: 32, 224 Size: 368, 64 Text: Report not selected. UseMnemonic: False
ActRun	Button	(Name): ActRun DialogResult: None Location: 232, 304 Size: 80, 24 Text: Run
ActClose	Button	(Name): ActClose DialogResult: Cancel Location: 320, 304 Size: 80, 24 Text: Close
ReportSelect	Form	(Name): ReportSelect AcceptButton: ActRun CancelButton: ActClose ControlBox: False FormBorderStyle: FixedDialog Size: 425, 376 StartPosition: CenterScreen Text: Library Reports

Adjust the tab order of the new controls by selecting the form, and then using the View→Tab Order menu command.

Although the administrator has probably given useful names to each report, the terseness of each report name may still confuse the user. Each report includes an optional full description. As the user selects reports from the list, an event handler updates the *FullDescription* label just below the main list. Add this event handler member to the class.

Insert Snippet
Insert Chapter 13, Snippet Item 3.

```
private void AllReports_SelectedIndexChanged(
   object sender, EventArgs e)
{
   // ----- Display a description of the report, if available.
   ReportItem reportEntry;

   // ----- Clear any previous description.
   FullDescription.Text = "No report selected.";
   if (AllReports.SelectedIndex != -1)
   {
      // ----- Locate the content and display it.
      reportEntry = (ReportItem)AllReports.SelectedItem;
      FullDescription.Text = reportEntry.Description;
```

```
        }
    }
```

Populate Reports from Configuration File

The *RefreshReportList* method loads the data from the report configuration file and processes the results. Eventually, the location of this file will be recorded in the application's configuration file, but we won't be adding that until a later chapter. For now, let's put in a hardcoded test file location, and mark it for later update.

> **Insert Snippet**
>
> Insert Chapter 13, Snippet Item 4.

```csharp
private void RefreshReportList()
{
    // ----- Load in the list of available reports.
    string configFile;
    XDocument configData;
    ReportItem reportEntry;

    // ----- Clear the existing list.
    AllReports.Items.Clear();

    // ----- Get the location of the configuration file.
    // TODO: Load this from the application's configuration.
    //       For now, just hardcode the value.
    configFile = @"c:\ReportConfig.txt";

    // ----- Load the configuration file.
    if (configFile.Length != 0)
    {
        if (System.IO.File.Exists(configFile))
        {
            try
            {
                // ----- Load in the file.
                configData = XDocument.Load(configFile);

                // ----- Process the configuration file.
                LoadReportGroup((XElement)configData.FirstNode, 0);
            }
            catch (Exception ex)
            {
                GeneralError("ReportSelect.RefreshReportList", ex);
            }
        }
    }

    // ----- If the configuration file resulted in no reports
    //       appearing in the list, add the default reports.
    if (AllReports.Items.Count == 0)
    {
        for (int counter = 1; counter <= Convert.ToInt32(
            ReportItemEnum.BuiltInStatistics); counter++)
        {
```

```
        // ----- Build the report entry.
        reportEntry = new ReportItem();
        reportEntry.Indent = 0;
        reportEntry.ItemType = (ReportItemEnum)counter;
        switch (reportEntry.ItemType)
        {
            case ReportItemEnum.BuiltInCheckedOut:
                reportEntry.DisplayText =
                    "Items Checked Out";
                break;
            case ReportItemEnum.BuiltInOverdue:
                reportEntry.DisplayText =
                    "Items Overdue";
                break;
            case ReportItemEnum.BuiltInMissing:
                reportEntry.DisplayText =
                    "Items Missing";
                break;
            case ReportItemEnum.BuiltInFinesOwed:
                reportEntry.DisplayText =
                    "Patron Fines Owed";
                break;
            case ReportItemEnum.BuiltInStatistics:
                reportEntry.DisplayText =
                    "Database Statistics";
                break;
        }

        // ----- Add the report entry to the list.
        AllReports.Items.Add(reportEntry);
    }
  }
}
```

Because the report configuration file allows nested report groups to any level, we need to use a recursive routine to repeatedly descend to each successive level. The *LoadReportGroup* routine, called by *RefreshReportList*, adds all report items and report groups within a starting report group. It's initially called from the reference point of the root *<reportList>* element. Each time it finds a child *<reportGroup>* element, it calls itself again, but this time starting from the reference point of the child *<reportGroup>* element.

Insert Snippet
Insert Chapter 13, Snippet Item 5.

```
private void LoadReportGroup(
    XElement groupNode, int indentLevel)
{
    // ----- Add the groups and items at this level,
    //       and recurse as needed.
    XElement detailNode;
    ReportItem reportEntry;
    int holdValue;
```

```
// ----- Process each item or group.
foreach (XElement scanNode in groupNode.Nodes())
{
   // ----- Build a content item for the list.
   reportEntry = new ReportItem();
   reportEntry.Indent = indentLevel;

   // ----- Get the display name.
   detailNode = (XElement)scanNode.Elements("displayText");
   if (detailNode == null)
      continue;
   reportEntry.DisplayText = detailNode.Value;

   if (scanNode.Name == "reportGroup")
   {
      // ----- Start a new display group.
      reportEntry.ItemType = ReportItemEnum.GroupLabel;
      AllReports.Items.Add(reportEntry);

      // ----- Recurse to child items.
      LoadReportGroup(scanNode, indentLevel + 1);
   }
   else if (scanNode.Name == "reportItem")
   {
      // ----- This is an item. Record its location.
      detailNode =
         (XElement)scanNode.Elements("reportPath");
      if (detailNode != null)
         reportEntry.ReportPath = detailNode.Value;

      // ----- Get any command-line arguments.
      detailNode =
         (XElement)scanNode.Elements("reportArgs");
      if (detailNode != null)
         reportEntry.ReportArgs = detailNode.Value;

      // ----- Get any item-specific flags.
      detailNode =
         (XElement)scanNode.Elements("reportFlags");
      if (detailNode != null)
      {
         // ---- "U" adds "-u loginid" to the command.
         if ((detailNode.Value.ToUpper().
               Contains("U") == true) &
               (LoggedInUserName.Length != 0))
            reportEntry.ReportArgs =
               (reportEntry.ReportArgs + " -u " +
               LoggedInUserName).Trim();
      }

      // ----- Store the full description.
      detailNode =
         (XElement)scanNode.Elements("description");
```

```
            if (detailNode != null)
                reportEntry.Description = detailNode.Value;

            // ----- So, what type of entry is it?
            if (scanNode.Attributes(
                "type").ToString() == "built-in")
            {
                // ----- Built-in program. Check for valid ID.
                if (int.TryParse(reportEntry.ReportPath,
                        out holdValue) == false)
                    holdValue = 0;
                if ((holdValue < 1) | (holdValue >
                        (int)ReportItemEnum.BuiltInStatistics))
                    continue;
                reportEntry.ItemType = (ReportItemEnum)
                    Convert.ToInt32(reportEntry.ReportPath);
                AllReports.Items.Add(reportEntry);
            }
            else if (scanNode.Attributes(
                "type").ToString() == "program")
            {
                // ----- EXE program-based report.
                if (reportEntry.ReportPath.Length == 0)
                    continue;
                reportEntry.ItemType =
                    ReportItemEnum.ExeProgram;
                AllReports.Items.Add(reportEntry);
            }
            else if (scanNode.Attributes(
                "type").ToString() == "url")
            {
                // ----- URL-based report.
                if (reportEntry.ReportPath.Length == 0)
                    continue;
                reportEntry.ItemType =
                    ReportItemEnum.UrlProgram;
                AllReports.Items.Add(reportEntry);
            }
        }
    }
}
```

Add the form's *Load* event, which loads in the content from the configuration file.

Insert Snippet
Insert Chapter 13, Snippet Item 6.

```
private void ReportSelect_Load(object sender, EventArgs e)
{
    // ----- Display the list of reports.
    RefreshReportList();
}
```

Running the Reports

Now that all of the groups and items appear in the list, we have to run the actual reports. The *ActRun* button's *Click* event handles this duty. For now, we will just add the framework to support the calling of each report. The built-in reports will be added in Chapter 21.

Insert Snippet

Insert Chapter 13, Snippet Item 7.

```
private void ActRun_Click(object sender, EventArgs e)
{
   // ----- Run the selected report.
   ReportItem reportEntry;

   // ----- Make sure a report is selected.
   if (AllReports.SelectedIndex == -1)
   {
      MessageBox.Show(
         "Please select a report from the list.",
         ProgramTitle, MessageBoxButtons.OK,
         MessageBoxIcon.Exclamation);
      return;
   }

   // ----- Different code for each type of entry.
   reportEntry = (ReportItem)AllReports.SelectedItem;
   this.Cursor = Cursors.WaitCursor;
   switch (reportEntry.ItemType)
   {
      case ReportItemEnum.GroupLabel:
         // ----- No report for group entries.
         MessageBox.Show(
            "Please select a report from the list.",
            ProgramTitle, MessageBoxButtons.OK,
            MessageBoxIcon.Exclamation);
         break;
      case ReportItemEnum.BuiltInCheckedOut:
         // ----- Items Checked Out
         // TODO: Write BasicReportCheckedOut();
         break;
      case ReportItemEnum.BuiltInOverdue:
         // ----- Items Overdue
         // TODO: Write BasicReportOverdue();
         break;
      case ReportItemEnum.BuiltInMissing:
         // ----- Items Missing
         // TODO: Write BasicReportMissing();
         break;
      case ReportItemEnum.BuiltInFinesOwed:
         // ----- Fines Owed by Patrons
         // TODO: Write BasicReportFines();
         break;
      case ReportItemEnum.BuiltInStatistics:
         // ----- Library Database Statistics
         // TODO: Write BasicReportStatistics();
```

```
        break;
    case ReportItemEnum.ExeProgram:
        // ----- Start a program.
        try
        {
            Process.Start(
                "\"" + reportEntry.ReportPath +
                "\" " + reportEntry.ReportArgs);
        }
        catch (Exception ex)
        {
            GeneralError(
                "ReportSelect.ActRun_Click.Exe", ex);
        }
        break;
    case ReportItemEnum.UrlProgram:
        // ----- Start a URL.
        Process.Start(reportEntry.ReportPath);
        break;
    }
    this.Cursor = Cursors.Default;
}
```

For external reports, the event handler calls the *Process.Start* method. This amazing method accepts either a standard command-line expression, or any valid URL or web page address.

We added some event handlers throughout this process, so now it's time to connect them to their underlying events. Add this block to the end of the *InitializeComponent* method.

Insert Snippet
Insert Chapter 13, Snippet Item 8.

```
this.ActRun.Click += this.ActRun_Click;
this.AllReports.SelectedIndexChanged +=
    this.AllReports_SelectedIndexChanged;
this.Load += this.ReportSelect_Load;
```

Finally, add a few *using* directives to the top of the form's source code so that some of the shortcuts we used in the code will compile. Add the following lines just after the existing *using* directives in the *ReportSelect.cs* file.

Insert Snippet
Insert Chapter 13, Snippet Item 9.

```
using System.Xml.Linq;
using System.Diagnostics;
using static Library.General;
```

Connecting the Select Report Form
To make the reports available to the user, we must enable a link to the report form from the main form. We included a distinct panel on that form just for printing reports. The *ActDoReports* button on that panel triggers a call to the new report selection form. Create a new event handler for the *ActDoReports* button and add the following code.

```
// ----- Show the reports form.
(new ReportSelect()).ShowDialog();
```

Now that we have a firm grasp on the world of XML, we'll let Visual C# do all the hard work of manipulating it for application configuration purposes.

Chapter 14

Application Settings

More than seven score years ago, President Abraham Lincoln began his famous Gettysburg Address with "Four score and seven years ago...." Why this poetic reference to the founding of America eighty-seven years earlier? He could have started the speech with "Last week, I was talking with members of my cabinet," or even, "These three confederate soldiers walked into a bar...." But he stuck with the decades-old anecdote.

Lincoln understood that his listeners, as humans, had a tie with the past, a fondness for the familiar, a love of fast sports cars, and a desire to see the stability of a former era restored. This is how people are. They like peace, not war. They like the status quo, not change. They like dinner on the table when they return home from a hard day at the office. They like short lines at the amusement park. They like seeing their favorite football team win once again.

People like to know that things are configured in a way that makes sense to them, set up in a way that is familiar and known. They expect this in life, and they expect this in their software. That's why Visual C# includes features that let you maintain user-specific and application-specific settings, to give the people what they want.

A Short History of Settings

Since that short yet dynamic speech by Lincoln, programmers have sought a convenient way to maintain configurable values in their applications. In the early days of MS-DOS development, it was a configuration free-for-all; each program provided its own settings system. Many applications needed no specialized configuration, but those that did often stored configuration settings together with the application's managed data, all in proprietary *.dat* files.

With the advent of mainstream Windows development, Microsoft introduced file-based settings management through its *application programming interface* (API). The "private profile" API calls (*GetPrivateProfileInt*, *GetPrivateProfileString*, *SetPrivateProfileString*, and a few others) supplied a standard way to store short configuration values in an open and easy-to-understand text file format. Microsoft used these "INI" files (named for the *.ini* file extension) for its own configuration, although today they largely exist for legacy support. Here's the content I found in the *win.ini* file from one of my older system's *Windows* folder.

```
; for 16-bit app support
[fonts]
[extensions]
[mci extensions]
[files]
[Mail]
MAPI=1
```

```
[CDWINSETUP]
AUTOUNLOAD=No
[MSUCE]
Advanced=0
CodePage=Unicode
Font=Arial
```

The format of an INI file was simple to understand. Each file included named sections defined within square brackets, as in *[fonts]*. Each section maintained a set of key-value pairs in the form *key=value*. The design was simple enough that anyone could use Notepad to make changes. It wasn't even that hard for a program to write its own INI-file management routines, but having them included in the Windows API made them that much more attractive.

But then came the clutter. With so many programs opting to store their configuration files in a known central location, the *Windows* folder quickly became the file equivalent of Grand Central Station at 5:00 p.m. on a Friday. Speed was an issue, too, since the constant parsing and rewriting of INI files consumed precious CPU resources.

Microsoft came up with a solution: the *registry*. This hierarchical database of key-value pairs cleaned up the filesystem and brought speed improvements to configuration management. It also added new administrator-defined security settings for access to the registry, and provided support for some limited strongly typed data. But the new API features weren't the most intuitive.

The registry threw technology at the configuration-values problem, but it wasn't a full triumph. With so many vendors stuffing gobs of data in the registry, bloat once again became an issue. And with the system managing all access to the registry, the larger the registry, the worse the performance.

.NET's initial release included application-specific configuration files, a sort-of return to those days of INI-file yesteryear. In some ways, *app.config* and *web.config* files were better than INI files since they contained structured XML content. But big whoop. INI files had structure, and you could update them in Notepad. .NET config files were notoriously difficult to update, either within a .NET application or externally in Notepad (due to some weird caching issues). Also, *.config* files had neither the security nor the strong data typing available in the registry.

Configuration settings have been giving programmers at least some level of angst since Windows first appeared. But a new and improved settings system, first added to Visual Studio in 2005, sought to change all that.

Settings in Visual C#

The settings system in today's Visual C# is a multi-file, XML-based, strongly typed, and easy-to-manage configuration approach. Its file-focused methodology includes these features and benefits.

- Data is stored in XML format for efficient processing by .NET libraries. Although it is not free-form text, XML is not overwhelmingly difficult when manual updates need to be made by mere mortals.

- The data stored in each settings-specific file is strongly typed, reducing errors from the processing of invalid data.

- Settings are managed on a per-application, per-user, and even per-assembly-version basis to promote security and reduce conflicts. You can also store multiple sets of settings per application as you require, such as one set of settings per document opened by your application. (I won't discuss it in this chapter, but you can search for "SettingsKey property" in the MSDN documentation for additional information on this feature.)

- Visual Studio includes a user-friendly management tool used to configure settings within an application.

But it's not all fun and games. As a developer, you have to do some of the work yourself, such as coming up with meaningful names for each setting ("MainFormLocation," "DatabaseConnection," etc.), and altering the behavior of your program as needed based on the stored settings.

The actual settings appear in XML files scattered throughout the filesystem.

- At design time, all the settings you create get stored in a *Settings.settings* file, stored in the *Properties* subdirectory of your source code folder. Here's the *Settings.settings* file as it exists so far in the Library Project.

```
<?xml version='1.0' encoding='utf-8'?>
<SettingsFile xmlns="http://schemas.microsoft.com/
      VisualStudio/2004/01/settings" CurrentProfile="(Default)"
      GeneratedClassNamespace="Library.Properties"
      GeneratedClassName="Settings">
  <Profiles />
  <Settings />
</SettingsFile>
```

- At runtime, all user-specific settings appear in a *user.config* file, typically stored in `C:\Users\<user>\AppData\Local\<company>\<appinfo>\<version>` for desktop applications, where `<user>` is the Windows username, `<company>` is the company name recorded in the assembly, `<appinfo>` is a combination of values that help to differentiate the settings based on use, and `<version>` is the four-part version number of the assembly. It seems like a difficult place to store settings, but it keeps things nice and ordered. (The location of the *user.config* file is a little different if you deploy an application using ClickOnce, a method described in Chapter 24, and for non-desktop targets.)

  You're probably wondering whether this contributes to disk bloat. Yes! Each time you bump up the version number of your application, .NET creates a new settings file to go with it. There's a way to mitigate this somewhat, but with typical hard drives approaching the terabyte range, no one's really complaining about disk space usage anymore.

- Some settings are application-focused, and apply to all users of the application on a particular workstation. These are stored in the *app.config* file that appears in the same folder as your assembly's executable. The settings appear in an XML branch named `<applicationSettings>` within this file. Application-focused settings cannot be modified by the application; you must manually update the *app.config* file to force a change.

The settings system is a great place to store *state*, things that you want the program to remember from the last time it was run, but that shouldn't be hardcoded into the source code.

Adding Settings to a Project

The Project Properties window within Visual Studio provides centralized control of an application's overall configuration. The Settings panel of this window, shown in Figure 14-1, provides access to the application's custom settings.

Figure 14-1. The Settings panel with no defined settings

To add a setting, type in its Name, select its data Type from the drop-down list, choose the Scope (User or Application), and enter its Value using whatever value editor is available for the selected type. The Type list includes many default selections, including the basic Visual C# data types, fonts, colors, and drawing-related sizes. Also included is a "(Connection string)" type that, when selected, enables a Connection Properties string builder in the Value column.

It's important that you select the correct type for each stored setting; otherwise, your workstation will explode. Actually, I think they fixed that in a later beta. It's really because all settings are strongly typed. If you set the type to *int*, you won't be able to stuff the word *None* in there as a special flag as you could have done with an INI file. You can choose any valid .NET type for the data type, although complex types without their own custom editors will require that you set their values through code.

What happens when you add a new setting to your Visual C# project? Let's find out. I'll add two settings to a new Windows Forms project: an *int* named *WarningLimit*, and a *System.Drawing.Font* named *NoticeFont* (see Figure 14-2).

Name	Type	Scope	Value
WarningLimit	int	User	25
NoticeFont	System.Drawing.Font	User	Arial, 14.25pt, style=Bold

Figure 14-2. The Settings panel with two new settings

As you already know, Visual Studio is just a user-friendly wrapper around .NET code, and the Settings panel is no different. So, the real changes occur somewhere in the code, or more correctly, in both code and the related *Settings.settings* file. If you head over to the Solution Explorer panel and expand Properties followed by *Settings.settings*, you will find that this XML file has its own Visual C# source code file, *Settings.Designer.cs*.

If you open the *Settings.Designer.cs* file, you find the following partial code.

```
namespace Library.Properties {
    internal sealed partial class Settings :
        System.Configuration.ApplicationSettingsBase {
        [System.Configuration.UserScopedSettingAttribute()]
        [System.Diagnostics.DebuggerNonUserCodeAttribute()]
        [System.Configuration.DefaultSettingValueAttribute("25")]
        public int WarningLimit {
            get {
                return ((int)(this["WarningLimit"]));
            }
            set {
                this["WarningLimit"] = value;
```

```
        }
    }

    [System.Configuration.UserScopedSettingAttribute()]
    [System.Diagnostics.DebuggerNonUserCodeAttribute()]
    [System.Configuration.DefaultSettingValueAttribute(
        "Arial, 14.25pt, style=Bold")]
    public System.Drawing.Font NoticeFont {
        get {
            return ((System.Drawing.Font)
                (this["NoticeFont"]));
        }
        set {
            this["NoticeFont"] = value;
        }
    }
  }
}
```

I excluded a lot of the extra code. It's amazing how much code Microsoft loads up in prewritten attributes, and unless you download the source code for .NET itself, it's not really possible to know what goes on inside. I can guess what the *DefaultSettingValueAttribute* attribute does for each setting (assigns the initial default value of the setting), but some of the others are mysteries. Oh well. Even the ancients didn't have answers for everything.

But the code that remains is quite clear. Visual Studio generates two properties within the *Settings* class, properties named—amazingly enough—*WarningLimit* and *NoticeFont*. Here's the property entry for *NoticeFont*.

```
public System.Drawing.Font NoticeFont
{
    get {
        return ((System.Drawing.Font)(this["NoticeFont"]));
    }
    set {
        this["NoticeFont"] = value;
    }
}
```

You won't find any private class members that store the hidden *WarningLimit* and *NoticeFont* values. Instead, somewhere else in this partial class is an indexer that gets and sets each defined property value, accessed through *this["something"]*.

The settings available through this indexer are loaded directly from the XML stored in the *Settings.settings* file. (This file is compiled into the application assembly; you don't have to distribute *Settings.settings* with the application.) Here's the content from that file with our two new configuration values.

```
<?xml version='1.0' encoding='utf-8'?>
<SettingsFile xmlns="http://schemas.microsoft.com/
    VisualStudio/2004/01/settings"
    CurrentProfile="(Default)"
    GeneratedClassNamespace="Library.Properties"
    GeneratedClassName="Settings">
  <Profiles />
  <Settings>
    <Setting Name="WarningLimit"
```

```
        Type="System.Int32" Scope="User">
      <Value Profile="(Default)">25</Value>
    </Setting>
    <Setting Name="NoticeFont"
        Type="System.Drawing.Font" Scope="User">
      <Value Profile="(Default)">
        Arial, 14.25pt, style=Bold</Value>
    </Setting>
  </Settings>
</SettingsFile>
```

Each setting contains distinct *Name*, *Type*, *Scope*, and *Value* attributes or entries, matching the four columns that appeared in the Visual Studio settings editor.

Properties.Settings

The code in *Settings.Designer.cs* exposes a member named *Default*, a static instance of the settings collection that is available to your project source code. As you add settings to your project, they become strongly typed class members of this *Properties.Settings.Default* instance. To access one, simply reference it directly in your code.

```
MessageBox.Show("The font for notices is: " +
    Properties.Settings.Default.NoticeFont.ToString());
```

(The output for this code appears in Figure 14-3.) The *Properties.Settings.Default.NoticeFont* is an actual instance of *System.Drawing.Font* that you can use like any other *Font* instance.

Figure 14-3. Be sure to take "notice" of this font

You can modify the value of any setting scoped as "User," and have the new value preserved for your next use of the application (i.e., for the current user's next use of the application).

```
Properties.Settings.Default.WarningLimit = 30;
```

Such changes to the user-specific settings remain in memory for use in your program, but they disappear when you close the program. To make these changes permanent, call the *Settings* instance's *Save* method.

```
Properties.Settings.Default.Save();
```

Settings come in three delicious flavors: default, persisted, and current. *Default settings* are those values defined by the programmer through the Visual Studio settings editor. *Persisted settings* include the saved changes to specific settings, and the default settings for those that have never been altered by the user. *Current settings* include any changes made to the settings during the current session, but not yet saved. You can play with these states using members of the *Properties.Settings.Default* object.

- The *Save* method, as mentioned previously, saves all current settings to a persisted state.
- The *Reload* method restores any current values with the persisted versions.

- The *Reset* method wipes out all current and persisted settings, and returns all configuration entries to their default values.

One of the strangest aspects of settings is that they are version-specific. If you release your application as version 1.0.0.0, and then later release version 1.1.0.0, each user will lose all of the previously persisted settings. Actually, they won't be lost, but they will be stuck in 1.0.0.0-land. If you always want to have the most up-to-date settings as modified by the user, you will have to make sure that older settings are upgraded when installing a new version. *Properties.Settings.Default* includes an *Upgrade* method that does the work for you. But if the user installs a newer version and upgrades the settings, makes changes to those settings, and then calls *Upgrade* again, any changes made since the last upgrade will be lost.

To get around this problem, the code should upgrade settings only when a new version appears. The easiest way to do this is to include a setting called something like *SettingsUpgraded* and set it to *false*. Check this flag before calling *Upgrade*. If it is still *false*, it is safe to call *Upgrade*. Once the code upgrades the settings, change *SettingsUpgraded* to *true*.

```
if (Properties.Settings.Default.SettingsUpgraded == false)
{
    Properties.Settings.Default.Upgrade();
    Properties.Settings.Default.SettingsUpgraded = true;
    Properties.Settings.Default.Save();
}
```

This need to upgrade settings whenever even minor version number changes are made to an assembly seems a bit over the top. But it's necessary to support .NET's goal of side-by-side installation. The user should be able to install two different versions of your application on the same workstation, and use each one without interference from the other. Storing version-specific settings helps to achieve this goal.

Bound Settings

Although using and updating your own custom configuration values can be exciting, even more exciting is that the fields in your Windows Forms and related controls can interact with the persisted settings automatically. By *binding* form- and control-specific properties to the settings system, Visual C# can save and restore user-controlled preferences within the user interface.

A typical use for bound settings is to have the application remember where a particular form appeared on the screen when the program was last run. The form's *Location* property maintains its on-screen position. Recording this value to the settings requires three steps. First, create a setting of type *System.Drawing.Point* to hold the persisted location value. Second, indicate in the form's properties that its *Location* value should persist to the new settings entry. Finally, call the settings collection's *Save* method before exiting the program to persist the changes.

Perform the first step by adding a new user-scoped *System.Drawing.Point* setting in the project properties' Settings panel. Let's name it *MainFormPosition*, and leave the Value field blank for now.

Back in the form editor, select the form object itself, and then access the Properties panel. Expand the "(ApplicationSettings)" property to locate the "(PropertyBinding)" subproperty. Clicking the "..." button for this entry displays the Application Settings dialog. This selection process appears in Figure 14-4.

Find the Location entry in the list, and choose "MainFormPosition" for its value. Now, each time you run the application containing this bound setting (and assuming that you persisted the settings from the previous run of the program), the modified form will remember its previous location.

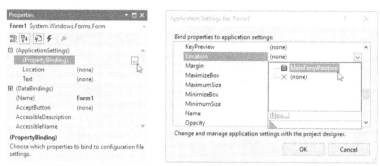

Figure 14-4. Bringing up the application settings dialog for a form

Summary

As with XML, the .NET settings system is one of those internal, behind-the-scenes, don't-let-the-boss-know features that makes your program great to use, but without all of the whiz-bang showing-off stuff. Personally, I found it a little hard to part with my precious INI files and all of their simplicity. But the automation attached to the settings system makes the migration painless.

Project

Of course, we will add settings to the Library Project in this chapter, but we'll also go back and start to use some of those settings in code that we previously entered as hardcoded values.

I really struggled over whether to use application-scoped or user-scoped configuration values for some of the rarely changing settings, such as the database connection string. I finally decided on the user area so that they could be modified through the features of the program. Application-scoped settings are read-only and can only be updated outside the program, so that idea is out. The expectation with application-scoped settings is that the system administrator will manage them, either by using Notepad on the XML file, or through some custom administrative tool. Since we aren't going to take the time in this book's project to write a separate administration tool, we'll keep everything at the user level and allow modification through the main Library program.

> **Project Access**
> Load the "Chapter 14 (Before) Code" project, either through the New Project templates or by accessing the project directly from the installation directory. To see the code in its final form, load "Chapter 14 (After) Code" instead.

Update Technical Documentation

Since the new settings are administrative in nature, we'll record them in our technical documentation. I've updated the Resource Kit for the Library Project with the settings details, and placed a new copy of that document (in Microsoft Word and PDF formats) in the *After* folder for this chapter. The new "User Settings" section in that document defines the user-scoped settings shown in Table 14-1. Unless otherwise indicated, all settings are strings.

Table 14-1. Library application settings

Setting Name	Description
DBConnection	A properly formatted connection string that identifies the SQL Server database used by the application. If missing, the application will prompt for the location of the database on startup.
HelpFile	The local path to an online help file for library patrons.
HelpFileAdmin	The local path to an online help file for library administrators.
HideLogin	A Boolean value that indicates whether the Login button in the upper-right corner of the main Library form should be hidden from view when in patron (non-administrative) mode.
MainFormPosition	The position of the upper-left corner of the main Library form, managed through the form's settings as described earlier in this chapter. This setting's data type is *System.Drawing.Point*.
ReceiptPostlude	When printing check-out receipts for patrons, this field contains any content that should appear at the end of the receipt.
ReceiptPrinter	The local path to the receipt printer used to print out patron receipts.
ReceiptWidth	The width, in characters, of each line on the receipt printer. This setting's data type is *int*.
ReportConfig	Indicates the UNC or drive letter-based location of the XML report configuration file. This file has the XML format described in the "Report Configuration File" section of the Resource Kit. This file indicates the reports available in the application.
SettingsUpgraded	When upgrading the application from an older release, this flag indicates whether the settings associated with that older release have already been upgraded into this new version. It defaults to *false* for all new releases. This setting's data type is *bool*.
UseReceipts	Indicates whether printed receipts are to be used at this workstation. If this field is missing, *false* is assumed. This setting's data type is *bool*.

Some of the entries in the table refer to features and technical content that won't be added until later chapters, so don't spend too much time thinking about features that you thought you already forgot.

Add the Settings

Since we know all of the settings we will add to the application, let's add them now. Open the project properties window and select the Settings tab. Add each setting to the application using Table 14-2 as a guide. If a setting in Table 14-2 has no listed value, leave the Value field blank as well in the settings editor.

Table 14-2. Default settings for the Library Project

Name	Type	Scope	Value
DBConnection	string	User	
HelpFile	string	User	
HelpFileAdmin	string	User	
HideLogin	bool	User	False
MainFormPosition	System.Drawing.Point	User	0, 0
ReceiptPostlude	string	User	
ReceiptPrinter	string	User	
ReceiptWidth	int	User	40
ReportConfig	string	User	

Name	Type	Scope	Value
SettingsUpgraded	bool	User	False
UseReceipts	bool	User	False

Make sure you type the setting names as listed. The application will not be able to match up incorrectly spelled names.

Positioning the Main Form

I showed you how to link a form's or control's property value to one of the settings earlier in this chapter, so let's do it for real in the project. We'll link the main form's Location property to the MainFormPosition setting. Just to refresh your memory, follow these steps to enable the link.

1. Open *MainForm.cs* in Design view.

2. Make sure the form itself is selected, not one of its subordinate controls.

3. In the Properties panel, expand the "(ApplicationSettings)" property.

4. Select the "(PropertyBinding)" subproperty, and click on the "..." button in its value area.

5. Locate the Location property in the binding list.

6. Select the MainFormPosition setting for the Location property's value. It should be the only setting available since it is the only one we defined as type System.Drawing.Point.

7. Click the OK button to enable the link.

Caching and Using Settings

Although all the settings are as close as typing "Properties.Settings.Default.*something*" in the code, some settings may initially be undefined, and using them could involve a lot of repetitive code that checks for valid settings. To reduce overall code and CPU cycles, we will cache some of the settings for easy use throughout the application.

Let's add three more global variables to cache some of the settings. Open the *General.cs* file, and add these three new class members.

> **Insert Snippet**
> Insert Chapter 14, Snippet Item 1.

```
public static string MainHelpFile;
public static string MainAdminHelpFile;
public static int FineGraceDays;
```

Let's give these variables initial values in the InitializeSystem method, where the code already initializes some other values. Add the following statements to that routine in the General class.

> **Insert Snippet**
> Insert Chapter 14, Snippet Item 2.

```
FineGraceDays = -1;

// ----- Locate the online help files.
MainHelpFile = Properties.Settings.Default.HelpFile + "";
MainAdminHelpFile =
    Properties.Settings.Default.HelpFileAdmin + "";
```

In an earlier chapter, we stored some settings in the SystemValue table that apply to all workstations that connect to the database. Since we're caching settings anyway, we should add some code to cache these database-stored values so that we don't have to keep opening and closing the database. Add the *LoadDatabaseSettings* method to the *General* class.

Insert Snippet

Insert Chapter 14, Snippet Item 3.

```
public static void LoadDatabaseSettings()
{
    // ----- Get some system-level values
    //       from database storage.
    string holdText;

    // ----- Get the default location.
    holdText = GetSystemValue("DefaultLocation");
    if (holdText.Length == 0)
        holdText = "-1";
    if (long.TryParse(holdText,
        out DefaultItemLocation) == false)
        DefaultItemLocation = -1L;

    // ----- Get the maximum number of search matches.
    holdText = GetSystemValue("SearchLimit");
    if (holdText.Length == 0)
        holdText = "-1";
    if (int.TryParse(holdText,
        out SearchMatchLimit) == false)
        SearchMatchLimit = -1;

    // ----- Get the number of days to wait
    //       before charging fines.
    holdText = GetSystemValue("FineGrace");
    if (holdText.Length == 0)
        holdText = "-1";
    if (int.TryParse(holdText,
        out FineGraceDays) == false)
        FineGraceDays = -1;
}
```

We will call this routine during application startup, just after we access and confirm the database. Add the following code to the *Main* method in *Program.cs*, just before the closing of the splash screen.

Insert Snippet

Insert Chapter 14, Snippet Item 4.

```
// ----- Load some settings that reside in the database.
LoadDatabaseSettings();
```

It's time to actually use a setting. The *HideLogin* setting indicates whether the Login button (*ActLogin*) on the main Library application form should appear when running in non-administrator (non-librarian) mode. The administrator can still bring up the login form through the F12 key, even if the button is hidden. In an environment where the patrons may be unknown, the system will be slightly more secure if the temptation of a Login button is removed.

The *UpdateDisplayForUser* routine in the *MainForm* class includes code for user mode (*LoggedInUserID == -1L*) and administrator mode (*LoggedInUserID != -1L*). In the user mode block (the first block), locate this line.

```
ActLogin.Visible = true;
```

Replace that line with the following code.

Insert Snippet

Insert Chapter 14, Snippet Item 5.

```
// ----- Show or hide the Login button per the settings.
ActLogin.Visible = !Properties.Settings.Default.HideLogin;
```

Adding Configuration Forms

It's time to add the forms that will manage all of the various application settings, both those stored locally in the user-focused settings file, and the system-wide settings stored in the database. Most of the settings are pretty simple—just basic strings, numbers, and Boolean flags—so it shouldn't overwhelm the administrator to have them all appear on a single form. But before we get to that form, we'll add a form that lets us manage the database connection.

I thought about calling up the connection properties dialog that Visual Studio uses to establish connection strings. I'm sure it's possible, but it provides way more flexibility than we need in this project. For instance, it supports the configuration of non-SQL Server databases, which is of no interest to the Library Project. Instead, we'll design a simpler form that collects only those data values that we need to build the Library connection string. The *LocateDatabase* form appears in Figure 14-5.

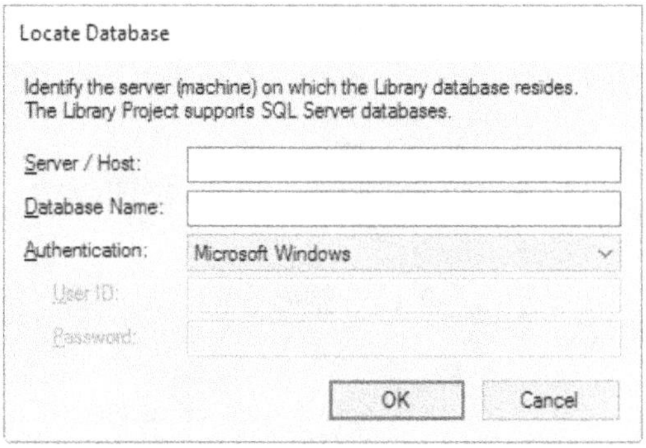

Figure 14-5. The new Locate Database form

I've already added the form and its controls to the project. Open the *LocateDatabase.cs* file to see the form. Four of the fields on this form are basic text entry fields (one with a password mask character). The fifth entry field, Authentication, lets the user select between Microsoft Windows authentication and SQL Server authentication.

Most of the form's code parallels what we've seen in many of the other forms already in the application. Go ahead and add in all of the form's code now.

Insert Snippet

Insert Chapter 14, Snippet Item 6.

Also, add the various event handler connections to the end of the *InitializeComponent* method for that form.

The significant work in this form occurs in the *Load* event, when the existing connection string is parsed out into distinct data entry fields, and in the *PromptUser* routine, where the parts are put back together.

There are many different ways you could chop up the connection string into its base parts. I took the basic divide-and-conquer approach, extracting out each semicolon- and equals sign-separated component. Here's the main block of code from the *Load* event handler that does the chopping and extracting.

```
for (int counter = 1; counter <=
   CountSubStr(connectionString, ";") + 1; counter++)
{
   // ----- Each comma-delimited part has
   //       the format "key=value".
   oneKey = connectionString.GetSubStr(";", counter);
   oneValue = oneKey.GetSubStr("=", 2).Trim();
   oneKey = oneKey.GetSubStr("=", 1).Trim().
      ToUpper().Replace(" ", "");

   // ----- Process each part.
   switch (oneKey)
   {
      case "DATASOURCE":
         // ----- Show the server host.
         RecordServer.Text = oneValue;
         break;
      case "INITIALCATALOG":
         // ----- Show the default database name.
         RecordDatabase.Text = oneValue;
         break;
      case "INTEGRATEDSECURITY":
         // ----- Only check for "true". False is assumed.
         if (oneValue.ToUpper() == "TRUE")
            RecordAuthentication.SelectedIndex =
            RecordAuthentication.Items.IndexOf(
            AuthenticationTypeWindows);
         break;
      case "USERID":
         // ----- A user ID forces SQL authentication.
         RecordAuthentication.SelectedIndex =
            RecordAuthentication.Items.IndexOf(
            AuthenticationTypeSQL);
         RecordUser.Text = oneValue;
         break;
      case "PASSWORD":
         // ----- A password forces SQL authentication.
         RecordAuthentication.SelectedIndex =
            RecordAuthentication.Items.IndexOf(
            AuthenticationTypeSQL);
         RecordPassword.Text = oneValue;
         break;
   }
}
```

Putting the parts together is less complicated. Here's the needed string concatenation code found in the *PromptUser* routine.

```
newConnection = "Data Source=" + RecordServer.Text.Trim() +
   ";Initial Catalog=" + RecordDatabase.Text.Trim();
if ((long)(ListItemData)RecordAuthentication.
   SelectedItem == AuthenticationTypeWindows)
{
   // ----- Use Windows security.
   newConnection += ";Integrated Security=true";
}
else
{
   // ----- Use SQL Server security.
   newConnection += ";User ID=" + RecordUser.Text.Trim() +
      ";Password=" + RecordPassword.Text.Trim();
}
```

Although the *LocateDatabase* form does all of the parsing and building of the connection string, it doesn't actually update the saved setting. Instead, it returns the newly built connection string, and relies on the calling code to save it.

Now, back to our single-form configuration editor, *Maintenance.cs*. This form does all of the direct modification of the values in both the database and the local *Properties.Settings* items. Figure 14-6 and Figure 14-7 show the two main panels of the Maintenance form. The centralized settings stored in the database are system-wide, and the workstation-specific values are those accessed through *Properties.Settings.Default*.

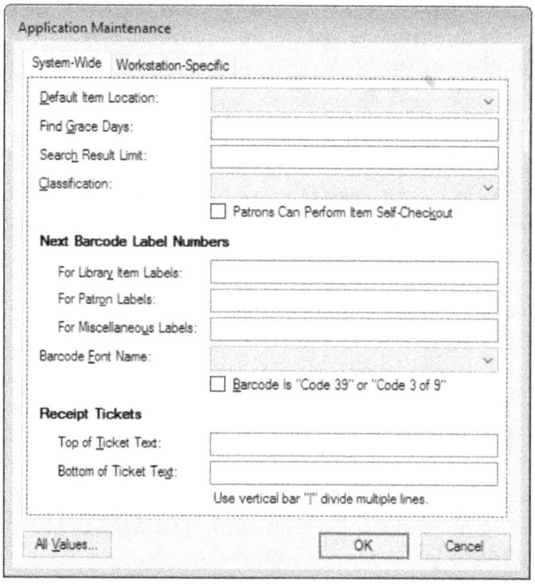

Figure 14-6. The new Maintenance form showing the System-Wide panel

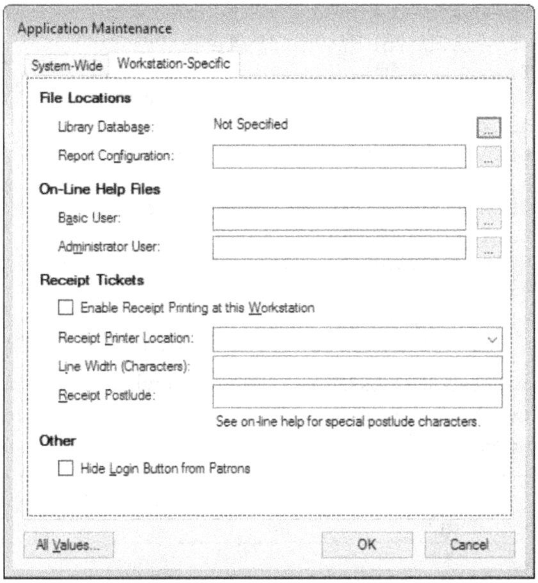

Figure 14-7. The new Maintenance form showing the Workstation-Specific panel

This form begins its work in its *Load* event handler, *Maintenance_Load*. This routine sets up the choices in some drop-down fields, including a list of fonts. The code loops through the collection of installed fonts made available through the GDI+ object *System.Drawing.Text.InstalledFontCollection*.

```
InstalledFontCollection allFonts =
   new InstalledFontCollection();
RecordFontName.Items.Add(new ListItemData(
   "<Not Selected>", -1L));
for (int counter = 0; counter <
      allFonts.Families.Length; counter++)
   RecordFontName.Items.Add(new ListItemData(
      allFonts.Families[counter].Name, (long)counter));
```

The routine also includes similar code to load a list of installed printers.

```
foreach (string installedPrinter in
      PrinterSettings.InstalledPrinters)
   RecordPrinterLocation.Items.Add(installedPrinter);
```

Once everything is set up, the *PopulateCurrentValues* procedure completes the initialization. Its code retrieves all the current values from both the database and the *Properties.Settings.Default* object, and stores those values in the various on-screen data entry fields. I've already added the database-specific code. Go ahead and add in the settings-specific code.

Insert Snippet
Insert Chapter 14, Snippet Item 8.

```
LibraryConnection =
   Properties.Settings.Default.DBConnection + "";
RecordDBLocation.Text = GetDBDisplayText(LibraryConnection);
RecordConfigLocation.Text =
   Properties.Settings.Default.ReportConfig + "";
```

```
RecordBasicHelp.Text =
    Properties.Settings.Default.HelpFile + "";
RecordAdminHelp.Text =
    Properties.Settings.Default.HelpFileAdmin + "";
EnableReceipts.Checked =
    Properties.Settings.Default.UseReceipts;
RecordPrinterLocation.Text =
    Properties.Settings.Default.ReceiptPrinter + "";
RecordPrinterWidth.Text =
    Properties.Settings.Default.ReceiptWidth.ToString();
RecordPostlude.Text =
    Properties.Settings.Default.ReceiptPostlude + "";
HideLogin.Checked = Properties.Settings.Default.HideLogin;
```

Most of the code in this form deals with basic user interaction while the form is in use. For example, the `ActDBLocation_Click` event handler displays the `LocateDatabase` form we added earlier. Add the relevant source code to that event handler.

> **Insert Snippet**
> Insert Chapter 14, Snippet Item 9.

```
// ----- Prompt for the database connection details.
string newConnection;

// ----- Prompt the user for the new setting.
newConnection = (new LocateDatabase()).PromptUser();
if (newConnection.Length == 0)
    return;

// ----- Store the new value.
LibraryConnection = newConnection;
RecordDBLocation.Text = GetDBDisplayText(LibraryConnection);
```

Several of the settings specify the locations of files used by the application, such as the online help files. The user can type in the path to the file directly, or use the Open File dialog to locate the file visually. To display this dialog, use an `OpenFileDialog` instance, filling in its various file-specific properties and calling its `ShowDialog` method. Here's the code already included in the `ActBasicHelp_Click` event handler that locates the non-administrative online help file.

```
// ----- Let the user browse for the basic help file.
//       Set up the file structure.
OpenFileDialog locateFileDialog;

// ----- Prepare the dialog.
locateFileDialog = new OpenFileDialog();
locateFileDialog.DefaultExt = "chm";
locateFileDialog.FileName = RecordBasicHelp.Text;
locateFileDialog.Filter =
    "Help Files (*.chm)|*.chm|" +
    "All Files (*.*)|*.*";
locateFileDialog.FilterIndex = 1;
locateFileDialog.Title = "Locate Help";

// ----- Prompt the user.
if (locateFileDialog.ShowDialog() != DialogResult.OK)
```

```
      return;

   // ----- Save the file path.
   RecordBasicHelp.Text = locateFileDialog.FileName;
```

Once the user has made the various setting changes, a click on the OK button saves each new setting to its storage area. I've included the database-focused saving code in the *SaveFormData* routine. I'll let you add the settings-focused code, near the end of that routine.

Insert Snippet
Insert Chapter 14, Snippet Item 10.

```
Properties.Settings.Default.DBConnection =
   LibraryConnection;
Properties.Settings.Default.ReportConfig =
   RecordConfigLocation.Text.Trim();
Properties.Settings.Default.HelpFile =
   RecordBasicHelp.Text.Trim();
Properties.Settings.Default.HelpFileAdmin =
   RecordAdminHelp.Text.Trim();
Properties.Settings.Default.HideLogin =
   HideLogin.Checked;
Properties.Settings.Default.UseReceipts =
   EnableReceipts.Checked;
Properties.Settings.Default.ReceiptPrinter =
   RecordPrinterLocation.Text.Trim();
Properties.Settings.Default.ReceiptPostlude =
   RecordPostlude.Text;

// ----- Save the receipt printer width.
if (RecordPrinterWidth.Text.Trim().Length == 0)
   Properties.Settings.Default.ReceiptWidth =
      DefaultReceiptPrinterWidth;
else
   Properties.Settings.Default.ReceiptWidth =
      Convert.ToInt32(RecordPrinterWidth.Text);
```

Although the Maintenance form provides a user-friendly interface to the database-stored settings, you probably remember that we already wrote code to update *SystemValue* table records through the *SystemValue.cs* file. In Chapter 12, we connected that form to the main form, but we're going to alter that logic. First, we'll add the call to the *SystemValue* form to the Maintenance form's *ActAllValues_Click* event handler.

Insert Snippet
Insert Chapter 14, Snippet Item 11.

```
// ----- Let the user edit the list of system values.
(new ListEditRecords()).ManageRecords(new SystemValue());

// ----- Refresh the display elements.
PopulateCurrentValues();
```

Then we'll change the *AdminLinkValues_LinkClicked* event handler back in *MainForm.cs*. Currently, it calls the *SystemValue* editor directly. Replace that part of the *LinkClicked* handler's code with code that calls the Maintenance form instead.

```
// ----- Access the maintenance portion of the program.
(new Maintenance()).ShowDialog();
```

Connecting to the Configured Database

When we originally wrote the *ConnectDatabase* routine in the *General* class, we added a hardcoded connection string just to get the program working.

```
// ----- Build the connection string.
// !!! WARNING: Hardcoded for now.
if (ActiveConnectionString.Length == 0)
    ActiveConnectionString = "Data Source=MYSYSTEM;" +
        "Initial Catalog=Library;Integrated Security=true";
```

Now that we have a user-configured connection string available, we will use that instead. The changes we must make to this routine are somewhat extensive, so just replace the function's existing content with the updated code.

```
// ----- Connect to the database.
//       Throw exception on failure.
SqlConnection libraryDB;
bool configChanged;

// ----- Initialize.
configChanged = false;

// ----- Obtain the connection string.
if (ActiveConnectionString.Length == 0)
{
    if ((Properties.Settings.Default.DBConnection +
        "").Trim().Length == 0)
    {
        // ----- Inform the user about the need to
        //       configure the database.
        if (MessageBox.Show(
            "This copy of the application has not been " +
            "configured to connect to the library database. " +
            "If you know the database settings, you can " +
            "configure it now. Would you like to proceed?",
            ProgramTitle, MessageBoxButtons.YesNo,
            MessageBoxIcon.Question) != DialogResult.Yes)
        return null;

        // ----- Prompt for the new connection details.
        ActiveConnectionString =
            (new LocateDatabase()).PromptUser();
        if (ActiveConnectionString.Length == 0)
            return null;
        configChanged = true;
    }
```

```
         else
         {
            ActiveConnectionString =
               Properties.Settings.Default.DBConnection;
         }
      }

      TryConnectingAgain:
      // ----- Attempt to open the database.
      try
      {
         libraryDB = new SqlConnection(ActiveConnectionString);
         libraryDB.Open();
      }
      catch
      {
         // ----- Perhaps it is just a configuration issue.
         if (MessageBox.Show(
            "The connection to the database failed, " +
            "possibly due to invalid configuration " +
            "settings. Would you like to change the " +
            "database configuration at this time?",
            ProgramTitle, MessageBoxButtons.YesNo,
            MessageBoxIcon.Question) != DialogResult.Yes)
            throw;

         // ----- Prompt for new details.
         ActiveConnectionString =
            (new LocateDatabase()).PromptUser();
         if (ActiveConnectionString.Length == 0)
            throw;
         configChanged = true;
         goto TryConnectingAgain;
      }

      // ----- Save the updated configuration if needed.
      if (configChanged == true)
         Properties.Settings.Default.DBConnection =
            ActiveConnectionString;

      // ----- Success.
      return libraryDB;
```

The basic gist of the code involves setting the *connectionString* variable to the persisted connection string, and using that to open the *LibraryDB* object. The new code obtains the connection string from *Properties.Settings.Default.DBConnection*. If for any reason the connection string is missing or fails to generate an open database connection, the user is prompted to supply or correct the connection string through our new *LocateDatabase* form.

Now that we're done playing with the settings, we need to ensure that any changes that took place while the program was running are persisted back to the permanent storage area. Since any legitimate changes to the settings will occur after the program is running and the user has had a chance to make those changes, let's tie the saving of the settings to the closing of the main form. Open the code for the *MainForm* class, locate the *MainForm_FormClosing* event handler, and add the following code to its handler body.

```
// ----- Save any updated settings.
Properties.Settings.Default.Save();
```

The last update ensures that the most recent settings applied by the user are retained when upgrading the Library application to a more current release, that is, a release with a more current assembly version number. Since we want this update, when required, to take place before the user has the chance to adjust any of the settings, we'll perform the update immediately when starting the application. Add the following code near the start of the *InitializeSystem* function in the *General.cs* file.

```
// ----- Ensure we have the latest settings.
if (Properties.Settings.Default.SettingsUpgraded == false)
{
    Properties.Settings.Default.Upgrade();
    Properties.Settings.Default.SettingsUpgraded = true;
}
```

The program is back to a condition where you can run it. The first time you run the program, it will prompt you to supply the database connection information. The values you supply will match the hardcoded version that used to be in the *ConnectDatabase* routine.

- Set Server/Host to *MYSYSTEM* or to the name of your actual SQL Server host.
- Set Database Name to *Library* or any other name you previously assigned to your library database.
- Set Authentication to Microsoft Windows if you use Windows integrated security. If you need to connect using SQL Server's security system, set this field to SQL Server, and enter a valid user ID and password.

In the next chapter, we'll focus on file manipulation techniques. Although we did update the settings file in this chapter, it was done indirectly through features provided by the framework. Chapter 15 will discuss more direct approaches to file manipulation.

Files and Directories

Software development in the twenty-first century has really turned programmers into a bunch of softies (no pun intended). In the old days of computers, developers had to solder programs into the computer by hand. Complex calculations could take days to set up, and one misplaced wire meant lead poisoning or worse. The suffering was real, and older issues of *Popular Electronics* are riddled with articles by former programmers who went crazy in their attempt to craft one more ballistics calculation algorithm.

Life improved tremendously for programmers when John von Neumann and others suggested that a computer could store internally the logic for an algorithm, and process it directly from memory instead of through hard-wired configurations. Engineers were soon putting their programs onto punch cards and paper tapes. The danger of lead poisoning was quickly replaced by the larger evil of paper cuts.

Punch cards were great—until you dropped your stack that took you hours or days to assemble. Some programmer somewhere dropped one too many card stacks and proclaimed, "That's it! I'm going to invent the hard disk and related technologies such as IDE and SCSI. Sure I'll become fabulously wealthy, but at least I won't have to deal with these stupid cards anymore."

And thus was born the filesystem, the structured storage of programs and information on a disk surface. Filesystems have been a part of Microsoft technologies since Bill Gates first wooed IBM. It's no coincidence that the "DOS" in "MS-DOS" stands for *Disk Operating System*. Bill knew how essential filesystems were, and so do you.

In this chapter, we'll talk about interactions with files and directories, the main units of storage and organization in the Windows filesystem. We'll also see some of the technologies and features .NET provides to manipulate files and their content. Just make sure you turn the pages carefully; I wouldn't want you to get a paper cut.

Manipulating Files through Streams

The .NET Framework includes an object-oriented approach to reading and writing files: *streams*. The abstract `Stream` class, found at `System.IO.Stream`, defines a generic interface to a chunk of data. It doesn't matter where that data is: in a file, in a block of memory, in a `string` variable—if you have a block of data that can be read or written one byte at a time, you can design a derived stream class to interact with it.

Stream Features
The basic features of a `Stream` object include the `Read` and `Write` methods that let you read or write bytes. As data is read from or written to a stream, the `Stream` object maintains a current position within the stream that you can adjust using the `Seek` method, or examine using the `Position` property. The

Length property indicates the size of the readable data. The class also exposes variations of these basic features to allow as much flexibility as possible.

Not every stream supports all features. Some streams are read-only, forward-only constructs that don't support writing or seeking. Other streams support all possible features. The features available to you depend on the type of stream you use. Since *Stream* itself is abstract, you must create an instance of one of its derived classes. .NET defines several useful streams ready for your use.

FileStream *class*

> The *FileStream* object lets you access the content of a file using the basic methods of the generic *Stream* class. *FileStream* objects support reading, writing, and seeking, although if you open a read-only file, you won't be able to write to it.

MemoryStream *class*

> A stream based on a block of raw memory. You can create a memory stream of any size, and use it to temporarily store and retrieve any data.

NetworkStream *class*

> This class abstracts data coming over a network socket. Whereas most of the derived stream classes reside in *System.IO*, this class sits in *System.Net.Sockets*.

BufferedStream *class*

> Adds buffering support to a stream to improve performance on streams with latency issues. You wrap a *BufferedStream* object around another stream to use it.

CryptoStream *class*

> This stream allows you to attach a cryptographic service provider to it, resulting in encrypted output from plain input, or vice versa. Chapter 11 includes examples that use this type of stream.

DeflateStream *and* GZipStream *classes*

> Let you use a stream to compress or decompress data as it is processed, all using standard compression algorithms.

Streams are useful on their own, but you can also combine streams so that an incoming network stream can be immediately encrypted, compressed, and stored in a block of stream memory.

Using a Stream

Using a stream is simple; first you create it, and then you start reading and writing bytes left and right. Here's some sample code I wrote that moves data into and out of a memory stream. It's loosely based on the code you'll find in the MSDN documentation for the *MemoryStream* class.

```
// ----- The Stream, or There and Back Again.
int position;
MemoryStream memStream;
byte[] sourceChars;
byte[] destBytes;
char[] destChars;
UnicodeEncoding asUnicode = new UnicodeEncoding();

// ----- Create a memory stream with room for 100 bytes.
memStream = new MemoryStream(100);
```

```
// ----- Convert the text data to a byte array.
sourceChars = asUnicode.GetBytes(
    "This is a test of the emergency programming system.");

try
{
    // ----- Store the byte-converted data in the stream.
    memStream.Write(sourceChars, 0, sourceChars.Length);

    // ----- The position is at the end of the written data.
    //       To read it back, we must move the pointer to
    //       the start again.
    memStream.Seek(0, SeekOrigin.Begin);

    // ----- Read a chunk of the text/bytes at once.
    destBytes = new byte[(int)memStream.Length];
    position = memStream.Read(destBytes, 0, 25);

    // ----- Get the remaining data one byte at a time,
    //       just for fun.
    while (position < memStream.Length)
    {
        destBytes[position] = (byte)memStream.ReadByte();
        position += 1;
    }

    // ----- Convert the byte array back
    //       to a set of characters.
    destChars = new char[asUnicode.GetCharCount(
        destBytes, 0, position)];
    asUnicode.GetDecoder().GetChars(destBytes, 0,
        position, destChars, 0);

    // ----- Prove that the text is back.
    MessageBox.Show(string.Join("", destChars));
}
finally
{
    memStream.Close();
}
```

The comments hopefully make the code clear. After creating a memory stream, I push a block of text into it, and then read it back out. (The text stays in the stream; reading it did not remove it.) Actually, the stream code is pretty simple. Most of the code deals with conversions between bytes and characters. If it looks overly involved, that's because it is.

Beyond Stream Bytes

For me, all that converting between bytes and characters is for the birds. When I write business applications, I typically deal in dates, numbers, and strings: customer names, order dates, payment amounts, and so on. I rarely have a need to work at the byte level. I sure wish there was a way to send this byte stuff down a programming stream of its own so that I wouldn't have to see it anymore.

Lucky me! .NET makes some wishes come true. Although you can manipulate streams directly if you really want to or need to, the *System.IO* namespace also includes several classes that provide a more programmer-friendly buffer between you and the stream. These classes—implemented as distinct readers and writers of stream data—provide simplified methods of storing specific data types, and retrieving them back again.

The readers and writers are designed for single-direction start-to-finish processing of data. After creating or accessing a stream, you wrap that stream with either a reader or a writer, and begin traversing the extent of the stream from the beginning. You always have access to the underlying stream if you need more fine-tuned control at any point.

There are three main pairs of readers and writers.

BinaryReader *and* BinaryWriter *classes*

>These classes make it easy to write and later read the core Visual C# data types to and from a (generally) non-text stream. The *BinaryWriter.Write* method includes overloads for writing *byte*s, *char*s, signed and unsigned integers of various sizes, *bool*s, *decimal*s and *double*s, *string*s, and arrays and blocks of *byte*s and *char*s. Curiously missing is an overload for *DateTime* values.

>The *BinaryReader* counterpart includes separate *Read* methods for each of the writable data types. The *ReadDouble* method returns a *double* value from the stream, and there are similar methods for the other data types.

StreamReader *and* StreamWriter *classes*

>These classes are typically used to process line-based text files. The *StreamReader* class includes a *ReadLine* method that returns the next text line in the incoming stream as a standard *string*. The related *StreamWriter.Write* method includes all the overloads of *BinaryWriter.Write*, and also has a version that lets you format a string for output. The reader includes features that let you read data one character at a time, one block at a time, or one entire file at a time.

StringReader *and* StringWriter *classes*

>This pair of classes provides the same features as the *StreamReader* and *StreamWriter* pair, but uses a standard *string* instance for data storage instead of a file.

One additional pair—*TextReader* and *TextWriter*—provides the base class for the other non-binary readers and writers. You can't create instances of them directly, but they do let you treat the stream and string versions of the readers and writers generically.

With these new tools, it's easier to process non-*byte* data through streams. Here's a rewrite of the simple memory stream code I wrote earlier, adjusted to use a *StreamReader* and *StreamWriter*.

```
// ----- The Stream, or There and Back Again.
MemoryStream memStream;
StreamWriter forWriting;
StreamReader forReading;
string finalMessage;
UnicodeEncoding asUnicode = new UnicodeEncoding();

// ----- Create a memory stream with room for 100 bytes.
memStream = new MemoryStream(100);
try
{
    // ----- Wrap the stream with a writer.
    forWriting = new StreamWriter(memStream, asUnicode);
```

```
    // ----- Store the original data in the stream.
    forWriting.WriteLine(
        "This is a test of the emergency programming system.");
    forWriting.Flush();

    // ----- The position is at the end of the written data.
    //       To read it back, we must move the pointer to
    //       the start again.
    memStream.Seek(0, SeekOrigin.Begin);

    // ----- Create a reader to get the data back again.
    forReading = new StreamReader(memStream, asUnicode);

    // ----- Get the original string.
    finalMessage = forReading.ReadToEnd();

    // ----- Prove that the text is back.
    MessageBox.Show(finalMessage);
}
finally
{
    memStream.Close();
}
```

That code sure is a lot nicer without all of that conversion code cluttering up the works. (We could simplify it even more by leaving out all of the optional Unicode encoding stuff.) Of course, everything is still being converted to bytes under the surface; the memory stream only knows about bytes. But *StreamWriter* and *StreamReader* take that burden away from us, performing all of the messy conversions on our behalf.

Reading a File via a Stream

Most *Stream* processing involves files, so let's use a *StreamReader* to process a text file. Although we already decided in Chapter 14 that INI files are a thing of the past, it might be fun to write a routine that extracts a value from a legacy INI file. Consider a file containing this text.

```
[Section0]
Key1=abc
Key2=def

[Section1]
Key1=ghi
Key2=jkl

[Section2]
Key1=mno
Key2=pqr
```

Now there's something you don't see every day, and with good reason! Still, if we wanted to get the value for *Key2* in section *Section1* (the "jkl" value), we would have to fall back on the *GetPrivateProfileString* API call from those bad old pre-.NET programming days. Or, we could implement a *StreamReader* in a custom function all our own.

```
public string GetINIValue(string sectionName,
        string keyName, string iniFile)
{
```

```csharp
// ----- Given a section and key name for an INI
//       file, return the matching value entry.
string oneLine;
string compare;
bool found;
int equalSign;

try
{
    // ----- Open the file.
    if (System.IO.File.Exists(iniFile) == false)
        return "";
    using (StreamReader readINI = new StreamReader(iniFile))
    {
        // ----- Look for the matching section.
        found = false;
        compare = $"[{sectionName.ToUpper().Trim()}]";
        while (readINI.EndOfStream == false)
        {
            oneLine = readINI.ReadLine();
            if (oneLine.ToUpper().Trim() == compare)
            {
                // ----- Found the matching section.
                found = true;
                break;
            }
        }

        // ----- Exit early if the section name
        //       was not found.
        if (found == false)
            return "";

        // ----- Look for the matching key.
        compare = keyName.ToUpper().Trim();
        while (readINI.EndOfStream == false)
        {
            // ----- If we reach another section, then
            //       the key wasn't there.
            oneLine = readINI.ReadLine().Trim();
            if (oneLine.Length == 0)
                continue;
            if (oneLine.StartsWith("[") == true)
                break;

            // ----- Ignore lines without an "=" sign.
            if (oneLine.Contains("=") == false)
                continue;
            equalSign = oneLine.IndexOf("=");

            // ----- See if we found the key.
            if (oneLine.Substring(0, equalSign).
                ToUpper().Trim() == compare)
            {
```

```
            // ----- Found the matching key.
            if (oneLine.Length == (equalSign + 1))
               return "";
            else
               return oneLine.Substring(
                  equalSign + 1).Trim();
         }
      }
   }

   // ----- If we reached here, the key was missing.
   return "";
}
catch
{
   // ----- Treat errors as having no key/value.
   return "";
}
}
```

This routine isn't an exact replacement for *GetPrivateProfileString*; it doesn't support a default return value, or perform file caching for speed. You could improve the routine with better error handling. But it does retrieve the value we seek, and it does it by reading the INI file one line at a time through a *StreamReader*.

```
MessageBox.Show(GetINIValue("Section1", "Key2", iniFilePath));
   // ----- Displays 'jkl'
```

File Management in .NET

In addition to the stream features describe above, the *System.IO* namespace includes several useful features for managing files and directories. Here are just some of the more common static methods used to manipulate the file system.

`Directory.CreateDirectory`

Creates a new directory, including all directories leading up to the final directory.

`Directory.Delete`

Deletes a directory. A variation of this method forces the removal even if the directory contains files.

`Directory.Exists`

Returns *true* if a specified directory does, in fact, exist.

`Directory.GetDirectories`

Returns a collection of subordinate directories given a parent path.

`Directory.GetFiles`

Just like *GetDirectories*, but returns subordinate files within a parent directory.

`File.Copy`

Makes a copy of a file and stores it in a new location, with a new name if requested.

`File.Delete`

Removes a specific file from the file system.

`File.Exists`

Returns *true* if a specified file exists.

`File.Move`

Moves a file from one place on the filesystem to another. If the destination is in the same directory, this method essentially performs a rename of the file.

`File.ReadAllText`

Reads the contents of a text file, ready for storage in a string variable or other target.

`File.WriteAllText`

Creates or replaces a file, filling it with all text from a string or another source.

`Path.Combine`

Given a directory name and a file name, this method combines them together, making sure all of the backslashes are in the right place. Or is it slashes? I always mix those up.

`Path.GetTempFileName`

Creates a zero-length file with a "tmp" file extension, and returns the full path to this new file. You can fill this file with whatever you wish, and delete it when you're done.

Summary

Managing and manipulating files isn't brain surgery. But with the filesystem as a major focus of any operating system, tools and methods for reading and updating files just seem to multiply like rabbits. The .NET Framework uses the *Stream* as its primary file interaction method, so this should help make things simpler. Of course, it piles dozens of wrapper classes on top of the basic stream, but that's another issue.

As for the management of files and directories, the classes and methods within the *System.IO* namespace provide enough goodies to let you walk all over your filesystem. Use the methods that meet your needs, and "file" the others away for future reference.

Project

I have some good news and some bad news. The bad news is that the Library Project does not make direct reads or writes of standard files, and has no need for file streams. That means we won't be adding any code to the project in this chapter at all. The good news is that we still have interesting things to talk about. Besides, I figured that since you had finished more than half of the book, you could use a break.

Project Access
Chapter 15 does not include any project templates, so don't bother looking in Visual Studio for them.

Obtaining a Barcode Font

The Library Project will include barcode printing support, but only if you have a barcode font installed on your system. It's no emergency, but you should obtain one before you reach Chapter 18, where we develop the barcode configuration code.

When you downloaded the code for this book, it didn't include a barcode font. It's all due to licensing issues and the like, you understand. But barcode fonts are easy to get. You can purchase a professional barcode font if you want to, and if you plan to deploy this project into an actual library setting, you probably should. But if you're only reading this book for the great humor, you can download one of the many free barcode fonts available on the Internet. Even if you don't plan to use the barcode printing features, I recommend that you download a free barcode font just so that you can try out some of the Chapter 18 features.

Once you've installed the font, you will need to tell the Library program to use it. The settings form we designed in the previous chapter included a selection field for this font. It's the Barcode Font Name field on the System-Wide tab of the Maintenance form. You can see it in the middle of Figure 14-6. I made it a system-wide setting because it seemed best to have all administrators in a single library using a common font.

If your font is a "Code 3 of 9" barcode font (also called "Code 39"), make sure you select the Barcode is "Code 39" or "Code 3 of 9" field on that same form. (The provider of the font will let you know whether it is a Code 3 of 9 font or not.) These fonts require an asterisk before and after the barcode number. Selecting this field will cause the Library program to add the asterisk characters automatically.

Well, I'm getting tired of talking about files, be they fonts or configuration files. In the next chapter, we'll go back into the world of code and its fraternal twin, data.

Chapter 16

Generics

When I was in high school, my family sometimes shopped at a local grocery warehouse named Fedmart. Signs on the window clearly stated that there was "no connection between Fedmart and the federal government," but people continued to shop there anyway. They had these small one-dollar frozen cheese pizzas that my mom would buy in bulk for me and my friends, teenage boys who didn't care much about what went down the esophagus.

Most of the store stocked the typical grocery products, but there was one aisle near the south border of the store that sold only "generic" products. Walking into this section was like walking into a black-and-white television; all of the product labels were plain clear or white, with simple black lettering. And they were cheap. They did the job, but just barely. You would never want to run out of name-brand ketchup in the middle of a celebratory barbeque with your friends, and offer up a bottle of generic ketchup as a replacement. Somehow I remember clearly reading the black lettering on the white label of that watery ketchup substitute, about how it met the federal ketchup standards. At that moment I had an epiphany, a sudden realization that would change the way I thought about life in these United States forever: the government has a federal ketchup standard!

Sadly, Fedmart closed down before I finished my senior year, leaving a vacuum in the generic ketchup and aluminum foil marketplace. But as a Visual C# programmer, you can still gain access to generics, through .NET's generics technology. *Generics*—the ability to use placeholders for data types—first appeared in Visual C# 2005 and the related .NET Framework 2.0. This chapter provides you with the "specifics" on generics.

What Are Generics?

In .NET, *generics* is a technology that lets you define data type placeholders within types or methods. Let's say you needed to define a class to track customer data, but you didn't want to enforce a specific format on the customer ID value. Part of your code needs to interact with customer objects using an *int* ID value, while another part of the code will use an alphanumeric key for the customer. You might ask, "Why don't you just include both types of identifiers as distinct fields in your customer record?" That wouldn't work because I am trying to come up with a reasonably simple example and answering that question would just distract me. So, here's the numeric version of the class.

```
class CustomerWithNumberID
{
    public int ID;
    public string FullName;
}
```

Here's the variation that uses a string ID.

```
class CustomerWithStringID
{
    public string ID;
    public string FullName;
}
```

Of course, you could define *ID* as *System.Object*, and stick anything you wanted in that field. But *System.Object* is considered "weakly typed," and there is nothing to stop you from mixing in *int* and *string* ID values for different instances in an array of customer objects.

What you want is a system that lets you define the class generically, and hold off on specifying the data type of *ID* until you actually create an instance of the class, or a complete collection of related class instances. With such a system, you could define a general-purpose version of the customer class.

```
class CustomerWithSomeID
{
    public [DataTypePlaceholder] ID;
    public string FullName;
}
```

Later, when it was time to create an instance, you could tell the language which data type to use for the placeholder.

```
CustomerWithSomeID<replace [DataTypePlaceholder]
    with int> oneCustomer
```

This is what generics let you do. Here's the actual Visual C# syntax that defines the nonspecific customer class.

```
class CustomerWithSomeID<T>
{
    public T ID;
    public string FullName;
}
```

The general placeholder, *T*, appears inside a set of angle brackets, just after the class name. (You don't have to name the placeholder *T*, but it's become a tradition when presenting sample code using generics.) As a data type, *T* can be used anywhere within the class definition where you don't want to define the data type up front. The class, and its *ID* member, are now ready for instantiation with an actual replacement data type for *T*. To create a new instance, try this code.

```
CustomerWithSomeID<int> numberCustomer;
```

When *<int>* is attached to the end of the class definition, Visual C# acts as though you actually declared a variable for a class that had an *int* member named *ID*. In fact, you did. When you create an instance of a generic class, the compiler defines a separate class that looks like a non-generic class with all of the placeholders replaced.

```
CustomerWithSomeID<int> customer1 =
    new CustomerWithSomeID<int>();
CustomerWithSomeID<int> customer2 =
    new CustomerWithSomeID<int>();
CustomerWithSomeID<string> customer3 =
    new CustomerWithSomeID<string>();
```

These lines define two instances of *CustomerWithSomeID<int>*, and one instance of *CustomerWithSomeID<string>*. *customer1* and *customer2* are truly instances of the same data type, but *customer3* is an instance of a completely different data type. Assignments between *customer1* and *customer2* will work, but you can't mix either of them with *customer3* without performing an explicit conversion.

```
// ----- This works just fine.
customer1 = customer2;

// ----- This will not compile.
customer3 = customer1;
```

As true compile-time data types generated automatically by the compiler, they exhibit all of the personality of other non-generic classes. Even Visual Studio's IntelliSense properly detects the substituted data type. Figure 16-1 includes a tool tip, just to the right of the instance member selection list, which properly identifies the *customer1.ID* member as *int*.

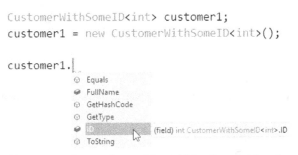

Figure 16-1. Congratulations, Mr. and Mrs. Generic: it's an int

Within the class definition, the *T* placeholder can appear anywhere, even within argument lists and local variable declarations.

```
class SomeClass<T>
{
    public T TransformData(T sourceData)
    {
        // ----- Add generic transformation code here.
        T workData;
        ...
    }
}
```

Generics work with structures and interfaces as well.

```
struct SomeStructure<T>
{
    public T GenericMember;
}

interface ISomeInterface<T>
{
    void DoWorkWithData(T theData);
}
```

Variations of Generic Declaration

If there were a minimum federal government data type placeholder requirement, the implementation of generics just described would certainly meet it. It's kind of nice to postpone the definition of data types until the last minute. But .NET generics don't stop there.

Multiple Placeholders

Generic placeholders—also known as *type parameters*—are like those knives you buy on late-night TV. You don't get one; you get more! As many as you need, it turns out. Each generic class can include multiple placeholders by listing them within the angle brackets.

```
class MultiTypes<T1, T2>
{
    public T1 Member1;
    public T2 Member2;
}
```

As before, you aren't required to use the boring names *T1* and *T2*. Whatever names you choose, include them as a comma-separated list within the brackets. When you're ready to create an instance, replicate the comma-delimited list in the same order, but using actual types. In this statement, *int* replaces *T1*, and *string* replaces *T2*.

```
MultiTypes<int, string> useInstance;
```

Data Type and Interface Constraints

The type parameters you include in a generic, such as *T*, accept any valid data type, including *int*, *string*, *System.Windows.Forms.Form*, or your own custom types. That is, *T* can be replaced by anything that derives from *System.Object*, which is everything. Consider this most generic of generic declarations.

```
class SomeClass<T>
```

With the ability to use any data type for *T*, it's as if the actual declaration specified *System.Object* as some sort of placeholder root.

```
class SomeClass<T> but only if T is
    System.Windows.Forms.Form or derived from it
```

The designers of C# generics likely pondered that specific syntax, but opted in the end for something a little shorter, yet with the same meaning. They chose the *where* keyword to indicate this type of data type restriction. If you don't include the *where* clause, Visual C# assumes you mean *System.Object*, but you can include any type you want.

```
class FormOnlyClass<T> where T:System.Windows.Forms.Form
```

By adding a specific class with the *where* clause, you enforce a *constraint* on the generic type, a limitation that must be met to use the type. In this case, the constraint says, "You may supply any class value for *T* as long as *it is or it derives from System.Windows.Forms.Form*." This means you can create an instance of *FormOnlyClass* using one of your application's forms, but not using non-*Form* classes.

```
// ----- This works.
FormOnlyClass<Form1> usingForm;

// ----- This doesn't work.
FormOnlyClass<int> usingForm;
```

When you add a constraint to a type parameter, it impacts the features you can use with that type parameter. Consider this generic class destined to work with forms, but not declared that way.

```
class WorkWithForms<T>
{
    public void ChangeCaption(T whichForm, string newCaption)
    {
        // ----- The following line will not compile.
        whichForm.Text = newCaption;
    }
}
```

In this class, the assignment to *whichForm.Text* will fail because the *WorkWithForms* class does not know that you plan to use it with forms. It only knows that you plan to use *T*, and *T* is, by default, of type *System.Object*. There's no *Text* property in the *System.Object* class; I checked.

If we change the definition of *WorkWithForms* to accept *Form* objects, the outlook for compiling this code changes dramatically.

```
class WorkWithForms<T> where T:System.Windows.Forms.Form
{
    public void ChangeCaption(T whichForm, string newCaption)
    {
        // ----- Yes! It now compiles.
        whichForm.Text = newCaption;
    }
}
```

Since *T* has to be a *Form* type or something derived from *Form*, Visual C# knows that all the members of the *Form* class, including *Text*, are available to all things *T*. Therefore, the assignment to *whichForm.Text* works.

In addition to classes, you can also use interfaces to constrain your generic types.

```
class ThrowAwayClass<T> where T:IDisposable
```

Instances of *ThrowAwayClass* can be created as needed, but only if the type supplied with the declaration implements the *IDisposable* interface.

```
// ----- This works. Pens use IDisposable.
ThrowAwayClass<System.Drawing.Pen> disposablePen;

// ----- This doesn't work, since the int data type
//       doesn't implement IDisposable.
ThrowAwayClass<int> disposableNumber;
```

But wait, there's more! See, I told you it was like shopping for knives on TV. Besides your run-of-the-mill types and interfaces, you can also include a *new()* expression within the *where* clause's generic placeholders.

```
class SomeClass<T> where T:new()
```

The *new()* expression says to the generic type, "Accept any type for *T*, but only if that type includes a constructor that requires no arguments." That is, *T* must include a default constructor. Once defined, you'll be able to create new instances of *T*—whatever type it actually turns out to be—in your generic type.

```
class SomeClass<T> where T:new()
{
    public void SomeSub()
    {
        T someVariable = new T();
```

```
        }
    }
```

If your generic class includes multiple type parameters, each parameter can include its own *where* clause with a distinct type or interface constraint.

```
class SomeClass<T1, T2> where T1:new() where T2:IDisposable
```

Simultaneous Constraints

It's nice that each of those knives you purchased can slice a watermelon, but what if you want to chop wood with that same knife, or use it to upgrade that electrical work you've been postponing? You're looking for a multifunctional tool, just like you find in each generic placeholder. If you need one placeholder to include a constraint for a specific class, an interface, and *new()* all at once, you can do it. After the constraint's colon separator, include the multiple constraints, delimited by commas. If you include the *new()* expression, it must be the last one in the list.

```
class SomeClass<T> where T:Form,IDisposable,new()
```

Now, any type you supply in the type's angle brackets when creating an instance of this class *must meet all of the constraints*, not just one of them. And here's something new: you can include more than one interface constraint at a time.

```
class SomeClass<T> where T:ISerializable,IDisposable
```

You can still include a class constraint and the *new()* constraint, even with those multiple interfaces. (You can't include more than one class constraint for a single placeholder.) If your generic type includes multiple type parameters, each of them can have its own multiple constraints set.

Generic Variance

You might remember when I mentioned that you can't directly assign a generic instance employing one specific data type to a variable defined using the same generic, but with a different data type within its angle brackets. That is, *FormFixer<Form1>* and *FormFixer<Form2>* can't interact directly. That seems kind of petty, don't you think? The good engineers at Microsoft thought so, too. So they introduced the concept of *variance* into generics. It only applies to generic interfaces and delegates (not classes or structures), but when used properly, it enables not-identical generic variables that nonetheless have a derived relationship to share instances.

```
// ----- This works when variance features are used.
IEnumerable<string> specificToText = GetTextData();
IEnumerable<object> somewhatGeneral = specificToText;
```

There are three forms of variance.

Covariance

> With covariance, you can assign a generic of a more derived type to a variable that was declared using a more base (that is, a more general) type. The sample code shown just above employs covariance. Covariant placeholders are sometimes used when specifying a method's return value as part of an interface declaration.

Contravariance

> Contravariance is the opposite, allowing you to assign a more general (a more base) instance to a variable that was created using a more derived placeholder type. It doesn't seem as helpful as covariance, but contravariant features are sometimes used when specifying parameters for interface methods.

If you don't want to make use of the variance features, it's known as invariant. Plain old generics are invariant by default, meaning that you can't mix and match unequal generic instances, even if the placeholders have a base-derived relationship.

To create a generic interface declaration using covariance, you include the `out` keyword just before the placeholder. Contravariant parameters use the `in` keyword. Invariant parameters, as the default, don't use any keyword.

```
interface IFlexible<out T1, in T2>
{
    // ----- Covariant return value.
    T1 ReturnFlex();

    // ----- Contravariant parameter.
    void FlexWork(T2 someData);
}
```

Covariant and contravariant parameters don't work with the `ref` keyword, and you can't use them with value types, which is fine since they can't be derived anyway. Unless you specifically need the level of flexibility offered by variant interfaces, you will likely never use them. I won't be using them in the Library Project, and as for more discussion on the matter, I think I'll stop right here. Some might call that invariant. I call it busy.

Nesting Generic Types
Generic types can include their own nested types.

```
class Level1<T1>
{
    public T1 Level1Member;
    class Level2<T2>
    {
        public T1 Level2Member1;
        public T2 Level2Member2;
    }
}
```

You can nest the generics as deeply as you need.

Non-Generic Types with Generic Members
If generic types seem a little scary or overwhelming, don't fret. You don't have to create a full generic type to use generic features. You can add generic support to just a single method within an otherwise normal class.

```
class SomeClass
{
    // ----- The class itself does not have the generic
    //        <> indicator, so it's not generic. But...

    public static void ReverseValues<T>
        (ref T first, ref T second)
    {
        // ----- This method is generic with its own <>.
```

```
        // ----- Reverse the contents of two variables.
        T holdFirst;

        holdFirst = first;
        first = second;
        second = holdFirst;
    }
}
```

Generic methods are useful when you need to have a local variable of the placeholder's type within the method (as is done with *holdFirst* here), but you don't know the type in advance. Using this shared *ReverseValues* method works like any other method, with the extra generic placeholder stuck in.

```
int x = 5;
int y = 10;
SomeClass.ReverseValues<int>(ref x, ref y);
MessageBox.Show(x.ToString());   // Displays 10
```

If you will be using the placeholder for one or more of the method arguments, Visual C# will infer the type based on the passed value. If Visual C# is able to guess the type in this way, you don't even need to specify the target data type when calling the generic method.

```
SomeClass.ReverseValues(ref x, ref y);
```

As with generic types, generic methods allow you to add constraints to the placeholders.

Overloading Generic Types and Members

Earlier I mentioned how the compiler essentially creates separate classes for each instance variation of a generic class that you create. This means that these two instances actually use completely different and generally unrelated classes.

```
SomeClass<int> numberVersion;
SomeClass<string> textVersion;
```

So, *SomeClass<int>* and *SomeClass<string>* are completely different classes, even though they have the same base name. In a way, Visual C# is *overloading* the class name for you, letting you use it in two (or more) different ways.

Generics also let you get involved in the class-overloading game. Normally, you can only create a single class with a given name—inside a particular namespace, that is. But with generics, you can reuse a class name, as long as the placeholders used among the classes are different enough, either in their number or in their applied constraints.

```
class SomeClass<T1>
{
    // ----- This is a generic class with one placeholder.
}

class SomeClass<T1, T2>
{
    // ----- This is a completely different generic
    //       class with two placeholders.
}
```

Visual C# will figure out which version to use based on data type parameters you include with the instance declaration.

```
SomeClass<int> simpleVersion;
SomeClass<int, string> complexVersion;
```

Generics and Collections

Generics really shine in the area of collections. The initial release of .NET had, among the thousands of possibly useful classes, a set of collection classes, all in the *System.Collections* namespace. Each collection lets you stuff as many other object instances as you want inside that collection, and retrieve them later. The collections differ in how you stuff and retrieve, but they all allow you to stick any type of object in the collection.

One of the collection classes is the *System.Collections.Stack* class. Stacks let you store objects like pancakes: the first object you add to the stack goes on the bottom, and each one you add goes on top of the previous object. When you're ready to eat a pancake—I mean, remove an item—it comes off the top. (This "last in, first out" system is sometimes called "LIFO.") The *Push* and *Pop* methods manage the addition and removal of objects.

```
Collections.Stack numberStack = new Collections.Stack();
numberStack.Push(10);
numberStack.Push(20);
numberStack.Push(30);
MessageBox.Show(numberStack.Pop().ToString()); // Displays 30
MessageBox.Show(numberStack.Pop().ToString()); // Displays 20
MessageBox.Show(numberStack.Pop().ToString()); // Displays 10
```

There is also a *Peek* method that looks at the topmost item, but doesn't remove it from the stack. The thing with stacks (and other similar collections) is that you don't have to put just one type of object into the stack. You can mix any ol' types of objects you want.

```
Collections.Stack numberStack = new Collections.Stack();
numberStack.Push(10);                    // Integer
numberStack.Push("I'm sneaking in.");    // String
numberStack.Push(this.Button1);          // Control
```

The stack doesn't care, since it's just treating everything as *System.Object*. But what if you needed to ensure that *only integers* were put into the stack? What if you wanted to limit a stack to any specific data type, but didn't want to write separate stack classes for each possible type?

This sure sounds like a job for generics to me. It sounded that way to Microsoft, too. So, it added a bunch of new generic collections to the framework. They appear in the *System.Collections.Generic* namespace. There are a few different classes in this namespace, including classes for linked lists, queues, chocolate chip cookies, and dictionaries. And hey, there's a class called *Stack<T>*. That's just what we need.

```
Collections.Generic.Stack<int> numberStack =
    new Collections.Generic.Stack<int>();
numberStack.Push(10);
numberStack.Push(20);
numberStack.Push(30);
```

Now, if we try to add anything other than an *int* to *numberStack*, an error occurs.

```
// ----- This won't work.
numberStack.Push("I'll try again.");
```

Generic Nullable Types

Back in Chapter 6, I introduced nullable types, a way to allow *null* to be used with value types.

```
int? numberOrNothing;
```

Although you can't tell from that source code line, nullable types are actually implemented using generics. The full version of *numberOrNothing*'s declaration is as follows.

```
Nullable<int> numberOrNothing;
```

Visual C# simply provided a shortcut for this syntax through the *?* suffix. You can use either syntax to declare your nullable instances.

Iterators

C#'s *foreach* statement lets you scan through a collection of objects, allowing you to linger and gaze on each member of the collection. You have a lot of options when it comes to collection sources. You can use the set of rows returned from the database query, something we've already seen in the Library Project code. You can also use any standard array or collection, including the generic collections discussed earlier in this chapter.

Beyond these mainstream collection sources, Visual C# includes *iterators* that let you craft "enumerable" collections on the fly, and have them available for consumption by loops or other collection-eating code. To create an iterator, build a standard function or property, and have it return a generic *IEnumerable* interface.

```
private IEnumerable<int> MyIterator()
{
}
```

Within the body of the routine, use the *yield return* statement to indicate what the next item in the collection will be. Your code can use the *yield return* statement as many times as it needs, until the end of the routine or a *return* statement is reached. If you want one or more of the code's *yield return* statements to be skipped in certain situations, the *yield break* statement will abort the collection building process early.

```
private IEnumerable<string> GetBillFaces(bool smallOnly)
{
    // ----- Faces shown on circulating US money.
    yield return "Washington";  // $1
    yield return "Jefferson";   // $2
    yield return "Lincoln";     // $5
    yield return "Hamilton";    // $10
    yield return "Jackson";     // $20
    if (smallOnly == true)
        yield break;
    yield return "Grant";       // $50
    yield return "Franklin";    // $100
}
```

The *yield return* statement acts somewhat like a standard *return* statement, but with the ability to disappear after it is used. If you use *GetBillFaces(true)* in a loop, the code will act as if it is calling the routine five times (once for each "small" bill), returning each subsequent *yield return* result.

```
foreach (string oneBill in GetBillFaces(true))
{
    // ----- Loops five times. Using GetBillFaces(false)
    //       would loop seven times, adding two names.
}
```

You don't need to include distinct *yield return* statements and literals, as any logic that includes *yield return* will generate a collection.

```
private IEnumerable<int> GetEvens(int maxEven)
{
    // ----- Yield a set of even numbers: 2, 4, 6...
    for (int counter = 2; counter <= maxEven; counter += 2)
        yield return counter;
}
```

Collection Initializers

Once you have an instance of a generic collection, you can start adding new items one by one.

```
List<string> planets = new List<string>();
planets.Add("Mercury");
planets.Add("Venus");
planets.Add("Earth");
```

You can also add multiple members at once as part of the collection declaration by including the list of initial items within curly braces just after the declaration.

```
// ----- Basic list.
List<string> planets = new List<string>()
    {"Mercury", "Venus", "Earth"};

// ----- Dictionary key-value pairs.
Dictionary<decimal, string> billPairs =
    new Dictionary<decimal, string>()
    {
        {1M, "Washington"},
        {5M, "Lincoln"},
        {10M, "Hamilton"}
    };
```

Basic arrays use this same initialization syntax.

```
string[] planets = {"Mercury", "Venus", "Earth"};
```

You can even combine collection and object initializers into some wonderfully complex declarations.

```
// ----- Assumes a BillType class with Value and Face members.
List<BillType> billPairs = new List<BillType>()
    {
        new BillType {Value = 1M, Face = "Washington"},
        new BillType {Value = 5M, Face = "Lincoln"},
        new BillType {Value = 10M, Face = "Jackson"}
    };
```

Summary

Having generics available for .NET development really makes Visual C# even more flexible and useful than all the hype you heard about it. You always had the ability to use placeholders for data—they're called *variables*. Generics provide that same placeholder functionality, but with data types instead of just plain data.

When you control all development aspects of an application, you might think that generics aren't for you. After all, you're not going to let an *int* variable slip into a collection of dates. But they are quite handy for enforcing standards within your code, which is always good.

Project

When a patron checks out a book or other library item, the due date is automatically calculated based on a number of days stored in the `CodeMediaType.CheckoutDays` database field. But what happens if that calculated date is a holiday, and the library is closed? The patron might not be able to return the book until the next day, and would incur a fine. This fine, though small, could start a chain reaction in the patron's life that would lead to poverty, despair, and an addiction to soap operas. Fortunately, this can all be avoided by adding a list of holidays to the project. If an item's return date falls on a documented holiday, the program adjusts the date forward until it finds a non-holiday date.

Project Access

Load the "Chapter 16 (Before) Code" project, either through the New Project templates or by accessing the project directly from the installation directory. To see the code in its final form, load "Chapter 16 (After) Code" instead.

Managing Holidays

As a small, standalone application that fully manages its own data, there isn't necessarily a pressing need for generics in the Library application. However, generics provide more advantages than just limiting the types of data stored in a class or collection. They also enhance data conversion and IntelliSense support, since Visual C# can tell immediately, for instance, what type of data will appear in a collection.

All holidays managed by the Library Project appear in the `Holiday` database table. The contents of this table will seldom change, and will be frequently accessed during the checkout process. To speed things up, we'll cache the data inside the application. And to simplify management of that cache, we'll store the holidays in a generic collection.

First, let's create the class that holds a single holiday entry. Add a new class to the project through the Project→Add Class menu command, and give it the name *HolidaySet.cs*. The familiar structure of an empty class appears.

```
public class HolidaySet
{
}
```

Add a `using` directive to the top of the *HolidaySet.cs* file, just before the class begins. This will provide easy access to some of the centralized features from the `General` class.

Insert Snippet

Insert Chapter 16, Snippet Item 1.

```
using static Library.General;
```

The `Holiday` database table includes two main fields used in calculating holidays: `EntryType` and `EntryDetail`. Let's store these as members of the class, and add a flag that ensures the entry is valid.

Insert Snippet

Insert Chapter 16, Snippet Item 2.

```
private string HolidayType;
private string HolidayDetail;
private bool IsValid;
```

We'll populate these private members through the class constructor.

Insert Snippet

Insert Chapter 16, Snippet Item 3.

```
public HolidaySet(string entryType, string entryDetail)
{
    // ----- Create a new holiday entry instance.
    int checkNum;

    HolidayType = "";
    if (entryType.Trim().Length > 1)
        HolidayType = entryType.ToUpper().
            Trim().Substring(0, 1);
    HolidayDetail = entryDetail;

    // ----- See if the details are valid.
    IsValid = true;
    switch (HolidayType)
    {
        case "A":
            // ----- The detail should be in mm/dd format.
            IsValid = CheckDateTime(entryDetail + "/2004");
            break;
        case "E":
            // ----- The detail is a number from 1 to 7.
            if (int.TryParse(entryDetail,
                out checkNum) == true)
            {
                if ((checkNum < 1) | (checkNum > 7))
                    IsValid = false;
            }
            else
                IsValid = false;
            break;
        case "O":
            // ----- The detail should be a valid date.
            IsValid = CheckDateTime(entryDetail);
            break;
        default:
            // ---- Invalid. This should never happen.
            IsValid = false;
            break;
    }
}
```

Clearly, the holiday entries have a coding system all their own, and it wouldn't be fair to force code elsewhere in the application to deal with all the complexities of holiday date comparisons. So, let's add a public method to the class that indicates whether a given date matches the holiday stored in an instance.

Insert Snippet

Insert Chapter 16, Snippet Item 4.

```
public bool IsHoliday(DateTime whatDate)
{
    // ----- Given a date, see if it matches
    //       the entry type in this instance.
```

```
      string buildDate;
      DateTime checkDate;
      int checkNum;

      // ----- If this record is invalid, then it is
      //       never a holiday match.
      if (IsValid == false)
         return false;

      switch (HolidayType)
      {
         case "A":
            // ----- Annual.
            buildDate = string.Format("{0}/{1}",
               HolidayDetail, whatDate.Year);
            if (DateTime.TryParse(buildDate,
                  out checkDate) == true)
               return (checkDate == whatDate);
            else
            {
               // ----- Must be 2/29 on a non-leap-year.
               return false;
            }
         case "E":
            // ----- Day of the week.
            if (int.TryParse(HolidayDetail,
                  out checkNum) == true)
               return (checkNum == (int)whatDate.DayOfWeek);
            break;
         case "O":
            // ----- See if this is an exact one-time match.
            if (DateTime.TryParse(HolidayDetail,
                  out checkDate) == true)
               return (checkDate == whatDate);
            break;
      }
      return false;
   }
```

We're done with that class. Now we just need a place to keep our cached holiday records. The *System.Collections.Generic* namespace includes a few different collection classes that we could use. Since the only thing we really need to do with the holidays once they are in the collection is scan through them looking for matches, the standard no-frills list seems best. Its class name is *List<T>*, and its primary feature, according to the .NET documentation, is that it lets you access members by index. That's fine.

Open the *General.cs* file and find where the global variables appear, somewhere near the top. Then add a definition for the global collection that will store all the holidays.

Insert Snippet
Insert Chapter 16, Snippet Item 5.

```
public static List<HolidaySet> AllHolidays;
```

There it is! There it is! The telling angle brackets of a generic declaration. This is a generic collection. Yeah! OK, party's over; let's move on.

Locate the *InitializeSystem* method, still in the *General.cs* file, and add the code that will initialize the global holiday cache.

Insert Snippet
Insert Chapter 16, Snippet Item 6.

```
AllHolidays = new List<HolidaySet>();
```

That's it for infrastructure. Let's add some routines that access this generic list. We need a routine that will tell us, *true* or *false*, whether a given date (the planned due date of a library item) matches any of the holidays or not. Add the function *IsHolidayDate* to *General.cs*.

Insert Snippet
Insert Chapter 16, Snippet Item 7.

```
public static bool IsHolidayDate(DateTime whatDate)
{
    // ----- See if the given date is a holiday.
    foreach (HolidaySet oneHoliday in AllHolidays)
    {
        if (oneHoliday.IsHoliday(whatDate))
            return true;
    }

    // ----- Not a holiday.
    return false;
}
```

This routine, *IsHolidayDate*, shows where generics really come in handy. It's all in the *foreach* statement that the magic occurs. In a normal collection, we wouldn't be sure what type of items were stored in the collection, be they *HolidaySet* or *string* or *int*. Well, *we* would know since *we* are the developer, but Visual C# plays dumb in this area, and assumes you mixed up the data types in one collection.

But because we tied the *AllHolidays* collection to the *HolidaySet* class using the *<HolidaySet>* data type indicator, C# now understands that we are only going to store items of *HolidaySet* in the *AllHolidays* collection. That means we don't have to explicitly convert items retrieved from the collection to the *HolidaySet* data type. If we weren't using a generic class, the code would look something like this.

```
HolidaySet oneHoliday;

foreach (System.Object scanHoliday in AllHolidays)
{
    oneHoliday = (HolidaySet)scanHoliday;
    if (oneHoliday.IsHoliday(whatDate))
        return true;
}
```

Since non-generic collections boil everything down to *System.Object*, we would have to explicitly convert each collection object to *HolidaySet* using a cast. But with a generic collection, C# takes care of it for us.

We still need to cache the holidays from the database, so add a *RefreshHolidays* method to *General.cs* that does this.

Insert Snippet
Insert Chapter 16, Snippet Item 8.

```
public static void RefreshHolidays()
{
    // ----- Load in the list of holidays.
    string sqlText;
    DataTable dbInfo;
    HolidaySet newHoliday;

    // ----- Clear the current list of holidays.
    AllHolidays.Clear();

    // ----- Get the holidays from the database.
    sqlText = "SELECT * FROM Holiday";
    try
    {
        dbInfo = CreateDataTable(sqlText);
    }
    catch (Exception ex)
    {
        GeneralError("RefreshHolidays", ex);
        return;
    }
    foreach (DataRow dbRow in dbInfo.Rows)
    {
        newHoliday = new HolidaySet(
            DBGetText(dbRow["EntryType"]),
            DBGetText(dbRow["EntryDetail"]));
        AllHolidays.Add(newHoliday);
    }
    dbInfo.Dispose();
}
```

You've seen a lot of code like this already, code that loads records from a database table into the program. I won't sport with your intelligence by explaining it to you line by line.

There are two places where we need to call *RefreshHolidays*: when the program first starts up, and later whenever changes are made to the list of holidays. We won't worry about other users changing the list; we'll just focus on when the local application updates the list. First, open the *Program.cs* file, and add this code to the *Main* startup procedure, just after the existing call to *LoadDatabaseSettings()*.

Insert Snippet
Insert Chapter 16, Snippet Item 9.

```
RefreshHolidays();
```

One down, and one to go. Open the *MainForm.cs* file, and locate the *AdminLinkHolidays_LinkClicked* event handler. This is the handler that lets the user edit the list of holidays. Add the same *RefreshHolidays()* line to the end of this code block.

Insert Snippet
Insert Chapter 16, Snippet Item 10.

```
// ----- Reload the holidays if they changed.
RefreshHolidays();
```

As you can see right in this routine, we already added the editor to manage the list of holidays. The only thing left to do is to actually access the holiday list when checking out items. We'll do that in a future chapter.

Chapter 17
LINQ

Many years ago my TV's remote control died. I had received this TV secondhand from my college-student friend—that should tell you about the quality of the set—and it was already a few years old. But I could still watch *Gilligan's Island*, so why complain? But when I contacted the manufacturer to get a replacement remote, they told me it was going to cost seventy-five bucks! The TV didn't cost anywhere near that, and I'm sure *Gilligan's Island* cost even less to produce.

The TV was pretty much useless without a remote control, so I went out and bought a *universal remote control*. These handy devices have the infrared codes for most common television manufacturers built right into the circuitry. Simply scan through all of the codes to find your TV set, and in a matter of minutes—and this demonstrates the modern miracle that is electronics—you will still not have the functionality you had with your original remote. I did lose all use of the closed-captioning system, but the power, channel, and volume buttons seemed to work.

Despite its deficiencies, the universal remote could control a TV, a VCR, and a DVD player, all through a common set of buttons. Imagine a universal remote control for your C# development. Well, stop imagining and start grabbing that *TV Guide*. Visual C# comes with the power of *LINQ*, a feature that lets you query unrelated data sources using a common "universal" syntax.

What Is LINQ?

LINQ, short for *Language Integrated Query*, is not just one, but somewhere around a million Visual C# and .NET technologies all working in tandem to make your programming life easier. Well, not easier in every case. As with any whiz-bang technology, there's good and bad.

The Good
LINQ exists because some weary programmers at Microsoft were tired of accessing data in their databases differently than they did their file-based data, or their in-memory object data, or their XML data. With LINQ, a single syntax lets you access all of these flavors of data, and more. The syntax itself is similar to SQL, the database query language already familiar to you, your programming associates, and a team of hackers at the NSA.

LINQ is able to support disparate data sources through the use of *providers*, custom LINQ libraries that know how to prepare a data source for use in LINQ queries. LINQ includes providers that interact with databases ("LINQ to ADO.NET," a collection of more specific providers that target different database sources, including SQL Server and .NET's own Entity Framework technology), in-memory object collections such as arrays or generic collections ("LINQ to Objects"), and XML ("LINQ to XML"). That's a great start, but the good news doesn't end there.

LINQ is extensible. That means you can enhance LINQ so that it can query any type of data you specify. LINQ to Spreadsheet, LINQ to Tab-Delimited-File, and LINQ to DVD-Chapter-Content are all possible. Is that a universal remote control I see in your programming language? As exciting as those possibilities are, I don't have space in this book to show you how to develop them, and that's where the bad news comes in.

The Bad

LINQ is a swell system for querying data—once you have established the connection between the query statements and the data. For some of the LINQ flavors, especially LINQ to Objects, there's not much to connect, so querying is a snap. For other LINQ varieties, especially of the database sort, you must create go-between classes that join your requests to the data. LINQ is a generic technology that can interact with any data once you provide the glue. And that glue can sometimes get very sticky.

As an example, consider LINQ to SQL. This LINQ implementation needs a class that represents the tables and records that you will query through LINQ. These classes aren't hard to create, and they look a lot like the original database tables. However, if you modify the structure of your table, you will need to modify the go-between class to take advantage of the table changes. It's a task that you would have needed to do anyway, even without LINQ, but it's something to keep in mind when considering the way that some programmers go gaga over LINQ.

The go-between nature of LINQ also means that some data processing may be slower when compared to accomplishing the same task without LINQ. Extra layers of data and code mean extra things for your computer to do. But that's already life in the world of the .NET Framework, so I wouldn't avoid LINQ because of it.

Supporting Technologies

LINQ is a big deal for Microsoft and for the .NET Framework. Most of the new features added to Visual C#'s 2008 edition were introduced primarily to support LINQ. Before we get into using LINQ, let's take a quick look at the technologies involved in making LINQ possible.

- Query expressions, the heart of data access through LINQ. This chapter discusses query expressions in detail.
- Lambda expressions, discussed in Chapter 9.
- Extension methods, covered in Chapter 12.
- Local type inference, discussed in Chapter 6.
- Anonymous types, something I'll introduce just after this list.
- Nullable types, discussed in Chapter 6.
- Partial methods, first appearing in Chapter 8.
- Object initializers, demonstrated in Chapter 9.
- Other new language and compiler features that must not have been important enough since they didn't get their own new cool-sounding names.

Anonymous Types

Anonymous types were added to C# to support LINQ, but you can use them in your own code as well. They are exactly what the name states: types without names. Well, that's not fully accurate. The types do have names, but they are generated automatically by the Visual C# compiler, and they never show up directly in your source code.

Consider a typical class designed to hold information on sushi selections.

```
class Sushi
{
   public string FishName;
   public decimal ServingCost;
}
```

Creating an instance of this class is straightforward.

```
Sushi tastyFood = new Sushi();
tastyFood.FishName = "maguro";
tastyFood.ServingCost = 3.5M;
```

Or, using the object initializer syntax I talked about back in Chapter 9, you can create the instance and fill in its fields, all in one statement.

```
Sushi tastyFood = new Sushi()
   { FishName = "maguro", ServingCost = 3.5M };
```

Anonymous types take this terse syntax one step further by leaving out the class name altogether.

```
var tastyFood = new
   { FishName = "maguro", ServingCost = 3.5M };
```

The *tastyFood* instance is now an instance of a class with two members, a string named *FishName* and a decimal value named *ServingCost*. The only thing it doesn't have is a class name that is known to you. But Visual C# knows what it is.

Just for fun I compiled that last block of code and looked up the name of the generated type. Here it is.

```
f__AnonymousType0`2<'<FishName>j__TPar','<ServingCost>j__TPar'>
```

Hmm. I still think sushi tastes better. What's really interesting is that the compiler created a generic type with two type parameter placeholders: the one with "FishName" inside the name, and the one with "ServingCost." Those names sure look a lot like members of the original unnamed class instance.

Anonymous types are major users of type inference. C# is guessing the data type of each member based on the data you supply with each name. In the sushi instances, the *ServingCost* member is of type *decimal* based on the decimal literal supplied with the instance definition.

LINQ to Objects

LINQ lets you query data from many different sources of data, and each LINQ-to-data interaction is managed by a *LINQ provider*. I listed the key providers included with Visual C# a little earlier; they all have the name "LINQ to *something*." For me, the most straightforward of the providers is LINQ to Objects, designed to interact with sets of in-memory objects. LINQ to Objects lets you process queries based on object collections, C# arrays, and any object that supports .NET's *IEnumerable* or *IEnumerable<T>* interfaces, including your own custom collections and iterators. (Various objects within the world of ADO.NET support these interfaces, but those types fall under the LINQ to DataSet provider, discussed a little later.)

When you run LINQ to Objects queries, the output of the query is a new set of objects that contains a subset of the original source object data. This lets you run queries by saying things like, "Hey LINQ, from this list of employees and their properties, give me just the names of those employees who were hired in the past ninety days." This results set, a collection based on *IEnumerable*, can be further queried or used as you would any other collection in your Visual C# code.

Before we get into some of the more complex LINQ providers, let's discover the syntax of LINQ queries using LINQ to Objects. In the next few sections, I'll use two small in-memory collections of books as my query source data. Here's the class definition for each book that includes a few reasonable members.

```
class Book
{
    public string Title;
    public string AuthorID;
    public int Pages;
}
```

Authors appear in a separate class. *Book* and *Author* instances match up through the common *AuthorID* field.

```
class Author
{
    public string AuthorID;
    public string FullName;
}
```

I'll create two small collections to manage the authors and books.

```
List<Author> Writers = new List<Author>
{
    new Author { AuthorID = "LT",
                 FullName = "Tolstoy, Leo" },
    new Author { AuthorID = "LW",
                 FullName = "Wallace, Lew" },
    new Author { AuthorID = "JB",
                 FullName = "Barrie, J. M." }
};

List<Book> Library = new List<Book>
{
    new Book { Title = "War and Peace",
               AuthorID = "LT", Pages = 1424},
    new Book { Title = "Anna Karenina",
               AuthorID = "LT", Pages = 976},
    new Book { Title = "Ben-Hur",
               AuthorID = "LW", Pages = 544},
    new Book { Title = "Peter Pan",
               AuthorID = "JB", Pages = 192}
};
```

To make our understanding of the output for each query easier, let's pretend that I've written a method that displays the results of any query in table form. I'll call this imaginary routine *ShowResults*.

Basic Query Expressions

LINQ expressions are built from *query clauses* that have the same feel as clauses in SQL statements at the database level. With the exception of the `from` clause, which must appear first, and the select clause, which is normally the final part of a query, the other clauses can generally appear in any order within the query.

The from Clause

Every basic LINQ query begins with the `from` keyword.

```
from bk in Library
```

By itself, the `from` clause is insufficient to generate query results, but it is the universal starting point for such queries. The `bk` variable included in the query is known as a *range variable* or *iteration variable*. (You don't have to use "bk"; I just chose that name at random. It's a variable, so give it any name you wish.) This variable provides a way to identify objects and object members from the source data within the query. Since `Library` is a collection, it wouldn't make sense to say `Library.Title` when referring to the title of just one book. Instead, you refer to `bk.Title`.

Personally, I find this `variable in source` syntax a little indirect. I much prefer the table-alias syntax used in SQL queries.

```
SELECT * FROM Library AS bk
```

The SQL `AS` keyword performs much the same function as the LINQ `in` keyword. Yet despite my internal tension, the `in` syntax prevails.

The select Clause

While you can't do much with a lone `from` clause, adding the `select` clause is all you need to make LINQ data queries a reality.

```
var bookBag = from bk in Library
              select bk;
ShowResults(bookBag);
// Results --> War and Peace    LT   1424
//             Anna Karenina     LT   976
//             Ben-Hur           LW   544
//             Peter Pan         JB   192
```

I stored the results of the query in the `bookBag` variable—the `var` keyword tells C# to infer the data type of the query output—but the query can also be used directly as an expression.

```
ShowResults(from bk in Library
            select bk);
```

The `select` keyword identifies the data fields to include in each returned data row. The query above includes just the range variable (`bk`), which returns all data members represented by that variable. Returning a single member from the range variable also works.

```
var bookBag = from bk in Library
              select bk.Title;
ShowResults(bookBag);
// Results --> War and Peace
//             Anna Karenina
//             Ben-Hur
//             Peter Pan
```

If you want to return more than one named member, you use the syntax that creates anonymous type instances, complete with the *new* keyword.

```
var bookBag = from bk in Library
              select new { bk.AuthorID, bk.Title };
ShowResults(bookBag);
' Results --> LT   War and Peace
'             LT   Anna Karenina
'             LW   Ben-Hur
'             JB   Peter Pan
```

The results set of this new query omits the page count found in the original data. That's because the LINQ query requested only the *AuthorID* and *Title* fields; the *Pages* member did not make it through the *select* clause. Also, notice that I reversed the order of the *AuthorID* and *Title* fields from the original class definition. This reversal is reflected in the printed results.

Behind the scenes, LINQ is creating a new anonymous type that includes two members: a string *AuthorID* field and a string *Title* field. One instance of this anonymous type is created for each resultant query record. These instances are then bundled up in a new collection that is based on *IEnumerable<T>*. This lets you use the query results in a new query, or in any code that would normally interact with a collection of results, such as a *foreach* statement.

```
var bookBag = from bk in Library
              select new { bk.AuthorID, bk.Title };
foreach (var oneResult in bookBag)
   MessageBox.Show(oneResult.Title);
// The Loop Displays --> War and Peace
//                       Anna Karenina
//                       Ben-Hur
//                       Peter Pan
```

In addition to migrating fields from the original objects over to the results set, you can use operators, functions, and methods to modify the results. This next example uses the *string* type's *ToUpper* method to alter the title name before compiling the results.

```
var capTitle = from bk in Library
               select bk.Title.ToUpper();
ShowResults(capTitle);
// Results --> WAR AND PEACE
//             ANNA KARENINA
//             BEN-HUR
//             PETER PAN
```

Since the *Title* field is a string, all string methods can be used as well, including the *ToUpper* method.

The Distinct Extension Method

Although LINQ is a fancy SQL-like syntax, the Visual C# compiler only knows about C#, and LINQ isn't technically C#. During the compilation process, each LINQ expression is converted into standard C# extension methods and lambda expressions, which we discussed in earlier chapters. As an example, let's revisit the query that returns all uppercase titles.

```
var capTitle = from bk in Library
               select bk.Title.ToUpper();
```

Behind the scenes, Visual C# uses LINQ's *Select* extension method, passing it a lambda expression that tells *Select* what to return for each output record.

```
var capTitle = Library.Select(bk => bk.Title.ToUpper());
```

If you include this line in your code, it will generate the exact same results as the LINQ query that it replaces. That's because it is the same, although the original query is gussied up in a nice LINQ syntax.

Because these are the same, you are welcome to build LINQ queries yourself using the extension method and lambda query way of doing things. LINQ includes several great features that can only be access through extension methods, including the *Distinct* feature. Like its SQL namesake, the LINQ version of *Distinct* eliminates duplicate records from a set of query results.

Consider the following LINQ query built using the expression method syntax. It's similar to the *capTitle* query we just looked at, but returns the *AuthorID* field for each record instead of an uppercase title.

```
var justIDs = Library.Select(bk => bk.AuthorID);
ShowResults(justIDs);
// Results --> LT
//             LT
//             LW
//             JB
```

By default, *Select* returns all records from the source. Getting complete information is a good thing, but sometimes it's too much of a good thing, especially when the information contains duplicates. In this sample, the results are complete, but *LT* appeared twice. Depending on your needs, that might be a bad thing. By adding the *Distinct* extension method, you can weed out the unneeded duplication.

```
var justIDs = Library.Select(bk => bk.AuthorID).Distinct();
ShowResults(justIDs);
// Results --> LT
//             LW
//             JB
```

The *Distinct* method looks at entire records for duplicates. A record is excluded only if *all fields* in that record exactly match *all fields* in another record.

If you don't like playing with lambda expressions, you can attach the *Distinct* method to the end of a standard LINQ query, and let C# worry about building the full extension-method-based expression.

```
var justIDs = (from bk in Library
               select bk.AuthorID).Distinct();
```

The where Clause

Whereas the *select* clause lets you weed out unwanted fields, the *where* clause lets you eliminate entire objects based on criteria you specify.

```
var bigBooks = from bk in Library
               where bk.Pages >= 1000
               select bk;
ShowResults(bigBooks);
// Results --> War and Peace    LT    1424
```

This query examines all incoming source records in the *Library* collection and includes a source object in the results only if it has a page count of 1,000 or more. The *where* clause can be complex, with multiple criteria joined with & and | operators, and grouped with parentheses.

```
var choices = from bk in Library
              where bk.Pages >= 1000 |
              (bk.Pages < 1000 &
              bk.Title.Contains("-") == true)
```

```
                select bk.Title;
    ShowResults(bigBooks);
    // Results --> War and Peace
    //              Ben-Hur
```

That last query also showed how you can include non-LINQ features, such as the `Contains` method, in your criteria, allowing you to restrict the results based on calculated results.

The orderby Clause

LINQ results, depending on the source of the data, are not guaranteed to appear in any particular order. To generate query results in a specific order, use the `orderby` clause. The `orderby` keyword precedes one or more source fields or calculated values, delimited by commas, and you can optionally include the `ascending` or `descending` keyword to reverse the sort order of each sorting field. (`ascending` is the default for each field.)

```
    var bookBag = from bk in Library
                  orderby bk.Pages descending
                  select new { bk.Pages, bk.Title };
    ShowResults(bookBag);
    // Results --> 1424    War and Peace
    //             976     Anna Karenina
    //             544     Ben-Hur
    //             192     Peter Pan
```

Joining Sources

If you were only ever going to query data from a single data collection or source, you probably would not have needed something like LINQ in the first place. When it does come time for you to merge results from different sources, LINQ again provides a SQL-like syntax for joining the sources. Actually, it provides two variations, paralleling the syntax variations supported by different SQL vendors.

The first syntax uses the `join` keyword to specify a field-specific link. The following query "inner joins" the `Library` and `Writers` tables at the expected `AuthorID` connection point.

```
    var bookBag = from bk in Library
                  join au in Writers
                  on bk.AuthorID equals au.AuthorID
                  orderby bk.Title
                  select new { bk.Title, au.FullName };
    ShowResults(bookBag);
    // Results --> Anna Karenina    Tolstoy, Leo
    //             Ben-Hur          Wallace, Lew
    //             Peter Pan        Barrie, J. M.
    //             War and Peace    Tolstoy, Leo
```

The special *on* and *equals* keywords assist in the join syntax. If your join involves multiple keys, you can build interim linking objects on the fly using the *new* declaration syntax.

```
    var results = from t1 in Table1
                  join t2 in Table2
                  on new { t1.Key1, t1.Key2 }
                  equals new { t2.Key1, t2.Key2 } // ...
```

All of the field names and types in each of these objects must match up. You can include field name aliases if needed.

```
var results = from t1 in Table1
              join t2 in Table2
              on new { t1.Key1, Key2 = t1.SecondKey }
              equals new { t2.Key1, t2.Key2 } // ...
```

The second join syntax lets you use multiple *from* clauses and a *where* clause to indicate the field links.

```
var bookBag = from bk in Library
              from au in Writers
              where bk.AuthorID == au.AuthorID
              orderby bk.Title
              select new { bk.Title, au.FullName };
// Same results as before
```

LINQ includes another join variation that generates *hierarchical query results*. In such queries, one of the fields in each resultant record will be a collection that contains multiple results. This syntax allows LINQ to return a list of all authors, one author per row, where each author record includes a "books" field, possibly with multiple values.

```
var authorBooks = from au in Writers
      join bk in Library
      on au.AuthorID equals bk.AuthorID
      into Published
      orderby au.FullName
      select new { au.FullName,
          Titles = (from pb in Published
          select pb.Title) };
ShowResults(authorBooks);
// Results --> Barrie, J. M.   Peter Pan
//             Tolstoy, Leo    War and Peace
//                             Anna Karenina
//             Wallace, Lew    Ben-Hur
```

This query has a somewhat strange syntax, but it successfully creates a results set with two fields per returned object: *FullName* (for the author name) and *Titles* (for the collection of book titles published by a specific author). For each returned record, the *Titles* member is a subordinate collection that can be processed like any other collection.

Skip and Take

The *Skip* extension method lets you skip over the first *x* records in the results set, effectively throwing them in the trash, like unwanted banana peels. The *Take* method does just the opposite, keeping only the first few records in the generated results. The following query skips over the first two records in the original data collection, returning just those records following the ignored values.

```
var someBooks = (from bk in Library
                 select new { bk.AuthorID, bk.Title })
                .Skip(2);
ShowResults(someBooks);
// Results --> LW   Ben-Hur
//             JB   Peter Pan
```

Related *SkipWhile* and *TakeWhile* extension methods let you use a Boolean expression instead of a number to indicate when to continue skipping or taking records.

Skip and *Take* are useful for paging results, as when showing just one page of results at a time from a larger set of queried results. Logic similar to the following could be used to show just the records destined for *CurrentPage*.

```
var onePageWorth = (from bk in Library
                    select new { bk.AuthorID, bk.Title })
                    .Skip(ItemsPerPage * CurrentPage)
                    .Take(ItemsPerPage);
```

One word of warning about *Skip* and *Take*: the order is important. In the previous query, if you place *Take* before *Skip*, you will get very different results.

Converting Results to Other Forms

Because the results of any LINQ query conform to the *IEnumerable<T>* interface, they are immediately ready to be used in other queries or in enumerable scans. If you need to access the records in a more traditional form for other purposes, LINQ provides a few conversion features that quickly move the results into either an array or a generic collection.

Each query result includes three extension methods that perform these conversions: *ToArray*, *ToDictionary*, and *ToList*. *ToArray* converts the results into a standard Visual C# array, with one result record stored in each array element.

```
var queryResults = from ...
var arrayVersion = queryResults.ToArray();
```

ToList performs a similar operation, creating a new *Generic.List* collection based on the results of the query. *ToDictionary* creates a *Generic.Dictionary* collection, but you must provide a function to *ToDictionary* that extracts the key. In most cases, a lambda expression that identifies the key field will suffice.

```
var authors = from au in Writers
              orderby au.FullName
              select au;
var authorDict = authors.ToDictionary(x => x.AuthorID);
MessageBox.Show(authorDict["LW"].FullName);
// Displays: Wallace, Lew
```

Aggregate Queries

Aggregate queries let you combine information from a larger query into a condensed collection or single result. The most basic aggregate queries use one or more of the *aggregate functions* in the form of extension methods, such as the *Sum* function in the following query.

```
var pages = (from bk in Library
             select bk.Pages).Sum();
MessageBox.Show(pages.ToString());   // Displays: 3136
```

Some aggregate functions use a lambda expression to guide the summary calculation. In the following code, the *All* function returns *true* when all individual records return *true* from a Boolean lambda expression. Since some books are under 1,000 pages, the following aggregation returns *false*.

```
var allBigBooks = (from bk in Library
                   select bk.Pages)
                   .All(pageCount => pageCount > 1000);
```

LINQ includes eight standard aggregate functions, shown in Table 17-1.

Table 17-1. Standard aggregate functions

Function	Description
`All`	Returns a Boolean value indicating whether the expression passed to it is true for all records.
`Any`	Similar to `All`, but returns `true` if just one of the records matches the supplied criteria expression.
`Average`	Returns the average numeric value from a set of records.
`Count`	Returns a count of records with `true` expression results. To return a count of all records in a query, use `Count(x => true)`.
`LongCount`	Same as `Count`, but returns a `long` instead of an `int`.
`Max`	Returns the maximum numeric expression from the set of records.
`Min`	Returns the minimum numeric expression from the set of records.
`Sum`	Returns the sum of the numeric expressions from the set of records.

Instead of wrapping an entire LINQ query in an aggregate expression method, you can also include aggregate expressions right in a standard non-aggregate query, although you need to guide the process by including the `into` keyword. We saw this keyword before when working with hierarchical queries. In aggregate queries, `into` creates a grouping context over which the query itself iterates to determine the aggregate result. The following query returns a count of books written by each author, using the `Count` aggregate function to add up the results for each author.

```
var authorBooks = from au in Writers
                  join bk in Library
                  on au.AuthorID equals bk.AuthorID
                  into NumBooks
                  orderby au.FullName
                  select new {
                      au.FullName, NumBooks =
                      NumBooks.Count(x => true) };
ShowResults(authorBooks);
// Results --> Barrie, J. M.    1
//             Tolstoy, Leo     2
//             Wallace, Lew     1
```

That query returned multiple groups of data, where each group was defined by an author name. You can generate aggregated results over an entire source collection by forcing all records into a single group. The following query accomplishes this via the *by* portion of the grouping context. The results are still grouped, and you will need to access the "first" record in the group to view the individual result members.

```
var pageInfo = from bk in Library
               group bk by true into AllBooks
               select new {
                   PageCount = AllBooks.Sum(x => x.Pages),
                   AvgPages = AllBooks.Average(x => x.Pages) };
// Displays: 784
MessageBox.Show(pageInfo.First().AvgPages.ToString());
```

LINQ to XML

Querying ordinary object instances is a blast, but the real power of LINQ comes from its ability to access data from a variety of sources, processing them using a common syntax. The *LINQ to XML* variation of this querying technology lets you access XML content from within standard LINQ queries.

Consider the small collection of books and authors introduced earlier in this chapter, stored within an XML document.

```
XDocument bookSet = new XDocument(
    new XDeclaration("1.0", "utf-8", "yes"),
    new XElement("booklist",
        new XElement("book",
            new XElement("title", "Anna Karenina"),
            new XElement("author", "Tolstoy, Leo"),
            new XElement("pages", 976)
        ),
        new XElement("book",
            new XElement("title", "Ben-Hur"),
            new XElement("author", "Wallace, Lew"),
            new XElement("pages", 544)
        ),
        new XElement("book",
            new XElement("title", "Peter Pan"),
            new XElement("author", "Barrie, J. M."),
            new XElement("pages", 192)
        ),
        new XElement("book",
            new XElement("title", "War and Peace"),
            new XElement("author", "Tolstoy, Leo"),
            new XElement("pages", 1424)
        )
    )
);
```

This block is now ready to process through LINQ, using the *XDocument* and *XElement* members such as *Descendants*, *Element*, and *Attribute*. The following query returns just the book titles from the source XML.

```
var titleList = from bx in bookSet.Descendants("book")
                select (string)bx.Element("title");
ShowResults(titleList);
// Results --> Anna Karenina
//             Ben-Hur
//             Peter Pan
//             War and Peace
```

LINQ for ADO.NET-Related Data

With ADO.NET's focus on querying data, it's understandable that ADO.NET has declared all-out war on its new enemy, LINQ. Oh wait, a truce was called in Beta 1. ADO.NET and LINQ now work very well together. In fact, ADO.NET sports three LINQ providers.

LINQ to Entities

Back in Chapter 10, I introduced .NET's ADO.NET Entity Framework. This interface between your programming code and a database lets you define a *logical* view of your system. For instance, you can create an entity called `Order` that includes your customer, vendor, order header, order detail, and product tables, all in one logical view. Related stored procedures can also be part of the package.

The framework does all of this magic by creating a set of go-between classes and related XML structural content that together manage the link between the logical and physical views of the data. Those classes can then be used in LINQ queries, and the author of the queries need not be concerned with trivial matters such as database connections and foreign key references. In reality, programmers have been writing code like this for years, abstracting the physical data model into a logical view that is easier to program against. The Entity Framework simply makes this process quicker and easier to set up.

The framework includes several tools that help you build the entities from the source database structures. One key tool is the ADO.NET Entity Data Model Designer, a visual drag-and-drop tool that makes creating entities as easy as creating Visual C# forms. I won't be discussing it here, but you can read all about it in the MSDN documentation.

LINQ to DataSet

LINQ supports queries of records within ADO.NET data tables. ADO.NET `DataTable` objects do not directly support the `IEnumerable` interface, and fields within these tables are, by default, untyped, which really makes LINQ angry. The *LINQ to DataSet* functionality overcomes both of these limitations so that querying of data sets works.

Back in "The where Clause" section of this chapter, we saw a LINQ example that used a `Book` class, extracting those titles that had 1,000 or more pages, or that included a hyphen in the book title. Let's keep that sample data, but pretend that the data now appears in an ADO.NET `DataTable` instance. The table will have four records (for the four books in our sample) and three columns: `Title`, `AuthorID`, and `Pages`. A LINQ to Objects query against a collection of `Book` records from this `DataTable` might look like the following.

```
var choices = from DataRow bk in LibraryTable.Rows
              where (int)bk["Pages"] >= 1000
              | ((int)bk["Pages"] < 1000
              & ((string)bk["Title"]).Contains("-"))
              select (string)bk["Title"];
```

This works, or more correctly, it's a workaround. We're constantly casting field values with unknown types into something usable, instead of using strongly-typed collections of data. LINQ to DataSet uses dataset-object-specific methods that coerce the ADO.NET objects into something that LINQ can interact with, and in a strongly typed fashion.

```
var choices =
    from DataRow bk in LibraryTable.AsEnumerable()
    where bk.Field<int>("Pages") >= 1000
    | (bk.Field<int>("Pages") < 1000
    & (bk.Field<string>("Title")).Contains("-"))
    select new { Title = bk.Field<string>("Title") };
```

It looks really different—more complicated, to be honest—but it is the same query. The *bookTable* *DataTable* instance is first forced to look like an *IEnumerable* instance through its *AsEnumerable* method. Then, as each field is involved in the query, its data type is declared through generic <> indicators, followed by the name of the field in quotes. Finally, because the query doesn't have direct access to field names, the results set is created using the object initializer syntax. It's much more roundabout than LINQ to Objects. But if you already have data sitting in ADO.NET in-memory objects, LINQ to DataSet is the way to go.

LINQ to DataSet also includes support for "typed" data sets, data sets that include the necessary metadata to fully describe the data type of each field. With typed data sets, you don't need to constantly hold LINQ's hand through casting; LINQ will figure out the field types on its own. For information about creating typed data sets, see the MSDN documentation.

LINQ to SQL

LINQ to SQL is the provider that lets LINQ queries interact with SQL Server databases. Since the Library Project uses SQL Server, we will spend a little more time on this technology. As with LINQ to Entities, LINQ to SQL works through go-between classes. Although you could provide a different logical view of your physical data tables using LINQ to SQL, there is more of an expectation that your LINQ to SQL objects will more closely resemble the underlying database tables.

LINQ to SQL includes a tool, the *Object Relational (O/R) Designer*, which helps create the go-between classes. You can take a quick peek at Figure 17-2 to see what it looks like, but I warn you, it's no Rembrandt. Still, it does a respectable job at making the needed database link. The O/R Designer is drag-and-drop simple, and is suitable for databases that aren't too terribly large. If you need to create the link classes for a database that has, say, hundreds of tables, you should read up on the *SqlMetal.exe* tool that comes with Visual Studio. You'll find full details in the MSDN documentation.

Using LINQ to SQL is done in five easy steps. You can follow along in a new Windows Forms project if you want.

1. *Add a new "dbml" file.* This file—actually, a few files that Visual Studio displays as one—describes your *data context*, the master class that contains link code for each database table that you will use in your application. To create this file from a Visual Studio project, use the Project→Add New Item menu command to display the Add New Item form. From the Data category, select the LINQ to SQL Classes template, change the name of the file to *Library.dbml* from the default, and click the Add button (see Figure 17-1).

Figure 17-1. Adding a new dbml class

A new `Library.dbml` item appears in your project, which opens the O/R Designer, shown in Figure 17-2. If you examine the properties of the designer's surface, you'll see that its name is `LibraryDataContext`.

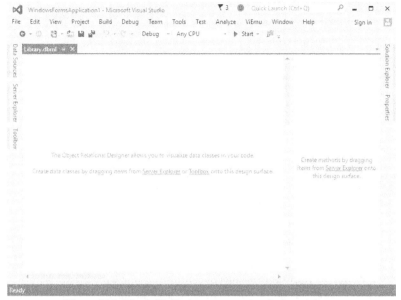

Figure 17-2. The O/R Designer; not much to look at right now

2. *Add tables to the O/R Designer.* Open the Server Explorer in Visual Studio. (Select the View→Server Explorer menu command to find it.) You should already see a link to the Library database in the Data Connections portion of the Server Explorer tree, since we created it in an earlier chapter. It will be called something like *mysystem.Library.dbo.* Expand that branch of the tree, and then the Tables branch below it. All of the tables in the Library database should appear.

   Drag and drop the `Activity` table from the Server Explorer to the left half of the O/R Designer. Sooner or later, an image of the table should appear on-screen (see Figure 17-3).

Figure 17-3. The familiar Activity table and its fields (properties)

3. *Build your application.* I've found that this step is necessary in some installs of Visual Studio, but not in others. It refreshes Visual C#'s view of the new `LibraryDataContext` classes. To build the application, select the Build→Build WindowsFormsApplication1 menu command.

4. *Open your custom data context.* The code generated by the O/R Designer defines the interaction between your program and the database, but you should still specify the database connection when you run your application, just in case anything changes down the road. Add a new `Button` control to `Form1`, then add the following code to that button's `Click` event handler.

```
// Assumes: using System.Data.SqlClient;
SqlConnection LibraryDB = new SqlConnection(
    "Data Source=MYSYSTEM;" +
    "Initial Catalog=Library;Integrated Security=true");
```

```
LibraryDataContext libraryLink =
    new LibraryDataContext(LibraryDB);
```

Replace *MYSYSTEM* in the code with the name of your own system or database instance, and update the security settings if you use SQL Server authentication.

5. *Write queries.* You're ready to design your LINQ queries. Here's some code that gets the first five activities from the *Activity* table and sorts them.

```
var activities = from act in libraryLink.Activities
                 where act.ID <= 5
                 orderby act.FullName
                 select act;
foreach (var oneItem in activities)
   MessageBox.Show($"{oneItem.ID}: {oneItem.FullName}");
// Messages --> 2: Manage author and name types
//               1: Manage authors and names
//               3: Manage copy status codes
//               4: Manage media types
//               5: Manage series
```

If you click the Show All Files button in the Solution Explorer, you can access the *.dbml* file's underlying designer file, *Library.designer.cs*. This file contains the generated go-between classes used by LINQ to SQL. As far as using the *Activity* table in our LINQ queries, here are the relevant parts of the auto-generated source code.

```
[System.Data.Linq.Mapping.Database(Name="Library")]
public partial class LibraryDataContext :
   System.Data.Linq.DataContext
{
   public System.Data.Linq.Table<Activity> Activities
   {
      get
      {
         return this.GetTable<Activity>();
      }
   }
}

[System.Data.Linq.Mapping.Table(Name="dbo.Activity")]
public partial class Activity
{
   private long _ID;
   private string _FullName;

   [System.Data.Linq.Mapping.Column(
      Storage="_ID", DbType="BigInt NOT NULL",
      IsPrimaryKey=true)]
   public long ID
   {
      get
      {
         return this._ID;
      }
      set
      {
```

```
            if ((this._ID != value))
                this._ID = value;
        }
    }

    [System.Data.Linq.Mapping.Column(
        Storage="_FullName", DbType=
        "VarChar(50) NOT NULL", CanBeNull=false)]
    public string FullName
    {
        get
        {
            return this._FullName;
        }
        set
        {
            if ((this._FullName != value))
                this._FullName = value;
        }
    }
}
```

The *LibraryDataContext* class implements a custom LINQ data context class that looks like, well, a mini version of my database. It contains references to those tables that I chose to include in the linkup. (All of the Library tables would have appeared in this class if I had dragged them to the design surface.) So, when I referenced *libraryLink.Activities* in the sample LINQ query, it was referencing the public *Activities* member from the data context.

The *Activity* table exposes distinct properties that match up with the underlying database fields. So really, it's no surprise that I'm able to query these classes through LINQ just like I do with any LINQ to Objects-type class. But there is that strange part about how the class actually gets the data from the database. That's the hidden LINQ to SQL part, handled through the base *DataContext* class and the associated attributes from the *System.Data.Linq.Mapping* namespace.

Deferred Execution

When you build a LINQ query, Visual C# does not process the query immediately. Instead, it *defers execution*, running the query only when you request a record from the results. This allows you to build up a query in parts, and not have it consume CPU cycles until you actually need the final data.

```
// WARNING: Simplistic example.
var someBooks = from bk in Library
                select new { bk.Title, bk.Pages };
var orderedTitles = from bk in someBooks
                    orderby bk.Title
                    select bk;
```

In this code, the ordering of the records doesn't happen until the second statement. But that doesn't matter since nothing was actually processed by the first statement. Remember that LINQ is really just converting your queries into extension methods and lambda expressions. The assignment of *someBooks* is doing something like this.

```
someBooks = Library.Select("Title, Pages");
```

The assignment of *orderedTitles* simply extends *someBooks*.

```
orderedTitles =
    Library.Select("Title, Pages").OrderBy("Title");
```

Actual processing occurs when you request a record from *orderedTitles*. By "processing" I mean that each extension method is executed on the original *Library* data source in order, from left to right. For *orderedTitles*, the original *Library* data is reduced through the *Select* method, and then further modified by the *OrderBy* method.

Having methods processed from left to right explains why the order of methods such as *Skip* and *Take* is so important. The following two expressions are not equivalent.

```
Library.OrderBy("Title").Take(2);
Library.Take(2).OrderBy("Title");
```

The first variation, the one with *OrderBy* appearing before *Take*, sorts the results first and then grabs the first two items from that sorted collection. The second expression takes whatever two items it finds at the top of the possibly unsorted collection, and then sorts just those two items by *Title*. If you start with more than two items in the original collection, there's a ridiculously large chance that the two expressions will produce dramatically different outcomes.

Summary

That was a fast overview of LINQ. It seems like a lot, but I covered only the basics. Besides querying data, you can also update the underlying data store through specially crafted LINQ statements. And the ability to craft your own LINQ provider means that the types of data stores that LINQ can process are unlimited.

The major downside of LINQ is that, especially for LINQ to SQL, the SQL statements and MSIL code that LINQ ultimately generates based on your query will probably not be as efficient as those that you could craft on your own. Some of your LINQ queries may run so slowly that you have no choice but to replace them with pre-LINQ alternatives. But for most common querying purposes, especially across divergent data sources, LINQ is a giant step forward.

Project

This chapter finally adds what many consider to be the heart of a library system: the lookup of books and other library items by patrons.

Project Access
Load the "Chapter 17 (Before) Code" project, either through the New Project templates or by accessing the project directly from the installation directory. To see the code in its final form, load "Chapter 17 (After) Code" instead.

Important Note about Visual Studio Bug
Beginning with the "Chapter 17 (After) Code" template, creating a new project using one of the Library templates may cause multiple errors to appear in Visual Studio. One of the errors says the following: "A custom tool 'MSLinqToSQLGenerator' is associated with file 'Library.dbml', but the output of the custom tool was not found in the project. You may try re-running the custom tool by right-clicking on the file in the Solution Explorer and choosing Run Custom Tool."

This error is caused by bug in Visual Studio that stems from adding an extra partial class file to a generated LINQ to SQL Object Relational Designer file, something that we will do in this chapter's project. Unfortunately, I can't prevent the error from appearing in template-generated projects.

However, correcting the error once the project exists is quite easy. To remove the error and successfully compile the project, perform one of the following two solution options.

Option 1: In the Solution Explorer panel, right-click on the *Library.dbml* file, then select Run Custom Tool from the shortcut menu that appears.

Option 2: Double-click on the error shown above in Visual Studio's Error List panel. When prompted to re-run the custom tool, click Yes.

Unfortunately, you may need to do this for any template-based projects from this chapter forward. If you open the chapter project directly from the installation folder, the error does not appear.

Looking Up Library Items

When we built the main Library form back in Chapter 7, we included fields that allowed a patron to search for library items. But that's about all we did; we didn't enable the fields or make them usable. We also didn't include any place to display a list of matching items. Let's complete those components in this chapter. We'll start with the matching items list.

I've added a form to the project named *ItemLookup.cs* that displays the results of a search for library items. It includes a few buttons at the top of the form, and three main display panels.

`PanelMatches`

Contains a large list box that displays non-item matches. For instance, it displays a list of matching author or publisher names as searched for by the patron. When this panel appears, the patron selects a match from the `MatchingGeneral` list, and clicks the Lookup button to display items tied to that selected author, publisher, or other entry.

`PanelItems`

Contains a large list box that displays items from the `NamedItem` database table. That is, it displays a list of library items matching some criteria. Selecting an item from the `MatchingItems` list and clicking the Lookup button displays the details of that item.

`PanelOneItem`

Contains a `WebBrowser` control that displays details about a single library item. The detail content is built using standard HTML, and may contain links that return you to the `PanelItems` panel with a new set of matching items displayed. For instance, if you are viewing the details of an award-winning (one can hope) Visual C# 2015 programming book and click on the publisher name for that item, the `PanelItems` panel appears, listing all items made by that publisher.

The form also includes a set of Back buttons (in the upper-left corner) that work like the Back button in your web browser, a Close button that returns to the main form, and a menu (`BackMenu`), used to support the Back button feature. Figure 17-4 shows the form with the `PanelItems` panel out in front, since it looks a little more interesting than the other two panels.

The associated source code weighs in at around 1,300 lines, much of it focused on filling in the two list boxes and the HTML detail content. The search performed on the main form calls into this lookup form through the `InitiateSearch` method. The actual database search for matching items occurs in the `PerformLookup` method, which is called by `InitiateSearch`. `PerformLookup` includes LINQ queries that travel to the *Library* database and back via the LINQ to SQL provider. Queries for all different types of searches are included: title, author, subject, keyword, publisher, series, barcode, and some ID number searches, mostly for internal use. The type of search performed determines which of the three panels gets displayed (via the `resultType` variable). An author search displays *PanelMatches* with a list of matching author names; a title lookup displays matching items on the *PanelItems* panel.

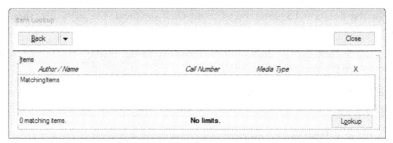

Figure 17-4. The panel of matching items, with column headings

Before we look at that LINQ code, we need to set some things up in the rest of the application to support these new LINQ queries. I've disabled the *ItemLookup.cs* file from compiling for now since it would just generate gobs of errors.

As amazing as LINQ to SQL is, it still requires the human touch (that's you) to help it locate the SQL Server database tables. We'll use the Object Relational Designer that we played with earlier in this chapter. Select the Project→Add New Item command from the Visual Studio menus. On the Add New Item form, select Data from the Categories list, select LINQ to SQL Classes from the Templates field, and set the Name field to `Library.dbml` before clicking the Add button. A blank O/R Designer window appears.

Open the Server Explorer and browse down to the Library database branch. From its Tables sub-branch, drag and drop the following tables onto the left half of the O/R Designer window.

- `Author`
- `CodeMediaType`
- `CodeSeries`
- `ItemAuthor`
- `ItemCopy`
- `ItemKeyword`
- `ItemSubject`
- `Keyword`
- `NamedItem`
- `Publisher`
- `Subject`

The designer will correctly analyze the relationships between the tables and show link lines between foreign references. You can rearrange the tables as needed to better see things, or put them in a heap if you like; I'm not your mother. But we do have to do a little renaming of the tables. The O/R Designer tries to be really smart, changing any plural table names it finds into their singular equivalent. (By tradition, singular names are preferred when designing database tables.) Unfortunately, it botched the conversion of the *CodeSeries* table, changing it to *CodeSery*. It's cute, but meaningless. Select that table and change its Name property to *CodeSeries* in the Properties panel.

That resets the table names to their roots, but it's still no good. The problem is that we used some of those table names for form names in the Library application. The conflicting classes are in different namespaces, so the code could compile, but we'd have to type a lot of namespaces when identifying these classes, and I'm just too lazy for that. To eliminate the conflicts, I arbitrarily decided to add the letter *Q* to the start of each LINQ to SQL table name. In the designer, select and rename each table, adding a *Q* to the start:

CodeSeries becomes *QCodeSeries*; *ItemAuthor* becomes *QItemAuthor*, and so on. When you are finished, you should have a designer view that looks something like Figure 17-5.

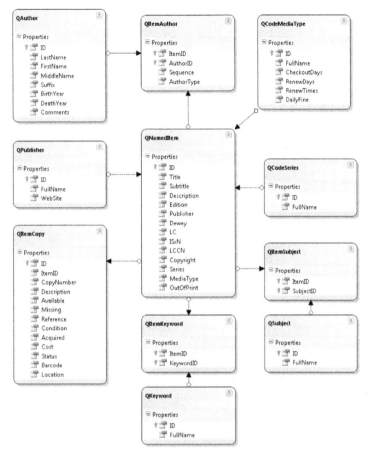

Figure 17-5. Why aren't they standing in a queue?

Despite working so hard to ensure that all the names avoid conflicts and that they are singular, when we use the library data context in our LINQ queries, we'll find that all of the class names for these LINQ-to-SQL-generated tables are somehow pluralized (*QPublishers* instead of *QPublisher*). Amazing.

The drag-and-drop of tables onto the O/R Designer window also stored information about the connection in an application setting. But as you may recall from Chapter 14, we already have a setting for that connection: *DBConnection*. No sense having two of them; it's not like database connections grow on trees. To share the connection string, we first need to remove the duplicate connection. Click on the background for the O/R Designer window. In the Properties panel, change the Connection property to *(None)*. Now we can add the connection. In the Solution Explorer, right-click on the *Library.dbml* file and select View Code from the shortcut menu. In the empty *LibraryDataContext* class that appears, insert the following code.

Insert Snippet
Insert Chapter 17, Snippet Item 1.

```
public LibraryDataContext() :
    base(Properties.Settings.Default.DBConnection)
```

```
{
    // ----- Use the user-supplied database connection.
    this.OnCreated();
}
```

Back in the project code for Chapter 12, we added an extension method to the *Data.DataRow* class that formats an author name from a database query.

```
public static string FormatAuthorName(this DataRow dbRow)
```

Unfortunately, this routine is usable only with *DataRow* objects. In the *PerformLookup* routine we're about to add, we'll need to format author names from a LINQ query of *QAuthor* table records. I guess we'll need another extension method for that type of object. Open the *General.cs* source code file and add a new *FormatAuthorName* method to the *General* class. Some of the code appears here.

Insert Snippet

Insert Chapter 17, Snippet Item 2.

```
public static string FormatAuthorName(this QAuthor author)
{
    // ----- Given an author record, return the formatted name.
    string authorName;

    // ----- Format the name.
    authorName = author.LastName + "";
    if (author.FirstName != null)
    {
        authorName += ", " + author.FirstName;
        if (author.MiddleName != null)
            authorName += " " + author.MiddleName;
    }
    if (author.Suffix != null)
        authorName += ", " + author.Suffix;

    ...some code omitted for brevity...

    // ----- Finished.
    return authorName;
}
```

If you compare this source code to the *DataRow* version, you'll find that this version is much cleaner since it references class members instead of database fields through a row instance. Thanks LINQ!

That's it for the LINQ support changes. Enable the *ItemLookup.cs* file (and its subordinate *ItemLookup.Designer.cs* file) by selecting it in the Solution Explorer panel and changing its Build Action property from None to Compile. Now let's return to the code in that file.

The *PerformLookup* routine consists mostly of a giant *if* statement, with different conditions for most of the different types of searches. The last *else* clause handles all of the searches that will fill in the list on the form's *PanelItems* panel. That's the list that shows actual items. It's got a lot of *if* statements, too. But what's really cool is its LINQ query. Instead of just being a simple query, it's a complex query that is built up little by little, thanks to deferred execution. The query starts with the basics, requesting matching records from the database's *NamedItem* table. (The *libraryDC* variable is the opened data context for the *Library* database.)

```
var itemQuery = from ni in libraryDC.QNamedItems
                select ni;
```

Next, if the user requested items of a specific media type ("just show me matching DVDs, not books"), the query is updated with the appropriate *where* clause.

```
if (LimitByMedia != -1L)
{
    // ----- Limit to a specific media type.
    itemQuery = from ni in itemQuery
                where ni.MediaType == LimitByMedia
                select ni;
}
```

The type of search also adjusts the query. For instance, a keyword search adds user-specified keywords as the criteria.

```
keywordSet = new List<string>();
keywordSet.AddRange(searchText.ToUpper().Split(new[] {","},
StringSplitOptions.None));
itemQuery = from ni in itemQuery
            let keySet = ((
                from ik in ni.QItemKeywords
                select ik.QKeyword.FullName.ToUpper())
            .Any(searchTerm =>
                keywordSet.Contains(searchTerm)))
            where keySet == true
            select ni;
```

That addition used an aggregate method, *Any*, within the main query. The *let* keyword, part of LINQ, assigns a subquery or other type of result to a temporary variable within the query (*keySet* in this case) so that it can be referenced elsewhere in the query.

Once the *where* clauses have been added, the entire query is sorted and used.

```
itemQuery = from ni in itemQuery
            orderby ni.Title, ni.Subtitle
            select ni;
```

Some of the LINQ queries in the *PerformLookup* routine are very straightforward. Here's the code that does a publisher-name search.

```
// ----- Prepare the query for a publisher lookup.
publishPattern = searchText.Trim();
if (publishPattern.Contains("*") == false)
    publishPattern += "*";
publishPattern = publishPattern.Replace("*", "%");
var publisherQuery = from pb in libraryDC.QPublishers
                     where SqlMethods.Like(
                         pb.FullName, publishPattern)
                     orderby pb.FullName
                     select pb;
```

It doesn't look that different from what you would expect in a SQL query, modified somewhat to fit the rules of C#'s LINQ query syntax.

After processing this query, the LINQ results are scanned, and records are moved into the *MatchingGeneral* list.

```
foreach (var publishItem in publisherQuery)
{
    MatchingGeneral.Items.Add(new ListItemData(
        publishItem.FullName, publishItem.ID));
    matches += 1;
}
```

This is just more of the same code you've seen in previous chapters. It loads the *ListBox* control with *ListItemData* objects, each containing a display name and an ID number from the database. That's fine for a list with simple display requirements. But if you look back at Figure 17-4, it's clear we want something a little more interesting for the list of matching items. We want columns, and columns require reasonable data.

To store this data, we'll make up a new class, called *MatchingItemData*, which works just like *ListItemData*, but has more data fields.

```
private class MatchingItemData
{
    public long ItemID; // NamedItem.ID
    public string Title;
    public string Subtitle;
    public string Author;
    public string MediaType;
    public string CallNumber;

    public override string ToString()
    {
        // ----- Build a simple display string.
        if ((Subtitle == null) || (Subtitle.Length == 0))
            return Title + ", by " + Author;
        else
            return Title + ": " + Subtitle + ", by " + Author;
    }
}
```

Since this class will be used only to display matching items on this form, I've made it a subordinate class within the larger *ItemLookup* form class. The *ToString* method outputs the text that appears in the list. We won't generate the actual columnar output until the next chapter. For now, we'll just display the title and author.

The *PanelMatches* and *PanelItems* panels each include Lookup buttons that initiate a new call to *PerformLookup* based on the item selected in the associated list. The Lookup button on the *PanelItems* panel retrieves the selected *MatchingItemData* object from the list, and performs the new search.

```
private void ActItemLookup_Click(
    object sender, EventArgs e)
{
    // ----- Look up the item with the selected ID.
    long itemID;

    // ----- Ignore if no match is selected.
    if (MatchingItems.SelectedIndex == -1)
        return;
    itemID = ((MatchingItemData)MatchingItems.
        SelectedItem).ItemID;
```

```
    // ----- Perform the lookup.
    if (PerformLookup(LookupMethods.ByDatabaseID,
        itemID.ToString(), false) == false)
      return;

    // ----- Store the history.
    AddLookupHistory(LookupMethods.ByDatabaseID,
      itemID.ToString());
  }
```

The call to *PerformLookup* starts the process all over again.

Maintaining Search History

Let's say you have a patron with a lot of time on his hands, and he wants to look up the book *War and Peace*.

- Starting from *InitiateSearch* and moving on to the *PerformLookup* code, the initial title search ("War and Peace") displays a list of matching titles on the *PanelItems* panel.
- The patron locates the book in this list, and clicks the Lookup button, which calls the *ActItemLookup_Click* event handler.
- This event handler in turn calls *PerformLookup* again, this time doing a precise lookup based on a database ID within the *NamedItem* table.
- The detail of the item appears on the *PanelOneItem* panel. (I'll discuss how it's done later in this chapter.)
- The detail includes a link to "Tolstoy, Leo," the long-suffering author of the book. When the patron clicks on this link, it initiates another call to *PerformLookup*, this time by author ID.
- We're back to the *PanelItems* panel, viewing a list of books and other items by Tolstoy, assuming he had time to write anything else.

The patron has now had an experience with three search panels: (1) a "general" list of titles matching the name "War and Peace"; (2) the "detail" display for the selected "War and Peace" item; and (3) an "items" list of books written by Leo Tolstoy. The history feature included in this form lets the patron return to any previous search page, just like the feature in your web browser.

It's possible that some of the searches performed could return hundreds of results. We don't want to store all of that content in memory, since it's possible the patron will never use the Back button. Instead, we will do just what your web browser does: store the minimum information needed to perform the query again. Your web browser maintains just the name and URL of visited paths in its "back" list. (File and image caching is not part of the history feature.) The *ItemLookup.cs* form needs to store only those values that *PerformLookup* needs to do the search again: the type of search, and the numeric or text criteria used in the search.

Patron history is accessed on a "last-in, first-out" basis. The most recent page viewed is the one the patron wants to see first when using the Back button. We discussed this type of last-in, first-out, or "LIFO," structure in Chapter 16: the stack. Each time the user views a panel, we'll make note of it, *pushing* just those values we will need later onto the stack. When the user wants to view history, we will *pop* the most recent lookup content off the stack and update the display.

The *ItemLookupHistory* class, another subordinate class within the *ItemLookup* class, stores the values we need to manage history in the stack.

```
    private class ItemLookupHistory
    {
      public string HistoryDisplay;
```

```
      public LookupMethods LookupType;
      public string LookupData;
   }
```

HistoryDisplay provides a short display name to help the user scan through history. *LookupType* and *LookupData* are the values that get passed to *PerformLookup*. It's all nice and neat. To make things even neater, we'll use a generic stack for actual storage. It's declared as a field of the *ItemLookup* class.

```
      private Stack<ItemLookupHistory> LookupHistorySet;
```

As the patron visits each panel, calls to the *AddLookupHistory* method populate the stack with each new visited item.

```
      private void AddLookupHistory(
         LookupMethods searchType, string searchText)
      {
         // ----- Add an item to the lookup history.
         ItemLookupHistory newHistory;
         string displayText;

         // ----- Build the text for display in the new item.
         displayText = BuildDisplayText(searchType, searchText);

         // ----- Build the new history item.
         newHistory = new ItemLookupHistory();
         newHistory.LookupType = searchType;
         newHistory.LookupData = searchText;
         newHistory.HistoryDisplay = displayText;
         LookupHistorySet.Push(newHistory);

         // ----- Update the back button.
         RefreshBackButtons();
      }
```

Later, when the patron clicks one of the Back buttons, the *BackMenuItems_Click* event handler examines the history stack, and calls *PerformLookup* as needed. And because we stored the *ItemLookupHistory* objects in a generic stack, we don't have to specifically convert them from *System.Object*; the program just knows what data type they are.

```
      private void BackMenuItems_Click(object sender, EventArgs e)
      {
         // ----- One of the back menu items was clicked.
         long whichItem;
         ItemLookupHistory scanHistory;

         // ----- Determine the clicked item.
         whichItem = Convert.ToInt64(DigitsOnly(
            ((ToolStripMenuItem)sender).Name));
         if (whichItem >= LookupHistorySet.Count)
            return;

         // ----- Get rid of the in-between items.
         for (long counter = 1L; counter <= whichItem; counter++)
            LookupHistorySet.Pop();
```

```
    // ----- Perform a lookup as requested.
    scanHistory = LookupHistorySet.Peek();
    if (PerformLookup(scanHistory.LookupType,
           scanHistory.LookupData, false) == false)
        return;
    RefreshBackButtons();
}
```

Showing Item Detail

The *BuildHTMLAndLinks* function builds the HTML content that appears on the *PanelOneItem* panel. This panel includes *SingleItemDetail*, a *WebBrowser* control included with .NET. It's basically a version of Internet Explorer that you embed in your applications. Normally, you supply it with a URL to display, but you can also provide custom content through the control's *DocumentText* property. The *ByDatabaseID* and *ByBarcode* lookup methods within the *PerformLookup* routine assign this property with content returned from *BuildHTMLAndLinks*.

```
    SingleItemDetail.DocumentText =
        BuildHTMLAndLinks(idQuery.ToArray()[0]);
```

The content supplied by this routine is standard HTML, but with some specially crafted links that let the library program perform additional lookups based on the details of the displayed library item.

Most of the HTML is boilerplate, and it seems a shame to waste brain cells doing string concatenation just to include it. So instead, I stored much of the HTML as a text file resource through the Resources panel of the project properties. On that panel, I clicked the Add Resource button, clicked the Add New Text File menu item, and entered *ItemLookupBody* as the name for the new text file (see Figure 17-6).

Figure 17-6. Adding a new text file resource

In the text editor window that appeared, I added the following HTML content.

```
<html>
<head>
<style type="text/css">
body { font-family: "Arial"; }
h1 { font-family: "Arial"; margin-top: 0px;
    margin-bottom: 0px; font-size: 18pt; font-weight: bold; }
h2 { font-family: "Arial"; margin-top: 20px;
    margin-bottom: 0px; font-size: 15pt; font-weight: normal; }
h3 { font-family: "Arial"; margin-top: 0px;
    margin-bottom: 0px; font-size: 15pt; font-weight: normal;
    font-style: italic; }
p { margin-top: 2px; margin-bottom: 2px;
    margin-left: 15px; font-family: "Arial"; font-size: 12pt; }
table { border: solid black 1px; margin-left: 15px; }
th { border: solid black 1px; background-color: black;
    color: white; white-space: nowrap; text-align: left; }
```

```
td { border: solid black 1px; white-space: nowrap; }
a:visited { color: blue; }
</style>
</head>
<body>
```

If you're familiar with HTML, you'll recognize most of the content as an embedded Cascading Style Sheet (CSS). Its various formatting rules will bring a specific and consistent look and feel to the browser content that appears within the item lookup form.

You can find the HTML content portion in the Solution Explorer, within the Resources branch. You've probably already noticed that the closing *</body>* and *</html>* tags aren't included. We'll attach those in the *BuildHTMLAndLinks* method. Since string concatenation is notoriously slow, I chose to use a *StringBuilder* class, a special string-like class that is custom-designed for speed when repeatedly adding content to a base string. You attach content to the end of the *StringBuilder* using its *Append* and *AppendLine* methods, and retrieve the entire string through the standard *ToString* method.

We'll begin the content with the boilerplate HTML listed previously. Since we added it as a resource, it already appears in the *Properties.Resources* object under the name we gave it.

```
StringBuilder detailBody = new StringBuilder();
detailBody.Append(Properties.Resources.ItemLookupBody);
```

Most of the code adds plain text to the *detailBody* string builder using its *AppendLine* method. Here's the code that adds the main book title.

```
detailBody.AppendLine("<h1>" +
    HTMLEncode(DBGetText(oneRow["Title"])) + "</h1>");
```

The *HTMLEncode* function, called in this block, is included in the *ItemLookup* class. It does some simple modification of special characters as required by HTML. It's called repeatedly throughout *BuildHTMLAndLinks*.

So, that's the HTML, but what about the links? If I put a standard link to, say, http://www.microsoft.com, the embedded browser will jump to that page when the link is clicked. But that doesn't help me do database lookups. The *WebBrowser* control doesn't really expose a link-clicked event, but it has a *Navigating* event that is close. This event fires whenever the browser is about to move to a new page. Fortunately, one of the data values passed to the event handler is the target URL. So, all we have to do is build a link that contains the information we need to perform the database lookup.

I decided to store the relevant database lookup details as a collection (similar to the history stack), and create fake URL-like links that indicate which item in the collection to use. After a lot of thought and contemplation, I decided on the format of my fake URL links.

```
library://x
```

In this URL template, *x* gets replaced by an index into the collection of links. It's simple, and it works. The collection of search details is a generic dictionary stored as a field within the form class.

```
private class SingleItemLink
{
    public LookupMethods LinkType;
    public long LinkID;
}

private Dictionary<long, SingleItemLink> ItemLinkSet;
```

Then back in the HTML-building code, I add fake URLs and *SingleItemLink* objects in tandem. Here's some of the code used to add in author links, given a data table with author name fields. (The *entryID* value supplies the *x* in *library://x*.)

```
foreach (DataRow dbRow in dbInfo.Rows)
{
    // ----- Add in this one author name.
    holdText = dbRow.FormatAuthorName();
    entryID += 1;
    detailBody.AppendLine("<p><a href=\"library://" +
        entryID + "\">" + HTMLEncode(holdText + " [" +
        DBGetText(dbRow["FullName"]) + "]") + "</a></p>");

    // ----- Add in an author link.
    newLink = new SingleItemLink();
    newLink.LinkType = LookupMethods.ByAuthorID;
    newLink.LinkID = DBGetLong(dbRow["ID"]);
    ItemLinkSet.Add(entryID, newLink);
    ItemLinks.Items.Add(new ListItemData("Author: " + holdText +
        " [" + DBGetText(dbRow["FullName"]) + "]", entryID));
}
```

When the user clicks on a link in the embedded web browser, it triggers the *Navigating* event handler.

```
private void SingleItemDetail_Navigating(
    object sender, WebBrowserNavigatingEventArgs e)
{
    // ----- Follow the clicked link.
    if (e.Url.Scheme == "library")
        FollowItemLink(Convert.ToInt64(e.Url.Host));
}
```

The *e.Url.Scheme* property returns the portion of the URL before the *://* characters, while *e.Url.Host* returns the first slash-delimited component just after these characters. That's where we stored the index into the *ItemLinkSet* dictionary. The *FollowItemLink* method extracts the lookup details from *ItemLinkSet*, and calls our trusty *PerformLookup* method, resulting in a new search that gets stored in the search history.

```
private void FollowItemLink(long entryID)
{
    // ----- Given a character position in the single
    //       item text panel, follow the link indicated
    //       by that item.
    SingleItemLink scanLink;

    // ----- Access the link.
    scanLink = ItemLinkSet[entryID];
    if (scanLink == null)
        return;

    // ----- Perform a lookup as requested.
    if (PerformLookup(scanLink.LinkType,
            scanLink.LinkID.ToString(), false) == false)
        return;
```

```
        // ----- Store the history.
        AddLookupHistory(scanLink.LinkType,
            scanLink.LinkID.ToString());
    }
```

Enabling the Search Features

The *ItemLookup* form is ready to use. We just need to call it from the search fields on the main form. The *PanelLibraryItem* panel in *MainForm.cs* includes several *ComboBox* selection controls, but there is no code to fill them in. Let's add that code now. Access the source code for *MainForm.cs*, and locate the *MainForm_Load* event. There's already some code there that adjusts the form elements. Append the new list-filling code to the end of this routine.

Insert Snippet

Insert Chapter 17, Snippet Item 3.

Here's the portion of that new code that fills in the list of search methods.

```
// ----- Load in the list of search types.
SearchType.Items.Add(new ListItemData(
    "Lookup By Title", (long)LookupMethods.ByTitle));
SearchType.SelectedIndex = 0;
SearchType.Items.Add(new ListItemData(
    "Lookup By Author", (long)LookupMethods.ByAuthor));
SearchType.Items.Add(new ListItemData(
    "Lookup By Subject", (long)LookupMethods.BySubject));
SearchType.Items.Add(new ListItemData(
    "Lookup By Keyword (Match Any)",
    (long)LookupMethods.ByKeywordAny));
SearchType.Items.Add(new ListItemData(
    "Lookup By Keyword (Match All)",
    (long)LookupMethods.ByKeywordAll));
SearchType.Items.Add(new ListItemData(
    "Lookup By Publisher",
    (long)LookupMethods.ByPublisher));
SearchType.Items.Add(new ListItemData(
    "Lookup By Series Name",
    (long)LookupMethods.BySeries));
SearchType.Items.Add(new ListItemData(
    "Lookup By Barcode", (long)LookupMethods.ByBarcode));
```

The Clear button on the search panel resets all of the search fields and prepares them for a new search. Add a new *ActSearchClear_Click* event handler by double-clicking on the Clear button on the form itself. Then add the following code to the handler.

Insert Snippet

Insert Chapter 17, Snippet Item 4.

```
// ----- Clear the current search criteria.
SearchType.SelectedIndex =
SearchType.Items.IndexOf((long)LookupMethods.ByTitle);
SearchText.Text = "";
SearchMediaType.SelectedIndex =
    SearchMediaType.Items.IndexOf(-1L);
SearchLocation.SelectedIndex =
    SearchLocation.Items.IndexOf(-1L);
```

Since the Library application will probably be used by many different patrons throughout the day, we should assume that a different person is using the program each time the form returns to the search panel. Let's simulate a click on the Clear button whenever the user views the search panel. Locate the existing *TaskLibraryItem* method, and add the following code to the end of the routine, just before the *SearchText.Focus()* statement.

Insert Snippet

Insert Chapter 17, Snippet Item 5.

```
ActSearchClear.PerformClick();
if (ActSearchLimits.Top == LabelMoreLimitsTop.Top)
    ActSearchLimits.PerformClick();
```

In the interest of being as user-friendly as possible, let's add some help text to the search panel that varies based on the search type selected in the Search Type drop-down list. Add a new *SearchType_SelectedIndexChanged* event handler, and then add its code.

Insert Snippet

Insert Chapter 17, Snippet Item 6.

I won't list it all here since it's rather repetitive. The code simply examines the current selection in the *SearchType* control, and sets the *LabelSearchHintsData* label to some helpful descriptive text.

We're getting close. The only thing left to do is to perform the search when the user clicks the Lookup button. Add an event handler for *ActSearch_Click*, and then add its code.

Insert Snippet

Insert Chapter 17, Snippet Item 7.

Most of this routine checks for valid input before calling the *ItemLookup* form through its *InitiateSearch* public method.

```
(new ItemLookup()).InitiateSearch(
    (LookupMethods)searchMethod,
    SearchText.Text.Trim(), mediaLimit, locationLimit);
```

You've done it, doctor. You've added a heart to the patient. The program is ready to run and use for item lookups! If you've already added some named items, you can locate them using any of the relevant search methods. Try doing a title search, using just the * wildcard character for the search criteria.

Although the search feature works, you will find that some of the display elements on the *ItemLookup* form don't work perfectly. We never did get those columns working on the item results panel. Improvements are coming soon. With the next chapter's focus on user interface techniques, we'll soon be able to customize the display to our heart's content.

Chapter 18

User Interface

A picture is worth a thousand words—or several thousand lines of source code, if you're generating a bitmap image of it. Writing code to manipulate images of varying color depths, or to trace out multilayer vector art, can be a nightmare of geometric contortions and linear algebra. It makes one yearn for those days of prescreen computers. The first programming class I took used a *DECWriter*, a printer-based terminal that had no screen, and included the graphics capabilities of a jellyfish. It was perfect for me. I couldn't draw a straight line anyway, and I didn't need some high-and-mighty "video display terminal" reminding me of it.

The graphics included in early display systems weren't much better. "Dumb terminals," such as the popular *VT100*, included some simple character graphics that displayed basic lines and blocks. Each graphic part was exactly one character in size, and any images you sought to display had to fit in a clunky 80 × 24 grid.

Fortunately for art aficionados everywhere, computers have come a long way in the graphics department. *GDI+*, the original .NET drawing system, includes complex drawing features that would make a DECWriter cry. Built upon the older Windows Graphics Device Interface (GDI) technology, GDI+ includes commands for drawing lines, text, and images in the Picasso-enhanced world of 2D graphics.

Beyond GDI+, .NET also provides support for the newer *Windows Presentation Foundation* (WPF), a rich user interface and multimedia presentation system based in part on XML. WPF includes display and interaction features that go way beyond GDI+, although there are a few GDI+ features absent from WPF. Although I will give a brief overview of WPF in this chapter, most of the content will revolve around GDI+.

Overview of GDI+

Before .NET, Windows programmers depended on the GDI system to draw pretty much anything on the screen, even if they didn't know that GDI existed. In addition to bitmap images, all controls, labels, window borders, and icons appeared on the screen thanks to GDI. It was a giant step forward from character graphics. GDI presented a basic set of drawing features from which you could potentially output any type of complex image. But it wasn't easy. The graphics primitives were—well—primitive, and you had to build up complex systems from the parts. Most programmers weren't into making things beautiful, so they tried to avoid the complexities of GDI. But sometimes you had to draw a line or a circle, and there was no way around it.

GDI+, new with .NET, builds on GDI, providing the basic primitives of GDI, but also supplying some more complex groupings of graphics features into easy-to-use functions. This simplicity has brought about a renaissance of programmer-initiated graphics work. Take a look at Figure 18-1, which shows an image that was drawn using the older GDI, and that same image generated with just a few quick commands in GDI+.

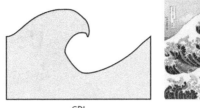

GDI   GDI+

Figure 18-1. The marvel that is GDI+

The GDI+ system makes its home in the `System.Drawing` namespace, and includes multitudes of classes that represent the drawing objects, surfaces, and embellishment features that enable display graphics. But it's not just about display. GDI+ generalizes bitmap and vector drawing on all available output surfaces: bitmaps or line drawings on the screen (including form and control surfaces), report output on a printer, graffiti on the back wall of your local supermarket, image content destined for a JPEG file—they are all the same to GDI+. All destinations use the same drawing methods and objects, making it easier for you to generalize your drawing code.

GDI+'s features include surfaces, coloring inks, drawing elements, and transformations.

- GDI+ generalizes drawing *surfaces* through the `System.Drawing.Graphics` class. This object represents a drawing canvas, with attributes for color depth and size (width and height). The canvas may link to a region of the workstation screen, an internal holding area for final output to the printer, or a general graphics canvas for manipulating content in-memory before outputting it to a display or file. Another type of surface, the *path* (`System.Drawing.Drawing2D. GraphicsPath`), is like a macro recorder for vector (line) graphics. Drawing done within a path can be "replayed" on a standard drawing surface, or used to supply boundaries for other drawing commands.

- Colors and inks appear in the form of *colors* (opaque or semitransparent color values), *brushes* (bitmap-based pseudo-pens used for fills and tiling), and *pens* (colored line-drawing objects with a specific thickness).

- *Drawing elements* include rectangles, ellipses, lines, and other standard or custom-edge shapes. They also include fonts, both bitmapped and outline-based versions.

- *Transformations* let you resize, rotate, and skew drawings as you generate them. When a transformation is applied to a surface, you can draw objects as though the transformation didn't exist, and the changes will adjust in real time.

The Windows Forms controls that you use in desktop applications generally take care of their own display features. However, some controls let you take over some or all of the drawing responsibilities. For instance, the `ListBox` control displays simple single-color text for each list item. However, you can override the drawing of each list item, providing your own custom content, which may include multicolor text or graphics. This ability to supply some of the drawing code to a control is known as *owner draw*, and it works through the same generalized `Graphics` object used for other drawing. We'll include some owner draw code in the Library Project.

In the interest of full disclosure, you should know that this chapter will cover probably only one percent of the available GDI+ features, if even that. GDI+ is complex and vast, and you could spend years delving into every little feature, just in time for your eventual switch over to WPF. I'll give you a brief overview of the GDI+ system so that you get a feel for some of the basics. If you need to manipulate images and text beyond what is listed here (and you probably will), try the MSDN documentation or another resource dedicated to deciphering GDI+.

Selecting a Canvas

Most drawing in .NET occurs in the context of a *Graphics* object. (For those familiar with pre-.NET development in Windows, this is similar to a *device context*.) *Graphics* objects provide a canvas on which you draw lines, shapes, bitmap images, and prerecorded drawing macros. *Graphics* objects do not contain the graphics surface itself; they are simply generic conduits to the actual canvas. There is always some surface behind the *Graphics* object, whether it is a portion of the screen, a *Bitmap* object, or the simulated surface of a printed page. Any drawing that is done to the *Graphics* object immediately impacts the underlying surface.

The *Graphics* object includes dozens of methods that let you draw shapes and images on the graphics surface, and perform other magical 2D activities. We'll cover many of them in this chapter.

Obtaining and Creating Graphics Objects

Getting a *Graphics* object for an on-screen form or control is as easy as calling the form's or control's *CreateGraphics* method.

```
Graphics wholeFormGraphics = this.CreateGraphics();
Graphics buttonOnlyGraphics = button1.CreateGraphics();
```

Some events, most notably the *Paint* event for forms and controls, provide access to a *Graphics* object through the event arguments.

```
private void pictureBox1_Paint(
    object sender, PaintEventArgs e)
{
    Graphics paintCanvas = e.Graphics;
}
```

You can also create a *Graphics* object that is unrelated to any existing display area by associating it to a bitmap.

```
Bitmap trueBitmap = new Bitmap(50, 50);
Graphics canvas = Graphics.FromImage(trueBitmap);
```

Remember, all changes made to the *canvas* instance will impact the *trueBitmap* image.

Disposing of Graphics Objects Properly

When you are finished with a *Graphics* object *that you create*, you must dispose of it by calling its *Dispose* method. (This rule is true for many different GDI+ objects.) Don't keep it around for a rainy day because it won't be valid later. You must, must, must dispose of it when you are finished with it. If you don't, it could result in image corruption, memory usage issues, or worse yet, international armed conflict. So, please dispose of all *Graphics* objects properly.

```
canvas.Dispose();
```

If you create a *Graphics* object within an event, you really need to dispose of it before exiting that event handler. There is no guarantee that the *Graphics* object will still be valid in a later event. Besides, it's easy to re-create another *Graphics* object at any time.

If you use a *Graphics* object that is passed to you from another part of the program (like that e.*Graphics* reference in the preceding *Paint* event handler), you should not dispose of it. Each creator is responsible for disposing of its own objects.

Choosing Pens and Brushes

A lot of graphics work involves drawing primitives: using lines, ellipses, rectangles, and other regular and irregular shapes to build up a final display. As in real life, you draw these primitives using a *Pen* object. For those primitives that result in a fillable or semi-fillable shape, a *Brush* object specifies the color or pattern to use in that filled area. GDI+ includes many predefined pens and brushes, or you can create your own.

Pens

Pens are line-drawing tools used with the drawing commands of a *Graphics* object. A basic pen has a solid color and a thickness.

```
// ----- A red pen five units wide.
Pen redPen = new Pen(Color.Red, 5);
```

As with *Graphics* objects, any *Pen* you create using the *new* keyword *must be disposed of properly* when you are finished with it.

```
redPen.Dispose();
```

Several predefined pens are made available through the *System.Drawing.Pens* class, all named by their color, as in *Pens.Red*. If you use one of these pens, you don't have to dispose of it.

You can create a lot of interesting pens that vary by line styles, end decorations, and color variations. The following code generates the image displayed in Figure 18-2.

```
private void pictureBox1_Paint(
    object sender, PaintEventArgs e)
{
    // ----- Draw some fancy lines.
    Pen usePen;

    // ----- Blank out the background.
    e.Graphics.Clear(Color.White);

    // ----- Draw a basic 1-pixel line using the title
    //       bar color.
    usePen = new Pen(SystemColors.ActiveCaption, 1);
    e.Graphics.DrawLine(usePen, 10, 10, 200, 10);
    usePen.Dispose();

    // ----- Draw a thicker dashed line with arrow and ball
    //       end caps. Each dashed segment has a triangle end.
    usePen = new Pen(Color.FromName("Red"), 5);
    usePen.DashCap = DashCap.Triangle;
    usePen.StartCap = LineCap.ArrowAnchor;
    usePen.EndCap = LineCap.RoundAnchor;
    usePen.DashStyle = DashStyle.Dash;
    e.Graphics.DrawLine(usePen, 10, 30, 200, 30);
    usePen.Dispose();

    // ----- A semi-transparent black pen with three line
    //       parts, two thin and one thick.
    usePen = new Pen(Color.FromArgb(128, 0, 0, 0), 10);
    usePen.CompoundArray =
        new float[] {0.0F, 0.1F, 0.4F, 0.5F, 0.8F, 1.0F};
```

```
    e.Graphics.DrawLine(usePen, 10, 55, 200, 55);
    usePen.Dispose();
}
```

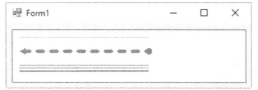

Figure 18-2. Yes sir, yes sir, three lines full

The code shows that there are a few different ways to specify a color, by either its predefined name (*Color.White* and *SystemColors.ActiveCaption*), a string name (using *Color.FromName*), or its Alpha-Red-Green-Blue value (*Color.FromArgb*). That last version lets you supply distinct values for the alpha blend (which sets the transparency level, from 0 for fully transparent to 255 for fully opaque), red, green, and blue components of the full color.

Most of the pen-specific properties I demonstrated here are somewhat self-explanatory. As with most of GDI+, the mind-numbing amount of available features makes it impossible to completely document in a small chapter, let alone provide a good night's sleep for authors designing such chapters. I will simply refer you to the online MSDN documentation for the *Pen* class to get all of the luscious details.

Brushes

Brushes are used for filling in spaces between drawn lines, even if you make those lines fully invisible. GDI+ includes a variety of brush types, including *solid brushes* (basic single-color brushes), *hatch brushes* (pattern brushes that are pleasant but general), *texture brushes* (where a custom bitmap is used for the brush), and *gradient brushes* (which slowly fade from one color to another across the brush). The *System.Drawing.Brushes* class includes some predefined solid brushes based on color name. As with pens, you must dispose of brushes that you create, but not the solid system-defined brushes.

The following block of code draws some simple rectangles with a variety of brush styles. The results appear in Figure 18-3.

```
private void pictureBox1_Paint(
    object sender, PaintEventArgs e)
{
    // ----- Draw some fancy rectangles.
    Brush useBrush;

    e.Graphics.Clear(Color.White);

    // ---- Draw a filled rectangle with a solid color.
    e.Graphics.FillRectangle(Brushes.Cyan, 10, 10, 150, 50);

    // ----- Draw a hatched rectangle. Use black for the
    //       background, and white for the pattern foreground.
    useBrush = new HatchBrush(HatchStyle.LargeConfetti,
        Color.White, Color.Black);
    e.Graphics.FillRectangle(useBrush, 10, 70, 150, 50);
    useBrush.Dispose();

    // ----- Draw a left-to-right linear gradient rectangle.
    //       The gradient's own rectangle determines the
```

```
//         starting offset, based on the Graphics surface
//         origin.
useBrush = new LinearGradientBrush(
   new Rectangle(200, 10, 75, 25), Color.Blue,
   Color.Yellow, LinearGradientMode.Horizontal);
e.Graphics.FillRectangle(useBrush, 200, 10, 150, 50);
useBrush.Dispose();

// ----- Use an image for the brush. I'm using the
//       "LookupItem.bmp" graphic used in the Library
//       Project.
useBrush = new TextureBrush(Image.FromFile(
   "LookupItem.bmp"));
e.Graphics.FillRectangle(useBrush, 200, 70, 150, 50);
useBrush.Dispose();
}
```

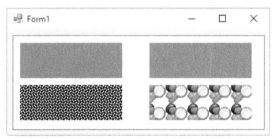

Figure 18-3. Kind of square, if you ask me

Flowing Text from the Font

Circles and squares are OK, but they don't always communicate much, unless you are Joan Miró. Most of us depend on text to say what we mean. Fortunately, GDI+ has features galore that place text on your graphics surface.

Before graphical user interfaces were all the rage, text wasn't really an issue; either you used the characters built into the system, or you used nothing. On the screen, each letter of the alphabet was designed into the hardware of the computer or monitor, and any particular character could appear only within each square of the predefined 80 × 24 grid. Printers were a little better, since you could backspace and retype over previously typed positions to generate either bold or underscore text. Still, you were generally limited to one font, or just a small handful of basic fonts embedded in the printer's memory.

Such limitations are a thing of the past. All text in Microsoft Windows appears courtesy of *fonts*, descriptions of character shapes that can be resized or stretched or emphasized to meet any text need. And because the user can add fonts to the system at any time, and from any third-party source, the variety of these fonts is amazing. But you already know all this. Let's get to the code.

To gain access to a font for use in your graphics, create an instance of the `System.Drawing.Font` class, passing it at least the font name and point size, and an optional style reference.

```
Font basicFont = new Font("Arial", 14, FontStyle.Italic);
```

Naturally, the list of available fonts varies by system; if you're going to go beyond the basic preinstalled fonts supplied with Windows, you should confirm that a named font is really available, and have a fallback option if it is not. You can get a list of all fonts by asking GDI+ nicely. All fonts appear in families, where each named family may have bold, italic, and other variations installed as separate font files. The following code block adds a list of all installed font families to a `ListBox` control.

```
var allFonts = new Drawing.Text.InstalledFontCollection();
foreach (Drawing.FontFamily oneFamily in allFonts.Families)
    listBox1.Items.Add(oneFamily.Name);
```

If the font you need isn't available and you aren't sure what to use, let GDI+ choose for you. It includes a few generic fonts for emergency use.

```
Drawing.FontFamily.GenericMonospace
Drawing.FontFamily.GenericSansSerif
Drawing.FontFamily.GenericSerif
```

Getting back to using fonts in actual drawing, the `Graphics` object includes a `DrawString` method that blasts out some text to the canvas.

```
private void pictureBox1_Paint(
    object sender, PaintEventArgs e)
{
    Font basicFont = new Font("Arial", 14, FontStyle.Italic);
    e.Graphics.DrawString("This is a test", basicFont,
        Brushes.Black, 0, 0);
    basicFont.Dispose();
}
```

Figure 18-4 shows the output for this code block. In most of the sample code in this chapter, I'll be outputting content to a `PictureBox` control named `pictureBox1` that I've placed on the form of a new Windows Forms application. I've also set that control's `BorderStyle` property to `FixedSingle`, and its `BackColor` property to `White` so that I can visualize the edges of the canvas. Drawing occurs in the `Paint` event handler, which gets called whenever the picture box needs to be refreshed, such as when another window obscures it and then goes away. In the remaining code examples, I won't be including the `void pictureBox1_Paint` method definition, just the code that goes inside it.

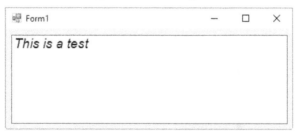

Figure 18-4. This is a test for sure

Of course, you can mix and match fonts on a single output canvas. This code includes text using Arial 14 and Arial 18.

```
Font basicFont = new Font("Arial", 14);
Font strongFont = new Font("Arial", 18, FontStyle.Bold);
float offset = 0.0F;
string showText;
System.Drawing.SizeF textSize;

showText = "This is some ";
textSize = e.Graphics.MeasureString(showText, basicFont);
```

```
e.Graphics.DrawString(showText, basicFont,
    Brushes.Black, offset, 0);
offset += textSize.Width;

showText = "strong";
textSize = e.Graphics.MeasureString(showText, strongFont);
e.Graphics.DrawString(showText, strongFont,
    Brushes.Black, offset, 0);
offset += textSize.Width;

showText = "text.";
textSize = e.Graphics.MeasureString(showText, basicFont);
e.Graphics.DrawString(showText, basicFont,
    Brushes.Black, offset, 0);
offset += textSize.Width;

strongFont.Dispose();
basicFont.Dispose();
```

The output of this code appears in the top box of Figure 18-5, and it's OK. But I want the bottom edges of the main body parts of each text block—that is, the *baselines* of each block—to line up properly, as shown in the lower box of Figure 18-5.

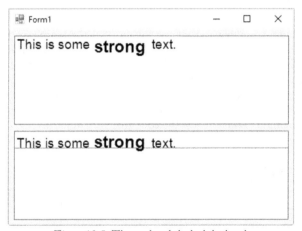

Figure 18-5. The good and the bad; both ugly

Doing all of the fancy font-lining-up stuff is kind of a pain in the neck. You have to do all sorts of measuring based on the original font design as extrapolated onto the pixel-based screen device. Then you connect the knee bone to the thigh bone, and so on. Here's the code I used to generate the second lined-up image.

```
Font basicFont = new Font("Arial", 14);
Font strongFont = new Font("Arial", 18, FontStyle.Bold);
float offset = 0.0F;
string showText;
System.Drawing.SizeF textSize;
float basicTop;
float strongTop;
float strongFactor;
float basicFactor;
```

```
// ----- The Font Family uses design units, probably
//       specified by the original designer of the font.
//       Map these units to display units (points).
strongFactor = strongFont.FontFamily.GetLineSpacing(
    FontStyle.Regular) / strongFont.Height;
basicFactor = basicFont.FontFamily.GetLineSpacing(
    FontStyle.Regular) / basicFont.Height;

// ----- Determine the location of each font's baseline.
strongTop = (strongFont.FontFamily.GetLineSpacing(
    FontStyle.Regular) - strongFont.FontFamily.GetCellDescent(
    FontStyle.Regular)) / strongFactor;
basicTop = (basicFont.FontFamily.GetLineSpacing(
    FontStyle.Regular) - basicFont.FontFamily.GetCellDescent(
    FontStyle.Regular)) / basicFactor;

// ----- Draw a line that proves the text lines up.
e.Graphics.DrawLine(Pens.Red, 0, strongTop,
    e.ClipRectangle.Width, strongTop);

// ----- Show each part of the text.
showText = "This is some ";
textSize = e.Graphics.MeasureString(showText, basicFont);
e.Graphics.DrawString(showText, basicFont,
    Brushes.Black, offset, strongTop - basicTop);
offset += textSize.Width;

showText = "strong";
textSize = e.Graphics.MeasureString(showText, strongFont);
e.Graphics.DrawString(showText, strongFont,
    Brushes.Black, offset, 0);
offset += textSize.Width;

showText = "text.";
textSize = e.Graphics.MeasureString(showText, basicFont);
e.Graphics.DrawString(showText, basicFont,
    Brushes.Black, offset, strongTop - basicTop);
offset += textSize.Width;

strongFont.Dispose();
basicFont.Dispose();
```

There's a lot more calculating going on in that code. And I didn't even try to tackle things like kerning, ligatures, or anything else having to do with typography. Anyway, if you need to perform complex font manipulation, GDI+ does expose all of the details so that you can do it properly. If you just want to output line after line of text using the same font, call the font's *GetHeight* method for each line displayed.

```
verticalOffset += useFont.GetHeight(e.Graphics);
```

Enough of that complex stuff. There are easy and cool things to do with text, too. Did you notice that text output uses brushes and not pens? This means you can draw text using any brush you can create. This block of code uses the Library Project's *LookupItem* bitmap brush to display some bitmap-based text.

```
Brush useBrush = new TextureBrush(
    Image.FromFile("LookupItem.bmp"));
Font useFont = new Font("Arial", 60, FontStyle.Bold);
```

```
e.Graphics.DrawString("Wow!", useFont, useBrush, 0, 0);
useFont.Dispose();
useBrush.Dispose();
```

The output appears in Figure 18-6.

Figure 18-6. The merger of text and graphics

Imagining Images

Probably more than anything else, the Internet has fueled the average computer user's need for visual stimuli. Web sites are awash with GIF, JPG, TIFF, and a variety of other image formats. Even if you deal with non-web applications, it's likely that you, as a programmer, will come into more frequent contact with graphical images. Fortunately, GDI+ includes features that let you manage and manipulate these images with ease.

The BMP file format is the native bitmap format included in Microsoft Windows, but it's not all that common in the web world. But none of that matters to GDI+. It can load and manage files using the following graphics formats.

- Windows bitmap ("BMP") files of any color depth and size.
- CompuServe Graphics Interchange Format ("GIF") files, commonly used for non-photo images on the Internet.
- Joint Photographic Experts Group ("JPEG") files, commonly used for photos and other images on the Internet. JPEG files are compressed internally to reduce file size, but with the possible loss of image quality.
- Exchangeable Image File ("EXIF") files, a variation of JPEG that stores professional photographs.
- Portable Network Graphics ("PNG") files, which are similar to GIF files, but with some enhanced features.
- Tag Image File Format ("TIFF") files, which are kind of a combination of all other file formats. Some government organizations store scanned images using TIFF.
- Metafiles, which store vector line art instead of bitmap images.
- Icon ("ICO") files, which are used for standard Microsoft Windows icons. You can load them as bitmaps, but there is also a distinct *Icon* class that lets you treat them in more icon-like ways.

Three primary classes are used for images: *Image* (an abstract base class for the other two classes), *Bitmap*, and *Metafile*. I'll discuss the *Metafile* class a little later.

Bitmaps represent an image as drawn on a grid of bits. When a bit in the grid is *on*, that grid cell is visible or filled. When the bit is *off*, the grid cell is invisible or empty. Figure 18-7 shows a simple image using such a bitmap grid.

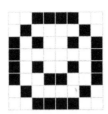

Figure 18-7. An 8 × 8 monochrome bitmap containing great art

Since a bit can support only two states, "1-bit bitmap files" are monochrome, displaying images using only black and white. To include more colors, bitmaps add additional *planes*. The planes are stacked on each other so that a cell in one plane matches up with that same position cell in all other planes. A set of eight planes results in an "8-bit bitmap image," and supports 256 colors per cell (because $2^{planes} = 2^8 = 256$). Some images include as many as 32 or even 64 bits (planes), although some of these bits may be reserved for alpha blending, which makes perceived transparency possible.

Unless you are a hardcore graphics junkie, manipulating all of those bits is a chore. Fortunately, you don't have to worry about it since it's all done for you by the *Bitmap* class. You just need to worry about loading and saving bitmaps (using simple *Bitmap* methods, of course), using a bitmap as a brush or drawing object (as we did in some sample code in this chapter already), or writing on the bitmap surface itself by attaching a *Graphics* object to it.

If you have a bitmap in a file, you can load it via the *Bitmap* class constructor.

```
Bitmap niceImage = new Bitmap("LookupItem.bmp");
```

To save a bitmap object to a file, use its *Save* method.

```
niceImage.Save("LookupItem.jpg", Imaging.ImageFormat.Jpeg);
```

Another constructor lets you create new bitmaps in a variety of formats.

```
// ---- Create a 50-50 pixel bitmap, using 32 bit-planes
//      (eight each for the amounts of red, green, and blue
//      in each pixel, and eight bits for the level of
//      transparency of each pixel, from 0 to 255).
Bitmap niceImage = new Bitmap(50, 50,
    Drawing.Imaging.PixelFormat.Format32bppArgb);
```

To draw a bitmap on a graphics surface, use the *Graphics* object's *DrawImage* method.

```
e.Graphics.DrawImage(niceImage, leftOffset, topOffset);
```

That statement draws the image to the graphics surface as is, but that's kind of boring. You can stretch and crop the image as you draw it, or even generate a thumbnail. I'll try all these methods using the image from the Library Project's "splash" welcome form (*SplashImage.jpg*).

```
Bitmap splashImage = new Bitmap("SplashImage.jpg");

// ----- Draw it at half width and height.
e.Graphics.DrawImage(splashImage, new RectangleF(10, 50,
    splashImage.Width / 2, splashImage.Height / 2));

// ----- Stretch it with fun!
e.Graphics.DrawImage(splashImage, new RectangleF(200, 10,
    splashImage.Width * 1.25F, splashImage.Height / 4));
```

```
// ----- Draw the middle portion.
e.Graphics.DrawImage(splashImage, 200, 100, new RectangleF(
    0, splashImage.Height / 3, splashImage.Width,
    splashImage.Height / 2), GraphicsUnit.Pixel);
```

Figure 18-8 shows the output for the previous block of code. But that's not all the drawing you can do. The *DrawImage* method includes thirty overloads. That would keep me busy for 37 minutes at least!

Figure 18-8. Three views of a reader: a masterpiece by the author

Exposing Your True Artist

OK, we've covered most of the basic GDI+ features used to draw images. Now it's all just a matter of issuing the drawing commands for shapes, images, and text on a graphics surface. Most of the time, you'll stick with the methods included on the *Graphics* object, all twelve bazillion of them. Perhaps I overcounted, but there are quite a few. Here's just a sampling.

Clear *method*

Clear the background with a specific color.

CopyFromScreen *method*

If the Prnt Scrn button on your keyboard falls off, this is the method for you.

DrawArc *method*

Draw a portion of an arc along the edge of an ellipse. Zero degrees starts at three o'clock. Positive arc sweep values move in a clockwise direction; use negative sweep values to move counterclockwise.

DrawBezier *and* DrawBeziers *methods*

Draw a Bézier spline, a formula-based curve that uses a set of points, plus directionals that guide the curve through the points.

DrawCurve, DrawClosedCurve, *and* FillClosedCurve *methods*

Draw cardinal curves (where points define the path of the curve), with an optional brush fill.

DrawEllipse *and* FillEllipse *methods*

Draw an ellipse or a circle (which is a variation of an ellipse).

`DrawIcon,` `DrawIconUnstretched,` `DrawImage,` `DrawImageUnscaled,` *and* `DrawImageUnscaledAndClipped` *methods*

Different ways of drawing images and icons.

`DrawLine` *and* `DrawLines` *methods*

Draw one or more lines with lots of options for making the lines snazzy.

`DrawPath` *and* `FillPath` *methods*

I'll discuss graphic paths a little later.

`DrawPie` *and* `FillPie` *methods*

Draw a pie slice border along the edge of an ellipse.

`DrawPolygon` *and* `FillPolygon` *methods*

Draw a regular or irregular geometric shape based on a set of points.

`DrawRectangle, DrawRectangles, FillRectangle,` *and* `FillRectangles` *methods*

Draw boring and exciting squares and rectangles.

`DrawString` *method*

We used this before to output text to the canvas.

`FillRegion` *method*

I'll discuss regions later in the chapter.

Here's some sample drawing code.

```
// ----- Line from (10, 10) to (40, 40).
e.Graphics.DrawLine(Pens.Black, 10, 10, 40, 40);

// ----- 90-degree clockwise arc for 40-pixel diameter circle.
e.Graphics.DrawArc(Pens.Black, 50, 10, 40, 40, 0, -90);

// ----- Filled 40x40 rectangle with a dashed line.
e.Graphics.FillRectangle(Brushes.Honeydew, 120, 10, 40, 40);
using (Pen dashedPen = new Pen(Color.Black, 2))
{
    dashedPen.DashStyle = DashStyle.Dash;
    e.Graphics.DrawRectangle(dashedPen, 120, 10, 40, 40);
}

// ----- A slice of elliptical pie.
e.Graphics.FillPie(Brushes.BurlyWood, 180, 10, 80, 40,
    180, 120);
```

And so on. You get the idea. Figure 18-9 shows the output for this code.

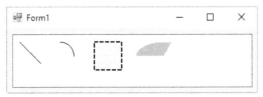

Figure 18-9. Some simple drawings

Paths: Drawings on Macro-Vision

The *Drawing2D.GraphicsPath* class lets you collect several of the more primitive drawing objects (such as lines and arcs, and even rectangles) into a single grouped unit. This full path can then be replayed onto a graphics surface as a macro.

```
using (GraphicsPath thePath = new GraphicsPath())
{
    thePath.AddEllipse(0, 0, 50, 50);
    thePath.AddArc(10, 30, 30, 10, 10, 160);
    thePath.AddRectangle(new Rectangle(15, 15, 5, 5));
    thePath.AddRectangle(new Rectangle(30, 15, 5, 5));

    e.Graphics.DrawPath(Pens.Black, thePath);
}
```

This code block draws a smiley face on the canvas (see Figure 18-10).

Figure 18-10. Drawing with a GraphicsPath object

That's cute. Fortunately, there are other uses for graphics paths, some of which I'll discuss in the next section.

Keeping It Regional

Usually, when you draw images, you have the entire visible canvas to work with. (You can draw images and shapes off the edge of the canvas if you want, but if a tree draws an image in the forest and no one is there to admire it, does it appear?) But there are times when you may want only a portion of what you draw to appear. Windows uses this method itself to save time. When you obscure a window with another one, and then expose the hidden window, the application has to redraw everything that appeared on the form or window. But if only a portion of that background window was hidden and then made visible again, why should the program go through the trouble of drawing everything again? It really has to redraw only the part that was obscured, the part that was in the hidden region.

A *region* specifies an area to be drawn on a surface. Regions aren't limited to boring rectangular shapes. You can design a region based on simple shapes, or you can combine existing regions into more complex regions. For instance, if you have two rectangular regions, you can overlap them and request a new combined region that contains (1) all of the original two regions; (2) the original regions but without the overlapped parts; or (3) just the overlapped parts. Figure 18-11 shows these combinations.

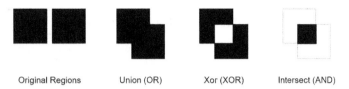

Original Regions   Union (OR)   Xor (XOR)   Intersect (AND)

Figure 18-11. Different combinations of regions

During drawing operations, regions are sometimes referred to as *clipping regions* because any content drawn outside the region is clipped off and thrown away. The following code draws an image, but masks out an ellipse in the middle by using (ta-da!) a graphics path to establish a custom clipping region.

```
// ----- Load the image. We'll show it smaller than normal.
Bitmap splashImage = new Bitmap("SplashImage.jpg");
GraphicsPath thePath = new GraphicsPath();

// ----- Create an elliptical path that is the size of the
//       output image.
thePath.AddEllipse(20, 20, splashImage.Width / 2,
    splashImage.Height / 2);

// ----- Replace the original clipping region that covers
//       the entire canvas with just the rectangular region.
e.Graphics.SetClip(thePath, CombineMode.Replace);

// ----- Draw the image, which will be clipped.
e.Graphics.DrawImage(splashImage, 20, 20,
    splashImage.Width / 2, splashImage.Height / 2);

// ----- Clean up.
thePath.Dispose();
```

The output for this code appears in Figure 18-12.

Figure 18-12. Ready to hang in your portrait gallery

Regions are also useful for *hit testing*. If you draw a non-rectangular image on a form, and you want to know when the user clicks on the image, but not on any pixel just off the image, you can use a region that is the exact shape of the image to test for mouse clicks.

Twisting and Turning with Transformations

Normally, anything you draw on the graphics canvas is laid down directly on the bitmap surface. It's like a giant grid, and your drawing commands are basically dropping colored inks directly into each grid cell. The `Graphics` object also gives you the ability to pass your drawing commands through a geometric transformation before their output goes to the canvas surface. For instance, a rotation transformation would rotate your lines, shapes, and text by the amount you specify (in degrees), and then apply the result to the surface. Figure 18-13 displays the results of the following code, which applies two transformations: (1) moving the (0, 0) origin right by 100 pixels and down by 75 pixels; and (2) adding a clockwise rotation of 270 degrees.

```
e.Graphics.DrawString("Normal",
    SystemFonts.DefaultFont, Brushes.Black, 10, 10);
e.Graphics.TranslateTransform(100, 75);
e.Graphics.RotateTransform(270);
e.Graphics.DrawString("Rotated",
    SystemFonts.DefaultFont, Brushes.Black, 10, 10);
e.Graphics.ResetTransform();
```

Figure 18-13. Normal and rotated text

Transformations are cumulative; if you apply multiple transformations to the canvas, any drawing commands will pass through all of the transformations before arriving at the canvas. The order in which transformations occur is important. If the code we just ran had reversed the `TranslateTransform` and `RotateTransform` statements, the rotation would have altered the x, y coordinates for the entire canvas world. The subsequent translation of (100, 75) would have moved up the origin 100 pixels and then to the right 75 pixels, at least in terms of the pre-rotated surface.

The `Graphics` class includes these methods that let you apply transformations to the worldview of the canvas during drawing.

`RotateTransform` *method*

Rotates the world view in clockwise degrees, from 0 to 359. The rotation can be positive or negative.

`ScaleTransform` *method*

Sets a scaling factor for all drawing. Basically, this increases or decreases the size of the canvas grid when drawing. Changing the scale impacts the width of pens. If you scale the world by a factor of two, not only do distances appear to be twice as far apart, but all pens draw twice as thick as when unscaled.

`TranslateTransform` *method*

Repositions the origin based on an *x* and *y* offset.

`MultiplyTransform` *method*

A sort of master transformation method that lets you apply transforms through a `Matrix` object. It has more options than just the standard transforms included in the `Graphics` object. For instance, you can apply a shearing transformation that skews all output in a rectangle-to-parallelogram type of change.

`ResetTransform` *method*

Removes all applied transformations from a canvas.

`Save` *method*

Saves the current state of the transformed (or untransformed) graphics surface to an object for later restoration. This allows you to apply some transformations, save them, apply some more, and then restore the saved set, wiping out any transformations applied since that set was saved.

`Restore` *method*

Restores a saved set of transformations.

Enhancing Controls through Owner Draw

A lot more GDI+ drawing features are included in .NET, but what we've seen here should be enough to whet your appetite. You can do a lot of fancy drawing with GDI+, but let's face it: you and I are programmers, not artists. If we were artists, we'd be raking in six figures using a floor mop to draw traditional abstract cubist Italian landscapes with Bauhausian accents.

Fortunately, there are practical semi-artistic things you can do with GDI+. One important drawing feature is *owner draw*, a sharing of drawing responsibilities between a control and you, the programmer. (You are the "owner.") The `ComboBox` control supports owner drawing of the individual items in the drop-down portion of the list. Let's create a `ComboBox` control that displays color names, including a small sample of the color to the left of the name. Create a new Windows Forms application, and add a `ComboBox` control named `comboBox1` to `Form1`. Make these changes to `comboBox1`.

1. Change its `DropDownStyle` property to `DropDownList`.
2. Change its `DrawMode` property to `OwnerDrawFixed`.
3. Alter its `Items` property, adding multiple color names as distinct text lines in the String Collection Editor window. I added Red, Green, and Blue.

Now, create an event handler for `comboBox1`'s `DrawItem` event, and use the following code for the handler.

```
private void comboBox1_DrawItem(
    object sender, DrawItemEventArgs e)
{
    // ----- Ignore the unselected state.
    if (e.Index == -1)
        return;

    // ----- Create a brush for the display color, based on
    //       the name of the item.
    SolidBrush colorBrush = new SolidBrush(Color.FromName(
        (string)comboBox1.Items[e.Index]));
```

```
// ----- Create a text brush. The color varies based on
//       whether this item is selected or not.
Brush textBrush;
if (((e.State & DrawItemState.Selected) ==
      DrawItemState.Selected) |
      ((e.State & DrawItemState.HotLight) ==
      DrawItemState.HotLight))
   textBrush = new SolidBrush(SystemColors.HighlightText);
else
   textBrush = new SolidBrush(SystemColors.ControlText);

// ----- Get the shape of the color display area.
Rectangle colorBox = new Rectangle(e.Bounds.Left + 4,
   e.Bounds.Top + 2, (e.Bounds.Height - 4) * 2,
   e.Bounds.Height - 4);

// ----- Draw the selected or unselected background.
e.DrawBackground();

// ----- Draw the custom color area.
e.Graphics.FillRectangle(colorBrush, colorBox);
e.Graphics.DrawRectangle(Pens.Black, colorBox);

// ----- Draw the name of the color to the right of
//       the color.
e.Graphics.DrawString((string)comboBox1.Items[e.Index],
   comboBox1.Font, textBrush, 8 + colorBox.Width,
   e.Bounds.Top + ((e.Bounds.Height -
   comboBox1.Font.Height) / 2));

// ----- Draw a selected rectangle around the item,
//       if needed.
e.DrawFocusRectangle();

// ----- Clean up.
textBrush.Dispose();
colorBrush.Dispose();
}
```

Run the code and play with the combo box, as shown in Figure 18-14.

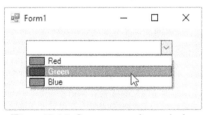

Figure 18-14. Our custom color combo box

Windows Presentation Foundation

Graphical user interfaces are a relatively new phenomenon. The first programmers didn't have all of the glitzy bling-bling that adorns many a modern UI. They had to make do with naval semaphore flags and Morse code. Here in the twenty-first century, having passed through the epochs of text-based and stick-figure interfaces, computers are finally able to present information in a way that totally confuses the end-user, yet in a beautiful and highly interactive style.

Microsoft's latest tool for building active, next-generation user interfaces is Windows Presentation Foundation, or WPF. As with LINQ, WPF melds together many different technologies into a unified whole. Some of those technologies have been with us for many years, such as Microsoft's Direct3D system that displays and manipulates 3D elements. WPF condenses all of these technologies, and makes them available through an XML-based descriptive language known as *XAML* (eXtensible Application Markup Language).

WPF includes features and elements that deal with many areas of presentation, including on-screen controls, 2D drawings (like GDI+), 3D graphics (from Direct3D), static images (such as JPEG pictures), interactive multimedia (video and audio), and WYSIWYG document presentation (similar to PDF documents). Individual elements and entire user interfaces can be animated automatically, or in response to user interactions.

When it comes time to display your WPF content, you can present it to the user in a few common ways. XAML files and related .NET code can be built into a standalone application, much like a typical .NET Windows Forms application, but with the amazing Cary Grant looks normally inaccessible to developers.

WPF can also be used to generate web-based applications hosted within a user's browser, and to manage the user interface details for mobile apps. In fact, elements that you design for use in desktop-style applications can be used on other platforms generally without any modifications. As expected, security limitations put a damper on some of the things you can do when running outside the traditional Windows environment.

The mobile app development features included in Visual Studio use XAML and a variation of desktop WPF to manage the user interface on supported devices. The Xamarin platform, especially when paired with the Xamarin.Forms UI layer, enables cross-platform features that are as easy to program as interfaces on desktop systems. If you have an interest in mobile development, you should read a book on Xamarin programming. Maybe I'll write one. Who knows?

WPF and XAML

One of the hallmarks of application design in WPF is the separation of logic from presentation. This is a common goal expressed in many newer technologies, including XML and ASP.NET. All application logic—all event handlers triggered by user input and system actions—is written in standard .NET code. The user interface can also appear as .NET code, with objects created out of the WPF-specific `System.Windows` namespace. But it's more common to design user interface elements and derived controls through XAML, an XML schema that can be generated by you in Visual Studio or Notepad, or by third-party tools.

Because XAML content can be built outside its application, a user interface design specialist with limited programming knowledge can build the UI components independently from the developer's work on the application logic. Microsoft offers a tool for such designers called *Microsoft Blend for Visual Studio*. Other vendors also offer tools to generate rich XAML content.

Visual Studio lets you create complete WPF applications based on XAML content. To build a WPF desktop application, start Visual Studio, create a new project, and from the New Project dialog select the WPF

Application template within the Visual C# Project type. Then click OK. Windows immediately creates a new WPF Forms project, displaying the starting form, *MainWindow* (see Figure 18-15).

Figure 18-15. Not too different from a Windows Forms application

The user interface is defined entirely by the XML set displayed at the bottom of the form. Currently, it defines the eventual application window itself.

```
<Window x:Class="WpfApplication1.MainWindow"
    xmlns="http://schemas.microsoft.com/winfx/2006/xaml/presentation"
    xmlns:x="http://schemas.microsoft.com/winfx/2006/xaml"
    xmlns:d="http://schemas.microsoft.com/expression/blend/2008"
    xmlns:mc="http://schemas.openxmlformats.org/
        markup-compatibility/2006"
    xmlns:local="clr-namespace:WpfApplication1"
    mc:Ignorable="d"
    Title="MainWindow" Height="350" Width="525">
    <Grid>

    </Grid>
</Window>
```

This code defines the window, *MainWindow*, which has as its real class *System.Windows.Window*. In fact, the much hyped XAML system is nothing more than ordinary XML content which your app uses to determine which classes to instantiate at runtime. The attributes of the XAML *Window* tag, including *Title*, *Height*, and *Width*, map back to properties of the same name in the *Window* class.

Let's spice up this form a little more. I'll add a button that includes a rainbow on the button's face, plus add a yellow glow around the button. I'll also add an event handler that shows a message box. As with standard Windows Forms applications, you use the controls in the toolbox to build your form. I'll drag a button onto the form's surface and use the XAML text area to bring new life to the window.

```
<Window x:Class="WpfApplication1.MainWindow"
    xmlns="http://schemas.microsoft.com/winfx/2006/xaml/presentation"
    xmlns:x="http://schemas.microsoft.com/winfx/2006/xaml"
    xmlns:d="http://schemas.microsoft.com/expression/blend/2008"
    xmlns:mc="http://schemas.openxmlformats.org/
        markup-compatibility/2006"
```

```
    xmlns:local="clr-namespace:WpfApplication1"
    mc:Ignorable="d"
    Title="MainWindow" Height="160" Width="411">
    <Grid>
      <Button Margin="95,26,99,35" Name="Button1">
        <Button.Foreground>White</Button.Foreground>
        <Button.FontSize>18</Button.FontSize>
        <Button.FontWeight>Bold</Button.FontWeight >
        <Button.Background>
          <LinearGradientBrush>
            <LinearGradientBrush.GradientStops>
            <GradientStopCollection>
              <GradientStop Color="Red" Offset="0" />
              <GradientStop Color="Orange" Offset="0.1425"/>
              <GradientStop Color="Yellow" Offset="0.285"/>
              <GradientStop Color="Green" Offset="0.4275"/>
              <GradientStop Color="Blue" Offset="0.57"/>
              <GradientStop Color="Indigo" Offset="0.7325"/>
              <GradientStop Color="Violet" Offset="0.875"/>
            </GradientStopCollection>
            </LinearGradientBrush.GradientStops>
          </LinearGradientBrush>
        </Button.Background>
        <Button.BitmapEffect>
          <OuterGlowBitmapEffect />
        </Button.BitmapEffect> Click Me
      </Button>
    </Grid>
  </Window>
```

I'll also add an event handler, using the same point-and-click simplicity that I've used in Windows Forms projects.

```
private void Button1_Click(object sender, RoutedEventArgs e)
{
    MessageBox.Show("Hello, World");
}
```

Running this program with the F5 key gives us the expected form and button, but oh, what a complex-looking button it is (see Figure 18-16).

Figure 18-16. Click somewhere on the rainbow

Although the colors don't appear in this grayscale book, the form does indeed have a rainbow button.

Microsoft's new Universal Windows Platform lets Visual Studio developers create applications that run on all Microsoft platforms. UWP applications use XAML as their user interface description language, and are developed through Visual Studio in much the same way as normal WPF applications.

Enhancing Classes with Attributes

Class-modifying attributes are something we discussed way back in Chapter 1, and they have nothing to do with GDI+. I just wanted to refresh your memory since they will be used in this chapter's project code.

Class- or member-modifying attributes appear just before the definition of the class or member, and within square brackets. This code attaches the *ObsoleteAttribute* attribute to the *SomeOldClass* class.

```
[ObsoleteAttribute]
class SomeOldClass
{
    ...class details here...
}
```

(You can leave the "Attribute" part of an attribute's name off if the first part of the name doesn't conflict with any Visual C# keyword.) Attributes appear as metadata in the final compiled assembly, and they are used by classes and applications that, by design, extract meaning from specific attributes. In this chapter's code, we'll make use of the *PropertyGrid* control, the control that implements the Properties panel within the Visual Studio development environment, and is often used to modify *Form* and *Control* properties. This control is available for your use in your own applications. To use it, assign a class instance to the control's *SelectedObject* property. Then, magically, all of the object's properties appear in the control's list of properties.

Nice as this is, it's not always desirable. Your object may have properties that should not be displayed. The *PropertyGrid* control is designed to be generic; it doesn't know about your object's needs, so it doesn't know which properties to exclude. That is, it doesn't know until you tell it through attributes. By adding specific attributes to your class's properties, you tell the *PropertyGrid* control how to treat members of your object. For instance, the *BrowsableAttribute* (in the *System.ComponentModel* namespace) attribute tells the *PropertyGrid* to include (*true*) or exclude (*false*) the property.

```
[Browsable(false)]
public string SecretProperty { get; set; }
```

I'll supply additional details about this when we use the *PropertyGrid* control later in this chapter.

Summary

Although many parts of GDI+ are pretty much wrappers around the old GDI system, GDI+ still manages to provide power and simplicity in a package that goes way beyond the original implementation. In business development, you won't always have a need to use the more interesting aspects of the *System.Drawing* namespace. But when you do, you'll encounter a simple and coherent system for displaying images, text, and custom vector elements on the screen or other output medium.

GDI+ is extremely stable, based as it is on technology going back decades. But it is probably only a matter of time before newer technologies supplant it. As Microsoft extends its .NET platform beyond the Windows operating system, opportunities for WPF and XAML style presentation abound. Look for them on a device near you.

Project

The Library Project has used features of GDI+ since the moment the first form appeared in the newly created project, but it all came for free through code included in the framework. Now it's time for you, the programmer, to add your own GDI+ contribution to the application. In this chapter's project code, we'll use GDI+ to enhance the normal display of a control through owner draw features. Plus, we'll finally begin to implement some of the barcode features I tempted you with in earlier chapters.

Although the main Library Project itself will not make use of WPF or XAML, we will use these newer display technologies for one of the Library program's helper applications. I'll walk you through the development of this small program in Chapter 22.

Project Access

Load the "Chapter 18 (Before) Code" project, either through the New Project templates or by accessing the project directly from the installation directory. To see the code in its final form, load "Chapter 18 (After) Code" instead.

Reminder about Visual Studio Bug

As a reminder, if you receive an error that mentions "MSLinqToSQLGenerator" when creating a template-based version of the chapter project, see the note in the Project section of Chapter 17 for instructions on how to eliminate the error.

Install the Barcode Font

If you haven't yet obtained a barcode font, now is the time to do it. The features included in this chapter's project code will require that you use such a font. You can find no-cost options from various web sites, or you can purchase a professionally designed barcode font. Make sure the font you obtain is a TrueType font.

Using Owner Draw

In the previous chapter, we added the *ItemLookup.cs* form with its multiple views of library items. One of those views included the `MatchingItems` control, a multicolumn list box displaying `Author/Name`, `Call Number`, and `Media Type` columns. Although we stored the column-specific data within each item already, we didn't actually display the individual columns to the user.

The thing about multicolumn lists and other limited-space text displays is that some of the text is bound to overrun its official area if you let it. For instance, the text in one list column may overlap into another column of text. In such cases, it has become the tradition to chop off the extended content and replace it with an ellipsis ("..."). So, we'll need a routine that will determine whether a string is too long for its display area, and perform the chopping and ellipsizing as needed. Add the `FitTextToWidth` method to the *General.cs* file's class code.

Insert Snippet
Insert Chapter 18, Snippet Item 1.

```
public static string FitTextToWidth(string origText,
   int pixelWidth, Graphics canvas, Font useFont)
{
   // ----- Given a text string, make sure it fits in
   //       the specified pixel width. Truncate and add
   //       an ellipsis if needed.
   string newText;

   newText = origText;
```

```
        if (canvas.MeasureString(newText,
            useFont).Width > pixelWidth)
        {
            while (canvas.MeasureString(newText + "...",
                useFont).Width > pixelWidth)
            {
                newText = newText.Substring(0, newText.Length - 1);
                if (newText.Length == 0)
                    break;
            }
            if (newText.Length != 0)
                newText += "...";
        }
        return newText;
    }
```

The *ItemLookup.cs* form has a web-browser-like Back button with a drop-down list of recent entries. The items added to this list may include long book titles and author names. Let's use the new *FitTextToWidth* method to limit the size of text items in this list. Open the source code for the *ItemLookup* form and locate the *RefreshBackButtons* method. About halfway through this routine is this line of code.

```
    whichMenu.Text = scanHistory.HistoryDisplay;
```

Replace this line with the following lines instead.

Insert Snippet
Insert Chapter 18, Snippet Item 2.

```
    whichMenu.Text = FitTextToWidth(scanHistory.HistoryDisplay,
        this.Width / 2, useCanvas, whichMenu.Font);
```

That will limit any menu item text to half the width of the form, which seems reasonable to me. That *useCanvas* variable is new, so add a declaration for it at the top of the *RefreshBackButtons* method.

Insert Snippet
Insert Chapter 18, Snippet Item 3.

```
    Graphics useCanvas = this.CreateGraphics();
```

Also, we need to properly dispose of that created graphics canvas at the very end of the method.

Insert Snippet
Insert Chapter 18, Snippet Item 4.

```
    useCanvas.Dispose();
```

Now let's tackle owner draw list items. *ListBox* controls allow you to use your own custom drawing code for each visible item in the list. You have two options when you are managing the item drawing by yourself: you can keep every item a consistent height, or you can make each list item a different height based on the content for that item. In the *MatchingItems* list box, we'll use the same height for every list item.

To enable owner draw mode, open the *ItemLookup* form design editor, select the *MatchingItems* list box on the form or through the Properties panel, and change its *DrawMode* property to *OwnerDrawFixed*.

Each matching list item will include two rows of data: (1) the title of the matching item, in bold; and (2) the three columns of author, call number, and media type data. Add the following code to the form's *Load* event handler that determines the entire height of each list item, and the position of the second line within each item.

Insert Snippet

Insert Chapter 18, Snippet Item 5.

```
// ----- Prepare the form.
Graphics formGraphics = null;

// ----- Set the default height of items in the matching
//       items listbox.
formGraphics = this.CreateGraphics();
MatchingItems.ItemHeight = Convert.ToInt32(
    formGraphics.MeasureString("A" +
    Environment.NewLine + "g",
    MatchingItems.Font).Height) + 3;
SecondItemRow = Convert.ToInt32(
    formGraphics.MeasureString(
    "Ag", MatchingItems.Font).Height) + 1;
formGraphics.Dispose();
```

I used the text "Ag" to make sure that the height included all of the font's ascenders and descenders (the parts that stick up and stick down from most letters). I think the calculation would include those values even if I used "mm" for the string, but better safe than sorry, I always say. Setting the *MatchingItems.ItemHeight* property here indicates the size of all items in the list. If we had decided to use variable-height items instead of fixed-height items, we would have handled the control's *MeasureItem* event. With fixed items, we can ignore that event, and move on to the event that does the actual drawing: *DrawItem*.

Here is what the code is going to do for each list item: (1) create the necessary brushes and font objects we will use in drawing; (2) draw the text strings on the list item canvas; and (3) clean up. Since list items can also be selected or unselected, we'll call some framework-supplied methods to draw the proper background and foreground elements that indicate item selections.

When we draw the multiple columns of text, it's possible that one column of text will be too long, and intrude into the next column area. This was why we wrote the *FitTextToWidth* function earlier. But it turns out that GDI+ already includes a feature that adds ellipses to text at just the right place when it doesn't fit. It's found in a class called *StringFormat*, in its *Trimming* property. Setting this property to *EllipsisCharacter* and using it when drawing the string will trim the string when appropriate. When we draw the string on the canvas, we will provide a rectangle that tells the string what its limits are. Here is the basic code used to draw one column of truncated text.

```
StringFormat ellipsesText;
ellipsesText.Trimming = StringTrimming.EllipsisCharacter;
e.Graphics.DrawString("Some Long Text", e.Font, someBrush,
    new Rectangle(left, top, width, height), ellipsesText);
```

The code we'll use to draw each list item in the *MatchingItems* list will use logic just like this. Let's add that code now to the *MatchingItems* control's *DrawItem* event handler.

Insert Snippet

Insert Chapter 18, Snippet Item 6.

```
// ----- Draw the matching items on two lines.
MatchingItemData itemToDraw;
```

```
Brush useBrush;
Font boldFont;
StringFormat ellipsesText;

// ----- Draw the background of the item.
if ((e.State & DrawItemState.Selected) ==
        DrawItemState.Selected)
    useBrush = SystemBrushes.HighlightText;
else
    useBrush = SystemBrushes.WindowText;
e.DrawBackground();

// ----- The title will use a bold version of the main font.
boldFont = new Font(e.Font, FontStyle.Bold);

// ----- Obtain the item to draw.
itemToDraw = (MatchingItemData)
    (MatchingItems.Items[e.Index]);
ellipsesText = new StringFormat();
ellipsesText.Trimming = StringTrimming.EllipsisCharacter;

// ----- Draw the text of the item.
e.Graphics.DrawString(itemToDraw.Title, boldFont, useBrush,
    new Rectangle(0, e.Bounds.Top, ItemColEnd.Left -
    MatchingItems.Left, boldFont.Height), ellipsesText);
e.Graphics.DrawString(itemToDraw.Author, e.Font, useBrush,
    new Rectangle(ItemColAuthor.Left, e.Bounds.Top +
    SecondItemRow, ItemColCall.Left -
    ItemColAuthor.Left - 8, e.Font.Height), ellipsesText);
e.Graphics.DrawString(itemToDraw.CallNumber, e.Font,
    useBrush, new Rectangle(ItemColCall.Left, e.Bounds.Top +
    SecondItemRow, ItemColEnd.Left - ItemColType.Left,
    e.Font.Height), ellipsesText);
e.Graphics.DrawString(itemToDraw.MediaType, e.Font, useBrush,
    new Rectangle(ItemColType.Left, e.Bounds.Top +
    SecondItemRow, ItemColType.Left -
    ItemColCall.Left - 8, e.Font.Height), ellipsesText);

// ----- If the ListBox has focus, draw a focus rectangle.
e.DrawFocusRectangle();
boldFont.Dispose();
```

See, it's amazingly easy to draw anything you want in a list box item. In this code, the actual output to the canvas via GDI+ amounted to just the four *DrawString* statements. Although this library database doesn't support it, we could have included an image of each item in the database, and displayed it in this list box, just to the left of the title. Also, the calls to e.*DrawBackground* and e.*DrawFocusRectangle* let the control deal with properly highlighting the right item (although I did have to choose the proper text brush). Figure 18-17 shows the results of our coding efforts.

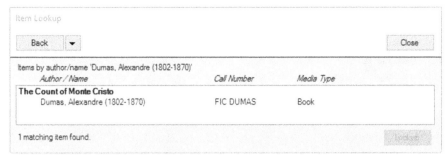

Figure 18-17. A sample book with two lines and three columns

Barcode Design

The Library Project includes generic support for barcode labels. I visited a few libraries in my area and compared the barcodes added to both their library items (such as books) and their patron ID cards. I found that the variety was too great to shoehorn into a single predefined solution. Therefore, the Library application allows an administrator or librarian to design sheets of barcode labels to meet their specific needs. (There are businesses that sell preprinted barcode labels and cards to libraries that don't want to print their own. The application also supports this method, since barcode generation and barcode assignment to items are two distinct steps.)

To support generic barcode design, we will add a set of design classes and two forms to the application.

BarcodeItemClass.cs

> This class file contains six distinct classes, one of which is a base class for the other five derived classes. The derived classes design the static text elements, barcode images, barcode numbers, lines, and rectangles that the user will add to the surface of a single barcode label.

BarcodePage.cs

> This is an editor form derived from *BaseCodeForm*, the same base form used for the various code editors in the application. This form specifies the arrangement of label sheets. The user will probably purchase label sheets from an office supply store. By entering the number of label rows and columns, the size of each label, and any spacing between and around each label, the user can output barcodes on pretty much any regular sheet of labels.

BarcodeLabel.cs

> Another editor based on *BaseCodeForm*, this form lets the user design a single barcode label by adding text, barcodes, lines, and rectangles to a preview area.

In a future chapter, we'll add label printing, where labels and pages are joined together in one glorious print job.

Since these three files together include a little more than 2,500 lines of source code, I will show you only key sections of each one. I've already added all three files to your project code, so let's start with *BarcodeItemClass.cs*. It defines each type of display item that the user will add to a label template in the *BarcodeLabel.cs* form. Here's the code for the abstract base class, *BarcodeItemGeneric*.

```
public abstract class BarcodeItemGeneric
{
    [Browsable(false)]
    public abstract string ItemType {get;}
    public abstract override string ToString();
}
```

Not much going on here. The class defines two required members: a read-only *string* property named *ItemType*, and a requirement that derived classes provide their own implementation for *ToString*. The other five derived classes in this file enhance the base class to support the distinct types of display elements included on a barcode label. Let's look briefly at one of the classes, *BarcodeItemRect*. It allows an optionally filled rectangle to appear on a barcode label, and includes member properties that track the details of the rectangle. Here's the code for the public *FillColor* property.

```
[Browsable(true), DescriptionAttribute(
    "Sets the fill color of the rectangle.")]
public Color FillColor {get; set;}
```

Like most of the other class members, it offers basic storage and retrieval of a value through an automatic property. Its declaration includes two attributes that will be read by the *PropertyGrid* control later on. The *Browsable* attribute says, "Yes, include this property in the grid," and *DescriptionAttribute* sets the text that appears in the bottom help area of the *PropertyGrid* control.

When you've used the Properties panel to edit your forms, you've been able to set colors for a color property using a special color selection tool built into the property. Just having a property defined using *System.Drawing.Color* is enough to enable this same functionality for your own class. How does it work? Just as the *FillColor* property has attributes recognized by the *PropertyGrid* control, the *System.Drawing.Color* class also has such properties, one of which defines a custom property editor class for colors. Its implementation is beyond the scope of this book, but it's cool anyway. If you're interested in doing this for your own classes, you can read an article I wrote about property grid editors a few years ago.[6]

Before we get to the editor forms, I need to let you know about four supporting functions I already added to the *General.cs* module file.

BuildFontStyle *function*

Font styles (such as bold and italic) are set in *Font* objects using members of the *System.Drawing.FontStyle* enumeration. But when storing font information in the database, I chose to store these style settings using letters (such as B for bold). This function converts the letters back to a *FontStyle* value.

ConvertPageUnits *function*

The label editors let you position items in a few different measurement systems, including inches and centimeters. This function converts measurements between the different systems.

DBFontStyle *function*

This is the opposite of the *BuildFontStyle* function, preparing a *FontStyle* value for insertion into a database record.

GetBarcodeFont *function*

This returns the name of the barcode font, if configured.

---

[6] Find the article on *Visual Studio Magazine*'s web site, http://www.visualstudiomagazine.com. The title is "Put Custom Property Editors on the Map," published on August 1, 2004. The associated code is written in Visual Basic, but it will look understandable for someone thinking in C#.

The *BarcodePage* form lets the user define a full sheet of labels. Not the labels themselves, but the positions of multiple labels on the same printed page. Figure 18-18 shows the fields on the form with some sample data.

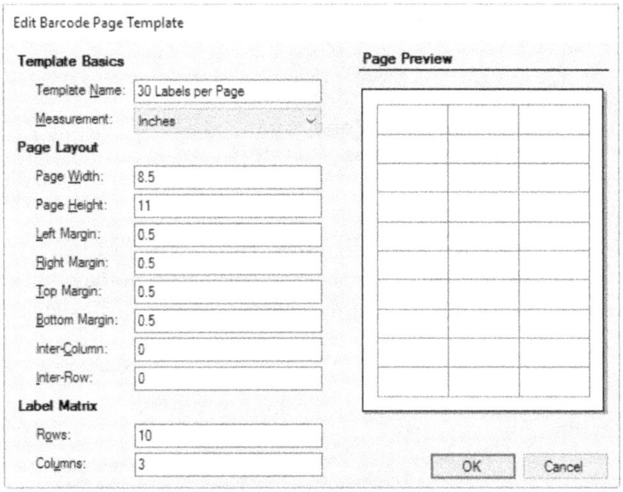

Figure 18-18. The BarcodePage form

Collectively, the fields on the form describe the size of the page and the size of each label that appears on the page. As the user enters the values, the Page Preview area instantly refreshes with a preview of what the page will look like.

As a code editor derived from *BaseCodeForm*, the logic in the form is already familiar to you; it manages the data found in a single record from the *BarcodeSheet* table. What's different is the GDI+ code found in the *PreviewArea.Paint* event handler. Its first main block of code tries to determine how you scale down an 8.5×11 piece of paper to make it appear in a small rectangle that is only 216×272 pixels in size. It's a lot of gory calculations that, when complete, determine the big-to-small-paper ratio, and lead to the drawing of the on-screen piece of paper with a border and a drop shadow.

```
e.Graphics.FillRectangle(SystemBrushes.ControlDark,
    pageLeft + 1, pageTop + 1, pageWidth + 2, pageHeight + 2);
e.Graphics.FillRectangle(SystemBrushes.ControlDark,
    pageLeft + 2, pageTop + 2, pageWidth + 2, pageHeight + 2);
e.Graphics.FillRectangle(Brushes.Black,
    pageLeft - 1, pageTop - 1, pageWidth + 2, pageHeight + 2);
e.Graphics.FillRectangle(Brushes.White,
    pageLeft, pageTop, pageWidth, pageHeight);
```

Then, before drawing the preview outlines of each rectangular label, it repositions the grid origin to the upper-left corner of the on-screen piece of paper, and transforms the world scale based on the ratio of a real-world piece of paper and the on-screen image of it.

```
e.Graphics.TranslateTransform(pageLeft, pageTop);
e.Graphics.ScaleTransform((float)useRatio, (float)useRatio);
```

There are a few more calculations for the size of each label, followed by a double loop (for both rows and columns of labels) that does the actual printing of the label boundaries (detail calculations omitted for brevity).

```
for (rowScan = 1; rowScan <=
   Convert.ToInt32(BCRows.Text); rowScan++)
{
   for (colScan = 1; colScan <=
      Convert.ToInt32(BCColumns.Text); colScan++)
   {
      leftOffset = ...
      topOffset = ...
      e.Graphics.DrawRectangle(Pens.Cyan, leftOffset,
         topOffset, oneWidthTwips, oneHeightTwips);
   }
}
```

The *BarcodeLabel* form is clearly the more interesting and complex of the two barcode editing forms. While the *BarcodePage* form defines an entire sheet of labels with nothing but emptiness in each label, *BarcodeLabel* defines what goes inside each of those labels. Figure 18-19 shows this form with a sample label.

Figure 18-19. The BarcodeLabel form

The *BarcodeLabel* form does derive from *BaseCodeForm*, so much of its code deals with the loading and saving of records from the *BarcodeLabel* and *BarcodeLabelItem* database tables. Each barcode label is tied to a specific barcode page template (which we just defined through the *BarcodePage* form), and stores its primary record in the *BarcodeLabel* table. This table defines the basics of the label, such as its name and measurement system. The text and shape items placed on that label are stored as records in the related *BarcodeLabelItem* table.

The *PrepareFormFields* routine loads existing label records from the database, creating instances of classes from the new *BarcodeItemClass.cs* file, and adds them to the *DisplayItems ListBox* control. Here's the section of code that loads in a barcode image (the actual displayed barcode) from an entry in the *BarcodeLabelItems* table.

```
newBarcodeImage = new BarcodeItemBarcodeImage();
newBarcodeImage.Alignment =
   (ContentAlignment)DBGetInteger(dbRow["Alignment"]);
```

```
newBarcodeImage.BarcodeColor =
    Color.FromArgb(DBGetInteger(dbRow["Color1"]));
newBarcodeImage.BarcodeSize =
    DBGetDecimal(dbRow["FontSize"]);
newBarcodeImage.Left = DBGetDecimal(dbRow["PosLeft"]);
newBarcodeImage.Top = DBGetDecimal(dbRow["PosTop"]);
newBarcodeImage.Width = DBGetDecimal(dbRow["PosWidth"]);
newBarcodeImage.Height = DBGetDecimal(dbRow["PosHeight"]);
newBarcodeImage.RotationAngle =
    (short)DBGetInteger(dbRow["Rotation"]);
newBarcodeImage.PadDigits =
    (byte)(DBGetInteger(dbRow["PadDigits"]));
DisplayItems.Items.Add(newBarcodeImage);
```

The user can add new shapes, text elements, and barcodes to the label by clicking on one of the five Add Items buttons that appear just below the *DisplayItems* control. Each button adds a default record to the label, which the user can then modify. As each label element is selected from the *DisplayItems* list box, its properties appear in the *ItemProperties* control, an instance of a *PropertyGrid* control. Modification of a label element is a matter of changing its properties. Figure 18-20 shows a color property being changed.

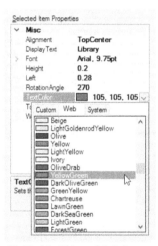

Figure 18-20. Modifying a label element property

As with the *BarcodePage* form, the real fun in the *BarcodeLabel* form comes through the *Paint* event of the label preview control, *PreviewArea*. This 300-plus-line routine starts out drawing the blank surface of the label with a drop shadow. Then it processes each element in the *DisplayItems* list, one by one, transforming and drawing each element as its properties indicate. As it passes through the element list, the code applies transforms to the drawing area as needed. To keep things tidy for each element, the state of the surface is saved before changes are made, and restored once changes are complete.

```
for (int counter = 0; counter <
    DisplayItems.Items.Count; counter++)
{
    // ----- Save the current state of the graphics area.
    holdState = e.Graphics.Save();

    ...main drawing code goes here, then...
```

```
// ----- Restore the original transformed state of
//       the graphics surface.
e.Graphics.Restore(holdState);
}
```

Each element type's code performs the various size, position, and rotation transformations needed to properly display the element. Let's take a closer look at the code that displays static text elements (code that is also called to display barcode text). After scaling down the world view to the label surface preview area, any user-requested rotation is performed about the upper-left corner of the rectangle that holds the printed text.

```
e.Graphics.TranslateTransform(X1, Y1);
e.Graphics.RotateTransform(textAngle);
```

Next, a gray dashed line is drawn around the text object to show its selected state.

```
pixelPen = new Pen(Color.LightGray, 1 / e.Graphics.DpiX);
pixelPen.DashStyle = DashStyle.Dash;
e.Graphics.DrawRectangle(pixelPen, X1, Y1, X2, Y2);
pixelPen.Dispose();
```

After setting some flags to properly align the text vertically and horizontally within its bounding box, the standard *DrawString* method thrusts the text onto the display.

```
e.Graphics.DrawString(textMessage, useFont,
   new SolidBrush(textColor),
   new RectangleF(X1, Y1, X2, Y2), textFormat);
```

We will somewhat duplicate the label drawing code included in the *BarcodeLabel* class when we print actual labels in a later chapter.

The only thing left to do is to link up these editors to the main form. Since I've had so much fun with these forms, I'll let you play for a while in the code. Open the code for *MainForm*, locate the event handler for the *AdminLinkBarcodeLabel.LinkClicked* event, and add the following code.

Insert Snippet
Insert Chapter 18, Snippet Item 7.

```
// ----- Let the user edit the list of barcode labels.
if (SecurityProfile[(int)LibrarySecurity.
   ManageBarcodeTemplates] == false)
{
   MessageBox.Show(NotAuthorizedMessage, ProgramTitle,
      MessageBoxButtons.OK, MessageBoxIcon.Exclamation);
   return;
}

// ----- Edit the records.
(new ListEditRecords()).ManageRecords(new BarcodeLabel());
```

Do the same for the *AdminLinkBarcodePage.LinkClicked* event handler. Its code is almost identical except for the class instance passed to *ListEditRecords*.

Insert Snippet
Insert Chapter 18, Snippet Item 8.

```
// ----- Let the user edit the list of barcode pages.
if (SecurityProfile[(int)LibrarySecurity.
```

```
            ManageBarcodeTemplates] == false)
        {
            MessageBox.Show(NotAuthorizedMessage, ProgramTitle,
                MessageBoxButtons.OK, MessageBoxIcon.Exclamation);
            return;
        }

        // ----- Edit the records.
        (new ListEditRecords()).ManageRecords(new BarcodePage());
```

Fun with Graphics

GDI+ isn't all about serious drawing stuff; you can also have some fun. Let's make a change to the *AboutProgram.cs* form so that it fades out when the user clicks its Close button. This involves altering the form's *Opacity* property to slowly increase the transparency of the form. From our code's point of view, no GDI+ is involved. But it's still involved through the hidden code that responds to the *Opacity* property.

Open the source code for the *AboutProgram.cs* file, and add the following code to the end of the *AboutProgram_Load* event handler.

Insert Snippet
Insert Chapter 18, Snippet Item 9.

```
// ----- Prepare the form for later fade-out.
this.Opacity = 0.99;
```

Although this statement isn't really necessary, I found that the form tended to blink a little on some systems when the opacity went from 100% (1.0) to anything else (99%, or 0.99, in this case). This blink was less noticeable when I made the transition during the load process.

In the event handler for the *ActClose.Click* event, include this code.

Insert Snippet
Insert Chapter 18, Snippet Item 10.

```
// ----- Fade the form out.
for (int counter = 90; counter >= 10; counter -= 20)
{
    this.Opacity = counter / 100.0;
    this.Refresh();
    System.Threading.Thread.Sleep(50);
}
this.DialogResult = DialogResult.Cancel;
```

This code slowly fades out the form over the course of 250 milliseconds, in five distinct steps. So that the form doesn't close abruptly before the cool fade-out, open the form designer, select the *ActClose* button, and change its *DialogResult* property to *None*.

Another thing we never did was to set the primary icon for the application. Although this isn't strictly GDI+, it does involve graphics display, which impacts the user's perception of the program's quality. I've included an icon named *Book.ico* in the project's file set. Open the project properties, select the Application tab, and use the Icon field to browse for the *Book.ico* file.

While testing out the icon, I noticed that the splash window appeared (with the default Visual Studio icon) in the Windows task bar. In fact, each opened form appeared in the task bar, right alongside the main form's entry. For dialog forms, this isn't really needed, since clicking on the task bar button for the main form will bring you to the active dialog. The task bar button behavior is controlled by each form's *ShowInTaskbar* property setting. I've taken the liberty of going through all dialog forms and setting this property to *False* when needed.

The Library application is really starting to bulk up with features. In fact, by the next chapter, we will have added more than ninety-five percent of its total code. I can see the excitement on your face. Go ahead, turn the page, and add to your coding enjoyment.

Chapter 19

Localization and Globalization

Bienvenue à chapitre dix-neuf! My apologies to those of you who don't speak French—and also to those who actually do. I took four full years of the language in high school, but for some reason, it didn't stick. I can still remember a few important sentences, such as *«Je suis un garçon»* and *«Où est le crayon?»*, but that's about it. We even read *Candide* and *Le Petit Prince* in class, but to no avail. I did take Japanese in college, and found it much easier to digest than French. So, perhaps I should instead say 第十九章にようこそ.

In an attempt to expand this book beyond the shores of English-speaking nations, I localized that previous paragraph. In an attempt to expand the appeal of your own applications beyond the English-speaking world, .NET provides features that let you *localize* your project in another language, even after your software has been compiled and released.

Coverage of all localization features in .NET would include lunar- and emperor reign-based calendars, and right-to-left writing systems. This chapter covers only some of the more common user interface localization features. Hopefully, it will entice you to push the language limits of your own applications, reaching out to *les étoiles.*

Defining Globalization and Localization

Microsoft has hundreds of for-sale and freely available software applications, and the company makes a lot of money worldwide providing these software products to consumers. Most of its products are developed in the United States, written by programmers who speak mainly English, directed by technical leads and product managers who make decisions in English, marketed by a sales team that plans out campaigns in English, and dogged by competitors and detractors who blast the motives and business practices behind each product in English. So, how is it possible that Microsoft can sell software to non-English speakers around the globe?

The key lies in the globalization and localization of its products. Sure, Microsoft or any other company could develop distinct yet identical products, each in a different language, and sell them in the appropriate markets. But that would be expensive and time-consuming. Instead, it writes a single program, and then enhances it with language- and culture-specific features.

Globalization is the process of preparing software so that it can be easily adjusted for each language and culture market. No foreign terms are added to software during the globalization process. Instead, the developers design the application so that all relevant English (in my case) terms and American cultural elements (such as currency displays in U.S. dollars) can be quickly and easily replaced by foreign substitutes, all without impacting the core software elements.

Windows applications have traditionally used *resources* to keep applications globally generic. Resources contain text strings, images, and other non-code elements that are replaced at runtime based on the active language and culture of the operating system. On a German-language system, the application loads its German-language resources (if available) and displays them instead of the default resources. The .NET Framework continues to use resources for this purpose, although it enhances resource development through XML-based resource files and tools.

Localization adds the actual non-native language and culture elements to an application. It is in this step that, say, English-language form labels get translated into Swahili, or some other target language. Visual Studio lets you localize an application within the development environment itself, or through external tools that translators who have no access to the application source code can use.

The good news for .NET developers is that Microsoft pretty much took care of the globalization part for you. You mainly need to focus on localizing your application. Your local community college offers foreign language instruction in a dozen or so languages, so I'll let you choose your first localization target.

Resource Files

Resource files are the key to language localization in .NET programs. Visual Studio will write the files for you, but it's good to know something about how they work, since you may want to craft your own resource files (if you have a lot of time on your hands). The life of a resource moves through three phases, as determined by the type of file in which it appears.

Source

> An application's resources start their lives in a resource source file. Before .NET, resources appeared in "resource script" files, which merged all the best of C-language development and UPPER CASE SCRIPT COMMANDS, and used an *.rc* file extension. In .NET, you use XML-based *.resx* files instead. Every new Windows Forms application already includes a *Resources.resx* file just waiting to be joyfully filled with your application resources.
>
> Beyond the core resource source files, other file types can be included as resources, although they are still referenced through the *.resx* file content. Common external resource files include image files (such as *.gif* and *.jpg* files) and plain-text files (*.txt*). The Library Project uses a file named *SplashImage.jpg* as a resource for the splash screen, and another file named *ItemLookupBody.txt* that contains HTML content used when displaying items through the *ItemLookup.cs* form.

Intermediate

> Once you have your resource sources ready, they are converted into an intermediate form, and stored with a *.resources* file extension, through a process called *resource generation*. Visual Studio normally does this step behind the scenes for you, but you can also use a tool supplied with the .NET SDK (called *resgen.exe*) to generate these files yourself. Intermediate resource files include binary content only, and are not designed for browsing in Notepad.

Compiled

> Intermediate resource files aren't much use to your deployed application. The term *intermediate* kind of gave this secret away, didn't it? Before employing the resources in your program, they need to be compiled into a DLL or EXE file. Perhaps you already knew that these files contained multiple sections, including distinct code and data sections. A compiled resource file contains only a data section with the resources; there is no code in a compiled resource file, although standard compiled code files may also include compiled resources.

In .NET, compiled resource files are satellite assemblies. They support your primary application assembly, and are not generally useful apart from that master assembly.

Figure 19-1 shows the lifetime of a resource through these three stages.

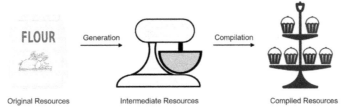

Figure 19-1. The edible life of a resource

Some standard resource types are stored in .NET resource (*.resx*) files.

Strings

We'll focus primarily on string resources in this chapter. Each string resource includes a name and a string value.

Images

Visual C# applications can include JPEG, GIF, TIFF, PNG, and BMP image files. Each image, as with all resources, includes an associated name, which may differ from the original name of the graphics file.

Icons

Program icons used with forms and the application itself appear as standard resources. Icons have an *.ico* file extension.

Audio

Resources can include named audio files, based on WAV audio content.

Files

If the file types listed so far don't meet your needs, you can include whole files of any type as a named resource.

Other

Beyond files, you can store the content of any valid .NET data type as a resource. The resources in a *.resx* file are actually strongly typed to .NET types, so there's really no limit to the kinds of data you can place there. You can also modify the underlying *.resx* file to include non-standard resources. Non-standard resources are beyond the scope of this chapter.

The project properties window includes a manager for application-wide resources (see Figure 19-2). The IDE also includes special editors that let you edit standard and a few non-standard resource types.

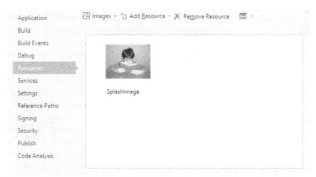

Figure 19-2. The resource manager for the Library Project in Visual Studio

The Properties.Resources Object

We discussed this in earlier chapters, but as a reminder, you can access a Windows Forms application's resources through the *Properties.Resources* object. If you have a string resource named *MainFormCaption*, the following reference returns its value.

```
Properties.Resources.MainFormCaption
```

All resources are strongly typed. In this case, *MainFormCaption* is of type *System.String*. The *SplashImage* image resource included in the Library Project is declared as type *System.Drawing.Bitmap*. Because each resource is strongly typed, you can use the *Properties.Resources* reference in your code just like any data of the resource's type.

In new Windows Forms applications, all application-wide resources appear in the *Resources.resx* file, found in the *Properties* directory within the application's source code directory. You can view it in Notepad if you want. It's a pretty big XML file that doesn't immediately interest me, except that it works! Here's the portion of the Library Project's *Resources.resx* file that specifies our two existing resources. (I've wrapped some of the lines to make it fit on the page.) I've highlighted the name of each resource, and their strong data types.

```
<data name="ItemLookupBody"
    type="System.Resources.ResXFileRef, System.Windows.Forms">
    <value>..\Resources\ItemLookupBody.txt;System.String,
        mscorlib, Version=4.0.0.0, Culture=neutral,
        PublicKeyToken=b77a5c561934e089;Windows-1252</value>
</data>
<data name="SplashImage"
    type="System.Resources.ResXFileRef, System.Windows.Forms">
    <value>..\Resources\SplashImage.jpg;System.Drawing.Bitmap,
        System.Drawing, Version=4.0.0.0, Culture=neutral,
        PublicKeyToken=b03f5f7f11d50a3a</value>
</data>
```

Each form you add to your project also has its own private resource file. The one for *Form1* is called *Form1.resx*. These files end up being a big plus in the localization of Windows Forms applications.

Behind the scenes, your application is taking an object-oriented approach to resource management. It's using the *System.Resources.ResourceManager* class to locate and return instances of each resource when you need them. And this same class makes decisions about which language-specific or culture-specific resources—from the dozens I'm sure you'll have added to your application—will be made visible to the user.

Localizing Forms within Visual Studio

There's no sense in postponing the introduction to the localization features of Visual Studio, since they are so easy to use. You already know about the application-wide project properties resource editor. Instead, let's look at the amazing part: localizing forms and controls right in the Visual Studio form editor. You might as well start up Visual Studio and try it out with me, because it's just so fun.

Here's a cute but relatively harmless Windows Forms application that writes your name upside down. I added some *Label* controls, a *TextBox* control, and a *PictureBox* control to a form, as shown in Figure 19-3.

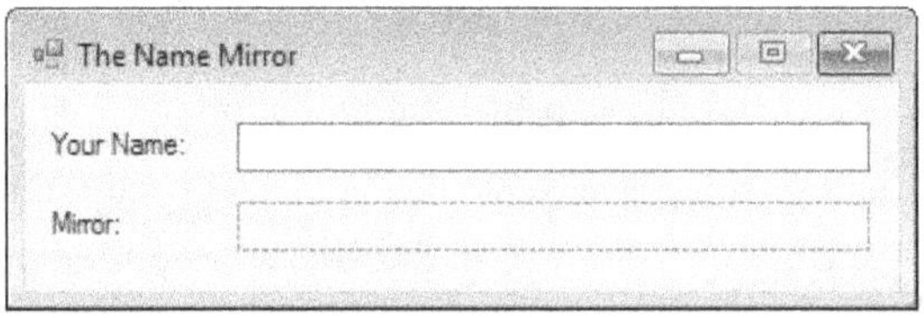

Figure 19-3. A typical Windows Forms application

Then I added the following event handlers to the form.

```
private void TextBox1_TextChanged(object sender, EventArgs e)
{
    // ----- Force a redraw.
    PictureBox1.Invalidate();
}

private void PictureBox1_Paint(object sender, PaintEventArgs e)
{
    // ----- Draw the blank background.
    e.Graphics.Clear(SystemColors.Window);
    e.Graphics.DrawRectangle(SystemPens.InactiveCaption, 0, 0,
        PictureBox1.Width - 1, PictureBox1.Height - 1);

    // ----- Change the orientation of the display.
    GraphicsState saveState = e.Graphics.Save();
    Matrix mirrorMatrix = new Matrix(1, 0, 0, -1, 0,
        PictureBox1.Height);
    e.Graphics.Transform = mirrorMatrix;

    // ----- Draw the text.
    e.Graphics.DrawString(TextBox1.Text, TextBox1.Font,
        SystemBrushes.WindowText, 1, 4);

    // ----- Put everything back.
    e.Graphics.Restore(saveState);
}
```

When you run the program, it creates a mirror image of whatever you type in the *TextBox* control using GDI+ features. Figure 19-4 shows me playing with the program instead of meeting this chapter's submission deadline.

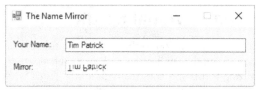

Figure 19-4. Look Ma, I'm upside down

As interesting as this program may be, it is neither fully globalized nor localized. It's *almost* globalized. All we need to do to fully globalize it is to throw the switch on the form that enables later localization. We do this through the form's `Localizable` property. Change this property from `False` to `True`. Ta-da! Your form is globalized!

Now for part two: localization. Here are the steps to localize the form.

1. Determine which language or language-culture combination you want to use for localization.

2. Select that language or language-culture from the form's `Language` property. When you open this property list, it includes languages alone, such as "French," and languages combined with a culture or country, as with "French (Canada)." The language-alone entries are known as neutral-language entries. You can use either type for localization. If you select, for instance, "French," users of your application in either France or French-speaking Canada will use the French resources. If you localize using "French (Canada)," French Canadian users will access the localized resources, but not French-language users in France.

3. Modify any of the properties of the form or its controls.

That's it. Whenever the form's `Language` property is changed to something other than `(Default)`, Visual Studio starts recording all form and control changes into a separate form-specific *and* language- or language-culture-specific resource file.

You can localize the form with multiple languages. Each time you change the `Language` property to another language or language-culture selection, the changes to the form or controls apply only to that selection. Whatever you change gets saved in a separate resource file.

Let's try it with the sample mirror program. I'm going to choose Japanese for the localization language. First, I set the form's `Language` property to "Japanese." The form momentarily blinks, but there is no other noticeable change. It looks just as it did in Figure 19-3.

Next, I change the `Text` properties of the form and of each label control to their Japanese language equivalents (see Figure 19-5).

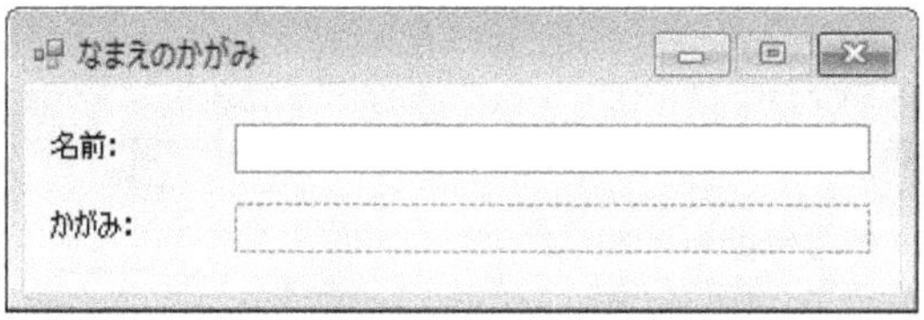

Figure 19-5. The name-mirror program in Japanese

Do you notice how the shorter Japanese language labels are farther away from the text and mirror display fields? Does it bother you as much as it bothers me? To get it out of my mind, I will resize the two fields a little larger by stretching them to the left, as I've done in Figure 19-6.

Figure 19-6. The Japanese version with adjusted fields

The amazing part is that if you set the form's `Language` property back to `(Default)`, not only will the labels return to English, but the resized text and mirror fields will return to their original sizes. Although I haven't checked out every property, the localization feature seems to impact all display elements of each control.

The program is now fully localized for English (the default language) and Japanese. Normally, the Japanese resources would be used only on a system running the Japanese version of Microsoft Windows. But we can force the program to use Japanese by changing its user interface culture. In the application's `Main` startup routine in the *Program.cs* file, I add the following code, just before displaying the form.

```
// ----- Prompt for language.
if (MessageBox.Show("Switch from English to Japanese?",
    "Foreign Names", MessageBoxButtons.YesNo,
    MessageBoxIcon.Question) == DialogResult.Yes)
  System.Threading.Thread.CurrentThread.CurrentUICulture =
    new System.Globalization.CultureInfo("ja-JP");
```

And sure enough, running the program and saying "Yes" to the "Switch to Japanese" prompt presents a form in Japanese, as shown in Figure 19-7. (If you answer "No" to the question, the default language, English, appears.)

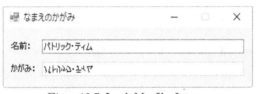

Figure 19-7. Look Ma, I'm Japanese

Let's look at the files created in this project. (Look in the installation directory of this book's code for the *Foreign Names* subdirectory. I've placed a copy of this mirror-text project there for you.) The source code directory includes a *Form1.resx* file, added by default to all new Windows Forms applications. But there is also a *Form1.ja.resx* file, the *Form1* resource file for the Japanese language. Visual Studio will compile this file into a language-specific resource when it builds the project. At that time, the code's *bin\Release* subdirectory will contain a further *ja* subdirectory with a file named *ForeignNames.resources.dll*. This is the satellite assembly that contains all of the Japanese language resources. If the application had included multiple forms, all of the Japanese resources for all forms would appear in that single DLL file.

Adding Resources outside Visual Studio

Visual Studio makes localization quite easy. But it's rare that the developer of a major application would also be fluent in multiple target languages. And you certainly don't want non-programmers gaining access to your forms and code in Visual Studio, where they can do who-knows-what to its logic.

To keep foreign-language eyes and fingers where they belong, Microsoft wrote the Windows Resource Localization Editor (*winres.exe*), and included it with Visual Studio. To start the program, use the Developer Command Prompt for VS2015 option from the Windows Start menu, and when the command window appears, type `winres`. (For non-developer systems that don't require the full Visual Studio experience, Microsoft offers "Targeting Packs" which install just the core .NET development tools, including *winres.exe*. See the MSDN web site for more information.)

When you are ready to have a translator convert a form to a specific language, you only need to provide them with access to *winres.exe*, and the form's *.resx* file (such as *Form1.resx*). The program simulates the display of the form as it appears in Visual Studio, and lets the translator modify any relevant form or control properties for a specific language. Figure 19-8 shows `ForeignNames`'s `Form1` in the Localization Editor.

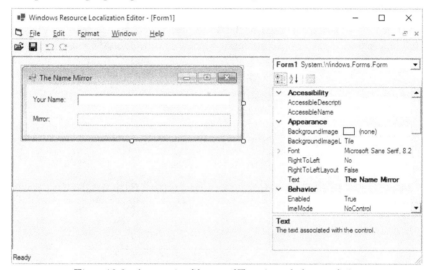

Figure 19-8. An amazing likeness of Form1, ready for translation

The program prompts for the target language or language-culture when you try to save changes. It outputs a language-specific *.resx* file (such as *Form1.ja.resx* for Japanese) that can be used in your application. Once you get the foreign resource files back from the translators, store them (the files, not the translators) in the project's source directory, and rebuild the project to generate the correct satellite assemblies.

Manually Compiling Resources

It's possible to generate the satellite assemblies manually from the source *.resx* files without rebuilding the entire project in Visual Studio. You will have to use the Developer Command Prompt (as mentioned above), and you will need access to the main assembly's EXE or DLL file. It's not for the faint of heart, and a single mistyped character could cost American taxpayers millions.

Figure 19-1 summarized the steps needed to move a *.resx* file into a satellite assembly. The "generate" and "compile" steps can be done using two command-line utilities: *resgen.exe* and *al.exe*. Doesn't that sound like great fun?

Resource File Generation

Once you have a *.resx* file available, either by creating it manually or by using the Windows Resource Localization Editor, you generate a *.resources* file using *resgen.exe*, the Resource Generator command-line utility. It accepts input and output filenames as its arguments.

```
resgen.exe Form1.ja.resx Form1.ja.resources
```

If you omit the output filename, *resgen* will simply replace the *.resx* extension with *.resources*.

If you have multiple foreign-language assemblies (for multiple forms, for instance), generate resource files for all of them. Then you will be ready to compile the satellite assembly.

Compiling Satellite Assemblies

.NET uses *al.exe*, the Assembly Linker program, to compile all of your .NET applications to their final assembly files. We'll use this same program to generate the satellite assemblies. Its command-line arguments were designed by a secret society, so getting them just right will take some work. Let's look at the command first, and then I'll explain it.

```
al.exe /target:lib
    /embed:Form1.ja.resources,ForeignNames.Form1.ja.resources
    /culture:ja /out:ForeignNames.resources.dll
    /template:bin\Release\ForeignNames.exe
```

You should enter these lines as one long line. I had to wrap them in the book because the publisher didn't want to do one of those fold-out pages that you see in some children's books. They didn't like my interactive pop-up Visual Studio environment idea, either, something about keeping the book at less than $100 per copy.

The options provided to *al.exe* work all of the magic.

`/target:lib`

> The `lib` part says, "Output a DLL-style file."

`/embed`

> This option indicates which source files you want to include in the output assembly. The first comma-delimited part indicates the source *filename*. The second part indicates the *name* by which this resource will be known in the application. The *name* must be in the format `basename.cultureName.resources`, where `basename` is the application name (for application-wide resources) or the class name (qualified with its namespace) for a specific class, such as `Form1`. Since my application and its default top-level namespace are both "ForeignNames," I've included that in the name component. You can add as many `/embed` options as you have resource files to include.

`/culture`

> Although you will eventually put the satellite assembly in a folder named for the target culture, Visual C# doesn't trust you. Instead, it wants a record of the culture embedded in the assembly itself. You do that through this command-line option.

`/out`

> This option specifies the output name of the satellite file. You really need to use the name *application.resources.dll* for the file, where *application* is the same as your application's name before the *.exe* part. If you don't do this, it won't work. Well, you could still get it to work by adjusting the application's *app.config* file, but that file is just plain scary, so you don't want to go there.

`/template`

> This is the option that says, "I'm making a satellite assembly, and the related primary assembly is *x*."

To use the satellite assembly, locate the directory that contains the main EXE assembly. Create a new subdirectory right there, giving it the name of the language or language-culture key used to create the assembly ("ja" in my case; "ja-JP" would have been an option if I created the assembly using "Japanese (Japan)"). Then put the new satellite assembly in that subdirectory.

Other Localization Features

Localization is more than just words on a screen. There are also issues of how you display times, dates, and monetary values to the user. The good news is that these features will work automatically if you *globalize* your program properly. Just as each .NET program maintains a user interface culture (which we played with in the sample program previously), it also has a general culture used for string manipulation of times, dates, financial values, and other similar culture-dependent things.

If you use core methods such as *DateTime.Parse* to extract date values, instead of scanning through a user-entered date string by hand, you get culture-specific date processing for free. Also for output, if you use the predefined formats for the type-specific *ToString* methods (and other similar string output methods), you get correct culture-specific formatting for no additional effort on your part. Let's try a quick sample that displays money using the local currency.

I'm creating a new Windows Forms application. I'll add the following code to *Main* startup routine.

```
if (MessageBox.Show("Switch from English to Japanese?",
        "Foreign Names", MessageBoxButtons.YesNo,
        MessageBoxIcon.Question) == DialogResult.Yes)
    System.Threading.Thread.CurrentThread.CurrentCulture =
        new System.Globalization.CultureInfo("ja-JP");
```

This code block is almost identical to the one we used in the previous sample, but I'm setting the *CurrentCulture* property instead of the *CurrentUICulture* property (the *UI* part is missing). This changes the string-manipulation culture instead of the user interface culture.

Now I'll add the following code to *Form1*'s class.

```
private void Form1_Load(object sender, EventArgs e)
{
    MessageBox.Show(500.ToString("C"));
}
```

Figure 19-9 shows the results of this code when run in both English and Japanese modes.

Figure 19-9. Spending money in two places at once

The Framework Class Library (FCL) includes even more culture management features in the *System.Globalization* namespace. The classes in this namespace let you manually adjust the output of culture-sensitive strings to meet your needs. Most of them are pretty esoteric and are intended for specific culture groups, so I won't be discussing them here.

Summary

It's a small world, after all. And the culture-specific features in .NET have helped to make it that way, at least for your software. I'm still amazed that I'm able to use Japanese on my English version of Microsoft Windows. And now it's not just Windows or Microsoft Office that can automatically shift with the current culture. Politicians can do it, too. Oops, I mean that your own applications can do it, too. By taking advantage of culture-specific resources and the automatic and manual formatting features included with .NET, you'll soon be selling your snazzy business application in six of the seven continents.

Project

I know you're expecting me to localize all of the forms in the Library Project into Greek, and it is a tempting idea. But in the interest of brevity (and my sanity), I'll leave that as an exercise for the reader. (Muffled laughter.)

What we will do in this chapter's project code is to enable the remaining patron-specific tracking and management features. Those features include the processing of fines for naughty patrons who don't return their library books on time. We'll use the generic currency formatting features discussed in this chapter to make the application as globally accessible as possible.

Project Access

Load the "Chapter 19 (Before) Code" project, either through the New Project templates or by accessing the project directly from the installation directory. To see the code in its final form, load "Chapter 19 (After) Code" instead.

Tracking Patron Payments

Let's create a class that exposes the important features of each set of payments applied to a specific checked-in item. Of course, they'll all be stored in the Library database. But keeping a summary of payments temporarily cached in memory simplifies some processing.

Add a new class item to the Library Project, giving it the name *PaymentItem.cs*. Define it using the following code.

Insert Snippet

Insert Chapter 19, Snippet Item 1.

```
public class PaymentItem
{
    // ----- Used to track and print payment tickets.
    public string ItemTitle;
    public long PatronCopyID;
    public decimal FeesPaid;
    public decimal BalanceDue;
}
```

Don't forgot to insert the *public* keyword just before the *class* keyword. Visual Studio doesn't insert it by default.

Each instance of this class identifies the collected fines and payments for a specific library item (*ItemTitle*) and for the patron who turned in the item late (*PatronCopyID*).

Calculating Patron Fines

We also need to know the total fines owed by a patron for all items, even when we're not showing the details. Add the *CalculatePatronFines* function to the *General.cs* module.

> **Insert Snippet**
>
> Insert Chapter 19, Snippet Item 2.

```
public static decimal CalculatePatronFines(long patronID)
{
    // ----- Given a patron ID, calculate the fines due.
    string sqlText;
    DataCommand sqlRun;

    // ----- Retrieve the fine records for the patron.
    sqlText = "SELECT SUM(Fine - Paid) FROM PatronCopy " +
        "WHERE Patron = @RecordID";
    sqlRun = new DataCommand(sqlText);
    sqlRun.AddLong("RecordID", patronID);
    try
    {
        return DBGetDecimal(ExecuteSQLReturn(sqlRun));
    }
    catch (Exception ex)
    {
        GeneralError("CalculatePatronFines", ex);
        return 0M;
    }
}
```

It's pretty basic code, actually, since the database does all of the work of adding up the values. I checked the database documentation and confirmed that *Fine* and *Paid* are required fields, and will never be *NULL*. This keeps the SQL code terse.

Patron Record Access

Before reviewing a patron's record, the user must identify the patron. This is done through a Patron Record Access form, sort of a login form for patrons. Each patron is assigned a password, which must be supplied before the patron can access his or her record. Administrators can access a patron's record without providing the password.

I've already added the *PatronAccess.cs* form to your project; it appears in Figure 19-10.

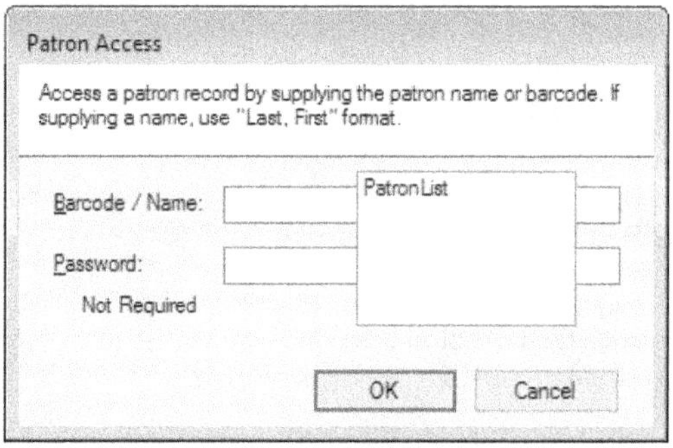

Figure 19-10. The Patron Access form

This form's code is a lot like that found in *ChangeUser.cs*, a form that provides administrative access to the program, and that we added back in Chapter 11. The Patron Access form behaves a little differently for administrators and regular patrons.

- Regular patrons must either provide their barcode, or supply their name (full last name, optional wildcards on the first name) *and* their password. If they use a partial name instead of a barcode, and a search of that name results in multiple matches, they will have to provide a more correct entry for their name. (If two patrons have the same name, they will have to depend on barcodes; but this program is for a *small* library, so name conflicts should be rare.)
- Administrators enter the patron's name or barcode, but no password is needed. If there are multiple name matches, the form presents all matching names in a list, and the administrator can select the correct entry from the list. This gives an administrator full access to all patron records. It's obviously important for an administrator to log out when finished using a workstation that is available to patrons.

The `PatronAccess` form's `SelectPatron` method provides the interface to the form for both administrators and ordinary patrons. The function returns the ID of the selected patron, or `-1` if the user didn't successfully access a patron record.

Patron Password Modification

Although administrators can change the password of each patron through the *Patron.cs* form, we don't want to give ordinary patrons access to that form and all of its raw, unadulterated power. But we still want the patrons to be able to change their own passwords, because it's the nice and secure thing to do. I've added the *PatronPassword.cs* form to your project to fulfill this purpose (see Figure 19-11).

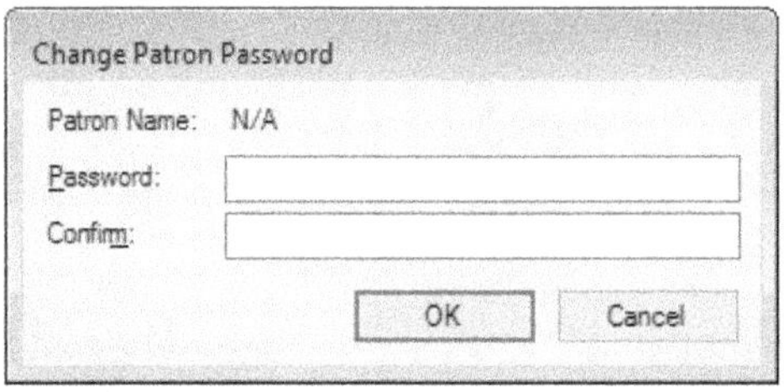

Figure 19-11. The Patron Password form

The form is basically a dramatically reduced subset of the full *Patron.cs* form. Since it needs to deal with only active patrons, it doesn't have a lot of the *Patron.cs* code that differentiates between new and existing patron records. The focus of the Patron Password form is the update statement that sets the patron's password, in the `SaveFormData` method.

```
sqlText = "UPDATE Patron SET [Password] = @NewPassword " +
    "WHERE ID = @RecordID";
sqlRun = new DataCommand(sqlText);
sqlRun.AddText("NewPassword", EncryptPassword(
    "patron", RecordPassword.Text.Trim()));
sqlRun.AddLong("RecordID", ActiveID);
try
{
    ExecuteSQL(sqlRun);
}
catch (Exception ex)
{
    GeneralError("PatronPassword.SaveFormData", ex);
```

```
        return false;
    }
    finally
    {
        this.Cursor = Cursors.Default;
    }
```

The word *Password* is a reserved keyword in SQL Server, so we need to "escape" it with square brackets when referring to the field in SQL statements.

Collecting Patron Payments

In a perfect world, patrons would never let their books and other library items reach the overdue state. Of course, in a perfect world, libraries would let you keep books you like indefinitely. And give me a break with those incessant overdue notices. What's up with that?

But for those small libraries that insist on charging fines for overdue items, the Library Project includes features for assigning and tracking fines. In a later chapter, we'll add the code that automatically calculates the fines for overdue items. Right now, we'll implement the form that lets you document patron payments and other financial adjustments to items in the patron's record.

I've added the `PatronPayment` form to the collection of project files, but it's not yet integrated into the project. Select the *PatronPayment.cs* file in the Solution Explorer, and then change its Build Action property (in the Properties panel) from None to Compile. Then do the same for its subordinate *PatronPayment.Designer.cs* file. Figure 19-12 shows the controls on this form.

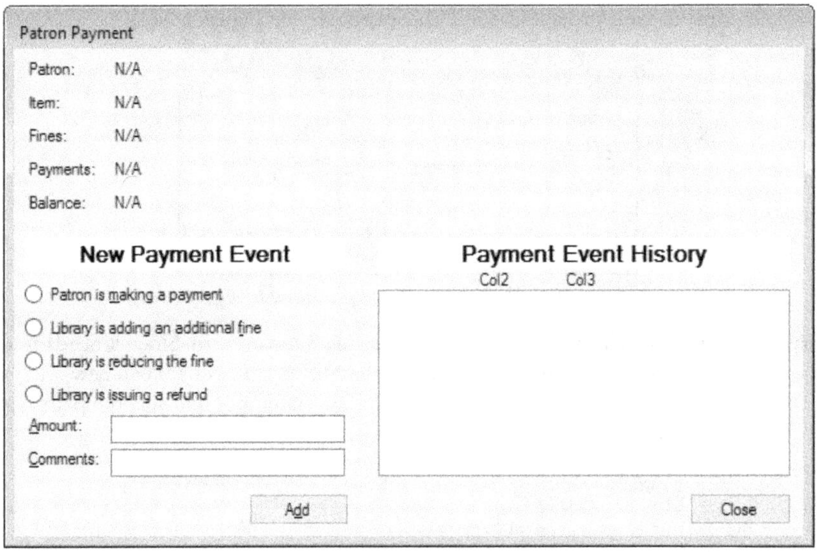

Figure 19-12. The Patron Payment form

Fines that are automatically added to an overdue item appear in the `PatronCopy.Fine` database field. Although that value is displayed on the Patron Payment form, it's not the primary focus of that form. Instead, the form exists to allow a librarian to enter charges and payments for a previously checked-out item, storing these updates in the `PatronPayment` database table. This table tracks four types of financial events for each item checked out by a patron.

- Additional fines imposed by a librarian or administrator. For example, a librarian may add the value of an item as a fine if it turns out that the patron has lost the item. Additional fine entries use the letter *F* in the `PatronPayment.EntryType` database field.
- Payments made by the patron for an overdue item. *P* is the entry type.
- A dismissal of some or all of the pending fines for an overdue item, indicated by a *D* entry type.
- If the entry type is *R*, the record indicates a refund paid to the patron by the library.

Each `PatronPayment` table record includes a transaction date, the amount of the transaction, optional comments, and the identity of the administrative user recording the entry. To make the code a little clearer, the letter codes in the database table are converted into enumeration values from the `EventEntryType` enumeration.

```
private enum EventEntryType: int
{
    NotDefined,
    PatronPayment,
    FineAdded,
    FineDismissal,
    RefundToPatron,
    OverdueFines
}
```

The `OverdueFines` entry allows the `PatronCopy.Fines` value to be part of the displayed financial history on the form.

The librarian uses the fields in the New Payment Event section of the `PatronPayment` form to add charge and payment records. All previously added records appear in the `EventHistory` list, in the Payment Event History section of the form.

The calling form (added later in this chapter) needs to pass in the `PatronCopy.ID` value to identify the proper record. But the plan is to have payments added on this form flow back to the parent form. The two forms will share a set of `PaymentItem` objects using the class we added a few sections earlier in this chapter. We'll store it in a class-level field as a generic set.

```
private List<PaymentItem> PaymentsOnly;
```

The entry point into the form will be a public method named `ManagePayments`. Add that code now to the `PatronPayment` class.

Insert Snippet
Insert Chapter 19, Snippet Item 3.

```
public void ManagePayments(
    long patronCopyID, List<PaymentItem> sessionPayments)
{
    // ----- Manage the payments for an item.
    ActivePatronCopyID = patronCopyID;
    PaymentsOnly = sessionPayments;
    this.ShowDialog();
}
```

This method records the patron-copy ID number and the collection of payments for that checked-out item. Processing then moves on to the form's *Load* event handler. It's in this routine that we will add our localized financial management code. In the `PatronPayment_Load` routine, scan down about one-third of the way through the method to the code that loads in the summary details from the database. Look for this line.

```
RecordItem.Text = DBGetText(oneRow["Title"]);
```

Just after that line, add the statements that will globally format currency values for the Fines, Payments, and Balance summary labels that appear near the top of the form.

Insert Snippet

Insert Chapter 19, Snippet Item 4.

```
originalFine = DBGetDecimal(oneRow["Fine"]);
RecordFine.Text = originalFine.ToString("C");
RecordPayments.Text =
   DBGetDecimal(oneRow["Paid"]).ToString("C");
balanceDue = originalFine - DBGetDecimal(oneRow["Paid"]);
RecordBalance.Text = balanceDue.ToString("C");
```

The rest of the *Load* event handler's code retrieves existing records from the *PatronPayment* table, plus the original overdue fine, if any, from the *PatronCopy.Fine* database field.

Later, when the user clicks the Add button to add a new financial event to the patron-and-item-copy entry, the *SaveEventData* routine—equivalent to the *SaveFormData* method in most of the other forms we've developed so far—saves the updated information in the database. This routine needs to save the new charge or payment in the *PatronPayment* table, plus update the charge and payment summary in the *PatronCopy* record. Add the code that writes out these records, just after the calculations for the *fineAmount* and *paidAmount* variables in the *SaveEventData* method.

Insert Snippet

Insert Chapter 19, Snippet Item 5.

```
// ----- Add the entry to the database.
try
{
   transInfo = TransactionBegin();

   sqlText = "INSERT INTO PatronPayment (PatronCopy, " +
      "EntryDate, EntryType, Amount, Comment, UserID) " +
      "OUTPUT INSERTED.ID VALUES (@NewCopy, GETDATE(), " +
      "@NewType, @NewAmount, @NewComment, @NewUser)";
   sqlRun = new DataCommand(sqlText);
   sqlRun.AddLong("NewCopy", ActivePatronCopyID);
   sqlRun.AddText("NewType", entryCode);
   sqlRun.AddDecimal("NewAmount", enteredAmount);
   sqlRun.AddText("NewComment", RecordComment.Text.Trim());
   sqlRun.AddLong("NewUser", LoggedInUserID);
   newID = DBGetLong(ExecuteSQLReturn(sqlRun, transInfo));

   sqlText = "UPDATE PatronCopy SET Fine = @NewFine, " +
      "Paid = @NewPaid WHERE ID = @RecordID";
   sqlRun = new DataCommand(sqlText);
   sqlRun.AddDecimal("NewFine", fineAmount);
   sqlRun.AddDecimal("NewPaid", paidAmount);
   sqlRun.AddLong("RecordID", ActivePatronCopyID);
   ExecuteSQL(sqlRun, transInfo);

   TransactionCommit(transInfo);
}
```

```
catch (Exception ex)
{
    if (transInfo != null)
        TransactionRollback(transInfo);
    this.Cursor = Cursors.Default;
    GeneralError("PatronPayment.SaveEventData", ex);
    return false;
}
```

I've wrapped up both database statements in a transaction to help ensure the integrity of the data. Once the database is up-to-date, it's time to update the screen. The on-screen list of charges and payments needs this new record. That list uses the local *EventHistoryItem* class, a variation of the application-wide *ListItemData* class that we usually use in *ListBox* controls. *EventHistoryItem* has fields that are specific to displaying financial information in the *EventHistory* list box. Craft the code that builds an *EventHistoryItem* record and adds it to the *EventHistory* list, immediately after the database update code we just added.

Insert Snippet
Insert Chapter 19, Snippet Item 6.

```
// ----- Add an item to the entry list.
historyItem = new EventHistoryItem();
historyItem.PaymentID = newID;
historyItem.EntryDate = DateTime.Today;
historyItem.PaymentAmount =
    Convert.ToDecimal(RecordAmount.Text);
historyItem.Comments = RecordComment.Text.Trim();
historyItem.EntryType = entryType;
EventHistory.Items.Add(historyItem);
```

This code block is followed by similar code that updates the *PaymentsOnly* list, the *List<PaymentItem>* instance that was passed in from the calling form. The code either updates the existing payment summary record, or adds a new record to the generic list.

```
// ----- Add a new payment.
onePayment = new PaymentItem();
onePayment.PatronCopyID = ActivePatronCopyID;
onePayment.ItemTitle = RecordItem.Text;
onePayment.FeesPaid = paidAmount;
onePayment.BalanceDue = fineAmount - paidAmount;
PaymentsOnly.Add(onePayment);
```

Before leaving this function, we need to refresh the three financial summary values near the top of the form, the ones we set when the form first loaded. Add this code just after the update to the *PaymentOnly* list.

Insert Snippet
Insert Chapter 19, Snippet Item 7.

```
// ----- Update the on-screen values.
RecordFine.Text = fineAmount.ToString("C");
RecordPayments.Text = paidAmount.ToString("C");
RecordBalance.Text = (fineAmount - paidAmount).ToString("C");
```

The *EventHistory* list is a variable-line-height owner draw control, similar to one we designed in Chapter 18. Its *MeasureItem* event handler sets the height of each list item (comments appear on a second line when available), and its `DrawItem` event handler does the actual drawing of each data column and the comments.

Managing All Fines and Payments

The Patron Payment form lets a librarian enter individual fines and payments, but the program still needs a form to manage all fines and payments for a single patron, a form that calls up the Patron Payment form when needed. The new *PatronRecord.cs* form fulfills this need. I've added this form to your project, although you need to enable it. Select it in the Solution Explorer, and change its Build Action property (in the Properties panel) from None to Compile. Then repeat this process for its *PatronRecord.Designer.cs* support file. Figure 19-13 shows the controls on this form.

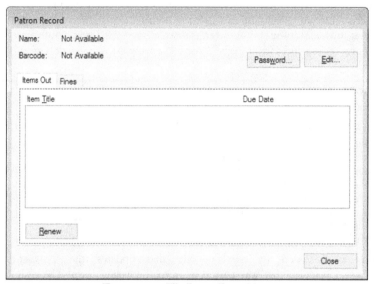

Figure 19-13. The Patron Record form

This form is available to both administrators and patrons, although some of the fields are hidden from patron view.

The Password button leads to the Change Patron Password form we added earlier in this chapter. The Edit button, available only to administrators, provides access to the full *Patron.cs* form. The main section of the Patron Record form displays a list of all items the patron currently has checked out. It includes a Renew button that lets a patron extend the due date for a checked-out item. We'll add the code for that feature in a later chapter.

The form also displays a summary of all pending fines and payments. Figure 19-14 shows the Fines tab and its fields.

The Print Balance Ticket button generates a printed receipt of all fines and payments for the patron. We'll add its code in a later chapter.

Most of the code in this form exists to manage fines and payments. To add a charge or payment, the librarian selects an item from the Fines list, and then clicks the Fines and Payments button. This brings up the just-added Patron Payment form.

Figure 19-14. The Fines panel on the Patron Record form

The two main lists on the Patron Record form will each forgo the standard *ListItemData* class, and instead will use a more property-rich class to support the display needs of each list. We'll add this *PatronDetailItem* as a separate public class since (as we'll see in a later chapter) it will be used elsewhere in the Library Project. Create a new class file named *PatronDetailItem.cs*, and use the following code for its content.

Insert Snippet
Insert Chapter 19, Snippet Item 8.

```
public class PatronDetailItem
{
    public long DetailID;
    public string TitleText;
    public DateTime DueDate;
    public decimal FineAmount;
    public decimal PaidAmount;
    public decimal BalanceDue;
}
```

As with the *PaymentItem* class earlier, don't forgot to insert the *public* keyword just before the *class* keyword.

Now back to the *PatronRecord* form. As you can tell from looking at the form, the Fines list displays several columns of currency values. Let's add the code that correctly formats the currency according to the regional monetary settings. First, locate the *RefreshPatronFines* method. This routine adds up all fines and payments, and displays the result through the *BalanceDue Label* control.

Near the top of this routine is a comment that states, "Clear the current list." Add the following code just after this comment.

Insert Snippet
Insert Chapter 19, Snippet Item 9.

```
Fines.Items.Clear();
totalBalance = 0M;
BalanceDue.Text = (0M).ToString("C");
this.Cursor = Cursors.WaitCursor;
```

We could have just set the *BalanceDue* field to "$0.00," but this would not be properly globalized. Using the *ToString* method with "C" as the formatting rule still results in "$0.00" when used in America, but properly adjusts for other cultures as well.

The *RefreshPatronFines* method does a whole bunch of calculations, and ends up with the remaining patron balance in the *totalBalance* local variable. Locate the comment that reads, "Show the total balance," and add the following code just after it.

Insert Snippet
Insert Chapter 19, Snippet Item 10.

```
BalanceDue.Text = totalBalance.ToString("C");
```

The Fines list, an owner draw *ListBox* implementation, also displays currency values. This is another list that forgoes the standard *ListItemData* class, using the *PatronDetailItem* class instead for its item management. Locate the *Fines_DrawItem* event handler, and the "Extract the details from the list item" comment within that handler. Add the following code just after the comment.

Insert Snippet
Insert Chapter 19, Snippet Item 11.

```
itemDetail = (PatronDetailItem)(Fines.Items[e.Index]);
titleText = itemDetail.TitleText;
fineText = itemDetail.FineAmount.ToString("C");
paidText = itemDetail.PaidAmount.ToString("C");
balanceText = itemDetail.BalanceDue.ToString("C");
if (itemDetail.BalanceDue == 0M)
    useNotice = useBrush;
```

This block properly formats each currency value. By default, all due amounts appear in red in the list. The last line in this code block resets the color to the neutral list item color if no balance is due.

Connecting Patron Features to the Main Form

That does it for the new patron-specific forms. Let's enable access to them through the main Library form. Wow! It's been awhile since I really looked at this form. I've forgotten what it looks like. Ah, yes. One of the main icons provides access to a patron's record (see Figure 19-15).

Figure 19-15. Accessing patron records from the main form

All we need to do is add an event handler for the Patron button. Locate the *ActAccessPatron_Click* event handler in the form's source code. Then add the following code to that handler.

Insert Snippet
Insert Chapter 19, Snippet Item 12.

```
// ----- Look up the record of an active patron.
long patronID;
```

```
// ----- Get the ID of the patron.
patronID = (new PatronAccess()).SelectPatron();
if (patronID == -1L)
    return;

// ----- Show the patron record.
(new PatronRecord()).ViewPatronRecord(patronID, true);
```

This code makes direct calls to two of the forms we added in this chapter: *PatronAccess* and *PatronRecord*. It first prompts the user to select a patron record, and then displays its details through the Patron Record form.

Dueling Patron Management Forms

Let's make one more change regarding patron records. Way back in an earlier chapter, we included a Manage Patron Items button on the *Patron.cs* form. This button existed to provide access to the future *PatronRecord.cs* form, but it's pretty much been dead weight until now. But with the *PatronRecord.cs* form in place, we're ready to make patron management history.

Open the source code for the *Patron.cs* form, and locate the *ActItems_Click* event handler. Then add the following code to it.

Insert Snippet
Insert Chapter 19, Snippet Item 13.

```
(new PatronRecord()).ViewPatronRecord(ActiveID, false);
```

This is all well and good, but you are probably thinking to yourself, "The Patron form now lets you open the Patron Record form. And that form has an Edit button that lets you once again open the Patron form. If you get a rogue librarian, there may be millions of patron management forms on the screen at once." And that's all true. So, we had to add some code to prevent that from happening. The second *false* argument to *PatronRecord.ViewPatronRecord* is a flag that says, "Don't show the Edit button on the Patron Record form." Similar code exists in the Patron Record form that stops the recursion.

```
private void ActEditPatron_Click...
{
    if ((new Patron()).EditRecordLimited(
        ActivePatronID) != -1L)...
```

The *EditRecordLimited* method hides the Manage Patron Items button on the *Patron.cs* form. Whichever form you start with, you can access the other form, but you won't be able to generate a new copy of the initial form.

There was a lot of new code in this chapter, but it was all very pedestrian. We could have made even more culturally sensitive changes. For example, the Due Date column in the list of checked-out items on the *PatronRecord.cs* form uses a hardcoded date format for its display.

```
dueDate = itemDetail.DueDate.ToString("MMM d, yyyy");
```

You could change the formatting code to "d" (the "short date" pattern) or another culture-neutral setting. Whichever method you choose really depends on your target audience. And if that target audience likes to see things spelled out on paper, the next chapter on printing is just for you.

Chapter 20

Printing

When Microsoft released its original version of MS-DOS, it included printing features that supported the most popular devices of that era: chisel and stone. Fortunately, printing has come a long way since then. These days, advanced color laser printers and even paperless printing systems (such as Adobe Acrobat) provide printer support that rivals that of professional four-color offset printing facilities.

Although the .NET Framework does not replace the print spooler system built into each copy of Windows, it makes it greatly accessible. As you'll read in this chapter, a printer is now treated like any other .NET drawing surface. The statements you use to draw on a form or control can be copied and pasted directly into your printing code.

This chapter provides a general discussion of .NET printing support. A discussion of report printing appears in the next chapter. If you are reading this chapter in a digital format, you can still rush right out and plunk down the funds for a hardcopy version of this book. Having that tactile response from the surface of the page should get you in the mood for this chapter's discussion of ink and paper.

Printing in Windows

Printers are a lot like people. Oh, I don't mean that they are cantankerous, or that they quickly run out of ink. Like the people of the world, printers speak many different languages. At the basic end of the language scale, some printers simply output the characters they receive. Others add *escape sequences*, special combinations of characters that enable enhanced features such as font selection and double-wide text. At the complex end of the scale are full object-oriented page description languages, such as PostScript, with commands that are somewhat similar to those in GDI+.

It would be every programmer's worst nightmare to adjust application code so that it targets all likely printers that a user may have. Each new printer language would mean another bout of development and testing. And printer makers are just giddy enough to come up with new language variations on a monthly basis.

Fortunately, Windows implements a system of printer-specific drivers that shield the developer from most printer variations. These drivers all speak a common language—let's call it "Printish"—which the driver translates into the printer's native tongue. As developers, we need only design software that speaks Printish.

The .NET Framework's printing system adds yet another level of language translation. .NET programs do not directly communicate with the printer drivers. Instead, they use GDI+ commands—the same commands used for screen updates—to output content to an in-memory printer canvas. The framework then converts these commands to Printish and sends the output on to the appropriate printer driver, and finally to the printer. Figure 20-1 shows a summary of the steps involved in .NET printing.

Application   .NET/GDI+   Printish   Driver   Printer

Figure 20-1. From programmer to canvas: printing with .NET

Printing in .NET

Having both screen and printer output generated through identical GDI+ commands means that I can make this a really short chapter, referring you back to Chapter 18 for details. But it also means that there needs to be a canvas—a *System.Drawing.Graphics* object—where the printer-specific GDI+ commands target their output. The *System.Drawing.Printing.PrintDocument* class provides you with the output canvas you need for both ordinary printing and print-preview output. There are two ways to use the *PrintDocument* class.

- Add a *PrintDocument* control to a form from the Windows Forms toolbox. This control appears by default in the toolbox's Printing section. Assign its properties and respond to its events as with any other control.
- Create a variable-housed instance of the *PrintDocument* class, and manually attach custom event handlers to its exposed events.

These are standard methods in .NET, but having a control variation makes the class that much more convenient. We'll get into the actual printing code a little later.

Four other printer-specific controls are available for Windows Forms projects.

PageSetupDialog

This control presents a standard Windows printer settings dialog that lets the user configure a specific print job, or all print jobs for the application. The control's *ShowDialog* method displays the form shown in Figure 20-2. The control also exposes properties related to the user's selection. Its *PageSettings* member exposes specific user preferences as defined on the form, and the *PrinterSettings* member identifies the selected printer and its properties. You can retain these members and later assign them to other printer-specific classes that include similar members.

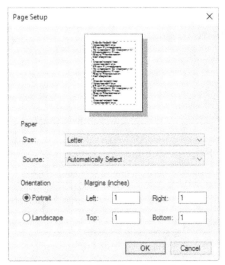

Figure 20-2. The Page Setup dialog

PrintDialog

Figure 20-3 shows this control's dialog, the standard dialog that appears in most programs when the user selects the File→Print menu command. This control also exposes a *PrinterSettings* member used to assign or retrieve the selected printer and related options.

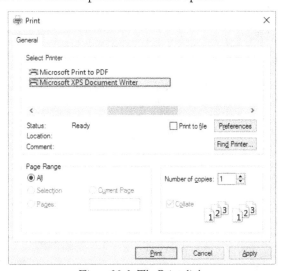

Figure 20-3. The Print dialog

PrintPreviewDialog

This control's dialog displays a preview of your printed document to the user. It includes standard preview presentation features, including zoom level and a pages-to-see-at-once control. The included Print button sends the preview content to the default printer (without prompting for printer selection). This control directly interacts with your *PrintDocument* instance, which drives the actual display content. Figure 20-4 shows the Print Preview dialog, although with no page-specific content.

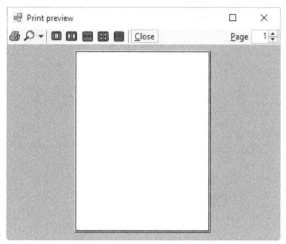

Figure 20-4. The Print Preview dialog

PrintPreviewControl

The *PrintPreviewDialog* control includes basic preview management features (such as the zoom feature) that meet the needs of most applications. Unfortunately, that control is a sealed black box, and you cannot easily add your own custom features to it, or remove features that you don't want. The *PrintPreviewControl* control provides an alternative interface that lets you fully customize the print preview experience. Instead of a full dialog, it implements just the page-display portion of the form. You must implement all toolbars and other features, and link their functionality with the preview control. I won't be discussing this control in this chapter. If you're interested in using this advanced control, you can find out more in an article I wrote about print preview more than a decade ago.[7] It's dated, but oh-so relevant.

Before you print, you need to know which printer your user wants to target for the output. You may also need to know about available features of the printer, such as whether it supports color. The *System.Drawing.Printing.PrinterSettings* class includes a shared *InstalledPrinters* string collection that lists the path to each configured printer. You can assign any of these strings to the *PrinterSettings.PrinterName* member, making the specific printer available within the application. The following code chunk lets the user select from the list of printers, and displays some basic information about the selected printer.

```
private void Form1_Load(object sender, EventArgs e)
{
   // ----- Display the list of printers.
   foreach (string scanPrinter in Drawing.Printing.
      PrinterSettings.InstalledPrinters)
      listBox1.Items.Add(scanPrinter);
}

private void button1_Click(object sender, EventArgs e)
{
```

---

[7] Find the article on *Visual Studio Magazine*'s web site, http://www.visualstudiomagazine.com. The title is "Take Control of Print Preview," published on July 1, 2004. The article includes Visual Basic sample code, but the core .NET concepts are identical in C#.

```
// ----- Display information about the selected printer.
Drawing.Printing.PrinterSettings selectedPrinter;

if (ListBox1.SelectedIndex == -1)
    return;
selectedPrinter = new Drawing.Printing.PrinterSettings();
selectedPrinter.PrinterName = listBox1.Text;
MessageBox.Show(selectedPrinter.ToString());
}
```

Printing a Document

Earlier we saw that many Windows components work together to generate your printed output. Within your .NET code, you will also use many components (classes) to drive the printing process. Four main steps are involved (at least directly) in printing a document from your code.

1. Create an instance of a *PrintDocument* class (or add it as a control to your form).

2. Set the *PrintDocument*'s various printer settings, either by using a *PrintDialog* (or related) class/control, or by using the default or manual settings.

3. Add an event handler for the *PrintDocument*'s *PrintPage* event. This event is called once for each page, and receives a *System.Drawing.Graphics* object for the printer canvas. Your event handler code prints a single page, and updates a flag telling the document whether there are more pages to come.

4. Call the *PrintDocument*'s *Print* method to start the ball rolling.

Let's try a little code to see how this printing beast eats. Or prints. Or whatever it does. How about a simple program that prints a five-page document on the user's selected printer? The output will be a large single-digit page number, perfect for the Sesame Street set. First, let's create a new Windows Forms application, and add a single button to *Form1* named *ActPrint*. We'll also add a *PrintDocument* control (named *CountingDoc*), and a *PrintDialog* control (named *UserPrinter*). Figure 20-5 shows the form and its supporting controls.

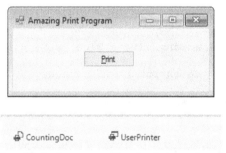

Figure 20-5. A program with only printing on its mind

These controls implement the first two steps of our four-step printing process. Next, we'll add the source code.

```
public partial class Form1 : Form
{
    private int WhichPage;
```

```
private void ActPrint_Click(object sender, EventArgs e)
{
   // ----- Prompt the user for printer settings,
   //       and start printing.
   UserPrinter.Document = CountingDoc;
   if (UserPrinter.ShowDialog() == DialogResult.OK)
      CountingDoc.Print();
}

private void CountingDoc_BeginPrint(object sender,
   Printing.PrintEventArgs e)
{
   // ----- Start the counting over.
   WhichPage = 1;
}

private void CountingDoc_PrintPage(object sender,
   Printing.PrintPageEventArgs e)
{
   // ----- Print a single page.
   Font hugeFont;
   StringFormat centeredText;

   // ----- Let's go overboard on the font: 256 points!
   hugeFont = new Font("Arial", 256);

   // ----- Center the text on the page.
   centeredText = new StringFormat();
   centeredText.Alignment = StringAlignment.Center;
   centeredText.LineAlignment = StringAlignment.Center;

   // ----- Print the number.
   e.Graphics.DrawString(WhichPage.ToString(), hugeFont,
      Brushes.Black, e.MarginBounds, centeredText);

   // ----- Draw the page margins to make it clear where
   //       they are.
   e.Graphics.DrawRectangle(Pens.Blue, e.MarginBounds);

   // ----- Limit the output to five pages.
   WhichPage += 1;
   e.HasMorePages = (WhichPage <= 5);
}
}
```

This code implements steps 3 (*ActPrint_Click*) and 4 (*CountingDoc_PrintPage*). The *ActPrint* button's *Click* event handler links the document and the Print dialog so that they both refer to the same settings. It then prompts the user to select a printer and various options through the *ShowDialog* call. If the user clicks the OK button on that dialog, it triggers a call to the document's *Print* method.

The action then moves to the events of the *PrintDocument* instance. I've implemented two of the events: a *BeginPrint* event handler that performs some initialization, and a *PrintPage* event handler that does the complex printing stuff. (Other events include *EndPrint*, used to clean up when printing is complete, and *QueryPageSettings*, where you can change the orientation and settings of each page of the document.) Actually, it's not all that complex, especially since we saw similar code in Chapter 18. The biggest difference is the amount of space available on a printed page, allowing us to play with fonts in the hundreds of point sizes.

Figure 20-6 shows page 2 of the output from this program. I printed to an Adobe PDF pseudo-printer and displayed the results in the Microsoft Edge browser. You can see in the upper-left corner that it did properly record five output pages.

Figure 20-6. This page is brought to you by the number 2

Print Preview

Adding a print preview interface is so easy, you should probably ask your boss for a really hard project to do first, and then come back when you're worn out. Let's build on our simple number-printing application, adding a new *Button* control named *ActPreview*. We will also add a *PrintPreviewDialog* control named *UserPreview*. Once these are in place, add the following preview button *Click* event handler.

```
private void ActPreview_Click(object sender, EventArgs e)
{
    // ----- Display a preview of the document.
    UserPreview.Document = CountingDoc;
    UserPreview.ShowDialog();
}
```

Hey, that's even simpler than the code that initiates printing to a real printer, even though print preview technology seems to be more complex than plain printing. There almost ought to be a law against code that simple. Fortunately, there's not. Figure 20-7 shows the preview window, after using the two-pages-at-once toolbar button.

Let's dwell just a little longer on how simple that code was. I can accept that the *PrintPreviewDialog* class includes a lot of amazing code for previewing printed output. But the remarkable part of the code is that we didn't have to rewrite the custom GDI+ drawing logic. The same set of GDI+ statements now drives the preview display and the actual output. All we had to do was assign the *PrintDocument* object to the correct dialog control.

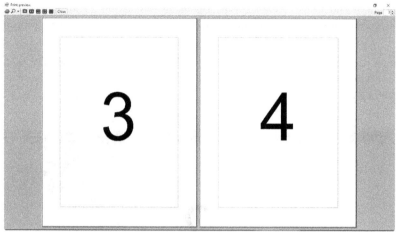

Figure 20-7. The preview displays multiple pages at once with no extra effort on our part

Counting and Numbering Pages

During the printing (or preview) process, the *PrintDocument*'s *PrintPage* event handler gets called once for each output page. But here's the tricky thing: when the *PrintPage* handler was called the first time, it was not to print "page 1" of the document, but instead to print "the first page in need of printing," whatever its page number. Search all you want through the members of the *PrintDocument* class, but you will never find a *PageNumber* property. The *PrintDocument* class does not know about the page numbers in your document, and—despite all of the nice things it does for you—it does not care. All it knows is that you have a bunch of pages to print, and it will call your *PrintPage* event handler until you say "enough!"

If you turn back to Figure 20-3, you'll see that the Print dialog includes a Page Range section, although most of its controls are disabled by default. The *PrintDialog* control includes three Boolean properties that let you enable specific controls in that section: *AllowCurrentPage*, *AllowSomePages*, and *AllowSelection*. Setting any of these properties to *True* enables the matching option control. Later, after the user has made a choice, you can query the *PrintDocument* object's *PrinterSettings.PrintRange* property to determine which choice it is.

Let's add code that enables page range selection. We'll still limit the allowed pages to just those numbered one to five, but the user will be able to choose a subrange within that set. Return to the *Click* event handler for the *ActPrint* button, and insert a few new lines of code (the ones in bold).

```
private void ActPrint_Click(object sender, EventArgs e)
{
    // ----- Prompt the user for printer settings,
    //       and start printing.
    UserPrinter.Document = CountingDoc;
    UserPrinter.AllowSomePages = true;
    CountingDoc.PrinterSettings.MinimumPage = 1;
    CountingDoc.PrinterSettings.MaximumPage = 5;
    CountingDoc.PrinterSettings.FromPage = 1;
    CountingDoc.PrinterSettings.ToPage = 5;
```

```
        if (UserPrinter.ShowDialog() == DialogResult.OK)
            CountingDoc.Print();
}
```

When the user clicks on the Print button this time, the Print Range section of the dialog has enabled the Pages field, and it's already filled in with the minimum and maximum pages in the range "1–5" (see Figure 20-8).

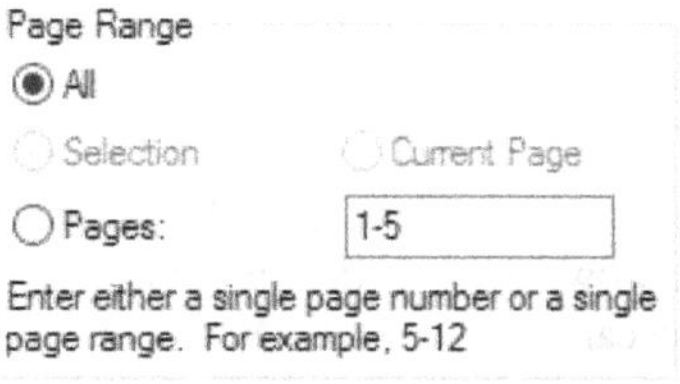

Page Range

◉ All

○ Selection   ○ Current Page

○ Pages: 1-5

Enter either a single page number or a single page range. For example, 5-12

Figure 20-1. Support for page ranges

If the user adjusts this field to "1–6," an error occurs stating that the valid range is somewhere within "1–5" only. But whether the user selects All Pages or 1–5 or 1–4 or 2–3 or Current Page or Selection, the *PrintPage* event handler will be called in exactly the same manner. In fact, the handler will be called dozens, even hundreds, of times until you tell it to stop. The user's selection impacts the *PrinterSettings.PrintRange* property and some other properties, but it does not directly impact the print process. It is up to you to alter the print behavior based on these settings.

Let's pretend that the user entered a print range of 2–3. We cannot let the *PrintDocument* fire the *PrintPage* event for all five pages because, even if we generated output for only pages 2 and 3, we would still get three other blank pages out of the printer. What we want is to have the event fire only twice, once for page 2 and once for page 3. We'll need to adjust the use of the *WhichPage* class-level tracking variable to compensate for the indicated range. First, let's change the *BeginPrint* handler to set the correct starting page number.

```
    private void CountingDoc_BeginPrint(object sender,
        Printing.PrintEventArgs e)
    {
        // ----- Start the counting over.
        WhichPage = CountingDoc.PrinterSettings.FromPage;
    }
```

In the *PrintPage* event handler, we must modify the code that determines when to quit the print process.

```
    WhichPage += 1;
    e.HasMorePages =
        (WhichPage <= CountingDoc.PrinterSettings.ToPage);
```

Since the print preview code shares the same document settings, we need to adjust the preview code to force it to always print all pages.

```
    private void ActPreview_Click(object sender, EventArgs e)
    {
        // ----- Display a preview of the document.
        UserPreview.Document = CountingDoc;
        CountingDoc.PrinterSettings.PrintRange =
            Printing.PrintRange.AllPages;
        UserPreview.ShowDialog();
    }
```

If you run the program and adjust the print range, you should get just the pages you requested. I've placed a copy of this program in the book's installation directory. You'll find it in the *Print Preview Test* subdirectory.

Printing in "Raw" Mode

Using GDI+ to generate printed pages is pretty straightforward. For complex pages, you may have to do a lot of positioning and measuring of text strings and whatnot, but it all boils down to "draw this text or this shape at this position."

Sadly, not all printers support the application-to-printer-via-GDI-and-Printish way of doing things. This is especially true of printers used to print thermal credit card receipts at your favorite pizza place. Although some of these printers may have Windows drivers, they were originally designed for direct communication with an application via their special escape-sequence languages. For such printers, you can write directly to the printer in "raw" mode, where you control exactly which characters get sent to the printer. (Actually, you don't have to go directly to the printer. You can still write to the printer's queue, and let Windows manage the scheduling of the print job.)

It is with even more sadness that I must inform you of .NET's lack of raw printer support. Although a DLL is included with Windows that enables this direct printing method, a managed .NET wrapper for it does not ship with the framework. You, and other overburdened programmers everywhere, must take up the charge yourselves.

Well, it's not all that bad. Microsoft and other developers have published code that maps the unmanaged DLL calls to managed equivalents. We'll be using a variation of some of this code in the Library Project in this chapter to support the printing of checkout slips, paper receipts that let a patron know which items were just checked out and when they are all due back.

Summary

I recommend that you peruse the printer-specific classes and controls discussed in this chapter. They include many properties that let you fine-tune the output of your printed page based on the user's specified settings. For instance, I promised you earlier in the chapter that you could discover whether a printer supported color. The `PrinterSettings.SupportsColor` property gives you a straight-up yes or no answer to this feature question. If you know that a printer does not support color, you can adjust your `PrintPage` code to present the page content in a slightly different format.

Project

As advertised, this chapter's project focuses on the printing of checkout and fine-payment receipts. But we'll also add all of the code that lets patrons and librarians check in and check out books and other library items.

> **Project Access**
> Load the "Chapter 20 (Before) Code" project, either through the New Project templates or by accessing the project directly from the installation directory. To see the code in its final form, load "Chapter 20 (After) Code" instead.

Supporting Raw Printing

In the interest of frank and honest discussion, I must tell you that I didn't come up with the basic code for raw printing in this section. Oh, some of the code is mine, both stylistically and imaginatively. But I didn't figure out all of the links between the application and the *winspool.drv* file. That code originally came from

Microsoft Knowledge Base article number 322090, which describes raw printing support from .NET applications. It uses a feature of .NET known as *interop* that allows .NET code to interoperate with older unmanaged COM-based components and applications.

Boy, am I glad that I got that off my chest. I mean, if anyone thought I was the one who came up with the code you are about to see, there would be angry mobs storming my house nightly, and general turmoil in the streets. The code, contained in the *RawPrinterHelper* class, is just plain ugly, as are the many support declarations.

Well, there's no sense in postponing it any longer. First, open the *NativeMethods.cs* file, and insert the *DOCINFOW* structure just before the *NativeMethods* class declaration.

Insert Snippet
Insert Chapter 20, Snippet Item 1.

```
[StructLayout(LayoutKind.Sequential,
    CharSet=CharSet.Unicode)]
public struct DOCINFOW
{
    [MarshalAs(UnmanagedType.LPWStr)]
    public string pDocName;
    [MarshalAs(UnmanagedType.LPWStr)]
    public string pOutputFile;
    [MarshalAs(UnmanagedType.LPWStr)]
    public string pDataType;
}
```

Next, add some interop declarations to the *NativeMethods* class itself. The code printed here is slightly condensed.

Insert Snippet
Insert Chapter 20, Snippet Item 2.

```
[DllImport("winspool.drv", EntryPoint="OpenPrinterW",
    SetLastError=true, CharSet=CharSet.Unicode,
    ExactSpelling=true, CallingConvention=
    CallingConvention.StdCall)]
public extern static bool OpenPrinter(
    string src, ref IntPtr hPrinter, int pd);

[DllImport("winspool.drv", EntryPoint="ClosePrinter"...]
public extern static bool ClosePrinter(IntPtr hPrinter);

[DllImport("winspool.drv", EntryPoint="StartDocPrinterW"...]
public extern static bool StartDocPrinter(
    IntPtr hPrinter, Int32 level, ref DOCINFOW pDI);

[DllImport("winspool.drv", EntryPoint="EndDocPrinter"...]
public extern static bool EndDocPrinter(IntPtr hPrinter);

[DllImport("winspool.drv", EntryPoint="StartPagePrinter"...]
public extern static bool StartPagePrinter(IntPtr hPrinter);

[DllImport("winspool.drv", EntryPoint="EndPagePrinter"...]
public extern static bool EndPagePrinter(IntPtr hPrinter);
```

```
[DllImport("winspool.drv", EntryPoint="WritePrinter"...]
public extern static bool WritePrinter(
    IntPtr hPrinter, IntPtr pBytes,
    Int32 dwCount, ref Int32 dwWritten);
```

Finally, create a new class named *RawPrinterHelper.cs*, and use the following code to replace the existing contents of the file.

Insert Snippet

Insert Chapter 20, Snippet Item 3.

```
using System;
using System.Runtime.InteropServices;

namespace Library
{
public class RawPrinterHelper
{
    // ----- The code in this class is based on Microsoft
    //       knowledge base article number 322090.
    //       Web: http://support.microsoft.com/?id=322090

    public static bool SendStringToPrinter(
        string targetPrinter, string stringContent,
        string documentTitle)
    {
        // ----- Send an array of bytes to a printer queue.
        //       Return True on success.
        IntPtr printerHandle = default(IntPtr);
        Int32 errorCode = 0;
        DOCINFOW docDetail = new DOCINFOW();
        Int32 bytesWritten = 0;
        bool printSuccess = false;
        IntPtr contentBytes = default(IntPtr);
        Int32 contentSize = 0;

        // ----- Set up the indentity of this document.
        docDetail.pDocName = documentTitle;
        docDetail.pDataType = "RAW";

        // ----- Convert the string to ANSI text.
        contentSize = stringContent.Length;
        contentBytes = Marshal.StringToCoTaskMemAnsi(
            stringContent);

        // ----- Open the printer and print the document.
        printSuccess = false;
        if (NativeMethods.OpenPrinter(targetPrinter,
            ref printerHandle, 0))
        {
            if (NativeMethods.StartDocPrinter(
                printerHandle, 1, ref docDetail))
            {
                if (NativeMethods.StartPagePrinter(
                    printerHandle))
```

```
            {
                // ----- Send the content to the printer.
                printSuccess = NativeMethods.WritePrinter(
                    printerHandle, contentBytes,
                    contentSize, ref bytesWritten);
                NativeMethods.EndPagePrinter(printerHandle);
            }
            NativeMethods.EndDocPrinter(printerHandle);
        }
        NativeMethods.ClosePrinter(printerHandle);
    }

    // ----- GetLastError may provide information on
    //       the last error. For now, just ignore it.
    if (printSuccess == false)
        errorCode = Marshal.GetLastWin32Error();

    // ----- Free up unused memory.
    Marshal.FreeCoTaskMem(contentBytes);

    // ----- Complete.
    return printSuccess;
    }
  }
}
```

Although ugly, the code is relatively clear-cut. The *SendStringToPrinter* method prepares a string for printing by forcing it to a standard ANSI format. It then uses the functions in the *winspool.drv* library (and declared in *NativeMethods.cs*) to open a new print job, and send the prepared content to it. There's a whole lot of "marshalling" going on in the code through members of the *Marshal* class. Since *winspool.drv* is an unmanaged library, all data must be shuttled indirectly between the managed Library application and the unmanaged *winspool.drv* library.

Printing Tickets

Now that we have a convenient class that will send any raw content to any specific printer, let's add some code to use it. First, we need to add a helper class for a portion of the ticket printing. Create a new class file named *CheckedOutItem.cs*, and replace its empty class template with the following code.

Insert Snippet
Insert Chapter 20, Snippet Item 4.

```
public class CheckedOutItem
{
    // ----- Used to store the details of each checked-out
    //       item on the main form, although it also
    //       supports receipt printing.
    public string ItemTitle;
    public int CopyNumber;
    public string Barcode;
    public DateTime DueDate;
}
```

We'll use this class to convey the details to be printed on the receipt when checking out items. Speaking of ticket printing, let's add the class that does the actual printing. Create a new class file named *TicketPrinting.cs*. Replace the entire contents of the file with the snippet code.

The code includes three static methods that drive printing: `PrintCheckoutTicket`, `PrintBalanceTicket`, and `PrintPaymentTicket`. These methods are called from other parts of the application when it's time to present a printed ticket to the user. The `TicketPrinting` class also includes a few other methods that support these three primary methods. Since these three methods are somewhat similar in structure, let's just look at `PrintCheckoutTicket`.

```csharp
public static void PrintCheckoutTicket(
   long patronID, ListBox checkedOutItems)
{
   // ----- Print out a ticket of what the patron checked
   //       out. The supplied ListBox control contains
   //       objects of type CheckedOutItem.
   int ticketWidth;
   System.Text.StringBuilder ticketText;
   decimal patronFines;
   CheckedOutItem itemDetail;
   string holdText;

   // ----- Ignore if there is nothing to print.
   if ((patronID == -1L) |
         (checkedOutItems.Items.Count == 0))
      return;

   // ----- Get the width of the ticket.
   ticketWidth = Properties.Settings.Default.ReceiptWidth;
   if (ticketWidth <= 0)
      ticketWidth = 40;

   // ----- Build the heading.
   ticketText = GetTicketHeader(patronID, ticketWidth);
   if (ticketText == null)
      return;

   // ----- Process each checked-out item.
   for (int counter = 0; counter <
      checkedOutItems.Items.Count; counter++)
   {
      // ----- Extract the detail from the list.
      itemDetail = (CheckedOutItem)
         (checkedOutItems.Items[counter]);

      // ----- Add the item name.
      holdText = itemDetail.ItemTitle;
      if (holdText.Length > ticketWidth)
         holdText = holdText.Substring(0,
            ticketWidth).TrimEnd();
      ticketText.AppendLine(holdText);

      // ----- Add the barcode number and due date.
      ticketText.AppendLine(LeftAndRightText(
         itemDetail.Barcode, "Due: " + itemDetail.
```

```
            DueDate.ToString("MMM d, yyyy"), ticketWidth));
        ticketText.AppendLine();
    }

    // ----- If there are fines due, print them here.
    patronFines = CalculatePatronFines(patronID);
    if (patronFines > 0M)
    {
        ticketText.AppendLine("Fines Due: " +
            patronFines.ToString("C"));
        ticketText.AppendLine();
    }

    // ----- Add the bottom display text.
    ticketText.Append(GetTicketFooter(ticketWidth));

    // ----- Send the ticket to the printer.
    try
    {
        RawPrinterHelper.SendStringToPrinter(
            Properties.Settings.Default.ReceiptPrinter,
            ticketText.ToString(), "Checkout Receipt");
    }
    catch (Exception ex)
    {
        GeneralError(
            "TicketPrinting.PrintCheckoutTicket", ex);
    }
}
```

The code builds a string (actually a *StringBuilder*) of display content, adding details about each checked-out item. Then it calls *SendStringToPrinter* to send the content to the configured receipt printer (*Properties.Settings.Default.ReceiptPrinter*).

We'll add the code that calls *PrintCheckoutTicket* later. Right now, let's add code that calls the two other methods. When the Payment Record form closes, we want to automatically print a receipt of all payments made while the form was open. Add the following code to the *ActClose_Click* event handler in the *PatronRecord* form, just before the code already found in that handler.

Insert Snippet
Insert Chapter 20, Snippet Item 6.

```
// ----- Print out a ticket if needed.
if (SessionPayments.Count > 0)
    TicketPrinting.PrintPaymentTicket(
        ActivePatronID, SessionPayments);
SessionPayments.Clear();
SessionPayments = null;
```

Then, add some code to the *ActBalanceTicket_Click* event handler, also in the *PatronRecord* class, that prints a balance ticket when the user requests it.

Insert Snippet
Insert Chapter 20, Snippet Item 7.

```
// ----- Print a ticket of all balances.
TicketPrinting.PrintBalanceTicket(ActivePatronID, Fines);
```

Printing Barcodes

The Library Project prints three types of barcodes: (1) item barcodes that you can stick on books, CDs, and anything else that can be checked out or managed by the system; (2) patron barcodes that can be made into patron identification cards; and (3) miscellaneous barcodes that a library can use for any other purpose. All three barcode types are printed through the new *BarcodePrint* form. Figure 20-9 shows the controls included on this form.

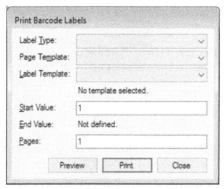

Figure 20-9. One form, three barcode types, many happy labels

I've already added this form to the project, including its code. Here's the code for the Preview button, which should look familiar after I beat its concepts into you throughout this chapter.

```
private void ActPreview_Click(object sender, EventArgs e)
{
    // ----- The user wants to preview the labels.
    PrintPreviewDialog barcodePreview;

    // ----- Make sure the user supplied valid data.
    if (VerifyFields() == false)
        return;

    // ----- Load in all of the page-specific
    //        details to be used in printing.
    if (LoadPageDetails() == false)
        return;

    // ----- Create the preview dialog.
    this.Cursor = Cursors.WaitCursor;
    PageSoFar = 0;
    PreviewMode = true;
    BarcodeDoc = new PrintDocument();

    // ----- Display the preview.
    BarcodeDoc.PrintPage += BarcodeDoc_PrintPage;
    barcodePreview = new PrintPreviewDialog();
    barcodePreview.Document = BarcodeDoc;
    barcodePreview.ShowDialog();
    BarcodeDoc = null;
```

```
      this.Cursor = Cursors.Default;
   }
```

The Print button's code is almost exactly the same, but it uses a *PrintDialog* instance instead of *PrintPreviewDialog*. It also keeps track of the final printed barcode number so that it can help avoid overlaps the next time they are printed.

The *BarcodeDoc_PrintPage* event handler does the actual barcode printing. Its code combines the *BarcodeLabel.PreviewArea_Paint* and *BarcodePage.PreviewArea_Paint* event handlers into one glorious printing machine.

To enable use of the barcode printing form, add the following statements to the *ActReportsBarcode_Click* event handler in the *MainForm* class.

Insert Snippet
Insert Chapter 20, Snippet Item 8.

```
// ----- Make sure the user is allowed to do this.
if (SecurityProfile[(int)LibrarySecurity.
   ManageBarcodeTemplates] == false)
{
   MessageBox.Show(NotAuthorizedMessage, ProgramTitle,
      MessageBoxButtons.OK, MessageBoxIcon.Exclamation);
   return;
}

// ----- Show the barcode label printing form.
(new BarcodePrint()).ShowDialog();
```

Renewal of Checked-Out Patron Items

For a library patron, the only thing more important than checking items out and in is being able to read those items. The Library Project won't help anyone with that, but it will do that check-in, checkout transaction thing through the code we add in this chapter. Let's start by adding the renewal code for currently checked-out items. The Renew button on the Patron Record form initiates the process. Add the code to the *PatronRecord.ActRenewItemsOut_Click* event handler that does the renewal.

Insert Snippet
Insert Chapter 20, Snippet Item 9.

The code does some calculations to determine the new due date (avoiding holidays), and then updates the database in a transaction.

```
transInfo = TransactionBegin();

// ----- Update the record.
sqlText = "UPDATE PatronCopy " +
   "SET DueDate = @TargetDate, " +
   "Renewal = @RenewalPos WHERE ID = @RecordID";
sqlRun = new DataCommand(sqlText);
sqlRun.AddDate("TargetDate", dueDate);
sqlRun.AddInteger("RenewalPos", renewsSoFar);
sqlRun.AddLong("RecordID", itemDetail.DetailID);
ExecuteSQL(sqlRun, transInfo);
```

```
// ----- Update the patron record.
sqlText = "UPDATE Patron " +
   "SET LastActivity = GETDATE() " +
   "WHERE ID = @RecordID";
sqlRun = new DataCommand(sqlText);
sqlRun.AddLong("RecordID", ActivePatronID);
ExecuteSQL(sqlRun, transInfo);

TransactionCommit(transInfo);
```

Support for Check-In and Checkout

If a library adds barcode labels to all of its items, check-in and checkout will be via a barcode reader. But a very small library using the program may not have the staff time available to apply barcodes to everything on the shelves. Therefore, the Library Project needs to support check-in and checkout by title. During checkout or check-in, the user enters either a barcode or a title (partial or complete). Non-numeric entries are assumed to be titles, and initiate a title search. The new *CheckLookup.cs* form, pictured in Figure 20-10, displays all matches for the entered title.

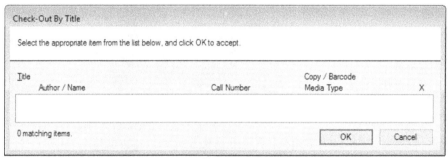

Figure 20-10. A title matching form for both check-in and checkout

Although the fields on the form initially indicate that they are for checkout only, the form does double duty, altering its visage for check-in purposes. Additionally, check-in listings are limited to only those items already checked out.

I've already added this form to the project, along with its source code. Most of the code queries the database for matching library items and displays the results using an owner draw list box. It is a subset of the code found in the *ItemLookup.cs* form. The only real difference between check-in and checkout occurs in the `PerformLookup` method. This code block starts to build the main item selection SQL command, and then ends it with these statements.

```
if (asCheckIn)
   sqlText += " AND IC.ID IN";
else
   sqlText += " AND IC.ID NOT IN";
sqlText += " (SELECT ItemCopy FROM PatronCopy " +
   "WHERE Returned = 0)";
```

So, the difference is "IN" versus "NOT IN."

The `CheckItemByTitle` function is the main interface to the form's logic.

```
public long CheckItemByTitle(
   bool checkIn, string searchText)
```

You pass this function the user-supplied title (*searchText*) and a flag indicating check-in or checkout, and it returns the *ItemCopy.ID* database field for the selected library item.

All of the remaining changes in this chapter occur in the *MainForm* class, so let's go there now. The *UpdateDisplayForUser* method adjusts the main form's features when an administrator logs in or out. One feature we didn't take into account before is the administrator-defined ability for patrons to check out their own items without librarian assistance. To support that feature, we need to change some of the code in the *UpdateDisplayForUser* method. About ten lines into the code, in the conditional section that sets up the display for patrons, you'll find these four lines.

```
LabelTasks.Visible = false;
LineTasks.Visible = false;
PicCheckOut.Visible = false;
ActCheckOut.Visible = false;
```

Replace these four lines with the following code.

Insert Snippet
Insert Chapter 20, Snippet Item 10.

```
// ----- See if patrons can check out items by themselves.
userCanCheckOut = GetBoolean(
    GetSystemValue("PatronCheckOut"));

LabelTasks.Visible = userCanCheckOut;
LineTasks.Visible = userCanCheckOut;
PicCheckOut.Visible = userCanCheckOut;
ActCheckOut.Visible = userCanCheckOut;
```

We also need to add similar security-related code to the *TaskCheckOut* method. Here are the first few lines of code from that method.

```
// ----- Update the display.
AllPanelsInvisible();
if (SecurityProfile[(int)LibrarySecurity.CheckOutItems])
    PanelCheckOut.Visible = true;
```

Replace these lines with the following code.

Insert Snippet
Insert Chapter 20, Snippet Item 11.

```
// ----- Check Out mode.
bool userCanCheckOut;

// ----- See if patrons can check out items by themselves.
userCanCheckOut = GetBoolean(
    GetSystemValue("PatronCheckOut"));

// ----- Update the display.
AllPanelsInvisible();
if (userCanCheckOut | SecurityProfile[
        (int)LibrarySecurity.CheckOutItems])
    PanelCheckOut.Visible = true;
```

The actual checkout of items occurs on the main form itself. First, a patron is identified, and then the items to check out get processed. Let's add a class-level variable to *MainForm* to keep track of the patron. And as long as we're adding definitions, we'll also add two constants that refer to images stored in the *MainForm.StatusImages* control. These constants will be used in some check-in-related code added a little later. Add the following code to the start of the class definition.

Insert Snippet
Insert Chapter 20, Snippet Item 12.

```
private long ActiveCheckOutPatron = -1L;

private const int StatusImageBad = 0;
private const int StatusImageGood = 1;
```

When the user identifies the patron to use for checkout, and then starts checking items out, the last step is a click of the Finish button, indicating the end of the checkout process for that patron. (Skip ahead to Figure 20-11 if you want to see the Finish button now.) However, there is nothing to stop the user from jumping to another part of the program, or from exiting the program completely, without first clicking the Finish button. We must anticipate this rude behavior so typical of software users. To ensure that checkout completes properly, we will add some code to three places in *MainForm* that should catch any such discourteous actions by the user. Add the following code to *the start* of these three methods: (1) the *MainForm_FormClosing* event handler; (2) the *ShowLoginForm* method; and (3) the *AllPanelsInvisible* method.

Insert Snippet
Insert Chapter 20, Snippet Item 13 *three times*.

```
// ----- Finish the in-process check-out if needed.
if (ActiveCheckOutPatron != -1L)
    ActFinishCheckOut.PerformClick();
```

Checking Out Items

All of the checkout code (except for the code in the *CheckLookup.cs* form) appears in the main form's class. Checkout is one of the eight main display panels accessed through this form (see Figure 20-11).

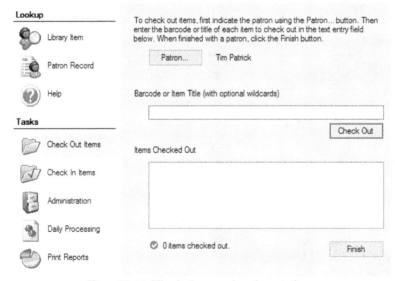

Figure 20-11. The checkout panel on the main form

Here's the process for checking out items from the checkout panel.

1. The user clicks the Patron button and identifies the patron who will check out items.
2. The user enters the title or barcode for each item to check out, and clicks the Check Out button for each one.
3. The user clicks the Finish button when checkout is complete.

Let's add the code for each of these three buttons. First, add code to the *ActCheckOutPatron_Click* event handler.

Insert Snippet
Insert Chapter 20, Snippet Item 14.

This code prompts the user for patron selection, and displays the remaining fields if successful. Here's the part of the code that does the prompting.

```
// ----- Get the ID of the patron.
patronID = (new PatronAccess()).SelectPatron();
if (patronID == -1L)
    return;

// ----- Get the patron name.
sqlText = "SELECT FirstName + ' ' + LastName " +
    "FROM Patron WHERE ID = @RecordID";
sqlRun = new DataCommand(sqlText);
sqlRun.AddLong("RecordID", patronID);
try
{
    patronName = DBGetText(ExecuteSQLReturn(sqlRun));
}
catch (Exception ex)
{
    GeneralError(
        "MainForm.ActCheckOutPatron_Click.Name", ex);
    patronName = "Unknown";
}

// ----- Is this patron active?
sqlText = "SELECT Active FROM Patron WHERE ID = @RecordID";
sqlRun = new DataCommand(sqlText);
sqlRun.AddLong("RecordID", patronID);
try
{
    if (DBGetBool(ExecuteSQLReturn(sqlRun)) == false)
    {
        MessageBox.Show("Patron '" + patronName +
            "' is marked as inactive.", ProgramTitle,
            MessageBoxButtons.OK, MessageBoxIcon.Exclamation);
        return;
    }
}
catch (Exception ex)
{
```

```
            GeneralError(
                "MainForm.ActCheckOutPatron_Click.Active", ex);
            return;
        }
```

Add code to the *ActDoCheckOut_Click* event handler, which processes each item through the Check Out button.

Insert Snippet
Insert Chapter 20, Snippet Item 15.

As I mentioned before, this code differentiates between numeric entry (barcodes) and other entries (titles).

```
    if (CheckDecimal(CheckOutBarcode.Text) == true)
    {
        // ----- Probably a barcode supplied.
        //       Get the related ID.
        sqlText = "SELECT ID FROM ItemCopy " +
            "WHERE Barcode = @TestBarcode";
        sqlRun = new DataCommand(sqlText);
        sqlRun.AddText("TestBarcode",
            DigitsOnly(CheckOutBarcode.Text));
        try
        {
            copyID = DBGetLong(ExecuteSQLReturn(sqlRun), -1L);
        }
        catch (Exception ex)
        {
            GeneralError("MainForm.ActDoCheckOut.Copy", ex);
            copyID = -1L;
        }
        if (copyID == -1L)
        {
            // ----- Invalid barcode.
            MessageBox.Show("Barcode not found.",
                ProgramTitle, MessageBoxButtons.OK,
                MessageBoxIcon.Exclamation);
            CheckOutBarcode.Focus();
            CheckOutBarcode.SelectAll();
            return;
        }
    }
    else
    {
        // ----- Lookup by title.
        copyID = (new CheckLookup()).CheckItemByTitle(
            false, CheckOutBarcode.Text.Trim());
        if (copyID == -1L)
            return;
    }
```

Eventually, after verifying that the item is available for patron use, the code checks out the item by updating the relevant records in the database.

```
    // ----- Perform the check-out in a transaction.
    transInfo = TransactionBegin();
```

```
// ----- Update patron copy record.
sqlText = "INSERT INTO PatronCopy (Patron, ItemCopy, " +
    "CheckOut, Renewal, DueDate, Returned, Missing, " +
    "Fine, Paid) VALUES (@NewPatron, @NewCopy, " +
    "@NewDate, 0, @NewDue, 0, 0, 0, 0)";
sqlRun = new DataCommand(sqlText);
sqlRun.AddLong("NewPatron", ActiveCheckOutPatron);
sqlRun.AddLong("NewCopy", copyID);
sqlRun.AddDate("NewDate", DateTime.Today);
sqlRun.AddDate("NewDue", untilDate);
ExecuteSQL(sqlRun, transInfo);

// ----- Update the patron record.
sqlText = "UPDATE Patron SET LastActivity = GETDATE() " +
    "WHERE ID = @RecordID";
sqlRun = new DataCommand(sqlText);
sqlRun.AddLong("RecordID", ActiveCheckOutPatron);
ExecuteSQL(sqlRun, transInfo);

TransactionCommit(transInfo);
```

The last of the three buttons is the Finish button. Add code to the *ActFinishCheckOut_Click* event handler.

Insert Snippet
Insert Chapter 20, Snippet Item 16.

This code simply resets the display fields in preparation for the next patron checkout.

The list box on the checkout panel needs to display two columns of data: (1) the due date; and (2) details of the item, such as title and barcode. These values were added to the list using the *CheckedOutItem* class we added a little earlier in the chapter. Add code to the *CheckedOutItems_DrawItem* event handler.

Insert Snippet
Insert Chapter 20, Snippet Item 17.

Checking In Items

Checking in items is much simpler since we don't need to identify the patron before processing starts. The barcode or title of the check-in item is sufficient to complete all processing. Figure 20-12 shows the check-in panel.

This panel includes a date indicating when the item will be checked in. Normally, that's today, but if library items are turned in through a nighttime drop box after business hours, the librarian might want to adjust the date to "Yesterday," just in case any of these items were turned in before midnight. Let's add some code so that the panel indicates "Today" or "Yesterday" or some other day when the date changes. Add the following code to the *CheckInDate_ValueChanged* event handler.

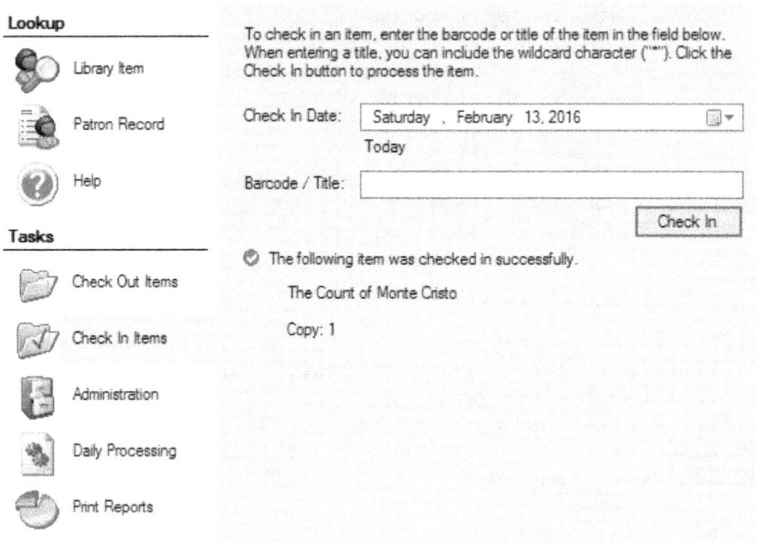

Figure 20-12. The check-in panel on the main form

Insert Snippet

Insert Chapter 20, Snippet Item 18.

```
// ----- Adjust the day in the display.
switch ((int)(DateTime.Today -
   CheckInDate.Value).TotalDays)
{
   case 0: // ----- Today
      CheckInDay.Text = "Today";
      CheckInDay.BackColor = SystemColors.Control;
      CheckInDay.ForeColor = SystemColors.ControlText;
      break;
   case 1: // ----- Yesterday
      CheckInDay.Text = "Yesterday";
      CheckInDay.BackColor = Color.Red;
      CheckInDay.ForeColor = Color.White;
      break;
   default: // ----- X days ago
      CheckInDay.Text = Convert.ToInt32(
         (DateTime.Today - CheckInDate.Value).
         TotalDays).ToString() + " days ago";
      CheckInDay.BackColor = Color.Red;
      CheckInDay.ForeColor = Color.White;
      break;
}
```

The actual check-in occurs when the user enters a barcode or title in the text field, and clicks the Check In button. Add code to the `ActDoCheckIn_Click` event handler.

Insert Snippet

Insert Chapter 20, Snippet Item 19.

After performing some lookups and confirmation checks, the code checks in the item through database updates.

```
// ----- Do the check-in in a transaction.
transInfo = TransactionBegin();

// ----- Update patron copy record.
sqlText = "UPDATE PatronCopy SET CheckIn = @NewDate, " +
    "Returned = 1 WHERE ID = @RecordID";
sqlRun = new DataCommand(sqlText);
sqlRun.AddDate("NewDate", CheckInDate.Value);
sqlRun.AddLong("RecordID", patronCopyID);
ExecuteSQL(sqlRun, transInfo);

// ----- Update the patron record.
sqlText = "UPDATE Patron SET LastActivity = GETDATE() " +
    "WHERE ID = @RecordID";
sqlRun = new DataCommand(sqlText);
sqlRun.AddLong("RecordID", patronID);
ExecuteSQL(sqlRun, transInfo);

TransactionCommit(transInfo);
```

That's it for the check-in and checkout procedures, and all ticket printing. It's pretty good code, but not yet perfect. What we haven't yet added is code to properly process fines on items before they are checked in, or as they are adjusted in other ways. We will postpone this logic until Chapter 22. Until then, let's look at another application printing feature: reports.

Chapter 21

Reporting

For the business application developer, reports are a fact of life. You may want to spend your time developing cool user interfaces or figuring out the core algorithms used in Generally Accepted Accounting Principles. But instead, you invest many boring hours each week turning out report after report. And these reports take a significant toll on the programming community. In America alone, the Centers for Disease Control and Prevention estimates nearly 850 report-related deaths each year—and that doesn't even count those who read the reports. I once had a customer that printed off twenty copies of a 600-page report every month for its top-level managers. Clearly stupefied by the amount of tree pulp used to generate this report, the staff was unable to come up with a more interesting name than "The Monthly Report."

If you are a business programmer, reports are in your future. But whereas your forebears had to deal with languages such as RPG III, you get to use .NET. Hey, reports won't be so bad after all. And even without resorting to third-party reporting tools, Visual Studio and .NET include several report-focused features and tools you can use right out of the box.

This chapter discusses some of those reporting resources, and delves a little deeper into the reporting controls used in the Library Project.

Report Options in .NET

Reporting involves displaying and printing basic or summarized data to the user for specific business purposes. Visual Studio offers a variety of tools that can help you accomplish this task, and you can always enhance these options using third-party tools.

PrintDocument-Based Printing

As we learned in the previous chapter, the .NET Framework includes a full object-based printing system that uses GDI+ commands to draw text and graphics on each printed page. Since you can put anything you want on each page, you could develop your own custom reports using this method. The responsibility for positioning each label and calculated field on the page, and determining when to move to a new page, will rest entirely on your shoulders. Still, the GDI+ commands are straightforward, and developing some basic reports using this method would not be overwhelming.

If you want to take this route for your reports, I refer you back to Chapter 20 and the basic printing concepts presented there.

HTML and Web Pages

Besides being a significant timewaster, the Internet (and its HTML-based page description language) is a great medium for data-report communication. The table-formatting tags in HTML (such as `<td>`) let you organize tabular output without much effort. Sure, it's a chore stringing all of those baby-size text strings together to build the page, but there are ways around that, too.

Back in Chapter 13, I discussed XSLT (XSL Transformations), a way to take XML-based data and reshape it into any form you want—including great works of art by Michelangelo, or nicely crafted HTML. However you obtain the HTML, you have a choice of display methods as well. The most direct method involves storing the generated HTML in a disk file, and starting the user's default browser to display it using standard .NET features.

```
Process.Start(@"c:\temp\MyReport.htm");
```

If you want the report to have a more integrated look in your application, you can display the HTML content in a web browser control. We did this in the project code for Chapter 17, when we displayed the details of a library item as HTML.

XPS Documents

Windows Presentation Foundation (WPF) is used primarily to make your user interface dance with color and action. But a portion of that technology exists to generate XML-based static documents known as *XPS* (XML Paper Specification). Just as you can generate reports using HTML, you can generate them using the XPS standard.

Chapter 18 includes a brief discussion of WPF, and you'll be building a sample WPF application in Chapter 22. If the generation of XPS-based reports is of interest to you, check out the relevant documentation on Microsoft's MSDN web site.

Reporting Services and Controls

Visual Studio includes a set of data management technologies bundled under the name "Microsoft SQL Server Data Tools." The entire package is based, in part, on Microsoft SQL Server Reporting Services, one of the key business analysis components provided alongside SQL Server. Among the tools in this set, you will find reporting components exposed through classes in the *Microsoft.Reporting* namespace, including the *ReportViewer* class.

The Library Project will use the *ReportViewer* class for its built-in reports. We'll spend most of this chapter discussing this class and its use in Windows Forms applications. You'll see how simple it is to add the class as a control to an existing project. Visual Studio also includes a distinct "Reports Application" project template that exists to build reporting apps with *ReportViewer* as the focus.

Crystal Reports

Crystal Reports, a popular third-party reporting tool, came bundled with Visual Studio during its first few release cycles, a practice that ended with Visual Studio 2010. Over the years, the ownership of Crystal Reports has changed hands almost as many times as I've changed the oil in my car. It is currently owned by the German software giant SAP.

Although Crystal Reports is no longer included with Visual Studio, SAP does offer a developer version for free that integrates into your Visual Studio projects. For more information on this reporting tool, visit SAP's web site, http://www.sap.com. Beyond Crystal Reports, there are various third-party reporting solutions that let you add reporting components directly into your Visual C# applications.

Integration with Microsoft Office

Microsoft offers a free Visual Studio add-on called "Office Developer Tools" that allows the managed world of .NET applications to interact with Microsoft Office applications. Once installed, your copy of Visual Studio will sport new project templates that target Microsoft Office products, SharePoint services, and hosted Office 365 environments.

Using Office Developer Tools, you can generate Word or Excel files that contain your custom reporting data. I won't be discussion this platform in this book. If you have an interest in Office development, visit Microsoft's Office Developer Tools web site, https://www.visualstudio.com/en-us/features/office-tools-vs.aspx.

Using Reporting Controls in .NET

Let's spend the remainder of this chapter discussing the standard reporting tools provided in Visual Studio: the *ReportViewer* class and its affiliated controls. The *ReportViewer* control integrates directly with Microsoft SQL Server Reporting Services, displaying whole pages generated by that server-based system. You might be using SQL Server Express Edition for your development, which does not include Reporting Services. Therefore, I'll focus on the control's "local" mode presentation. This lets you display any data from any source you choose on each report display page, including from SQL Server.

Depending on the options you selected when installing Visual Studio 2015, your system might be missing the components needed to use *ReportViewer*. When properly installed, you will find a Reporting section within the available Visual C# project templates when viewing the New Project dialog in Visual Studio. If no such template group exists, follow these instructions to add Microsoft SQL Server Data Tools to your copy of Visual Studio 2015.

1. Open the Windows Settings page of the Windows Control Panel, and activate the Programs and Features option.
2. In the list of installed applications, select your Visual Studio installation (such as Microsoft Visual Studio Community 2015), then click the Change button above the list.
3. When the Visual Studio configuration program appears, choose Modify to access the Features panel.
4. In the Select Features list, within the Windows and Web Development branch, select the Microsoft SQL Server Data Tools option. Then click Update.

In the vein of "those who can, do; those who can't, teach," let me walk you through the steps needed to visually design a simple report using the *ReportViewer* class. We'll create a report that lists the records in the Library Project's *Activity* table, a table that will have data in it even if you haven't used the Library program yet. This works best if you follow along in front of your computer, because reading about report design is a lot like reading about brain surgery: it's more interesting if you actually do it. Start by creating a new Windows Forms application called "SimpleReport."

Adding the Data Source

Add a data source to the project that refers to the *Activity* database table. We already did this back in Chapter 10, in the "Creating a Data Source" section. Select the Project→Add New Data Source menu command, and use the Data Source Configuration Wizard to locate your Library database. When you reach the list of database objects, check the box next to the *Activity* table, and click the Finish button. You should now have a data source named *LibraryDataSet*. Figure 21-1 shows the elements added to the Solution Explorer and the Data Sources panel by this action.

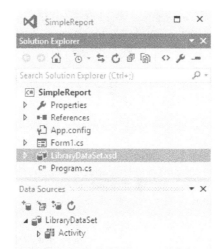

Figure 21-1. The LibraryDataSet as a data source, and as an XML .xsd file

Adding a Report Design Surface

Use the Project→Add New Item menu command to add a new "Report" item. Figure 21-2 shows the item template in the Add New Item dialog.

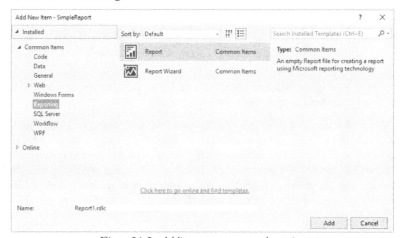

Figure 21-2. Adding a new report to the project

Click the Add button to insert the report into the project. A new *Report1.rdlc* file appears in your project, and its designer opens automatically. "RDLC" is short for "Report Definition Language – Client," and files of this type contain XML content that describes the layout of a locally designed report. Figure 21-3 shows the designer for the added *Report1.rdlc* file, plus the controls in the toolbar that you can add to the report surface. I will refer to reports created through this designer as "RDLC reports" throughout the rest of this chapter.

Figure 21-3. The report designer and related toolbar

Designing the Report Surface

If you've written reports in Microsoft Access or in some other common reporting tool, you are probably familiar with "banded" reports. These reports have separate bands or stripes that represent a portion of the printed page. Bands include page headers and footers, report headers and footers, the record detail section, and group headers and footers used to visually and logically group the detail entries. As the report runs, an imaginary horizontal page-wide line runs from the top to the bottom of the page. As the line hits each band, the report processes the fields in that band until there are no more records to process.

RDLC reports are a little bit different from those banded reports. There are only three bands: page header, page footer, and everything else (a band called "Body"). Instead of adding bands for records and groups, you add fields to *data regions*. These special controls process the records linked to the report according to the shape of the data region. There are four data region controls in the toolbox.

Table

> This region presents an unlimited number of data rows, but with a predefined set of data columns. It's designed for tabular presentation of data records, with each column generally displaying a single source or calculated data field. Each row of the table represents a source data record.

Matrix

> This control is similar to the `Table` region, but it allows for a flexible number of data columns.

List

> The `List` region provides a free-form display section for each incoming record. You can add any number of fields or display controls to the record section.

Chart

> The `Chart` region uses the collected data of the report to present line, bar, and pie charts to the user.

Records from data sets are always tied to a data region. If your report includes data from multiple distinct data sources, each data source will link to exactly one report region, and all regions appear in the Body band. We'll use a `List` data region for this sample report. Go ahead and add the `List` control from the Toolbox to the Body band on the report surface. When the Dataset Properties panel appears, select the LibraryDataSet as the Data Source. This should automatically fill in the Available Datasets field with the Activity table. Enter `LibraryDataSet_Activity` as the Dataset Name. Finally, click the OK button.

You can now add other items either to the band surface itself, or to the *List* control surface. Items added to the *List* control are reprocessed for each record in the incoming data source. These items can be either controls from the toolbox, or database fields displayed in the Datasets branch of the Report Data panel, which should now be visible within Visual Studio.

Expand the Datasets branch, and the LibraryDataSet_Activity item within it, exposing the ID and FullName members of the data set. Drag the FullName item to the *List* control surface. Figure 21-4 shows the display just after performing this drag operation.

Figure 21-4. A List control with a field from the data set

When we dragged the field to the *List* control, Visual Studio added a *TextBox* control to the list's surface, and set the control's content expression to *[FullName]* (displayed within the control image itself). This expression indicates what content to include from each source record when the report runs.

I'm going to resize the *List* control, the text box, and the Body band so that the *FullName* text box field is pretty much all there is in the report (see Figure 21-5).

Figure 21-5. A resized version of the report

The report is ready to use. As we designed the report surface, Visual Studio was busy generating XML and storing it in the *Report1.rdlc* file.

Using a Report Control

The RDLC file is only an XML definition of a report; it doesn't have any ability to display itself. To view the report, we must add a report control to a form that knows how to properly merge the XML design content with the data from the specified data source. Return to *Form1*, and add a *ReportViewer* control to its surface from the toolbox (it's in the Reporting section of the toolbox on my system).

The added control includes a small "smart tags" button in its upper-right corner. Clicking this button displays the ReportViewer Tasks fly-out window, as shown in Figure 21-6.

The *ReportViewer* control presents a form-based experience for displaying reports. Most of the control is a blank area where the report appears. It also includes a toolbar used to navigate through the pages of the report. The user can initiate an export or a printout of the report through these controls. If you don't need the toolbar or one of its controls, use the various *Show...* properties of the *ReportViewer* control to hide the unneeded elements.

Figure 21-6. The ReportViewer control on the form surface

The report viewer is generic and report-independent. If you have several RDLC files in your project, you can display any of them (one at a time) through the same report viewer. We have only one report in our project, so let's connect it (*SimpleReport.Report1.rdlc*) to the viewer by using the Choose Report task from the report viewer's smart tags button. Also, click on the Dock in Parent Container task in the fly-out window to expand the report to the form's size.

The RDLC report, the data from the data source, and the `ReportViewer` control are all joined in one glorious report display by the magic of data binding. When you linked the report to the viewer control, three more controls appeared on the form: `LibraryDataSet`, `ActivityBindingSource`, and `ActivityTableAdapter`. `LibraryDataSet` is a reference to the actual data source we added earlier. The other two controls wrap up that data in a form that can be bound to the report viewer. Although you can't see it in the designer, the hidden form code connects up these controls and the XML report to the viewer.

```
reportDataSource1.Name = "LibraryDataSet_Activity";
reportDataSource1.Value = this.ActivityBindingSource;
this.reportViewer1.LocalReport.DataSources.Add(
    reportDataSource1);
this.reportViewer1.LocalReport.ReportEmbeddedResource =
    "SimpleReport.Report1.rdlc";
```

Yeah, I don't really get it, either. But that's OK. Visual Studio connected it all up for us.

Running the Report

Press F5 and see the results of your efforts. In Figure 21-7, I adjusted the view by clicking on the Page Layout toolbar button, and setting the zoom level to Page Width.

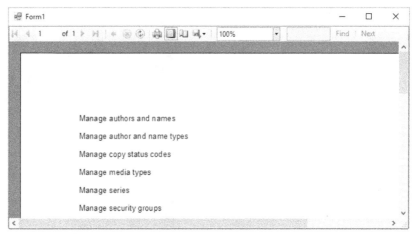

Figure 21-7. Reporting the essential contents of the Activity table

Well, that report is fine as far as `Activity` table reports go, but we could spruce it up a bit more.

Adding a Page Header and Footer

I think the report needs a meaningful title at the top of each page, plus a page number in the bottom-right corner. Let's return to the RDLC report designer and add them. Once there, right-click on the background of the report (not the *Body* element, but the window-colored background area that surrounds it), as shown in Figure 21-8.

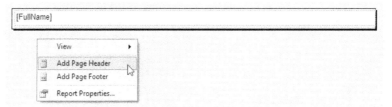

Figure 21-8. Adding page headers and footers

From this menu, select Page Header, then bring up the menu again and select Page Footer. Each new band appears on the report surface.

Whether it's static, unchanging text or text that's dynamically generated from a data source, the `TextBox` control is the control of choice for showing text content. Add a `TextBox` control from the toolbox to both the header and footer sections. Click inside the header's text box, and type the following expression.

```
="The Activity Table Report"
```

You can use the Properties panel to adjust the look of this control, including its display font, or to give it a name. And you might want to give it a meaningful name since, as you might have noticed by now, the content you entered in that field has been replaced by the meaningless text «*expr*». Setting the *Name* property will at least give you some clue as to what the field is for when you select it.

In the footer text box, add this text expression.

```
="Page " & Globals!PageNumber
```

> **Note**
>
> If you feel a nagging sense of discomfort from that last source code line, there's a good reason for it: that expression is written using Visual Basic. Right about now you may be thinking, "Darn it, I chose the wrong language; Visual Basic is so much more awesome than C#. Even the SQL Server reporting tools use it." What you're feeling is called Programmer's Remorse, and it's quite common. The feeling will pass. In the meantime, here are some things you should know about these Visual Basic expressions: (1) string concatenation uses the & operator instead of +; (2) the ! symbol is a shortcut for looking up items by key from a dictionary-like collection; and (3) Visual Basic includes some built-in functions, like *Left*, used to manipulate strings and other expressions.

The *Globals* pseudo-object includes a few members that you can use in the report. How did I know to use *Globals!PageNumber*? I built the expression visually using the Expression Editor. To access it, right-click on the *TextBox* control and select Expression from the shortcut menu. The editor, shown in Figure 21-9, lets you build up a new expression (or modify an existing expression) using lists of functions and field names. The actual functions just happen to be Visual Basic functions, but their common names should make them recognizable to C# developers.

Figure 21-9. The Expression Editor

Support for Grouping and Sorting

Grouping of data is common in printed reports. To add grouping to our report, we need to embed our existing *List* control (the detail record) within another *List* control (the group), and set various properties on the group *List* control to determine the method of data grouping.

Let's try it. Add another *List* control (called *Tablix2* by default) to the report body, and give it twice the height as the existing *List* control (called *Tablix1*). Then, drag *Tablix1* (the detail record) into *Tablix2* (the new group), placing it toward the bottom. Your report should look like Figure 21-10.

Figure 21-10. A grouping list added to the report

To configure the group, click on the group surface. At the bottom edge of the editor, you should see a Row Groups panel, with a single "(Details1)" entry. Double-click on that entry to bring up the Group Properties form. With the General tab selected, locate the Group Expressions area and click the Add button. Enter the following text in the Group On field that suddenly appears.

```
=Left(Fields!FullName.Value, 1)
```

This expression tells the *Tablix2* control to group its detail results by the first character of the first name field.

On this same form, select the Advanced panel, and enter the following text in the Document Map field.

```
="Letter: " & Left(Fields!FullName.Value, 1)
```

The document map enables a clickable hyperlink list into the different groups of the report. When we run the report a little later, we'll see this map just to the left of the report display surface.

The records in the *Activity* table are ordered for the convenience of the programmer (me). But the report user probably wants to see them sorted in some reasonable fashion. Select the Sorting panel, click the Add button on that panel, and add the following text to the Sort On field that appears.

```
=Fields!FullName.Value
```

As expected, this will sort the data by the *FullName* field. Click the OK button to save these changes, and return to the report surface.

We still need to add something that will make each group stand out. Add a *TextBox* control to the *Tablix2* grouping control. Put it in the upper-left corner of that parent control, and type the following text into it.

```
=Left(Fields!FullName.Value, 1)
```

I also set its *BackgroundColor* property to Black, its Color property to White, and its Font property to "Calibri, 12pt, Normal, Bold, None" just for looks.

Running the report gives the results in Figure 21-11. Notice the document map along the left edge of the window, and the grouped single-letter titles before each grouped section.

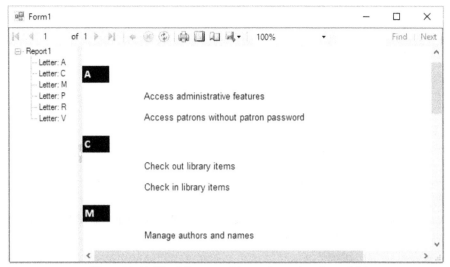

Figure 21-11. The full report, with grouping and sorting enabled

Enhanced Style Formatting

Probably the coolest feature of RDLC reports is that many of the properties for items placed on the report surface can include conditional expressions. This means that you can conditionally alter, say, the visual properties of a *TextBox* control based on the value of a field in the current record.

In the "Project" section of this chapter, we'll write a report that uses due dates for items currently checked out. If the item is past due, I want to show the due date in red. Normally, a *TextBox* control's *Color* property (which controls font color) is set to Black. To have that field respond to overdue items, I will replace the default value with the following expression.

```
=IIf(Fields!DueDate.Value < Today, "Red", "Black")
```

Visual Basic's *IIf* function is similar to C#'s *?:* ternary operator, returning a value based on a Boolean test expression.

Using Custom Data

Although it is very common to generate reports from databases, you can actually use data from virtually any source. When using the *ReportViewer* control, any data source that implements the *IEnumerable* interface is good enough. That includes all collections, arrays, and LINQ query results. The report isn't that picky, as long as the data is formatted as it expects. For the report we just made, we can ditch the actual data and supply our own fake data. This intercepting and substituting of data is like something out of a spy thriller. But we must follow a few rules to make it work.

- When we dragged the *Activity.FullName* field from the data source to the report surface, the report (actually, the *Tablix1* control) got this funny idea that all data had to come from a data source named *LibraryDataSet_Activity*, the name we entered when setting up the data set properties. Any data source we use in place of the real one must keep this name.
- The fake data source must include the *FullName* field, since that is what the report fields expect.

Those rules aren't so bad. So, here's what we need to do: create a fake data source, intercept the report just before it tries to get the data from the Library database, and insert our own data instead.

For a fake data source, we'll need a class that includes at least a *FullName* property.

```
public class FakeActivityRecord
{
    public FakeActivityRecord(long whatID,
        string whatFullName)
    {
        this.ID = whatID;
        this.FullName = whatFullName;
    }

    public long ID { get; set; }
    public string FullName { get; set; }
}
```

The exposed fields must be properties, and not just public fields; the report viewer doesn't recognize standard member fields.

If you look at the source code for *Form1*, you'll find that the following code was added to the *Form_Load* event handler when we linked the report viewer with the RDLC report.

```
this.ActivityTableAdapter.Fill(this.LibraryDataSet.Activity);
this.reportViewer1.RefreshReport();
```

It's that first line that loads the data from the Library database's *Activity* table and links it to the report. We need to replace those two wizard-generated lines with code that cuts off the real data at the pass.

```
// ----- Create a fake table of fake records.
List<FakeActivityRecord> fakeSource =
    new List<FakeActivityRecord>();

// ----- Add each of the fake records.
fakeSource.Add(new FakeActivityRecord(1, "Do some work"));
fakeSource.Add(new FakeActivityRecord(2, "Take a nap"));
fakeSource.Add(new FakeActivityRecord(3, "Write a program"));

// ----- The report was already bound to the true
//       data source. Delete it.
this.reportViewer1.LocalReport.DataSources.Clear();

// ----- Build a new data source. Remember, it must have
//       the same name.
Microsoft.Reporting.WinForms.ReportDataSource
    fakeReportSource = new
    Microsoft.Reporting.WinForms.ReportDataSource();
fakeReportSource.Name = "LibraryDataSet_Activity";
fakeReportSource.Value = fakeSource;

// ----- Connect the data source to the report, and we're done.
this.reportViewer1.LocalReport.DataSources.Add(
    fakeReportSource);
this.reportViewer1.RefreshReport();
```

Figure 21-12 shows the report with the fake data on display.

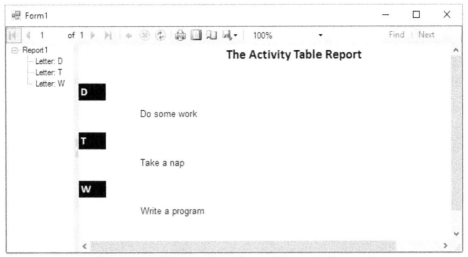

Figure 21-12. This fake data will not self-destruct in five seconds

Supplying Custom Data Sources

Substituting data at the last second is fine and all, but what if you want to design a report that doesn't depend on a database at all? You can do that, too, by supplying a fully custom data source. RDLC reports require some sort of data source schema at design time; you just can't supply fully custom data on the fly when running the report. But you can supply a custom schema based on a class in your application.

For the class, we'll stick with the `FakeActivityRecord` we created in the previous section. Then we will design a data source from this class. Select the Project→Add New Data Source menu command. When the Data Source Configuration Wizard has appeared in the past, you have always selected Database as the source for the data. This time, select Object, as shown in Figure 21-13.

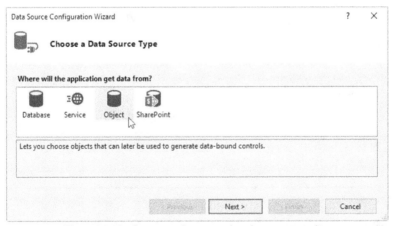

Figure 21-13. Creating a data source based on a custom object

When you click the Next button, a hierarchy of all the classes in your application appears. Expand the SimpleReport branch and locate and select the `FakeActivityRecord` class. (Its location will vary based on where you chose to add it in your test application.) Click the Finish button. `FakeActivityRecord` now appears as a data source in the Data Sources panel.

Now you can drag and drop this data source's `FullName` field onto a new RDLC report design surface. Add a new report to your project (not a form with a report viewer, but an RDLC report), and follow the same steps we used previously to design the first report. This time, use `SimpleReport` as the Data Source, and choose `FakeActivityRecord` from the Available Datasets field.

To test this new report, I removed the original `Form1` from the project and added a brand-new `Form1`. I also added a `ReportViewer` control to its surface and docked it, but I did not link it to the RDLC report. This keeps things a lot cleaner as there are no binding source controls and whatnot to worry about. Then I added this code to the form's `Load` event handler.

```
// ----- Link to the RDLC report design.
this.reportViewer1.LocalReport.ReportEmbeddedResource =
    "SimpleReport.Report2.rdlc";

// ----- Create a fake table of fake records.
List<FakeActivityRecord> fakeSource =
    new List<FakeActivityRecord>();

// ----- Add each of the fake records.
fakeSource.Add(new FakeActivityRecord(1, "Breakfast"));
fakeSource.Add(new FakeActivityRecord(2, "Lunch"));
fakeSource.Add(new FakeActivityRecord(3, "Dinner"));

// ----- Build a new data source.
Microsoft.Reporting.WinForms.ReportDataSource
    fakeReportSource = new
    Microsoft.Reporting.WinForms.ReportDataSource();
fakeReportSource.Name = "SimpleReport_FakeActivityRecord";
fakeReportSource.Value = fakeSource;

// ----- Connect the data source to the report,
//       and we're done.
this.reportViewer1.LocalReport.DataSources.Add(
    fakeReportSource);
this.reportViewer1.RefreshReport();
```

It's pretty similar to the previous custom code, although the data source name is now `SimpleReport_FakeActivityRecord`, the name I entered when defining the new data set (although you can call it whatever you want).

I've saved a copy of both custom reports in the installation directory for the book's source code samples. Look in the subdirectory named *Simple Report*. Before running the report that draws its data from the database, you need to update the *LibraryDataSet* so that it refers to your own SQL Server instance instead of *MYSYSTEM*.

Summary

Although this chapter included many pretty pictures and a lot of instructions, we only scratched the surface of the features available in the reporting controls included with .NET. I think I bruised my brain when I tried to study up on every available feature, but perhaps your brain is better prepared for the task. Still, if you don't find it exactly to your liking, you can use one of the other reporting features I listed at the start of the chapter, or even opt for a different third-party solution.

Reports are an important part of the business developer's daily life. Finding the right reporting tool (and getting comfortable with its features) is not only a good suggestion, it is a necessity in the world of report-hungry software users.

Project

When we last left the Technical Resource Kit document for the Library Project, it listed five built-in reports.

- Report #1: Items Checked Out Report
- Report #2: Items Overdue Report
- Report #3: Items Missing Report
- Report #4: Fines Owed by Patrons Report
- Report #5: Library Database Statistics Report

We'll add these five reports to the project in this chapter. Before we write any code, we need to figure out how we're going to get the data. Since the data will come from the Library database, we just need to craft the SQL statement for each report that will link to the designed report.

The fifth "Statistics" report will list things such as the number of items, the number of patrons, and other similar statistical values from the Library database. Since this data can't really come from a single SQL statement, we'll extract the data from the database and build a custom data source that feeds into the report.

Crafting the SQL Statements

The first "Items Checked Out" report lists the patron name and item title for every item currently checked out by the patron. It involves the *Patron* table (to get the patron name), the *PatronCopy* table (the checkout event), the *ItemCopy* table (the actual item checked out), and the *NamedItem* table (where the item title appears). We'll also include the *CodeMediaType* table, which tells us whether the item is a book, a CD, or some other media type.

Microsoft SQL Server Management Studio includes a visual Query Designer that we can use to design the query. Figure 21-14 shows the five needed tables as linked together by the designer.

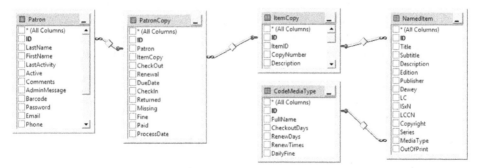

Figure 21-14. The five tables in the checked-out items query

Whether you use the Query Designer or build the SQL statement by hand, you eventually come up with something similar to the following, which we'll use within the Library application.

```
/* ----- Report #1: Items checked out report. */
SELECT PA.LastName + ', ' + PA.FirstName AS PatronName,
    PA.Barcode AS PatronBarcode,
    PC.DueDate, IC.CopyNumber, IC.Barcode AS ItemBarcode,
```

```
        NI.Title, CMT.FullName AS MediaName
    FROM Patron AS PA
        INNER JOIN PatronCopy AS PC ON PA.ID = PC.Patron
        INNER JOIN ItemCopy AS IC ON PC.ItemCopy = IC.ID
        INNER JOIN NamedItem AS NI ON IC.ItemID = NI.ID
        INNER JOIN CodeMediaType AS CMT ON NI.MediaType = CMT.ID
    WHERE PC.Returned = 0
        AND PC.Missing = 0
        AND IC.Missing = 0
    ORDER BY NI.Title, IC.CopyNumber, PA.LastName, PA.FirstName
```

This query links up all of the tables, and then requests every record that has not been returned (*PC.Returned = 0*). It ignores any item marked as missing (*PC.Missing = 0 AND IC.Missing = 0*). This query will eventually drive the report. But for now, keep in mind that RDLC reports don't actually need a real SQL statement or database table for the report schema. We can also build a compatible schema by hand using a class. This turns out to be a lot cleaner since we won't have a lot of dataset-related files strewn throughout the project source code. (The *LibraryDataSet* data source we created in the sample report earlier in this chapter added four source files and nearly 50KB of source code to the project, not counting the RDLC report! The class-based data source didn't add any code other than the class definition itself, and a little bit of XML in the RDLC file.)

As for the data source schema, we can extrapolate it from the *SELECT* clause of the SQL query. If we were to design a class with a matching schema, it would look like this.

```
class Report1Schema
{
    public string PatronName { get; set; }
    public string PatronBarcode { get; set; }
    public DateTime DueDate { get; set; }
    public int CopyNumber { get; set; }
    public string ItemBarcode { get; set; }
    public string Title { get; set; }
    public string MediaName { get; set; }
}
```

The next two reports are for "Overdue Items" and "Missing Items." For me, the schema for Report #1 is exactly what I want to see in these other two reports, so let's use Report #1's SQL statement as a starting point. All we need to do is change the *WHERE* clause. For the overdue items report, use this *WHERE* clause.

```
WHERE PC.Returned = 0
    AND PC.Missing = 0
    AND IC.Missing = 0
    AND PC.DueDate < GETDATE()
```

The missing items report will use this *WHERE* clause.

```
WHERE PC.Missing = 1
    OR IC.Missing = 1
```

The fourth report displays the amount of fines still owed by patrons, so it will require a different schema. Here's its SQL statement, which uses some aggregate grouping features.

```
/* ----- Report #4: Fines owed by patron. */
SELECT PA.LastName + ', ' + PA.FirstName AS PatronName,
    PA.Barcode AS PatronBarcode,
    SUM(PC.Fine - PC.Paid) AS FinesDue
FROM Patron AS PA
```

```
       INNER JOIN PatronCopy AS PC ON PA.ID = PC.Patron
   GROUP BY PA.LastName + ', ' + PA.FirstName, PA.Barcode
   HAVING SUM(PC.Fine - PC.Paid) > 0
   ORDER BY PatronName
```

Here's the schema that goes with Report #4.

```
class Report4Schema
{
    public string PatronName { get; set; }
    public string PatronBarcode { get; set; }
    public decimal FinesDue { get; set; }
}
```

For the final report, we'll just use a schema with two string values: a statistic name, and its related value. Here's its schema.

```
class Report5Schema
{
    public string EntryName { get; set; }
    public string EntryValue { get; set; }
}
```

Well, that's enough preparation. Let's start coding.

Project Access

Load the "Chapter 21 (Before) Code" project, either through the New Project templates or by accessing the project directly from the installation directory. To see the code in its final form, load "Chapter 21 (After) Code" instead.

Adding Report Schemas

The *ReportSchemas.cs* file, already added to the project, includes the three schemas used for the five built-in reports. Just to remind us of the members, here are the public property definitions included in each class.

```
public class ReportSchemaPatronItems
{
    // ----- Used for the following reports:
    //          Report #1: Items checked out report
    //          Report #2: Items overdue report
    //          Report #3: Items missing report
    public string PatronName {get; set;}
    public string PatronBarcode {get; set;}
    public DateTime DueDate {get; set;}
    public int CopyNumber {get; set;}
    public string ItemBarcode {get; set;}
    public string Title {get; set;}
    public string MediaName {get; set;}
}

public class ReportSchemaPatronFines
{
    // ----- Used for the following reports:
    //          Report #4: Fines owed by patron
    public string PatronName {get; set;}
    public string PatronBarcode {get; set;}
    public decimal FinesDue {get; set;}
```

```
    }

    public class ReportSchemaStatistics
    {
        // ----- Used for the following reports:
        //            Report #5: Library database statistics report
        public string EntryName {get; set;}
        public string EntryValue {get; set;}
    }
```

Once the schema classes are in the project, you will need to build the project before those classes can be used in RDLC reports as data sources. In the Library Project, build the project now with the Build→Build Library menu command. All three schemas should then appear as sources in the Data Sources panel (see Figure 21-15). If the Data Sources panel is closed, open it using the View→Other Windows→Data Sources menu command.

Figure 21-15. The three data source schemas

Adding Reports

Since we already jointly created an RDLC report earlier in the chapter, I went ahead and added the five built-in reports for you.

ReportCheckedOut.rdlc

This file implements Report #1, the "Items Checked Out" report. It uses the *ReportSchemaPatronItems* class schema, and includes three columns in the main data list: patron name/barcode, item name/barcode/details, and due date. For the item name field, I wanted to present additional information when available. The item name, copy number, and media type are required values, but item barcode is optional. Here's the format I desired.

```
    Item Name (#CopyNumber, MediaType, Barcode)
```

To get this result, I had to concatenate the various source fields together, and use a Visual Basic conditional function (*IIf*) to optionally include the barcode and its comma (entered all on a single line).

```
    =Fields!Title.Value & " (#" & CStr(Fields!CopyNumber.Value) &
        ", " & Fields!MediaName.Value &
```

```
IIf(IsNothing(Fields!ItemBarcode.Value), "",
    ", " & Fields!ItemBarcode.Value) & ")"
```

The *CStr* function forces its argument to a string, while the *IsNothing* function returns *true* if the expression is *null*. As mentioned earlier, the due date field has an expression in its *Color* property that turns the text red when the item is overdue.

ReportOverdue.rdlc

This report shows a list of all overdue items in the system. Since everything will be overdue, I set the due date field to always use red for its font color. Other than that and the title, the report is basically identical to the checked-out items report.

ReportMissing.rdlc

This report shows a list of all items marked as missing. Even though the schema includes a due date field, I don't use it in this report. The rest of the report is basically identical to the checked-out items report.

ReportPatronFines.rdlc

This report lists all patrons that still owe fines, and the amount of the fine due. It uses the *ReportSchemaPatronFines* class schema. The field that displays the fine has a "C" in its *Format* property. This formatting code forces the decimal value to display as currency using the culture settings on the local system. This *Format* property uses the same codes as those recognized by the *string.Format* method.

ReportStatistics.rdlc

Report #5 displays record counts from some of the tables in the Library database. This is the only report that uses the *ReportSchemaStatistics* class schema. The report itself displays two strings per record: a name and a value. It depends on the calling code to format those fields properly.

Adding a Report Viewer

It's time to add a *ReportViewer* control. Since a single *ReportViewer* control can display any type of RDLC report, we'll just add a single form to handle all five built-in reports.

Add a new form named *ReportBuiltinViewer.cs* to the project. Set its *Text* property to *Library Report* and its *WindowState* property to *Maximized*. Also, load the project's icon (*Book.ico*) into the *Icon* property. You'll find a copy of this file in the project installation directory. If you want, you can size the form to some reasonable starting point for a report, but each report will start out maximized when used.

Add a *ReportViewer* control named *ReportContent* to the form, and set its *Dock* property to *Fill*. Set both the *ShowBackButton* and *ShowDocumentMapButton* properties to *False*.

The code we will add to this form is a variation of code we wrote earlier in this chapter. The code that starts each report will pass to this form the name of the report RDLC file, the name of the data schema used, and the actual data. Since these reports will be modeless (you can keep them open while still using other parts of the Library program), we can't let the calling code wait around for the user to close the report before we discard the report data. We'll let the report dispose of the data itself. To do this, we need to keep a reference to that data. Add the following statement to the *ReportBuiltinViewer* form class.

Insert Snippet
Insert Chapter 21, Snippet Item 1.

```
private object StoreDataTable;
```

Remember, reports can use a variety of data source formats, including true database connections, arrays, and collections. Reports #1 through #4 will use a *DataTable* instance, and Report #5 will pass a generic *List* collection.

While we're up near the top of the file, insert a new *using* directive just after the existing collection of directives, one that will provide easy access to reporting features.

Insert Snippet
Insert Chapter 21, Snippet Item 2.

```
using Microsoft.Reporting.WinForms;
```

The best time to dispose of the data is when the report is closing. Add a *FormClosing* event handler to the form. Then add the following code to it, which confirms that the data supports the disposal process before calling the *Dispose* method.

Insert Snippet
Insert Chapter 21, Snippet Item 3.

```
// ----- Get rid of the data.
if (StoreDataTable is IDisposable)
    ((IDisposable)StoreDataTable).Dispose();
```

The code that opens this display form will pass in the essential report values through a public method named *StartReport*. Add its code now.

Insert Snippet
Insert Chapter 21, Snippet Item 4.

```
public void StartReport(string whichReport,
    string whichDataSchema, object whichData)
{
    // ----- Run one of the built-in reports. whichReport
    //       is the name of the RDLC report file, in the
    //       format "Library.xxx.rdlc." whichDataSchema
    //       provides the name of the schema to use, in
    //       the format "Library_xxx." whichDataSet is the
    //       actual data to link to the report, which must
    //       match the schema.
    ReportDataSource customDataSource = new ReportDataSource();

    // ----- Connect the viewer, the report, and the data.
    ReportContent.LocalReport.
        ReportEmbeddedResource = whichReport;
    customDataSource.Name = whichDataSchema;
    customDataSource.Value = whichData;
    ReportContent.LocalReport.DataSources.Add(
        customDataSource);

    // ----- Display the report.
    StoreDataTable = whichData;
    this.Show();
}
```

This code tells the viewer which report to use as an embedded resource, and then attaches the data as a custom data source. "Local" in these property names indicates a local (client) report instead of a "server" report that runs within SQL Server.

When we were playing with the reports before, we saw that the default display mode was the fill-the-entire-screen-with-page-content mode. Personally, I like to see those fake page boundaries. The *ReportViewer* control doesn't include a property that lets us change this default view (why not?), but we can still adjust the initial display style through methods on the control. When we added the report viewer to the form, Visual Studio also added the following statement to the form's *Load* event handler.

```
ReportContent.RefreshReport();
```

Add the following code just before that statement.

Insert Snippet
Insert Chapter 21, Snippet Item 5.

```
// ----- Generate and display the report.
ReportContent.SetDisplayMode(DisplayMode.PrintLayout);
ReportContent.ZoomMode = ZoomMode.Percent;
ReportContent.ZoomPercent = 100;
```

Adding Built-in Reports

I forget how long ago we added the *ReportSelect.cs* form that drives reporting, but it is already there in the project. In case you forgot what it looked like (I did), Figure 21-16 gives us a refresher.

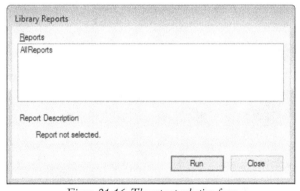

Figure 21-16. The report selection form

We previously added support for our five built-in reports in this form's code. In a tribute to the never-ending reality of forgetting to finish all of the code, we need to add some code that we overlooked earlier. If you use an XML report configuration file to populate the report list, and you provide a description for each report in the XML, each entry displays that description in the lower half of the report selection form. But if you don't use a configuration file, and just depend on the form to add the five built-in reports by default (which it does), the form won't display associated descriptions, because we forgot to add them. Add a function to the *ReportSelect* class that returns a short description for each of the five reports.

Insert Snippet
Insert Chapter 21, Snippet Item 6.

```
private string GetBuiltinReportDescription(
    ReportItemEnum whichReport)
{
```

```
// ----- Return a predefined description for the
//       built-in reports.
switch (whichReport)
{
    case ReportItemEnum.BuiltInCheckedOut:
        return "Displays all items currently checked " +
            "out, sorted by name.";
    case ReportItemEnum.BuiltInOverdue:
        return "Displays all overdue items, " +
            "sorted by name.";
    case ReportItemEnum.BuiltInMissing:
        return "Displays all missing items, " +
            "sorted by name.";
    case ReportItemEnum.BuiltInFinesOwed:
        return "Displays all unpaid fines owed by " +
            "patrons, sorted by patron name.";
    case ReportItemEnum.BuiltInStatistics:
        return "Displays some record counts from the " +
            "Library database.";
    default:
        return "There is no description for this report.";
}
}
```

We'll call this code from two places. The first is in the *LoadReportGroup* method. This code loads in the XML report configuration file. If that file includes one of the built-in reports, but doesn't supply a description with it, we'll supply the description ourselves. About halfway through that code, you'll find these lines.

```
// ----- So, what type of entry is it?
if (scanNode.Attributes("type").ToString() == "built-in")
```

A few lines below this is the following statement.

```
reportEntry.ItemType = (ReportItemEnum)Convert.
    ToInt32(reportEntry.ReportPath);
```

Add the following code just after that statement.

Insert Snippet
Insert Chapter 21, Snippet Item 7.

```
if (reportEntry.Description.Length == 0)
    reportEntry.Description =
        GetBuiltinReportDescription(reportEntry.ItemType);
```

The second need for the built-in descriptions appears in the *RefreshReportList* method. This method makes the call to *LoadReportGroup* to retrieve the XML configuration. But if after that the report list is still empty, *RefreshReportList* adds in the five default reports, which each require a description. Near the end of the method, within a *for* loop, you'll find this closing statement.

```
// ----- Add the report entry to the list.
AllReports.Items.Add(reportEntry);
```

Add the following code just before that statement.

Insert Snippet
Insert Chapter 21, Snippet Item 8.

```
reportEntry.Description =
    GetBuiltinReportDescription(reportEntry.ItemType);
```

OK, that's it for the fix-up code. Now back to writing the actual reports. The code to start each of the five reports already exists in the *ReportSelect* form's *ActRun_Click* event handler. Most of that code includes a *switch* statement that acts as a switchboard for the selected report. Here's the part that calls the five built-in reports.

```
case ReportItemEnum.BuiltInCheckedOut:
    // ----- Items Checked Out
    // TODO: Write BasicReportCheckedOut();
    break;
case ReportItemEnum.BuiltInOverdue:
    // ----- Items Overdue
    // TODO: Write BasicReportOverdue();
    break;
case ReportItemEnum.BuiltInMissing:
    // ----- Items Missing
    // TODO: Write BasicReportMissing();
    break;
case ReportItemEnum.BuiltInFinesOwed:
    // ----- Fines Owed by Patrons
    // TODO: Write BasicReportFines();
    break;
case ReportItemEnum.BuiltInStatistics:
    // ----- Library Database Statistics
    // TODO: Write BasicReportStatistics();
    break;
```

Clearly, this code isn't accomplishing much. Change each of the *TODO* lines, removing the *TODO: Write* portion of the statement and the initial comment symbol. Here is one of the lines to be updated.

```
// TODO: Write BasicReportCheckedOut();
```

Change the code to the following instead.

```
BasicReportCheckedOut();
```

Do that for each of the five TODO lines.

Exposing these five method calls means that we have to write those methods, darn it. These methods will retrieve the data for the report, and send that data to the report viewer, along with the name of the RDLC file. They're actually quite short and simple, considering the beautiful reports you will get out of them. Let's start by adding the *BasicReportCheckedOut* method to the *ReportSelect* class.

Insert Snippet
Insert Chapter 21, Snippet Item 9.

```
private void BasicReportCheckedOut()
{
    // ----- Run built-in report #1: Items checked out report.
    string sqlText;
    DataTable reportData;
    ReportBuiltinViewer reportForm;

    // ----- Retrieve the data as a dataset.
    sqlText = "SELECT PA.LastName + ', ' + " +
```

```
            "PA.FirstName AS PatronName, " +
            "PA.Barcode AS PatronBarcode, " +
            "PC.DueDate, IC.CopyNumber, " +
            "IC.Barcode AS ItemBarcode, " +
            "NI.Title, CMT.FullName AS MediaName " +
            "FROM Patron AS PA " +
            "INNER JOIN PatronCopy AS PC ON PA.ID = PC.Patron " +
            "INNER JOIN ItemCopy AS IC ON PC.ItemCopy = IC.ID " +
            "INNER JOIN NamedItem AS NI ON IC.ItemID = NI.ID " +
            "INNER JOIN CodeMediaType AS CMT " +
            "ON NI.MediaType = CMT.ID " +
            "WHERE PC.Returned = 0 " +
            "AND PC.Missing = 0 " +
            "AND IC.Missing = 0 " +
            "ORDER BY NI.Title, IC.CopyNumber, " +
            "PA.LastName, PA.FirstName";
        try
        {
            reportData = CreateDataTable(sqlText);
        }
        catch (Exception ex)
        {
            GeneralError(
                "ReportSelect.BasicReportCheckedOut.Retrieve", ex);
            return;
        }

        // ----- Check for no data.
        if (reportData.Rows.Count == 0)
        {
            reportData.Dispose();
            MessageBox.Show("No items are checked out.",
                ProgramTitle, MessageBoxButtons.OK,
                MessageBoxIcon.Exclamation);
            return;
        }

        // ----- Send the data to the report.
        reportForm = new ReportBuiltinViewer();
        try
        {
            reportForm.StartReport(
                "Library.ReportCheckedOut.rdlc",
                "Library_ReportSchemaPatronItems", reportData);
        }
        catch (Exception ex)
        {
            GeneralError(
                "ReportSelect.BasicReportCheckedOut.Start", ex);
        }
    }
```

The code retrieves the report-specific records from the database, and makes sure that at least one record was included. (We could have added the SQL statement to the Library database as either a stored procedure or a view, and called that instead. For the purposes of this tutorial, it was simpler to store the statement directly in code.) It then calls the report viewer, passing the name of the RDLC file, the schema name (in the format *ProjectName_ClassName*), and the data table.

Next, add the *BasicReportOverdue* and *BasicReportMissing* methods. I won't show the code here since, except for the name of the RDLC file and the *WHERE* clause in the SQL statement, they are identical to *BasicReportCheckedOut*.

Insert Snippet
Insert Chapter 21, Snippet Item 10.

Add in the *BasicReportFines* method, which handles built-in Report #4.

Insert Snippet
Insert Chapter 21, Snippet Item 11.

This routine is also quite similar to the *BasicReportCheckedOut* method, but it uses the SQL statement we designed earlier for patron fine retrieval. It also uses a different schema and report name.

```
reportForm.StartReport("Library.ReportPatronFines.rdlc",
    "Library_ReportSchemaPatronFines", reportData);
```

The last method to add to *ReportSelect.cs* is *BasicReportStatistics*, which handles built-in Report #5. It's a little different from the other four because it gathers data from six different tables, one at a time. In each case, it retrieves a count of the number of records in a database table. The results are then stored in a generic collection (*Generic.List*), where each list entry is an instance of *ReportSchemaStatistics*, the class we used for the fifth report's data schema. What a coincidence!

Here's the code for *BasicReportStatistics* for you to add now to the *ReportSelect* form class.

Insert Snippet
Insert Chapter 21, Snippet Item 12.

```
private void BasicReportStatistics()
{
    // ----- Run built-in report #5:
    //          Library database statistics report.
    string sqlText;
    List<ReportSchemaStatistics> reportData;
    ReportSchemaStatistics oneEntry;
    ReportBuiltinViewer reportForm;
    int resultValue;
    const string tableSets = "Author,Publisher,Subject," +
        "NamedItem,ItemCopy,Patron";
    const string tableTitles = "Authors,Publishers," +
        "Subject Headings,Items,Item Copies,Patrons";

    // ----- Build the report data. It's all counts from
    //          different tables.
    reportData = new List<ReportSchemaStatistics>();
    for (int counter = 1; counter <=
        CountSubStr(tableSets, ",") + 1; counter++)
    {
        // ----- Process one table.
        sqlText = "SELECT COUNT(*) FROM " +
            tableSets.GetSubStr(",", counter);
```

```
    try
    {
        resultValue = DBGetInteger(
            ExecuteSQLReturn(sqlText));
    }
    catch (Exception ex)
    {
        GeneralError(
            "ReportSelect.BasicReportStatistics." +
            tableSets.GetSubStr(",", counter), ex);
        return;
    }

    // ----- Add it to the report data.
    oneEntry = new ReportSchemaStatistics();
    oneEntry.EntryName =
        tableTitles.GetSubStr(",", counter);
    oneEntry.EntryValue = resultValue.ToString();
    reportData.Add(oneEntry);
}

// ----- Send the data to the report.
reportForm = new ReportBuiltinViewer();
try
{
    reportForm.StartReport(
        "Library.ReportStatistics.rdlc",
        "Library_ReportSchemaStatistics", reportData);
}
catch (Exception ex)
{
    GeneralError(
        "ReportSelect.BasicReportStatistics.Start", ex);
}
}
```

Since we really need to get the same information (*COUNT(*)*) for each of the six tables involved, I implemented the code as a loop, and built the SQL statement for each one as I passed through the loop. A friendly table name and the record count are then stored in the generic list, which is eventually sent to the report.

You can now run the application and use the five built-in reports. You must log in as a librarian or administrator, and then access the Print Reports panel on the main form.

Believe it or not, we're almost finished with the application. The only big thing left to do is to process past-due patron items to see whether fines are required. We'll add this code in the next chapter, and also take a look at licensing.

Chapter 22

Licensing Your Application

Proper .NET content licensing can mean the difference between marketplace dominance and financial bankruptcy. And I'm just talking about trying to understand the license agreement that comes with Visual Studio. You still have to figure out a licensing method for your own application before you send it to your customers.

Licensing and license agreements are an essential means of protecting the intellectual property you've worked so hard to develop. How does licensing work? The key is found in the roots of the word itself: *license* comes from "li-" (to tell a lie) and "-cense" (from "cents" as in "pennies"). Together, these roots mean "to tell lies about small units of currency." The confusion brought about in trying to figure out what this means keeps the bad guys perplexed and occupied long enough so that they don't steal your application.

If this method doesn't work, there are software solutions, some of which I'll review in this chapter. Part of the discussion focuses on designing a licensing system that will appear in the Library Project. The .NET Framework does include classes for component licensing, but they exist primarily for designers of controls used by other programmers within the Visual Studio IDE, and not for end-user applications. We will not be covering these licensing features in this chapter. If you're curious about such features, start by reading about the License Compiler (*lc.exe*) in the MSDN documentation.

For apps destined for distribution through the Windows Store, Microsoft has crafted a set of standard licensing terms that apply to all such apps. Although the general concepts in this chapter apply to this standard license, I will not be discussing Windows Store app distribution or licensing.

Software Licensing Options

Back in the early days of software, licensing wasn't an issue: if you could get to the computer, it was because you were authorized. All user interaction with the system was through the programmers and technicians. If some user wanted to steal something, it would be in the form of twenty tons of steel, wires, and vacuum tubes. Fun? Yes. Easy? No.

Today, it's a different story. Most users are non-technical, and some are unethical. So, now we have licensing agreements backed up by teams of lawyers. But we also have software, software that can delicately enforce some of the rules. For a particular piece of software, there is still the question, "How much licensing enforcement code do I add to my application?" The amount of software control you include will fall somewhere in the Freedom-Security continuum shown in Figure 22-1.

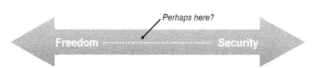

Figure 22-1. The licensing enforcement continuum: where are you on it?

If you go for the Freedom end of the spectrum ("convenient for users and hackers"), you will have to go on the trustworthiness of your users, and any armed guards you have dispatched to their offices, to keep the program in compliance. At the Security end of the scale ("secure for programmers and highly paid law firms"), the software implements practices and policies that ensure that only licensed users of the application ever use or install it; no armed guards needed.

The rest of this section discusses some possible options you could choose within the Freedom-Security range.

License Agreement Only

The License Agreement Only method clearly opts for freedom over security. When you supply the user with software, it comes with a carefully crafted license agreement that lays out the terms of use for both the user and the software supplier. It generally gives the user certain rights as to installation, use, and distribution of the software.

When you write an application for use only within a specific organization or by a small group of users with whom you will have regular contact, the License Agreement Only method may be just what you need. In fact, I would bet that most Visual C# applications are in this vein. Many, and probably most, applications designed for the Windows platform target a specific organization or line of business, tied to a specific custom database. Such systems often require very little in the way of license enforcement, since the application is useless when carried outside the building where it was meant to reside.

Even if your software achieves widespread distribution, this licensing scheme may still be the way to go. Many open source applications, including a major operating system that rhymes with "Plinux," use the Free Software Foundation's GNU General Public License (http://www.fsf.org/licensing/licenses/gpl.html) as their primary licensing and distribution policy.

Generated General License Key

If you need a bit more control over the distribution, installation, and use of an application, you can impose a *generated general license key*—basically a password that allows the application to be installed or used. Such keys are often entered at the start of the installation process, with the user prompted for a specific key. Without the key, it's goodbye installation.

The software vendor will need a way to generate a good set of unique installation keys. There are a couple of options.

- Just generate a sequential serial number, and mix into it a product ID and version number. The great thing about such a key is that it is easy to generate. The installation program doesn't need to perform any complex verification logic on the key. It only needs to ensure that the general format is correct. In a way, it's not much more secure than using just a license agreement, since anyone who knows the general format can make up a new key without first getting permission.

- Use a hashed or scrambled key, based on some original serial number or formula that can be verified by the installation program. A well-crafted hashing algorithm can generate a wide range of keys, but make it difficult for others who don't know the formula to generate their own fake keys. Although I am not privy to Microsoft's internal processes, this appears to be the method it uses for its twenty-five-character product keys, including those that target Visual Studio. Although it is difficult for keys to be invented out of whole cloth, the public nature of the keys makes them subject to sharing. For some of its products, Microsoft has combined a product key with some sort of verification or registration process to enhance security.

- Supply a hashed or encrypted key based on a serial number that is (secretly) supplied with the installation program or distribution media. When the user enters the key, it is unencrypted or otherwise prepared, and then compared with the serial number. Only if it matches will the software installation complete properly.

Generated Custom License Key

A custom-generated license key is similar to a general generated key, but uses personal information supplied by the user as part of the generation process. Such a key is more interactive, and requires that the end-user specifically communicate with the software vendor (or an application on its web site) to complete the installation process.

During the purchase or installation process, the user makes specific information (such as the owner's name and the date of purchase) available to the software vendor. The vendor then uses public-private key encryption (asymmetric cryptography) to either fully encrypt or digitally sign the relevant information. The encrypted signature is then returned to the end-user for installation. The installation process uses the public portion of the key pair to either decrypt the content or ensure that the signature is valid.

We will use this license key method in the Library Project, so I'll have more to say about it a little later.

License Key with Hardware Identity or Lock

For paranoid software vendors, or for those who have a legitimate need to keep a tight rein on their installation base, there are solutions that involve regular access to hardware or services to confirm that previously installed software is legal and valid. One popular method uses a dongle, typically a USB port-based device that the software must have access to each time it runs. The software vendor supplies a dongle with the licensed software, and may encode it with date-based or use-based limits.

With the prevalence of the Internet, software vendors also have the option of real-time verification over the Web. Each time the program runs, it could access a known vendor site to engage in a usage verification process. Such a system allows for ongoing monitoring of the software by vendors who may have a business or governmental reason to limit use of the software.

For one of my customer projects, I must access a third-party web site on a monthly basis and download proprietary data for use with that vendor's software. The vendor requires that I always access their web site from a specific machine with a specific IP address. It will refuse to supply the data if I attempt to connect from any other machine. If I have a real need to use a fresh IP address (if, for example, I change Internet service providers), I must submit paperwork to the vendor informing them of the new IP address. It seems pesky, and it is an irritation. But the data they supply is unique and valuable, and they feel they have a business need to protect that investment. Since my customer requires the data, I have no choice but to comply with the monthly verification procedures.

Controlled Access

The highest level of security requires a blatant distrust of the user, although there may be a good reason for this. For highly sensitive applications, the software vendor may make their product available to only a limited number of customers, and then only on a lease basis. As part of the lease agreement, the customer agrees to have a trained staff member of the software vendor on-site, running and maintaining the application for the customer. At the very least, the vendor will require that one of its employees be immediately available to the customer whenever the application is used.

In a world of instant-download mobile software applications, it seems unconscionable that such a system could exist. But in high-risk situations, security concerns are raised to such a level that neither party is willing to fully assume the risks of installing and using the application apart from the other.

Although I was tempted to use this system for the Library Project, I think we'll stick with our original plan of employing a custom-generated license key.

License Agreements

A *license agreement* is a document wherein the party of the first part hereby and does amicably render to the party of the second part certain rights, quid pro quos, treasury bonds, and other benefits; in exchange, the party of the second part will do the same for the party of the first part without respect for any other party or festival.

Let's try that again. A license agreement tells a user, "Go ahead, install and use the software, but you have to follow these rules." Although they are often written in legalese, they can also appear in a real language, such as English. They also range in granted rights, from "You can use this, but when you're finished, you must destroy all copies," to "Use it, and feel free to pass a copy of the program and its source code to your friends and relations."

The Library software provided with this book comes with a license agreement. (I've included it in Appendix B, "Software License Agreement.") When you installed the sample code, you agreed to the terms of the license agreement, including the part about supporting my family financially well into my retirement years. But enough about me; let's talk about license agreements you may want to use for your applications.

If you're developing a DVD catalog program for your cousin Fred, you can probably skip the license agreement part. But any software you craft in a business capacity for use outside your own company should include some sort of agreement between you (or your company) and the user of the software. This agreement could be defined as part of the contract that established the software development project (this is typical for software consulting), or you could include the agreement as a component of the software (common for off-the-shelf programs).

Whichever method you choose, it is important that you state it in written form because it can save you grief down the road. I once had a customer who insisted that I fork over a copy of the source code for an application I wrote for them so that they could enhance it and sell the new version to other businesses (the nerve!). Fortunately, we had a written contract that stated the rules of engagement. They were entitled to a copy of the source code for archive purposes, but they could not use it or derive products from it without written consent from me. This granted a level of safety for them while still providing the means for me to provide the best support possible for their organization. Fortunately, it all came to a happy conclusion, and since that early-1990s code doesn't even run anymore, it's a moot point.

A license agreement usually exists to protect the rights of the software vendor, but it would be useless if it didn't also grant meaningful rights to the user—and some of the rights can be rather generous. Did you know that the standard consumer licensing agreement for Microsoft Office 365 Home edition allows you to install the product simultaneously on up to ten different systems (five PCs and five tablets) using a single licensed copy of the program? It's not a complete install-fest. All devices must belong to the same family, and what is that family doing with five tablets? But it's still a meaningful benefit to the typical user.

The legal minds at my publisher want to remind you that Tim Patrick does not have a sufficient understanding of the law, and cannot advise you on the contents of any licensing agreement you may want to craft for your projects.

Obfuscation

I hinted a little about Visual Studio's obfuscation support in Chapter 5, but it's high time we actually took a look at the features. Visual Studio includes a stripped-down version of Dotfuscator from a company named PreEmptive Solutions (not a part of Microsoft—yet). To access the program, use the Tools→PreEmptive Dotfuscator and Analytics menu command in Visual Studio. The main interface appears in Figure 22-2.

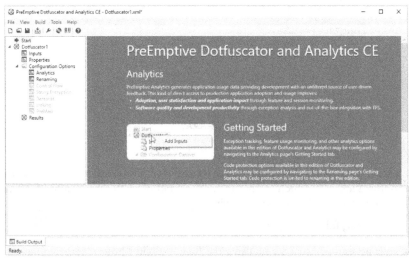

Figure 22-2. It's time to obfuscate!

Even though this is the basic version of the product, you can see that it has a gazillion options. If you want to dive into its enhanced features for your project, that's fantastic. I'll just cover the basic usage here.

Let's recall quickly why you would want to obfuscate your code, or even use the word *obfuscate* in mixed company. Here's some code from the Library Project.

```
public static string CenterText(string origText, int textWidth)
{
    // ----- Center a piece of text in a field width.
    //       If the text is too wide, truncate it.
    string resultText;

    resultText = origText.Trim();
    if (resultText.Length >= textWidth)
    {
        // ----- Truncate as needed.
        return origText.Substring(0, textWidth).Trim();
    }
    else
    {
        // ----- Start with extra spaces.
        return new string(' ', (textWidth -
            origText.Length) / 2) + resultText;
    }
}
```

This code is quite easy to understand, especially with the comments and the meaningful method and variable names. Although .NET obfuscation works at the MSIL level, let's pretend that the obfuscator worked directly on Visual C# code. Obfuscation of this code might produce results similar to the following.

```
public static string A(string AA, int AAA)
{
    string AAAA;

    AAAA = AA.Trim();
    if (AAAA.Length >= AAA)
    {
        return AA.Substring(0, AAA).Trim();
    }
    else
    {
        return new string(' ',
            (AAA - AA.Length) / 2) + AAAA;
    }
}
```

In such a simple routine, we could still figure out the logic, but with more effort than in the original version. Naturally, true obfuscation goes much further than this, scrambling the readability of the code at the IL level, and confounding code readers and hackers alike.

To obfuscate an assembly, follow these steps.

1. Build your project in Visual Studio using the Build→Build [Project Name] menu command.

2. Start Dotfuscator using the Tools→PreEmptive Dotfuscator and Analytics menu command in Visual Studio.

3. Select the Inputs node of the project tree and click the Add Input button, the one that has a green plus sign on it.

4. Browse for your compiled application, and click the OK button. The assembly to use will usually be in the *bin* or *bin\Release* subdirectory within your project's source code directory.

5. Select the Build→Build Project menu command to generate the obfuscated assembly. You will be prompted to save the Dotfuscator project file (an XML file) before the build begins. Save this file to a new directory. When the build occurs, it will save the output assembly in a *Dotfuscated* subdirectory in the same directory that contains the XML project file.

6. The build completes, and the results appear in the Build Output panel. Your obfuscated file is ready to use. The process also generates a *Map.xml* file that documents all the name changes made to types and members within your application. It would be a bad thing to distribute this file with the assembly. It is for your debugging use only.

To prove that the obfuscation took place, use the IL Disassembler tool that comes with Visual Studio to examine each assembly. (Open the Developer Command Prompt for VS2015, then type `ILDASM` on the command line.) Figure 22-3 shows the global variables included in the Library Project's *General.cs* file. The obfuscated version of these same variables appears in Figure 22-4.

```
ActiveConnectionString : private static string
AllHolidays : public static class [mscorlib]System.Collections.Generic.List`1<class Library.HolidaySet>
DefaultItemLocation : public static int64
DefaultLicenseFile : public static literal string
FineGraceDays : public static int32
LoggedInGroupID : public static int64
LoggedInUserID : public static int64
LoggedInUserName : public static string
MainAdminHelpFile : public static string
MainHelpFile : public static string
MatchNone : public static literal int32
MatchPresent : public static literal int32
MaxLibrarySecurity : public static literal valuetype Library.General/LibrarySecurity
NotAuthorizedMessage : public static literal string
ProgramTitle : public static literal string
SearchMatchLimit : public static int32
SecurityProfile : public static bool[]
UseDBVersion : public static literal int32
```

Figure 22-3. Global variables before obfuscation

```
a : public static literal string
b : public static literal string
c : public static literal int32
d : public static literal string
e : public static literal int32
f : public static literal int32
g : public static literal valuetype e/b
h : public static int64
i : public static string
j : public static int64
k : public static bool[]
l : public static int64
m : public static int32
n : public static string
o : public static string
p : public static int32
q : public static class [mscorlib]System.Collections.Generic.List`1<class Library.HolidaySet>
r : private static string
```

Figure 22-4. Global variables after obfuscation

I will not be performing obfuscation on the Library Project through this book's tutorial sections. Feel free to try it out on your own.

The Library Licensing System

The tools and procedures we will use to design the Library Project's licensing system can be built from features discussed in previous chapters.

- The license file contains XML content. (Chapter 13)
- The license appears as a separate file in the same directory as the *Library.exe* assembly. The Library software reads content from the license file. (Chapter 15)
- The license includes a digital signature, which is based on public-private key encryption. (Chapter 11)

Designing the License File

The Library Project's license file contains some basic ownership and rights information related to the user who purchased the software. Here's the XML content I've come up with.

```
<?xml version="1.0" encoding="utf-8"?>
<License>
```

```
<Product>Library Project</Product>
<LicenseDate>1/1/2000</LicenseDate>
<ExpireDate>12/31/2999</ExpireDate>
<CoveredVersion>1.*</CoveredVersion>
<Licensee>John Q. Public</Licensee>
<SerialNumber>LIB-123456789</SerialNumber>
<Signature>
  Digital signature appears here (not shown)
</Signature>
</License>
```

That seems sufficient. The process that builds the digital signature also stores the encrypted signature within the XML content.

Generating the License File

In the "Project" section of this chapter, we'll build a new application that exists solely to generate license files for the Library application. It will have three primary components.

1. Generate and manage the public and private keys used in the signature process.

2. Prompt the user for the license date, expiration date, covered version, licensee name, and serial number for a single license. These are the values that appear in the license file's XML content.

3. Output the XML license file and digitally sign it using the private key.

As promised way back in Chapter 7, this new tool will be developed using Windows Presentation Foundation (WPF) and XAML instead of with Windows Forms. The core XML and file management features needed to generate the license file are the same no matter which user interface library you employ.

Installing the License File

The "Project" section of this chapter will show you how to generate a generic license file. This XML file will be distributed and installed with the Library application using the setup program that we will build in Chapter 24. The file will be named *LibraryLicense.lic* (by default) and will always appear in the same directory as the *Library.exe* application file.

If I were developing a real application for paying customers, and I had a web site that supported a web service, here is one design for installing the license file that I might use.

1. Run the setup program to install the application on the user's workstation.

2. During installation, the setup program prompts the user for the license details that will ultimately appear in the XML license file.

3. The setup program contacts the web service on my vendor web site, and passes the user-supplied values to that registration service.

4. The registration service returns a digitally signed XML file that contains the licensing content.

5. The setup program installs this file along with the application.

6. If for any reason the licensing process does not complete successfully during setup, the main application contains identical licensing code, and can communicate with the registration service itself.

Using the License File

Whenever the Library application runs, it reads in the XML license file and performs many checks to ensure that the license is valid for the current application installation. If the license is invalid for any reason, the application blocks access to the enhanced administrative features included in the Library system.

Summary

Since you will often spend dozens or hundreds of hours designing and developing a quality Visual C# application, it is important to use appropriate licensing and obfuscation technology to protect your work. Licensing is another one of those common programming tasks that didn't make it into the .NET Framework as an easy-to-use class—unless you are building and distributing design-time controls, or distribution your app through the Windows Store. For the rest of us, it's make-it-up-as-you-go time. Fortunately, .NET has great support tools, so adding licensing support isn't too difficult.

Project

In this chapter's project code, we'll implement two of the four licensing steps discussed in the section "The Library Licensing System" earlier in this chapter: *generating the license file* and *using the license file*. The design we created previously is good enough for our needs, although we still need to record it in the project's technical documentation. We won't formally install the license file until we create the setup program in Chapter 24.

Update Technical Documentation

Since we'll be adding a new external file that will be processed by the Library Project, we need to document its structure in the project's *Technical Resource Kit*. I've already applied the changes to that document. Since this is the last change we'll make to the Resource Kit, you can find the completed document in the *Final Project Documents* folder of the project installation directory.

In addition to documenting the individual tags of the license file's XML content, the Resource Kit updates also reveal that a license-specific setting now appears in the project settings for the Library program. The setting is called `LicenseFileLocation`, and contains the full path to the license file.

Library License Helper Application

Generating license files and digital signatures by hand using Notepad would be...well, let's not even think about it. Instead, we'll depend on a custom application to create the files and signatures for us. I've already developed that custom tool for you. You'll find it in the installation directory for this book's code, in the *Library Licensing* subdirectory.

This support application includes two main forms, called "windows" in a WPF application. The first (*KeyLocationWindow.xaml.cs*, shown in Figure 22-5) locates or creates the public-private key files used in the digital signature process.

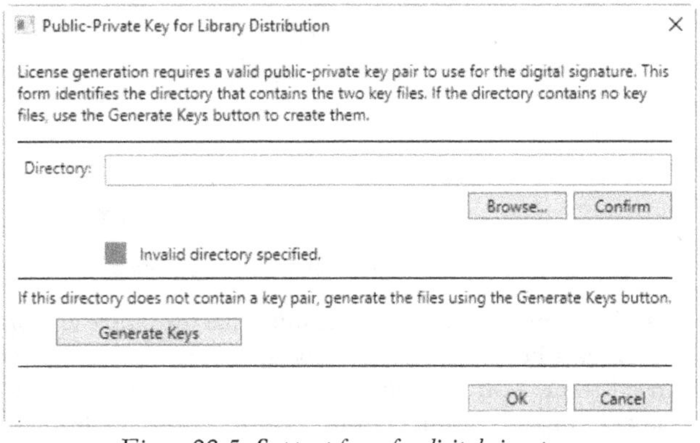

Figure 22-5. Support form for digital signatures

Most of the form's code helps to locate and verify the folder that will contain the two key files (one private, one public). Some of the code in the *ActGenerate_Click* event handler creates the actual files.

```
RSA twoPartKey;
string publicFile;
string privateFile;

...some code skipped here, then...

// ----- Generate the keys.
twoPartKey = new RSACryptoServiceProvider();
twoPartKey = RSA.Create();

// ----- Save the public key.
System.IO.File.WriteAllText(publicFile,
    twoPartKey.ToXmlString(false));

// ----- Save the private key.
System.IO.File.WriteAllText(privateFile,
    twoPartKey.ToXmlString(true));
```

That's really simple! The *System.Security.Cryptography.RSA* class and the related *RSACryptoServiceProvider* class do all the work. All you have to do is call the *RSA.Create* method, and then generate the relevant XML keys using the *ToXmlString* method, passing an argument of *false* for the public key and *true* for the private key. If you want to look at some sample keys, open the *License Files* subdirectory in this book's source installation directory. You'll find two files, one for the public key and one for the private key. I'd print one of them here, but it all just looks like random characters.

The other support form is *MainWindow.xaml.cs*, which generates the actual end-user license file, and appears in Figure 22-6.

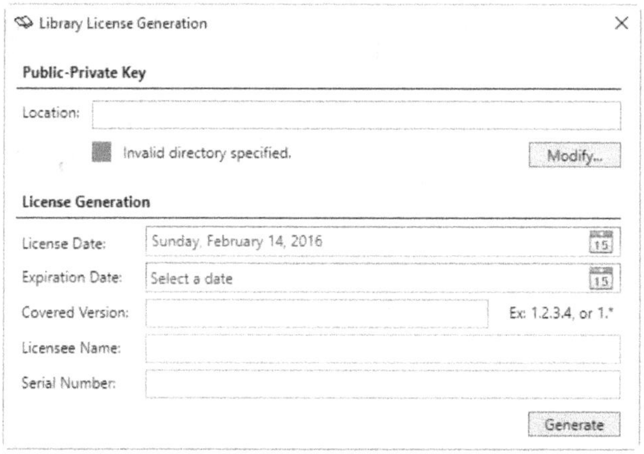

Figure 22-6. Support form for license file generation

As with the first form, most of this form's code simply ensures that the public and private key files are intact, and that the user entered valid data before generation. The *ActGenerate_Click* event handler is where the real fun is. First, we need some XML content, which we build in the *BuildXmlLicenseContent* method. It creates the content element by element, using "the new way" we learned about in Chapter 13.

```
    return new XDocument(
        new XDeclaration("1.0", "utf-8", "yes"),
        new XElement("License",
            new XElement("Product", ApplicationProductName),
            new XElement("LicenseDate", LicenseDate.SelectedDate.
                Value.ToString("M/d/yyyy")),
            new XElement("ExpireDate", ExpirationDate.SelectedDate.
                Value.ToString("M/d/yyyy")),
            new XElement("CoveredVersion",
                CoveredVersion.Text.Trim()),
            new XElement("Licensee", LicenseeName.Text.Trim()),
            new XElement("SerialNumber",
                SerialNumber.Text.Trim())
        )
    );
```

Then comes the digital signature, via the *SignXmlLicenseContent* function. Unfortunately, the .NET features that do the signing don't play well with the *XDocument* class. Instead, we need to convert the XML object back to "the old way" for it to work.

```
XDocument licenseXMLNew = BuildXmlLicenseContent();
XmlDocument licenseXML = new XmlDocument();
licenseXML.LoadXml(licenseXMLNew.ToString());
```

Old XML in hand, we're ready to add the digital signature. This happens in the *SignXmlLicenseContent* method. The core of that routine's logic appears here.

```
// ----- Add a digital signature to an XML document.
string privateKeyFile;
RSA privateKey;
SignedXml signature;
Reference referenceMethod;

// ----- Load in the private key.
privateKeyFile = System.IO.Path.Combine(
    KeyLocation.Text, PrivateKeyFilename);
privateKey = RSA.Create();
privateKey.FromXmlString(
    System.IO.File.ReadAllText(privateKeyFile));

// ----- Create the object that generates the signature.
signature = new SignedXml(sourceXML);
signature.SignedInfo.CanonicalizationMethod =
    SignedXml.XmlDsigCanonicalizationUrl;
signature.SigningKey = privateKey;

// ----- The signature will appear as a <reference>
//        element in the XML.
referenceMethod = new Reference("");
referenceMethod.AddTransform(
    new XmlDsigEnvelopedSignatureTransform(false));
signature.AddReference(referenceMethod);

// ----- Add the signature to the XML content.
signature.ComputeSignature();
sourceXML.DocumentElement.AppendChild(signature.GetXml());
```

Digital signing occurs via the *SignedXml* class (in the *System.Security.Cryptography.Xml* namespace). This class uses a few different signing methods; the one I chose (*XmlDsigCanonicalizationUrl*) is used for typical XML and ignores embedded comments.

This signature appears as tags and values in the XML output, added through the *AppendChild* statement near the end of the routine. Since we don't want the signature itself to be considered when we later scan the XML file for valid content, the *SignedXml* class adds the signature as a *<reference>* tag. This occurs in code by adding a *Reference* object that is programmed for that purpose. It's added through the *signature.AddReference* method call.

Once we have the signature in the XML content, we write it all out to a file specified by the user via the standard *XmlDocument.Save* method (in the *ActGenerate_Click* event handler).

```
licenseXML.Save(LicenseSaveLocation.FileName);
```

Here's a sample XML license file that includes a digital signature. This is the one that I have included in the *License Files* directory in the book's source installation directory (with some lines wrapped to fit this page).

```
<?xml version="1.0"?>
<License>
  <Product>Library Project</Product>
  <LicenseDate>1/1/2000</LicenseDate>
  <ExpireDate>12/31/2999</ExpireDate>
  <CoveredVersion>1.*</CoveredVersion>
  <Licensee>John Q. Public</Licensee>
  <SerialNumber>LIB-123456789</SerialNumber>
  <Signature xmlns="http://www.w3.org/2000/09/xmldsig#">
    <SignedInfo>
      <CanonicalizationMethod Algorithm=
        "http://www.w3.org/TR/2001/REC-xml-c14n-20010315" />
      <SignatureMethod Algorithm=
        "http://www.w3.org/2000/09/xmldsig#rsa-sha1" />
      <Reference URI="">
        <Transforms>
          <Transform Algorithm="http://www.w3.org/2000/09/
            xmldsig#enveloped-signature" />
        </Transforms>
        <DigestMethod Algorithm="http://www.w3.org/2000/09/
          xmldsig#sha1" />
        <DigestValue>Dn6JYIBI/qQudmvSiMvuOvnVBGU=
          </DigestValue>
      </Reference>
    </SignedInfo>
    <SignatureValue>NULghI4WbzDLroIcf2u9aoybfSjXPJRN5
      0UMrCPYa5bup+c7RJnqTM+SzP4jmfJWPPs7pOvDC/fbdNY
      VMaoyXW0jL3Lk8du3X4JXpW3xp9Nxq31y/Ld8E+RkoiPO6
      KRGDI+RRZ8MAQda8WS+L2fMyenRAjo+fR9KL3sQ/hOfQX8=
    </SignatureValue>
  </Signature>
</License>
```

The digital signature appears as the scrambled content within the *<SignatureValue>* tag. Now, if anyone tries to modify any of the license values, the license will no longer match the signature, and the entire license will become invalid.

Instead of using a digital signature, we could have encrypted the entire licensing file with the private key, and later used the public key to decrypt it and examine its contents. But I like the digital signature better, since it allows anyone to open the license file and check the parameters of the license itself while still preventing any changes.

Dealing with WPF

The original implementation of the Library License helper application was done using Windows Forms, just like the main Library program. When I ported the tool to WPF format, I did so with minimal flair, replicating as closely as possible the look, feel, and workflow of the original program. And yet, it took a significant amount of effort to build the app's XAML counterpart. As mentioned before, the core, non-UI logic was basically identical to what appeared back in Windows Forms. But the differences in form development are significant, and there are other tickles here and there that make the simultaneous management of both types of programs a bit of a pain.

The friendly *MessageBox.Show* method is one such source of conflict. In Windows Forms, a standard message communique looks like this.

```
// ----- In the System.Windows.Forms namespace.
MessageBox.Show("Hi there!", messageTitle,
    MessageBoxButtons.OK, MessageBoxIcon.Information);
```

Here's the same call using WPF.

```
// ----- In the System.Windows namespace.
MessageBox.Show("Hi there!", messageTitle,
    MessageBoxButton.OK, MessageBoxImage.Information);
```

It's not that different. Just the removal of "s" from the end of one class name (*MessageBoxButtons*), and the change from *MessageBoxIcon* to *MessageBoxImage*. The question is: why? Microsoft designed Windows Forms, in part, as a way of bringing standardization to Windows development. Why didn't they retain the names they worked so hard to standardize?

It gets even worse when dealing with forms (now called "windows") and controls. In Windows Forms, the display text for each element uses the property name *Text*. Whether it's the form caption, or the title on a button, or the main text in a label or text box, *Text* is your consistent go-to property.

Not so in WPF. The text in labels and buttons use the *Content* property. Window titles call it *Title*. The *TextBlock* control (which I use to get around the non-wrapping aspect of label controls) shows its text through the *Text* property. So inconsistent, and so hard to find in WPF's already-difficult and non-keyboard-friendly Properties panel.

There are other development surprises when moving from Windows Forms. When assigning a form's *DialogResult* property in Windows Forms, you have options for OK, Cancel, Yes, No, plus a few others. Lots of variety to choose from. In WPF, that identically named property is a Boolean value, so just True and False.

Not that I'm complaining. WPF and XAML enable user interface functionality that far exceeds the features found in Windows Forms, at least with the same amount of coding. There are a lot of pluses when using it. But it has some cumbersome aspects as well. Take a gander through the code and see how many differences you can find from the Windows Forms samples you've seen thus far.

Adding the License to the Library Program

Let's return to the Library application, a kind, friendly, Windows Forms project.

The program will adjust its behavior depending on whether it is licensed or not. But to make that determination, it needs to ensure that the contents of the licensing file are valid and haven't been tampered with. To do this, it needs a way to unscramble the signature and compare it with the rest of the license to make sure it matches. We built the signature using the private key; we must unscramble it using the public key.

We could store the public key in its own file outside the program, but then it might get lost (just like my real keys). Instead, we'll store the public key as an application resource, found externally in the source code's *Resources* folder. I've already added the resource to your copy of the program, and named it `LicensePublicKey`. With this key embedded in the application, *any regeneration of the public and private keys will require modification of this resource.* In code, we refer to the XML content of the public key using its resource name.

```
Properties.Resources.LicensePublicKey
```

Some of the security features use classes found in the `System.Security.Cryptography.Xml` namespace. This is not one of the namespaces included by default in new Visual C# applications, so we'll have to add it ourselves. In the Solution Explorer panel, right-click on the References item in the hierarchy, then select Add Reference from the shortcut menu. In the Reference Manager, select Assemblies/Framework from the choices along the left edge. Locate and select System.Security from the list of framework assemblies, and finally click OK.

Next, we'll add a license-specific setting. Open the project properties and access its Settings tab. Add a new string user setting and enter `LicenseFileLocation` for its name. We'll use this setting to store the path to the license file. Save and close the project properties window.

Our general licensing needs throughout the application are pretty simple. We only need to know the current status of the licensing file, and have access to a few of the licensing values so that we can display a short message about the license. We may need to do this in various parts of the program, so let's add some useful centralized processing code to the *General.cs* class. Open that file now.

Right at the top, the code already includes a reference to the `System.Security.Cryptography` namespace, since we include code that encrypts user passwords. But this doesn't cover the standard or secure XML stuff. So add two new `using` directives as well.

```
using System.Xml;
using System.Security.Cryptography.Xml;
```

We'll use an enumeration to indicate the status of the license. Add it now to the `General` class.

```
public enum LicenseStatus: int
{
    ValidLicense,
    MissingLicenseFile,
```

```
    CorruptLicenseFile,
    InvalidSignature,
    NotYetLicensed,
    LicenseExpired,
    VersionMismatch
}
```

Let's also add a simple structure that communicates the values extracted from the license file. Add this code to the *General* class.

Insert Snippet
Insert Chapter 22, Snippet Item 3.

```
public struct LicenseFileDetail
{
    public LicenseStatus Status;
    public string Licensee;
    public DateTime LicenseDate;
    public DateTime ExpireDate;
    public string CoveredVersion;
    public string SerialNumber;
}
```

By default, the license file appears in the same directory as the application, using the name *LibraryLicense.lic*. Add a static constant to the *General* class that identifies this default name.

Insert Snippet
Insert Chapter 22, Snippet Item 4.

```
public const string DefaultLicenseFile =
    "LibraryLicense.lic";
```

All we need now is some code to fill in the *LicenseFileDetail* structure. Add the new *ExamineLicense* function to the *General* class.

Insert Snippet
Insert Chapter 22, Snippet Item 5.

```
public static LicenseFileDetail ExamineLicense()
{
    // ----- Examine the application's license file,
    //       and report back what's inside.
    LicenseFileDetail result = new LicenseFileDetail();
    string usePath;
    XmlDocument licenseContent;
    RSA publicKey;
    SignedXml signedDocument;
    XmlNodeList matchingNodes;
    string[] versionParts;
    int holdPart;
    int comparePart;
    string appPath;
    Assembly currentAssembly;

    // ----- See if the license file exists.
    result.Status = LicenseStatus.MissingLicenseFile;
```

```
usePath = Properties.Settings.
   Default.LicenseFileLocation;
if (usePath.Length == 0)
{
   // ----- Look in the application's directory.
   currentAssembly = Assembly.GetEntryAssembly();
   if (currentAssembly == null)
      currentAssembly = Assembly.GetCallingAssembly();
   appPath = System.IO.Path.GetDirectoryName(
      currentAssembly.Location);
   usePath = System.IO.Path.Combine(
      appPath, DefaultLicenseFile);
}
if (System.IO.File.Exists(usePath) == false)
   return result;

// ----- Try to read in the file.
result.Status = LicenseStatus.CorruptLicenseFile;
try
{
   licenseContent = new XmlDocument();
   licenseContent.Load(usePath);
}
catch
{
   // ----- Silent error.
   return result;
}

// ----- Prepare the public key resource for use.
publicKey = RSA.Create();
publicKey.FromXmlString(
   Properties.Resources.LicensePublicKey);

// ----- Confirm the digital signature.
try
{
   signedDocument = new SignedXml(licenseContent);
   matchingNodes = licenseContent.
      GetElementsByTagName("Signature");
   signedDocument.LoadXml((XmlElement)
      (matchingNodes[0]));
}
catch
{
   // ----- Still a corrupted document.
   return result;
}
if (signedDocument.CheckSignature(publicKey) == false)
{
   result.Status = LicenseStatus.InvalidSignature;
   return result;
}
```

```
// ----- The license file is valid. Extract its members.
try
{
   // ----- Get the licensee name.
   matchingNodes = licenseContent.
      GetElementsByTagName("Licensee");
   result.Licensee = matchingNodes[0].InnerText;

   // ----- Get the license date.
   matchingNodes = licenseContent.
      GetElementsByTagName("LicenseDate");
   result.LicenseDate = Convert.ToDateTime(
      matchingNodes[0].InnerText);

   // ----- Get the expiration date.
   matchingNodes = licenseContent.
      GetElementsByTagName("ExpireDate");
   result.ExpireDate = Convert.ToDateTime(
      matchingNodes[0].InnerText);

   // ----- Get the version number.
   matchingNodes = licenseContent.
      GetElementsByTagName("CoveredVersion");
   result.CoveredVersion = matchingNodes[0].InnerText;

   // ----- Get the serial number.
   matchingNodes = licenseContent.
      GetElementsByTagName("SerialNumber");
   result.SerialNumber = matchingNodes[0].InnerText;
}
catch
{
   // ----- Still a corrupted document.
   return result;
}

// ----- Check for out-of-range dates.
if (result.LicenseDate > DateTime.Today)
{
   result.Status = LicenseStatus.NotYetLicensed;
   return result;
}
if (result.ExpireDate < DateTime.Today)
{
   result.Status = LicenseStatus.LicenseExpired;
   return result;
}

// ----- Check the version.
versionParts = result.CoveredVersion.Split(
   new[] {"."}, StringSplitOptions.None);
currentAssembly = Assembly.GetEntryAssembly();
if (currentAssembly == null)
   currentAssembly = Assembly.GetCallingAssembly();
```

```
for (int counter = 0; counter <
   versionParts.Length; counter++)
{
   if (int.TryParse(versionParts[counter],
      out holdPart) == true)
   {
      // ----- The version format is
      //       major.minor.build.revision.
      switch (counter)
      {
         case 0:
            comparePart = currentAssembly.
               GetName().Version.Major;
            break;
         case 1:
            comparePart = currentAssembly.
               GetName().Version.Minor;
            break;
         case 2:
            comparePart = currentAssembly.
               GetName().Version.Build;
            break;
         case 3:
            comparePart = currentAssembly.
               GetName().Version.Revision;
            break;
         default:
            // ----- Corrupt version number.
            return result;
      }
      if (comparePart != holdPart)
      {
         result.Status =
            LicenseStatus.VersionMismatch;
         return result;
      }
   }
}

// ----- Everything seems to be in order.
result.Status = LicenseStatus.ValidLicense;
return result;
}
```

That's a lot of code, but most of it just loads and extracts values from the XML license file. The signature-checking part is relatively short.

```
publicKey = RSA.Create();
publicKey.FromXmlString(
   Properties.Resources.LicensePublicKey);
signedDocument = new SignedXml(licenseContent);
matchingNodes = licenseContent.
   GetElementsByTagName("Signature");
signedDocument.LoadXml((XmlElement)(matchingNodes[0]));
if (signedDocument.CheckSignature(publicKey) == false)
```

```
{
    // ----- Invalid.
}
```

The *SignedXml* object—which we also used to generate the original license file—needs to know exactly which XML tag in its content represents the digital signature. You would think that having an element named `<Signature>` would be a big tip-off, but perhaps not. Anyway, once you've assigned that node using the *SignedXml.LoadXml* method, you call the *CheckSignature* method, passing it the public key. If it returns *true*, you're good. I mean, not in a moral sense; the code doesn't know anything about you. But the signature is valid.

Display the License on the About Form

When we added the About form to the project a few hundred pages ago, we included a *Label* control named *LabelLicensed*. It currently always displays "Unlicensed," but now we have the tools to display a proper license, if available. Open the source code for the *AboutProgram.cs* form, and add the following statements to the start of the *AboutProgram_Load* event handler.

Insert Snippet
Insert Chapter 22, Snippet Item 6.

```
// ----- Prepare the form.
LicenseFileDetail licenseDetails;

// ----- Display the licensee.
licenseDetails = ExamineLicense();
if (licenseDetails.Status == LicenseStatus.ValidLicense)
    LabelLicensed.Text =
        "Licensed to " + licenseDetails.Licensee +
        Environment.NewLine +
        "Serial number " + licenseDetails.SerialNumber;
```

Figure 22-7 shows the *AboutProgram* form in use with details displayed from the license file.

Figure 22-7. Displaying a valid license

Just for fun, I changed the version number in my license file from "1.*" to "2.*" without updating the digital signature. Sure enough, when I displayed the *AboutProgram* form again, it displayed "Unlicensed," since the check of the signature failed. How did I test the code this early? I copied the *LibraryLicense.lic* file from the book's installed *License Files* subdirectory and placed that copy in the *bin\Debug* subdirectory of the project's source code. Later on, you'll be able to put the file anywhere you want and browse for it, but we're getting ahead of ourselves.

Enforcing the License

At some point, a missing or invalid license should have a negative impact on the use of the application. When that happens, we should give the user a chance to correct the problem by locating a valid license file. We'll do this through the new *LocateLicense.cs* form. I've already added the form to your project. It appears in Figure 22-8.

Figure 22-8. The gentle way to enforce a product license

This form starts up with a call to its public *ChangeLicense* function, which returns *true* if the user changes the license. Most of this form's code manages the display, presenting detailed reasons why a license is valid or invalid using the results of the *ExamineLicense* function. If for any reason the license is invalid, a click on the Locate button lets the user browse for a better version.

```
private void ActLocate_Click(object sender, EventArgs e)
{
    // ----- Prompt the user for a new license file.
    OpenFileDialog locateLicenseDialog;

    locateLicenseDialog = new OpenFileDialog();
    locateLicenseDialog.Filter =
        "License Files|*.lic|XML Files|*.xml|All Files|*.*";
    locateLicenseDialog.Title = "Open License File";
    if (locateLicenseDialog.ShowDialog() != DialogResult.OK)
        return;

    // ----- Store the new path.
    Properties.Settings.Default.LicenseFileLocation =
        locateLicenseDialog.FileName;
    LocationModified = true;

    // ----- Update the display.
    DisplayLicenseStatus();
    LicensePath.Text = Properties.Settings.
        Default.LicenseFileLocation;
}
```

The *LocationModified* form-level variable gets sent back to the caller as a trigger to refresh the status of the license.

For the Library Project in particular, I didn't see a point in enforcing the license on startup, since it's not the patrons' fault that the library stole this important work of software. Instead, I delay the verification process until an administrator or librarian tries to access the enhanced features of the application. Then, if the license check fails, the user should be able to browse the disk for a valid license file.

I think the best place to add the license check is just after the administrator successfully supplies a password. If we checked before that point, it would give ordinary patrons the ability to browse the disk, which is probably a no-no, since anyone and her uncle can walk up and use a patron workstation. Open the source code for the *ChangeUser.cs* form, locate the *ActOK_Click* event handler, and locate the "Successful login" comment.

```
' ----- Successful login.
LoggedInUserID = DBGetLong(dbRow!ID)
LoggedInUserName = DBGetText(dbRow!LoginID)
...
```

Just *before* this block of code, add the following license-checking code.

Insert Snippet

Insert Chapter 22, Snippet Item 7.

```
// ----- Don't allow the login if the program is unlicensed.
while (ExamineLicense().Status != LicenseStatus.ValidLicense)
{
    // ----- Ask the user what to do.
    if (MessageBox.Show("This application is not properly " +
        "licensed for administrative use. If you have " +
        "access to a valid license file, you can verify it " +
        "now. Would you like to locate a valid license " +
        "file at this time?", ProgramTitle,
        MessageBoxButtons.YesNo, MessageBoxIcon.Question) !=
        DialogResult.Yes)
    {
        dbInfo.Dispose();
        dbInfo = null;
        return;
    }

    // ----- Prompt for an updated license.
    (new LocateLicense()).ChangeLicense();
}
```

This code gives the user an unlimited number of chances to locate a valid license file. Once the license is validated, the code moves forward and enables administrative access.

Daily Item Processing

The last major set of code to be added to the Library Project isn't related to licensing, but it's important nonetheless: the processing of fines for overdue items. We'll add a common method that will perform the processing, and then call it where needed throughout the application.

Add the new *DailyProcessByPatronCopy* method to the *General* class.

Insert Snippet

Insert Chapter 22, Snippet Item 8.

```
public static void DailyProcessByPatronCopy(
    long patronCopyID, DateTime untilDate)
{
```

```
// ----- This routine does the most basic work of
//       processing overdue fines. All other daily
//       processing routines eventually call
//       this routine.
string sqlText;
DataCommand sqlRun;
DataTable dbInfo;
DataRow oneRow;
int daysToFine;
DateTime lastProcess;
decimal fineSoFar;

// ----- Get all of the basic values needed
//       to process this entry.
sqlText = "SELECT PC.DueDate, PC.ProcessDate, " +
   "PC.Fine, CMT.DailyFine " +
   "FROM PatronCopy AS PC " +
   "INNER JOIN ItemCopy AS IC ON PC.ItemCopy = IC.ID " +
   "INNER JOIN NamedItem AS NI ON IC.ItemID = NI.ID " +
   "INNER JOIN CodeMediaType AS CMT " +
   "ON NI.MediaType = CMT.ID " +
   "WHERE PC.ID = @RecordID " +
   "AND PC.DueDate <= @TargetDate " +
   "AND PC.Returned = 0 " +
   "AND PC.Missing = 0 AND IC.Missing = 0";
sqlRun = new DataCommand(sqlText);
sqlRun.AddLong("RecordID", patronCopyID);
sqlRun.AddDate("TargetDate", DateTime.Today);
try
{
   dbInfo = CreateDataTable(sqlRun);
}
catch (Exception ex)
{
   GeneralError(
      "DailyProcessByPatronCopy.Retrieve", ex);
   dbInfo = null;
}
if ((dbInfo == null) || (dbInfo.Rows.Count == 0))
{
   // ----- Missing the patron copy record. Oh well.
   //       It was probably because this item was
   //       not yet overdue, or it was missing, or
   //       something valid like that where fines
   //       should not increase.
   dbInfo.Dispose();
   dbInfo = null;
   return;
}
oneRow = dbInfo.Rows[0];

// ----- If we have already processed this record
//       for today, don't do it again.
if (Convert.IsDBNull(oneRow["ProcessDate"]) == false)
```

```
{
    if (DBGetDate(oneRow["ProcessDate"]) >= untilDate)
    {
        dbInfo.Dispose();
        dbInfo = null;
        return;
    }
    lastProcess = DBGetDate(oneRow["ProcessDate"]);
}
else
{
    lastProcess = DBGetDate(oneRow["DueDate"]);
}

// ----- Fines are due on this record.
//       Figure out how much.
daysToFine = (int)(untilDate -
    DBGetDate(oneRow["DueDate"])).TotalDays -
    (int)(lastProcess -
    DBGetDate(oneRow["DueDate"])).TotalDays -
    FineGraceDays;
if (daysToFine < 0)
    daysToFine = 0;
fineSoFar = 0M;
if (Convert.IsDBNull(oneRow["Fine"]) == false)
    fineSoFar = DBGetDecimal(oneRow["Fine"]);
fineSoFar += DBGetDecimal(oneRow["DailyFine"]) *
    (decimal)daysToFine;
dbInfo.Dispose();
dbInfo = null;

// ----- Update the record with the latest fine
//       and processing information.
sqlText = "UPDATE PatronCopy " +
    "SET ProcessDate = @NewDate, " +
    "Fine = @NewFine WHERE ID = @RecordID";
sqlRun = new DataCommand(sqlText);
sqlRun.AddDate("NewDate", untilDate);
sqlRun.AddDecimal("NewFine", Math.Round(
    fineSoFar, 2).ToString());
sqlRun.AddLong("RecordID", patronCopyID);
try
{
    ExecuteSQL(sqlRun);
}
catch (Exception ex)
{
    GeneralError(
        "DailyProcessByPatronCopy.Update", ex);
}
}
```

This code examines a *PatronCopy* record—the record that marks the checking out of a single item by a patron—to see whether it is overdue, and if so, what penalty needs to be added to the record. Each record includes a *ProcessDate* field. We don't want to charge the patron twice on the same day for a single overdue item (no, we don't), so we use the *ProcessDate* to confirm which days are uncharged.

There are a few places throughout the application where we want to call this processing routine without bothering the user. The first appears in the *PatronRecord* form, the form that displays the fines a patron still owes. Just before showing that list, we should refresh each item checked out by the patron to make sure we display the most up-to-date fine information. Open that form's source code, locate the *PatronRecord_Load* event handler, and add the following code, just before the call to *RefreshPatronFines(-1L)* that appears halfway through the routine.

Insert Snippet

Insert Chapter 22, Snippet Item 9.

```
// ----- Make sure that each item is up-to-date.
for (int counter = 0; counter <
    ItemsOut.Items.Count; counter++)
{
    newEntry = (PatronDetailItem)(ItemsOut.Items[counter]);
    DailyProcessByPatronCopy(
        newEntry.DetailID, DateTime.Today);
}
```

The overdue status for an item must also be refreshed just before it is checked in. Open the source code for the *MainForm* form and locate the *ActDoCheckIn_Click* event handler. About halfway through its code, you'll find a comment that starts with "Handle missing items." Just before that comment, insert the following code.

Insert Snippet

Insert Chapter 22, Snippet Item 10.

```
// ----- Bring the status of the item up-to-date.
DailyProcessByPatronCopy(patronCopyID, CheckInDate.Value);
```

Checkout needs to refresh the patron's fines as well, just before letting the patron know whether there are, in fact, any fines due. Move to the *MainForm.ActCheckOutPatron_Click* event handler, and locate a comment that starts with "Show the patron if there are any fines due." As usual, it's about halfway through the routine. Insert the following code just before that comment.

Insert Snippet

Insert Chapter 22, Snippet Item 11.

```
// ----- Bring the patron record up-to-date.
sqlText = "SELECT ID FROM PatronCopy " +
    "WHERE Returned = 0 AND Missing = 0 " +
    "AND DueDate < @TargetDate AND (ProcessDate IS NULL " +
    "OR ProcessDate < @TargetDate) AND Patron = @RecordID";
sqlRun = new DataCommand(sqlText);
sqlRun.AddDate("TargetDate", DateTime.Today);
sqlRun.AddLong("RecordID", patronID);
try
{
    dbInfo = CreateDataTable(sqlRun);
}
catch (Exception ex)
{
```

```
        this.Cursor = Cursors.Default;
        GeneralError(
            "MainForm.ActCheckOutPatron_Click.Date", ex);
        dbInfo = null;
    }
    if (dbInfo != null)
    {
        foreach (DataRow dbRow in dbInfo.Rows)
            DailyProcessByPatronCopy(DBGetLong(
                dbRow["ID"]), DateTime.Today);
        dbInfo.Dispose();
        dbInfo = null;
    }
```

In addition to automatic fine processing, the Library Project also allows an administrator or librarian to perform daily processing of all patron items at will. This occurs through the Daily Processing panel on the main form (see Figure 22-9).

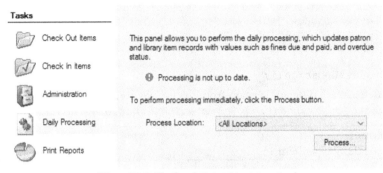

Figure 22-9. Daily administrative processing

Currently, the panel doesn't do much of anything, so let's change that. The first task is to update the status label that appears at the top of the panel. Add a new method named *RefreshProcessLocation* to the *MainForm* form's class.

Insert Snippet
Insert Chapter 22, Snippet Item 12.

I won't show its code here, but it basically checks the *CodeLocation.LastProcessing* database field either for all locations, or for the user-selected location, and updates the status display accordingly.

The user selects a location for processing with the *ProcessLocation* drop-down list, but we haven't yet added any code to populate that list. Find the *TaskProcess* method in the main form's source code, and add these declarations to the top of its code.

Insert Snippet
Insert Chapter 22, Snippet Item 13.

```
    string sqlText;
    DataTable dbInfo;
```

Then add these statements to the end of the method.

Insert Snippet
Insert Chapter 22, Snippet Item 14.

```
// ----- Refresh the list of locations.
ProcessLocation.Items.Clear();
ProcessLocation.Items.Add(new ListItemData(
    "<All Locations>", -1L));
ProcessLocation.SelectedIndex = 0;
sqlText = "SELECT ID, FullName " +
    "FROM CodeLocation ORDER BY FullName";
try
{
    dbInfo = CreateDataTable(sqlText);
}
catch (Exception ex)
{
    GeneralError("MainForm.TaskProcess", ex);
    return;
}
foreach (DataRow dbRow in dbInfo.Rows)
    ProcessLocation.Items.Add(new ListItemData(
        DBGetText(dbRow["FullName"]),
        DBGetLong(dbRow["ID"])));
dbInfo.Dispose();
dbInfo = null;
RefreshProcessLocation();
```

Each time the user selects a different location from the list, we need to update the status display. Add the following code to the *ProcessLocation_SelectedIndexChanged* event handler.

Insert Snippet
Insert Chapter 22, Snippet Item 15.

```
// ----- Update the status based on the current location.
RefreshProcessLocation();
```

Daily processing occurs when the user clicks on the Process button. Add the following code to the *ActDoProcess_Click* event handler.

Insert Snippet
Insert Chapter 22, Snippet Item 16.

```
// ----- Process all of the checked out books.
string sqlText;
DataCommand sqlRun;
DataTable dbInfo;
long locationID;

this.Cursor = Cursors.WaitCursor;

// ----- Get the list of all items that
//       likely need processing.
sqlText = "SELECT PC.ID FROM PatronCopy AS PC " +
    "INNER JOIN ItemCopy AS IC " +
    "ON PC.ItemCopy = IC.ID WHERE PC.Returned = 0 " +
    "AND PC.Missing = 0 AND IC.Missing = 0 " +
    "AND PC.DueDate < @TargetDate " +
    "AND (PC.ProcessDate IS NULL " +
    "OR PC.ProcessDate < @TargetDate)";
```

```
if (ProcessLocation.SelectedIndex != -1)
{
    locationID = (long)(ListItemData)
        ProcessLocation.SelectedItem;
    if (locationID != -1L)
        sqlText += " AND IC.Location = @RecordID";
}
else
{
    locationID = -1L;
}
sqlRun = new DataCommand(sqlText);
sqlRun.AddDate("TargetDate", DateTime.Today);
if (locationID != -1L)
    sqlRun.AddLong("RecordID", locationID);
try
{
    dbInfo = CreateDataTable(sqlRun);
}
catch (Exception ex)
{
    GeneralError(
        "MainForm.ActDoProcess_Click.Retrieve", ex);
    dbInfo = null;
}
if (dbInfo != null)
{
    foreach (DataRow dbRow in dbInfo.Rows)
        DailyProcessByPatronCopy(DBGetLong(
            dbRow["ID"]), DateTime.Today);
    dbInfo.Dispose();
    dbInfo = null;
}
this.Cursor = Cursors.Default;
MessageBox.Show("Processing complete.", ProgramTitle,
    MessageBoxButtons.OK, MessageBoxIcon.Information);

// ----- Update the processing date.
sqlText = "UPDATE CodeLocation " +
    "SET LastProcessing = @TargetDate";
if (locationID != -1L)
    sqlText += " WHERE ID = " + locationID.ToString();
sqlRun = new DataCommand(sqlText);
sqlRun.AddDate("TargetDate", DateTime.Today);
if (locationID != -1L)
    sqlRun.AddLong("RecordID", locationID);
try
{
    ExecuteSQL(sqlRun);
}
catch (Exception ex)
{
    GeneralError(
        "MainForm.ActDoProcess_Click.Update", ex);
```

```
    }

    // ----- Update the status display.
    ProcessStatus.Text = "        Processing is up to date.";
    ProcessStatus.ImageIndex = StatusImageGood;
```

To try out the code, run it, locate a valid license file, and test out the different administrative features.

This marks the end of primary coding for the Library Project. Congratulations! But there's still plenty to do, as you can tell by the presence of three more chapters. Now would *not* be the time to close the book and call it a day. But it would be a good time to learn about online help, the topic of the next chapter.

Chapter 23

Online Help

If there's one thing I've learned in nearly thirty-five years of programming, it's that users often need some help to run software on their systems. Programmers need help, too, but getting back to computers: it's rare that you find a technically conversant user. If you write applications that target businesses and departments within organizations (that's what I do), you find that the users are very skilled at their jobs, but not necessarily skilled at using a computer. This is shocking, yet true, even in this era where everyone carries a supercomputer in their pockets and purses. That's why it is imperative that you make your programs as straightforward to use as possible.

One way you can expand understanding of your application is by including online help. These ready documents act as the first wave of support for your users' software needs. Of course, they seldom read it, and so you (or your technical support staff) will actually become the first wave of support. But it's somewhat refreshing to be able to say, "Did you check the online help, which covers this issue in detail?"

In this chapter, we'll discuss the online help options available to you in Visual C# and focus in on HTML Help, Microsoft's old yet still relevant help system for Windows PCs.

Windows Online Help Options

Online help has been a part of Windows since its initial release, back in the days when applications and operating systems still shipped with printed manuals and never required more than two floppy disks. I really miss that time. That sense of touch; the cold, smooth pages in my hands. I remember the first Windows software I ever purchased, a newly released Personal Information Manager. It had everything I needed, including a 400-page user's guide and reference manual. Sheer delight.

Those days are gone, replaced by online help systems and HTML readme files. Now you buy books such as this one to bring back that included-user's-guide feeling. But you can do a lot with online help, especially these days with the ability to include dynamic, active content in online help pages.

WinHelp

The original Windows help system was *WinHelp*. It included simple formatted help pages with hyperlinks to other pages. The WinHelp development process used specially formatted Rich Text Format (RTF) files as its source content, producing an *.hlp* file and a supporting *.cnt* contents file that together provided users with basic help for their applications.

WinHelp met the needs of Windows users for years. However, it is not officially supported in Windows 10.

HTML Help

When the Internet started sweeping the world with its ability to generate beautifully formatted pages through the common HTML tag-based language, Microsoft decided to upgrade its help system to one that used standard HTML documents: *HTML Help*. As its name implies, HTML Help is truly HTML-based. Anything that generates HTML can generate HTML Help content: third-party web-page designer tools, word processors, your own custom applications, even Notepad. As expected, some vendors designed tools specifically targeting the HTML Help system.

HTML Help is better than WinHelp, due to its dependence on HTML and other related technologies. Each page of your online help file is a separate HTML page/file. Hyperlinks to other help pages are standard HTML hyperlinks. And HTML Help employs many of the features used in common web pages, including Cascading Style Sheets (CSS) and JavaScript.

Compiled HTML Help files have a *.chm* extension, and a single file includes primary content, the table of contents, and a predefined index of terms. We will use HTML Help technology to add online help content to the Library Project. I'll skip the details of the system until a little later in the chapter.

Microsoft Help 2 and Microsoft Help Viewer

Microsoft continued to enhance its help offerings. *Microsoft Help2* arrived with the original release of the .NET system in 2002. Its *.hxs* files (and other supporting files) merged HTML with XML to provide an enhanced content experience beyond what HTML Help offered.

Microsoft Help 2 never caught on much beyond Visual Studio and Office products. Eventually, Microsoft upgraded the technology to *Microsoft Help Viewer*, released with Visual Studio 2010. A big selling point of the new system was that the help pages could be displayed in any standard web browser, instead of being limited to a proprietary help application.

Other Methods

Not every application uses Microsoft-defined help systems. In fact, a lot of desktop applications today either limit themselves to an HTML readme file, or direct users to the support area of a vendor web site. With the rise of mobile and cloud-hosted applications, this level of simple, centralized documentation is the likely future for many systems.

Designing HTML Help

HTML Help files are built from multiple source files.

- *Content files*, especially standard HTML files, communicate core information to the user, either through static text and graphics or through advanced web-page-style behaviors and scripts normally available in web pages.
- *The Help Contents file* uses *.hhc* for its file extension. Using standard HTML `<ul>` and `<li>` tags, the file specifies the hierarchical table of contents used by the help file.
- *The Help Keywords file* uses an *.hhk* file extension, and documents the index used to access help pages from specific predefined keywords.
- *The Help Project file*, using an *.hhp* file extension, defines an entire help project and its target *.chm* file. This INI-style text file identifies all the other files that will be compiled into the target help file. It also defines a few project-wide options.

You can build the primary content files by hand using any standard HTML tool you wish, as long as the output format matches what is expected by the HTML Help Compiler (supplied by Microsoft). For the content files, it generally doesn't matter what tool you use since standard HTML is sufficient. Any hyperlinks that you include in the content that refer to other help pages in the same directory will become standard help links in the compiled help file.

The non-content files require a very precise format; they are all based on HTML, except the Help Project file, which is an INI file. You will either design these files by hand using the expected format, or use a tool that can generate these files for you.

Microsoft provides a free tool that helps you create the non-content files, and joins together the content files with them for final compilation. You can download *HTML Help Workshop* directly from Microsoft's web site. Go to the Microsoft Download Center at https://www.microsoft.com/downloads and search for "HTML Help Workshop." You will receive a few results, but the first one in the list (when sorted by popularity) should be the one you need. Figure 23-1 shows the main page of the HTML Help Workshop application with an active project file open.

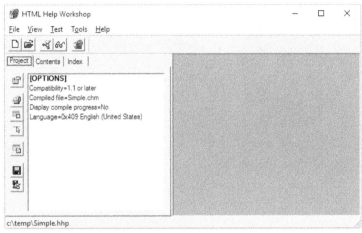

Figure 23-1. Giving help to those who really need it

In the rest of this section, we'll use HTML Help Workshop to build a simple HTML Help file that contains two pages: a welcome page and a more-information page. You can find this sample help project in the *HTML Help Sample* subdirectory of the book's installation directory.

Content Files

Our mini project includes two content files: *welcome.htm* and *moreinfo.htm*. Ever the technology maven, I crafted them in Notepad. Here's the content for *welcome.htm*.

```html
<html>
  <head><title>Welcome to My Help</title></head>
  <body>
    Welcome to My Help. For more information,
    <a href="moreinfo.htm">click here</a>.
  </body>
</html>
```

The *moreinfo.htm* file is a lot like it.

```html
<html>
  <head><title>My Help Additional Info</title></head>
  <body>
    Not much more to say. For a greeting,
    <a href="welcome.htm">click here</a>.
  </body>
</html>
```

You can add graphics files (such as JPEG and GIF files) and link them in as you normally would in a web page. Be sure to store the graphics files in the same directory (or subdirectory) as the main file for easy access.

Help Project File

Let's generate the remaining files through HTML Help Workshop. Start it up, and use the File→New menu command to create a new project. Using the New Project Wizard, identify the location and name of your new *.hhp* file. I'll create a file named *Simple.hhp* in the same folder as the two content files. The wizard prompts you for files already created. Check the HTML Files (.htm) field, as shown in Figure 23-2.

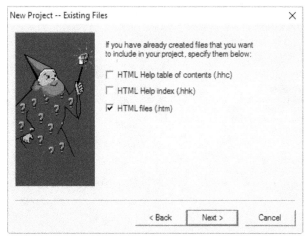

Figure 23-2. Locate the files now, or you can do it later

Add the two HTML files in the next step and complete the wizard. The project file is created with references to your two files.

The project is pretty empty; it doesn't even have a window title defined for the compiled help file. You can set the title and other general settings through the project options, accessed through the topmost button in the toolbar that runs on the left side of the main window. You can also double-click on the [OPTIONS] item in the project details list. When the option window appears, enter `Simple Help` in the Title field, and then click OK.

Here is what the project file contains at this point.

```
[OPTIONS]
Compatibility=1.1 or later
Compiled file=Simple.chm
Default topic=welcome.htm
Display compile progress=No
Language=0x409 English (United States)
Title=Simple Help

[FILES]
welcome.htm
moreinfo.htm

[INFOTYPES]
```

The file will change as we add the other two non-content files, but not by much.

Compiling the file right now (using the File→Compile menu command) and running it displays a very simple help window, as shown in Figure 23-3.

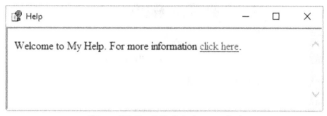

Figure 23-3. A little help; very little

Help Contents File

A table of contents will help the user peruse this massive online help experience. To add a contents file, click on the Contents tab on the left side of the main form, and respond to the prompt that you wish to create a new file, naming it *Simple.hhc*. The form changes to display a table-of-contents editor. Another way to create the contents file is by using the File→New menu command, and choosing Table of Contents from the New selection form. This is less direct, as it doesn't immediately connect the contents file with the project.

Use the new toolbar buttons running down the left side of the window to add and modify content entries. First, use the top button (Contents Properties) to edit the options for the table of contents. On the Table of Contents Properties form, uncheck the Use Folders Instead of Books field and click OK.

The next two buttons—the book button (Insert a Heading) and the page/question mark button (Insert a Page)—are the main buttons used to add new entries to the contents. I clicked the Insert a Page button to get to the Table of Contents Entry form shown in Figure 23-4.

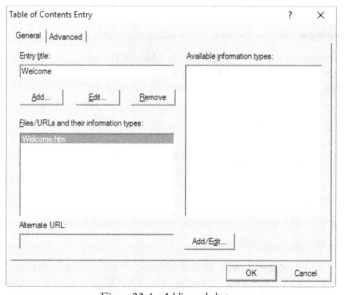

Figure 23-4. Adding a help page

As shown in the figure, I set the entry title (`Welcome`), and selected the Welcome to My Help (*welcome.htm*) file through the Add button. I did the same for the *moreinfo.htm* file, giving it a title of `More Information`. I also added a heading entry using the Insert a Heading toolbar button on the main form, naming it `Other`

Pages. I used the arrow toolbar buttons to move the *moreinfo.htm* entry into this heading section. Then I took a much-needed break and looked at my completed table of contents in Figure 23-5.

Figure 23-5. The full table of contents

If you compile and run the file, it now includes the table of contents in a separate panel, plus a toolbar (see Figure 23-6).

Figure 23-6. New and improved TOC; same great content

Help Keywords (Index) File

An index file lets the user access specific pages by searching for a concept or subject from a list. There is a many-to-many relationship between these keywords and the help pages: one keyword can lead to one or more pages, and a single page can be the target of multiple keywords.

Create an index by clicking on the Index tab on the left half of the main form, and respond to the prompt that you want to create a new index file, calling it *Simple.hhk.* As with the Contents editor, the Index editor includes a small vertical toolbar. Use the second button in the toolbar, the one with the key image, to create new keyword entries. I will add three keywords.

- `basic`, linking to *welcome.htm*
- `advanced`, linking to *moreinfo.htm*
- `everything`, linking to both pages

The Index Entry editor form works just like the Table of Contents Entry form, allowing you to specify the target pages for each keyword.

Saving and compiling the project adds index features to the compiled help file.

Formatting Help Windows

On my system, running the compiled help file displayed the content in a little window in the upper-right corner of the screen. But my help content is important; I want it to appear much closer to the middle of the screen, and in a larger window. Fortunately, you can control the windows used to display the content. Return to the Project tab and click on the third toolbar button down on the left side of the window. This Add/Modify Window Definitions button lets you define one or more windows to use for distinct help pages in your file. When prompted, add a New Window Type named `SimpleWindow`.

The Window Types dialog that appears has many options for getting just the window you want, although you're probably being too picky if you need more than, say, 243 different window types. The Position tab is a lot of fun. It includes an Autosizer button that lets you drag a window to the desired size. Adjust the size to something reasonable, add a Title Bar Text of *Simple Help* back on the General tab, and click OK. Since this is the only defined window, it becomes the default, and will be used for the main help display the next time you compile and run the file.

Accessing HTML Help

Visual Studio provides two primary methods of integrating online help into desktop applications. The first uses the *HelpProvider* control, found in the Components section of the Visual Studio Toolbox. The second uses the *Help.ShowHelp* method of the Windows Forms package. Both methods let you display specific pages or portions of a compiled HTML Help file.

HelpProvider Control

The *HelpProvider* control can be added to a form to enable access to online help. It provides two primary online help experiences: (1) standard access to compiled HTML Help files; and (2) pop-up help. Both methods put the focus on individual controls of a form, and on the specific help features to be tied to each control.

Accessing HTML help files

To use the *HelpProvider* control with compiled HTML Help files, set the control's *HelpNamespace* property to the location of a valid help file. Then adjust the properties of other controls on the form to refer to specific features within the help file. The *HelpProvider* control impacts other controls by adding several additional properties to each. Figure 23-7 shows the four additional properties (*HelpKeyword*, *HelpNavigator*, *HelpString*, and *ShowHelp*) automatically added to a *Button* control.

Figure 23-7. Adding help support to individual controls

The *HelpNavigator* property added to each control defines what features of the help file to access when the user presses the F1 key while that control has the focus. To access a specific page within the help file (such as *welcome.htm*), you set the target control's *HelpNavigator* property to *Topic* and set the related *HelpKeyword* property to the filename of the page (*welcome.htm*).

The *HelpNavigator* property for a control can be set to access non-page sections of the online help file as well. The value *TableOfContents* displays the file's contents outline; *Index* jumps to the keyword index. There are a few other choices as well.

Showing pop-up help

The *HelpProvider* control also enables pop-up help on individual controls. This help variation causes a small tool tip window to appear just above a control, displaying a short message that provides usage information for that control, as shown in Figure 23-8.

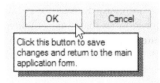

Figure 23-8. Pop-up help on a button control

Pop-up help works when you enable the pop-up button in the form's title bar. To set pop-up help for a control, follow these steps.

1. Add a *HelpProvider* control to the form, but don't bother setting its *HelpNamespace* property to a file.

2. Set the form's *HelpButton* property to *True*.

3. Set the form's *MaximizeBox* and *MinimizeBox* properties to *False*.

4. Set the *HelpString on helpProvider1* property to some informational text on each control that will display its own pop-up help.

The user displays pop-up help by first clicking on the question-mark "help" button in the form's title bar, and then clicking on a control.

ShowHelp Method

The *System.Windows.Forms.Help.ShowHelp* method displays specific portions of a compiled HTML Help file based on the arguments passed to the method. It's quite similar to the file-based help portion of the *HelpProvider* control, but in method form. To display a specific page within a help file, use this syntax.

```
Windows.Forms.Help.ShowHelp(this, "Simple.chm",
    HelpNavigator.Topic, "moreinfo.htm");
```

The first argument is a reference to the form calling the method.

A common way to use this method is to monitor the form for the F1 key, and call *ShowHelp* from the form's *KeyDown* event handler.

```
private void Form1_KeyDown(object sender, KeyEventArgs e)
{
    // ----- Call online help.
    if (e.KeyCode == Keys.F1)
        Windows.Forms.Help.ShowHelp(this, "Simple.chm",
            HelpNavigator.Topic, "moreinfo.htm");
}
```

You must set the form's *KeyPreview* property to *True* to trigger the form-level *KeyDown* event. Otherwise, all keys go to the active control and bypass the form-level events.

The *ShowHelp* method offers a lot more control over the user's online help experience since you (and not the *HelpProvider* control) determine exactly when to access the help file.

Summary

If it is your plan to stand over the shoulder of each user and give running verbal instructions while they sit before your software, by all means skip the writing of any online help or other user documentation. But if you plan to have a life, make it easier by including usage support right in the application. These are not the bad old days when you had to provide your own method of online help display, or needed to dig through the Windows API library to find the function that accessed the help file. This is .NET! It has all the help features you need built right in.

Crafting compiled HTML files is not too difficult with the HTML Help Workshop tool. But if you will work on any sizable help file, or if you want to add enhanced features consistently, you should think about plunking down a few hundred dollars on a third-party help development tool.

Project

Once you have access to an online help file, you have access to every page of it. That's usually a good thing, because users are curious. (I mean that they are inquisitive and not merely objects of curiosity.) But in the case of the Library Project, that curiosity could lead to topics that are really no business of ordinary patrons. Most of the features in the Library application are for administrative use only. To keep things as calm as possible, the Library Project includes two online help files.

- *LibraryBasic.chm*, a patron-focused help file that describes only the parts of the program the patron can access
- *LibraryAdmin.chm*, a file targeting administrators and librarians that fully describes the features of the application

This section builds both of these online help files, and integrates them into the Library application.

Building the Help Files

I've written the content for both online help files for you. You'll find it all in the *Online Help* subdirectory in the primary install directory for this book, with distinct directory branches for Basic and Admin files.

Most of the HTML files have a one-to-one link with specific forms in the application. For instance, the *ItemLookup.htm* file contains the online help content for the *ItemLookup.cs* form in the application. And this help page shows up in both the basic and administrative versions of the file. When the user presses F1 from the Item Lookup form, the application tries to show the online help page *ItemLookup.htm*. If the user is a standard patron, it accesses this page in the *LibraryBasic.chm* file; administrative users access the same page name, but from the *LibraryAdmin.chm* file instead.

Each help source folder contains *.hhp*, *.hhc*, and *.hhk* files that define the project, the contents, and the index details, respectively. The administrative version also includes a few GIF graphics files.

I've already compiled each file and placed a copy of the *.chm* file in these directories.

Adding Help Support to the Application

To keep things simple and somewhat centralized, we'll employ the `ShowHelp` method described earlier to display online help for each form in the application. Because of the busywork nature of the changes involved in this chapter's project code, I've already made all of the updates to the project. Most of the changes involve making the same change to every form in the project, all of which I'll describe soon.

Project Access

Load the "Chapter 23 (After) Code" project, either through the New Project templates or by accessing the project directly from the installation directory. This chapter does not include a "Before" variation of the project code.

The *Maintenance.cs* form already provides a way for the administrator to specify the location of each online help file. It updates two settings through the `Properties.Settings.Default` object.

```
Properties.Settings.Default.HelpFile =
    RecordBasicHelp.Text.Trim();
Properties.Settings.Default.HelpFileAdmin =
    RecordAdminHelp.Text.Trim();
```

Those settings also get stored in two global variables.

```
MainHelpFile = RecordBasicHelp.Text;
MainAdminHelpFile = RecordAdminHelp.Text;
```

That means we only need to call *ShowHelp* from each form and access one of the two files whenever the user presses F1.

But what if the administrator never uses the *Maintenance.cs* form to configure the locations of the help files? Since the help files will probably be installed in the same folder as the *Library.exe* program file, we should look there automatically. The *InitializeSystem* method in *General.cs* already sets the two global variables to the values stored in the settings.

```
// ----- Locate the online help files.
MainHelpFile =
    Properties.Settings.Default.HelpFile + "";
MainAdminHelpFile =
    Properties.Settings.Default.HelpFileAdmin + "";
```

Just in case these settings don't exist, I included some code just after these lines to provide default access to the files.

```
if ((MainHelpFile.Length == 0) |
    (MainAdminHelpFile.Length == 0))
{
    // ----- Try looking in the current directory.
    currentAssembly = Assembly.GetEntryAssembly();
    if (currentAssembly == null)
        currentAssembly = Assembly.GetCallingAssembly();
    appPath = System.IO.Path.GetDirectoryName(
        currentAssembly.Location);

    if (MainHelpFile.Length == 0)
        MainHelpFile = System.IO.Path.Combine(
            appPath, "LibraryBasic.chm");
    if (MainAdminHelpFile.Length == 0)
        MainAdminHelpFile = System.IO.Path.Combine(
            appPath, "LibraryAdmin.chm");
}
```

Since we need to continuously adapt to the current user state of the application (whether the user is a patron or an administrator), a centralized routine that displays help from the correct file seems best. Here's the code for *OnlineHelp*, a new method in the *General.cs* file.

```
public static void OnlineHelp(
    Form whichForm, string contextName)
{
    // ----- Show the online help. Differentiate between the
    //       basic and the administrative online help usage.
    string fileToUse;
```

```
    // ----- Which file to use.
    if (LoggedInUserID == -1L)
        fileToUse = MainHelpFile;
    else
        fileToUse = MainAdminHelpFile;
    if (fileToUse.Length == 0)
    {
        MessageBox.Show(
            "Online help is not properly configured.",
            ProgramTitle, MessageBoxButtons.OK,
            MessageBoxIcon.Exclamation);
        return;
    }

    // ----- Show the online help.
    try
    {
        Help.ShowHelp(whichForm, fileToUse,
            HelpNavigator.Topic, contextName);
    }
    catch
    {
        MessageBox.Show(
            "An error occurred while trying to access " +
            "the online help file.", ProgramTitle,
            MessageBoxButtons.OK, MessageBoxIcon.Exclamation);
    }
}
```

The biggest task in this chapter involves going to each form in the project and making these two changes.

- Set the form's *KeyPreview* property to *True*.
- Add a call to *OnlineHelp* from the form's *KeyDown* event handler.

Here's the code added to the *ChangeUser.cs* form.

```
private void ChangeUser_KeyDown(
    object sender, KeyEventArgs e)
{
    // ----- F1 shows online help.
    if (e.KeyCode == Keys.F1)
        OnlineHelp(this, "ChangeUser.htm");
}
```

A few of the forms process online help requests a little differently from the others. *AboutProgram.cs* doesn't include its own online help page. Instead, it displays *Welcome.htm*. *Splash.cs* doesn't show any online help since the user isn't really supposed to interact with it. *ReportBuiltInViewer.cs*, the form that shows each of the five built-in reports, displays help for a related form via *ReportSelect.htm*. The *CheckLookup.cs* form has two associated online help pages: one for checkout and one for check-in of items. Its *KeyDown* event handler chooses the right page based on the current mode of the form.

```
    // ----- F1 shows online help.
    if (e.KeyCode == Keys.F1)
    {
        if (CheckInMode == true)
            OnlineHelp(this, "CheckLookup_In.htm");
```

```
    else
        OnlineHelp(this, "CheckLookup_Out.htm");
}
```

The *MainForm.cs* form is even more diverse, choosing from among nine distinct online help pages when in administrative mode. Each panel on the main form is like a whole separate form, so I added an online help page for each panel. Code in the form's *KeyDown* event handler shows the right page based on the currently displayed panel.

```
if (PanelLibraryItem.Visible == true)
    OnlineHelp(this, "MainForm_Library.htm");
else if (PanelPatronRecord.Visible == true)
    OnlineHelp(this, "MainForm_Patron.htm");
else if (PanelHelp.Visible == true)
    OnlineHelp(this, "MainForm_Help.htm");
else if (PanelCheckOut.Visible == true)
    OnlineHelp(this, "MainForm_Out.htm");
else if (PanelCheckIn.Visible == true)
    OnlineHelp(this, "MainForm_In.htm");
else if (PanelAdmin.Visible == true)
    OnlineHelp(this, "MainForm_Admin.htm");
else if (PanelProcess.Visible == true)
    OnlineHelp(this, "MainForm_Daily.htm");
else if (PanelReports.Visible == true)
    OnlineHelp(this, "MainForm_Print.htm");
else
    OnlineHelp(this, "MainForm_Basic.htm");
```

The Help panel on the main form includes buttons designed to jump to the table of contents and index of the current online help file. I added event handlers for these buttons. The code for both *MainForm.ActHelpContents_Click* and *MainForm.ActHelpIndex_Click* is just like the code in the generic *OnlineHelp* routine, except for the final call to *ShowHelp*.

```
private void ActHelpContents_Click(
    object sender, EventArgs e)
{
    // ----- Show the online help table of contents.
    ...
    Help.ShowHelp(this, fileToUse,
        HelpNavigator.TableOfContents);
    ...
}

private void ActHelpIndex_Click(
    object sender, EventArgs e)
{
    // ----- Show the online help index.
    ...
    Help.ShowHelp(this, fileToUse, HelpNavigator.Index);
    ...
}
```

Once the online help (*.chm*) files are in place, and once the application is properly configured to locate those files on the workstation, the user can access help from any form by pressing the F1 key. Figure 23-9 shows help accessed from the Library Items panel of the main form.

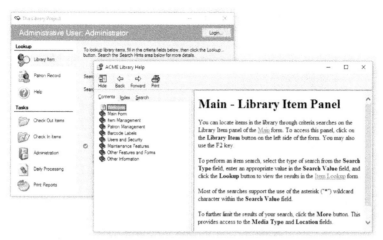

Figure 23-9. Answering the call for help

Speaking of correctly configuring the *.chm* files, we still have to figure out how to get the entire application—including the online help files—onto the client workstation, and at a cost that will put food on the table. We'll look at these deployment issues in the next chapter.

Chapter 24

Deployment

Although Aesop lived thousands of years ago, he has much to tell us about software development. His story of the boy who cried wolf is a perfect example. It concerns a young shepherd boy who tricks nearby villagers repeatedly by shouting, "Wolf!" when no such danger exists. The trick was good for a few laughs, but then the boy found out the consequences of his actions: he couldn't get any villagers to buy his sheep and he had to eat them all by himself. Yuck! If only the boy had learned how to properly deploy his flock into the hands of the villagers instead of making up wolf-based lies, he would never have come to such a tragic end.

So, Aesop clearly shows us how important deployment is. And Microsoft took this lesson to heart by including several different options right in Visual Studio that let you install your compiled applications and supporting files onto a target workstation or device. We'll look at these methods in this chapter, and use one of the methods to build a setup program for the Library Project.

What's Involved in Deployment?

In the days before Microsoft Windows, deployment wasn't so difficult. Many programs were nothing more than an MS-DOS executable file, with perhaps one or two supporting data and help files. That was it. Once you copied those files into some folder on the client workstation and updated the *PATH* environment variable, you were done.

Microsoft Windows applications (and large and complex MS-DOS programs) were not as easy to install. They often had these DLL file things hanging off them—files that had to be put in the proper places. And sometimes you didn't know what that proper place was, since a third-party vendor may have supplied the DLL without sufficient documentation. Then there were the configuration files, supporting data files, user-specific and workstation-specific changes to the system registry, shortcuts on the desktop and in the Start menu, uninstall settings and programs, two sets of forms (in triplicate) to the Library of Congress, online help files, the readme and license agreement files for the distribution CD, special fonts that may be required for the program, and on and on and on.

I don't think I mentioned even half of the files you need to deploy a full-bodied Windows application, but you can already see how involved it is. Fortunately, Visual Studio will share the burden with you in exchange for some simple, though sometimes indirect, configuration on your part.

Depending on the type of application you are building, your desired installation target, and the edition of Visual C# you have installed on your system, the deployment features in Visual Studio typically provide you with the core functionality you need to distribute standard desktop, web-based, and mobile applications. If your deployment needs are complex, or if you fall outside of the standard use cases, there are Microsoft-created and third-party setup-and-deployment options you can obtain instead, some of which include advanced features such as scripting support.

Deployment Methods within Visual Studio

Writing your own installation application has always been an option for the savvy developer. But after spending what seemed like centuries writing the perfect application, it was a bit of a letdown to develop a tiny program that copied file X to location Y. Fortunately, the earliest releases of Visual C# included support for the Windows Installer platform, with its all-powerful *.msi* files. While the installation project templates included with Visual Studio provided access to only the most basic Windows Installer features, it was often sufficient for most desktop applications.

These days, Visual Studio includes several deployment methods, a tribute to the different types of applications, the different types of users, and the different types of secure environments that a programmer may need to target. Read through each of the available methods to see which one best meets the needs of your program. I've already made my selection for the Library Project, which I'll reveal in a public ceremony about halfway through this chapter.

Direct ASP.NET Deployment

ASP.NET is Microsoft's official web development platform, and a gigantic part of Visual Studio. Although I haven't covered web application or web service programming in this book, you'll be glad to know that if you choose to create such programs in Visual Studio, the platform already includes the tools you need to deploy your site to a web server.

When you are ready to deploy your web site, Visual Studio includes a Build→Publish menu command that gets the ball rolling. Often, you will direct the publishing process to dump your site files out to a directory, ready for migration to your target server. But you can also automate remote FTP deployments for uploading your site to a Microsoft Azure host. For advanced deployments, the publishing process exposes script-based installation rules that you can modify to your heart's content, as long as you don't include fatal typos.

That's the extent of my ASP.NET presentation. You can find out more about ASP.NET Core 1.0 development and the deployment of ASP.NET systems on the Microsoft MSDN web site.

XCopy Deployment

Compiled .NET assemblies contain a manifest that fully describes the assembly and its needs. This means that you can copy any assembly to another system that has the correct version of the .NET Framework installed, and as long as the other files the assembly needs are copied as well, the program will run. This is called "XCopy deployment," because you can use the command-line *XCopy* command to move the files.

You may be thinking, "Well, duh! An EXE assembly is a real Windows program. Of course it will run when I copy it to a new system." Well, that's true. But it wasn't true in the Wild West days of pre-.NET applications. Many applications in those days used COM ("Component Object Model") libraries, which had to be configured in the Windows Registry before they could be accessed at runtime. Depending on the language used to develop the Windows app, certain Microsoft-supplied runtime libraries would also need to be installed. The .NET Framework is a requirement for .NET programs, but since the framework is managed automatically by the Windows Update system, this is not as big of a headache.

What I've taken too many sentences to say is that in most cases, you can install a .NET desktop or console application on a workstation just by copying the program, and maybe a few support files, to a directory. I'm not saying that this is how you should install programs. Actually, I would be shocked—shocked!—if I discovered any of my programming friends using this method in a real business environment. But .NET makes this deployment option available to you if you don't want to be my friend anymore.

If you do use XCopy deployment, you probably won't have any issues with security or administrative limitations that may be imposed on the workstation. Chances are, if you're installing software using the

XCopy command or by dragging-and-dropping files, it's probably because you are friends with the owner of the workstation, and it's really none of my business who you want to have as your friends.

Windows Installer Deployment

Windows Installer Projects used to be the official installation system provided with Visual Studio. For years, they served as the base system for standard Visual Studio-generated installation packages. And then, one day, they all went away.

For reasons that still boggle the mind, Microsoft removed Windows Installer Projects from Visual Studio 2012. Perhaps it had to do with the inclusion of InstallShield Limited Edition, which first appeared in Visual Studio 2010, and which I'll discuss below. But between 2012 and 2014, users who wished to upgrade from Visual Studio 2010 had to give up their cherished Installer Projects.

Visual Studio 2015 still does not come with intrinsic support for Windows Installer Projects. However, in 2014, Microsoft responded to demands to bring these types of projects back, and began offering an installer enhancement to Visual Studio as a separate free download from its web site. For the Library Project, we will download, install, and use this technology. But first, let's learn a little about what it does.

Windows Installer Projects target the conveniently named Windows Installer technology, a core part of Microsoft's deployment story since Windows 2000. Before Windows Installer, each installation package vendor pretty much did things as they saw fit. But this meant that installed products sometimes clobbered one another, since one software package didn't necessarily look out for files installed by another tool. Repairing such damage was difficult for the user, who usually didn't even know which files were installed or updated.

Microsoft sought to change that with Windows Installer. One of the key features of the system is its database of installed and updated files. It also supports a full uninstall/restore and rollback capability so that any failure can be fully undone, restoring the system to its previous state. Other features include support for patching, rebooting, custom enhancements, some limited user interface and prompt design, the ability to repair or "heal" a previously installed but damaged program, and install-on-demand, which keeps features or full applications on the installation media until the user tries to use that feature.

The heart of the Windows Installer system is the "MSI" file (with an *.msi* file extension), the single file that contains all the files and instructions needed to install, update, and uninstall a software product. When enhanced with Windows Installer Project templates, Visual Studio can create setup projects based on the MSI standard, although you can't use some of the more advanced features of Windows Installer through Visual Studio. Still, if your needs are simple—and most business-level software projects written in Visual C# have simple installation needs—the Windows Installer Project template is probably all you require.

Because we'll be using this technology for the Library Project, go ahead and download the needed update from the MSDN web site. Access MSDN's product gallery (http://visualstudiogallery.msdn.microsoft.com), and search for "Installer Projects 2015." Hopefully, the first result should be the one you want. Download and install the extension. Don't you think that installing an installer is weird?

Building a setup project is just as easy as creating regular Visual Studio projects. But first, we need something to set up. For the discussion in this section, I've created a desktop application. Well, not a very good one. I simply created a new *WindowsFormsApplication1* project with its default *Form1*, and saved it to my *C:\temp* folder. All it does when you run it is display *Form1*.

To create an MSI installation file for a Visual C# project, open that project in Visual Studio and use the File→Add→New Project menu command to add a setup project to the entire solution that contains your original project. Figure 24-1 shows the Add New Project dialog. Under the Other Project Types→Visual

Studio Installer template branch, select the Setup Wizard template to create a setup program for the active solution. Set the Name and Location fields according to your needs, and then click OK.

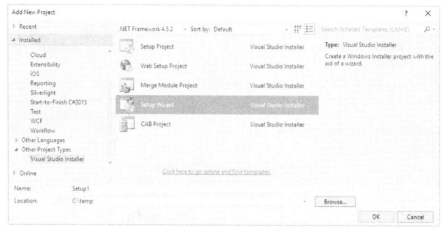

Figure 24-1. Adding a setup project to your solution

The Setup Wizard appears, leading you through five steps to peace, harmony, and a working MSI file.

Step 1

The first wizard step just says "Welcome," so click Next and get on with post-welcome activities.

Step 2

Step 2 asks you for the type of setup project to generate. Personally, I think it could have figured this out from the content of the already-loaded projects, but if the wizard did everything, why would the world need programmers like us? There are four choices, shown in Figure 24-2.

Figure 24-2. Choosing the type of setup program

The first two choices create full setup files for either desktop or web-based applications. (The web-based setup would be delivered to a web site administrator for installation on the server.) *Merge modules* let you create a portion of an installation that can later be merged into a full MSI file. This is a good choice if you are designing a library that will be used for multiple applications, but it is useless on its own. The CAB file option creates an archive of files that can be installed using slightly older file distribution technology. Since I'm targeting a desktop application, I'll choose the Create a Setup for a Windows Application option, and then click Next.

Step 3

Although you can create a setup program that simply installs miscellaneous files scavenged from your hard disk, you usually build a setup project based on the files or compiled output of other projects. The third wizard step prompts you to include elements from the other projects found in the active Visual Studio solution. I've chosen to include the compiled EXE file from my desktop project, as shown in Figure 24-3.

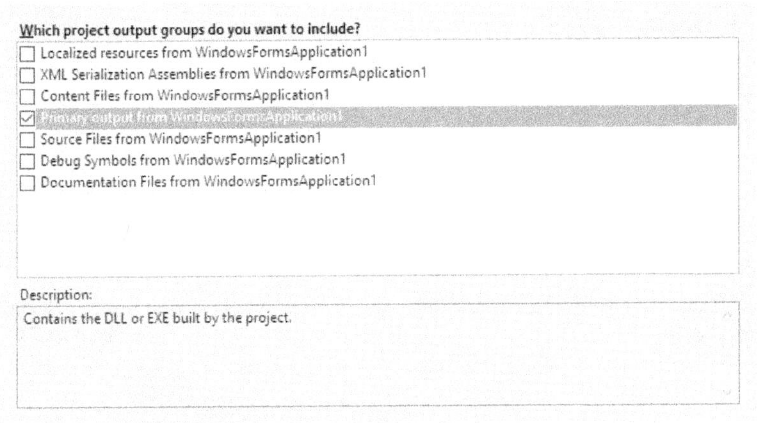

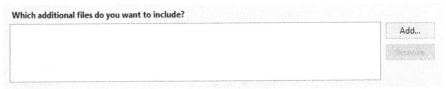

Which project output groups do you want to include?
- ☐ Localized resources from WindowsFormsApplication1
- ☐ XML Serialization Assemblies from WindowsFormsApplication1
- ☐ Content Files from WindowsFormsApplication1
- ☑ Primary output from WindowsFormsApplication1
- ☐ Source Files from WindowsFormsApplication1
- ☐ Debug Symbols from WindowsFormsApplication1
- ☐ Documentation Files from WindowsFormsApplication1

Description:
Contains the DLL or EXE built by the project.

Figure 24-3. Choosing project elements to include in the setup

I generally don't want to include my source code in the setup project, so I'll leave that element unchecked. But the Content Files item may be useful. If my project had a compiled online help file (with a *.chm* file extension), I could have added it as a standard content file to the main project via the Project→Add Existing Item menu command. That file would be classified as Content, and could move into this setup project through the Content Files selection. But there are other ways to include online help in the installation, which we'll see in the next step. For now, I'll stick with the Primary Output selection, and click the Next button.

Step 4

In this step, you can add any other non-project-specific files you want to the setup project (see Figure 24-4). Readme files, online help content, license agreements, pictures of your kids, and pretty much anything else can be included here. I've got nothing more to add. Click Next.

Which additional files do you want to include?

[Add...]
[Remove]

Figure 24-4. Add those other files that have always wanted a chance at setup project stardom

Step 5

The final step displays a summary of the choices you made (see Figure 24-5). Well, that wizard was pretty easy. We had to do work in only three of the five steps. Click Finish to complete the wizard.

Figure 24-5. Confirming our choices for the setup project

After the wizard

Once the wizard completes, the primary interface for Visual Studio setup project design appears in the development window. Figure 24-6 shows Visual Studio displaying the newly generated setup project for *WindowsFormsApplication1*, another project that also appears in the Solution Explorer panel.

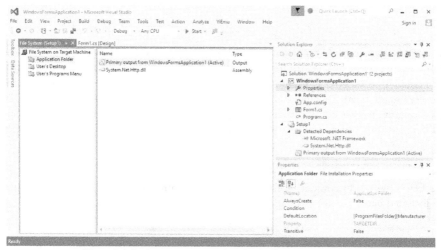

Figure 24-6. A setup project within the development environment

The main window in Figure 24-6 is one of several "editors" that let you customize the setup project. You can access each editor through the View→Editor menu command, or by using the toolbar buttons in the Solution Explorer panel.

File System Editor

That's the editor you already saw in Figure 24-6. It presents a standard folder/item view of portions of the target system's filesystem. Through this hierarchy, you place files (the EXE output from your main project, help files, configuration files, shortcuts to any of these files, etc.) into special folders (Application folder, Desktop, 32- or 64-bit Program Files, Fonts, the Start Menu folder, and others). If you don't see a folder you want in the File System on Target Machine panel, use the Action→Add Special Folder menu command to include it in the list. Besides the standard special folders, the Add Special Folder menu includes a Custom Folder option that lets you create a specific folder anywhere on the target system.

Registry Editor

This editor displays a truncated hierarchy of the registry hives. Any keys or values added here will be created in the user's registry during installation.

File Types Editor

This editor lets you define associations between a file extension (such as *.txt*) and specific programs or actions. Any custom action, such as Open or Print, can be linked to any command text you wish, including commands that target the primary assembly being installed.

User Interface Editor

The default setup project includes a few forms that prompt for things such as installation location and confirmation that the installation should occur. You can insert additional dialog boxes into the flow of the installation. But beware: you will not be adding full Visual C#-enabled forms. Instead, you will choose from a few predefined dialogs (such as the License Agreement dialog, or the 4 Radio Buttons dialog), and set the dialog properties to configure the display text of each dialog field or prompt. Each user entry field or control includes a named value that you use in the other editors to limit a specific installation action. For instance, you could monitor the value of a user-prompted checkbox, and if the user didn't check it, you could withhold the installation of certain files that were associated with that checkbox.

Custom Actions Editor

If you need the ultimate level of control, you can add a custom action, a call to an external program or script, that runs at a certain point in the install (or uninstall) process.

Launch Conditions Editor

If the target workstation must be in a certain state before you can successfully install the project, this editor lets you define the limiting conditions. By default, the installer adds the .NET Framework as an installation condition; the framework must be installed before the project can be installed. You can look for specific files or registry keys that must be present before installation begins. For instance, you might want to confirm that the target database drivers are on the system before you install a database-dependent application.

Generating the MSI file

Once you've set up your project through the various editors, you output the final MSI file by building the solution via the Build→Build Solution menu command. The MSI file appears in the location specified in the setup project's properties (Project→Properties). This file contains all the instructions and content required to fully install the application on the target workstation.

InstallShield Deployment

InstallShield is a popular third-party installation tool. If you paid for a Visual Studio 2015 license, then you also received a complimentary copy of InstallShield Limited Edition for Visual Studio. If instead you downloaded the free Community Edition of Visual Studio, you got zilch. With Microsoft pushing the Community Edition as the replacement of choice for individuals and small businesses that previously purchased Visual Studio Professional Edition, there's a good chance that you're using this freebee. It was this broad reach of the Community Edition that prompted me to use the older Windows Installer option for the Library Project.

The general concepts behind InstallShield deployment projects are exactly the same as those for Windows Installer projects. You indicate the files to deploy, where to deploy them, and specify other configuration and dependency needs on the target system. Just be aware of the word "Limited" in the product name. The features are restricted, and if you require advanced installation scenarios, you will need to hand over a purchase order from your company's accounting department to get the proper version.

ClickOnce Deployment

Visual Studio includes a deployment method called *ClickOnce*. It is designed to provide the ultimate in setup deployment ease for desktop (Windows Forms and WPF) applications. It still involves a wizard, but for basic installations, that's all there is to it. Once your application is published through ClickOnce, the user can install it directly from a web site or other stored location.

This sounds like a standard MSI installation, but it is different in several ways.

- ClickOnce deployments can be installed even if the current user does not have local administrative privileges. Many software installs affect key files in the Windows system folders, or in other important but restricted directories. If you are a developer, it's likely that you never experience this problem because you are the administrator on your own workstation. But in IT department-managed organizations with many users, there is a benefit to reducing the privilege level of individual users. One negative side effect of this is that an administrator must be present to install some software products. But that's not the case with ClickOnce. Is your entire IT department out to lunch? (I mean that literally.) No problem. Any ClickOnce-published application can be installed by any user. The software is installed in a "sandbox" that protects the system and other applications from the ClickOnce-installed program's villainous intents.

- A ClickOnce-deployed application can trigger its own automatic software updates. If configured in this way, the program will check the original deployment location for a new version each time it runs. If there is a new version, it will be installed automatically without the user having to do a thing.

- ClickOnce applications are designed for ease of installation. With an MSI-deployed application, you need to obtain the MSI file and process it through the Windows Installer system. Although you also have to download a ClickOnce deployment, it happens more or less transparently. A ClickOnce-published application can be configured so that it looks like an extension of a web page: click a link, and the program immediately runs, displaying its main form to the user.

That sounds great. But it's not all peaches and cream. Since ClickOnce-enabled applications (by default) run in their own sandbox, they are limited in their access to some local resources. Also, to fully support all of the automatic-updating features, you must add code to your application that performs the actual update. (The `System.Deployment` namespace provides access to these features.)

To deploy your project via ClickOnce, use the Build→Publish menu command in Visual Studio. After asking you some very basic questions about where the user will obtain the deployment file (from a web site, a network folder, or a media drive), Visual Studio generates the installation file and makes it immediately available for use.

Of course, that method gives you only the most basic installation options. It makes the primary EXE or DLL of your project (and its dependencies) available for installation on the target workstation, but that's about it. If you want more control over the publishing process and the components it will include, use the Publish tab of your project's properties, as shown in Figure 24-7.

This panel includes fields that let you set the version number for the published installation package. If you modify this version number and republish the application, the custom deployment code you added to the application can detect the new version and initiate an update from the distribution location.

Figure 24-7. The world of publishing, just a mouse click away

Windows Store Deployment

If you plan to distribute your desktop or mobile application through the Microsoft Windows store, you must create a Windows Store deployment. The full packaging and deployment process is quite involved, requiring that you establish credentials with Microsoft, and follow all of the submission requirements before your app becomes available to the masses. Since I'm not covering Windows Store projects in this book, I'll let you research the deployment process for such apps on your own.

Summary

It's really nice that Visual Studio provides a few different deployment methods for your custom applications. Visual C# and the larger Visual Studio environment were designed as general-purpose programming systems that allow you to solve almost any development problem facing you or your users. But that doesn't mean that every single feature in the system is applicable to all environments. By having a few different deployment options available, Visual Studio is even more general-purpose than before, and I think that's just great. Sure, you have to take five minutes and decide between MSI, ClickOnce, and Windows Store targets. But in most projects, the needs of the users will push you in one specific direction.

Project

Although I could have created a ClickOnce deployment for the Library Project, the needs of the application seemed more in line with a traditional MSI installation. The Library application is meant to be a permanent feature on the target workstation, so it's likely that someone with IT knowledge or administrative privileges will perform the actual installation. As it is a licensed product, there is little chance that I would be putting copies of the Library installation out on my public web site. A CD or network-based distribution—common for MSI installations—is the expected medium. Also, since it's a quality piece of software from a trusted vendor (that's me), there isn't a need for a protective sandbox. Still, the application does include several files, including two online help files, so an *XCopy* installation would be a burden. All in all, a standard MSI installation is the best deployment option.

Planning the Deployment

The Setup Wizard, described above, automatically adds my project assembly to the MSI file, but I am sure other files are needed to properly deploy the Library Project. A quick look through the previous chapters reveals the following list of file requirements.

The .NET Framework

> This must be installed on the target system to run the Library application. The setup program will need to automatically install the framework if it isn't already on the target system.

Library.exe

> This is the primary assembly. The install would be useless without it.

LibraryBasic.chm and *LibraryAdmin.chm*

> These online help files will be installed in the same folder as the primary application.

The barcode font

> If you have obtained distribution rights for a barcode font, your setup program can copy it directly to the target system's *Fonts* folder.

LibraryLicense.lic

> Ah, the license file—remember that this hand-generated file needs to be custom-crafted for each customer purchasing the Library application. Compiling it directly into the setup program seems extreme, since I would have to regenerate Setup for each customer. Instead, I will put the file on the distribution source (such as the install CD), and have the user locate it when running the Library program.

ACME Library Resource Kit.pdf

> This administrator-level file shouldn't be installed by default on a customer workstation. But we'll include it on the distribution media.

Database Creation Script.sql

> If I were developing a full end-user application, I would build a separate setup system for the server portion, focusing mainly on the database setup. Since this book is designed as an introduction only, I will just copy the database build script to the distribution media and assume that a qualified IT representative or database administrator will take charge of this installation step.

Readme.htm

> The CD should include an informational file right at the root that will tell the user how to use the files on the CD. I haven't written this file yet, but I will before the chapter ends.

The generated Setup file will include only the first four items in that list (three if you are excluding the font), and the first two are added automatically by the Setup Wizard. This won't be too difficult.

Building the Setup Project

Earlier in the chapter, we added a new setup project to an existing project, combining them into a single solution. It is possible to build a setup project that appears alone within Visual Studio. In such projects, you need to browse for the target assembly (*release\Library.exe*) to include it in the Setup output. However, the Setup Wizard doesn't do much for you if you go that route. So, for the Library application, let's add a new setup project to a main project already loaded into Visual Studio.

> **Project Access**
>
> Load the "Chapter 23 (After) Code" project through the New Project templates. Then save the project to a folder where you want to build the complete Setup solution. I have also included a "Chapter 24" project in the installation directory, but not as a project template. Its folder already contains a linked setup project. If you want to view this finished solution, open the *Library.sln* file in the *Chapter 24* folder.

The first few steps parallel those we performed earlier in this chapter. Once you have the Library program loaded and saved to its target folder, add a new setup project using the File→Add→New Project menu command. As described above, select Setup Wizard as the template, enter `LibrarySetup` for the Name, and use the just-saved Library project's folder as the Location. Apply the following settings within the wizard.

- In step 2, select Create a Setup for a Windows Application.
- In step 3, select Primary Output from Library from the list.
- In step 4, locate and add the *LibraryBasic.chm* and *LibraryAdmin.chm* files. In this book's installation directory, you can find them in the subdirectory named *Online Help*.

Complete the wizard and use the File→Save All menu command. When prompted to save the solution file (*Library.sln*), just store it in the Library project directory, which should already be selected.

As before, the setup project opens to the File System Editor. Before making any changes within the editor, let's set some Setup-wide properties. Click on LibrarySetup in the Solution Explorer panel, and modify the following properties in the Properties panel.

- Set the `Author` property to `Tim Patrick` or your own name.
- Set the `Manufacturer` property to `ACME`.
- Set the `ManufacturerURL` property to `http://www.owanipress.com`, or any web site you wish to use.
- Set the `ProductName` property to `ACME Library`.
- Set the `Title` property to `ACME Library Setup`.

Since the File System Editor is open, let's make a few changes there. When we added the *Library.exe* assembly through the wizard, it figured out all of the required dependencies. Not only do the main program and help file items appear in the Application Folder section, but several additional DLLs appear, all used to support the main application (see Figure 24-8).

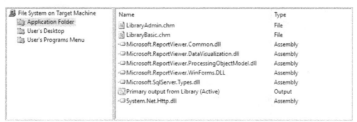

Figure 24-8. A lot more files than we bargained for

Since these DLLs are supplied by Microsoft as part of .NET, it doesn't make much sense to store them in my own application's installation directory. They should go in the Global Assembly Cache (GAC), the special system folder that maintains shared .NET assemblies. The GAC isn't one of the folder choices displayed in the editor, but it can be. Make sure that the File System on Target System item in the left-hand panel of the File System Editor is selected, and then use the Action→Add Special Folder→Global Assembly Cache

Folder menu command. A new folder, Global Assembly Cache Folder, appears in the left-side panel. Select the Application Folder item again, and then drag the various DLL items into the new Global Assembly Cache Folder item, as shown in Figure 24-9.

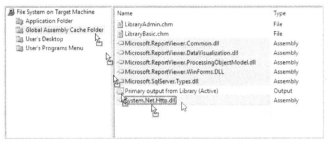

Figure 24-9. Make these DLL files someone else's responsibility

Let's add two shortcuts to the user's system during installation: one on the desktop and one in the Start menu's Programs section. Both shortcuts point to the main *Library.exe* assembly. The Setup Wizard anticipated our needs by adding the *User's Desktop* and *User's Programs Menu* folders to the File System Editor. All we have to do is add a shortcut to each folder.

Let's start with the desktop. Select the *User's Desktop* folder and then right-click in the right-side panel (where the files would appear). From the context menu, choose the Create New Shortcut menu command. (This same command is available from the main Action menu when the right-side panel is active.) The Select Item in Project dialog, shown in Figure 24-10, appears. Choose the Application Folder from the Look In field, then select Primary Output from Library (Active) from the item list. Click the OK button. The new shortcut appears in the right-side panel, waiting for you to give it a more meaningful name. Give it the name *ACME Library*.

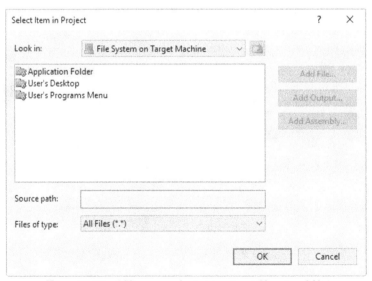

Figure 24-10. Adding a new shortcut to a target file system folder

To create the same shortcut in the Start menu, follow all the steps in the previous paragraph, but start from the *User's Programs Menu* folder instead of the *User's Desktop* folder.

Adding those shortcuts was a good idea, but whenever I install new software, I always immediately delete any shortcuts that get added to the desktop. Adding an icon to the Start menu makes sense, but I like keeping a nice, clean desktop. Laugh if you want, but keeping that desktop free from clutter is what helps make me a world-famous author and developer.

What we need is a way to alter the behavior of the setup program so that it doesn't create the desktop icon if the user doesn't want one. The setup project provides a way to do this. First, we need to add a prompt where the user indicates a desktop-icon preference, and then we need to act on that preference. The first step involves altering the user interface of the setup program. Such changes occur through the User Interface Editor. Display this editor with the View→Editor→User Interface menu command. The User Interface Editor appears, as shown in Figure 24-11.

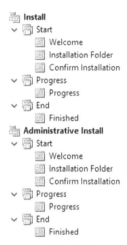

Figure 24-11. The user interface editor displays each dialog and each prompt

The User Interface Editor is divided into two main installation types: Install and Administrative Install. The administrative branch is used only when an administrator wants to store the setup image on a shared network folder. It doesn't allow the types of changes we want to make. So, let's focus on the standard Install branch, which manages standard user installations on a client workstation. Both branches include step-by-step prompts that appear to the user during the setup process. Custom data collection prompts can be added only to the Start entry in the Install main branch.

During actual setup, the user interface prompts the user in a wizard-like fashion. During the initial Start phase, the setup program collects the user's desires for the remainder of the process. Once this section ends, the installation proceeds until it completes or fails. What we want to do is insert a new step in the wizard process, displaying a checkbox to the user that asks whether the desktop icon should appear or not. Additional data collection fields such as these are added through new dialogs. And there just happens to be a dialog that includes a customizable checkbox. In the Install branch, right-click on the Start item and select Add Dialog from the context menu. The Add Dialog window, shown in Figure 24-12, displays the available dialogs. Select the Checkboxes (A) item from the list and click OK.

The new Checkboxes (A) item appears in the Install/Start section. Use the mouse to drag it up until it appears between the Welcome and Installation Folders dialogs. The Checkboxes dialog lets you display up to four checkbox selections with custom captions. Make sure it is selected in the dialog outline, and then use the Properties panel to set this new dialog's properties.

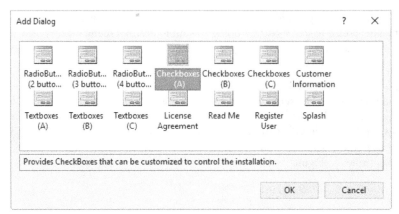

Figure 24-12. A few different dialog options are available for setup customization

- Set the `BannerText` property to `Installation Options`. This text appears near the top of the dialog window, displaying a large main title.

- Set the `BodyText` property to `Select the options you wish to use for this installation`.

- Set the `Checkbox1Label` property to `Add an icon for ACME Library to the desktop`. This defines the custom text for the first checkbox control.

- Set the `Checkbox1Property` property to `LIBRARY_DESKTOP_LINK`. This gives the checkbox a name that we can use later to alter the install process.

- Set the `Checkbox1Value` property to `Checked`. This tells the installation to include the desktop icon by default.

- Set the `Checkbox2Visible`, `Checkbox3Visible`, and `Checkbox4Visible` properties to `False`, hiding the other three unused checkboxes.

During the setup process, the user sees the new dialog prompt in Figure 24-13. It includes the banner text, the body text, and the single checkbox as configured in the custom dialog's properties.

Now it's time to use that checkbox setting. Close the User Interface Editor and return to the File System Editor. Select the *User's Desktop* folder in the left-side panel, and then go to the Properties panel. One of the few listed properties is `Condition`, which lets you define a Boolean condition that, when true, installs the associated files on the user's desktop. However, if the condition is false, no associated files will be placed on the user's desktop during installation. Set this property to the following text.

```
LIBRARY_DESKTOP_LINK
```

This is the name we gave to the first checkbox back in the dialog design. During installation, the setup program checks the user's selection, and alters the desktop update as requested.

One thing I won't be adding to my version of the setup program is the barcode font. Sadly, I have not acquired a license to distribute a third-party font to you or anyone else reading this book. The good news is that I just saved you $10 on the cost of the book. The bad news is that I will have to tell you how to add the font, but not actually do it.

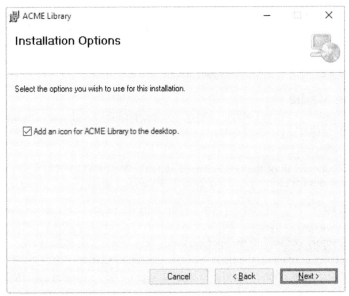

Figure 24-13. The sparse but useful checkbox dialog in action

Actually, you can probably already guess how to do it. The *Fonts* folder is one of the special folders available in the File System Editor. When the File System on Target Machine item on the left-side panel is active, use the Action→Add Special Folder→Fonts Folder menu command. Then add the original font file (a TrueType *.ttf* file) to the *Fonts* folder section. You won't be able to add this font directly from your own *Windows\Fonts* folder. Instead, you will need to get the original *.ttf* file and use that. On the target workstation, the setup program properly installs and registers the font for use in Windows.

The setup project is complete. The only thing left to do is to generate the MSI file. You might not have noticed it, but Visual Studio includes different compilation configurations in every project. The two default configurations are Debug and Release, and they each generate a different set and flavor of final output files when you compile your application. Normally, your project is set to Debug, but you can change it by using the Configuration Manager. In Visual Studio, select the Build→Configuration Manager menu command to display the manager's form (see Figure 24-14). In this form, change the Active Solution Configuration setting from Debug to Release, then click the Close button.

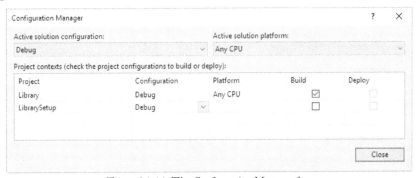

Figure 24-14. The Configuration Manager form

It's time to build the MSI file. Right-click on the LibrarySetup root in the Solution Explorer panel, and select Build from the context menu. In just a few seconds, your MSI file will be baked and ready to eat. You'll find it in the setup project's *Release* subdirectory. This directory also includes a *Setup.exe* file that acts as a bootstrapper. Any standard Windows 10 system will work with just the plain MSI file, but providing a *Setup.exe* file may add a level of comfort to novice users.

The Distribution Media

I hate it when users come over to my office and try to copy the MSI file directly from my hard drive. I find that providing the file on a CD tends to improve the vendor-customer relationship. So, let's build a CD for client use.

The distribution CD contains all of the content needed by the library IT staff to support the application. It contains distinct directories for each type of content. Here's what I am planning to put in the root of the CD.

- *Readme.htm*, an HTML file that displays information about the contents of the CD.
- *Database*, a directory containing the database creation script, *Database Creation Script.sql*.
- *License*, a directory containing the specific user's license file, *LibraryLicense.lic*.
- *Setup*, a directory containing the main MSI file, *LibrarySetup.msi*.
- *Technical*, a directory containing the technical support documentation, *ACME Library Resource Kit.pdf*.

I've put all these directories and their files in the book's installation directory, in a subdirectory named *Library CD Contents*. You can scan through the *Readme.htm* file in that folder to see the welcoming manner in which we offered the application to the end user.

I want this readme file to appear automatically when the user inserts the CD into the workstation drive. This requires one additional file named *autorun.inf* at the root of the CD. This simple INI-style file supports the Auto Run feature used by Windows CDs (when permitted on the target workstation). Here is the content of the file that will display the *Readme.htm* file automatically.

```
[Autorun]
Open=explorer.exe Readme.htm
```

Copying all of these directories and files to a CD and adding a pretty label should result in a happy librarian.

We're quickly approaching the end of the book. Only one chapter remains. Turn the page to find out what exciting content you'll find there.

Chapter 25

Project Complete

You've done it! You've completed the Library Project and met with acclaim from users and fellow programmers alike. And you've also accomplished something that few thought was possible: you slogged through all twenty-five chapters of this book. You're probably anxious to get on with your life as a highly paid software consultant, working just six months per year as the programmer that other programmers call when systems fail. Well, I won't keep you too long. But there are a few more issues to discuss concerning the Library Project and programming in general.

The Library Project

The Library Project is filled with features that target small library-style organizations. But it may not meet everyone's needs. And that's OK. The users know your address and phone number; you'll hear from them. When they call, you can tell them that the software wasn't designed for everyone; no software can be. All software, even general-purpose applications such as Visual Studio, can never meet the needs of every person or organization. What is important is that the features included in the project meet the needs of the intended audience. That audience may be the card-catalog-using public, or it may just be a small library with one part-time staff member.

Still, there is always room for improvement. Because the Library Project's real target audience was you—the student of Visual C# and .NET—it did not have all the features that most libraries would require. Looking quickly back through the source code, I came up with at least the following changes that could be made to the project to bring a lot more value to library administrators and users.

Error handling

> When an error does occur, most of the Library code simply reports the error and moves on. The application's *GeneralError* method is little more than a noisy klaxon, offering ominous warnings, but little in the way of long-term guidance. Some error-prone methods ignore problems completely. In general, the code could do a better job of processing error results. Some errors are more fatal than others, and specific errors should include additional options that the user can access to better recover from the fault.

Multithreading

> Beyond the extremely short discussion of asynchronous programming in Chapter 9, this book did not discuss or encourage the use of the multithreading features included in the .NET Framework. Processor-intensive activities tend to kill the responsiveness of the user interface, but there are ways to mitigate the impact. In the Library Project, two specific areas would benefit from the use of background worker threads, either by employing the *async* keyword, or by using the features of the *System.Threading* namespace directly: (1) searching for library items through the *ItemLookup*

form; and (2) processing overdue and fine data for a single day at all locations through the `MainForm.ActDoProcess_Click` event handler.

User interface and presentation

Although I included some cute graphics on the main Library Project form and the Splash form, I didn't do much beyond that. Mostly it was an issue of time and effort, but I also have very little talent for the graphic arts. The program could use an update in its general look and presentation. And with the new graphics features available through the Windows Presentation Foundation (WPF), you could enable some really amazing effects with little programming effort.

User interface consistency

Although I tried to be careful, there are probably labels, controls, and error messages that use two different names for the same thing. Perhaps I used the word *book* or *DVD* when I should have used the more general term *item*. Although tracking down such inconsistencies is a lot of work, it increases the level of professionalism in your application. It also makes the task of foreign-language translation easier when localizing the program.

Testing new databases

The *LocateDatabase.cs* form builds a connection string from the fields supplied by the user, but it does not test the connection to see whether it works. Providing an option to test the entered values could reduce long-term errors. An even better option would be to let the user search for the database, similar to the way that SQL Server itself sniffs out and presents located servers and databases.

Numeric title searches

The checkout and check-in features let you locate an item either by name or by barcode. If you enter a number, the program assumes that you have entered a barcode and retrieves the matching item. But some book titles are numeric. For instance, David McCullough's book *1776* would cause the program some difficulty if each copy did not include its own barcode. An enhancement to the program would provide the user additional disambiguation options when a numeric entry matched both a barcode and a title.

Enhanced item searches

Although I have much reason to be impressed by my item lookup code, the program could do so much more. When you use the card catalog systems at larger libraries, the lookup features include proximity searches that return results that are alphabetically close to the search terms provided by the user. SQL Server also has a full-text search option that could be used to broaden the item lookups.

Reserves and holds

I thought about adding a "reserves" feature to the Library Project so that patrons could add their names to a waiting list for checked-out library items, and have those items placed aside by the library staff when they were returned by the previous patron. Although this would be a cool and useful feature for a library, it didn't add any pedagogic value to the book, so I left it out. But I still hear the software sniffling and crying once in a while when it thinks of the feature that might have been. This would be a great enhancement for Version 2.0.

Incomplete item history

On the *PatronRecord.cs* form, the Fines list shows a patron's previously checked-out library items only if those items had once been overdue and had incurred fines. Items that were returned on time cannot be displayed in the list using the current form logic. A satisfying change would add a "Show all returned items" checkbox that would include these checked-in items. This would allow a librarian to charge for things such as damage on items that were otherwise free of fines.

Return of missing items

If an item is marked as missing, the library staff may charge the patron for the loss of the book. If the patron later returns that item, the librarian can process a reimbursement to the patron. But the program could make this task easier by automatically marking the item as eligible for such a refund. This would require a new field in the *PatronCopy* database table to track this status.

Barcode design interaction

The *BarcodeLabel.cs* form is, I think, pretty amazing with its graphics preview of the barcode. But the preview is unidirectional only; the user is not able to select a display element by clicking on that element in the preview. Instead, it is necessary to click on the related item in the *DisplayItems* list. Enhancing the program to detect clicks on the preview and to translate those clicks into item selections would make the program work much more like other applications that support basic drawing features.

Database setup features

Although we built the setup program for the main Library application, we skimped on the server side, only providing the database creation scripts as text files on the installation media. A more professional system would provide a separate installation program that could build and configure a new database from an existing SQL Server installation.

Support for library standards

Just as the software development world has standard formats and protocols such as XML, library systems also share common standards. Two accepted standards are MARC (Machine-Readable Cataloging, a standard card catalog data format) and the Z39.50 interface (a communications protocol used for inter-computer searches and data retrieval). Incorporating these standards into a small library system may be overkill, but they would bring a much higher level of automation and convenience to the library staff.

Bug fixes

I probably left a few bugs in the application. No, wait. I think I put them in there on purpose to test you, to see whether you were learning and growing in your programming skills. Did you find them?

These are just some of the improvements that I thought of off the top of my head. If I had gone all the way down to my shoulders, I could have come up with even more. If your software will target the general population of users, you will probably release updates on a regular schedule, such as annually, and charge appropriately for the improved features. If you wrote the application for one specific customer, the updates may be more frequent, even weekly or daily in some cases. Whatever the audience size, your opportunities for improving and enhancing the software will be regular and ongoing.

The Programming Mindset

As you enter deeper into the world of software development, you will quickly discover that the application-building process is about much more than syntax, statements, and logic. It is also about who you are as a programmer. The way that you think about software, and the care with which you approach the task of programming, have a direct impact on the quality of the code you write. This is certainly true in other areas of life. If you are a portrait painter, but you don't take your strokes seriously, or if you are sloppy in your use of paints and brushes, it will show in the low quality of your work.

In one of my previous books, *The Visual Basic .NET Style Guide* (Prentice Hall), I wrote about three traits that provide a strong basis for the programming life.

Discipline

> The act of self-training with a goal of increasing order, focus, and quality in your projects and work ethic

Planning

> The careful analysis and implementation of procedures and standards that scream out for quality

Ethics

> The inner character drive that shows itself through public and private honesty in attitudes and actions

If you are deficient in any of these three areas of your programming life, your applications and code will also be deficient by a similar factor. I have tried to sprinkle some humor and fun throughout the pages of this book. But on this point, I make no jokes. You need these three elements in your work life.

If you are serious about a career in software development, take the time to ask yourself questions that focus on these three aspects. Do I employ regular discipline in the way that I craft my software? Do I create reasonable and reliable plans, and then stick to them during a project? Do I exhibit ethical standards in the way I communicate with my customers, my employer, my coworkers, and even myself? If you are not able to answer these questions to your satisfaction, find resources that can help you overcome the lapses. It will make your programming work so much easier, and it will positively impact the other areas of your life as well.

Summary

Now you've really reached the end of the book. You can read through the appendixes and the index if you're still hungry for more. But a better solution would be to find out if I've come out with the next edition of the book and buy it. Ha!

I thank you for taking the time to read through *Start-to-Finish Visual C# 2015*. I wrote it so that you might expand your understanding and expertise of a very practical and enjoyable subject: Visual C#. And *enjoyable* is the key word. Nobody has to be a computer programmer, no matter what historians say. You should take on the role of a Visual C# developer only if you truly take pleasure in helping other people become more productive through specialized or general software. If, even after reading this book, you find coding to be a bore and sheer drudgery, I recommend the food services industry as an alternative.

For those of you still excited about C# programming, have as much fun with it as possible. Microsoft is constantly updating the language and its Visual Studio shell so that you can really enjoy yourself as you program. Why do you think Microsoft put in all of those animation features? Take time to go beyond the mundane in your code and in your user interfaces. Challenge yourself by trying out new features within the language and in the framework. And above all, smile each time you successfully complete a project. Your author, and your users, will thank you.

Installing the Software

You are holding more than just a book. You are holding an idea. No wait, that's what you get when you hold a philosophy book. In this case, what you also get is software—free software. And it's all found on the publisher's web site for this book.

http://www.owanipress.com/STFCS2015

When you download and run the setup program provided on the web site, the following items are added to your system.

- A directory structure with all chapter-specific source code and documentation.
- A set of Visual Studio *project template* files. Each template creates a new project based on "before" or "after" source code images for most chapters in the book. Once you install the templates, you will have the option of accessing chapter-specific projects using the File→New→Project menu command in Visual Studio.
- A directory of *code snippets* that let you follow along with the action in each chapter's "Project" section, all without the need to retype every line of code printed in the book.

The installation requires approximately 50MB of disk space. This appendix discusses the download and installation procedures.

Download the Software

To obtain the software for the book, browse to the book's web site.

http://www.owanipress.com/STFCS2015

Locate the Download Code link on this page and click it. When prompted, save the download file to your system using the standard file download features of your browser. You can save the file, named *Start-to-Finish Visual C# 2015.exe*, to a temporary area of your system. Once you complete installation, you will no longer need this file, unless you wish to retain it as a backup.

Install the Software

Double-click or run the downloaded *Start-to-Finish Visual C# 2015.exe* file. When prompted, indicate the target directory to use for the installation of all project files. Once the files are extracted, a readme file appears describing the final installation steps.

Install Project Templates

The book's installation folder includes a directory called *Templates*, containing the chapter-specific templates that integrate directly with Visual Studio. To use these templates, you must first copy the template files into Visual Studio's project template directory within your user account. To locate this directory, click the Windows Start button, then type the following.

```
%USERPROFILE%
```

This will open your user directory, typically located at *C:\Users\YourName* on Windows 10 systems. Within this directory, browse to the following subdirectory.

```
Documents\Visual Studio 2015\Templates\ProjectTemplates\Visual C#
```

In this location, add a new subdirectory with the following name.

```
Start-to-Finish C#2015
```

Copy all files from the book's *Templates* directory into this newly created directory. The next time you start Visual Studio and use the File→New→Project menu command, the template files will be installed.

Install Code Snippets

Code snippets are installed from within the Visual Studio application. Start Visual Studio, and run the Tools→Code Snippets Manager menu command. The Code Snippets Manager window appears, as shown in Figure A-1.

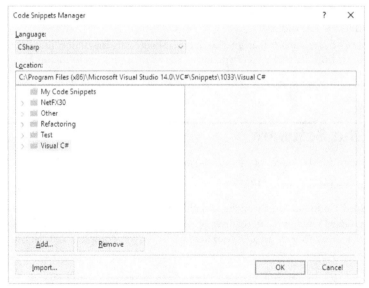

Figure A-1. The Code Snippets Manager

Click the Add button and browse to the directory where you extracted this book's downloaded content. Browse within the *Code Snippets* directory, select the *Start-to-Finish C#2015* subdirectory, and click the Select Folder button. When control returns to the Code Snippets Manager form, click the OK button to complete the installation.

Barcode Support

The web site that hosts the project content also contains information on locating and obtaining barcode font information. You may use one of the barcodes mentioned on this site with the project code, or you may obtain your own valid barcode font.

Software License Agreement

When you download and install the software provided with this book, you agree to the terms of the software license agreement.

Terms of Use

The source code and software components provided with *Start-to-Finish Visual C# 2015* (collectively known as the "software") are designed for use with that book, and are available only to those who obtain and use the book. As such, the software is covered by the copyright and licensing of the book itself. However, there are a few additional terms and conditions that should make the software even more useful to your development and learning activities.

Using the software with the book

You may install and use the software in conjunction with your reading of the text. If you use multiple workstations in your tutorial endeavors, feel free to install the software on each of those systems.

Distributing the supplied software

You may not package, distribute, sell, or otherwise make available to others the partial or complete applications provided with the book. Claiming that this work is your own, and attempting to distribute or sell it as such, is wrong and an all-around bad idea.

Using portions of the software in your projects

You may use portions of this software in your own applications and development projects. If you include significant portions of the software in your derived work, please give credit where credit is due, and make it known that your application employs the useful content provided with *Start-to-Finish Visual C# 2015*.

Acknowledgments

The software was developed by Tim Patrick, author of *Start-to-Finish Visual C# 2015*. Tim Patrick and Owani Press gladly make this software available to you for your education and enjoyment.

Warranty

No warranty is provided with the software. Although every attempt has been made to keep the software safe and benign when installed on any target system, such safety is not guaranteed. Tim Patrick and Owani Press shall not be liable for any harm or damage that comes to your system or to any data stored on your system as a result of installing this software.

Other terms and conditions

There may be additional terms and conditions instituted on the download web site where you obtained this software. Please read those carefully as they contain important information concerning downloads accessed from the web site.

Enjoy

I hope that these terms and conditions didn't scare you off. The software exists to help you learn and to advance your understanding of Visual C# software development concepts. I think you'll find the software to be quite useful in your training, so download and enjoy.

Index

catch keyword, 210
char type, 30, 114
class, 5, 7, 173
class keyword, 173
ClickOnce, 552
closure class, 204
Code Access Security (CAS), 239
code snippet, 54
CodeLens, 15
column, 71
Command class, 219
comment, 34
Common Language Runtime (CLR), 5, 27
Common Language Specification (CLS), 6, 31
Common Type System (CTS), 7, 25
compile, 13, 91, 169
compiler constant, 94
condition, 25, 39, 47
Connection class, 219
connection string, 226
const keyword, 33, 117, 174
constant, 117, 174
constraint, 75, 350
constructor, 22, 32, 119, 183
continue statement, 43
contravariance, 352
control, 21, 96, 140, 148, 433
Convert class, 130
covariance, 352
culture, 438
data binding, 80, 225
data conversion, 129
Data Definition Language (DDL), 73
Data Manipulation Language (DML), 73
data set, 220, 375
data structure, 111
data type, 7, 29, 75, 111, 350
DataAdapter class, 219
database, 71, 217
DataReader class, 219
DataRelation class, 220
DataSet class, 220
DataTable class, 220
DateTime type, 30
Debug object, 213
decimal type, 30, 114
default constructor, 32, 183
default keyword, 32, 41
delegate, 7, 50, 177

delegate keyword, 49, 156, 177
deployment, 69, 545
derived class, 171
descending keyword, 370
designer file, 21, 105
destructor, 183, 185
dialog, 106, 158
directive, 94
Distinct LINQ method, 369
Document Type Definition (DTD), 293
documentation, 80
double type, 30, 114
else keyword, 39
encapsulation, 171
encryption, 240, 505
Entity Framework (EF), 229, 375
enum keyword, 118, 174
enumeration, 7, 117, 174
error handling, 206, 561
escape sequence, 116
event, 7, 49, 141, 155, 177
event handler, 20, 49, 101, 141, 155
event keyword, 49, 155, 177
Exception class, 213
explicit keyword, 268
expression, 37, 122
Extensible Application Markup Language (XAML), 413, 510
Extensible Markup Language (XML), 77, 291, 510
Extensible Stylesheet Language (XSLT), 296
extension method, 272
extern keyword, 167, 177
false literal, 28, 115
field, 3, 33, 174
finally keyword, 211
float type, 31, 115
flow control statement, 25, 47
for statement, 41, 127
foreach statement, 42
form, 19, 96, 140, 144, 433
Framework Class Library (FCL), 8, 90
from keyword, 367
Func delegate, 202
function, 26, 38, 45, 175
garbage collection, 183
GDI+, 395, 452
generic method, 354
generics, 347

get accessor, 46, 175
Global Assembly Cache (GAC), 10, 90, 555
global keyword, 52
global variable, 188
globalization, 429
goto statement, 47
hash, 244, 504
hexadecimal, 115
icon, 107, 404
if statement, 39
implementation, 5, 172
implicit keyword, 268
import, 53
in keyword, 353, 367
index, 75
indexer, 176
inference, 122
inheritance, 171, 179
initialization, 117, 128, 190, 357
instance, 5, 173
instance member, 178
instantiation, 32, 182
int type, 30, 114
interface, 4, 7, 171, 172, 177, 186
interface keyword, 186
Intermediate Language (IL), 6, 91
internal keyword, 120
invariance, 353
is operator, 126
iterator, 177, 356
join, 72, 79
join keyword, 370
jump, 25
label, 47
lambda expression, 201, 372
Library project, 59
license agreement, 569
licensing, 503
lifetime, 121
LINQ, 363
literal, 27, 115
local variable, 33, 120
localization, 430
long type, 30, 115
loop, 25, 41, 47
Main procedure, 6, 143
managed code, 5, 23
manifest, 10, 91
member, 3, 171, 174

member access, 182
MessageBox.Show method, 26, 190
metadata, 10, 91, 104
method, 3, 38, 171
modal form, 158
mutex, 166, 168
namespace, 8, 51, 173
namespace statement, 53, 173
narrowing conversion, 129
nested loop, 43
nested type, 7, 177
new keyword, 21, 32, 119, 181, 182, 351, 368
normalization, 72
null keyword, 29
null propagation, 191
nullable type, 29, 128, 356
obfuscation, 13, 92, 507
object, 3, 169
object type, 29, 30, 115
object-oriented programming (OOP), 3, 169
online help, 531
operand, 35, 123
operator, 35, 122
operator keyword, 264
operator overloading, 263
optional argument, 38, 179
orderby keyword, 370
out keyword, 45, 131, 353
overloading, 38, 172, 178, 354
override keyword, 180
overriding, 171
owner draw, 411, 417
parameter, 44, 228
params keyword, 191
parentheses, 37
Parse method, 130
partial keyword, 21, 173, 189
partial method, 188
Pascal casing, 121
pass by reference, 44
pass by value, 44
polymorphism, 172
primary key, 72
print preview, 457
printing, 451
private keyword, 120
procedure, 26
project management, 65
project methodology framework, 65

yield break statement, 356

Also Available from Owani Press

C#–Visual Basic Bilingual Dictionary

Built on Microsoft's powerful .NET Framework, C# and Visual Basic are complete equals in terms of coding power and application development possibilities. In today's multi-platform environment, an understanding of both languages is a job requirement. *The C#-Visual Basic Bilingual Dictionary* unifies the languages by providing clear, functional equivalents for all syntax and grammar differences.

* **Complete coverage of all language keywords.** Nearly 900 dictionary-like entries cover every Visual Basic and C# keyword and grammar feature, including VB's "My" namespace.

* **Examples in both languages.** Hundreds of code samples in both C# and Visual Basic make translations between the languages clear and easy to understand.

* **Full support for Roslyn.** Each chapter covers the latest language features from Visual Studio 2015 and Microsoft's "Roslyn" compiler.

Whether you work on a team that uses both languages, or just need to understand a technical article written in that "other" language, the *C#-Visual Basic Bilingual Dictionary* is an essential resource for developers crafting Microsoft software solutions.

Now Available!

owanipress.com

www.ingramcontent.com/pod-product-compliance
Lightning Source LLC
Chambersburg PA
CBHW082107070326
40689CB00052B/3744